VIKINGS

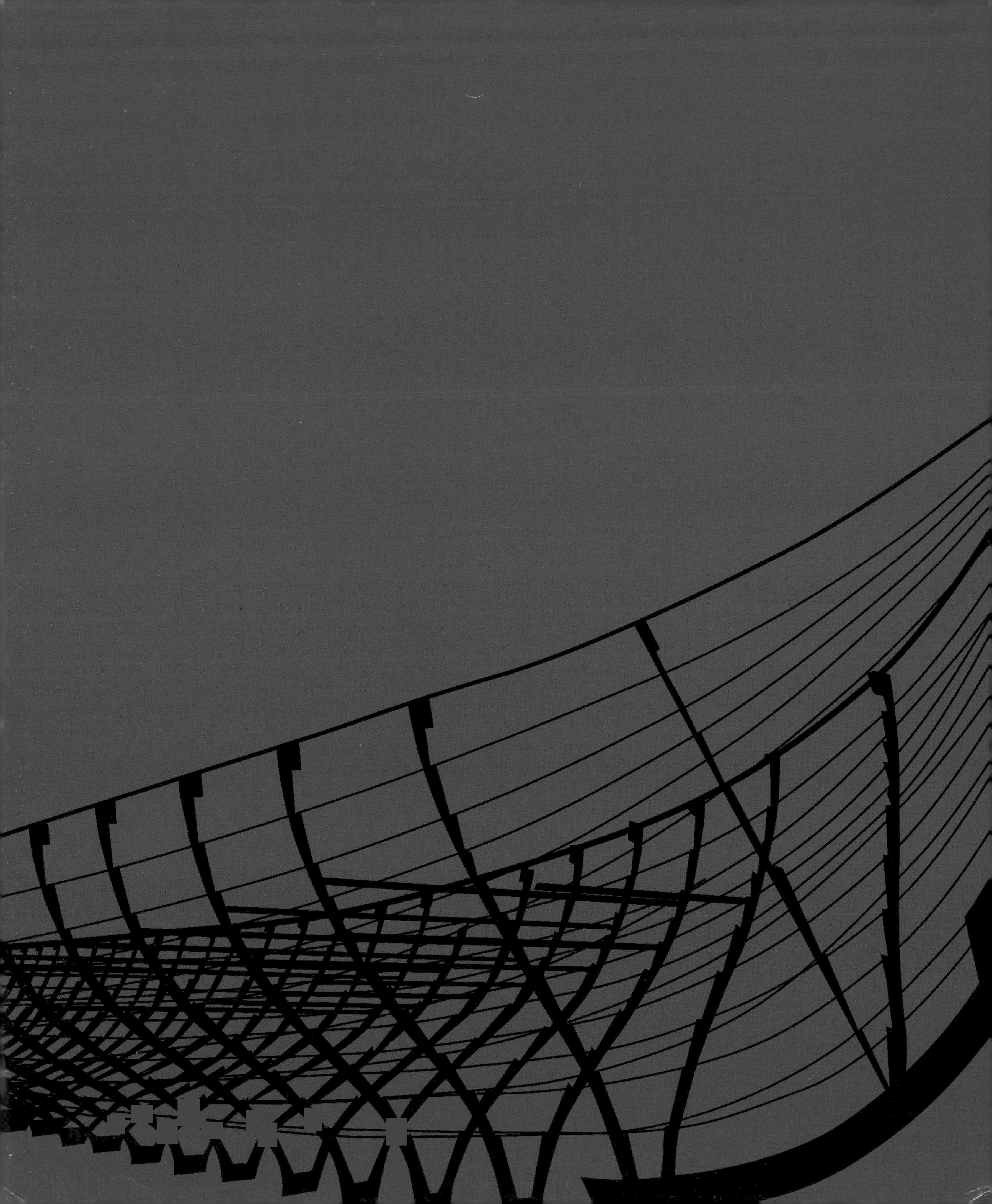

VIKINGS

LIFE AND LEGEND

EDITED BY

GARETH WILLIAMS
PETER PENTZ
MATTHIAS WEMHOFF

Cornell University Press
Ithaca, New York

This publication accompanies the exhibition *Vikings: life and legend* organized by the National Museum of Denmark, the British Museum and the Museum für Vor- und Frühgeschichte, Staatliche Museen zu Berlin.

First published in the United Kingdom in 2014
by The British Museum Press
A division of The British Museum Company Ltd
38 Russell Square, London WC1b 3QQ
britishmuseum.org/publishing

First published in the United States of America in 2014 by Cornell University Press

First printing, Cornell Paperbacks, 2014

A catalog record for this book is available from the Library of Congress
ISBN 978-0-8014-7942-7

Papers used by The British Museum Press are recyclable products made from wood grown in well-managed forests and other controlled sources. The manufacturing processes conform to the environmental regulations of the country of origin.

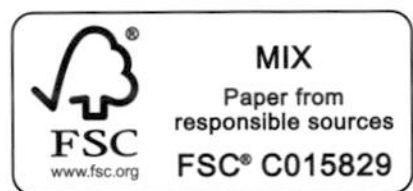

Designed by Will Webb Design
Printed in Italy by Printer Trento SRL

Paperback printing 10 9 8 7 6 5 4 3 2 1

Contents

The Sea Stallion from Glendalough, a full-scale reconstruction of the warship Skuldelev 2, which was built near Dublin *c.* 1042 and sunk at Skuldelev near Roskilde in Denmark a generation later.

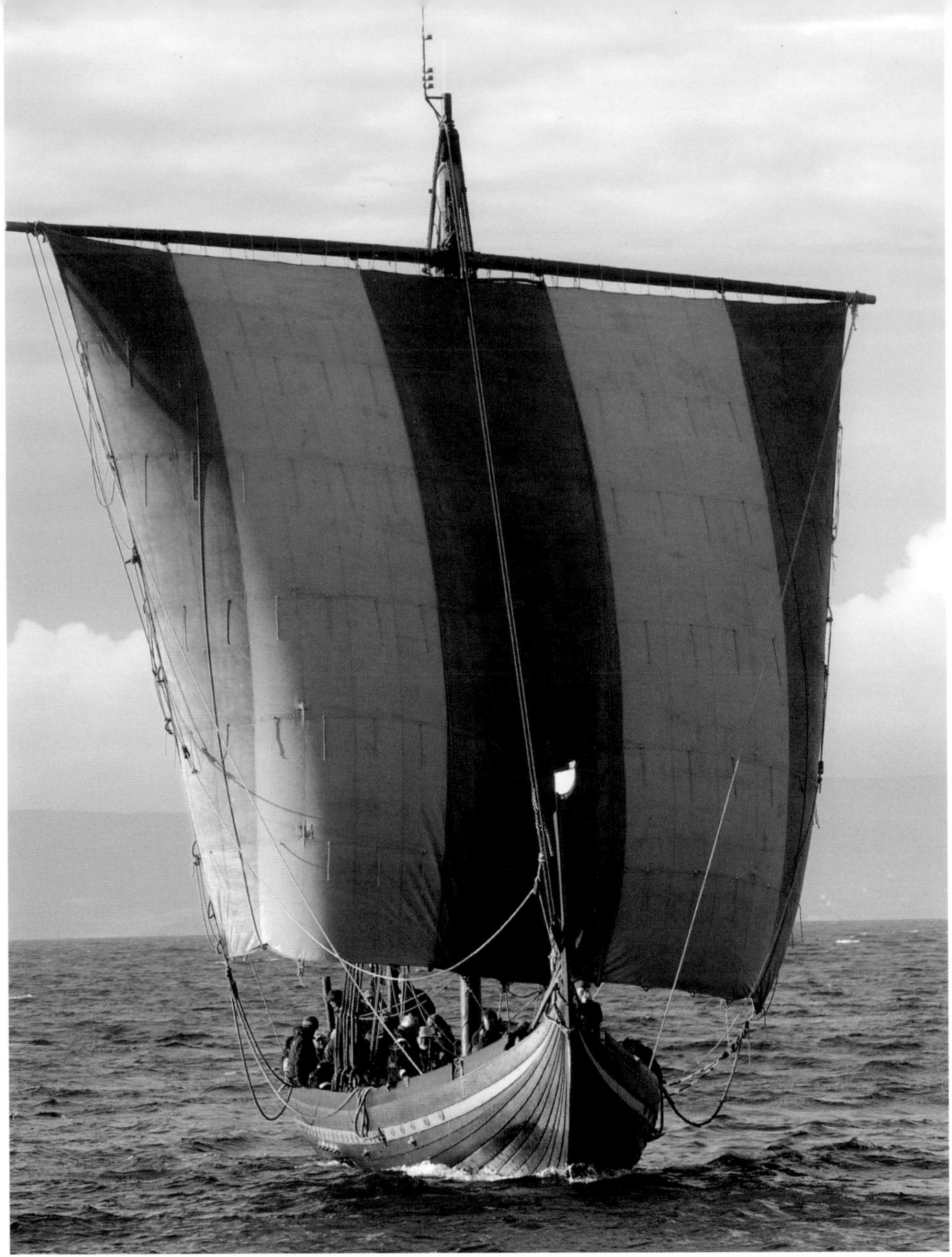

Foreword

Her Majesty Queen Margrethe of Denmark

IS THERE ANY PERIOD IN OUR DISTANT PAST that fascinates us more than the Viking Age, I wonder? We know about it from the epic sagas as well as from remains found in the ground and at the bottom of our coastal waters, but first and foremost from reconstructed Viking ships. It is here the past comes alive. Once you have seen a Viking ship at sea or even been on board one, you will never forget it (fig. 1).

Vikings: life and legend is the largest international Viking exhibition to be held for many years. It was masterminded by three international museums, and many new finds and much new knowledge have been added since the last time the Viking Age was reviewed. The biggest new find, quite literally, is the wreck of the just over 37-metre-long ship, Roskilde 6, from the harbour at Roskilde, which is the central piece of the exhibition.

At no other time in Scandinavian history were ships, seafaring and society so closely bound together as in the Viking Age. Without ships, there would have been no Viking Age. But they were not just a means of transport and were not only found on the sea. On the contrary, they were present everywhere: in art, in beliefs and as symbols. Ships and their need for a crew may even have formed the basis of the administrative division of land and have left their mark on the architecture. Building a vessel of this kind required power over things and people.

What did the people on board the great ship, the royal ship – because it probably was a royal ship – think? Those who sailed in it, those who built it and those who remained behind? Not to mention those who watched anxiously as the longships steered in towards the shore. Was it the enemy arriving? The many new finds have given us further knowledge about the people of the Viking Age, their thoughts and deeds. Yet we certainly do not know everything, and such information may throw light on the darkness. It is here, at the transition between knowledge and darkness, in the twilight, that the imagination steps in and dreams begin.

On a small piece of wood found in the Norwegian city of Bergen, at some time in the early Middle Ages, somebody captured and scratched a fleeting image (fig. 2). The picture shows a war fleet in all its power and glory. Stem by stem lie the beautiful ships, some with dragons' heads gazing longingly up towards the wind vanes, the Viking pennants that show where the ships will be borne by the wind.

This little work of art is carved on a stick of juniper wood. Juniper, which belongs to the cypress family, is the most widespread of conifers. This was also the case in the Viking Age. Juniper grew where no other trees were found, from the dry mountain slopes of the Mediterranean to the windswept islands of the Faeroes, even by the icy sea in treeless Greenland – all over the wide Viking world. The artist, who was also evidently a master of carving runes, wrote on the stick: *Hér ferr hafdjarfr* (Here sails the Sea-Brave). The Sea-Brave could have been the ship from Roskilde harbour in its prime!

It is the world's longest Viking ship, built of Norwegian timber, felled during the early part of the reign of Cnut the Great (d. 1035), at the time of the North Sea empire. We also know that the ship ended its travels at Roskilde on the Danish island of Zealand. By then the Viking Age was over, and from the shore close to the gigantic hulk people had only to look up to see one or two of Denmark's first stone churches in Roskilde.

We cannot be certain of which seas' foam sprayed the 5-metre high prow and to which shores the Sea-Brave sailed in peace or war. The answer is blowing in the same winds that filled the ship's enormous sail a thousand years ago. But when reality gives us no answers, the imagination takes over. Dreams go beyond the boundaries set by our knowledge and give the answers reality refuses to give us. And these dreams and answers belong to us alone.

The magic and fascination of the Viking Age live on!

A depiction of a fleet of ships carved into wood, from Bergen, Norway. Although the carving dates from the late 13th century, the dragon heads and wind vanes on the prows of some of the ships have parallels in the Viking Age.
Wooden stick. L c. 25 cm
University Museum of Bergen, Bergen

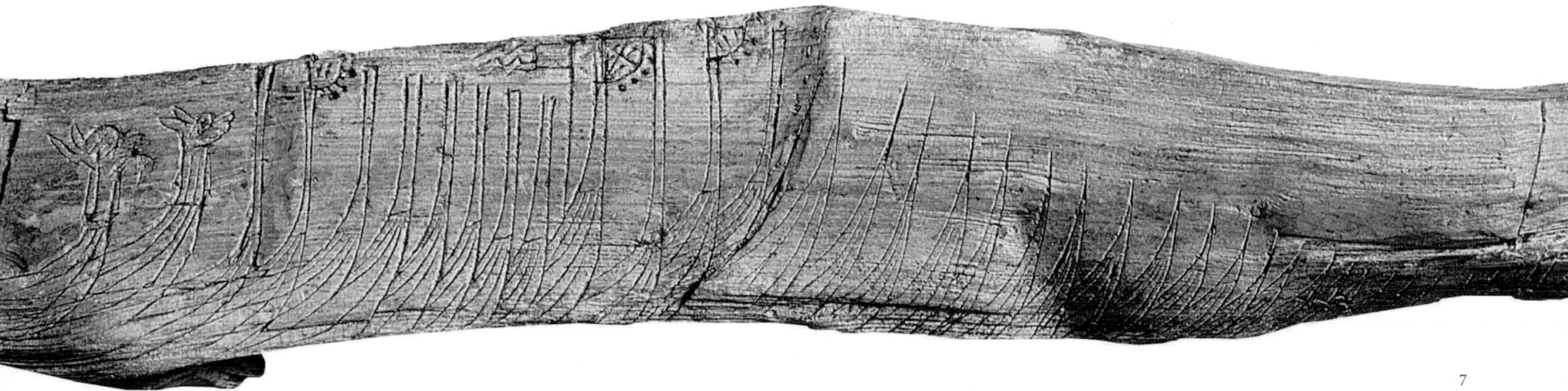

Directors' foreword

What we call the 'Viking Age' today lasted from about 800 to 1050. This span of around 250 years was a crucial period for the vast area of Northern Europe that includes the countries bordering the Baltic Sea to the east, the North Sea and the North Atlantic as well as the Irish Sea and the English Channel. The Vikings left a lasting impression, be it in a practical, historical or even ideological sense, on a large number of nations that make up our world today.

For most of that area the Viking Age was a period of transformation out of which emerged the medieval Christian kingdoms we still recognize in present-day states and nations. Throughout their existence the Vikings of the North were adventurers, farmers, traders, conquerors and sailors, and much more. They were certainly both peaceful and fierce – fighting or bargaining their way through as far as Constantinople in the East, Greenland and North America in the North, the British Isles and Northern France in the West as well as into Spain and the Mediterranean.

One thing remains clear – it was the sea and the rivers that connected people and cultures and it was all made possible by the Viking ship, considered one of the outstanding achievements of the Viking Age.

Therefore, it is entirely appropriate that the largest Viking ship ever found is the centrepiece and the connecting icon of our special exhibition on the Vikings to be held in Copenhagen, London and Berlin. The ship, here presented to the public for the very first time, is of exceptional quality and represents a major investment by a magnate or even a king – an expression of high technological skills and know-how. It is certainly a warship but also a symbol of power, and of the maritime society of the Vikings, and it is at the core of the themes running through the exhibition and this book that accompanies it.

The exhibition was created to show the wealth of established and new evidence about the Vikings, and to demonstrate their wide range of contacts both inside and outside the Viking world. The Vikings were cultural transformers and promoters, as well as settlers and empire builders on a level corresponding to their European counterparts. Since the last major Viking exhibitions in our three capitals some twenty or thirty years ago, much new evidence has emerged that has decisively changed our perception of Viking-Age society and history. Complex sites of vast dimensions, such as the royal monuments and the enclosure in Jelling in Denmark, have changed our understanding of the Viking society's elite and new research methods, such as isotope analysis, have shed light on the movement of people, among them the men serving King Harald Bluetooth as mercenaries. New hoards, such as the Vale of York hoard, as well as single finds of gold and silver, both from archaeological sites and through metal detecting, have revealed the widespread contacts and the complexity of the different layers of economy and exchange in the Viking Age, while studies of the Norse gods in a wider context of beliefs has led to a rethinking of the character of belief and ritual in the Viking Age. The discovery of the magnificent Viking ship from Roskilde provides further testimony of the scale of the technical achievements of the late Viking Age.

How we present our research and knowledge to the public is another field undergoing change. New virtual techniques and ways of display are brought in to enhance the experience and curiosity of the public and thereby help to fulfill the aim of our museums. However, museums still need the necessary space for an exhibition of this size, especially given the challenges presented by a Viking ship some 37 metres long.

The emphasis within the exhibition and this book on cultural interactions between the Vikings and their neighbours reflects not only the partnership between our three museums, but also the fact that each of our museums combines a mixture of global, regional and national collections, supported by a strong tradition of research, collecting and the dissemination of knowledge. This project has drawn also on the collections and expertise of many other institutions in several different countries, and we wish to express our gratitude not only to the project teams in our own museums for their magnificent efforts, but to all the friends and colleagues from across the Viking world, without whose co-operation and support this exhibition would not have been possible.

Michael Eissenhauer, Staatliche Museen, Berlin
Neil MacGregor, British Museum, London
Per Kristian Madsen, National Museum of Denmark, Copenhagen

British Museum Director's foreword

The last major exhibition on Vikings at the British Museum took place in 1980. Since then discoveries of new material in Britain, Scandinavia and elsewhere, and a wealth of international research have transformed our understanding of the Viking Age. Such changes reflect many wider developments, including the welcome growth of dialogue and collaboration with colleagues and institutions in Russia and other countries in Eastern Europe. The closer relations have implications beyond the current exhibition alone, but have undoubtedly helped to increase our understanding of history and archaeology at the eastern end of the Viking world: and *Vikings: life and legend* includes a number of important finds from Eastern Europe never previously shown in the United Kingdom. Closer to home, museum collections and academic knowledge have been enhanced and enriched by the proper use of modern metal detectors in the hands of skilled amateur archaeologists. Britain and Denmark lead the world in the systematized reporting and recording of such finds, through the twin processes of the Treasure Act and the Portable Antiquities Scheme in Britain, both administered by the British Museum, and the corresponding *Danefæ* system in Denmark, administered by the National Museum of Denmark. Both museums, as well as regional museums in both countries, have acquired important new finds across many different periods as a result, including stunning new Viking material presented in this exhibition.

The British Museum has spent over four years preparing *Vikings: life and legend*, working closely with colleagues from the National Museum of Denmark in Copenhagen and the Museum für Vor- und Frühgeschichte in Berlin. The British Museum wishes to express its gratitude to our partner museums for a successful and inspiring collaboration, which has underpinned the whole project. A version of the exhibition has already appeared in Copenhagen, and another will follow in Berlin after the exhibition in London. Particular thanks must go to the National Museum of Denmark for taking the lead (with support from Augustinusfonden) in the conservation and the preparation for display of the warship Roskilde 6, which occupies a central place both physically and conceptually in the exhibition. Excavated in the mid-1990s this is one of the most significant recent discoveries from the Viking Age, as the longest Viking ship so far discovered. This find has a dual significance for the British Museum. Firstly, it dates from the reign of King Cnut, who ruled both Denmark and England nearly 1,000 years ago. Secondly, there could be few more suitable objects for the inaugural show in the Sainsbury Exhibitions Gallery at the heart of the British Museum's newly opened World Conservation and Exhibitions Centre. At just over 37 metres long, Roskilde 6 highlights why we needed a purpose-built gallery for special exhibitions. Prior to this, there was nowhere in the British Museum that such a large and splendid object could have been displayed and this, together with the design of the exhibition, highlights the exciting opportunities now opened up to the Museum by the new space.

Finally *Vikings: life and legend* would never have been possible without the generous support of BP. This BP exhibition is part of an ongoing partnership with the British Museum and on behalf of the Museum I would like to offer my heartfelt thanks.

Neil MacGregor
Director, British Museum, London

Sponsor's foreword

As a global business, BP is very pleased to support *Vikings: life and legend*, a fascinating exhibition that casts a new light on a group of people who had a profound influence on the world of their time, spanning four continents.

This will be the first major UK exhibition on the Vikings in over thirty years – and also the first to be staged in the British Museum's new Sainsbury Exhibitions Gallery.

It reminds us of the scale of Viking exploration – from modern-day North America to the Middle East and Eastern Europe as well as the North Atlantic region.

It provides a fresh insight into the role of the Vikings, exploring how they interacted with people they encountered and the multi-faceted influences that arose from their extensive cultural contacts.

It also highlights major recent finds, including the very impressive 'Roskilde 6', the longest Viking ship yet discovered, and the beautiful – and instructive – Vale of York Hoard of coins and other items.

BP has a long-standing relationship with the British Museum and our support for *Vikings: life and legend* is part of a wider programme that helps to connect communities with excellence in arts and culture worldwide.

We very much hope you enjoy this account of the exhibition.

Bob Dudley
Group Chief Executive BP

The Viking world.

With southern Scandinavia placed in the centre of the world, rather than tucked away in the top corner as on most modern maps of Europe, the limits of the Viking world are easier to understand. North America, Central Asia and North Africa are all roughly the same distance from the Viking homelands. The zones shaded in red show areas of Viking settlement.

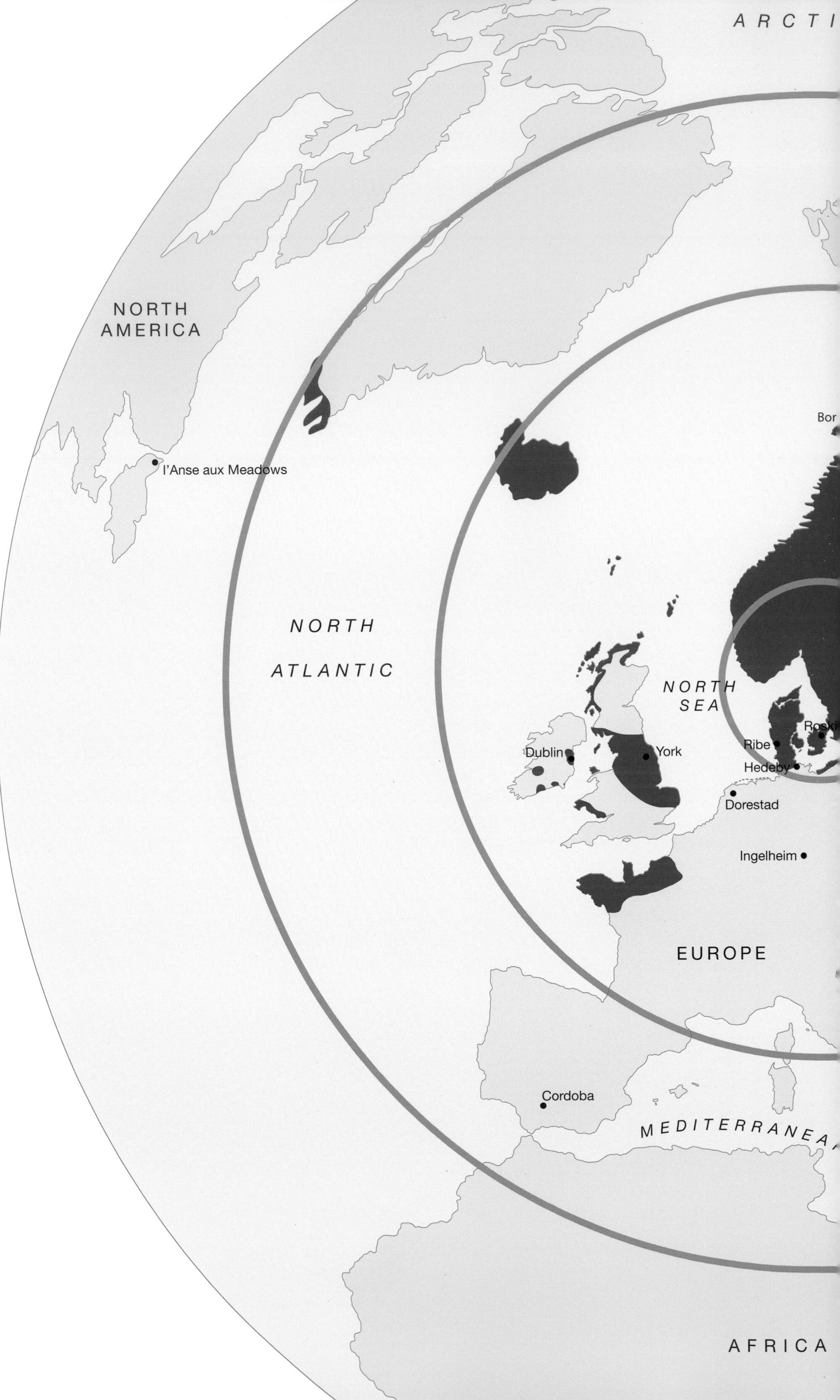

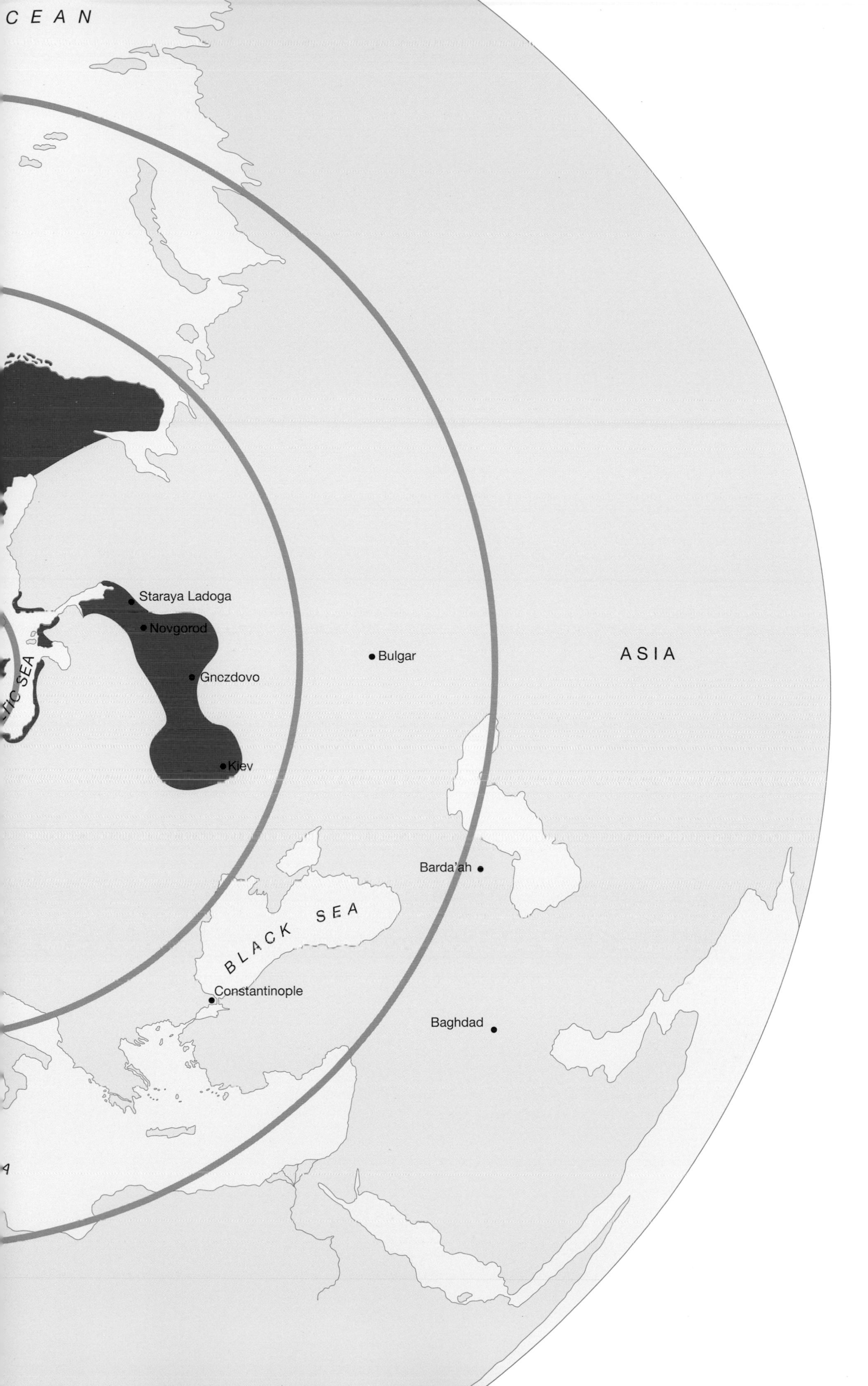
CEAN
Staraya Ladoga
Novgorod
Gnezdovo
Kiev
TIC SEA
Bulgar
ASIA
Barda'ah
BLACK SEA
Constantinople
Baghdad

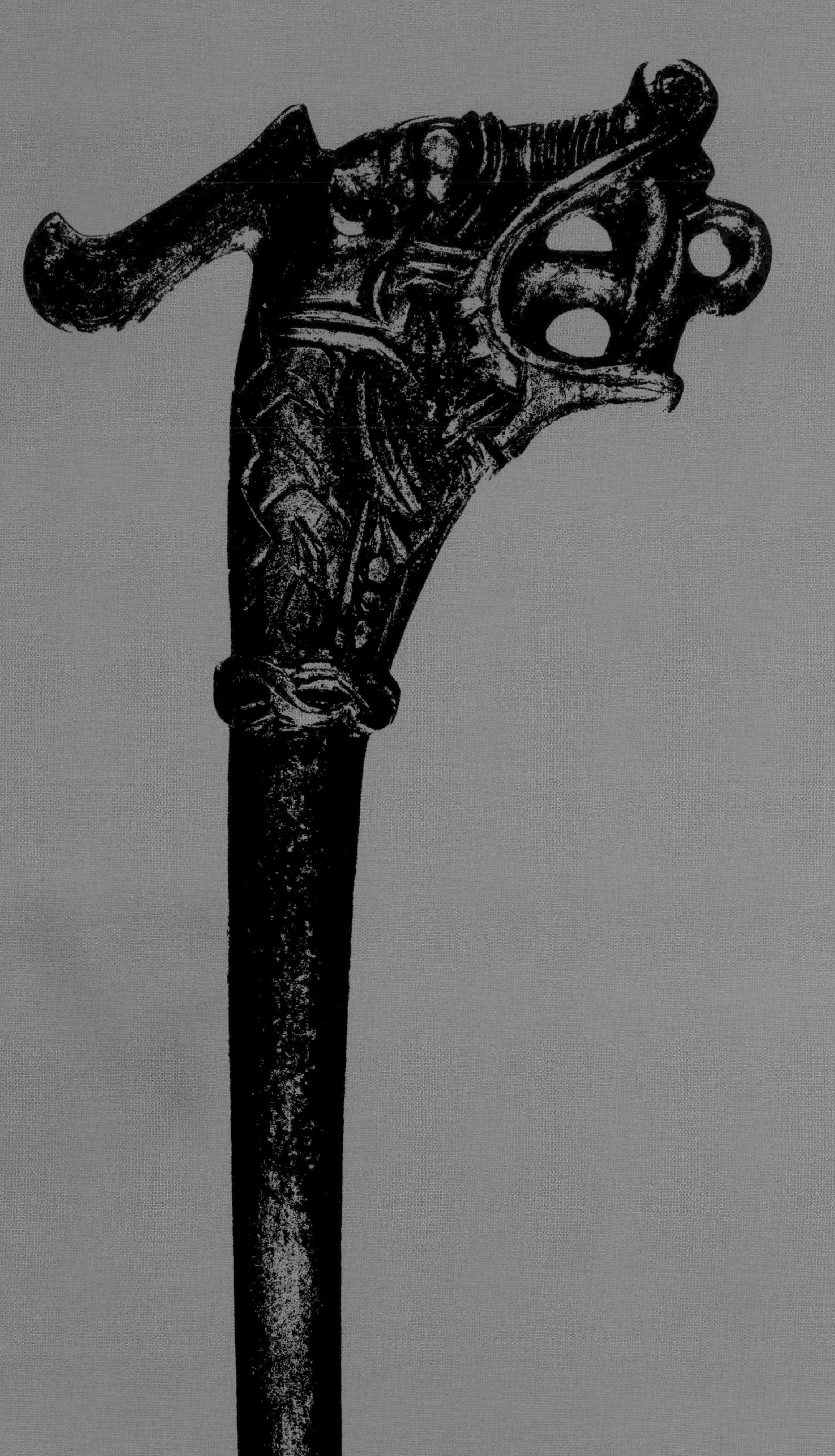

INTRODUCTION

Gareth Williams

They journeyed boldly;
Went far for gold,
Fed the eagle
Out in the east,
And died in the south
In Saracenland

GRIPSHOLM RUNE-STONE (*c.* 1050)

INTRODUCTION

THIS BOOK, AND THE EXHIBITION that it accompanies, is concerned with the Viking Age, a period between the late eighth and late eleventh centuries during which there was an unprecedented movement of people out from the Scandinavian homelands. This expansion led to interaction with a number of cultures, not only in northern Europe but also spread between North America in the west, Central Asia in the east, and North Africa in the south. The character of these contacts varied, and a nineteenth-century view of the Vikings purely as raiders and killers was broadened in the late twentieth century to include recognition of the achievements of Scandinavians in the Viking Age as traders, settlers, craftsmen, poets, explorers, shipbuilders and sailors. This reflects a wealth of archaeological discoveries, especially since the 1970s, but also a more careful reading of the existing historical evidence, much of it compiled by other peoples with whom the Vikings came into contact. For all of the peaceful achievements of the Viking Age, some of those encounters were undoubtedly violent and this is reflected in the accounts of those they fought. The repeated focus on such attacks should warn us against too peaceful an interpretation of the Vikings.

Structure

Two core themes run throughout this book. The first is that the events and developments of the Viking Age cannot be understood purely in the context of Scandinavia, or even of northern Europe. The Vikings had an extensive network of external contacts and as a result of those contacts they exercised varying degrees of influence on the different peoples with whom they interacted, while a range of external factors impacted on developments within the Vikings' Scandinavian homelands. This is discussed in more detail in Chapter 1, but the theme of cultural interaction, and the influences and changes that resulted from interaction, also underpins the remaining chapters.

The second core theme relates to the object that, both literally and metaphorically, forms the focus of the accompanying exhibition. The warship known as Roskilde 6 was built around 1025, lost perhaps twenty or thirty years later (the precise date is uncertain), and was discovered in 1996–7, in the course of the construction of the 'Museum Island' of the Viking Ship Museum, which is situated in the harbour area of Viking and medieval Roskilde in Denmark. Roskilde 6 is by some way the largest Viking ship so far discovered, with a reconstructed length of just over 37 metres, and has been specially conserved and mounted for the exhibition (see pp. 228–37). The construction of the ship coincides with a period in which the modern countries of Denmark, Norway and Sweden were taking shape, and more particularly with the reign of King Cnut (1016–35). Following in the footsteps of his father Svein Forkbeard, king of the Danes (*c.* 986–1013), Cnut conquered England in 1016 and shortly thereafter secured control of Denmark as well. He went on to conquer Norway in 1028 and coin inscriptions suggest that he exercised some sort of over-kingship in Sweden, although Sweden had kings of its own at the time.[1] Cnut was still a comparatively young man at the time of his death and his sons were unable to maintain his empire, which quickly fragmented after he was gone. The largest known Viking ship thus dates from the time of the largest ever Viking kingdom, which spanned the North Sea in a way that has never been paralleled before or since. Roskilde 6, and Viking ships more generally, relate in different ways to the themes explored in this book.

Unlike many books and exhibitions, the aim here is not to produce an overview of all aspects of the Viking Age, but rather to explore themes that emphasize aspects of the Viking Age in which there have been important recent archaeological discoveries, or in which new academic research has changed our understanding of existing material. The four themes – Contacts & Exchange, Warfare & Military Expansion, Power & Aristocracy, and Belief & Ritual – are covered in separate chapters, each of which relates to different aspects of Roskilde 6 and other Viking ships. For Contacts & Exchange, the emphasis is on maritime culture: it was the Vikings' skill in shipbuilding and seamanship that permitted them to develop a network of cultural and trading contacts spanning four continents. For Warfare & Military Expansion, the important thing is that Roskilde 6 is a true 'longship', a purpose-built warship of the sort that enabled Cnut to conquer the neighbours of the Danes and to build his North Sea empire. For Power & Aristocracy, the focus is on the scale of the ship. Not only is Roskilde 6 the largest Viking ship discovered archaeologically to date, but also her size places her at the upper end of the ships described in the historical sources. The resources required to build such a ship almost certainly indicate that she was built at royal command, either as a royal ship or for service in the national ship-levy (see p. 113). In the case of Belief & Ritual, there are two links. Although Roskilde 6 was a wreck rather than a burial, boats and ships were closely connected with passage to the afterlife in the Viking Age, whether directly through burials, in iconography or in poetry and mythology. Furthermore, Roskilde 6 was built in the early eleventh century, a period in which Christianity was coming to supplant the more established belief systems of the region, and close to the date of the martyrdom of King Olaf the Saint (d. 1030), Norway's national saint. In the exhibition the ship is a constant presence, just as maritime technology was central to the Viking Age, and the importance of Viking ships is reflected in the concluding chapter of this book: Ships & the Vikings.

Vikings: what's in a name?

The word 'Viking' is used to mean a variety of different things. In Old Norse, the words *víkingr* and *víking* had quite specific meanings relating to raiding and piracy (see p. 79), but 'Viking' is also widely used today to refer to the peoples and culture of Scandinavia in the 'Viking Age' (800–1050), and sometimes even as an ethnic label. The origins of the word (also known in the Old English form *wicing*) are obscure. It may come from the word *vík,* meaning a bay or coastal inlet, an element preserved in place names, such as Reykjavík, Iceland (Smoke Bay); Lerwick, Shetland (Mud Bay); and Uig, Lewis (Bay) (fig. 1). On this basis it has been suggested that the term may have originated with pirates who frequented such inlets, from which they emerged to attack passing ships. Alternatively, it could refer to the inhabitants of one particular bay, in which case the Oslo Fjord in south-eastern Norway, which is still also known by the alternative name of *Viken* (The Bay), would be the most likely candidate, although there is nothing to single this area out as a focus of Viking

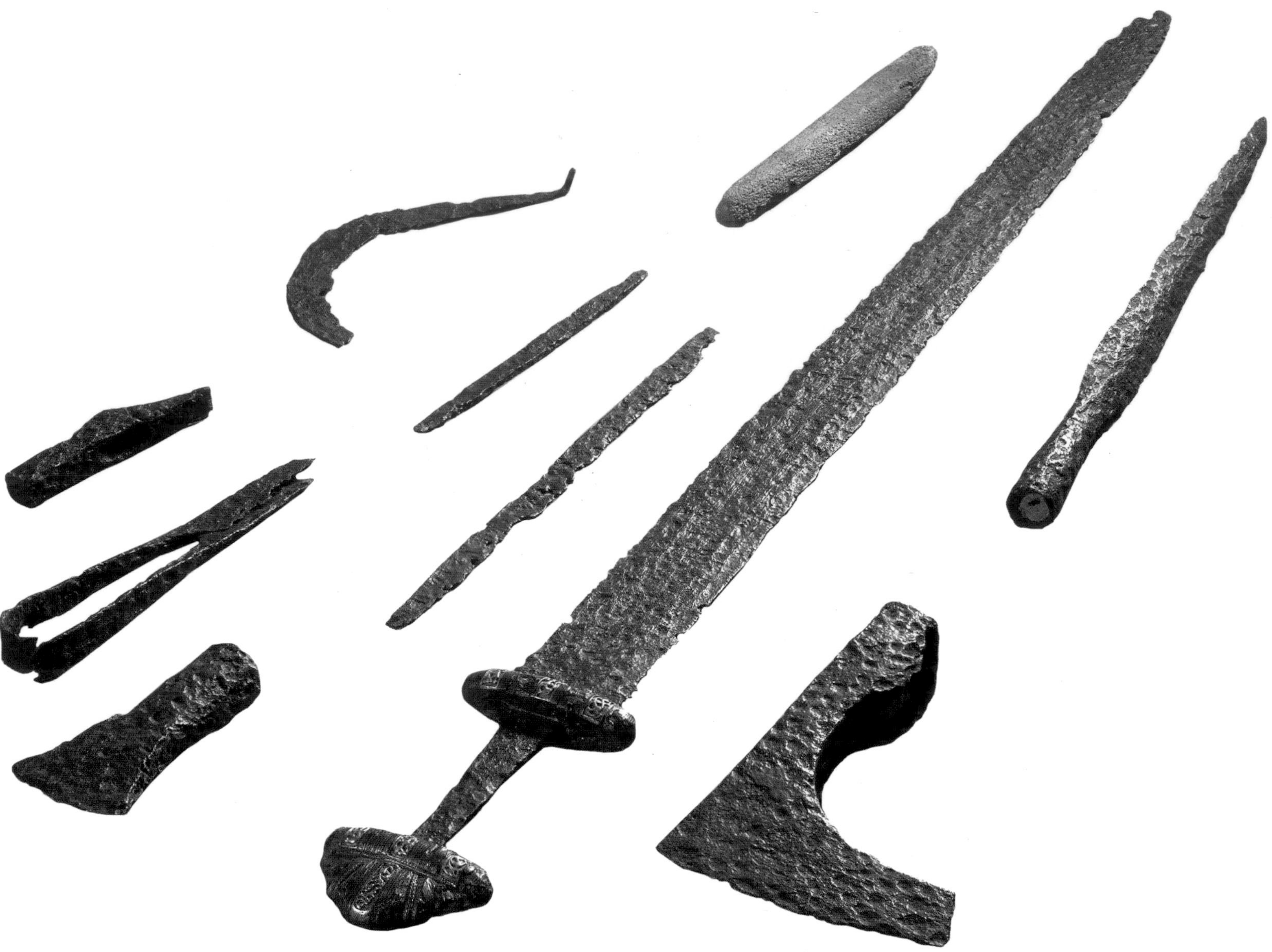

1.
Weapons were important symbols of cultural identity for Viking warriors and were often buried with the dead. These objects were recovered from a burial at Steinsvik in northern Norway. The vik part of the place name means 'bay' or 'inlet'.

Carolingian sword, Scandinavian spearhead and axe, 800–50. Steinsvik, Tjeldsund, Nordland, Norway.
Iron, copper alloy, silver. Sword L 100.1 cm
Museum of Cultural History, University of Oslo, Oslo

activity.[2] A third possibility is that it is a type of trading centre or emporium found around the North Sea as in the Latin *vicus* or Old English *wic,* another element that survives in place names such as Wijk bij Duurstede (Netherlands; fig. 2), Quentovic (France) and Ipswich (England), and that in the Viking Age featured in the names of other major centres in England, including *Hamwic/Hamwih* (Southampton), *Eoforwic* (York) and *Lundenwic* (London). These trading centres were typically located on coasts or on navigable rivers and seem to have been, at least in part, entry-points for foreign trade goods, which could then be distributed across wider networks of smaller centres, although different models have been proposed for how they functioned.[3]

This derivation from *wic* has the advantage that it indicates something of the diversity of modern interpretations of the Vikings. Was the original *wicing* the peaceful trader of post-1970s Viking studies, coming to (or from) the *wic* for legitimate purposes, as demonstrated by the evidence for trade as early as the mid-eighth century between Ribe in western Denmark and trading centres in England and Frisia (modern Netherlands)? Or was the *wicing* more the archetypal pirate, who attacked such centres, as in the repeated assaults on Dorestad?[4] Or was he simply a foreigner of indeterminate origin who might visit such

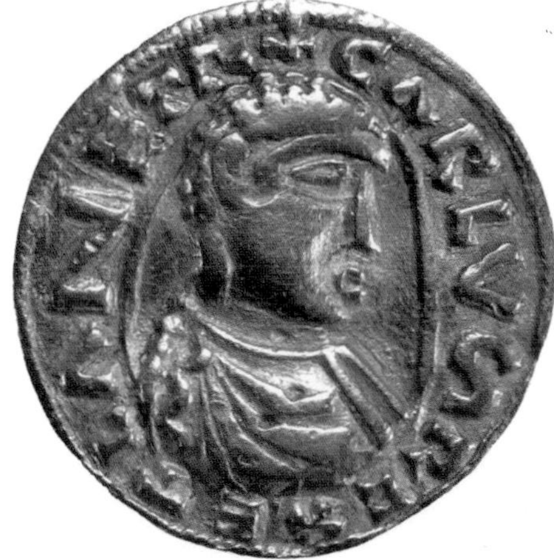

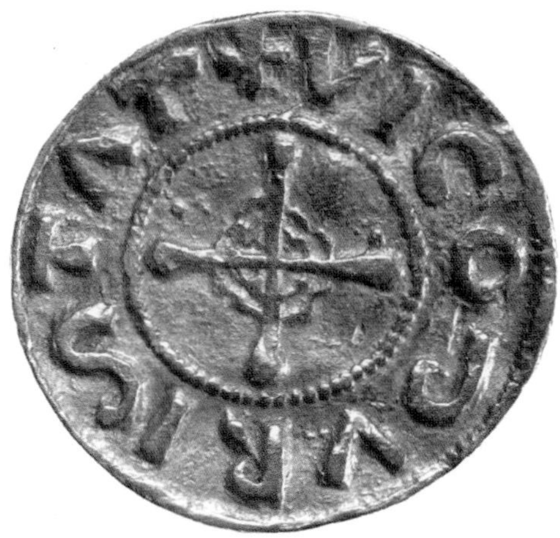

2.
Gold solidus from the reign of the Frankish Emperor Charlemagne (king of the Franks 759–814, emperor 800–814). The reverse of the coin bears the inscription VICO DURISTAT, revealing that it was minted at the trading settlement at Dorestad (modern Wijk bij Duurstede) in the Netherlands.
Gold. Diam. 2.05 cm
British Museum, London

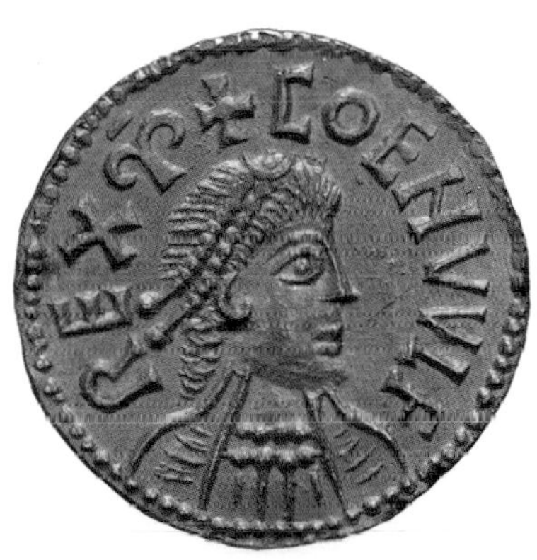

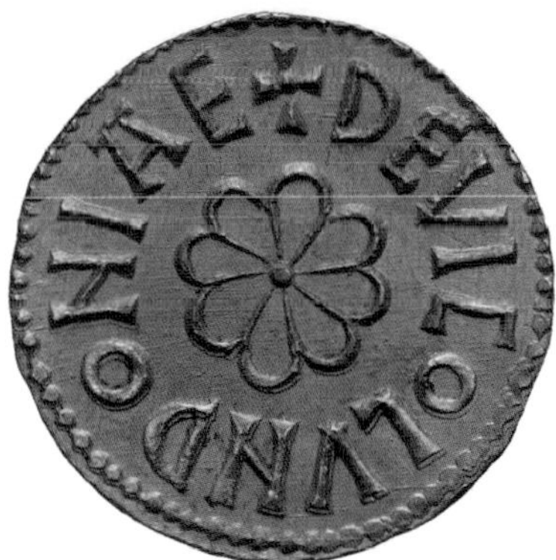

In England, Charlemagne's contemporary Coenwulf of Mercia (796–821) also celebrated London's status as a *wic* or *vicus*. This coin carries the caption IN VICO LVNDONIAE '[minted] in the trading centre of London'.
Gold. Diam. 2.0 cm
British Museum, London

places for either peaceful or violent purposes (see chapter 2)? Distinctions between raiding and trading are sometimes blurred, as in the case of the slave trade. Prisoners were acquired through raiding and sold on through trading, and there is no particular reason to doubt that the same people were responsible for both activities. If the origins of the word Viking do relate to *wics,* this sort of ambiguity may have led to the shift to the more violent meaning that the word certainly acquired in Old Norse.

Despite the emphasis on raiders and traders, the bulk of the population of Scandinavia was involved in farming, whether as landowners, free labourers or thralls (slaves), while others were engaged in a wide range of crafts and domestic activities. None of this can be described as 'Viking' activity according to any meaningful definition of Old English or Old Norse usage. Is it therefore appropriate to describe these people as Vikings, or even to describe the period as the Viking Age? This has been a recurrent question in Viking studies for decades. The fact that it is still necessary to ask it reflects both widespread recognition that the term is not entirely appropriate and the difficulty of devising a suitable alternative. For example, 'Late Iron-Age Scandinavia' is an accurate enough description of the Viking homelands from an archaeological perspective, but excludes the Viking expansion overseas and is unlikely ever to engage the popular imagination.

An alternative that has often been suggested is to use modern national labels of identity such as Danish, Norwegian and Swedish, but these are as misleading as the term 'Viking'. As discussed in more detail below (pp. 150–5), these kingdoms, and their identities, emerged comparatively late in the Viking Age, and the boundaries of these kingdoms at that point did not correspond to the modern borders. Before these larger kingdoms emerged all three were fragmented into smaller kingdoms, but the names and borders of these are often more obscure.

Western European sources tend most often to refer to Viking raiders as 'pagans' or 'heathens', emphasizing their non-Christian identity rather than any ethnic identity (fig. 3). Other terms, such as the Irish distinction between 'White Foreigners' and 'Black Foreigners', have sometimes been explained as a differentiation between Vikings of Norwegian and Danish origin respectively. However, this is an interpretation rather than established fact and only one of a number of possible options.[5] The term 'Danes' is also used, but this is particularly problematic. In some cases, as in Frankish annals of the eighth and ninth centuries, it refers to a specific kingdom of the Danes, which developed in the course of the Viking Age into the kingdom of Denmark, although its boundaries probably shifted on a number of occasions between the eighth and the eleventh century, and there are different opinions of exactly what areas formed 'Denmark' and the 'kingdom of the Danes' when they

3.
Thor's hammers are the most widespread surviving symbol of non-Christian Viking beliefs.

Pendant suspending three small hammers, symbols of the god Thor, probably 10th century. Fugledegård, north-west Zealand, Denmark.
Iron. L c. 3 cm
National Museum of Denmark, Copenhagen

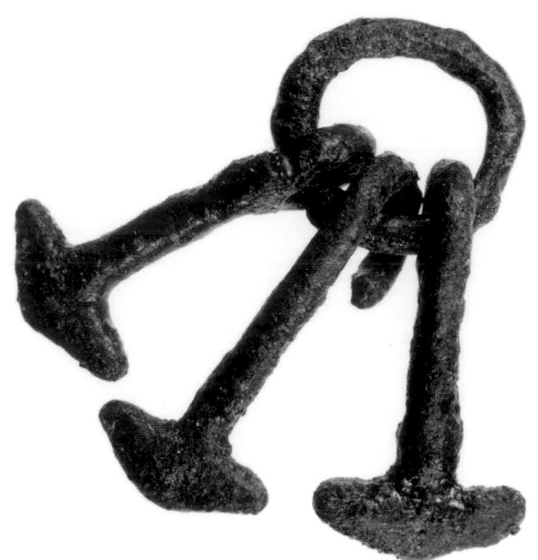

first appear in the historical sources. 'Dane' is also used in a more general sense in Frankish and Old English sources, with a meaning closer to modern 'Scandinavian', or perhaps 'western Scandinavian', and the term *dansk töngu* (Danish tongue or language) was used of Old Norse and Old Icelandic as well as Old Danish.[6] However, 'Danish' was used generically not just of language but of people. The same is true of various forms of the name 'Northmen', which sometimes apply specifically to people from what became the kingdom of Norway, sometimes (following the grant of the county of Rouen to Northmen in 911) to Normans, and sometimes more generally to Scandinavians, or to Scandinavian settlers in other areas. Frankish sources of the ninth century indicate that the people called 'Northmen' by the Franks called themselves 'Danes' and 'Svear', raising a wider issue of different names being applied to the same group.[7] Likewise, the name 'Rūs', which appears in a number of versions in both eastern and western sources, probably originated as the name of a people in Sweden (possibly a sub-group of the Svear, who gave their name to Sweden), but is used of the population of the Viking Age towns of Russia and Ukraine, including Scandinavians and Slavs (see pp. 53, 81–3), and more generically for Scandinavians.[8] One must also consider that Scandinavia was composed of many small kingdoms and peoples, and even after these were absorbed into the larger kingdoms of Denmark, Norway and Sweden, the inhabitants of, for example, Vestfold in southern Norway, may have continued to be identified by themselves and others as people of Vestfold, rather than as Norwegians.[9] The use of modern national labels has also encouraged in the past a narrowly ethnic interpretation of Viking-Age Scandinavia, ignoring the presence of other ethnic groups in Scandinavia at the time (see pp. 33–4), including Slavs (fig. 4) and Finno-Ugrians (peoples speaking a group of languages originating between the Baltic and the Urals, and today including among others Finns, Estonians and the Sámi of northern Scandinavia).

The fact that no alternative label is without its problems contributes to the continued use of 'Vikings' as a general term, and it is in this wider sense that the word is used in this book and the accompanying exhibition. This does not mean that all Vikings were the same. On the contrary, they were highly diverse in terms of their ethnic, political, cultural and religious identities, and our aim is to explore something of that diversity, rather than simply reflecting the features that the peoples of Scandinavia had in common. 'Vikings' in this sense thus implies no more than a convenient shorthand name for the inhabitants of Scandinavia, and of Scandinavian settlements overseas, in the period *c.* 800–1050, a period characterized at least in part by the Viking raids from which the Viking Age takes its name.

4.
Part of a silver hoard including Slavic-style jewellery discovered in Sweden, 11th century. Runsberga, Gårdslösa, Öland, Sweden.
Silver. Earrings W c. 4 cm
Statens Historiska Museum, Stockholm

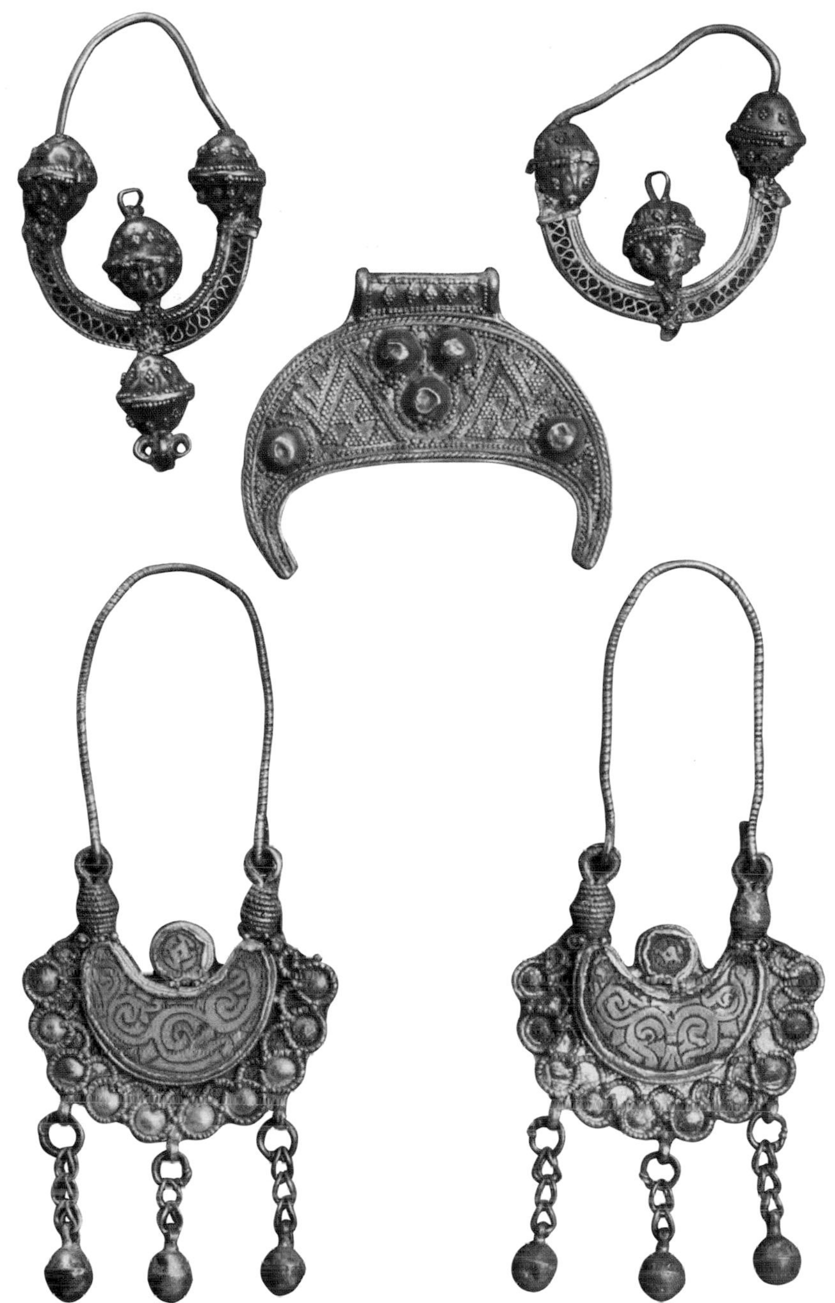

The Viking world

The word 'Viking' is immediately associated with northern Europe, and modern illustrations of the Viking Age tend to portray a Nordic stereotype, with Vikings typically tall and blonde. Although the origins of the word 'Viking' seem to refer to an activity rather than a specific people or ethnic group, the Viking stereotype reflects a fairly widespread view of the Vikings as representing a purely Scandinavian (or at least purely Germanic) native tradition, with shared roots across the Scandinavian countries of Denmark, Norway and Sweden, and with an external impact largely confined to northern Europe and the North Atlantic (fig. 5). This view has been particularly popular with nationalists, taking its most extreme form in the appropriation of Viking imagery and

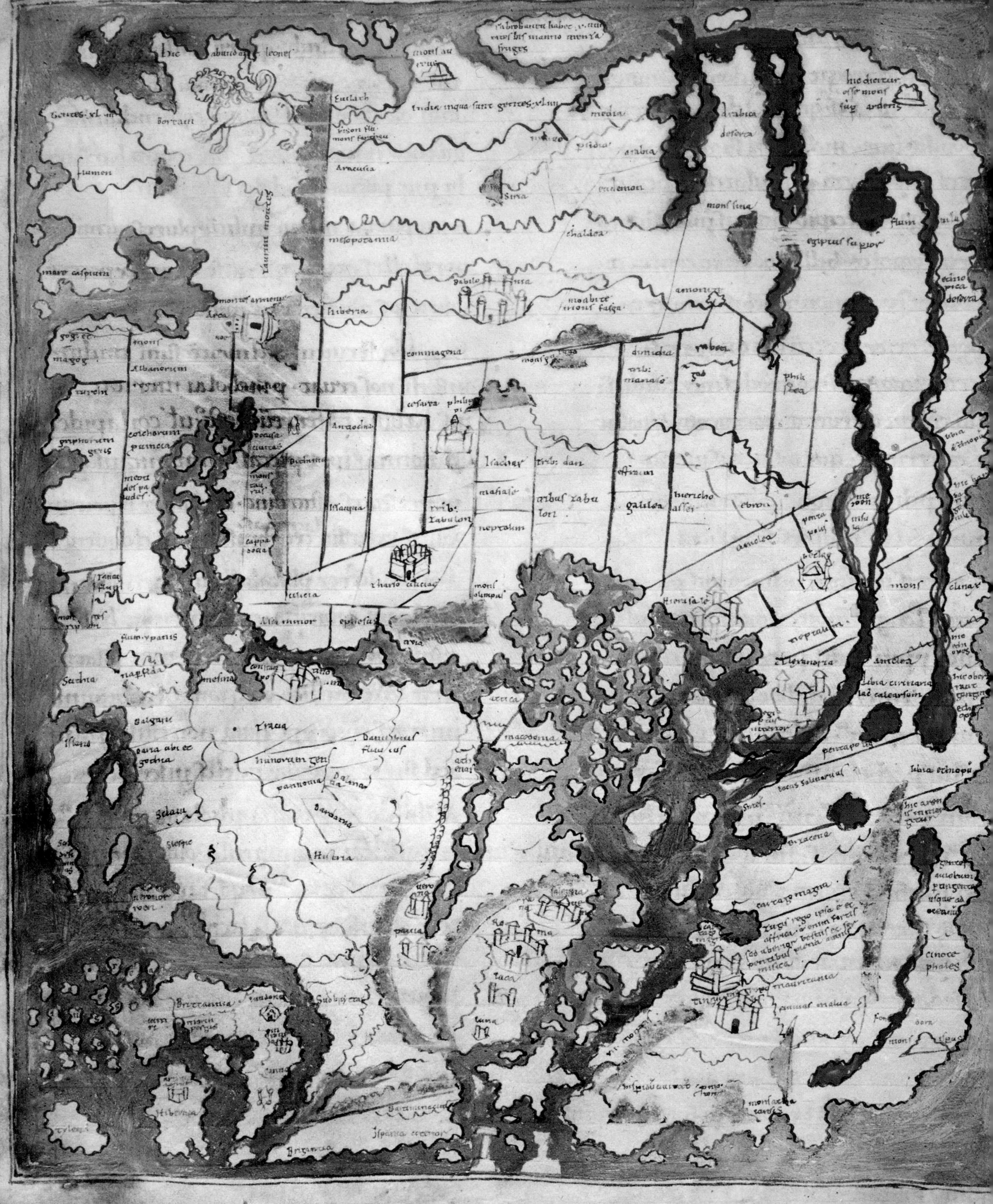

India in qua sunt gentes .xliiii.
media
arabia
Siria
chaldea
mesopotamia
mare caspium
mons sina
egiptus superior
hiberia
commagena
Antiochia
Isauria
cappadocia
cilicia
Asia minor
ephesus
galilea
Hierusalem
Alexandria
pentapolis
Tracia
Danubius fluvius
pannonia
Barbaria
Histria
macedonia
Roma
cartago magna
mauritania
cinocephales
Brittannia
Hibernia
Ispania citerior

5.
This map represents a view of the known world as it was understood in Britain in the first half of the 11th century. East is 'up'. The Scandinavian peninsula appears as an island near the bottom left-hand corner, labelled 'Thule', and the Jutland peninsula of Denmark is clearly visible below and to the right.

Anglo-Saxon world map, 1025–50. Probably from Canterbury, England.
Pigment on vellum. L 26 cm, W 21.5 cm
British Library, London

6.
Oval brooches of Scandinavian type from a female burial, second half of the 10th century. Grave 124, Kiev, Ukraine.
Copper alloy. L 11 cm
State Historical Museum, Moscow

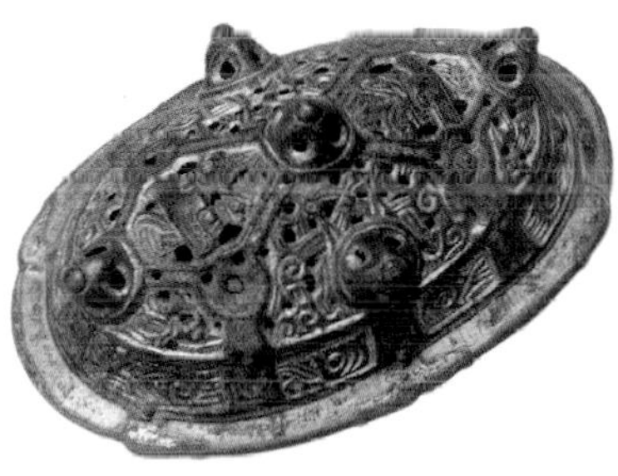

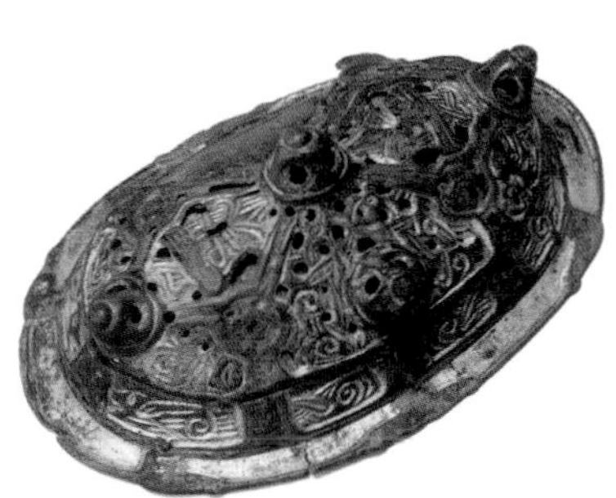

Nordic mythology as part of the image of pan-Germanic Aryan purity and supremacy promoted in Nazi Germany.[10] Elsewhere, the Viking past has sometimes been denied equally vigorously. Under the Soviet Union, an emphasis on Scandinavian influence on the early formation of states in Russia and Ukraine was seen as undermining the accepted view of the purely Slavic origins of city states such as Novgorod and Kiev, and the so-called 'Normannist' interpretation met with official disapproval (fig. 6). Meaningful academic dialogue on the subject across the Iron Curtain was difficult in any case, and understanding was also hampered by the range of different languages in which scholarly literature was published.[11]

Interpretation of the past is inevitably informed by the character of the society making the interpretation, and the academic view of the Viking phenomenon since the late twentieth century has been less narrow for a number of reasons. While opinion may remain divided as to just how far cultural diversity within any given society is a good thing, people have become used to the idea that society can be ethnically and culturally diverse across even a relatively small geographical area. The fact that such diversity is nothing new is demonstrated clearly by the science of historical DNA studies.[12] At the same time, the expansion of email and the internet, combined with the removal of some of the former political restrictions on international scholarship, means that the exchange of information and ideas, and indeed the loan of museum objects, across the whole of the Viking world is easier than ever before. Finally, recent decades have seen a wealth of new discoveries, both in Scandinavia and elsewhere, which point beyond any possible doubt to interaction between the Viking homelands and their neighbours, near and far.

Like most other defined periods in archaeology or history, the Viking Age was a period not of stasis, but of development and transition. This is visible in many different ways, both internally and externally. A large number of small local kingdoms emerged across the period into the forerunners of the modern kingdoms of Denmark, Norway and Sweden, and new systems of kingship and administration were adopted to support these larger kingdoms. Long-distance trading routes were established and, as a response to trade, Scandinavia saw the adoption of urban settlement and monetary economics (figs 7–9). A variety of different local belief systems were replaced, at least in terms of the formal position adopted by various rulers, by the unifying force of Christianity. Migration from Scandinavia led to settlement across many areas from Russia to North America whether through conquest or more peacefully. In some cases this led to lasting connections, in others it did not, but in almost all it left a legacy of some sort, whether linguistic, cultural or archaeological. Even in areas where Viking impact was minimal, and in some instances limited to the more negative aspects of raiding and plunder, the peoples of Scandinavia who previously had been unknown or at best largely ignored, started to enter the consciousness of their neighbours. As a result, there are surviving accounts of the Vikings from a range of different perspectives.

These accounts and a constantly growing body of archaeological evidence mean that it is possible to look at the Vikings in a more global perspective. Scholars may remain divided on exactly how to analyse the evidence and in areas of Viking settlement it is possible to put forward a variety of models. These include not just the extreme positions of mass migration and genocide at one end and small elites ruling subjected populations of another race at the other, but a number of more nuanced understandings of interaction, influence and coexistence. However, whichever interpretation is followed (and the same need not necessarily apply to all parts of the Viking world), there is no denying the existence of the evidence itself, which points both to an increased Viking influence in varying degrees across the greater Viking world, and to external influences entering Scandinavia from many directions that between them contributed to the developments noted above.

Weights, often highly decorative, were used in trade and exchange.

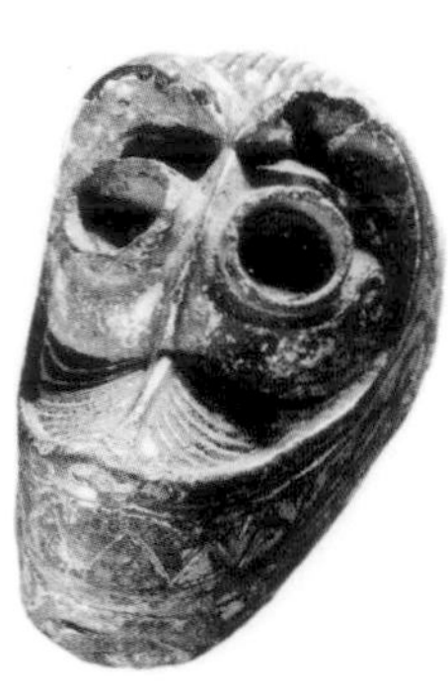

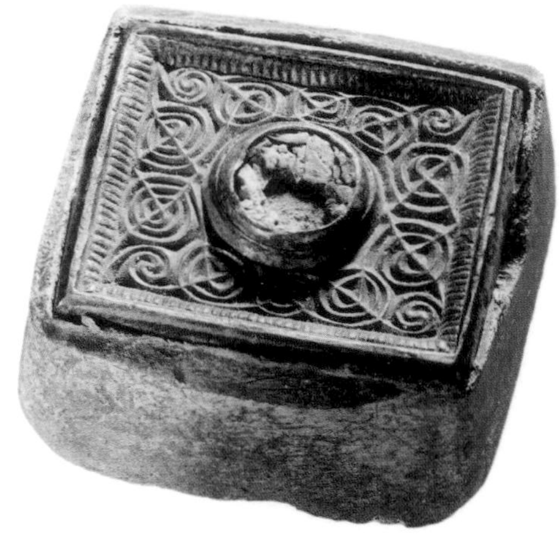

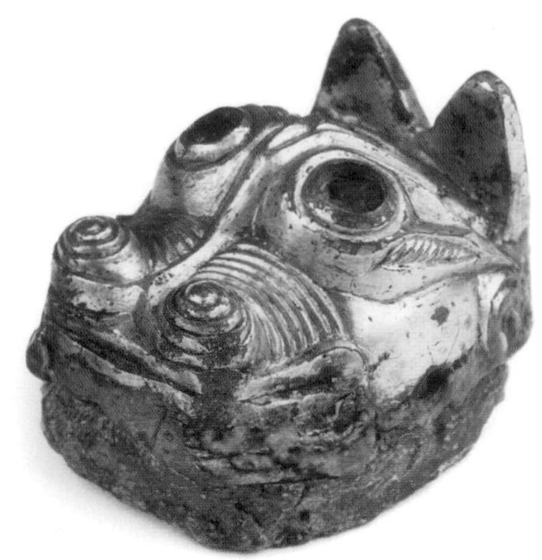

Viking weights made in England or Ireland, incorporating local metalwork.

7. (above left)
Animal head weight, late 9th century. Berg, Buskerud, Norway.
Lead, gold, silver, gilt copper alloy.
L 3.4 cm, H 1.6 cm
National Museum of Denmark, Copenhagen

8. (above centre)
Lead weight with precious metal inset, late 9th century. Berg, Buskerud, Norway.
Lead, gold, silver, gilt copper alloy.
L 4 cm, W 3.5 cm
National Museum of Denmark, Copenhagen

9. (above right)
Animal head weight, 9th century. Kilmainham-Islandbridge, Dublin, Ireland.
Lead, gilt copper alloy. L 3.28 cm, W 2.53 cm, H 2.24 cm
National Museum of Ireland, Dublin

Understanding the Vikings

Knowledge and understanding of the Viking Age is based on a variety of forms of evidence, which differ in quality and quantity due to cultural traditions and states of preservation. Literacy in Scandinavia was largely limited to the runic alphabet and was typically used for relatively short inscriptions. These include monumental stones, but also personal names scratched on individual items, graffiti and charms (as runes were linked with magic, as well as providing a functional alphabet).[13] Finds from the twelfth and thirteenth centuries from Bergen in Norway indicate that by that time runic literacy was widespread and applied to all sorts of everyday matters.[14] Runic inscriptions on scraps of wood served a number of functions, including short letters and notes, effectively the emails and post-it notes of the day (figs 10–11). While it is possible that runes were being used in the same way in the Viking Age, there is currently no evidence to suggest this. The surviving runic inscriptions from the Viking Age nevertheless provide fascinating snippets of information on a range of subjects, including some major historical events (see pp. 158–9), as well as direct evidence of Viking travels to distant places such as *Grikland* (land of the Greeks, i.e. the Byzantine empire), *Serkland* (land of the Saracens, i.e. anywhere in the Islamic Caliphate and probably other areas around the Caucasus and eastern Russia too) and England, which in the Viking Age might have seemed equally exotic in eastern Sweden. Despite these details, the rune-stones do not give a narrative history of the Viking Age from within Scandinavia.

Such a narrative is provided by the sagas, written texts in Old Norse (mostly compiled in Iceland but occasionally also in Norway), and by a few 'histories' in Latin, from both Denmark and Norway. In many cases, these probably genuinely preserve elements of historical fact, but all of the surviving examples date from the late twelfth century or after, well beyond the Viking Age.[15] Quite apart from obvious anachronisms, the insertion of fabulous events into otherwise apparently historical accounts and the desire of the authors or compilers to tell a good story, to reflect specific cultural or political agendas, and, in some instances, to include well-established patterns and motifs, there is a fundamental problem in guessing how far actual historical information may have been preserved. To what extent the events became distorted between the time of their happening and their description in the sagas written several generations later is hard to define (fig. 12). Sagas thus cannot be accepted as reliable historical evidence for the Viking Age (they become more useful for later periods), but neither can they be completely ignored. Contained within many of the

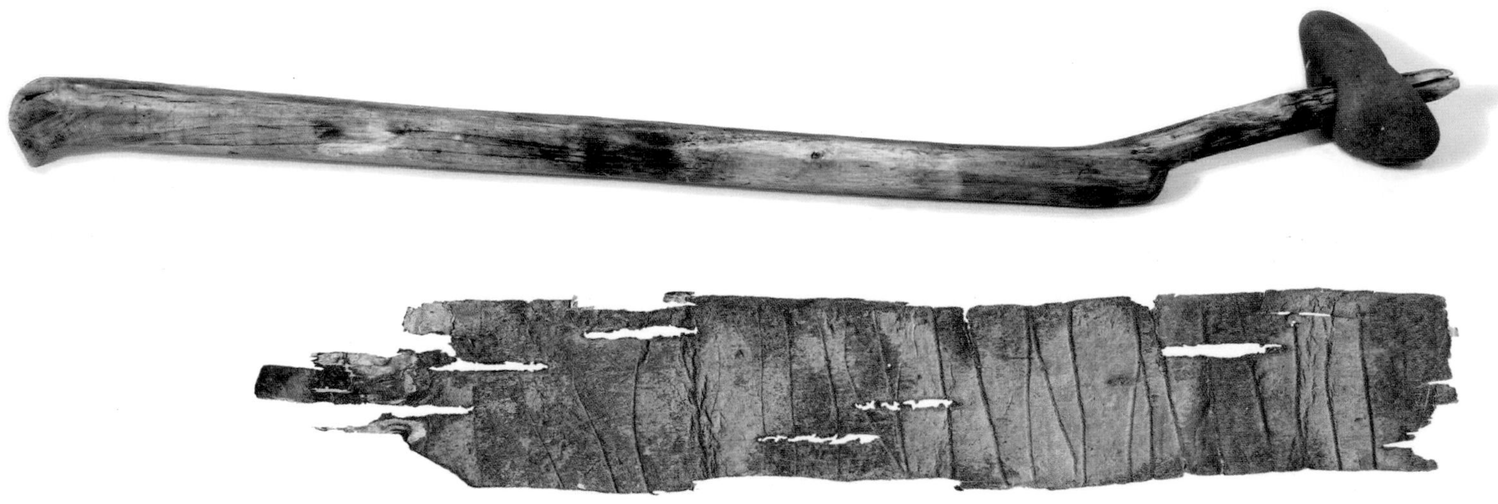

10.
This stick was found with the warship Roskilde 6. It has a piece of flint inserted into one end and a bird's head carved at the other. It also carries a runic inscription, part of which reads. 'Sakse carved these runes'. The purpose of the stick is unclear, but it may have had some kind of magical significance.

Carved stick with stone head, 1050–1100. Roskilde harbour, Zealand, Denmark.
Wood, stone. L 46 cm
Roskilde Museum, Roskilde

11.
This inscription on birch bark comes from Smolensk in Russia. The words loosely translate as 'Visgeirr took this plot [of land]', perhaps referring to the foundation of a Scandinavian trading centre in Smolensk.

Runic letter on birch bark, 12th century. Smolensk, Russia.
Bark. L 13.2 cm
State Historical Museum, Moscow

sagas are poems in the style known as skaldic verse, usually attributed to specific skalds, or poets, who were often eyewitnesses, or at least contemporaries, of the events described in the poems. The rigid structures of metre and alliteration within verse forms mean that individual words could not be altered without changing the structure of the poem, and such poems, learned by rote, are therefore more likely than free prose to have been passed down by oral tradition unmodified over two or three centuries. The meaning of skaldic verse is often somewhat obscure, since it typically describes events partly through a combination of metaphors and references to Nordic mythology. Nevertheless skaldic poems provide important accounts of a number of historical events, as well as a mine of information for language and terminology relating to a wide range of objects and activities.[16]

More in the way of contemporary evidence can be derived from some of the societies with whom the Vikings came into contact. Although the natives of North America and the Vikings' neighbours around the Baltic and in Russia were no more literate than the Vikings themselves, the Christian kingdoms of Europe all had educated churchmen (while the majority of the population were unable to read), and literacy was more widespread in the Byzantine empire and across the Islamic world. Written accounts survive from all these areas and these provide the historical framework for our understanding of the Viking Age. Annals and chronicles record major events and their dates, sometimes in detail but more often very briefly, while mention of the Vikings can also be found in letters, sermons and accounts of the lives of kings and saints. They also feature in geographical compilations, such as a text inserted into an Old English translation, assembled at the court of Alfred the Great, king of the West Saxons (871–99), of the *History against the Pagans* by the Roman author Orosius. The original Latin text contains a description of the geography of Europe, and this has been supplemented by the addition of journeys in Norway and Denmark by Ohthere (*Óttarr* in Old Norse), a chieftain from arctic Norway, and across the southern coast of the Baltic by someone with the Anglo-Saxon name of Wulfstan.[17] There are also several references to the Vikings, both in Scandinavia and abroad, in the works of geographers from the Islamic world (see pp. 70–1). Contemporary sources from both east and west offer valuable insights into the Vikings, but even so they must be used with caution, as their descriptions may be coloured by religious and political agendas, or simply by imperfect knowledge, as well as on occasion by deliberate borrowings from earlier literature.

Another important source of evidence, both inside and outside Scandinavia, is archaeology (fig. 13). The material remains of the Vikings include entire settlement sites (including towns, fortresses, farms and estate centres), individual buildings and structures,

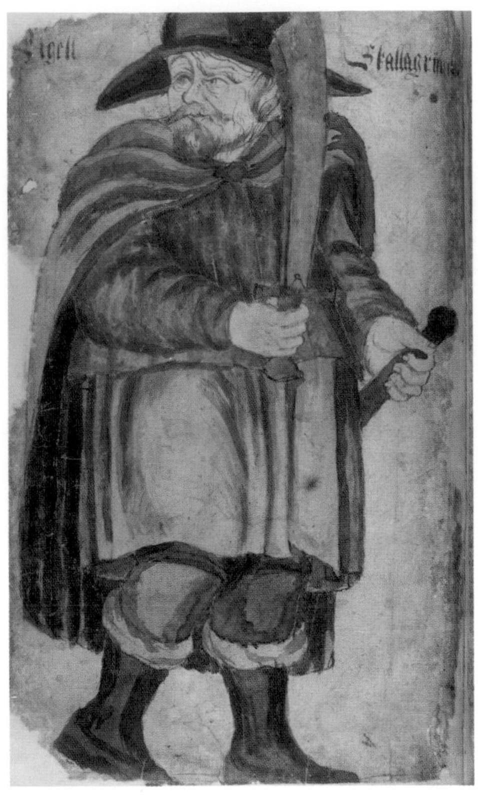

12.
According to the later medieval saga of his life, Egil Skallagrimsson was both a ferocious Viking warrior and a gifted skald. Having killed the son of King Erik Bloodaxe and been sentenced to death for the crime, the saga tells that Egil won his life and freedom by composing an exceptionally fine poem in praise of the king.

Egil Skallagrimsson, as depicted in an Icelandic manuscript, 1600s, Iceland.
Árni Magnússon Institute, Reykjavík

ships and other forms of transport, and a wide variety of tools, weapons, trade goods, household items, personal ornaments and even items of clothing and shoes. The state of preservation varies considerably, depending on the original materials and the environment in which they were preserved, but archaeological remains allow us to trace Viking-Age occupation and activity, as well as internal and external cultural contacts, even when the historical record is too thin to provide much information. Furthermore, archaeology is constantly supplying new information. Fresh excavations are taking place all the time, whether purely for research or ahead of building developments, and, in addition to traditional excavation, the systematic recording of metal-detected finds in Denmark and England in particular has resulted in a massive expansion of certain types of material, such as silver hoards, base-metal personal ornaments and dress-fittings.[18] Refinements in archaeological techniques have also permitted the re-interpretation of existing material, either through re-excavation of established Viking sites, through the application of improved dating techniques, or through comparisons with new material. Thus archeology is constantly changing our interpretation and understanding of the Viking Age.

Numismatics (the study of coins) spans history and archaeology, as coins are both historical texts (if short ones) and archaeological objects. The fact that coins combine inscriptions and iconography, and also carry information about the issuing authorities, means that they are a valuable source of information about political, religious and cultural identities in the time and place that they were issued. As archaeological objects, they provide a useful index of the movement of wealth, whether through raiding or trading. Like other archaeological objects, coins are appearing all the time, which is rare for historical texts, and can thus provide a source of new historical information (fig. 14).

The Viking expansion overseas can also be traced through less tangible sources, including language and place names. Unsurprisingly, Viking settlers took their language with them when they travelled and this is visible to varying degrees in different places. In areas in which all or most of the population was of Scandinavian origin, and which were comparatively little exposed to later settlement from other areas, the Old Norse language dominated and has to a great extent survived. Modern Icelandic and Faroese are closer in many ways to their Old Norse origin than modern Norwegian. In other areas with more mixed populations, the influence of Old Norse is limited and takes the form of loan-words into other languages. These include words that have entered the language as a whole

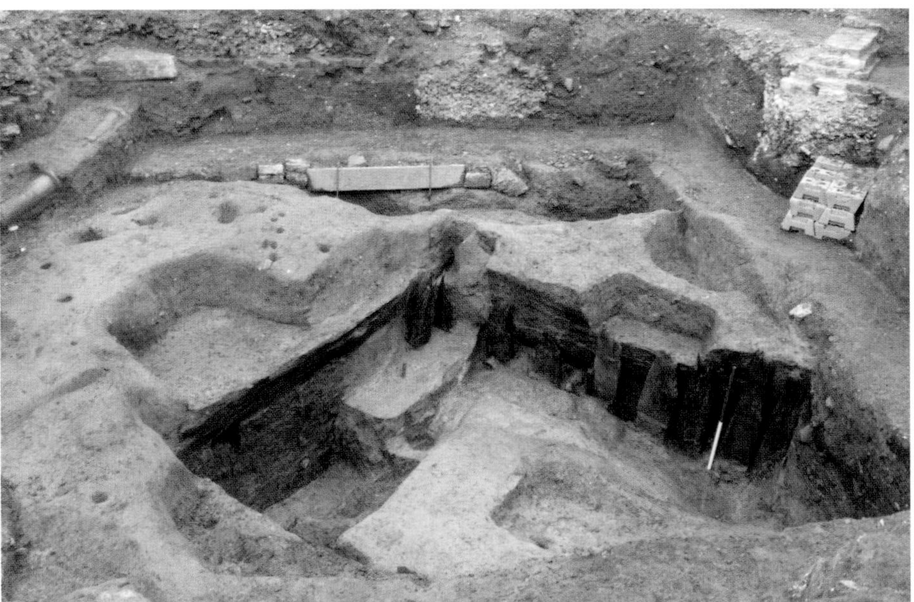

13.
Recent excavations at Hungate in York, England. The Hungate excavations took place between 2007 and 2012 and uncovered a Viking street, including a building constructed from reused ship timbers.

(e.g. 'egg', 'sister' and 'window' in modern English) and those that appear as dialect words in areas with higher concentrations of Viking settlement (e.g. 'fell' for 'hill', and 'beck' for 'stream' in northern England). These influences are apparent not just in spoken language, but in place names. In some areas, such as Shetland (where Norse has had a strong influence on dialect), almost all of the place names are of Old Norse origin, indicating a very heavy level of Viking settlement. In others, including parts of western Scotland, much of northern and eastern England, and Normandy, Old Norse elements appear alongside other local languages, while in others, such as Russia, the very small number of Scandinavian place names points to a much more limited scale of Viking settlement.[19]

14.
In Britain, Viking conquerors assimilated Christian ideas remarkably quickly. This coin was issued a generation after Edmund, the last English king of East Anglia, was martyred by Vikings in 870.

Silver penny commemorating St Edmund, issued by the Scandinavian rulers of East Anglia, *c.* 895–910. Cuerdale, Lancashire, England.
Silver. Diam. 1.9 cm
British Museum, London

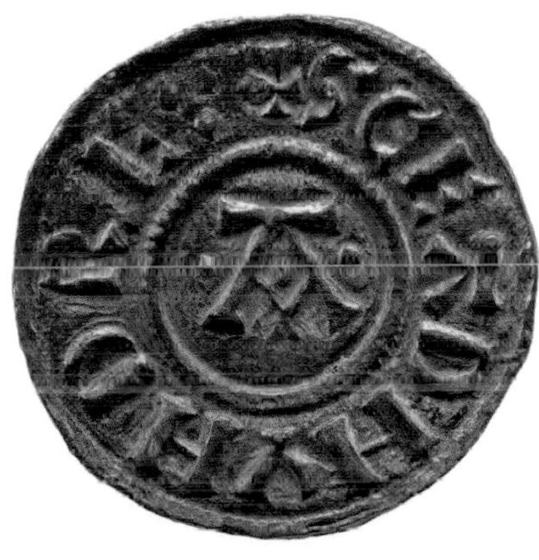

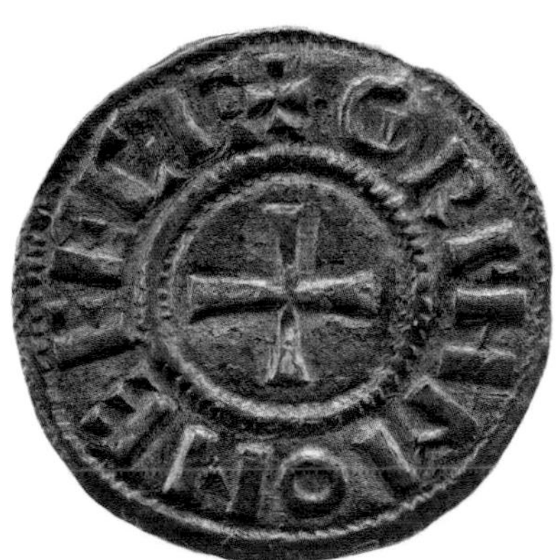

The end of the Viking Age

There is no absolute end date for the Viking Age, but by the mid-eleventh century, a number of fundamental changes had taken place in Scandinavian society. The kingdoms of Denmark, Norway and Sweden had emerged in place of the many smaller nations that existed at the beginning of the Viking Age, and Christianity had been established by the rulers of all three. The westward expansion across the North Atlantic had reached its full extent with the settlement of Greenland and the failure of the settlement of Vinland in North America (see p. 43), while links with the Islamic Caliphate, which dominated the eastern trade, had been disrupted by the Khazars (see pp. 48–9). Even the raiding for which the Vikings are so infamous seems to have been scaled down after this period, although it did not disappear altogether.

From an English perspective, the year 1066 makes a convenient cut-off point. Harald Hardruler of Norway (1046–1066) had certainly been a Viking in his youth, and his invasion of the north of England – culminating in his defeat and death at Stamford Bridge near York – is often seen in the same light as earlier raids on England, although this attack should perhaps be seen more in terms of 'national' warfare than Viking raiding. At the same time, William the Conqueror (1066–87) was descended from the 'Northmen' who gave their name to Normandy. His fleet, as portrayed on the Bayeux Tapestry, was made up of recognizably 'Viking' ships, and his army at Hastings was a loose coalition of allies and adventurers in addition to his own Norman followers, much like the forces with which the Danish Svein Forkbeard and Cnut had conquered England half a century before.

None of these points are as simple as indicated above. Centralized royal power in Sweden collapsed in the mid-eleventh century, and with it the official status of Christianity. Even in other areas where Christianity was the 'official' religion promoted by rulers, this did not mean that all other religions had disappeared completely by this time. Occasional trips to North America seem to have continued later into the Middle Ages, while contacts with the east were preserved through political ties with the emerging Russian state and through Scandinavians continuing to serve in the Byzantine army. The events of 1066 were momentous for England, but had less direct impact elsewhere, with the Western Isles of Scotland remaining under Norwegian rule until 1266, and the Northern Isles until 1468–9. Even in England, Harald's attack in 1066 was not the last Scandinavian raid, with assaults by Svein Estrithsson of Denmark (1047–74) in 1069 and 1072, while Harald's grandson Magnus Barelegs of Norway (1095–1103) raided repeatedly in Ireland, Scotland and around the Irish Sea.

By 1050 (or 1066) Scandinavia had been altered significantly by the external contacts established during the Viking Age, and while the heyday of Scandinavian influence overseas was over by this time the legacy of the Vikings is evident in many areas across the wide reaches of the Viking world.

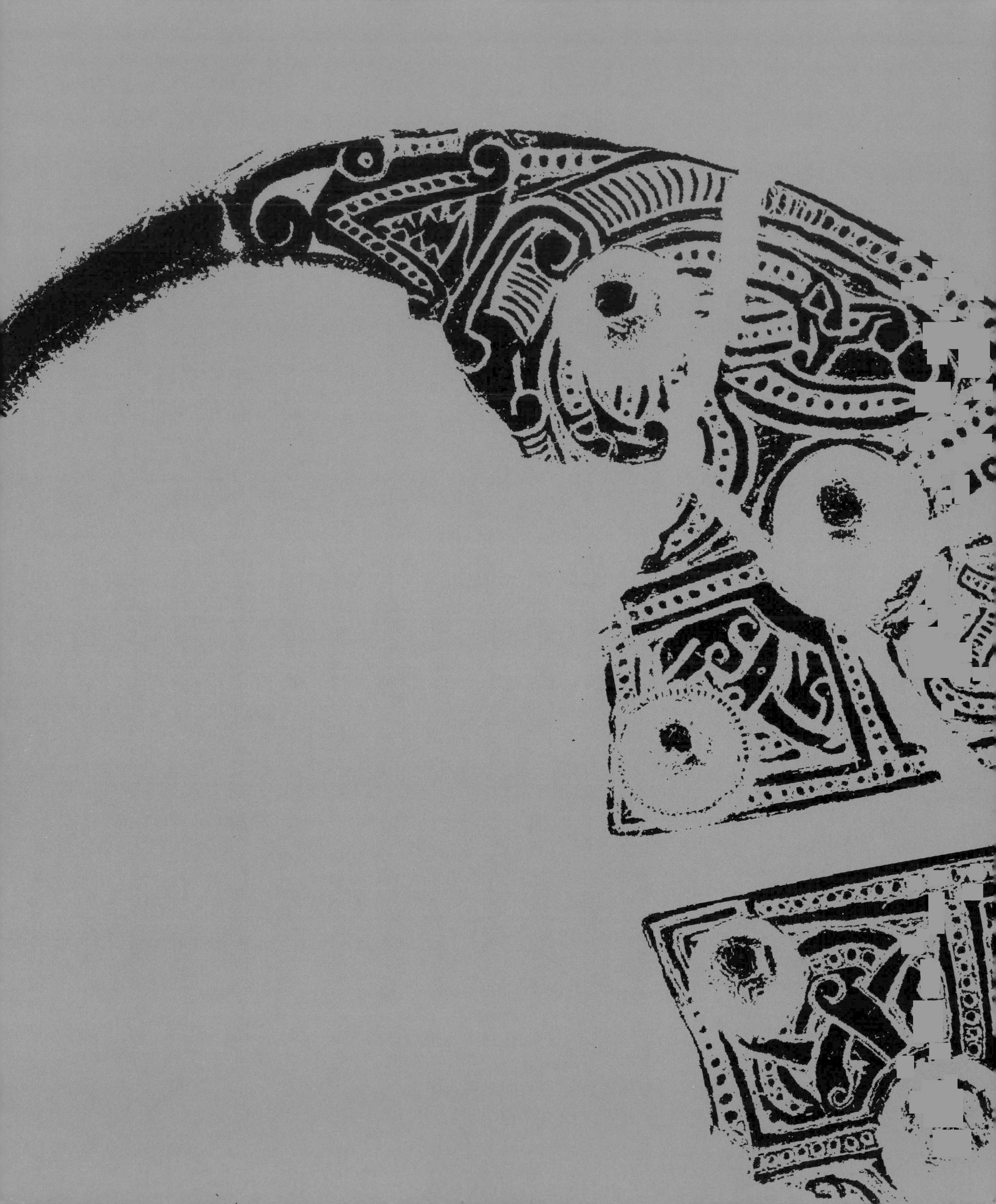

1

CONTACTS & EXCHANGE

Sunhild Kleingärtner & Gareth Williams

Ohthere said that the district in which he lived is called Hålogaland. He said that no one lived to the north of it. Then there is a port in the southern part of the land which is called Sciringes healh. To this he said that it was not possible to sail in one month, if one camped at night and each day had a favourable wind…

OHTHERE'S VOYAGE (*c.* 890)

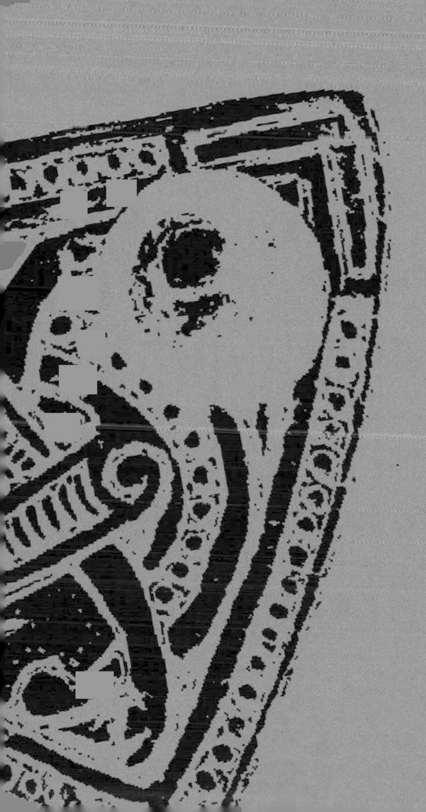

CONTACTS & EXCHANGE

ONE OF THE MOST REMARKABLE THINGS about the Viking Age is the scale of the world the Vikings inhabited and the diversity of the peoples with whom they came into contact. The period from the late eighth to the early eleventh centuries saw a physical expansion of the Viking world beyond Scandinavia in the form of trade, raiding and conquest, and peaceful settlement, and with it a much greater degree of contact and interaction with the different cultures that inhabited the lands that the Vikings visited and in some cases occupied. This expansion started from a number of small kingdoms and would develop in the course of the period into the forerunners of the modern countries of Denmark, Norway and Sweden. The effects of the expansion were felt most strongly in the surrounding areas: around the Baltic to the east, and around the North Sea and adjoining areas in the west. However, the Viking phenomenon was not limited to northern Europe. While Scandinavia may be seen as peripheral to other great cultures – for example, lying beyond the boundaries of the Roman empire – the Viking Age saw the development of a network of contacts spanning four continents, from Central Asia in the east to Greenland

1.
This slate appears to have been used to practise stone carving techniques. The type of decoration is purely Scandinavian (the 'Urnes' style), but the object was found (and probably made) in Ireland. It demonstrates that artistic fashions, as well as people and goods, travelled widely in the Viking Age. Late 10th or early 11th century. Killaloe, Co. Clare, Ireland.
Stone. L 8.9 cm, W 7.7 cm
British Museum, London

and North America in the west, from the Arctic Circle in the north to the Mediterranean coast of Africa in the south.

The peoples of the Viking homelands were themselves more culturally and ethnically diverse than is often realized, but the combination of raiding, trading, conquest and settlement that characterized the Viking Age brought them into contact with radically different peoples in other parts of the wider Viking world. These contacts resulted in economic exchange, including both raiding and trading, and a variety of social exchanges, including alliances, gift-giving, political marriages, and even the acceptance of Viking rulers as godsons by Christian kings such as the Frankish emperor Louis the Pious (814–40) and Alfred the Great of Wessex (871–99).[1] Such exchanges had a direct influence on many aspects of Scandinavian society, while the same period also saw an unprecedented degree of Scandinavian influence elsewhere. This interaction with outsiders took place not only as a result of the Viking expansion, but also because foreigners from different areas visited the Viking homelands. These visitors included traders, migrants, missionaries and diplomats, while attacks from neighbouring areas remind us that Scandinavians were not always the aggressors in a time when violence was still very much a standard tool of international politics.

The nature and the significance of contact and interaction with other peoples varied considerably across the extended Viking world and chronologically within the period (fig. 1). These contacts developed for a range of reasons. These included long-term interaction and change, such as the gradual adoption of Christianity across much of Scandinavia, and of first bullion-based then coin-based economies and temporary adjustments and experiments, such as the establishment of Viking kingdoms in England in the late ninth to mid-tenth centuries, or the very short-lived and unsuccessful settlement of the North American mainland around 1000. Whether or not making contact with others led to cultural interaction depended on a variety of factors, including the time and space within which the meeting took place, the attitudes of the cultures involved, their relative degree of technical sophistication, and the nature of the contacts, not least whether these were peaceful or violent. The form of the interaction was also conditioned by the physical environment in which it took place, with drastically different geographical and climatic situations around the Viking world. This chapter provides an introduction to the Viking world and the reach of their network of contacts. It also explores some of the forms of interaction and exchange that took place with other cultures.

The Viking homelands

The Scandinavian homelands were themselves diverse: geographically, politically, economically and culturally. This diversity was to some extent dictated by the landscape. Although the whole of Scandinavia can be considered to be part of northern Europe, the massive peninsula that forms most of modern Norway and Sweden extends for a total of 1880 km from the northern tip of Norway to the southernmost tip of Sweden. The northern parts of this land mass fall within the Arctic Circle, but this accounts for only a relatively small proportion of Norway and Sweden, with a milder climate in the south. Denmark, further south, is milder still (fig. 2).

A line of mountains known as the 'Keel' runs down the middle of the Scandinavian peninsula, dividing the bulk of Norway to the west from the Oslo Fjord and Sweden to the east. On the west of the Keel, the mountains in many places extend close to the sea, with fjords (inlets from the sea) dividing different ranges of mountains and only a relatively narrow strip of habitable land next to the coast and on the sides of the fjords. A series of

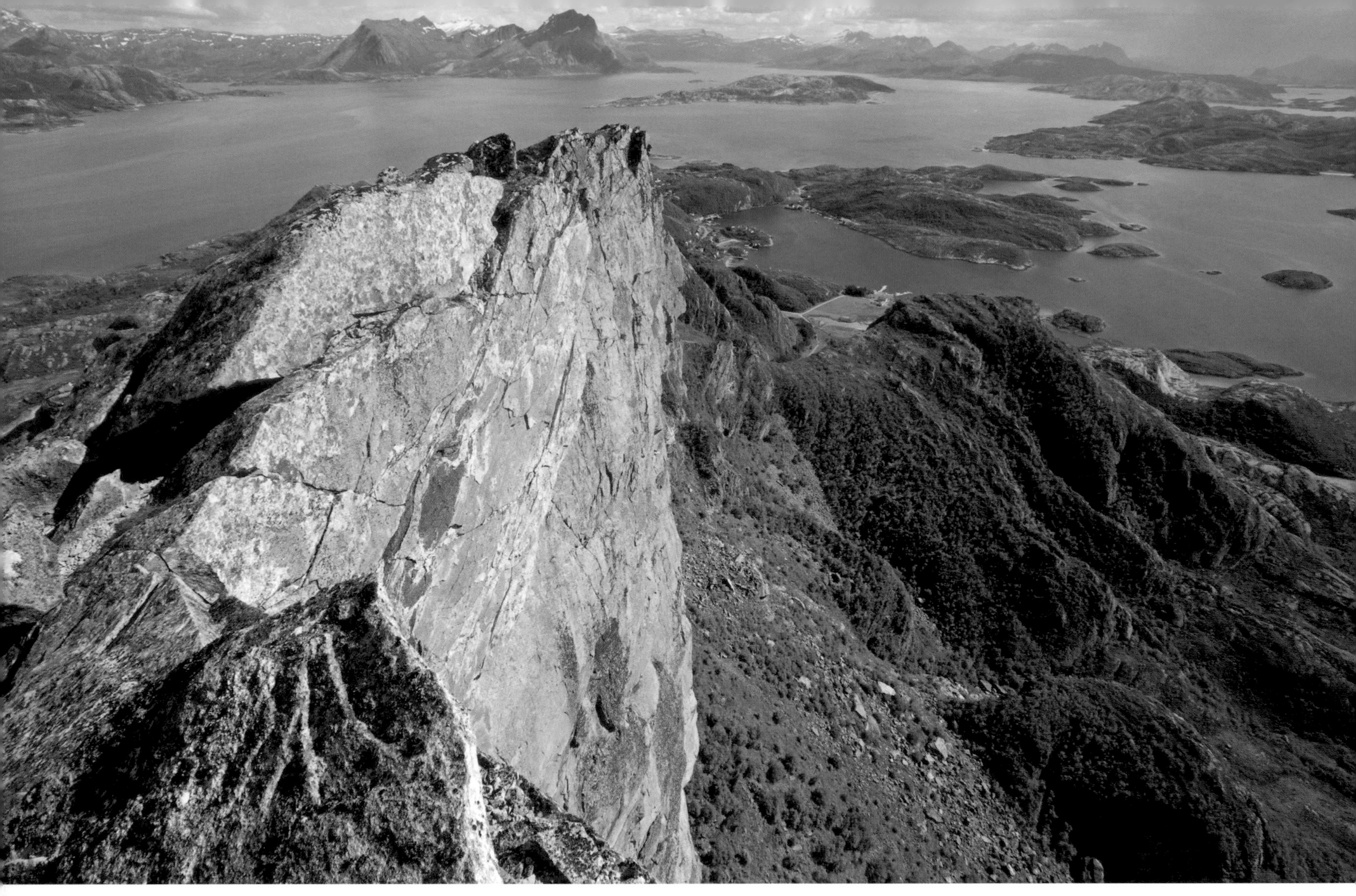

2.
The fractured geography of Norway's western coastline creates natural harbours and sheltered inlets ('fjords') that were perfectly suited to the development of a maritime culture. Helgeland, Nordland, Norway.

islands lie off the west coast and these provide a protected sailing route along some stretches of the coast. It is this coastal sailing route, the 'northern way', which gives us the name of Norway. The mountains were not completely impassable – skis, skates and sledges were all known in the Viking Age – but they provided a natural division of the landscape into distinct communities. As with the other Scandinavian kingdoms, Norway was unified only towards the end of the Viking Age (see pp. 150–5), and at the beginning of the period was divided into several smaller kingdoms.[2] Within these, local chieftains might exercise virtually complete independent rule.

East of the Keel, eastern Norway and Sweden are less mountainous, but nevertheless fragmented. Another range of mountains extends down the spine of the southern part of Sweden, and while Sweden lacks the mountainous fjords of western Norway, smaller fjords, rivers and lakes divide the landscape, and large tracts of forest again meant that the population was split into a series of separate communities rather than distributed across the whole country. For much of the Viking Age, the population was primarily comprised of two peoples: the Svear in the east (whose name is preserved in the name Sweden), based in Uppland and around the Mälar Valley, and the Götar in the south (whose name is preserved in modern Gothenberg), although these were in two separate groups in the east and the west. Two other distinct populations were found off the Swedish coast on the islands of Öland and Gotland. As in Norway, these groups largely reflect geographical fragmentation rather than fundamental cultural differences, although some regional variations can be

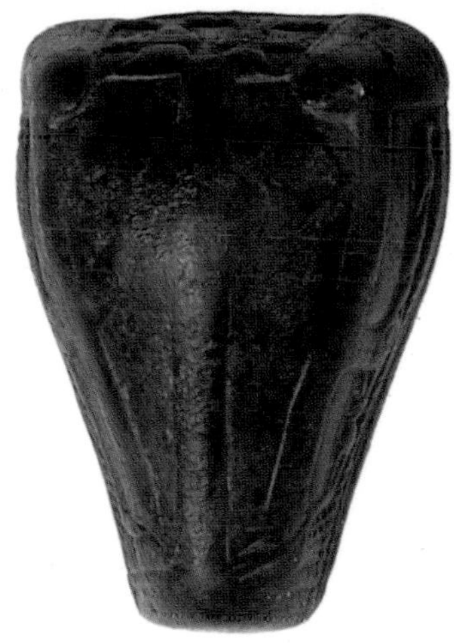

3.
One of a pair of animal-head brooches from a female burial, characteristic of Gotlandic female dress. Grave 218A, Ire, Hellvi, Gotland.
Copper alloy
Gotlands Museum, Visby

observed, such as the taste in Gotland for small brooches shaped like animal heads as an essential part of female dress (fig. 3), rather than the larger oval brooches found elsewhere in female graves across the Viking world (see p. 64).

Denmark lacks the mountains of northern Scandinavia but is broken up by natural borders (fig. 4). The Jutland peninsula is connected to mainland Europe by a narrow neck of land, with a river to the east and a bog to the west. The gap between was blocked even before the beginning of the Viking Age (although we do not know how effectively) by the large defensive structure known as the Danevirke, which combined wooden palisades with earth ramparts and ditches along a distance of around 30 kilometres. However, Jutland is only a relatively small part of Denmark, with the rest formed of islands of various sizes. Some of these certainly had distinct identities, such as Bornholm, believed to be the territory of the Burgendes, from the late ninth century.[3] Kings of the 'Danes' are recorded from before the Viking Age, but it is seldom clear what this meant in terms of territory before the mid-tenth century. Modern Denmark may or may not have been fully unified earlier than this, and at times Danish rulers exercised authority in Vestfold on the western side of the Oslo Fjord in southern Norway. In the later Viking Age Danish kings certainly controlled parts of what is now southern Sweden fairly continuously, and rulers such as Harald Bluetooth (*c.* 958–85) and Cnut the Great (1016–35) could claim authority over the whole of Norway and, in the latter case, possibly briefly also over Sweden.

The language used to describe different peoples and areas both by contemporary writers and modern scholars can be confusing. It is possible to draw clear distinctions between Danes, Norwegians and Swedes in terms of political identities, and these identities were beginning to emerge as early as the ninth century, but people across all three modern countries spoke variants of the 'Danish tongue', even though this was already dividing into separate languages and dialects. Contemporary accounts written outside Scandinavia may refer to 'Danes' or 'Northmen' (among other less flattering terms such as 'heathens' and 'pirates'), but it is not always clear that these terms were intended to convey ethnic or cultural differences.[4]

The population of Scandinavia in this period was not exclusively Nordic, or 'Danish'-speaking, but included a number of peoples speaking Finno-Ugrian languages (see p. 20).

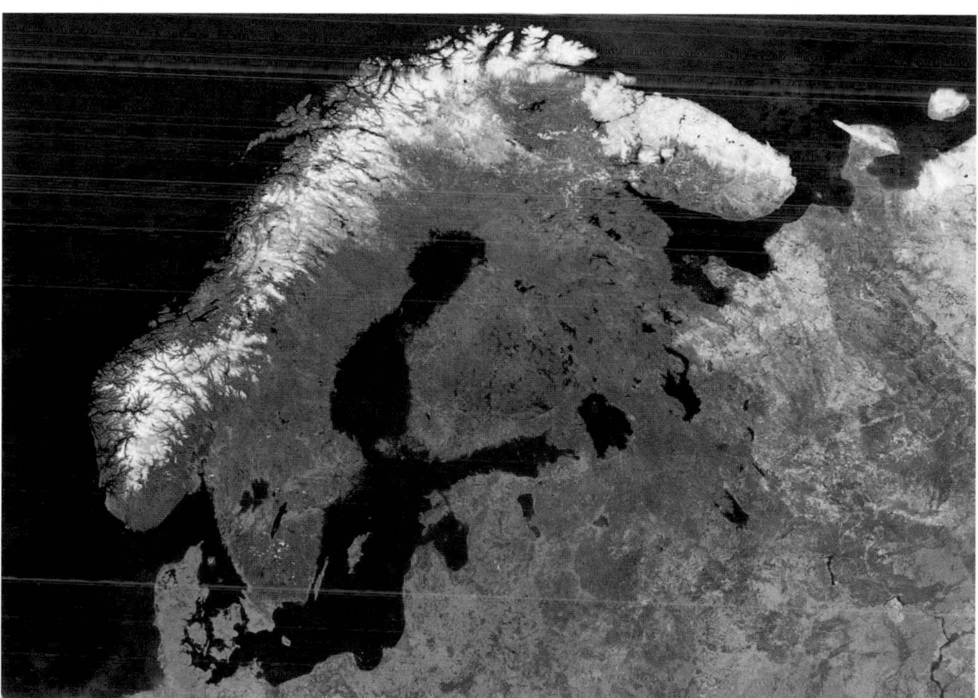

4.
Satellite image of Scandinavia.

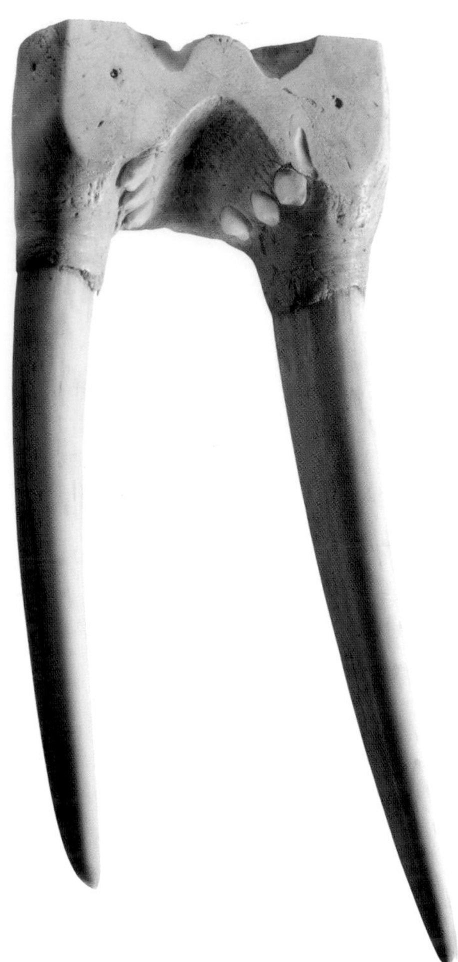

5.
Walrus skull piece with two tusks. Greenland.
Walrus bone, ivory. H 47 cm, W 19.5 cm
Private collection

The account of Ohthere, dating from the late ninth century (see p. 26), includes reference to a variety of peoples in northern Norway and adjoining areas, including the Finnas, Terfinnas, Cwenas and Beormas. Ohthere was sufficiently well informed to distinguish between these groups, but also to note similarities: 'The Finnas and the Beormas [from northern Russia], it seemed to him, spoke practically one and the same language'. He describes what he himself observed of the different peoples, but was too cautious simply to repeat what they said of themselves: 'The Beormas told them [or him] many stories about their own land and about the lands that were around them, but he did not know what there was of truth in it, because he did not see it himself.'[5] The various peoples mentioned by Ohthere probably included the ancestors of the modern Sámi people of northern Norway and Sweden, and the Finns of Finland, and perhaps other peoples whose identities have been entirely lost.[6] Unfortunately, the nomadic lifestyle of these peoples, and the fact that they were not as obliging to modern archaeologists as other groups with more elaborate burial rituals, means that they are impossible to distinguish today. Later accounts written in the form of sagas (see p. 25) tended to refer to them all as Finnas, just as contemporary Anglo-Saxon accounts may have failed to distinguish between different groups of Scandinavians (referring to them all, in general, as 'Danes').

Geographical and cultural diversity led to diverse forms of economy throughout the region. Some living in the Scandinavian homelands relied on arable and pastoral farming, while others exploited reindeer for meat, milk and furs, or traded in furs, walrus tusks, amber and other natural resources (fig. 5). The beginnings of specialized production and long-distance trade are also visible before the Viking Age began, but the number of major trading centres was limited to only a few at the beginning of the period, such as Ribe in western Denmark and Helgö in Sweden, and the development of trade and urbanization on a larger scale was very much a product of the Viking Age (see p. 49).

Despite this fragmentation and diversity in many respects, there were also common characteristics found across societies in different regions. These included shared or at least overlapping approaches to belief and ritual as discussed in detail in chapter 4. There were similarities in social structure and hierarchies too. This was reflected by the presence in the landscape of so-called 'central places', sites that combined the roles of lordly residence and local power centre with elements of pre-urban production and trade, and sometimes also with ritual functions (see pp. 124–8, 156–7, 198–9). With the exception of the nomadic peoples of northern Norway and Sweden, there were similar levels of technological development and production skills across much of Scandinavia, even if differences in taste sometimes led to the development of distinct local styles of design and ornamentation.

One further key point in common among many pre-Viking Scandinavian societies was their maritime nature – seas, fjords, rivers and lakes were the main means of transportation and contact, rather than barriers. The importance of maritime culture is reflected not just in river- and sea-going vessels, but also in graves and houses. Boats and ships were central to society, so it is perhaps unsurprising that burial in boats and ships was relatively common, with ship shapes formed of stones placed around some graves for which actual vessels were not used. Similarly, the bow-sided longhouses found across the Viking world – whether built in timber, stone or turf – are reminiscent of the shape of ships (fig. 6). The necessity for effective boats and ships led to a series of developments in shipbuilding and surviving examples are among the most striking and impressive remains from the Viking Age. Their technological progress and significance is discussed in more detail in chapter 5, but it is important to note here their central role in the expansion of the Viking world.

The maritime character of Scandinavian society led to the exploitation and control of waterways locally and regionally, both for economic and defensive purposes. Artificial barriers played a pivotal role, not in order to block seaways altogether, but as a way of

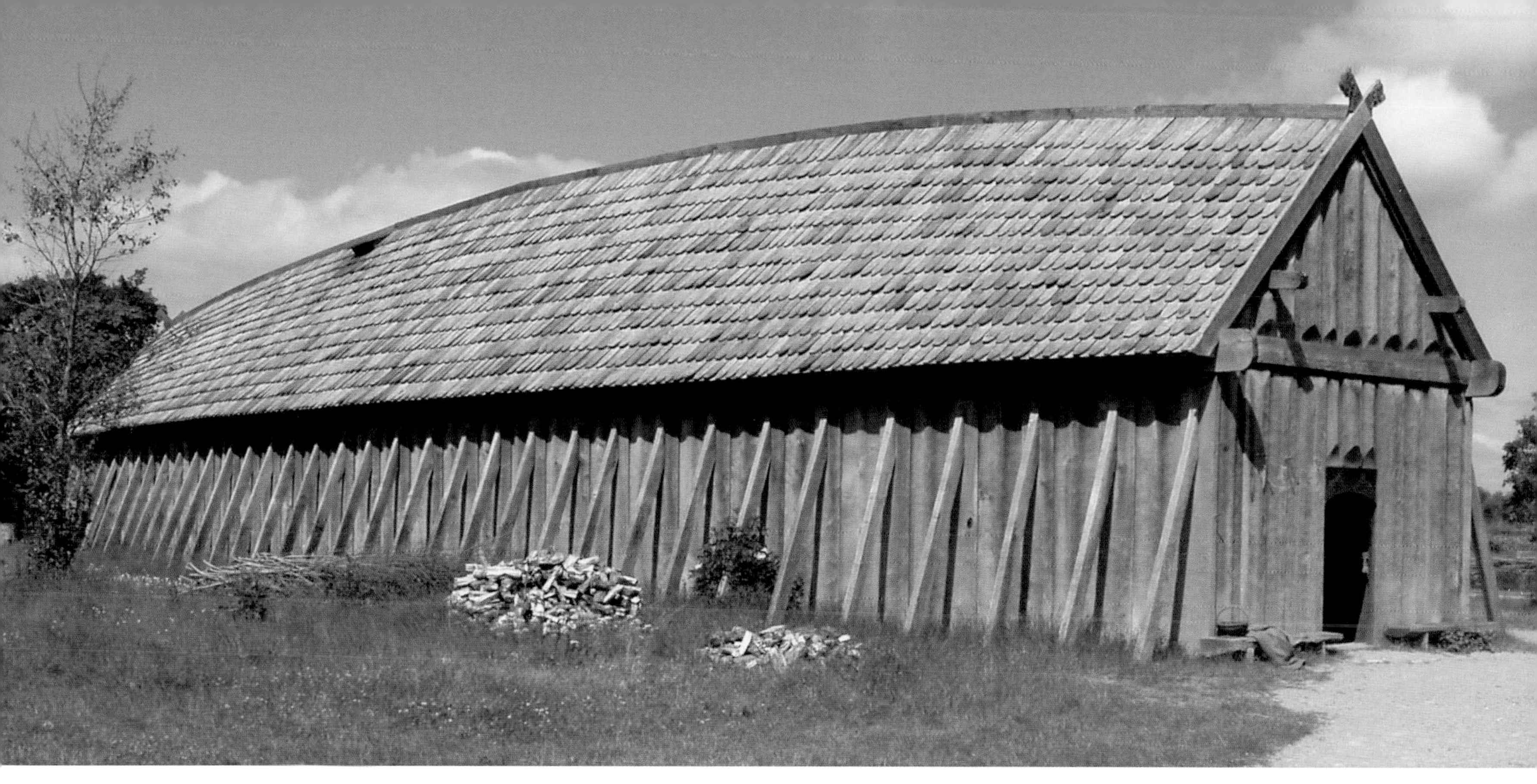

6.
Reconstruction of a Viking longhouse at the Vikinge Center, Ribe, Denmark, based on a house of *c.* 980 excavated at Gammel Hviding in Jutland, Denmark.

managing the movement of ships. Control of the resources needed for building and outfitting ships was also important, and the command of waterways and maritime resources can be linked to the growth of larger kingdoms and military organization.

This maritime society was a central element in driving and facilitating the Viking expansion, since the Viking homelands were bordered by the North Sea and the Atlantic in the west, and the Baltic in the east, with only very limited land boundaries in southern Jutland and in northern Norway/Sweden. Since there was already trading contact across both the Baltic and the North Sea by the late eighth century, the Viking Age saw the expansion of existing links with neighbours overseas, with whom there were opportunities for repeated interaction, both peaceful and violent. Although the speed of transport by sea was very dependent on weather, under ideal conditions all of the areas and peoples around the North Sea and the Baltic could be reached within a few days' sail no further by sea from the nearest part of the Viking homelands than the journey from the northern to the southern tip of Norway, or from the westernmost to the easternmost parts of Denmark. This meant that the Vikings were in contact with a number of peoples who can be considered near neighbours.

Near neighbours

Immediately to the south of Denmark lay the kingdom of the Franks. The Franks were originally comprised of several West Germanic tribes, but these gradually joined together into a single kingdom that expanded to its greatest size during the reign of Charlemagne (king of the Franks 759–814), who assumed the title of emperor in 800 and ruled over what is referred to by modern historians as the Carolingian empire. This empire developed into the greatest European power of its day, extending across most of western Europe from the North Sea to the Mediterranean, although this was later divided into smaller kingdoms.[7]

7.
Containers like this would have been used to transport large quantities of goods by river and sea. This barrel was probably used to transport wine, but then reused to line a well.

Transport vessel, 800–1050. Hedeby, modern Germany.
Rhenish spruce. H 210 cm, Diam. 75 cm
Archäologisches Landesmuseum, Schloss Gottorf, Schleswig

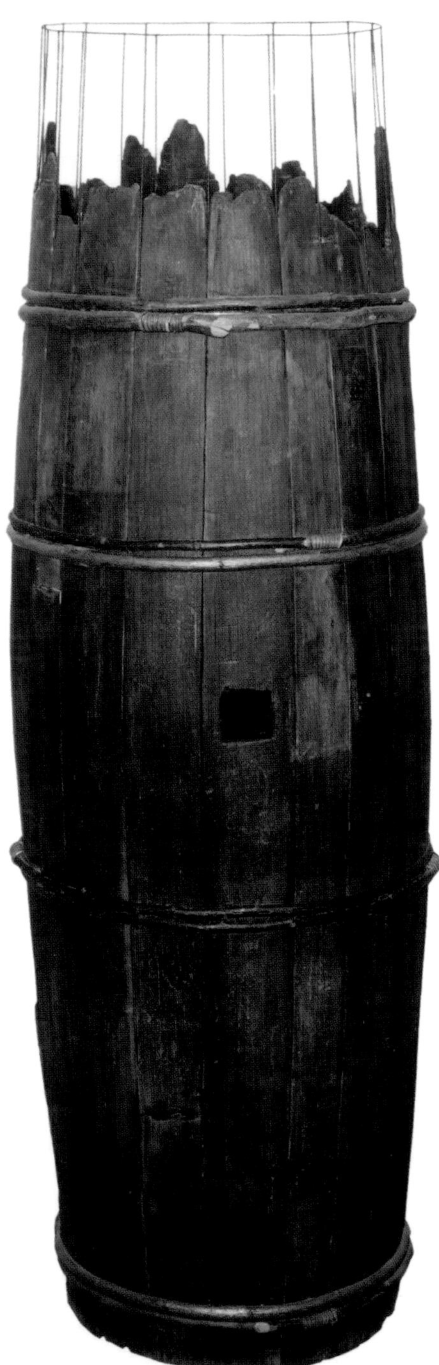

The Christian Frankish rulers travelled around their kingdom rather than having a single capital, requiring a huge number of royal buildings, estates and servants, supported by a well-organized literate administration.

The Carolingian empire was characterized by a mixture of sacral and secular power, motivated by the conscious imitation of the Roman empire. This is reflected in rituals, insignia and high-status buildings in stone, including imperial palaces, churches and cloisters.[8] Due to the demand from the elite for objects of prestige, one section of the economy was based on long-distance trade in luxury goods, with its focus in centres of royal and religious power as well as coastal trading centres (fig. 7).[9] This attracted foreign traders, including Scandinavians, but also provided a target for Viking raids. Long-distance trade led to specialized production for export, as shown by the industrialized manufacture of Rhenish ceramics or the exploitation of basalt-lava quarries.

In contrast to the ruling elite and traders, most of the Frankish population lived in wooden farmsteads in rural areas and worked as peasants in agriculture. This increasing social differentiation is mirrored in the formation of a land-holding system where ownership of large estates was in the hands of the aristocratic minority who rented land to tenants. A clear social distinction can also be read in the location of burials, which are situated inside or around churches within Christian cemeteries: the closer to the altar, the more important the burial.

The Anglo-Saxons originated in Denmark, northern Germany and the Netherlands, and settled in England in the fifth and sixth centuries. A variety of smaller tribal groupings gradually combined into larger kingdoms, which adopted Christianity one by one in the late sixth and seventh centuries. This brought with it a model of Romanized Christian kingship shared with other Germanic peoples including the Franks. Early settlement was concentrated in the south and east, but by the time of the first Viking raids in the late eighth century, Anglo-Saxon settlement extended across most of modern England, although settlement in highland and other marginal areas was limited (fig. 8).[10] England did not become unified until the tenth century and this took place in part because the Vikings conquered several of the Anglo-Saxon kingdoms. At the beginning of the Viking Age, there were five main kingdoms in England: Northumbria, Mercia, East Anglia, Kent and Wessex. During this period Kent fell under the domination first of Mercia then of Wessex and had disappeared as an independent kingdom before the Viking conquests of the late ninth century (see p. 85).[11]

Like the Franks, the Anglo-Saxons had a strong social hierarchy, with a relatively small aristocracy dominating the holding of land and power. The Church was also rich and powerful, and churches and monasteries played an active part in the development of trade. While there were few settlements in England that could be considered towns by the beginning of the Viking Age, a large number of trading centres can be identified both in historical sources and through archaeology, and it seems likely that many of these were controlled by the Church.[12] Long-distance trade extended from eastern England around the North Sea to Ribe in western Denmark as early as the first half of the eighth century.

The English landscape has some similarities with parts of Scandinavia: the agricultural land of eastern England has more in common with Denmark, while the highland areas of the north-west are similar to Norway. The Old English language originally came from the same roots as Old Norse, although these had already moved apart by the eighth century. The extent to which the two languages were mutually intelligible remains the subject of debate, but it is likely that there was some shared understanding.[13]

The other inhabitants of Britain and Ireland were linguistically more distinct from the Vikings. These were a variety of peoples speaking Celtic languages in Scotland, Ireland, Wales and parts of western England. They fall into three main groups: the Irish, the British and the Picts. The Irish inhabited the whole of Ireland, which was divided into a number of

8.
The distribution of inhabitants in Britain and Ireland at the beginning of the Viking Age.

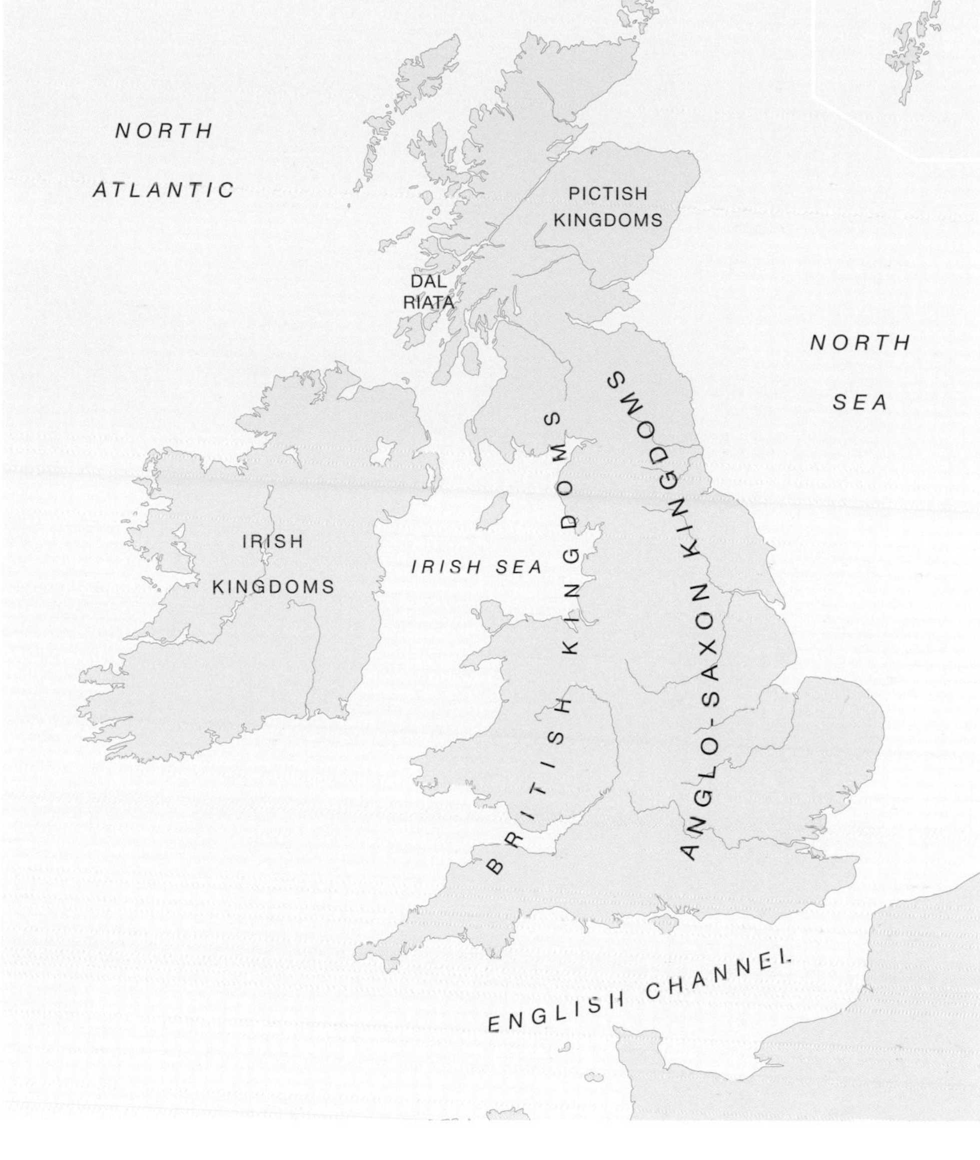

9
Pictish symbol stone, 7th–9th century. Burghead, Moray Firth, Scotland.
Stone, H 53 cm, W 55 cm
British Museum, London

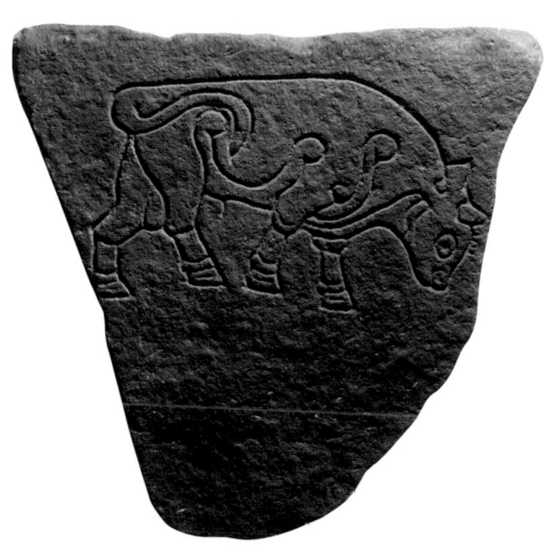

small kingdoms, although a tradition of high kings meant that at any point one of these kingdoms was likely to be dominant and exercising some sort of lordship over the others. Settlement from Ireland in the pre-Viking period had also established the kingdom of Dal Ríata in what is now western Scotland. To the south, extending from south-west Scotland down through north-west England and Wales to Cornwall, were a number of separate British kingdoms speaking a different branch of Celtic languages, which gave rise to Cornish and Welsh. In northern and eastern Scotland were the Picts, who have often been characterized as a completely distinct ethnic group, although the rarity of surviving Pictish written sources makes this interpretation problematic, and recently it has been suggested that the Picts were more closely related to other Celtic peoples than was previously recognized. Like the Irish, a number of smaller Pictish kingdoms were apparently ruled by an over-king (fig. 9).[14]

All of these kingdoms became Christian before the Viking Age, but in other respects there are similarities with Scandinavian society. There were no towns, and no monetary economy, although as in England some monasteries may have acted as trading centres. Wealth was primarily based on land and livestock, but precious metals also indicated status

10.
Very large brooches like this were used to indicate status. Their form and extravagant size were copied, with modification, by Scandinavian settlers.

Pictish brooch with interlaced ornamentation, 8th century. Rogart, Sutherland, Scotland.
Silver. Diam. 7.7 cm, L 13.3 cm
National Museums Scotland, Edinburgh

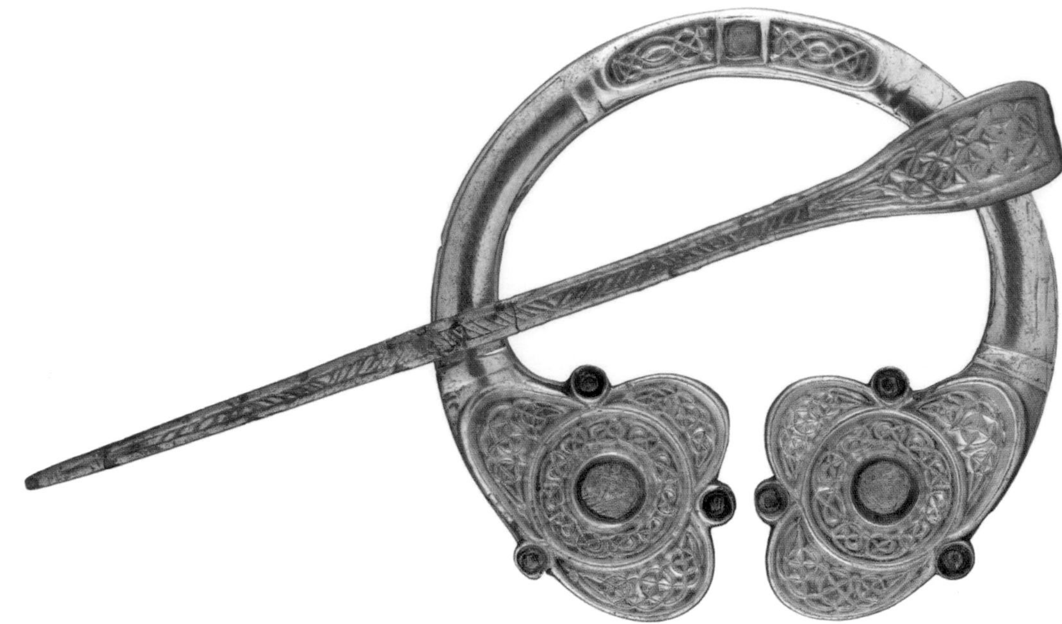

(fig. 10) and were used in a variety of forms of social exchange, such as the giving of arm-rings and other status-objects as publicly visible rewards for loyal service or valour in battle (see pp. 128–31).

The land occupied by these different peoples was almost as varied as in Scandinavia, with areas of good farmland but also sparsely inhabited highland regions in Scotland (fig. 11), Wales and north-west England. Together with dense forest, lochs and islands, these highland regions created natural borders between many societies and, as in Scandinavia, transport by water was often easier than by land. This again led to the development of maritime cultures, although different shipbuilding traditions gave rise to technology that was less well suited to large-scale expansion than Viking ships.[15]

To the east of the Carolingian empire lay the territory of the non-Christian Slavs, comprised of several tribes. The Slavs had a tradition of personal ornament that was distinct from the Carolingians and Vikings, including earrings, temple rings (rings worn suspended over the temples from a female headdress; fig. 12), beads, crescent-shaped pendants and *gombíky* – spherical pendants made from a variety of metals, often gilded. Much of this jewellery was silver, but items of gold and bronze are also known.[16] There were also differences in shipbuilding traditions, as Scandinavians preferred iron nails, while Slavs favoured wooden ones. Nevertheless, close maritime contacts with Scandinavia are reflected in the form of coastal trading centres. With wide sandy beaches, estuaries sheltered waters and lagoons, the southern Baltic coast provided an ideal environment for the establishment of coastal trading stations by offering protection for the ships against the weather. Natural resources such as salt, furs, wood and possibly agricultural surplus could easily be brought to the coast via inland waterways. These raw materials as well as amber seem to have played a key role, as these places were already established before the flow into the Baltic of Islamic silver coins, known as dirhams, started in the late eighth century (see pp. 54–7).[17] In addition to hack-silver (fragmented silver bullion) the Slavs possibly used slightly concave dishes of iron, known as Silesian bowls, as a medium for some forms of social exchange.

As well as unfortified agricultural settlements, a large number of monumental circular timber-framed earthwork enclosures are known, although it is not clear what they were used for.[18] These have been seen in connection with the elite, owing to the large resources

12. (opposite)
Pair of Slavonic headdress 'temple' rings, late Viking Age. Bakkegard, Bornholm, Denmark
Silver. 2.78 g; 3.85 g
National Museum of Denmark, Copenhagen

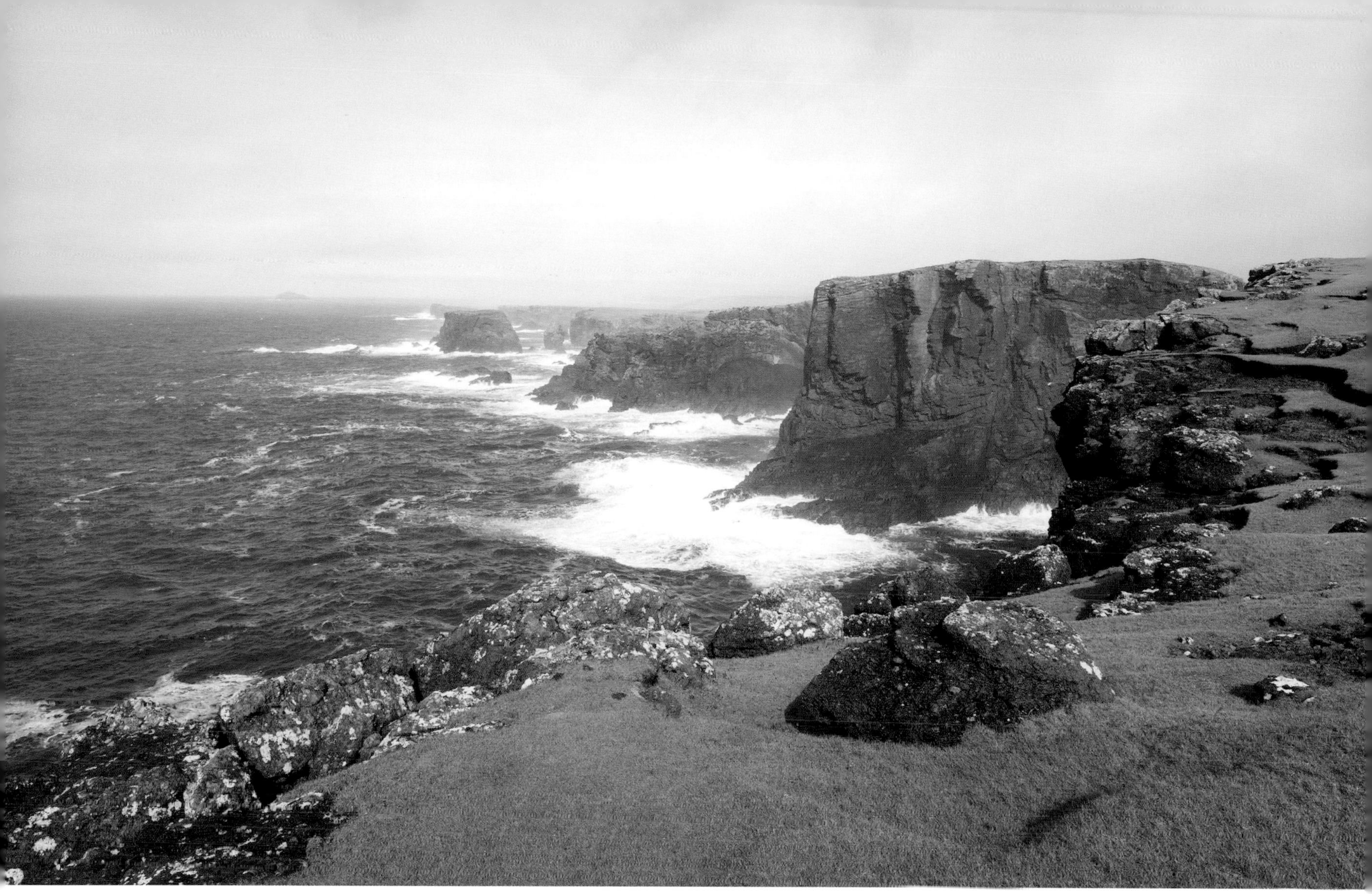

11.
The coastline of Shetland. Shetland is a group of islands that lies 170 km north of mainland Scotland.

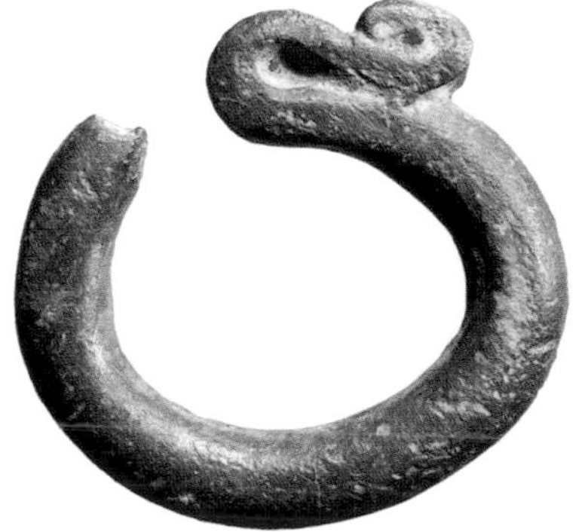

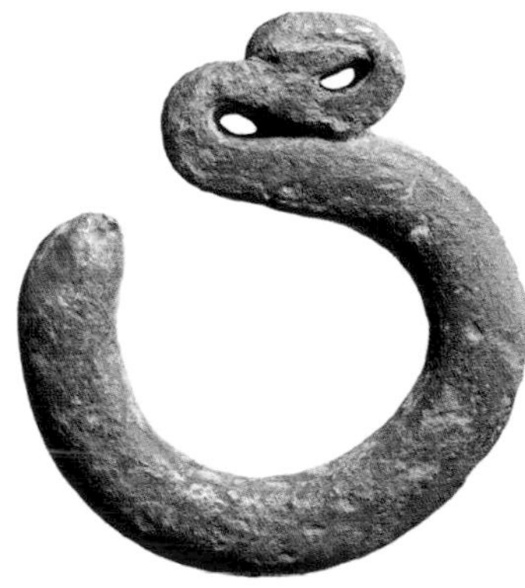

required for their construction. Their function may well have depended on contemporary political circumstances. The older ones might have been storage centres for agricultural surplus; some others might have served as military stations built for political reasons. A number of valuable items have been found at later examples and, as central points in the regional economy, they might have been used as collection points for tribute and as centres for the redistribution of goods.

Several tribes described as Balts, situated in today's Latvia and Lithuania as well as north-western Russia, lived and operated in a similar way to the Slavs. These are characterized by small settlements and timber-framed earthwork enclosures,[19] which from the tenth century onwards increasingly attracted traders and craftsmen. An early Scandinavian presence is demonstrated by items found in graves and a picture stone (a stone with carved illustrations) in the area around Grobiņa, as well as by two boat graves on the island of Saarema, where forty armed men were buried.[20] After the mid-ninth century Latvian burials no longer show Scandinavian influence, although it can be found from this

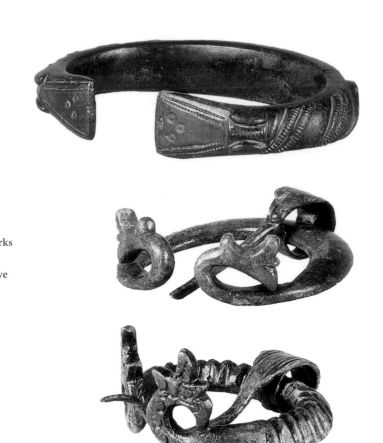

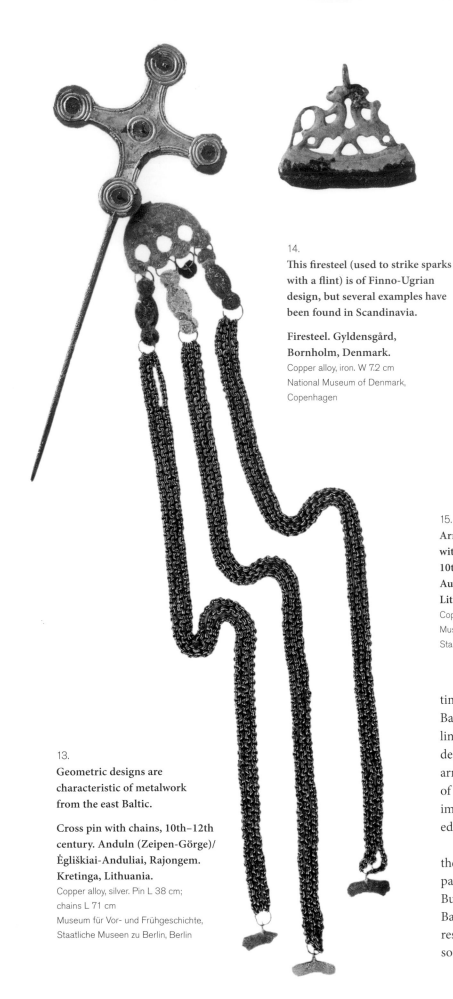

14.
This firesteel (used to strike sparks with a flint) is of Finno-Ugrian design, but several examples have been found in Scandinavia.

Firesteel. Gyldensgård, Bornholm, Denmark.
Copper alloy, iron. W 7.2 cm
National Museum of Denmark, Copenhagen

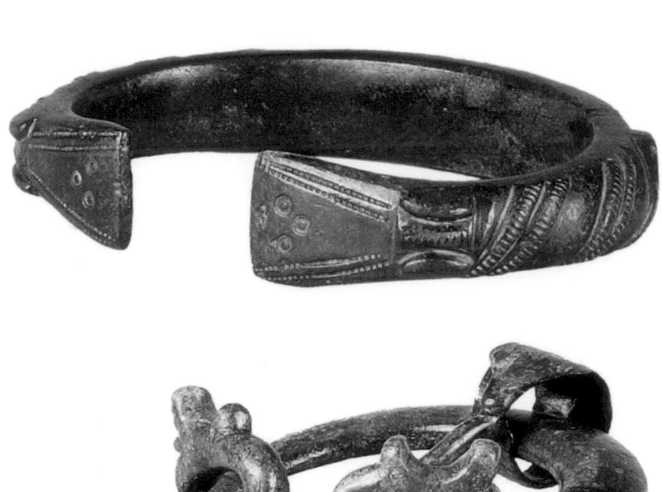

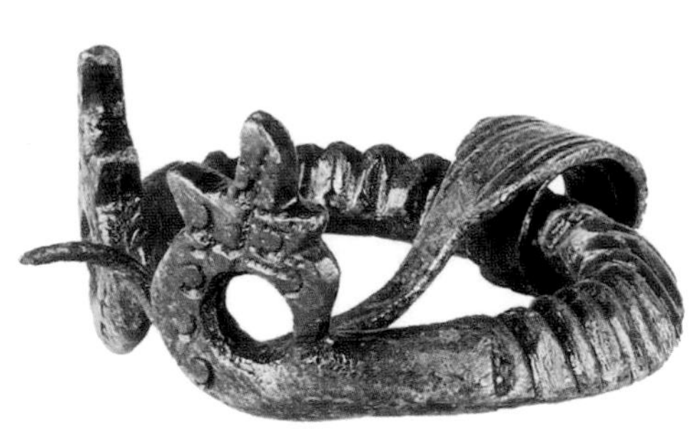

15. (top right)
Arm-ring of Baltic type with animal-head terminals, 10th–13th century. Oberhof/ Aukdtkiemiai, Raj. Klaipėda, Lithuania.
Copper alloy. Diam. 7.7 cm
Museum für Vor- und Frühgeschichte, Staatliche Museen zu Berlin, Berlin

16–17.
Two penannular brooches of Baltic type with animal-head terminals, 13th–15th century. Stangenwalde bei Rossitten, Kurische Nehrung/ Rybatschi, Kaliningradskaja Obl., Russia.
Copper alloy. Diam. 6.2 cm, 5.2 cm
Museum für Vor- und Frühgeschichte, Staatliche Museen zu Berlin, Berlin

13.
Geometric designs are characteristic of metalwork from the east Baltic.

Cross pin with chains, 10th–12th century. Anduln (Zeipen-Görge)/ Ėgliškiai-Anduliai, Rajongem. Kretinga, Lithuania.
Copper alloy, silver. Pin L 38 cm; chains L 71 cm
Museum für Vor- und Frühgeschichte, Staatliche Museen zu Berlin, Berlin

time in the burial mounds of Wiskiauten (see p. 72). Jewellery of the Balts, featuring geometric decorative motifs of circles, triangles and lines, differs very much from the zoomorphic (animal-shaped) decorated jewellery of the Vikings (figs 13–14). Nevertheless, arm-rings and brooches with stylized animal heads indicate a level of interaction between the Balts and the Scandinavians, as do local imitations of a type of oval brooch with an eyelet along the lower edge to suspend beads and other items (figs 15–17).

The Balts worshipped the spirits of natural elements, especially the earth but also mountains, water and forests; they remained pagans into the thirteenth century and in some areas even later. Burial goods suggest that horses played an important role for the Balts and the curved shape of their stirrups bears a stronger resemblance to those used by nomadic peoples of the steppes in southern Russia than those of west European origin.

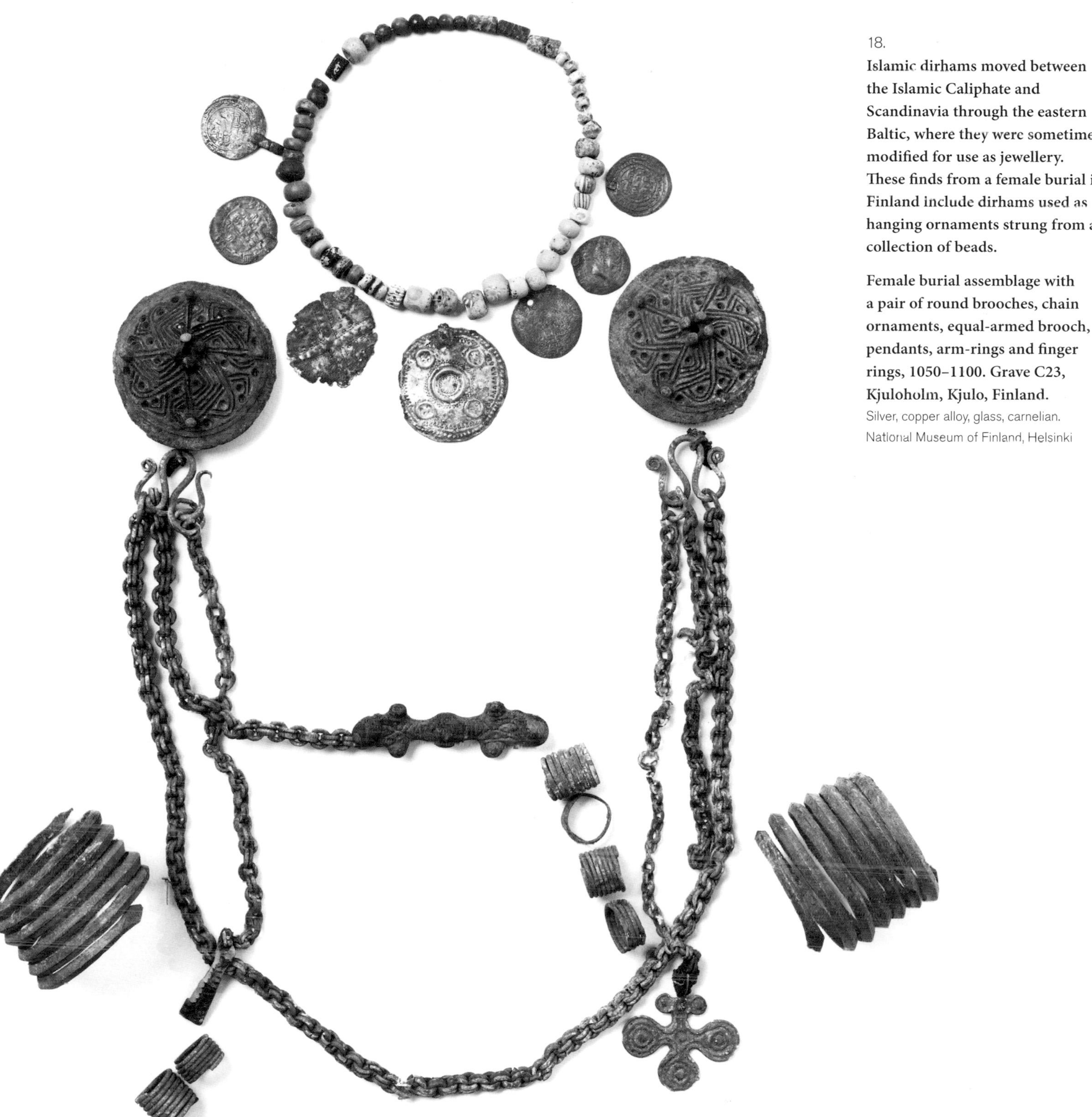

18.
Islamic dirhams moved between the Islamic Caliphate and Scandinavia through the eastern Baltic, where they were sometimes modified for use as jewellery. These finds from a female burial in Finland include dirhams used as hanging ornaments strung from a collection of beads.

Female burial assemblage with a pair of round brooches, chain ornaments, equal-armed brooch, pendants, arm-rings and finger rings, 1050–1100. Grave C23, Kjuloholm, Kjulo, Finland.
Silver, copper alloy, glass, carnelian. National Museum of Finland, Helsinki

Judging from burials containing bones, claws and teeth from bears, as well as imitations of claws and teeth in clay and bronze worn as amulets in combination with chains, the bear seems to have been an important animal for the Finns, probably as a result of Russian influence (see p. 175). Today's Finland was shaped in the late Iron Age by an agricultural base economy of peasant farmers, who lived on independent farms without centralized authority. Due to its iron production and its situation between the Baltic and the Russian river system, Finland played the role of a transit area. This is reflected in finds of Frankish swords with zoomorphic decorated hilts and hoards with coins of Islamic and west European origin (fig. 18). Finno-Ugrians occupied lands from the northern part of Scandinavia around the north and north-eastern side of the Baltic. They thus came into close contact with Scandinavians both in the Viking homelands and in what is now the northern part of Russia, including the important trading centre of Staraya Ladoga (see pp. 49, 53).[21]

Distant contacts

Sea-faring vessels allowed the Vikings to expand their territories and to make cultural contacts further afield. The Viking expansion carried travellers across the North Atlantic and down the Atlantic coast of western Europe to the Mediterranean, and through the river systems of Russia and eastern Europe to the Black Sea and the Caspian Sea.

Across the North Atlantic, contact with other cultures was limited, but exploration provided opportunities for largely peaceful settlement. The Faeroes, Iceland and Greenland were apparently almost entirely deserted prior to the Vikings' arrival in the late ninth century, with the exception of a small number of Irish monks seeking isolation from the world, who left when they arrived. The Faeroes are a group of mountainous islands, suited more to pastoral farming and fishing than to arable agriculture, while Iceland had areas of good farmland around the coast, although the central glacier and more mountainous areas limited the scope for settlement inland (fig. 19).[22]

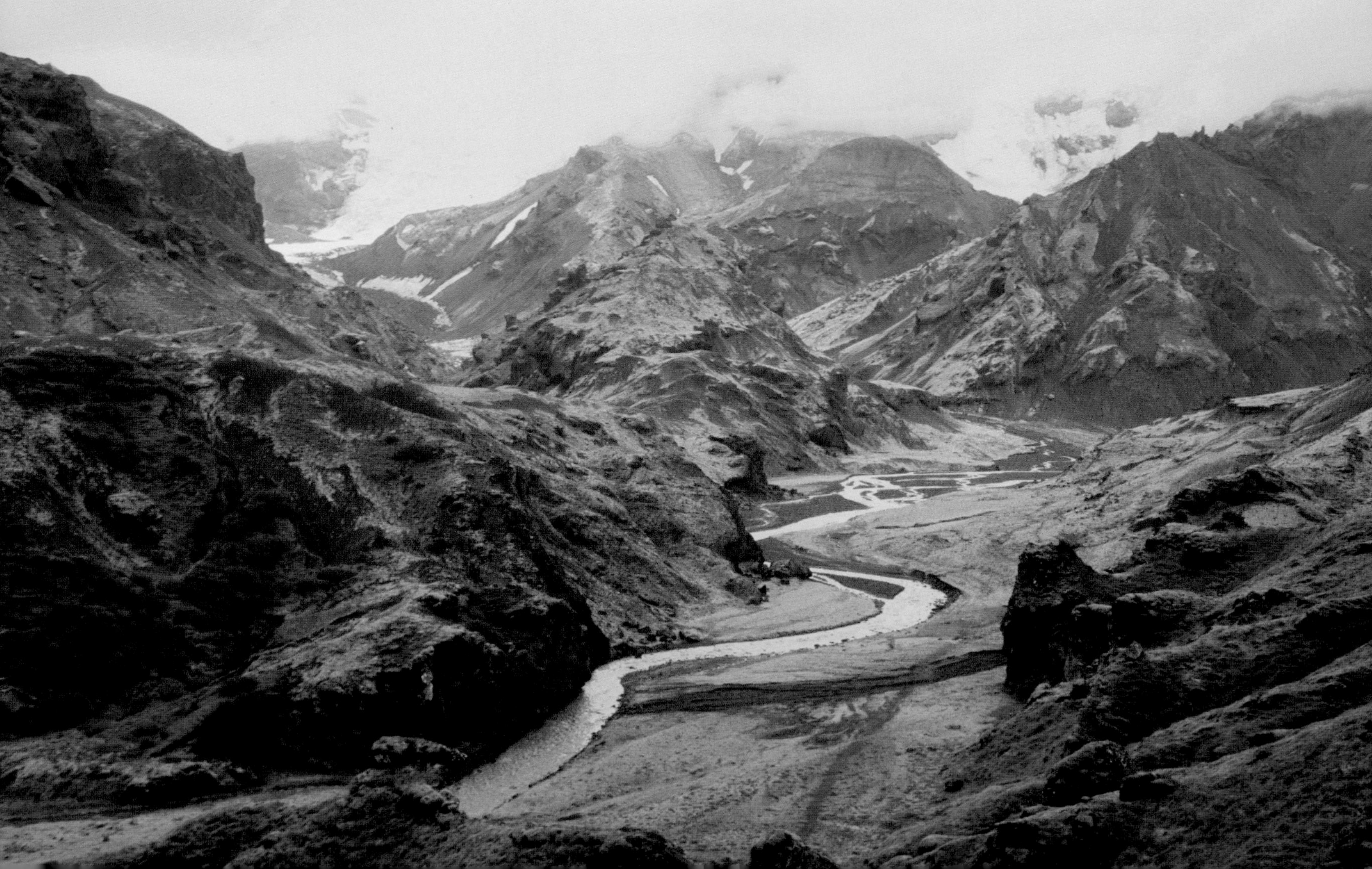

19.
The dramatic and distinctive open landscape of Iceland was formed partly as a result of Viking settlement. Demand for timber and animal pasture led to rapid deforestation. Þórsmörk Valley, Iceland.

20.
Whale bone was a readily available resource for settlers in the North Atlantic.

Whale bone axehead, 11th–13th century. Sandnæs (Kilaarsarfik), Nuuk, Sermersooq, Greenland.
Whale bone. L 13.9 cm
National Museum of Denmark, Copenhagen

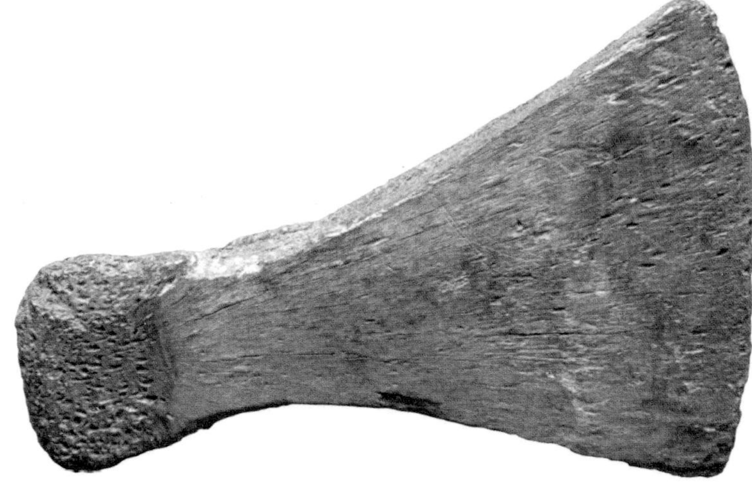

The landscapes of the North Atlantic settlements may not seem particularly hospitable, but the late Viking Age had a warmer climate than at present – the naming of Greenland appears to have been a genuine attempt to draw people to a new land, rather than a joke – although the main value of Greenland seems to have been as a source for sealskins, walrus hides (used to make rope) and walrus tusks. The settlement of the North Atlantic was largely led by chieftains from western Norway and the Viking settlements in Scotland, where there was a limited supply of good land, so the new lands to the west provided opportunities to establish large estates, maintaining or increasing the social status of the settlers (fig. 20).[23]

Unlike the Faeroes and Iceland, North America was already populated. Peoples of the Dorset culture inhabited parts of north-eastern Canada and possibly also the north-western part of Greenland, while ancestors of the Innu and Beothuk inhabited Labrador and Newfoundland. Unlike other groups with whom the Vikings came into contact, these had little impact on Viking culture, in part because of the limited scale of their interaction.[24] Viking settlement in Greenland took place in two relatively small areas, while the one recorded attempt in 'Vinland' in North America was unsuccessful, as the settlers provoked the hostility of the native population. It is not clear if the settlement discovered at L'Anse aux Meadows (fig. 21) at the northern end of Newfoundland relates to this unsuccessful

21.
Reconstruction of the excavated turf buildings from the Viking settlement at L'Anse aux Meadows, Newfoundland, Canada.

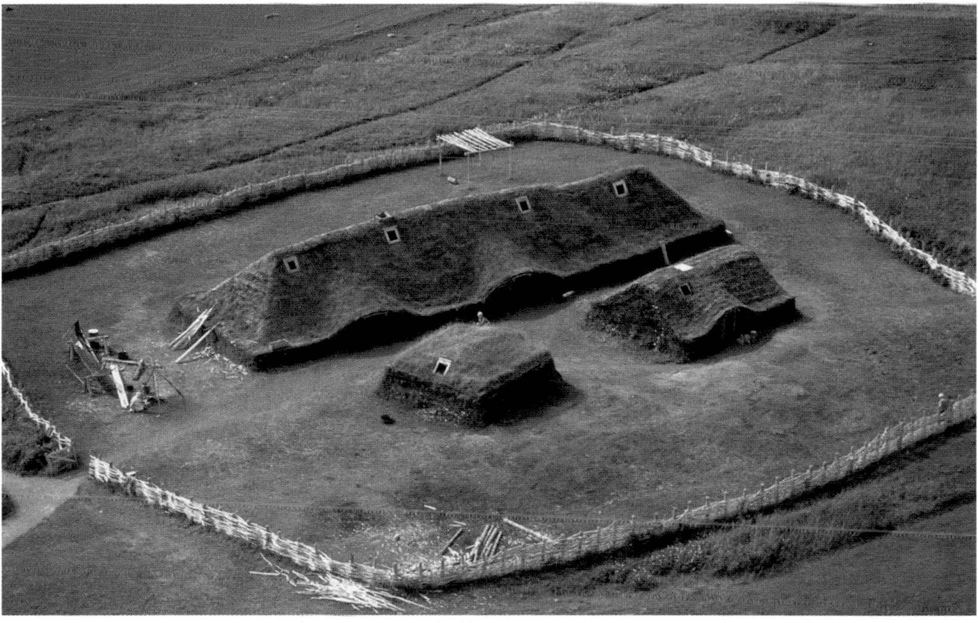

attempt. There were later journeys from Greenland to fetch timber, but contacts with inhabitants of North America were probably relatively few and far between. In addition, the natives of eastern Canada were hunter-gatherers, with less developed technologies than the Vikings, so there was little of interest for the Vikings to imitate. The influence of the Vikings on these peoples was also minimal and not entirely positive – a small number of finds point to limited trade with the Dorset people, but it has been suggested that European diseases brought by the Vikings may have contributed to the demise of the Dorset people in northern Greenland.[25]

At the opposite extreme, both geographically and culturally, were the two great empires at the south-eastern edge of the Viking world. The Byzantine empire during the Viking Age was largely confined to south-eastern Europe and Asia Minor, with its capital at Constantinople (modern Istanbul), and was subject to constant threats from external enemies, among them Arabs and a variety of semi-nomadic tribes, such as the Bulgars, the Volga Bulgars (a distinct group), the Khazars and the Pechenegs (see below). Threats could sometimes be reduced by entering into alliances, and Byzantine emperors at different times allied themselves with the various peoples mentioned above, as well as with the Viking rulers of Kiev in the tenth century. Nonetheless, the need to defend the empire required considerable attention and as a consequence the Viking Age saw repeated shifts in the northern frontiers of the empire. The Byzantine empire was a powerful one that tried to maintain and expand its political influence and at the same time to promote Christian belief. These interests meant that Byzantium naturally looked north to the regions between

22.
Hagia Sophia, the great Christian church – dedicated in 360 – that formed the spiritual heart of the imperial city of Constantinople. The present building dates from 532–7. Minarets and buttress walls are Turkish additions after 1453.

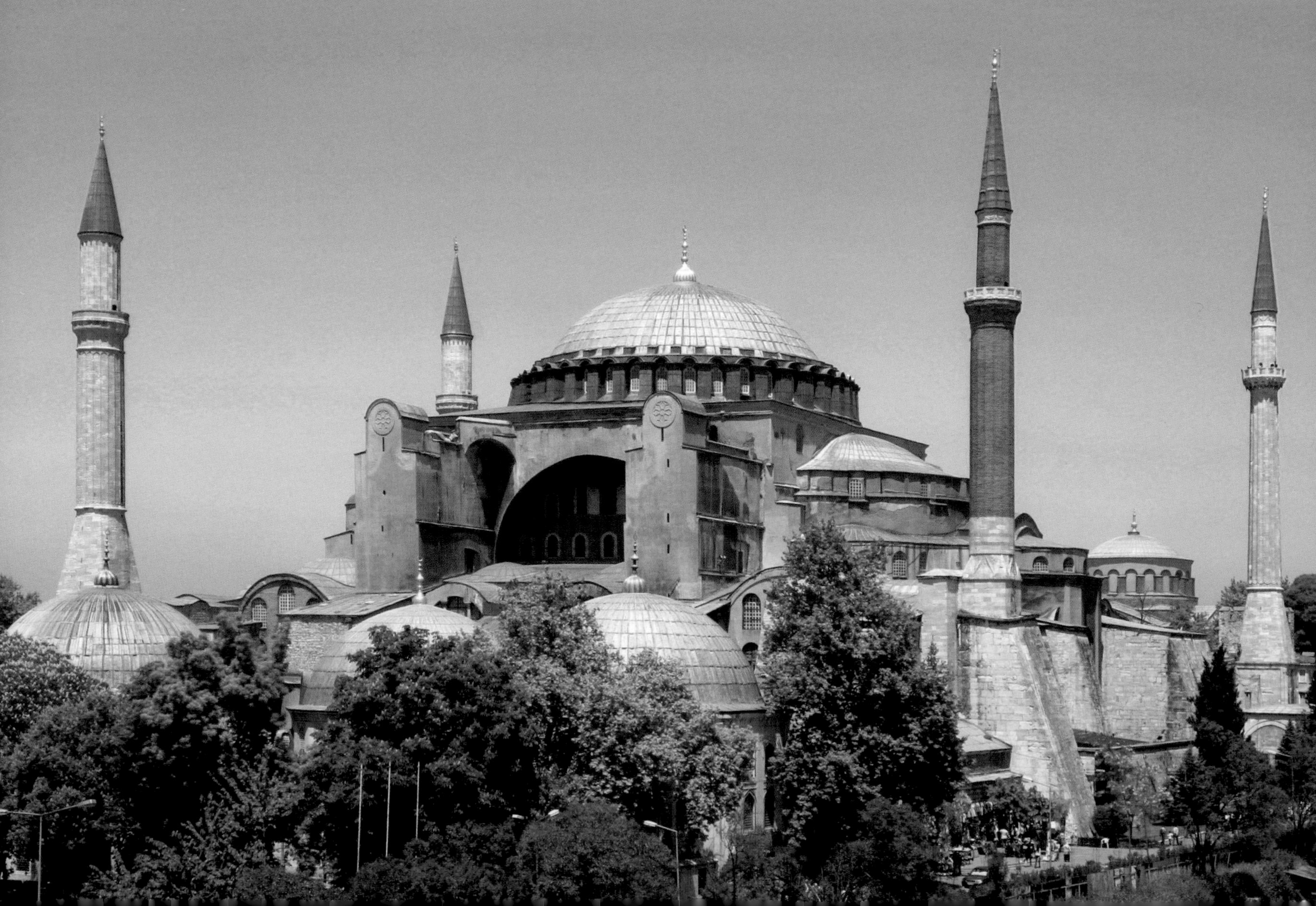

23.
Byzantine flask, 8th–9th century. Southern Italy.
Ivory. H 23 cm
British Museum, London

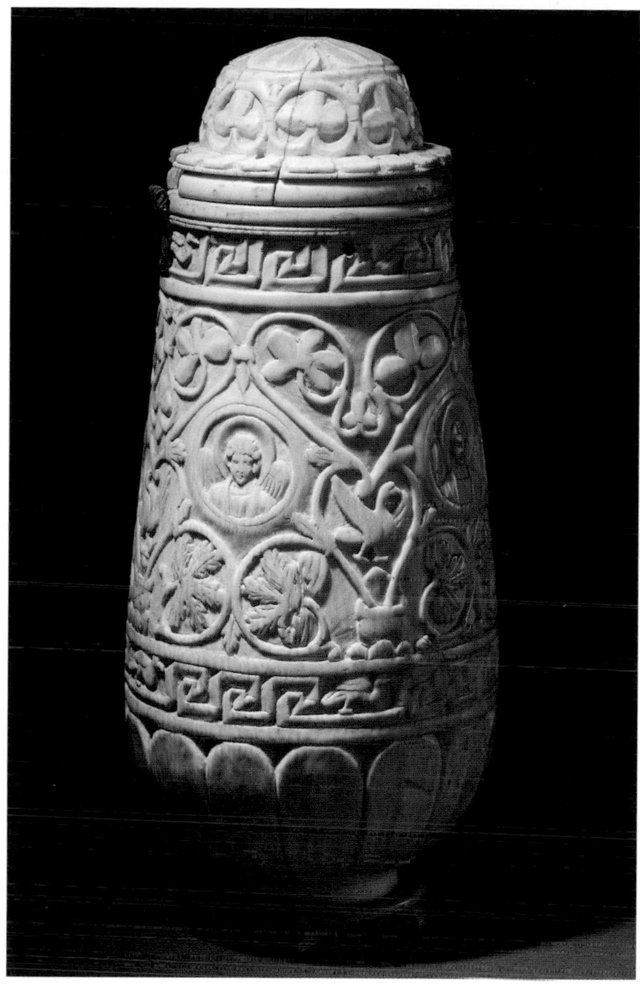

the Black Sea and the Baltic, encouraging contact with the Viking world once the Viking expansion began.[26]

Constantinople itself was a magnificent metropolis with stone buildings and aqueducts, and the empire as a whole was distinct from northern Europe in the early Viking Age due to its large towns and urban economy. This was largely a monetary economy, but finite supplies of metals for coinage meant that Byzantine emperors were more reticent about letting large amounts of coins leave the empire than their Islamic neighbours. Nevertheless, the wealth of Byzantium provided a market for Scandinavian trade.

Based on Roman state structures as well as Roman traditions and identity, centralized secular and ecclesiastical power were omnipresent, as represented by the royal palace and several churches as well as imperial and Christian iconography on coins and seals. The Byzantine emperor was at the centre of a large and well-organized state apparatus, more developed and sophisticated even than the Frankish and Anglo-Saxon courts, and infinitely more advanced than anything in Scandinavia or around the Baltic (figs 22–23).[27]

The Byzantine empire also had a highly developed military, both in terms of a structured army and the use of military technology. In addition to the land army, the large military and commercial naval fleets of the Byzantines dominated the Black Sea and allowed a strong presence in the Mediterranean, while their exclusive use of the petroleum-based projectile weapon known as Greek Fire gave them an automatic advantage over other naval forces, including the Vikings (see p. 82). External threats on various borders placed a heavy burden on the military structure, while the emperors also saw a need for troops whose loyalty was to the emperor personally rather than to particular court factions or families

24.
Limestone with carved Arabic inscription, 10th–11th century. Hama, Syria.
Limestone, H 24.5 cm, L 25 cm
National Museum of Denmark, Copenhagen

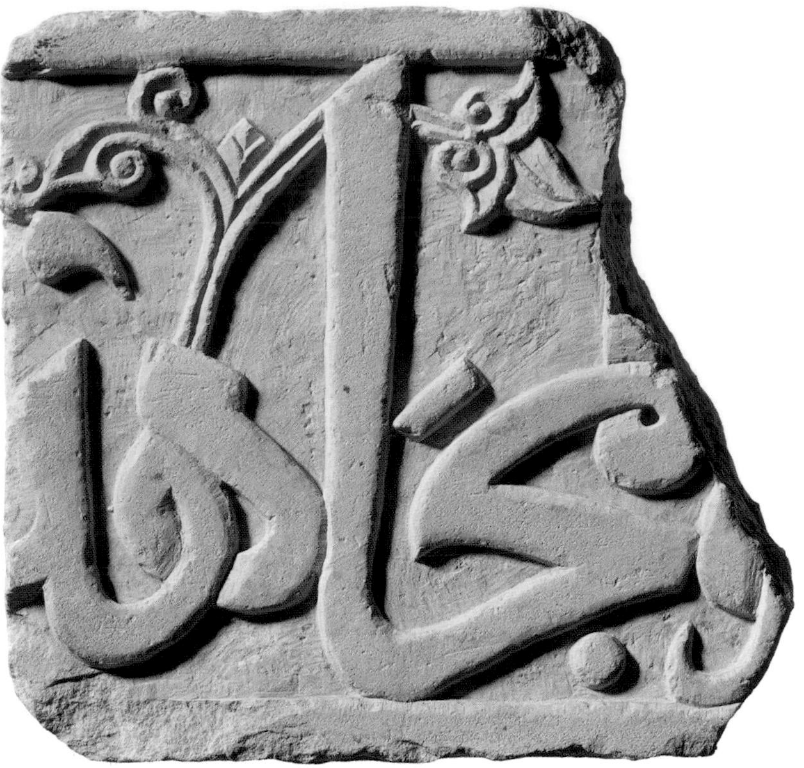

who might challenge for imperial power. Both situations created a demand for mercenaries from outside the empire, which the Vikings were well placed to satisfy.

The other vast and powerful empire with which the Vikings had contact was the Islamic Caliphate, which extended from Central Asia in the east and across the whole of the Middle East and the North African coast to Morocco and Spain in the west (fig. 24). This meant that the Vikings had access to the Caliphate both by the Atlantic route to Spain and North Africa, and via the river routes to the Middle East and Central Asia.[28]

Based on access to vast amounts of silver and gold, the Caliphate had a sophisticated coin-based economy. It possessed large commercial fleets and good ports for maritime trade, but also had extensive trade links by land, and there were many towns and cities both inland and in coastal regions. Situated on the western end of the Silk Road, it was rich in oriental spices, silk and other exotic luxury goods (fig. 25). Carnelian and rock crystal mined in the Caliphate and in India were widespread, especially in the eastern part of the empire and along the trade routes connecting to the Baltic (fig. 26). So, for the Vikings, the Islamic Caliphate represented a link to further trading partners.

Like Byzantium, the Islamic Caliphate was interested in the expansion of political and religious influence, and secular and sacral leadership were united in the person of the caliph. Madīnat-al-Salām (Baghdad), the political and cultural centre of the Caliphate, was characterized by mosques and other buildings bursting with pomp and wealth, and was far larger than any city in Europe, let alone the small settlements in Scandinavia. In many repects the Caliphate enjoyed its heyday in the ninth century, but it was already beginning to fragment and struggles and organizational changes in the civil service, combined with competition between rival dynasties, resulted in the foundation of independent emirates and kingdoms with only formal allegiance to the caliph in Baghdad.

Although many tend to equate 'Islamic' with 'Arabic', and the Arabic language was widely used (for example on coins), the Caliphate was ethnically diverse. Especially in the

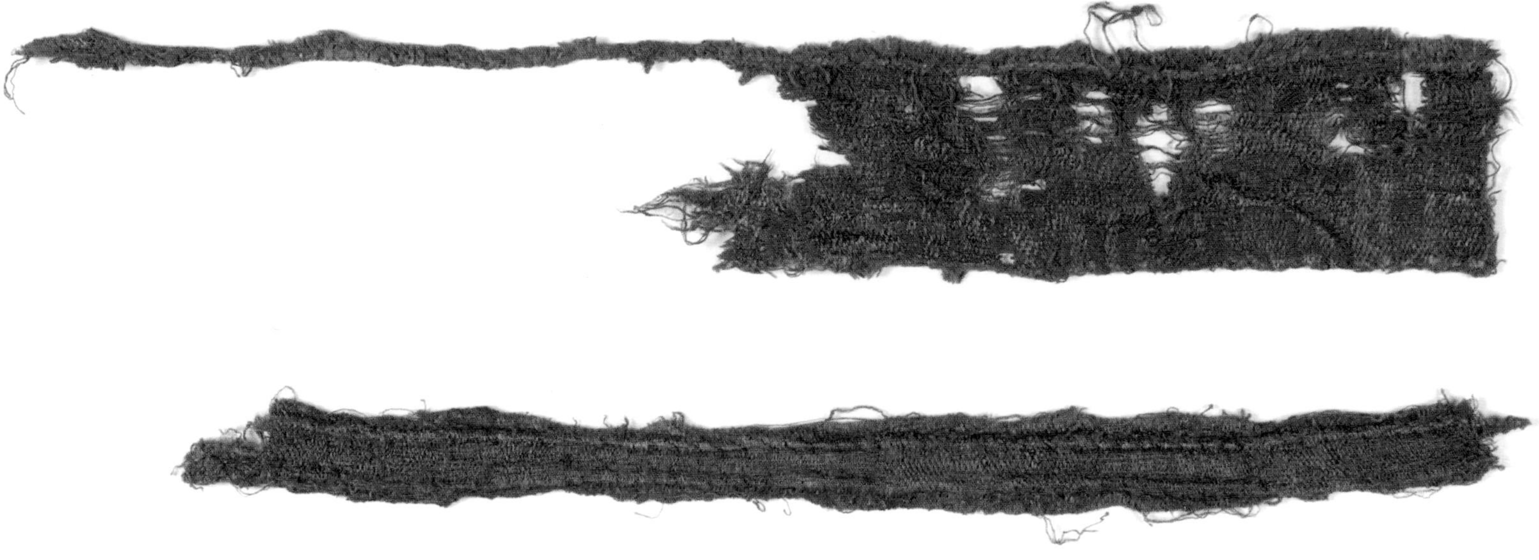

25.
Fragments of silk found in Dublin, a centre of Viking trade, probably late 10th–early 11th century. Fishamble Street, Dublin, Ireland.
Silk. L 22 cm; L 19.5 cm
National Museum of Ireland, Dublin

26.
Examples of semi-precious stone beads and one silver bead made using filigree technique, 9th–10th century. Found at the Viking-Age settlement of Janów Pomorski/ Truso, Poland.
Carnelian, rock crystal, amethyst, silver.
Museum of Archaeology and History in Elblag

later Viking Age, contact with the Islamic world was primarily with eastern dynasties, such as the Sāmānids from northern Afghanistan, who claimed descent from the Sasanians of Persia, and the Saffārids in Iran, rather than with the Abbasid caliphs in Madīnat-al-Salām. Under both the Sāmānids and the Saffārids the Persian language was revived, while the Persian administrative tradition became the source of Islamic bureaucratic practice across the Caliphate under the Abbasids (fig. 27).

The land between the eastern Baltic and the northern borders of both the Byzantine empire and the Caliphate was occupied by a number of groups of Turkic origin, who had arrived in the area as nomads but had settled to varying degrees, in some cases establishing lasting areas of political authority including diplomatic relations with Byzantium and/or the Caliphate. The most important of these groups was the Khazar khāqānate. With their capital at Itil, near the mouth of the Volga, the Khazars were no longer entirely nomadic but held a substantial territory north of the Black Sea, the Caucasus and the Caspian Sea, with the potential to control the river routes to the Baltic. Like the Caliphate, the eastern end of the khāqānate was connected to the Silk Road, providing trading links east into South and East Asia. The khāqānate itself produced honey, slaves and furs for trade. In the pre-Viking period the Khazars were allied with Byzantium but in the ninth and tenth centuries were under the influence of the Caliphate. Despite this, the Khazar elite converted to Judaism from their traditional shamanistic religion in the course of the ninth century, although the population as a whole combined a variety of faiths, as well as several different ethnic groups.[29]

27.
The eastern Abbasid Caliphate and its neighbours in the 9th–11th centuries.

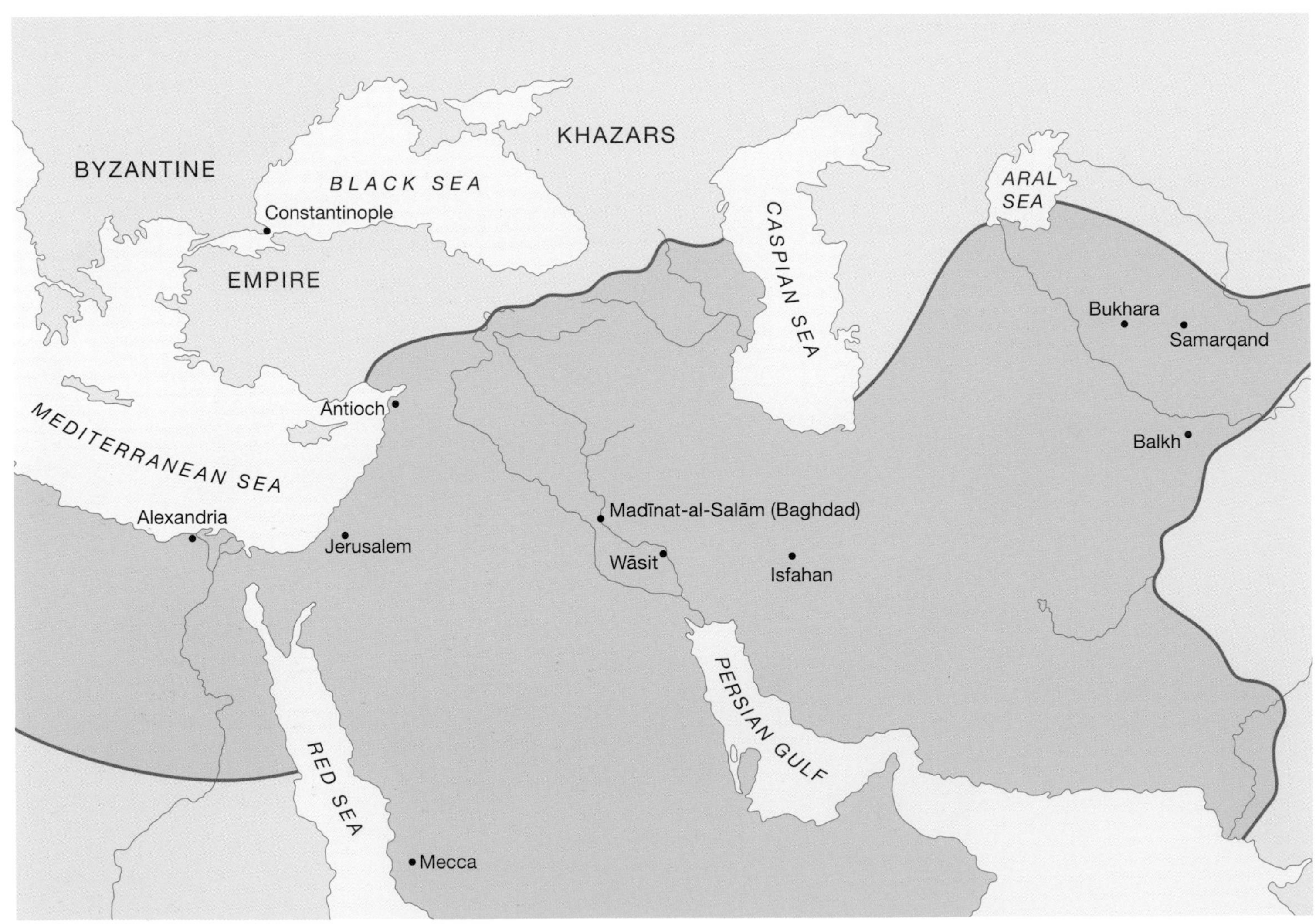

The Judaism of the Khazars set them apart from the other main group of Turkic semi-nomads with whom the Vikings had contact, the Volga Bulgars. These were based around the upper Volga and therefore were well placed either to engage in trade with the Vikings or to interfere with their trade further south. For much of the ninth and tenth centuries the Volga Bulgars were dominated by the Khazars, but in order to strengthen their own position against the Khazars they sought closer relations with the Caliphate, adopting Islam and issuing dirhams of Islamic type, although their main currency is recorded to have been marten skins (see p. 54).[30]

A third group of semi-nomads, the Pechenegs or Patzinaks, occupied the territory to the west of the Khazars and south of the Volga Bulgars, and were thus positioned across the trade routes between eastern Europe and Byzantium. They were also predominantly of Turkic origin, but the population combined a variety of faiths and ethnic groups. They were at times allied with the Byzantine empire and with the emerging Rūs states to the north, but at other periods there was open warfare between the Pechenegs and the Kievan Rūs, which was disruptive to trade between the territories of the Rūs and Byzantium.[31]

Trade and exchange

One of the major drivers for the start of the Viking movement outside Scandinavia, and in turn for making contact with and interacting with other cultures, was the desire to generate wealth. While the Vikings are best known for doing this through plunder, tribute and conquest (see chapter 2), they also did so through trade, and the development of long-distance trade routes is one of the most distinctive features of the Viking Age. A limited degree of trade beyond the borders of Scandinavia was already established before the beginning of the Viking expansion at the end of the eighth century. On the eastern side of Scandinavia, the island of Helgö on Lake Mälaren was home to a pre-urban trading centre with contacts across the Baltic and beyond from the sixth century onwards, although this was replaced by another settlement at nearby Birka in the ninth century. A trading centre was established at Staraya Ladoga in Russia by the mid-eighth century and archaeology suggests that this was inhabited by a mixture of Scandinavians, Slavs and Balts (fig. 28).[32]

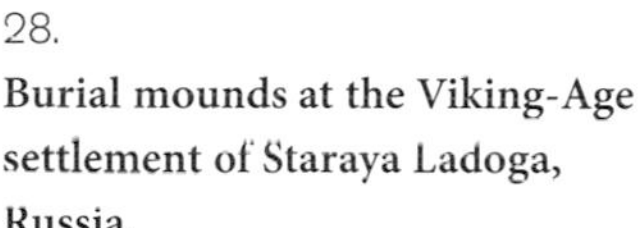

28.
Burial mounds at the Viking-Age settlement of Staraya Ladoga, Russia.

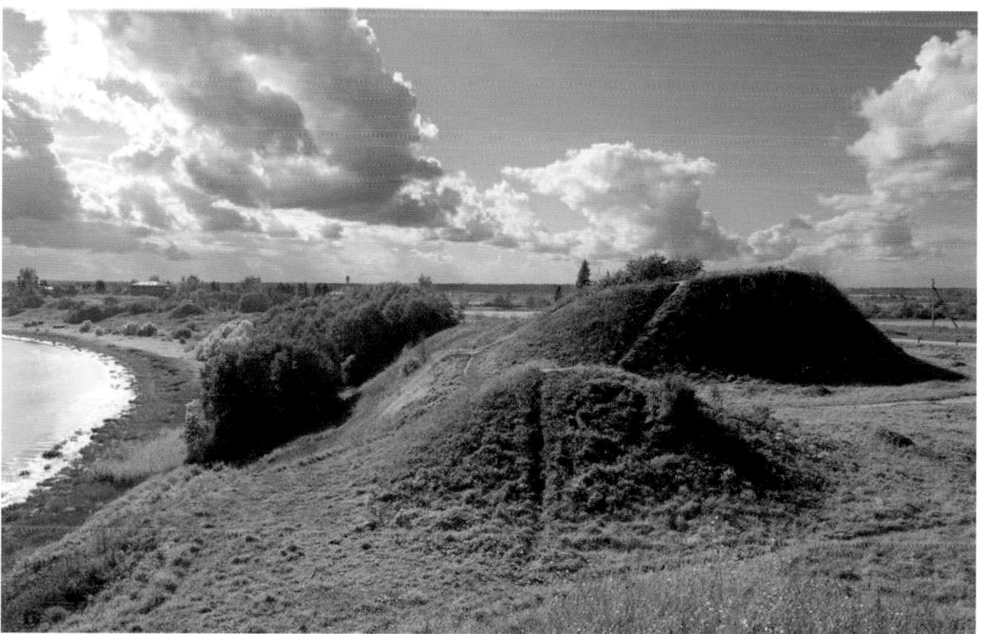

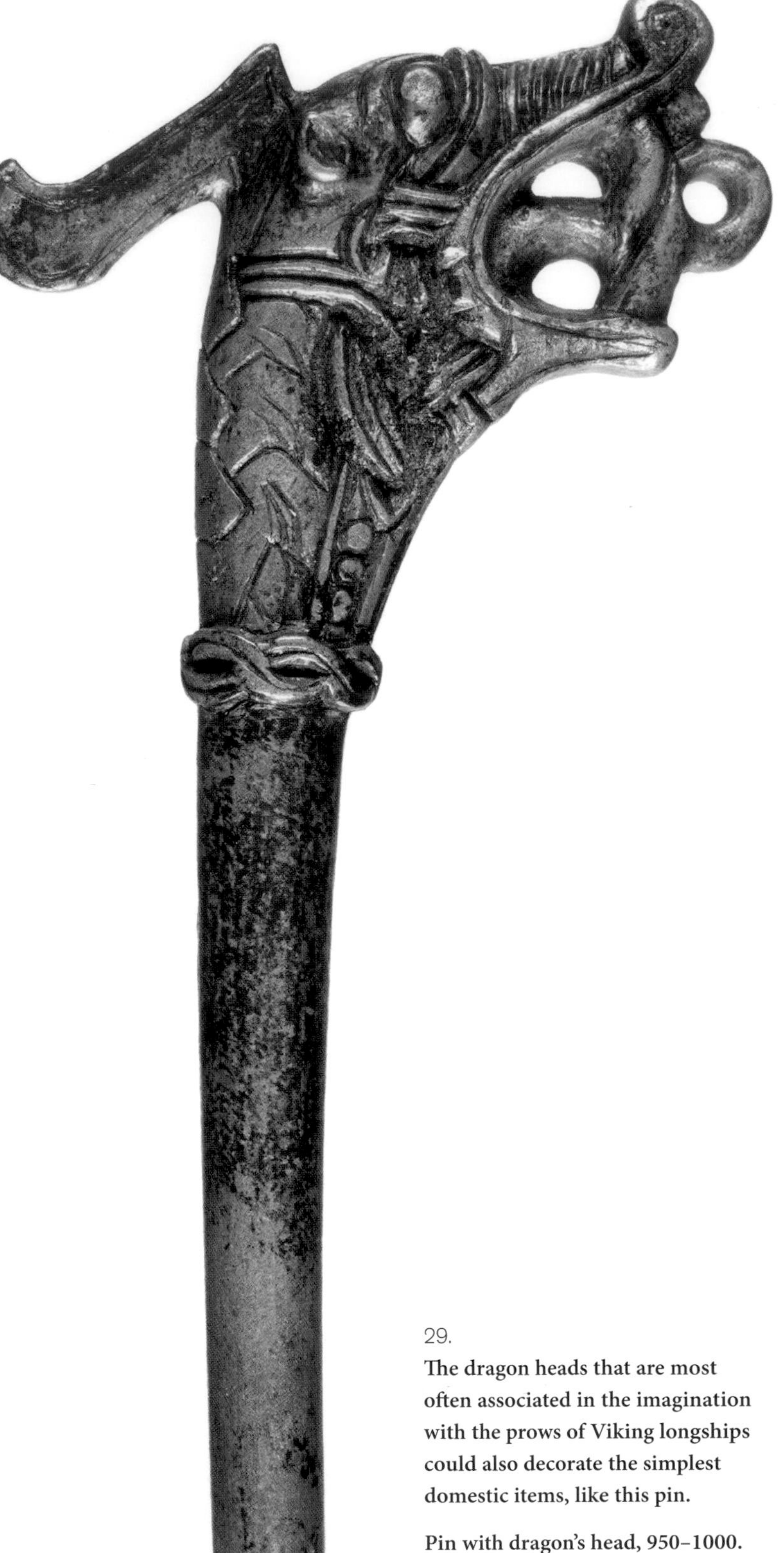

29.
The dragon heads that are most often associated in the imagination with the prows of Viking longships could also decorate the simplest domestic items, like this pin.

Pin with dragon's head, 950–1000. Hedeby, modern Germany.
Copper alloy. L 16.2 cm
Archäologisches Landesmuseum, Schloss Gottorf, Schleswig

On the other side of Scandinavia, Ribe in western Jutland was also established as a trading centre in the early eighth century, as the eastern end of a trading and monetary network that stretched around the North Sea via Frisia (modern Netherlands and north-western Germany) to eastern England. It is likely that these contacts built the familiarity with the coastlines of north-western Europe and specifically with monasteries and other wealthy trading centres that enabled the success of the early raids.[33] Arguably the earliest account of a Viking raid, at Portland in Dorset, describes the death of a West Saxon royal official who treated the Vikings as if they were traders and was killed for his trouble. Indeed, the event may have begun as a trading expedition that turned violent, rather than being planned as a raid.[34] Furthermore, peaceful trade apparently continued alongside violent raids throughout the Viking Age. Raiders on the Loire in 862 negotiated a truce over the winter that included the right to hold a market in which they could trade with the local people, and Viking camps in Britain and Ireland in the ninth century routinely seem to have combined military and economic functions (see pp. 120–1). The reign of Alfred the Great of Wessex (871–99) saw one of the main peaks of Viking raiding in England, but he also entertained at his court the Norwegian chieftain Ohthere who described his travels in northern Norway and his journey from there to the trading centre of Hedeby in southern Denmark, via the trading centre of *Sciringes healh* [Kaupang] in southern Norway (fig. 29). Although his purpose in visiting Alfred is not described, it is likely that this was also for the purpose of trade in luxury goods from northern Norway. Ohthere's account mentions how he took tribute from the Finnas in various types of furs, feathers, whale bone and ropes of walrus or seal-hide, and particularly mentions the importance of walruses 'because they have very fine bone in their teeth – they brought some of the teeth to the king'.[35] Similarly, while the numerous hoards of Anglo-Saxon coins in Scandinavia from the late Viking Age derive in part from raiding on England, many of them probably also were obtained from trade.[36]

There is not always a clear division between violent raiding and peaceful trading. The Islamic world traded in slaves with the Vikings and the Slavs, and the Vikings themselves kept unfree servants, known as thralls. Accounts of Viking raids in Britain and Ireland frequently record the taking of large numbers of prisoners and these were almost certainly taken for slaves or for ransom. Recent studies of DNA in Iceland show that while the male genes are almost exclusively from Scandinavia, the female genes have a strong Irish/Scottish component, and this has been explained by the presence of female Irish thralls, as mentioned in saga accounts of the settlement of Iceland.[37] Certainly slaving was one aspect of Viking activity in Ireland and excavation finds from Viking Dublin include a slave collar and shackle (figs 30–31). Control of trade could also be forceful. The major trading centre of Hedeby on the southern border of Denmark was established in part through the

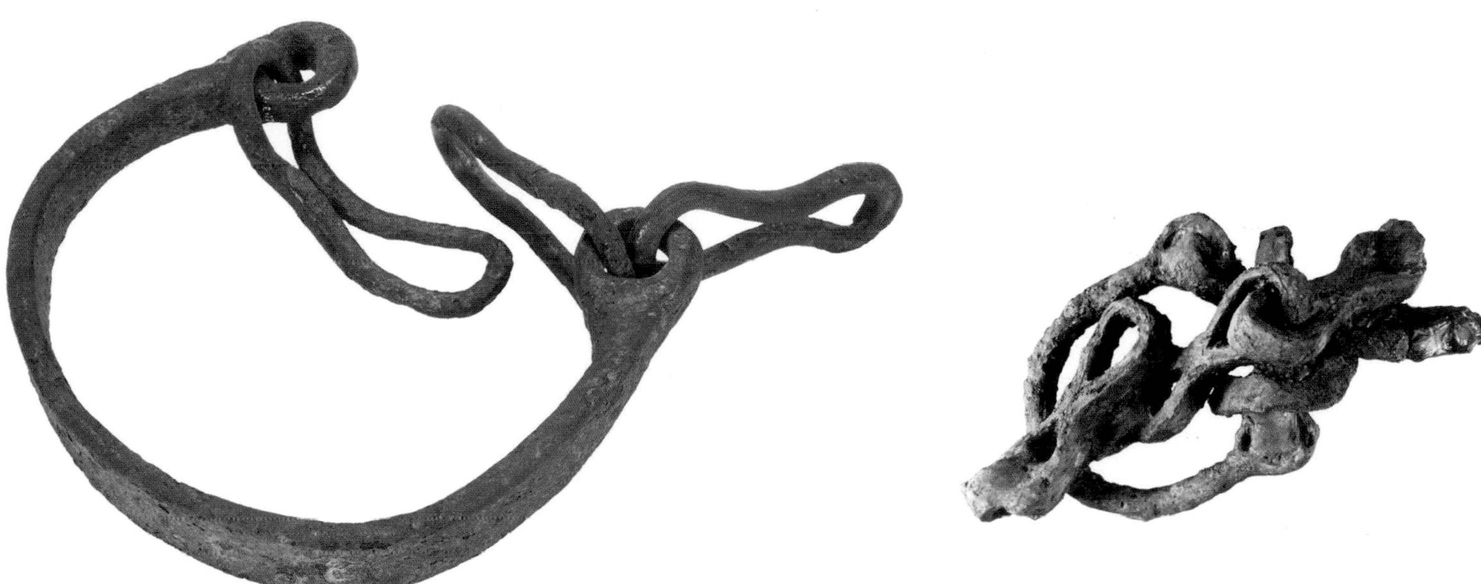

30. (above)
Slave collar, c. 10th–12th century. St John's Lane, Dublin, Ireland.
Iron. W 15 cm
National Museum of Ireland, Dublin

31. (above right)
A number of other sites besides Dublin have been linked with the Viking slave trade. This slave lock is from northern Germany.

Ankle shackle. Parchim Löddigsee, Mecklenburg, Germany.
Iron.
Archäologisches Landesmuseum, Schloss Gottorf, Schleswig

forcible relocation of traders from the Slavic centre of Reric, a short distance along the Baltic coast but outside Danish political control.[38]

Trade took place both on a local level and over long distances, and involved luxury goods and more basic commodities. These included foodstuffs, but also raw materials for the manufacture of jewellery, tools and weapons (fig. 32). Since the distribution of metal sources across the Viking world was uneven, this probably meant the movement of various metals in the form of bars, as well as other materials found only in particular places. For example, amber from the Baltic, jet from north-east England and walrus tusks from the North Atlantic were all transported around the Viking world (figs 33–35). Slate from Ovruč (Ukraine) has been found in northern Germany, while Baltic amber is known from places as far apart as Ireland, Central Asia and the Far East.[39] Imports to Scandinavia included weapons (see pp. 102–3), wine, glassware, quern stones (for grinding grain), pottery and both precious and non-precious metals. Exports included falcons, amber, hides and, above all, furs. Dried fish, which became a main element in Scandinavian trade in the later Middle Ages, seems to have become important only at the end of the Viking period, as changes in fishing practices made fishing on a commercial scale possible for the first time.

Trading centres varied dramatically in size and character. A limited number grew into what have been labelled as 'nodal points' for long-distance trade, forming a network of

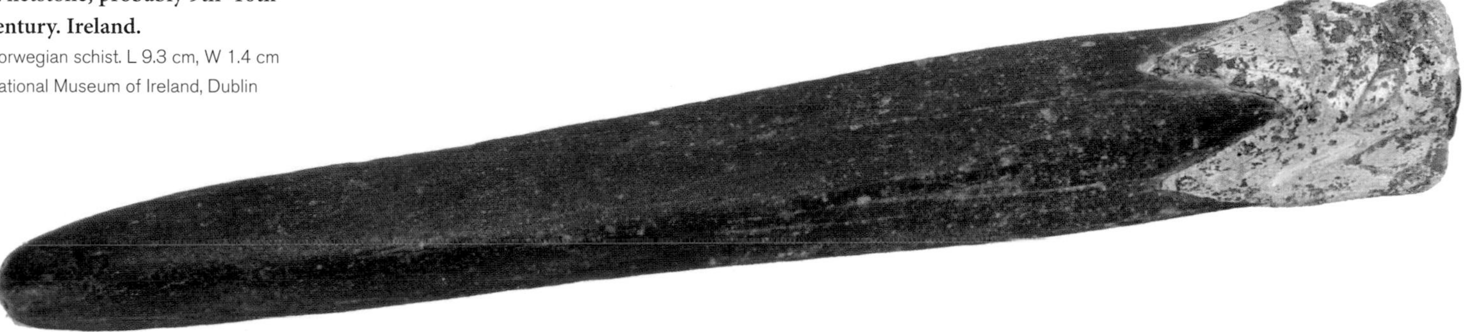

32.
Whetstones are used for the sharpening of bladed tools and weapons. This one was found in Ireland, but is made from Norwegian stone.

Whetstone, probably 9th–10th century. Ireland.
Norwegian schist. L 9.3 cm, W 1.4 cm
National Museum of Ireland, Dublin

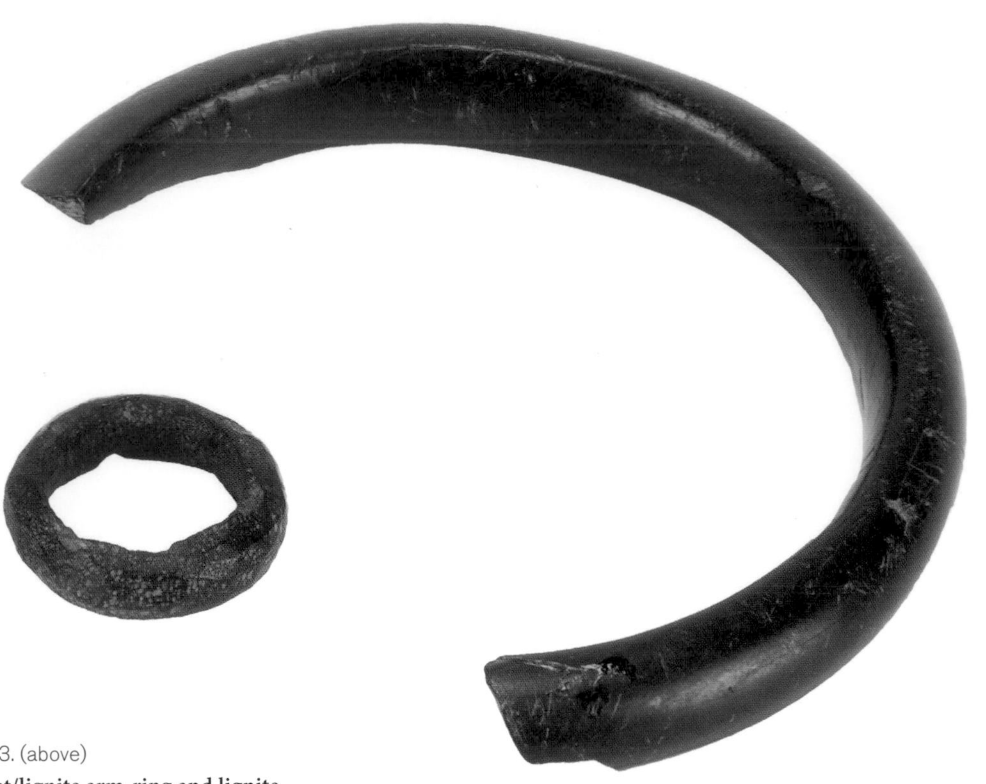

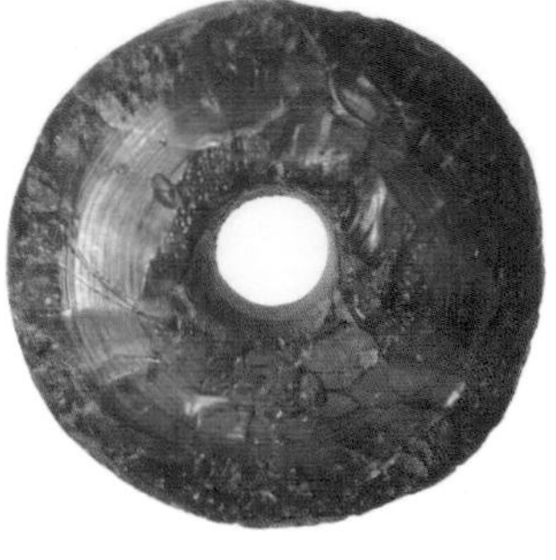

33. (above)
Jet/lignite arm-ring and lignite finger ring, probably 10th–11th century. Fishamble Street, Dublin, Ireland.
Jet/lignite. Finger ring Diam. 2.3 cm; arm-ring L 4.2 cm; L 5.69 cm
National Museum of Ireland, Dublin

34. (above)
Faceted bead, made from translucent yellow-red amber, 9th–10th century. Janów Pomorski/Truso, Poland.
Amber. Diam. 2.1 cm
Museum of Archaeology and History in Elblag

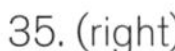

35. (right)
Raw amber from the Viking-Age trading site at Janów Pomorski/Truso, Poland.
Museum of Archaeology and History in Elblag

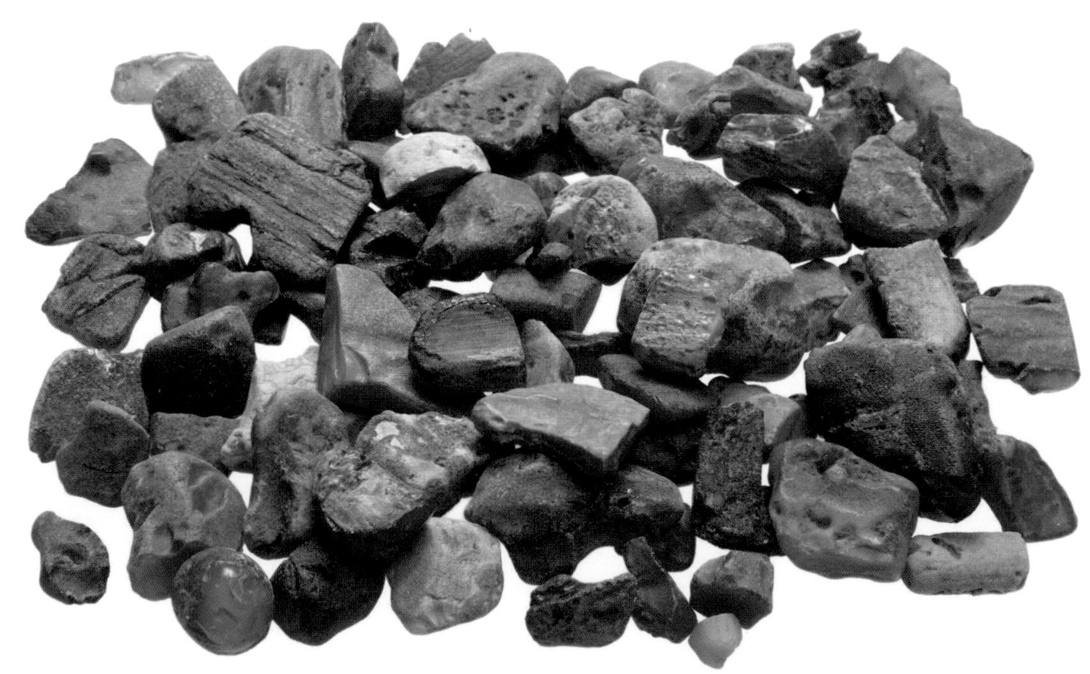

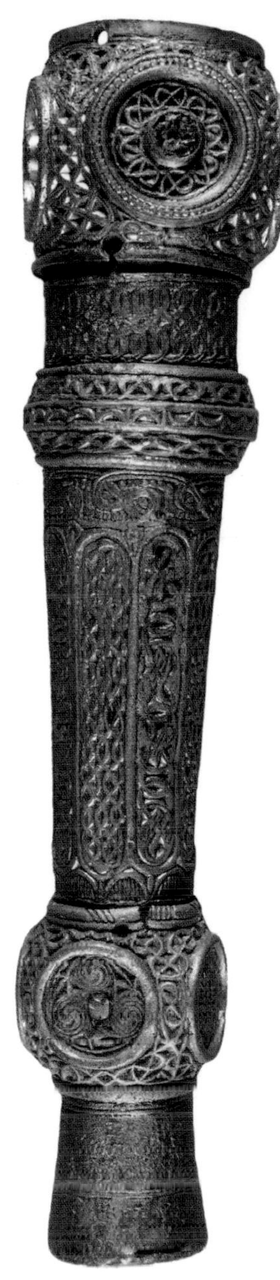

36.
At the beginning of the Viking Age, Ireland and Scandinavia shared a similar level of artistic technological expertise, despite fundamental cultural differences. Ireland, unlike Scandinavia, had been Christian for several hundred years.

Base of a crozier (bishop's crook), 8th century. Ireland.
Gilt copper alloy, amber. L 19.9 cm
National Museum of Ireland, Dublin

centres along established trade routes. Within Scandinavia, the principal trading sites in the early Viking Age were Hedeby and Ribe in Denmark, Åhus and Birka in Sweden, and Kaupang in the Oslo Fjord, and together with Truso (Janów Pomorski) in Poland and Staraya Ladoga in Russia they dominated trade in the Baltic.[40] These then linked into a larger network of smaller trading places that engaged in trade of a more local nature. Both production and exchange also continued at high-status residences and other so-called 'central places'. True towns were a feature of the late Viking Age, associated with the development of royal authority as much as trade (see pp. 150–5), when planned towns functioned as centres of power and administration – a situation with parallels in late Anglo-Saxon England and Ottonian Germany. Denmark saw the establishment of a few towns in the tenth century and a wider network in the eleventh, most notably Århus, Roskilde, Schleswig (which replaced Hedeby), Ribe, Ålborg, Odense and Lund (now in southern Sweden). In Sweden, Birka was replaced by Sigtuna in the late tenth century, while Norway witnessed the growth of a number of towns in the eleventh century, including Oslo, Bergen and Trondheim.[41]

A line of trading centres along the Russian river systems also gradually developed into towns: Gnezdovo, Gorodische, Chernigov, Novgorod and Kiev. In Ireland, the first wave of settlement was based on small fortified camps known as *longphuirt*, which combined military and economic functions (see pp. 120–1), but these were replaced in the tenth century by a handful of towns, with surrounding hinterlands (fig. 36). A similar transition from trading centres to towns took place in England in the tenth century, both in Anglo-Saxon and Viking territories. However, urbanization was not an essential part of Viking trade. As yet, no Viking towns have been discovered in Scotland, despite the fact that both the Northern and Western Isles lay along established trade routes between Ireland and Scandinavia, while saga evidence suggests that Vikings arriving in Iceland would simply trade from the estates of local chieftains who offered hospitality and protection.[42]

As discussed above, Viking-Age trade was based on a combination of luxury goods and commodities. Initially there was minimal use of coinage and bullion as means of exchange. Coins were used in Ribe in the eighth century as a result of Anglo-Saxon and Frisian influence, and in Hedeby from the early ninth century under Carolingian influence, but these local experiments made little impact elsewhere.[43] Exchange outside the main trading centres may have been based partially on barter of one type of goods for another, with the exchange rate depending on the individual circumstances.

However, current thinking suggests that there may also have been extensive use of 'commodity money', where items with an intrinsic value of some sort are given a quasi-monetary function, both as a means of exchange and as a measurement of value, providing a mechanism for the pricing of other commodities. Such systems leave little clear trace in the archaeological record and the dearth of historical sources for Scandinavia means that the existence of commodity money cannot be clearly established in the Viking Age. However, the Vikings would certainly have encountered such systems in Russia, where

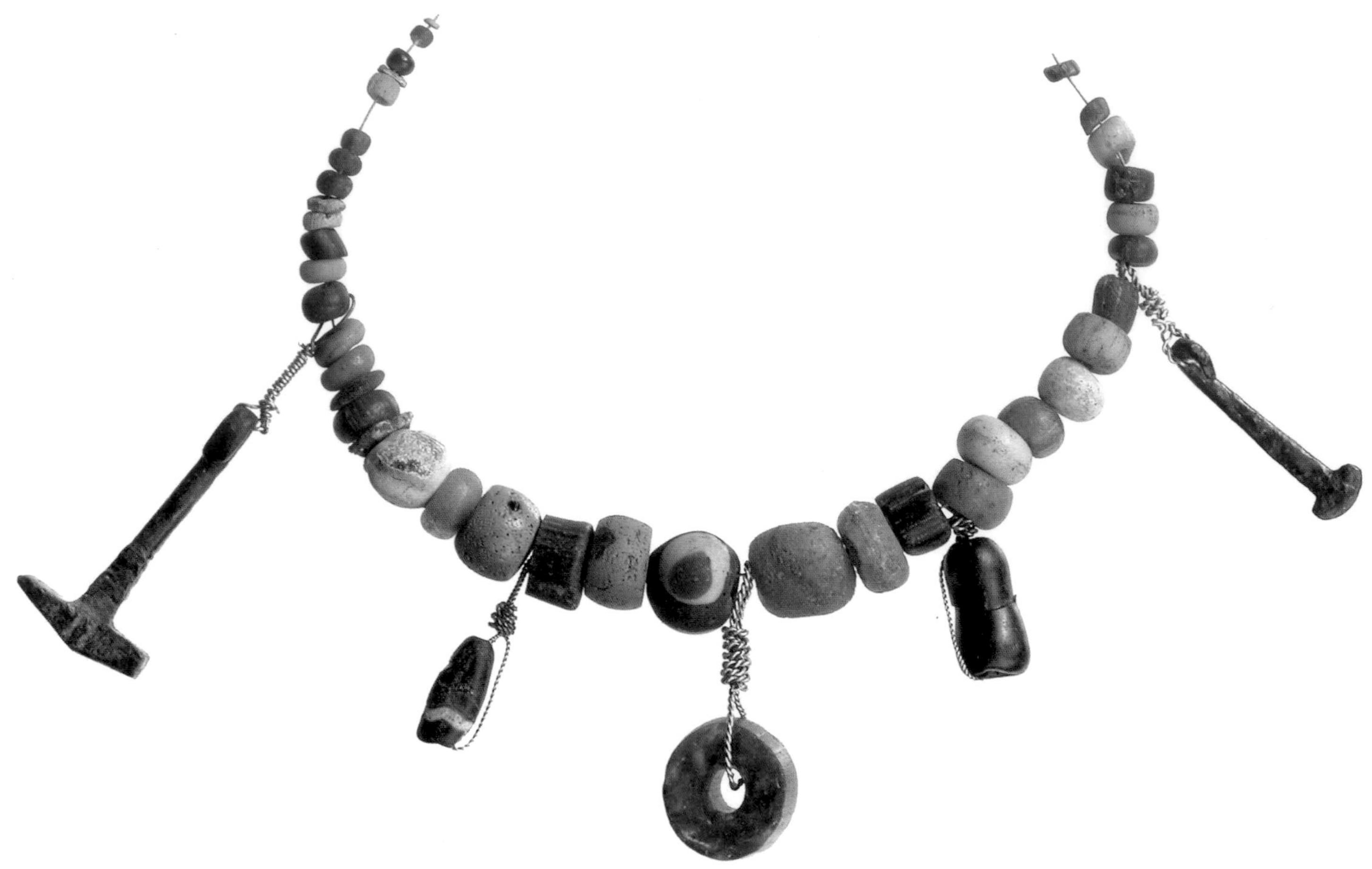

37.

Glass beads and two iron pendants made into a necklace, 9th–10th cenutury. Janów Pomorski/Truso, Poland.

Glass, iron.
Hammer-shaped pendant (left) L 3.25 cm;
Hammer-shaped pendant (right) L 2.75 cm
Museum of Archaeology and History in Elblag

Arabic sources indicate the monetary use of glass beads (worth one silver dirham) and marten skins (worth two and a half dirhams). Glass beads are common finds in Viking trading centres in Scandinavia and may have fulfilled a similar function there (fig. 37).[44]

A fundamental shift took place in the ninth century, with the adoption of silver as a means of exchange. At the beginning of the Viking Age, precious metals were almost exclusively confined to social rather than economic functions. Gold and silver were important in the display of personal wealth, and gifts and the exchange of precious metal objects underpinned a variety of social relationships (see pp. 128–33, 138–40). This created a demand for precious metals as raw material for the manufacture of status items that was met by a massive influx of Islamic silver coins, with well over 100,000 recorded from Viking-Age Scandinavia (figs 38–41). New hoards are being discovered all the time. The supply of dirhams was intermittent as it was susceptible to the interruption of trade caused by the Khazars and Volga Bulgars and dried up entirely in the late tenth century, although the discovery of new sources of European silver meant that it was easily replaced in Scandinavia by Anglo-Saxon and German coins.[45]

Coins were thus initially valued to some extent as a raw material, but the durability of silver and gold made them more suited to a monetary role than many other commodities, while the Islamic world, Byzantium, the Carolingian empire and the Anglo-Saxon kingdoms all provided examples of coin use. It is likely that these examples, and especially that of Islamic coinage, sparked the use of bullion in exchange (figs 42–45). Although bullion lacked the formal quality control linked with coinage, it provided a highly flexible system. A variety of methods could be used to test the purity of the metal, including 'nicking' and 'pecking' the surface to test the hardness of the alloy and also to reveal plating

The social and symbolic importance of Islamic coins as an indicator of wealth and status is made particularly apparent by the profusion of imitation dirhams produced in Scandinavia during the Viking period.

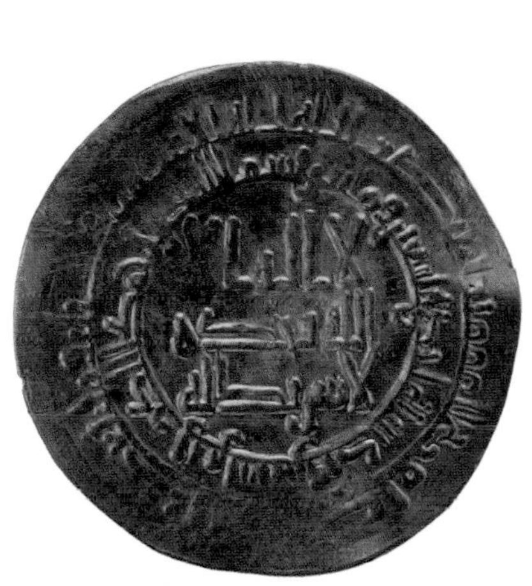

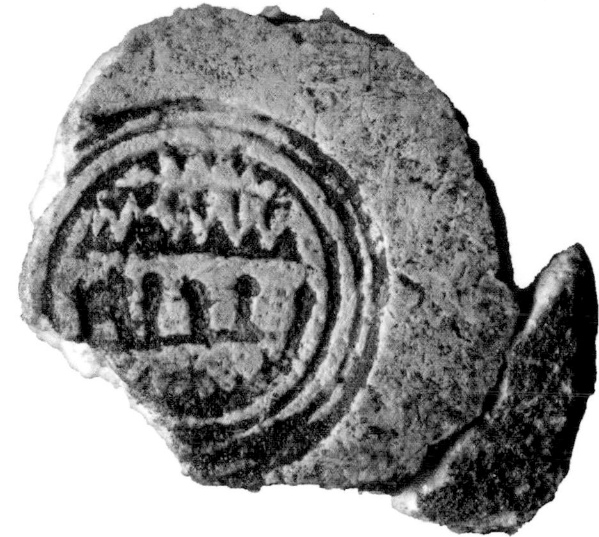

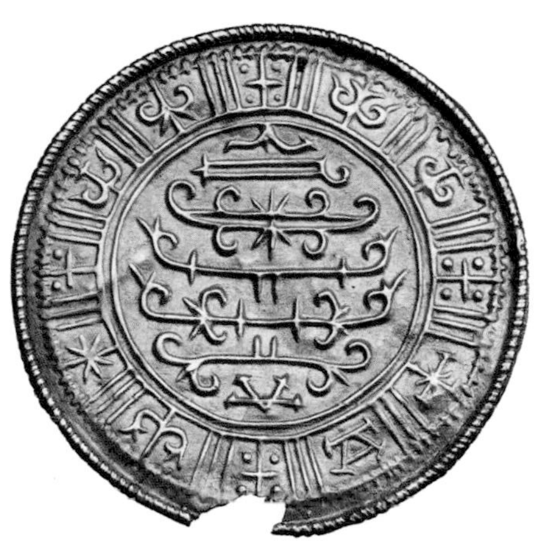

38.
Silver dirham of Ismail b. Ahmad (892–907), minted in Samarkand in AH 291 (902–3). Vale of York hoard, buried c. 927–8. North Yorkshire, England.
Silver. Diam. 2.2 cm
British Museum, London

39.
Fragment of a Scandinavian mould for making imitation Islamic coins. Hedeby, Germany.
Antler. L 3.3 cm, W 2.6 cm, H 1 cm
Archäologisches Landesmuseum, Schloss Gottorf, Schleswig

40.
Gold bracteates (thin single-sided circular ornaments) were produced as jewellery in Scandinavia from the fifth century onwards. This example is decorated with a pattern inspired by Islamic Kufic calligraphy.

Pseudo cufic bracteate. Gotland, Sweden.
Gold.
National Museum of Denmark, Copenhagen

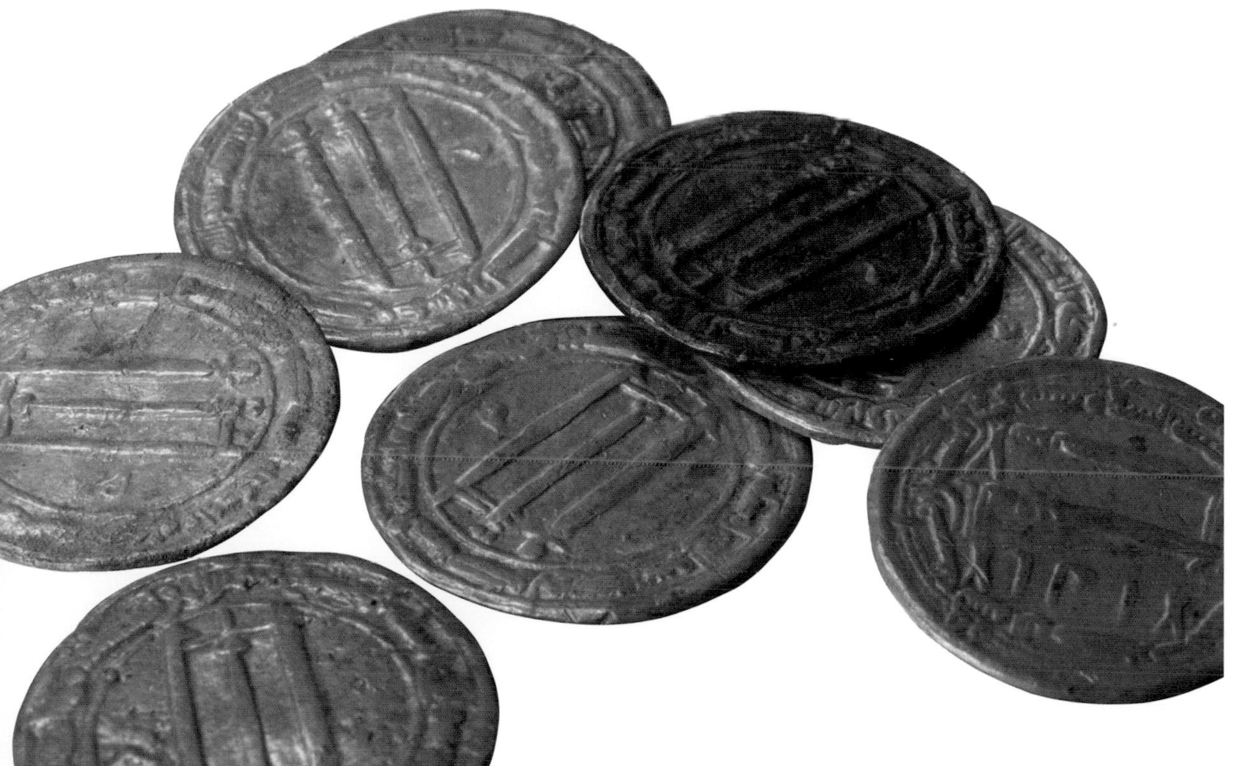

41.
Nine identical contemporary imitations of a silver dirham of Harun al Rashid, 807/808, Baghdad. Hedeby harbour, Germany.
Tin/lead alloy. Diam. 2.2 cm
Archäologisches Landesmuseum, Schloss Gottorf, Schleswig

42. (right)
In the Viking bullion economy, precious metal was melted down and turned into portable ingots.

Mould and silver ingot. Birka, Uppland, Sweden.
Silver, stone. Mould L 11 cm
Statens Historiska Museum, Stockholm

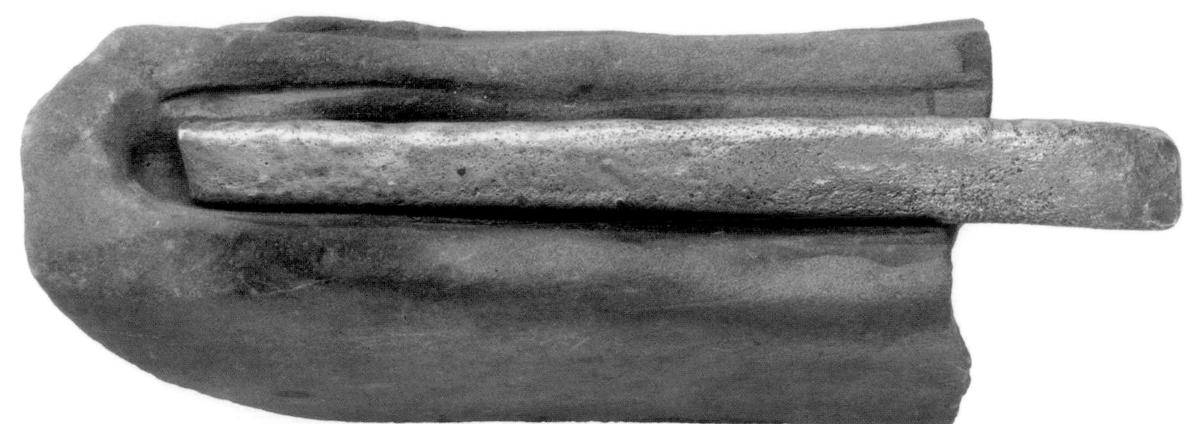

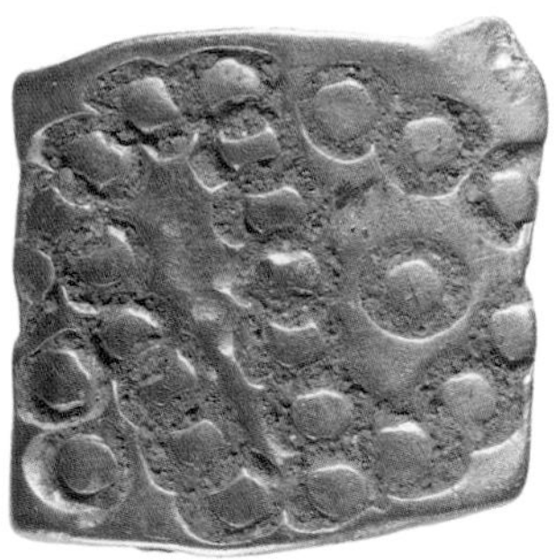

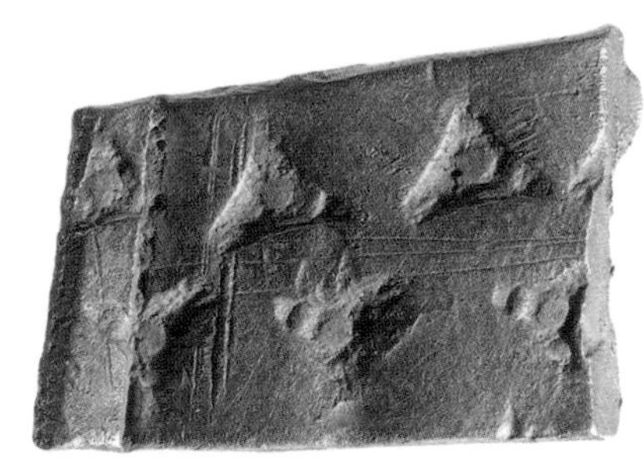

43. (above)
Hack-gold with stamped ornament, late 800s–1000. Aldbrough, Yorkshire, England.
Gold. L 1.1 cm
British Museum, London

44. (above)
Hack-gold with stamped ornament, late 800s–1000. Torksey, Lincolnshire, England.
Gold. L 1.1 cm
British Museum, London

45. (below)
Gold ingot, probably 9th–11th century. Askeaton, Co. Limerick, Ireland.
Gold. L 4 cm
National Museum of Ireland, Dublin

47. (right)
This silver hoard contains ingots and arm-rings that have been nicked on the edges to test the silver quality.

Hoard of arm-rings and ingots, 900–1100. Skomentnen/Skomętno, Woj. Warmińsko-Mazurskie, Poland.
Silver. Arm-rings Diam. 8.5–9.5 cm; ingots L 5.7–14.5 cm
Museum für Vor- und Frühgeschichte, Staatliche Museen zu Berlin, Berlin

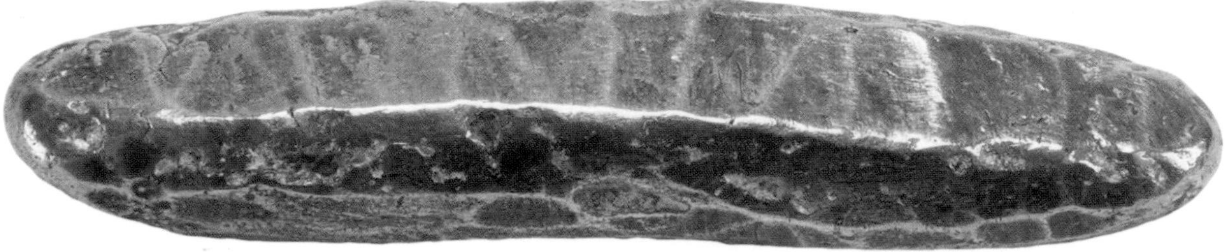

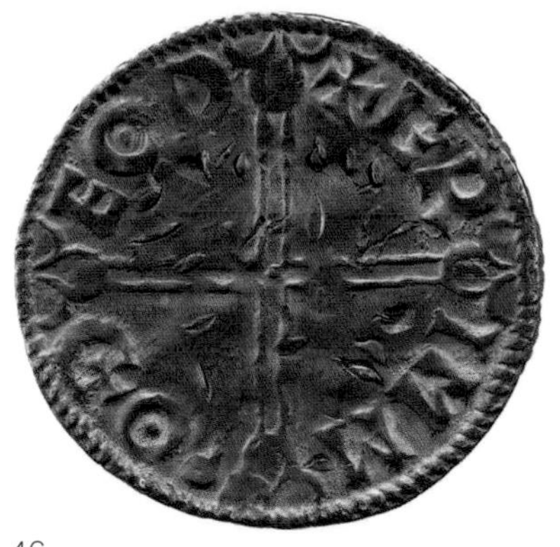

46.
The surface of this Anglo-Saxon coin shows characteristic 'pecks', where the point of a knife has been dug into the metal to test the purity.

Silver penny of Æthelred II, Long Cross type (978–1013 and 1014–1016).
British Museum, London

(fig. 46), while the value could be measured by weight. The bullion economy included coins, both whole and fragmentary, but also larger ingots and cut fragments of ingots, jewellery, plate, etc. – known collectively as hack-silver (fig. 47). Whereas coins in this period came in a very limited range of denominations, bullion could be used in any quantity: the tiniest fragments of hack-silver are much smaller and lighter than coins and therefore better suited to low-value transactions, while the largest ingots weighed over 1 kilogram each and could only have been used for major purchases or convenient storage.[46]

The use of bullion required the measurement of weight and here too we can see the influence of the Islamic world (fig. 48). Two types of weights in particular seem to have been imported along with the dirhams. These are cubo-octahedral weights, sometimes known as 'dice weights', and oblate spheroids, or 'barrel weights', both of which were produced in various sizes, with markings indicating the weights that they represented (fig. 49). Imported weights were used, but local imitations were also produced, in some cases with pseudo-Arabic inscriptions on the barrel weights. These weights are found across the whole of the Viking world as far west as Ireland, and became widespread in the late ninth century. At the same time, the Vikings in Britain and Ireland began producing their

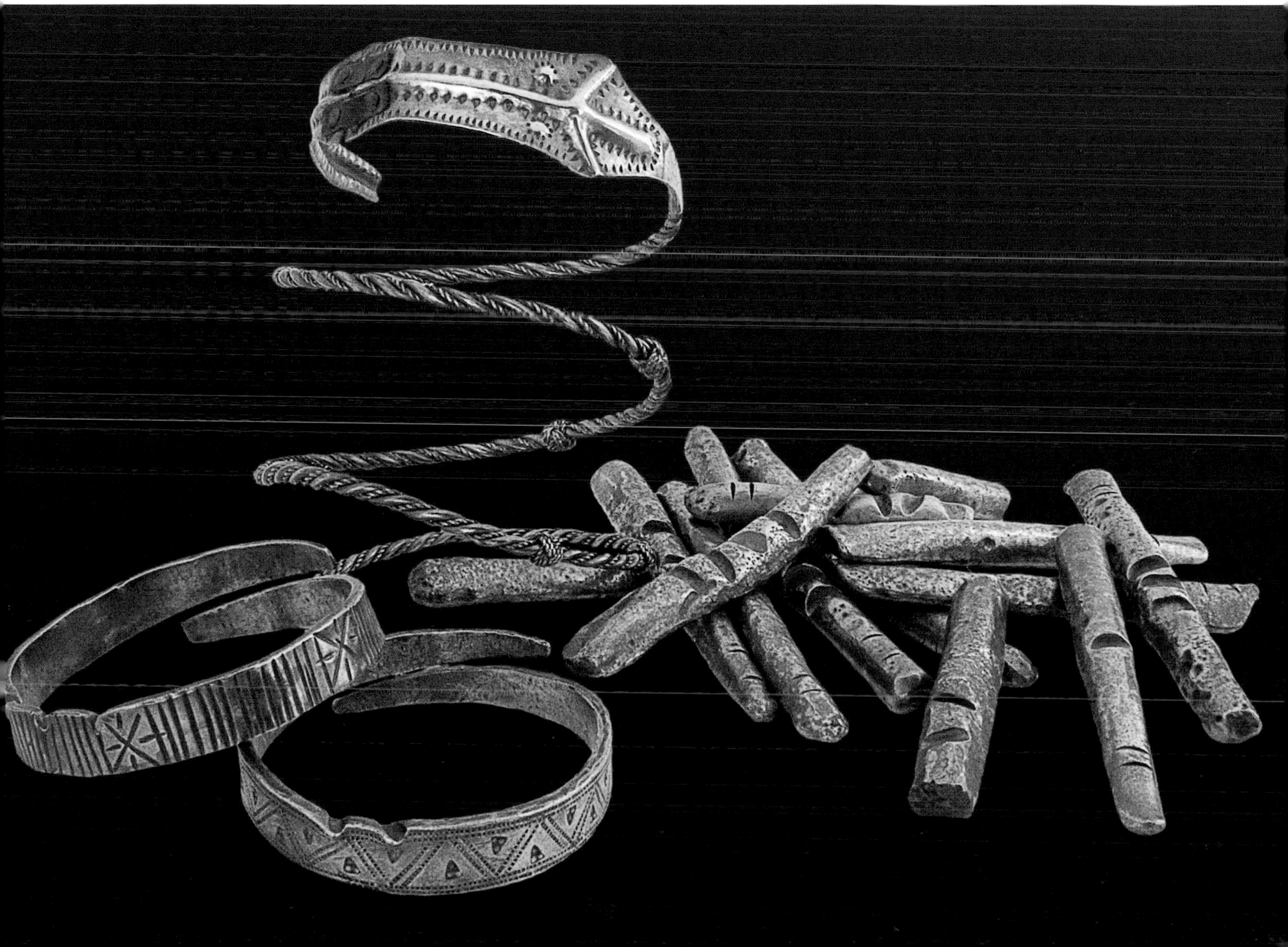

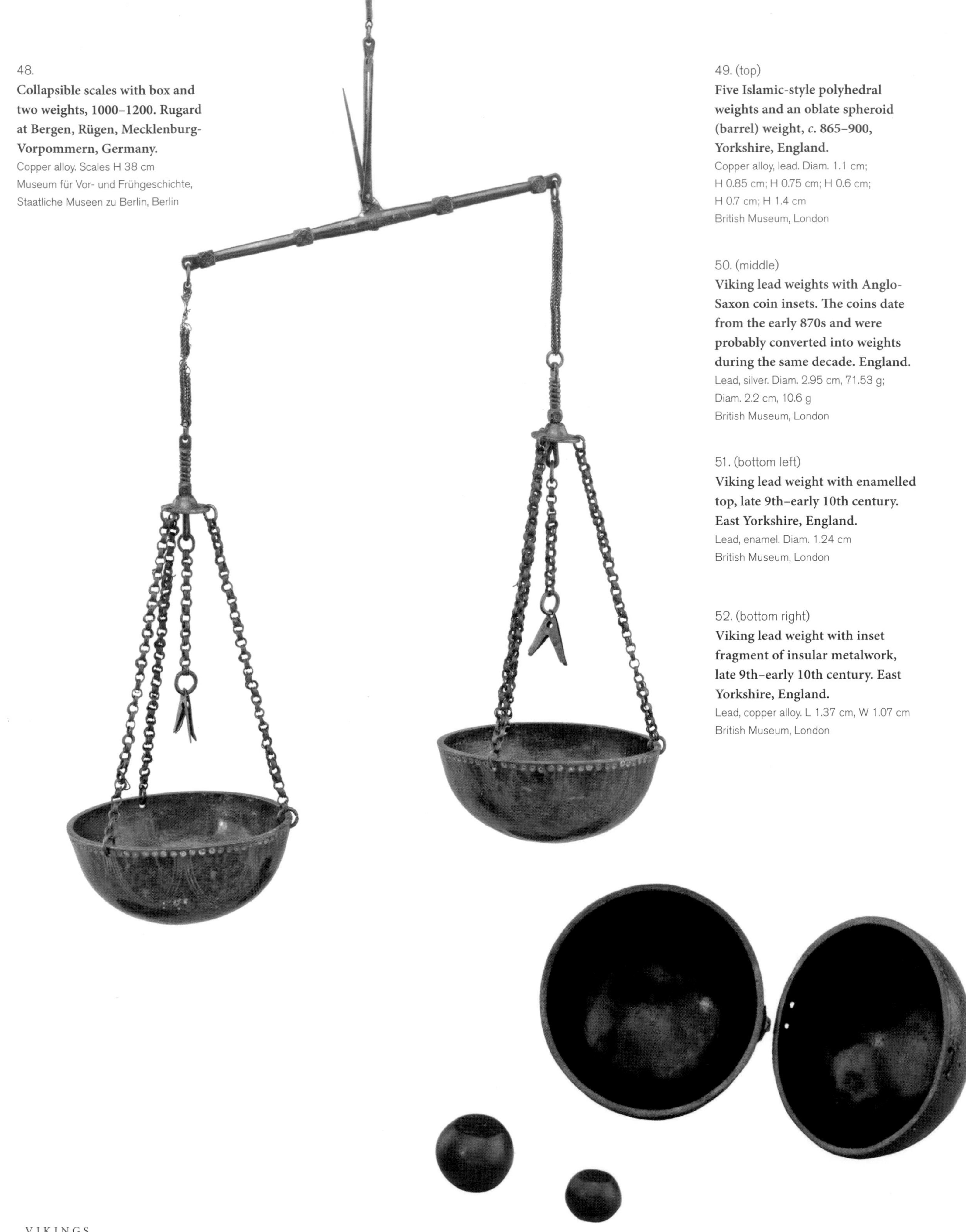

48.
Collapsible scales with box and two weights, 1000–1200. Rugard at Bergen, Rügen, Mecklenburg-Vorpommern, Germany.
Copper alloy. Scales H 38 cm
Museum für Vor- und Frühgeschichte, Staatliche Museen zu Berlin, Berlin

49. (top)
Five Islamic-style polyhedral weights and an oblate spheroid (barrel) weight, *c.* 865–900, Yorkshire, England.
Copper alloy, lead. Diam. 1.1 cm; H 0.85 cm; H 0.75 cm; H 0.6 cm; H 0.7 cm; H 1.4 cm
British Museum, London

50. (middle)
Viking lead weights with Anglo-Saxon coin insets. The coins date from the early 870s and were probably converted into weights during the same decade. England.
Lead, silver. Diam. 2.95 cm, 71.53 g; Diam. 2.2 cm, 10.6 g
British Museum, London

51. (bottom left)
Viking lead weight with enamelled top, late 9th–early 10th century. East Yorkshire, England.
Lead, enamel. Diam. 1.24 cm
British Museum, London

52. (bottom right)
Viking lead weight with inset fragment of insular metalwork, late 9th–early 10th century. East Yorkshire, England.
Lead, copper alloy. L 1.37 cm, W 1.07 cm
British Museum, London

A variety of weights were used by Vikings in Britain.

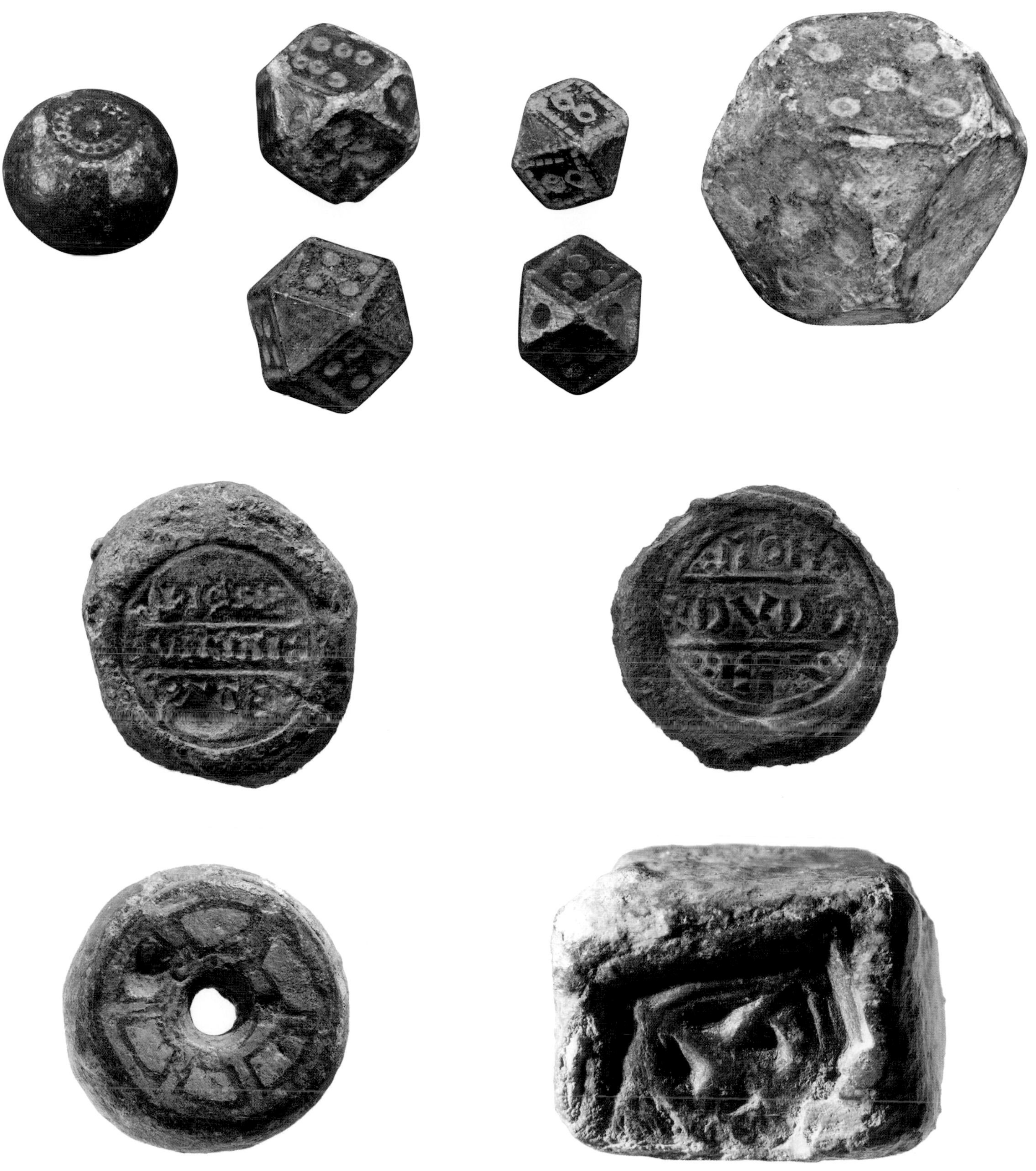

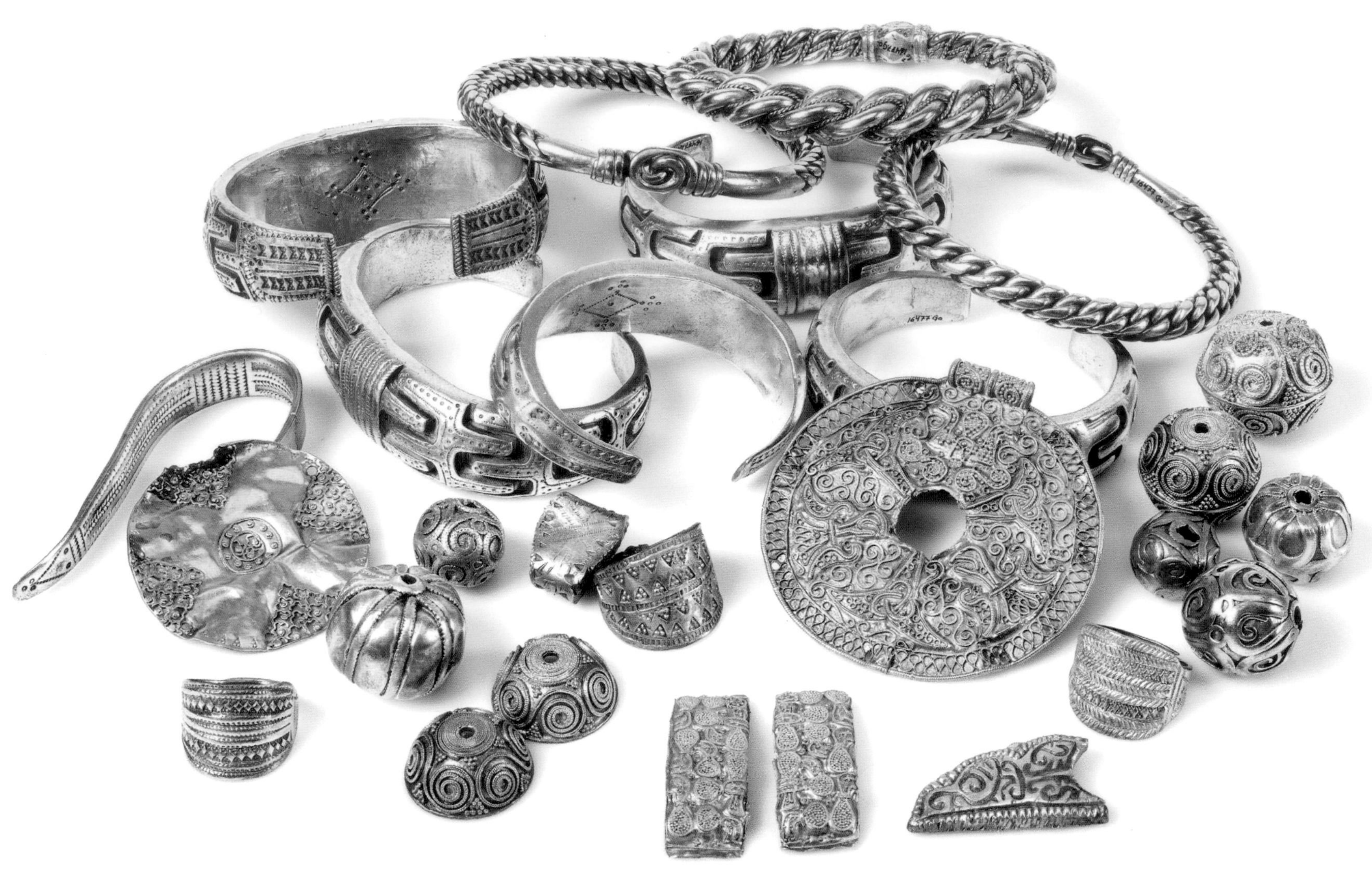

53.
Silver hoard of Scandinavian and Baltic objects, including five arm-rings of standardized weight among other items. Malmsmyr, Rone, Gotland, Sweden.
Statens Historiska Museum, Stockholm

own weights for use with silver. These were lead weights decorated either with enamelling or with insets of coins or cut-up ornamental metalwork. This meant that, unlike the dice weights and barrel weights, each of the decorative lead weights was unique, so there was no danger of them being switched in the course of a transaction (figs 50–52). Both types of weights broadly followed weight standards derived from the Islamic world (and ultimately from the Roman ounce), but opinion is divided on how controlled and consistent weight standards were across the Viking world as a whole.[47]

The relationship between the bullion value of silver and its role in display and social exchange was most explicit in the production of weight-adjusted jewellery (fig. 53). Neck-rings from northern Russia and imitations of the type from Scandinavia, together with different types of arm-rings from Scandinavia, Ireland and Scotland, all seem to have been produced to be consistent with multiples of the ounce, although the exact standard of the ounce apparently varied across time and from region to region. The origins of such standardized jewellery can perhaps be seen in the account of the Arab writer ibn Fadlān of how Rūs traders symbolized their wealth through neck-rings:

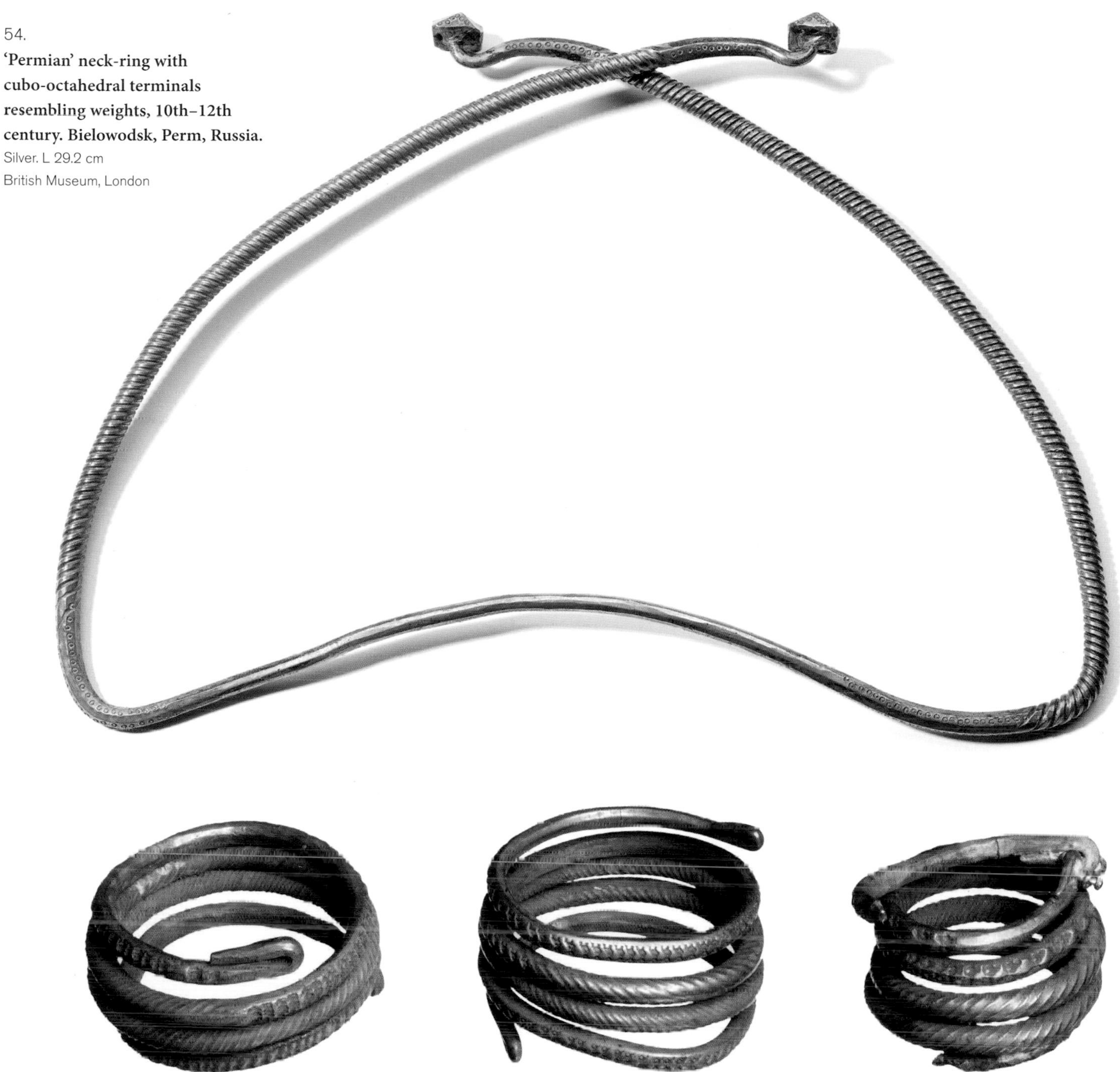

54.
'Permian' neck-ring with cubo-octahedral terminals resembling weights, 10th–12th century. Bielowodsk, Perm, Russia.
Silver. L 29.2 cm
British Museum, London

55.
Neck-rings of standardized weight from Russia and Scandinavia were sometimes coiled into arm-rings.

Hoard of three spiral arm-rings, 9th century. Hoffmanslyst, East Jutland, Denmark.
Silver. Diam. 3.9 cm; 3.9 cm; 3.47 cm
National Museum of Denmark, Copenhagen

> Round their necks [Rūs women] wear torques of gold or silver, for every man, as soon as he accumulates 10,000 dirhams, has a torque made for his wife. When he has 20,000 he has two torques made, and so on. Every time he increases his wealth by 10,000 he adds another torque to those his wife possesses, so that one woman may have many torques around her neck.[48]

A standardized neck-ring would thus symbolize possession of a far greater amount of wealth, and the relationship with weights is reinforced by the use of decorative terminals on the Russian neck-rings, with shapes derived from the cubo-octahedral weights used for weighing silver (figs 54–55).[49]

The Viking Age saw the gradual introduction of coinage across most of the Viking world, although it seems to have been little used in the North Atlantic islands.[50] This in part reflects the monetary influence of the Vikings' neighbours, although both native and imported coinage typically circulated as bullion alongside other forms of silver, rather than within a tightly regulated coin-based economy as seen in late Anglo-Saxon England or the Islamic world. However, the adoption of coinage was closely linked with the adoption of Christianity and the development of royal authority, and coinage will be discussed in more detail in these contexts in later chapters (see pp. 151–4).[51]

Cultural exchange

Trading is only one form of exchange and interaction is visible in other respects across the Viking Age. Written sources tell us about individual Scandinavian traders in both the east and west, and Islamic merchants having contacts with the Rūs in Russia and Scandinavia. However, we also hear of Anglo-Saxon and Frankish missionaries in the north, Scandinavian settlers in the west and political envoys from various places moving around the Viking world. Contact could be violent, as in the case of the monastery of Lindisfarne, off the Northumbrian coast, which was attacked by Vikings in 793.[52] It could also occur in a gentler manner through trade and travel, as well as through royal weddings, such as those between Viking and Slavonic nobles in the tenth century (see p. 133).[53]

Even before the raid on Lindisfarne took place, trading links were being established through southern Scandinavia across the North Sea and the Baltic, and thus between several different cultural groups. The centres that supported such trade also permitted the exchange of a wide range of ideas, religious views, technical skills and even fashions of clothing and hairstyles. Thus even the attack on Lindisfarne might be interpreted as divine retribution for copying the ungodly hairstyles of the Vikings.[54] The importance of such centres is shown both by the recording of repeated raids and by their role as a focus for Christian missionary activity.

Raiding and trading provided short-term (if potentially repeated) interaction, while other activities offered opportunities for more prolonged contact. For example, Vikings serving in the Varangian Guard (a regiment within the Byzantine military with defined ranks and salaries, which functioned both as an elite guard for the emperor and as a field unit in various wars on the fringes of the empire; see p. 98) in Constantinople might find themselves at the heart of the Byzantine court for years. Missionaries and diplomats might spend a long or a short time in the places they visited, but even a brief spell could be enough to form impressions that could then be passed on to others. The *Life of Ansgar*, the biography of a missionary in Denmark and Sweden in the mid-ninth century, and the account of the Moorish envoy al-Tartushi, who visited Hedeby in the late tenth century (see p. 71), provide interesting information to the modern historian about Frankish and Arabic perspectives on the Vikings (even if they are somewhat low on useful factual information), but they were also intended to be shared at the time they were written.[55]

One interaction that led to a long-term relationship with profound consequences was the conversion of Scandinavian rulers to Christianity. Although Christian missionaries were active in Scandinavia from the early ninth century, it is striking that some Scandinavian rulers were baptized not in their homelands but abroad. In 826 Harald Klak was baptized on the Continent, becoming the first Danish king to accept Christianity, while as late as 1013 the Norwegian Olaf Haraldsson received baptism in northern France.[56] This special kind of contact with the outer world is likely to have been used for strengthening external alliances and therefore the ruler's internal position as well,[57] bringing adjustments not just to personal beliefs but to the ruler's role within society and the structures of kingship. It was also reflected in more directly visible ways, for example by the adoption of royal robes and regalia in the style of Carolingian kings, and the public expression of the king's royal identity in Carolingian style through monuments and coins (see pp. 140, 151–3, 156–7). The material influence of Christianization extended beyond kings and aristocrats. For instance, the spread of Frankish-style round brooches in the ninth century suggests wider effects on Scandinavian dress as a result of Christian influence.[58]

Cultural interaction was not limited to the elite and to envoys at foreign courts. Settlement overseas often involved high-status leaders – there were, after all, kings of Dublin, princes of Kiev, dukes of Normandy, earls of Orkney and so on – but the settlers represented a wide variety of social status, including lesser chieftains, farmers and thralls (slaves). Areas of permanent Viking settlement are reflected in the widespread distribution of place names of Scandinavian origin, as seen across much of northern and eastern England, parts of Scotland, Ireland and Wales, and in Normandy (fig. 56). In some cases, such as Shetland, there are almost no pre-Viking place names, while in parts of England

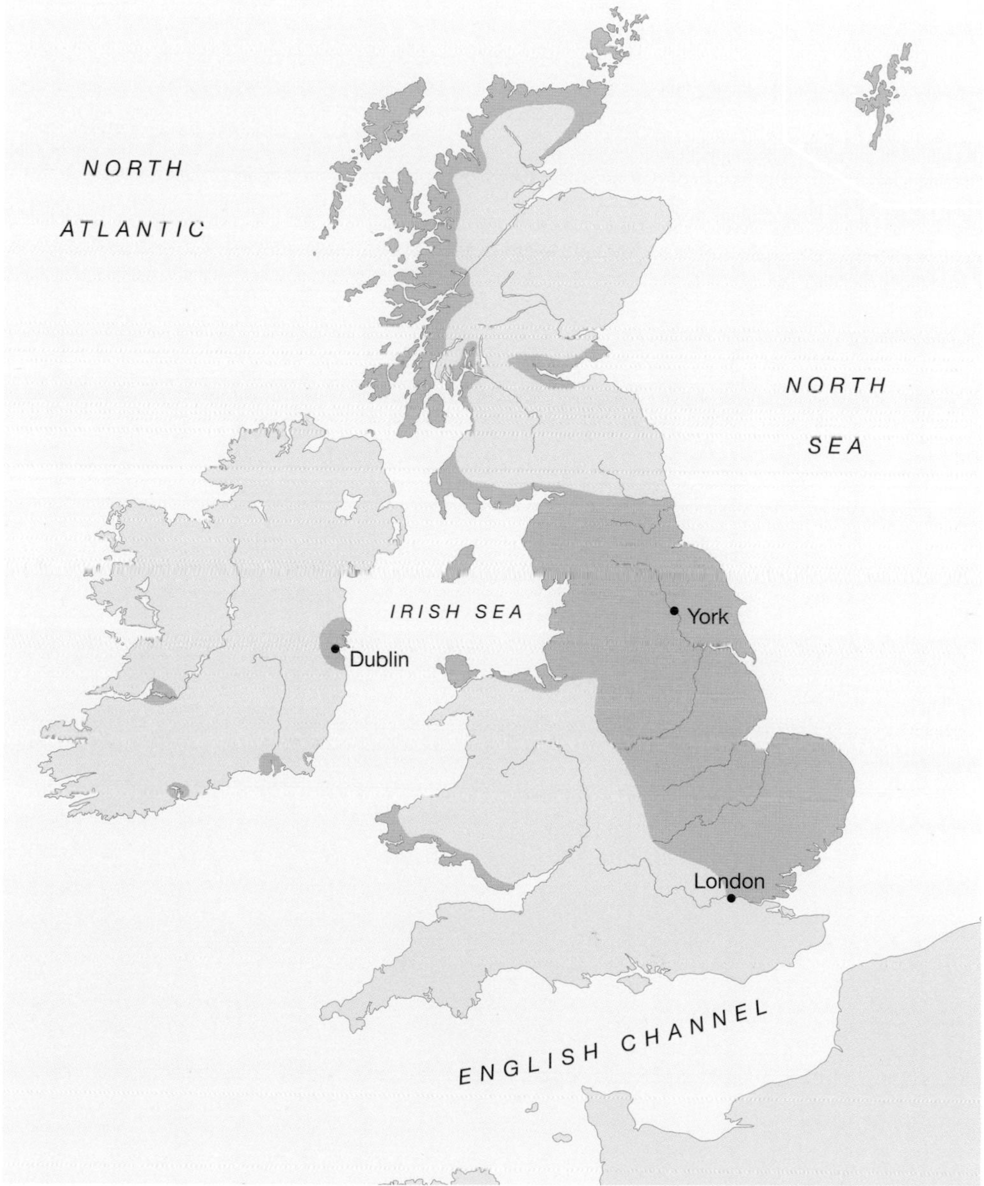

56.
Regions of Britain and Ireland with evidence for strong Scandinavian influences, usually including Viking-Age settlement.

and Normandy, Viking and native place names exist side by side. In other areas the patterns are more complicated, as in western Scotland and the Isle of Man, where a resurgence of Gaelic after the Viking Age means that it can be difficult to determine whether Celtic place names are pre-Viking or post-Viking. It also worked the other way round: Slavonic place names known from the Danish isles and southern Sweden indicate permanent settlement of people from across the Baltic. There are similar issues of language, with individual words borrowed from one language to another. Given the maritime nature of Viking society, it is perhaps unsurprising that Old Norse vocabulary relating to ships was widely borrowed by other languages.

Another recent source of information about the movement of peoples has been the application of science. Strontium isotope analysis of teeth can establish where individuals lived when they were growing up, while DNA analysis of skeletal remains can match individuals with the dominant DNA patterns in different ethnic groups, although the certainty with which individuals can be assigned to specific groups is often overstated. The same applies to the use of DNA to study the genetic roots of modern populations. Since the techniques identify only a single line of ancestry among the many millions that make up each person, they are of limited value with regard to the individual. However, where there is a shared trend across a significant proportion of the population of a region, the results can be informative, such as the evidence suggesting strong Norwegian elements in the Northern and Western Isles of Scotland, and in north-west England.[59]

There are similar issues with the distribution of archaeological objects. Small items used as souvenirs or gifts could easily be moved from one place to another, and a single find may not indicate cultural influence, or even necessarily direct contact. A bronze Buddha figure found in Helgö in Sweden and a Norwegian penny found in Maine, USA both probably reached their final destination after passing through the hands of intermediaries. However, where a group of objects are found out of place together, for example the contents of an isolated grave, this probably points to direct contact. When a whole pattern of objects are found reflecting a particular culture with its origin elsewhere, this suggests either settlement or at least strong cultural influence. For example, boat graves are typical of Viking-Age Scandinavia (see pp. 178–9) and provide indicators of Viking presence across the Viking world. Similarly, paired oval brooches are typical of Viking female graves, and very similar brooches can be found in the many areas of Viking contact (fig. 57). However, such designs also sparked local imitation, leading to the creation of distinct types representing a new identity combining local and Scandinavian elements, as found, for example, in the brooch sets of Latvia in the late Viking Age.

This sort of cultural mixing is reflected in a wide variety of objects. Some combine foreign forms, such as swords with Frankish blades and hilts decorated in a range of Scandinavian styles (fig. 58).[60] There are also numerous hybrid art styles. For example, silversmiths in Ireland took traditional Irish brooch forms and modified them to Viking tastes in a style that has become known as Hiberno-Viking or Hiberno-Scandinavian (fig. 59).[61] A similar mixture of styles is found in England, where widespread finds of low-value copper alloy jewellery in both Scandinavian and Anglo-Scandinavian styles suggests that settlers were not always limited to the elite.[62]

We can also see customization and reuse of objects across cultures. The Hunterston brooch is a pre-Viking Scottish brooch with purely Celtic decoration. On the back, someone has scratched the runic inscription translated as 'Mælbrigða owns this brooch'. The name is Celtic (and Christian), the language and runic alphabet Norse, demonstrating that this pre-Viking object continued to be valued in a mixed Scottish-Viking society (fig. 60).[63]

Runic and other inscriptions underline the wide range of different kinds of contacts spanning large distances. Runes commonly appear in personal inscriptions on more or less

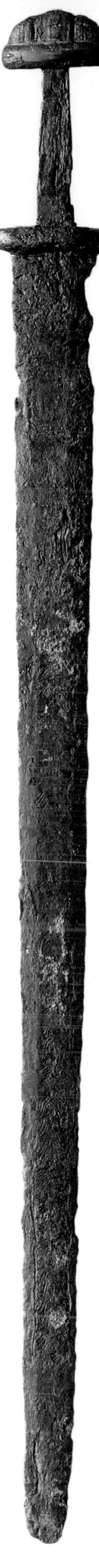

57. (below)
Oval brooches with strings of beads, 9th century. Lilleberge, Namdalen, Nord-Trøndelag, Norway.
Copper alloy, glass. Brooch L 10.4 cm
British Museum, London

58. (left)
The blade of this sword is Frankish; the hilt fittings are of Scandinavian workmanship.

Double-edged sword, Mannheim type, *c.* 800. Sjørring Volde, Thy, Denmark.
Iron. L 91.5 cm
National Museum of Denmark, Copenhagen

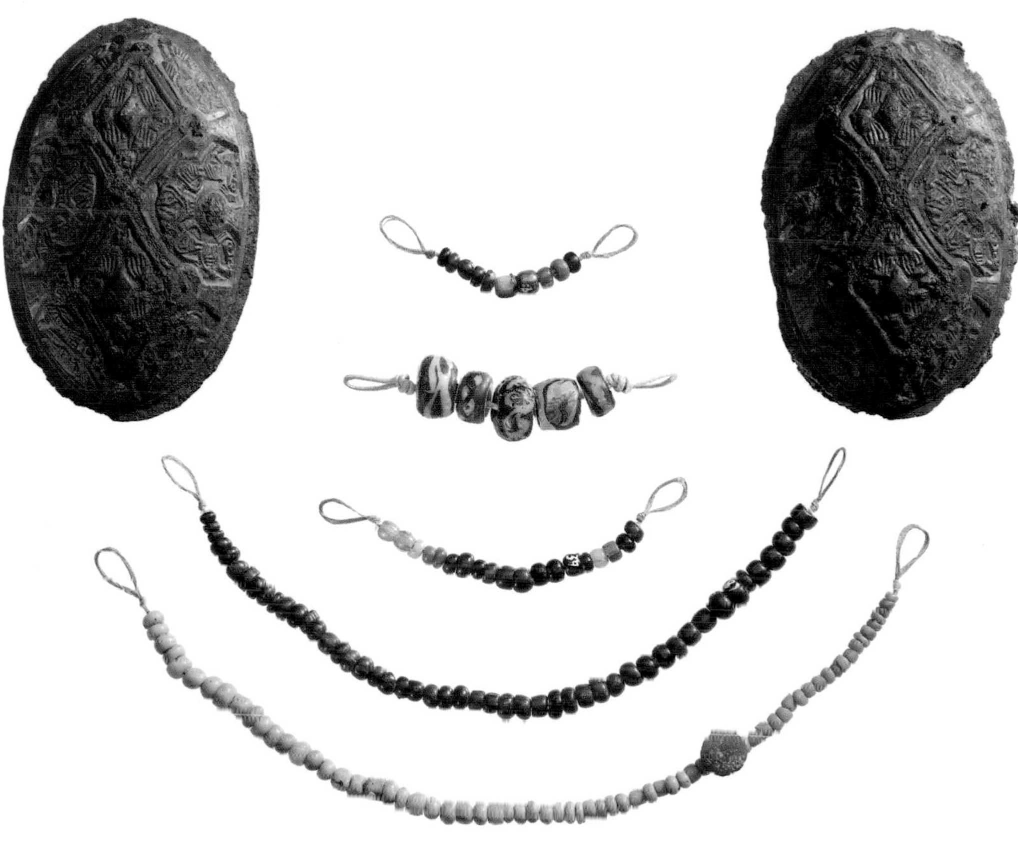

standardized Scandinavian memorial rune stones.[64] These are concentrated in Scandinavia, but are known from as far apart as Britain and Russia. Such stones commemorate the dead and sometimes mention notable achievements. In some cases these include long-distance travel. Swedish rune stones honour travellers to England, Grikland (Byzantium) and Serkland (Russia, the Caucasus and the Caliphate). Runes also appear in less formal inscriptions, both in the Scandinavian homelands and overseas. These include runic graffiti on monumental structures such as the megalithic site of Maes Howe in Orkney, the stone lion from Piraeus or the walls of Hagia Sophia, but runes are found on more portable objects too, such as a futhark (the opening letters of the runic alphabet) on a brooch from Penrith in Cumbria (fig. 61), or even on objects as small as coins. Other forms of graffiti also appear on coins, with Thor's hammers and crosses incised on Islamic dirhams, probably representing a conscious rejection of Islam.[65]

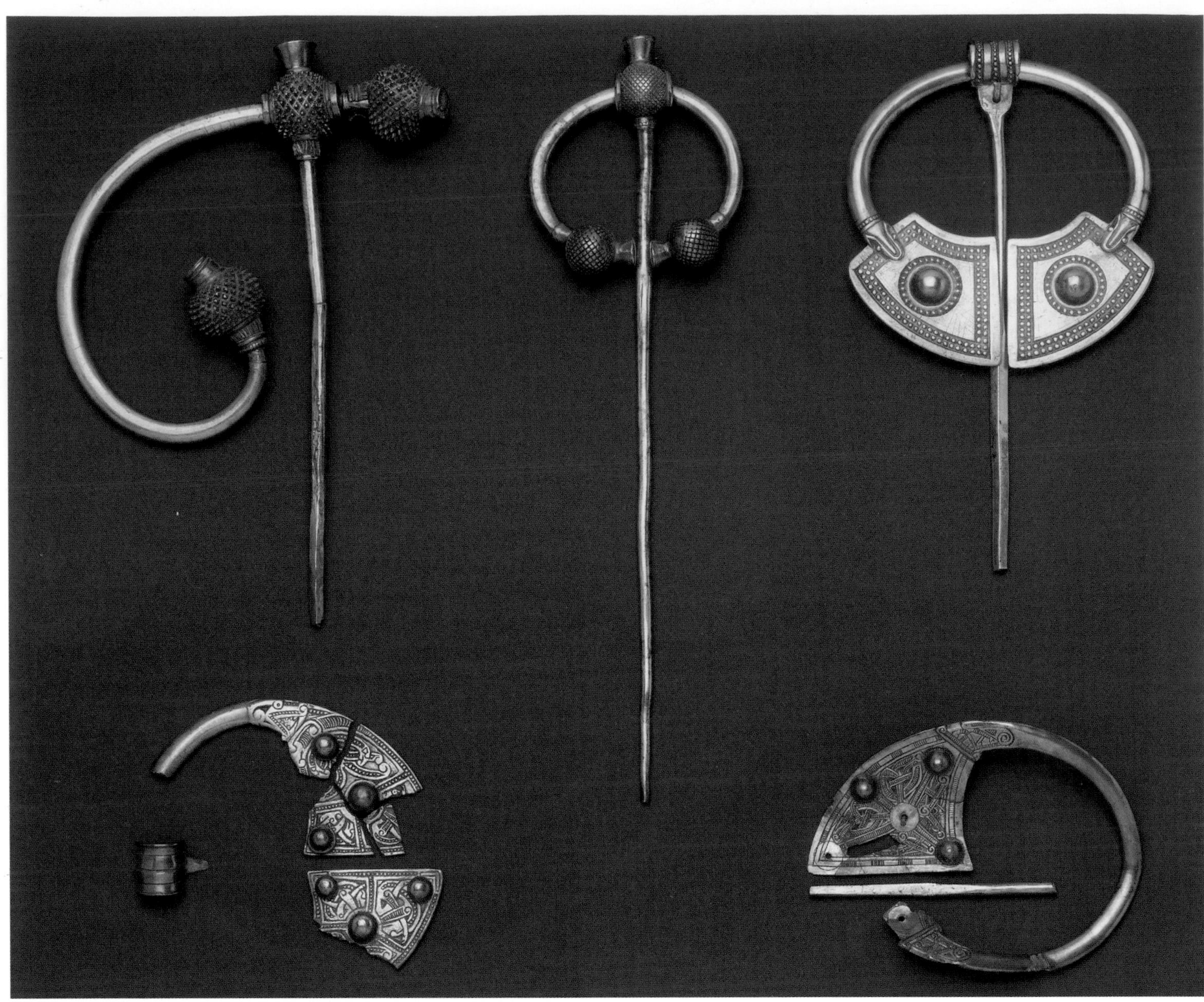

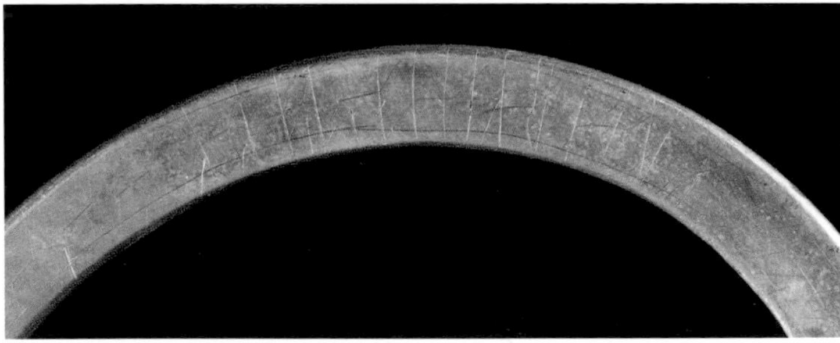

61.
The runes on this brooch read 'futhark', the opening letters of the runic alphabet. The sound 'th' is represented by a single rune, Þ.

Details of a brooch, *c.* 900, from near Penrith, Cumbria, England.
Silver. Diam. (of complete brooch) 10.4 cm
British Museum, London

59. (above)
So-called 'Hiberno-Scandinavian' ornaments combine Scandinavian and Irish elements, and are found all around the Irish sea, not just in Ireland.

Hoard of brooches, *c.* 900, from near Penrith, Cumbria, England.
Silver. Central brooch L 26 cm
British Museum, London

60. (right)
This pre-Viking brooch carries the inscription 'Mælbrigða owns this brooch'. The inscription is in Old Norse and in the runic alphabet, but the name is Celtic, indicating a fusion of cultures.

Brooch, *c.* 700, Hunterston, Ayrshire, Scotland.
Gold, silver, amber. Diam. 12.2 cm
National Museums Scotland, Edinburgh

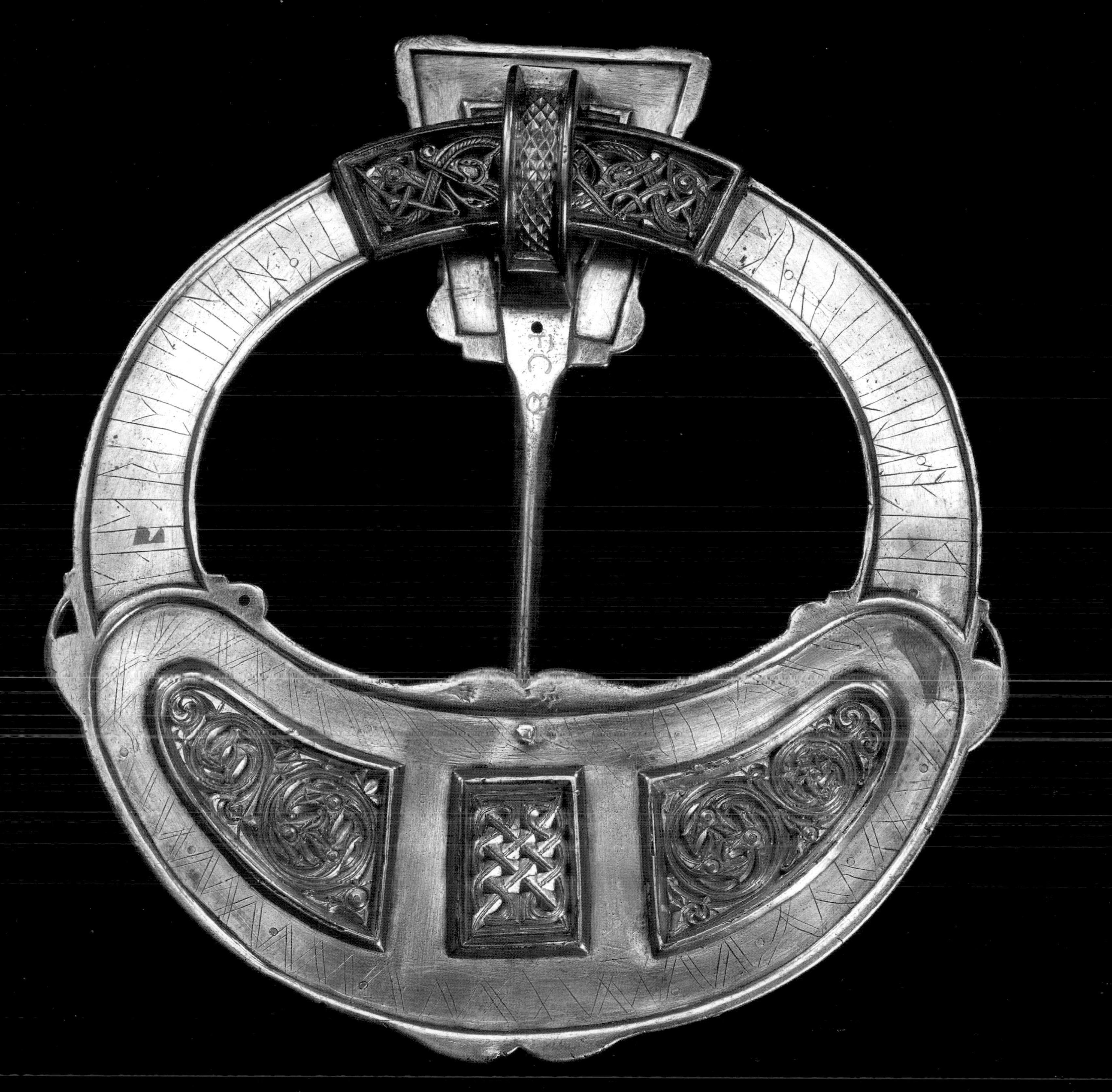

62. (below)
Silver hoard with jewellery of Slavic manufacture alongside pendants decorated in the Scandinavian 'Borre' style, 10th–11th century. Lyuboyezha, Ilmensee region, Russia.
Novgorod State Museum, Novgorod

63. (opposite)
A Carolingian cup, 9th century, was used as a container for a hoard of gold and silver arm-rings, hack-silver, ingots and coins. The hoard contains objects from as far away as Afghanistan and Uzbekistan.

The Vale of York hoard, 10th century. North Yorkshire, England.
Silver-gilt, gold, silver. Cup H 9.2 cm, Diam. 12 cm
British Museum, London/Yorkshire Museum, York

Perhaps the most striking examples of the mixing of contacts around the Viking world are found in hoards of precious metal. These can show a range of geographical origins and possible activities leading to the movement of different objects. A group of tenth- and eleventh-century silver ornaments known as the Lyuboyezha hoard (fig. 62), found near Lake Ilmen (Russia), contains a variety of complete and fragmented items of jewellery, including pendants of Slavic, Scandinavian and oriental origin, as well as three ancient Indian coins gilded and used as pendants.[66] Similarly, the Vale of York hoard, buried in the late 920s, contains Islamic dirhams and a cut fragment of a Russian neck-ring, which probably reflect long-distance trade, but also a gilt-silver liturgical vessel almost certainly looted from a Frankish church, and arm-rings from both Scandinavia and the Irish Sea area that are more likely to represent gift-giving and social exchange. With items from as far apart as Ireland and Afghanistan, obtained from both raiding and trading, and objects referring to Christianity, Islam and the worship of Thor, this single hoard represents the broad scope for the exchange of goods and cultures and the range of peoples with whom the Vikings came into contact (fig. 63).[67]

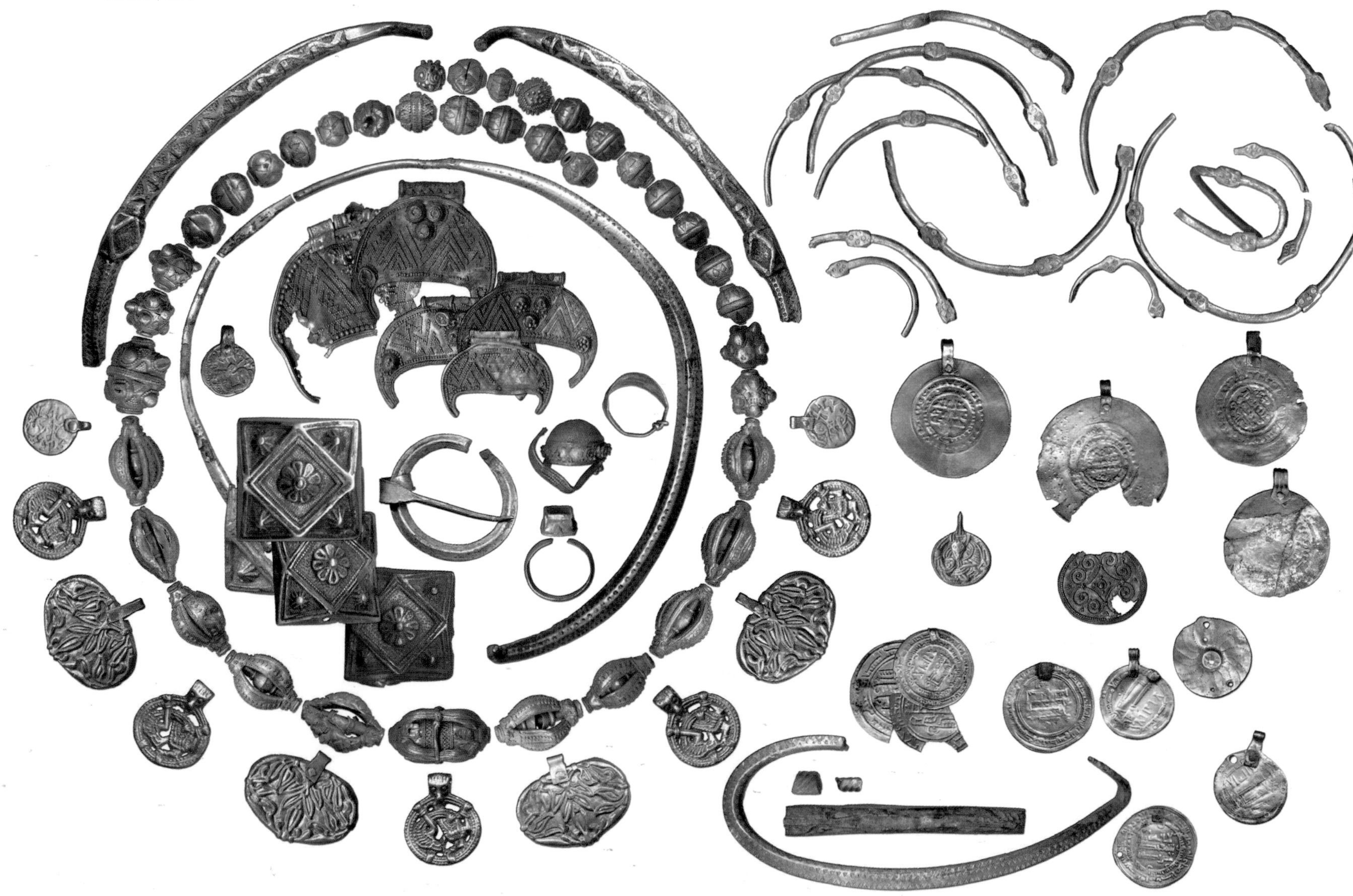

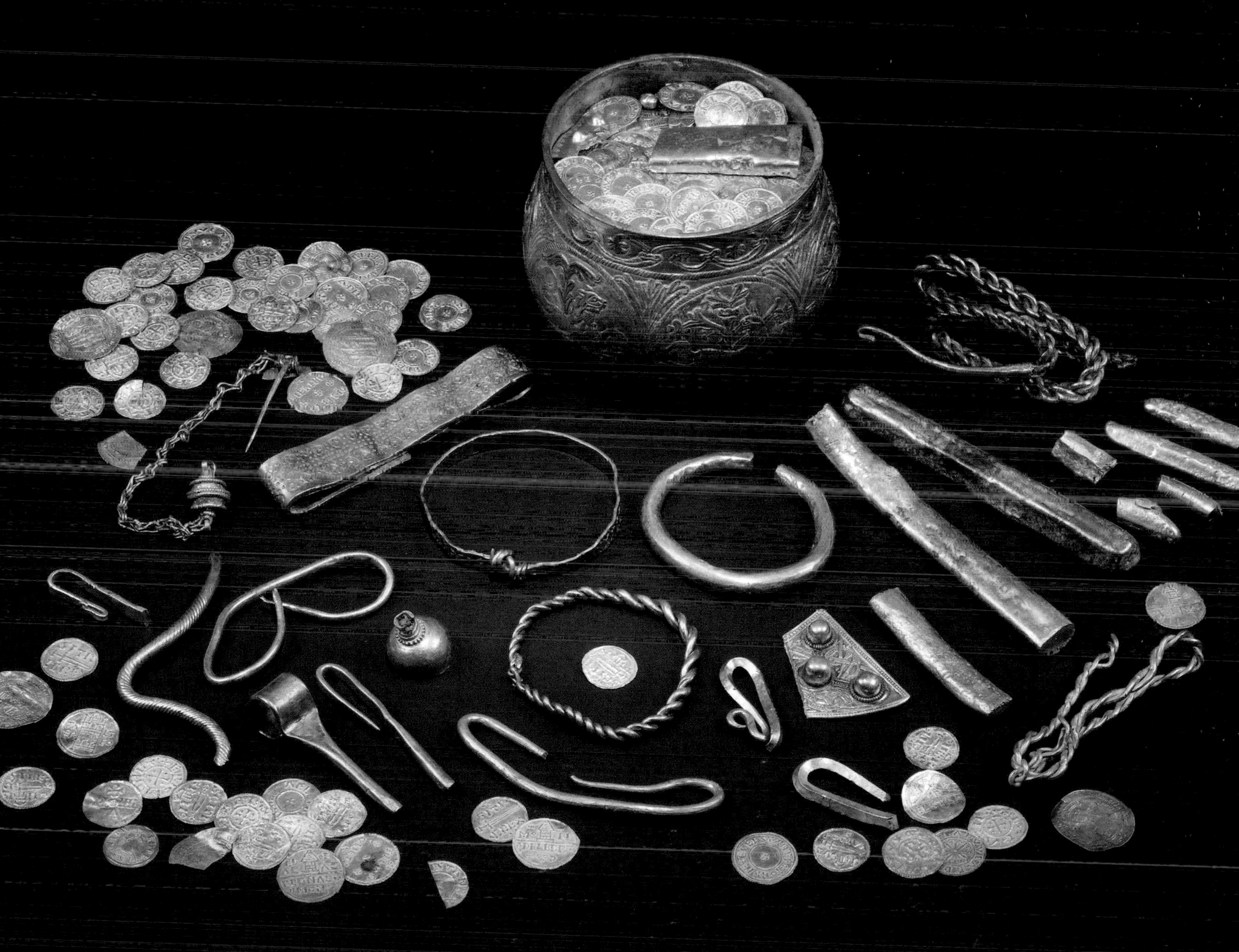

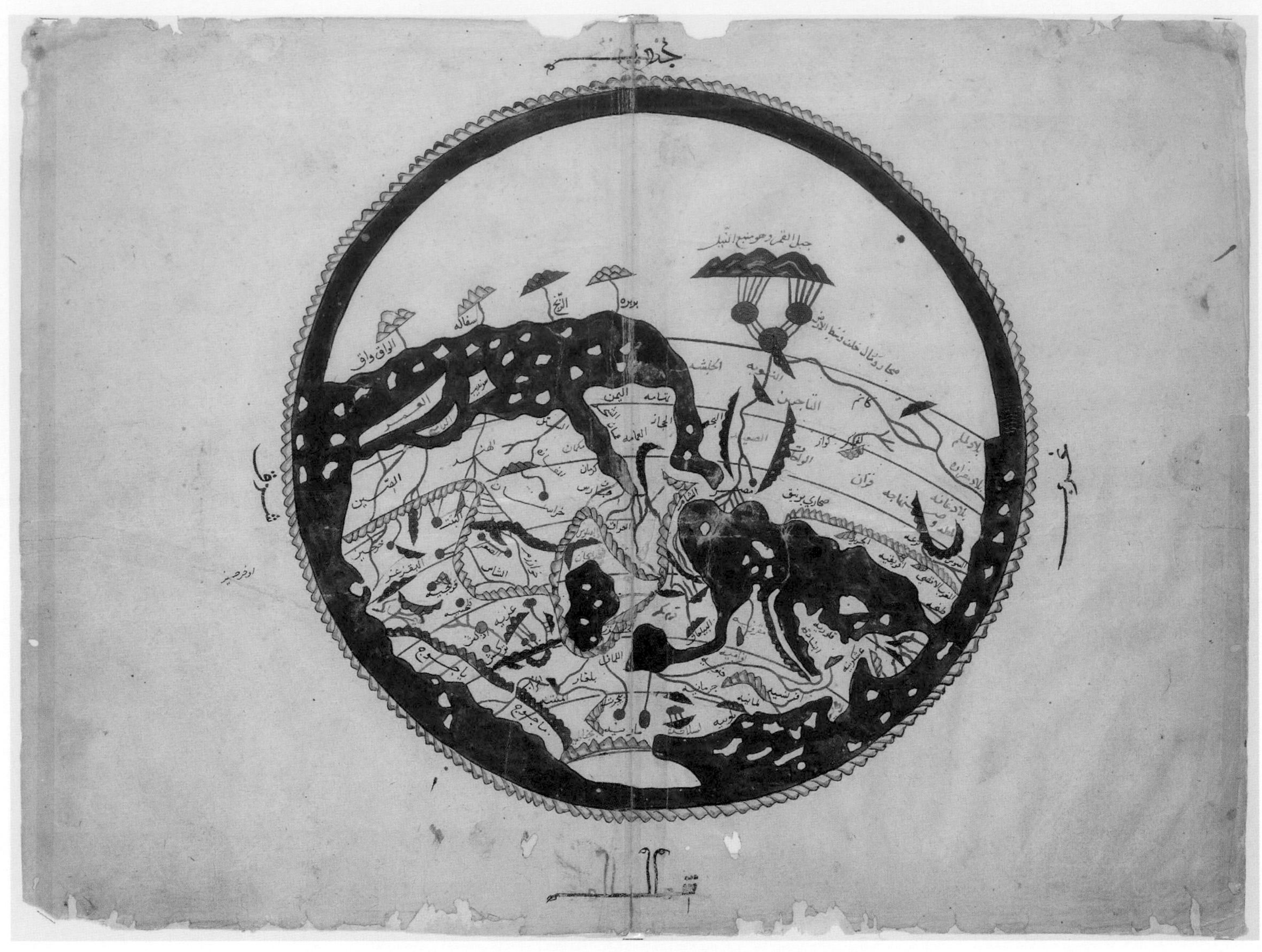

Vikings in Arabic sources

Gareth Williams

The Viking world intersected with the Islamic world in two different regions. In the south the Vikings had contact with Muslim Spain and Morocco, which had broken away from the Caliphate. In the east they had trading contacts with the Middle East and Central Asia. Although the Caliphate was ethnically and to some extent linguistically and culturally diverse, literacy in Arabic existed across the whole of the region. As a result, references survive in Arabic sources to contact with the Vikings in both the east and the west (fig. 1).[1]

Some are straightforward accounts of Viking raids. Ibn Hayyān, a historian from Al-Andalus, describes in detail a raid on southern Spain in 844, which was the first recorded Viking raid into the Mediterranean, although others followed. The Vikings are described as *majūs* (Persian *magus/magi),* a term normally used in Arabic sources of this period to describe followers of the Zoroastrian religion in Iran and surrounding areas, but here used in the more general sense of 'unbelievers'.[2] Another account, by the historian Miskawayh, describes the short-lived conquest of Bardha'a in the Caucasus by Viking Rūs (see pp. 82–3).[3]

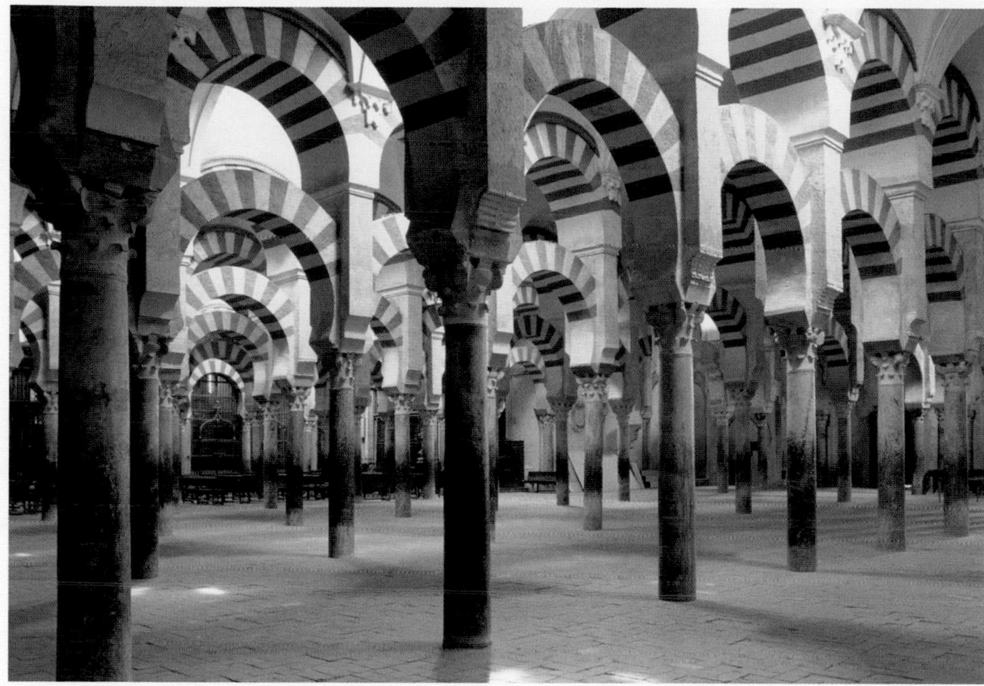

1. (opposite)
15th-century copy of Muhammad al-Idrisi's world map of 1154. North is at the bottom of the map.
Bodleian Library, Oxford

2. (left)
The interior of the Great Mosque of Cordoba, completed as a mosque in 987, but incorporating elements of an earlier building.

The Vikings also feature in Arabic geographical accounts. These brought together information on societies beyond the Caliphate, either on the basis of the writers' own personal experience or through the reports of diplomats, traders and other travellers. Like the work of modern anthropologists, these often included comments on the appearance, customs and religious beliefs of the peoples with whom the writers came into contact.

Several of these narratives mention the Rūs, the part-Viking inhabitants of what are now Russia and the Ukraine. Different accounts disagree on specific details and this probably reflects in part the diversity of cultures among the Rūs. However, like the term Saqāliba (normally indicating Slavs), the name is not applied consistently and the accounts are not always entirely reliable.[4]

One colourful account that often appears in histories of the Vikings is that of the scholar ibn Dihya (d.1235), which describes a diplomatic mission by one al-Ghazāl from Muslim Spain (fig. 2) to an unidentified Viking settlement and his encounters there. These included an attempt to humiliate the visitor by forcing him to kneel in order to go through a low doorway (sometimes taken as an indication of Viking humour), and an undiplomatically close relationship with the wife of the Viking ruler. Recent scholarship suggests that the details are borrowed from other stories with no Viking connection and that it tells us nothing about the Vikings at all.[5] Even so, individual points in Arabic accounts can sometimes be confirmed by other evidence, such as the Persian geographer ibn Rusta's account of the baggy trousers of the Rūs (confirmed by illustrations on stone carvings from Gotland) and of burials with grave goods that broadly correspond with Viking burial practice.[6]

The best known account of the Rūs is that of Ahmad ibn Fadlān, who was part of a diplomatic mission in 921–2 from the caliph Muqtadir (908–32) to the king of the Volga Bulgars. He describes his journey from Baghdad east to Bukhara (Uzbekistan) and then north-west to Kazan' on the River Volga (Russia). He concludes with a rather mixed description of a group of Rūs whom he met somewhere on the Volga, commenting on their height ('like palm trees'), colouring and resistance to cold. He states that he has 'never seen bodies more perfect than theirs', but he was shocked by their sexual habits and their low standards of hygiene, describing them as 'the filthiest of God's creatures'. Nevertheless, he provides useful observations on weapons, dress and customs, including details of trading (see p. 60). What has particularly captured popular imagination is his description of a Viking funeral, in which a dead chieftain's slave-girl was dramatically sacrificed and then burned together with him in his ship to accompany him in the afterlife (see pp. 181–2).[7]

Most Arabic accounts of the Vikings commented on the Vikings abroad, but we also have one of the Viking homelands. Ibrahim ibn Yaqub al-Tartushi, a traveller from Islamic Spain, visited Hedeby in the late tenth century. He mentions the presence of a small Christian community among a mostly pagan population, whom he describes as 'worshippers of Sirius' and discusses religious feasts and animal sacrifice. He also mentions that the main food was fish, that both men and women wore eye-make-up, that women could freely divorce their husbands and that the singing of the people of Hedeby was particularly ugly to hear, 'like the barking of dogs, and even more like a wild animal than that'.[8] Although this detail is not recorded in other Arabic sources, the general impression it gives of the Vikings as somewhat barbaric is typical of the perspective from the more sophisticated Caliphate.

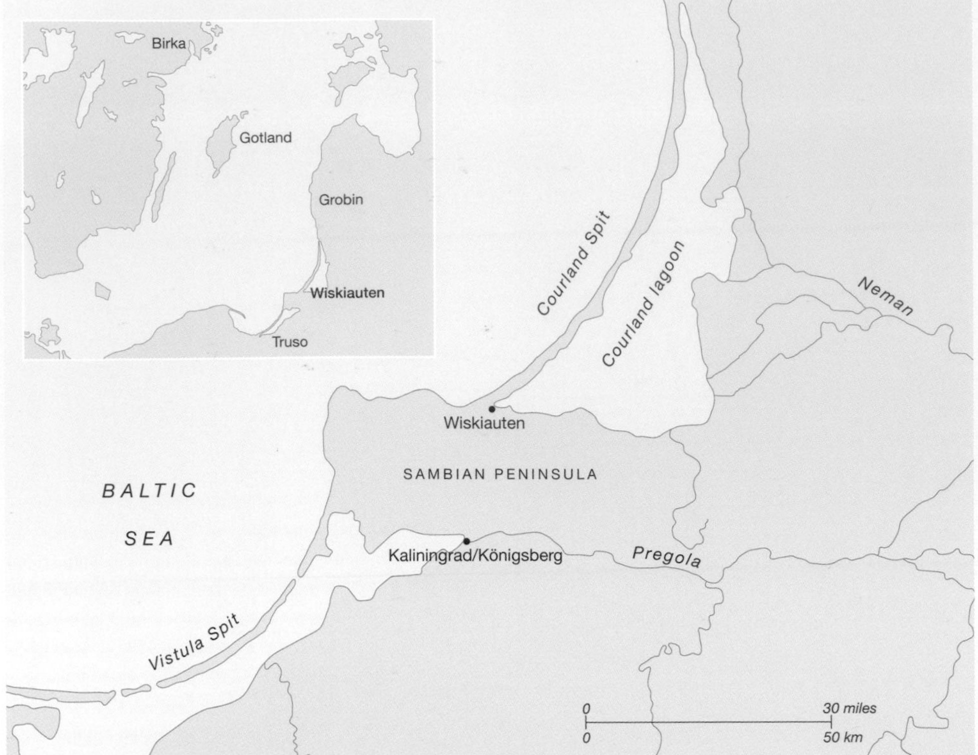

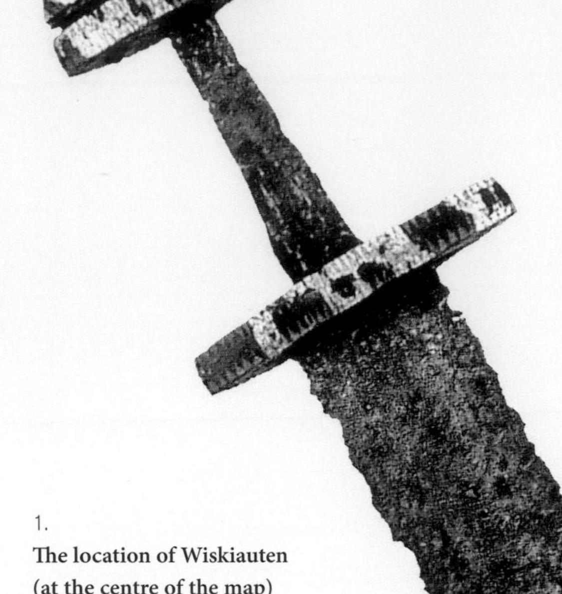

1.
The location of Wiskiauten (at the centre of the map) in the Baltic Sea.

Wiskiauten: a trading site on the southern coast of the Baltic?

Timo Ibsen

Wiskiauten is situated at the foot of the Courland Spit, 3 kilometres south of the Baltic Sea in Russia's Kaliningradskaja Oblast, near the town of Selenogradsk (fig. 1). The site was discovered in 1865 by German archaeologists and is known for its cemetery, which contains 500 burial mounds dated to the years 850–1050. These are squeezed into a small forest named Kaup, close to a former extension of the Courland lagoon. More than 300 mounds have so far been excavated, but the material has not yet been fully published.[1]

The mounds, with diameters of up to 12 metres and a height of 1.5 metres, contained the remains of men and women, both cremated and buried. Items were found in the graves (grave goods), most of which originated from Scandinavia (fig. 2). The presence of forty-four oval brooches of characteristic Scandinavian style in female graves has led to the interpretation that there was a Scandinavian trading centre at this point on the southern coast of the Baltic.[2] The written sources suggest that Danish Vikings raided the Sambian peninsula on the south-eastern shore of the Baltic, but do not mention any specific location.

Other trading centres, like Truso in the Vistula estuary in Poland or Grobina in Latvia, are seen as sites of multicultural interaction, typically situated in natural protected harbours that were easily accessible by Viking-Age ships. They were part of a trading network connecting people from all around the Baltic. In the case of Wiskiauten, we can assume that the rich amber reservoirs of the Sambian peninsula – more than 90 per cent of the world's amber is deposited here – attracted traders from Scandinavia.[3] Judging by grave goods, style of dress and burial traditions, they probably mostly came from Gotland and Birka in Sweden, but there are also a few Danish and Baltic elements in the graves.

In the Viking Age the area around Wiskiauten was inhabited by the Baltic tribe of the Prussians, who buried their deceased in flat graves, often combined with horse burials. A smaller group of these Prussian graves was found in the eastern part of the Kaup forest in the 1930s and has recently been re-examined by a joint Russian-German research project.[4] These graves, containing men

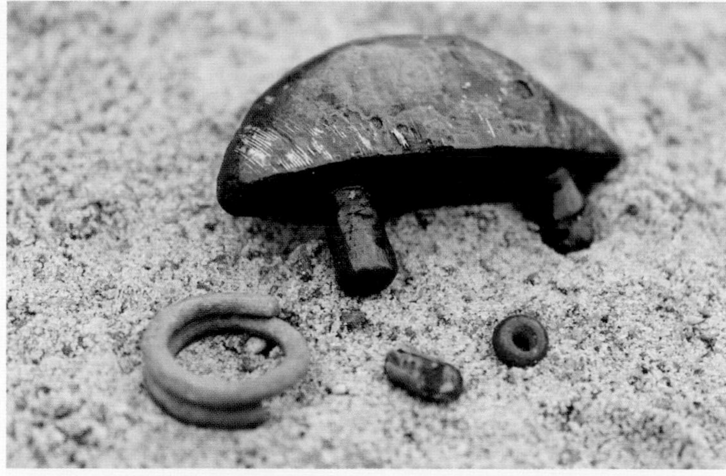

and horses, are later than the burial mounds and date from the eleventh and twelfth centuries. This suggests that the related settlement, which was presumably in the near vicinity, probably survived after the Vikings departed in the middle of the eleventh century until the thirteenth century, when the knights of the Teutonic Order conquered the Balt region (later known as Prussia, now in modern Poland and Russia).

Since 2005, more than 150 hectares of land around the cemetery have been scanned with geophysical survey methods.[5] A series of twenty-two excavations covering a total of 2,250 square metres uncovered ground plans of wattle-and-daub houses, production pits, waste pits, fireplaces, single finds and other indications of settlement activity, dating from the middle of the first millennium AD to the mid-thirteenth century. They show the existence of several smaller settlement units without any defensive structures, probably indicating that trade was mostly conducted in a peaceful manner. The dwelling sites are widespread across the whole settlement area, with no particular concentration.

The excavations have identified three main phases of settlement. During the first phase, from the fifth to the mid-ninth century, local Prussians were living on the banks of two small streams, both running towards the open water north and east of the cemetery. The second phase is contemporary with the mound cemetery of the ninth and tenth centuries. Excavations close to the shore of the former water basin unearthed cultural layers, houses and pits with a range of finds that can be connected loosely to the Vikings. However, the absence of typical Scandinavian artefacts in the settled area – except for a few stray finds (fig. 3) – does not clearly indicate a Viking settlement, and most of the finds appear to be of local origin. The final phase covers the mid-eleventh century to the first half of the thirteenth century, and is represented by typical ornaments and jewellery of the local Prussian culture (fig. 4).

The site of Wiskiauten probably served as a minor trading centre, mostly inhabited by Prussians from the fifth to the thirteenth century, visited or even partially inhabited by Scandinavians over a period of 150 to 200 years. It was never as important as other big sites, such as the famous Hedeby, Wolin, Birka, Truso or Staraya Ladoga, but was certainly one of the stations of the super-regional trading network that the Scandinavians established all around the Baltic Sea.

2. (left)
Viking sword, 10th century. Wiskiauten/Mochovoe, Rajon Zelenogradsk, Russia.
Iron, silver, copper. L 73 cm
Museum für Vor- und Frühgeschichte, Staatliche Museen zu Berlin, Berlin

3. (above right)
Pommel from sword hilt, 10th century. Wiskiauten/Mochovoe, Rajon Zelenogradsk, Russia.
Iron with silver inlay. W 7.0 cm, H 2.8 cm
Kaliningrad Regional Museum of History and Arts, Kaliningrad

4. (below right)
Prussian jewellery, 11th–12th century. Wiskiauten/Mochovoe, Rajon Zelenogradsk, Russia.
Bronze. Horse shoe fibula fragment 5.0 x 3.1 cm; finger-ring 2.4 x 2.2 cm; ring brooch Diam. 4.2 cm; belt hook fragment 3.2 x 1.4 cm; complete belt hook 6.1 x 1.5 cm
Kaliningrad Regional Museum of History and Arts, Kaliningrad

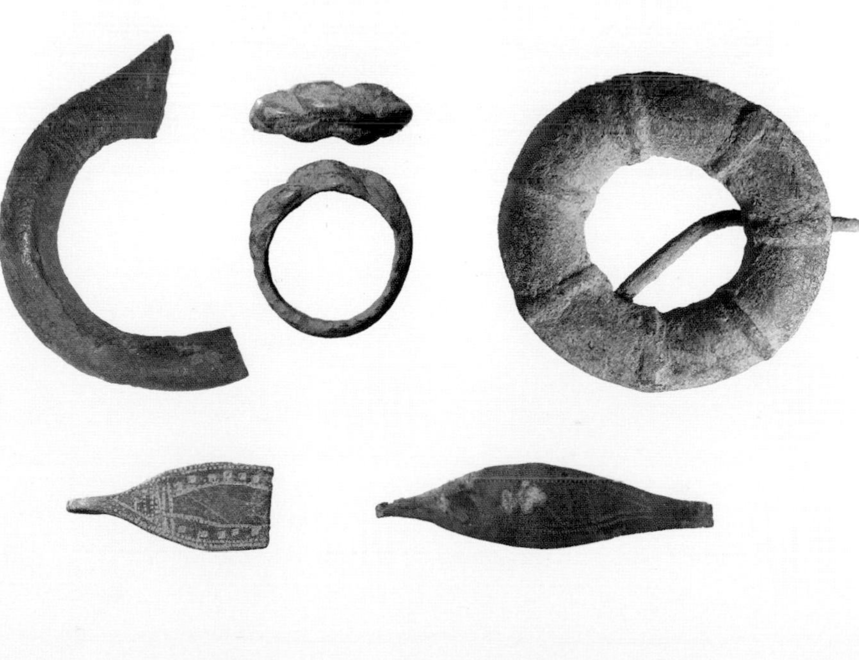

Reuse of foreign objects

Sunhild Kleingärtner

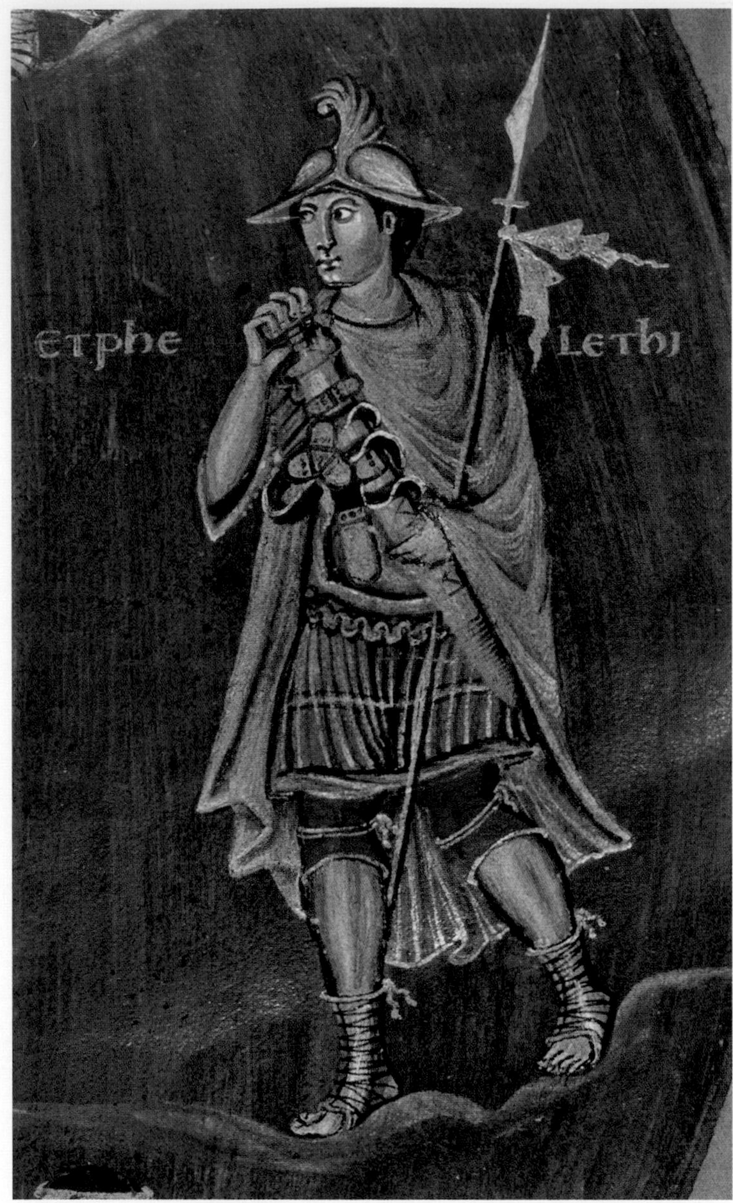

There are various, often pragmatic, reasons for reusing objects, one of which is to make economical use of resources. This is especially important when particular raw materials are scarce or specific techniques are not available. Evidence from the Viking homelands shows that objects of foreign origin were often reused in a new context. This might sometimes have been for purely practical reasons, as in the case of the settlement at Hedeby (Haithabu) in Schleswig, where silver fir wood barrels from the Rhineland, originally used for transporting wine, were reused as wells.[1]

In the Viking Age, foreign objects were also used specifically to display wealth and status. These notably include cloverleaf brooches worn by women, which have a basic shape indicating that they developed from the mounts found on Carolingian sword belts (fig. 1).[2] In addition, Eastern mounts from belts originally worn by men were used as pendants on women's necklaces (fig. 2).[3] One function of weapons and belts was to display the status of those who wore them,[4] so it can reasonably be assumed that this is why mounts of this particular type were adapted for use as articles of costume.

Viking-Age jewellery also incorporated objects that had been used as a means of payment in the regions where they originated. These include coins, which were fitted with clasps on the back so that they could be worn as brooches, or were pierced or fitted with loops so that they could be hung on necklaces (fig. 3).[5] Although coins from all over the Viking world were adapted for this purpose, the Islamic coins known as dirhams were particularly widely used, and we have written evidence of dirhams as a form of jewellery in the report of the Arab traveller ibn Fadlān.[6] The finds from Kullaberg in Scania, southern Sweden (fig. 4), provide clear evidence of the connection between Arab coins, used for payment in other parts of the world, and the shapes of local rings.[7] The influence of coinage on neck- or arm-rings, which in the Viking Age were often given as a mark of social alliance[8], emphasized the value of these objects and underlined their function as symbols of status. An even closer fusion of these two functions can be found in the combination of jewellery and weights. Permian rings, and the circular and horseshoe-shaped brooches that are widespread in the Baltic region, are often decorated with cubo-octahedral ends mimicking the shape of dice weights (fig. 5)[9] adopted from the Near East (see p. 59).

When not actually in use, these objects were sometimes buried in the ground to protect them from capture by third parties.[10] Sets of drinking vessels have also been found buried. These too arrived from outside Scandinavia and were reused in a very particular way. Each set consists of a number of small silver bowls with one larger decorated silver vessel (see p. 146). The larger bowls were originally for religious worship, probably in the celebration of the Eucharist in Christian churches.[11] However, the way they are found buried together with a number of smaller bowls leads us to conclude that in Scandinavia they were used instead as drinking vessels of high material value to symbolize sovereignty. They must have been of particular worth to their owners, as they were not only of foreign

1.
Carolingian soldier as depicted in the Vivian Bible. Note the cloverleaf belt mount depicted near the hilt of the soldier's sword. Vivian Bible, *c.* 845–846. Tours, France.
Vellum. L 49.5 cm W 34.5 cm
Bibliothèque Nationale, Paris

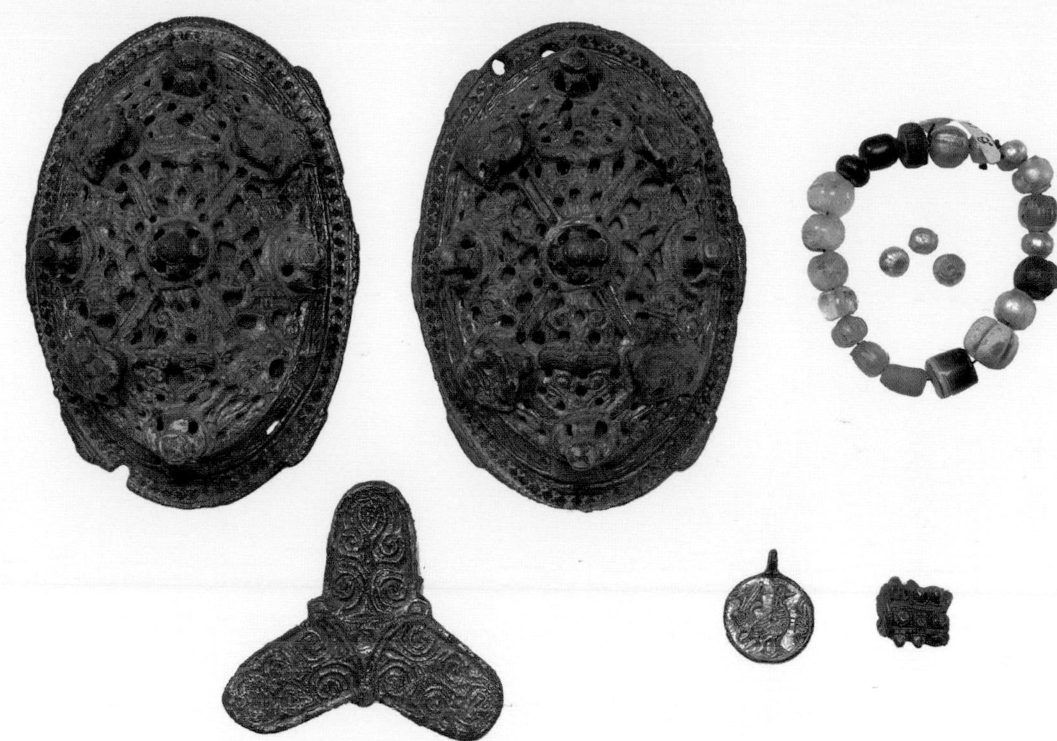

2.
Female grave assemblage, including a Carolingian trefoil strap mount reused as a brooch along with Scandinavian brooches, 10th century. Birka, Uppland, Sweden. Stockholm
Copper alloy, glass, silver, agate, rock crystal. Oval brooches L 10.8–10.9 cm
Statens Historiska Museum, Stockholm

origin and made of very high-quality materials, but were also individually produced, which gave them great rarity value. We can therefore assume that the rarity of an object increased in value many times between its place of origin and the place where it was found in the new context.

When objects of foreign origin were adopted, it was probably not where they came from that was important, but rather the fact that they were rare and exotic or indicated status and wealth. The unusual but apparently systematic reuse of these objects shows that it was not a question of the chance adoption of random items, but a deliberate reuse or remodelling of specific pieces to express an independent Viking-Age identity. By owning objects of foreign origin, certain people created a visual distinction between themselves and others within their society, in order to further underline their higher social standing. The use of these objects is therefore an example of wealth worn for show and a demonstration of the increasing complexity of society during the Viking Age.[14]

3.
Folded dirham with suspension ring, 10th century. Grisebjerggård, Zealand, Denmark.
Silver. 0.85 g
National Museum of Denmark, Copenhagen

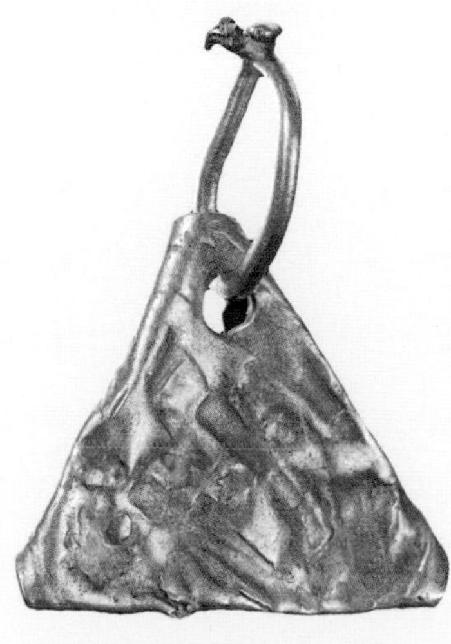

4.
Arm-ring with attached smaller rings and folded dirhams, 10th century. Kullaberg, Brunnby, Scania, Sweden.
Silver. W c. 8.0 cm
Statens Historiska Museum, Stockholm

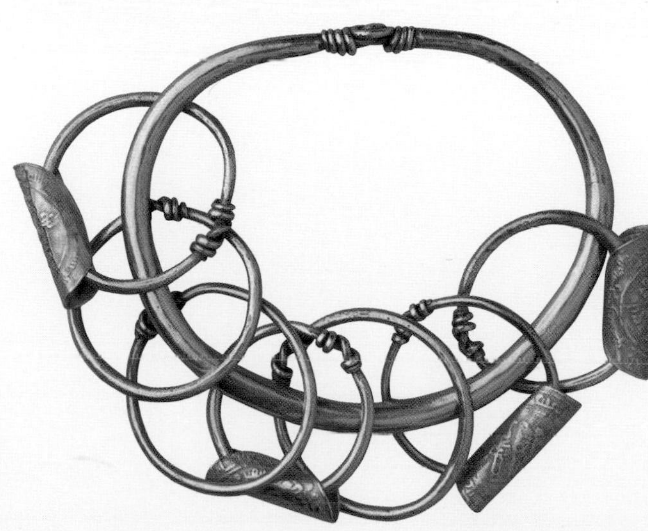

5.
Silver Sassanid drachma, possibly of the Persian King Chosroes II (591–628), adapted as a pendant.
Silver.
Landesamt für Kultur und Denkmalpflege Mecklenburg-Vorpommern, Schwerin

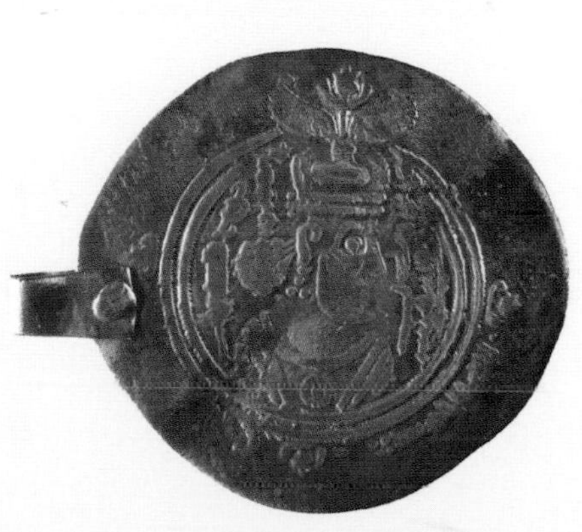

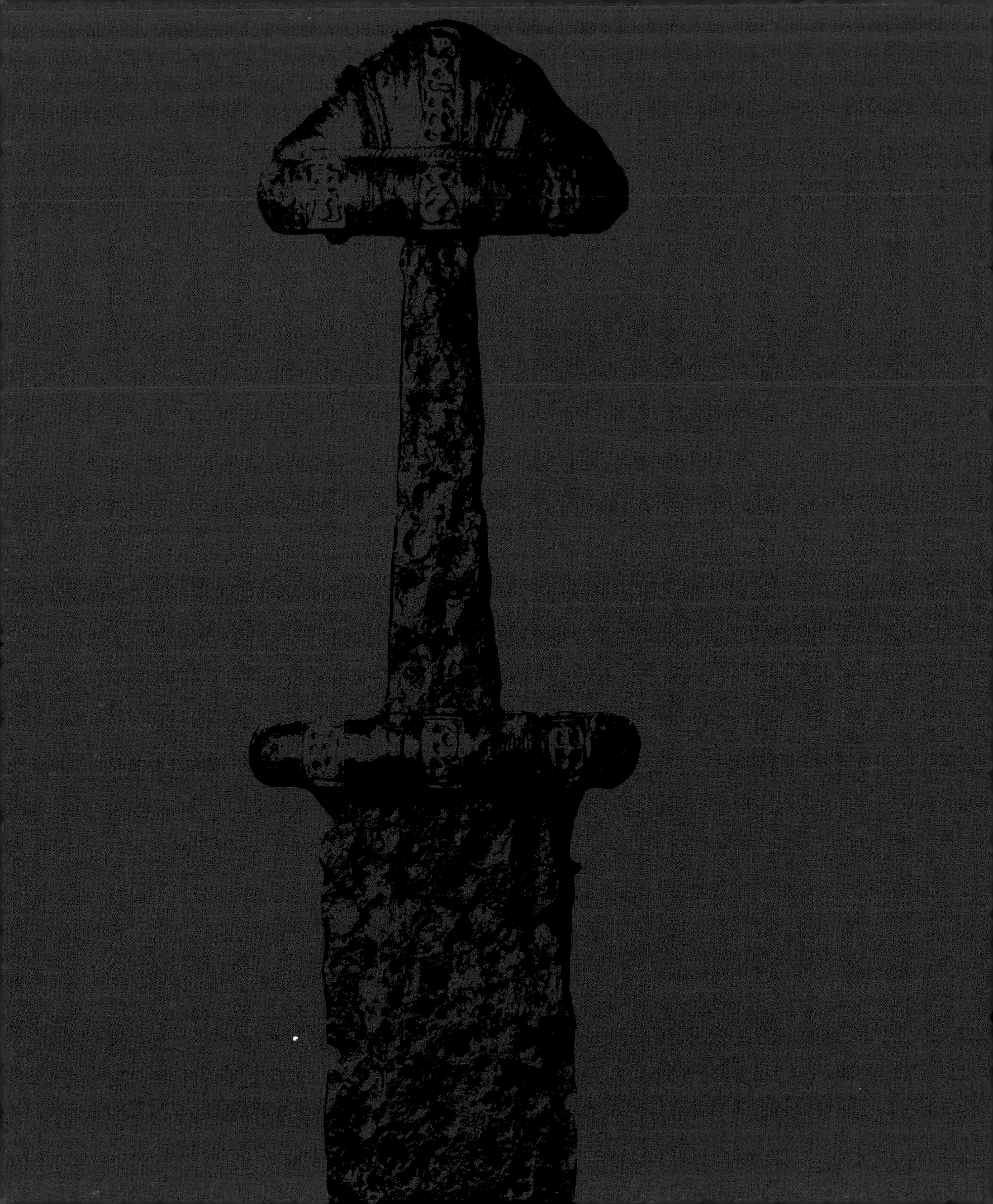

2
WARFARE & MILITARY EXPANSION

Gareth Williams

Time running on, she rode the waves now,
hard in by headland. Harnessed warriors
stepped on her stem; setting tide churned
sea with sand, soldiers carried
    bright mail-coats to the mast's foot,
war-gear well-wrought; willingly they
    shoved her out,
thorough-braced craft, on the craved
    voyage.
Away she went over a wavy ocean,
boat like a bird, breaking seas…

BEOWULF, 210–218 (8th–11th century)

WARFARE & MILITARY EXPANSION

THE TRADITIONAL VIEW OF VIKINGS, established since the nineteenth century, is based around Viking warriors and Viking raids. This interpretation has its origins in Anglo-Saxon, Frankish and Irish accounts from the period, mixed in with the stories told in the Icelandic sagas of the late twelfth and thirteenth centuries, together with a substantial element of nineteenth-century Romanticism. According to this view, the overseas expansion from Scandinavia that began in the closing years of the eighth century was essentially a violent one. Viking marauders descended on the coasts of western Europe in their longships, destroying and plundering, and eventually turning to conquest as the size of the raiding forces grew ever larger (fig. 1). These Viking warriors were particularly violent, bloodthirsty and treacherous (but also sometimes heroic), and defeated their enemies time after time through a combination of cunning, superior weapons and armour, and greater skill and savagery on the battlefield, as well as the unparalleled mobility provided by their ships. Unlike their victims, they were not Christian, but worshipped a pantheon of heathen

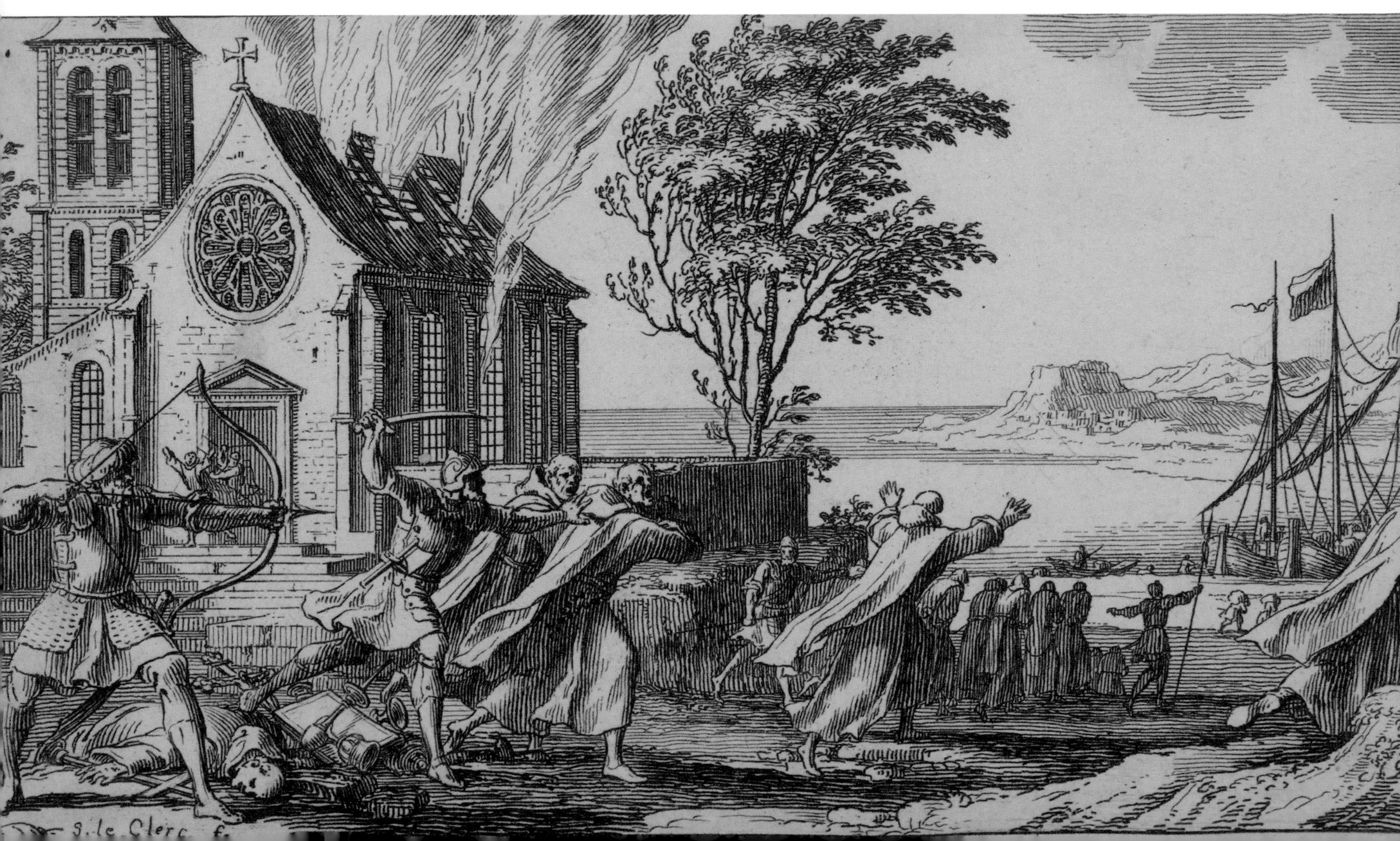

1.
Ideas about Vikings in recent centuries have emphasized their violence, especially towards the Church. A broader view of Viking society developed in the late 20th century.

Vikings attacking an English monastery, Sébastien Leclerc (1637–1714), *c.* 1705. France.
Book illustration (print on paper).
L 18 cm, W 14 cm
British Museum, London

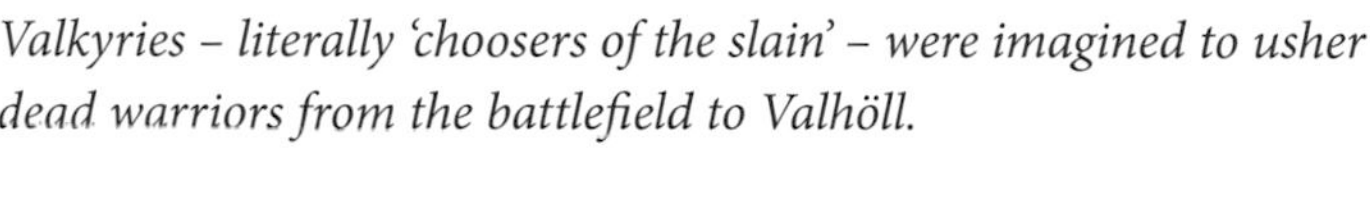

Valkyries – literally 'choosers of the slain' – were imagined to usher dead warriors from the battlefield to Valhöll.

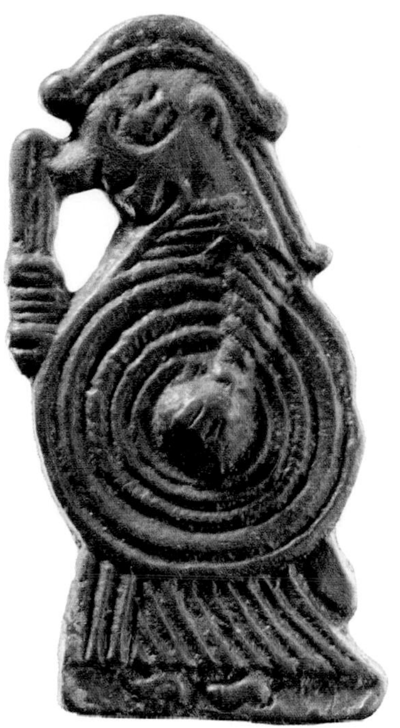

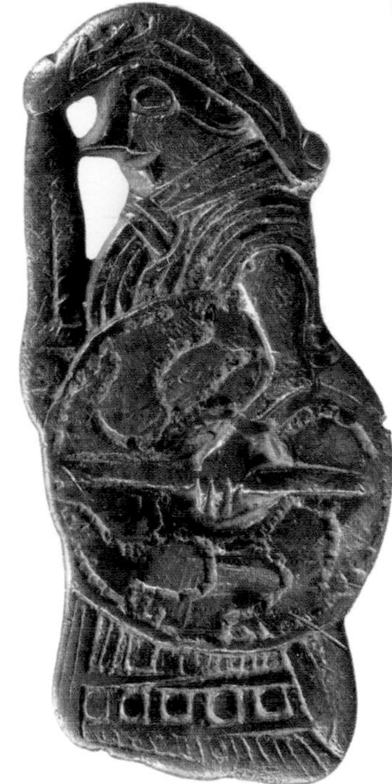

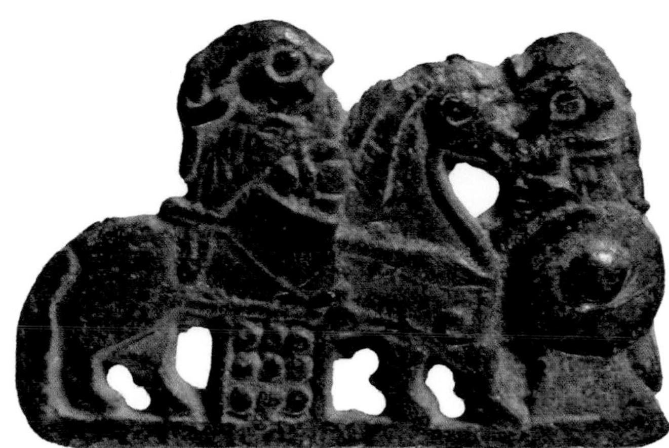

Scandinavian female figures, usually interpreted as Valkyries.

2.
Valkyrie brooch, 9th century. Galgebakken, Vrejlev, Vendsyssel, Denmark.
Silver. H 3.82 cm
National Museum of Denmark, Copenhagen

3.
Valkyrie figure, 9th century. Wickham Market, Suffolk, England.
Silver. H 4 cm
Colchester and Ipswich Museum Service

4.
Valkyrie brooch, 9th century. Fugledegård/Bulbrogård, north-west Zealand, Denmark.
Copper alloy. H 3.5 cm
National Museum of Denmark, Copenhagen

gods, and glorified war. They had no respect for the sanctity of churches and monasteries, broke holy oaths, carried out a wide range of atrocities, lacked any moral restraint, and wished for nothing more than a glorious death in battle to ensure that they would spend the afterlife in Valhöll (the hall of the slain, called Valhalla by the Victorians), feasting, drinking and fighting while waiting to take part in the great battle of Ragnarök at the end of the world (figs 2–4).

Like most stereotypes, this picture of the Vikings is a mixture of fact and fiction. The Vikings were neither unusually atrocious nor universally successful in battle, and since the 1960s historians have interpreted both contemporary historical sources and the later sagas more critically, rather than simply accepting the more extreme versions at face value. At the same time, this exclusively violent picture of the Vikings has been partially overtaken by a more peaceful view of the Viking Age. Study of the sagas, together with extensive archaeological excavation of sites from around the Viking world, has led to a change of focus on to what can be seen as some of the positive achievements of the Viking Age: exploration and the peaceful settlement of the North Atlantic; long-distance trade and the development of towns; maritime technology and shipbuilding; craftsmanship and an appreciation of beautiful objects; complex societies governed by law; poetry and, later, written literature. All of these activities combine to give us a much more rounded idea of the Viking Age, and it is now generally recognized that Viking warriors made up only a small and not particularly representative proportion of Scandinavian society as a whole.

While a broader view of the Viking Age is a good thing, it is important not to forget that it was the warlike aspects of Scandinavian society from the late eighth to eleventh centuries that give us the concept of 'Vikings' and the 'Viking Age'. Although the exact origins of the word are debated (see p. 17), the masculine noun *víkingr* in Old Norse meant a pirate or raider, and the feminine noun *víking* meant a raiding expedition. Neither form is commonly recorded from the Viking Age itself, but both appear in contemporary poetry and runic inscriptions from Scandinavia, as well as in later sagas. In the sagas, at least,

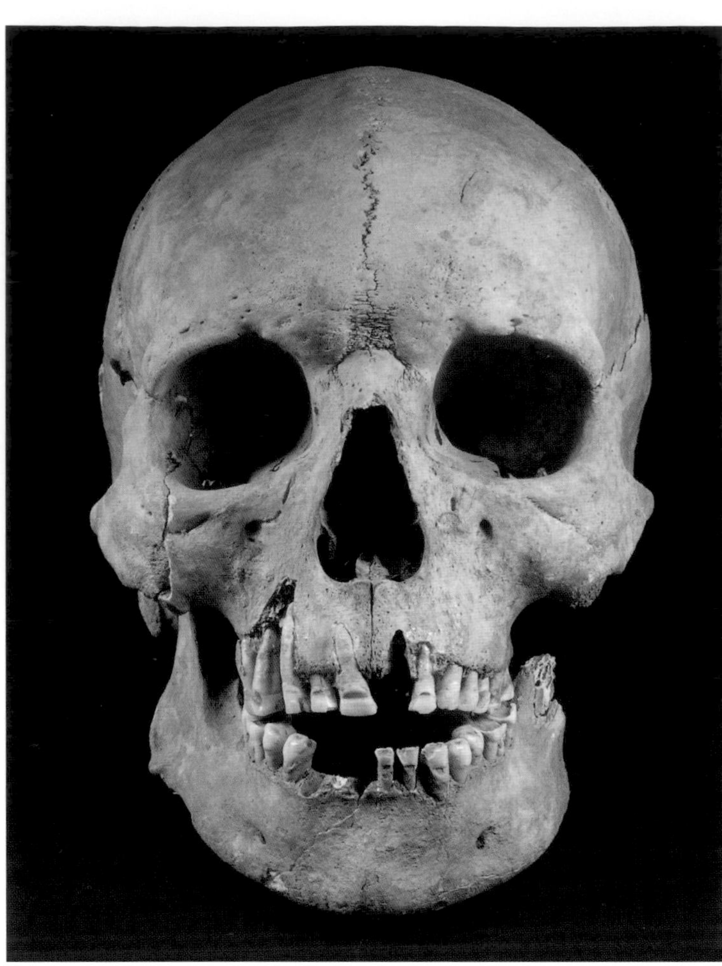

6–8. (opposite)
Weapons and amulets from a warrior grave of Scandinavian character in Russia.

Grave 4, Gnezdovo, Obl. Smolensk, Russia.

Frankish sword with VLFBERH+T inscription, 10th century.
Iron, copper alloy. L 98.5 cm

Scandinavian-type spearhead with damascened blade, 10th century.
Iron, copper alloy. L 52.3 cm

Thor's hammer ring, 10th century.
Iron, copper alloy. L 15.3 cm, W 15.9 cm
State Historical Museum, Moscow

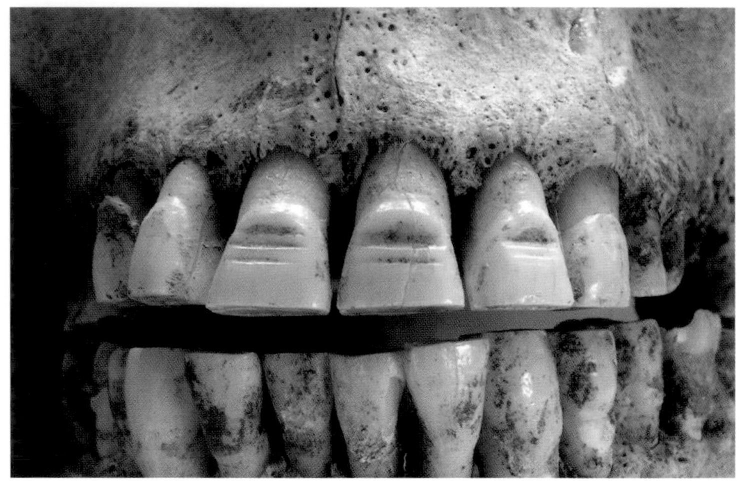

5.
Male skulls with filed teeth, 900–1050.
Köpingsvik, Gotland, Sweden.
Gotlands Museum, Visby

the term often carries negative overtones, and it seems that being considered a 'Viking' was not entirely respectable, even in a society in which the status of warrior was highly respected. At the same time, the runic inscriptions indicate that Viking expeditions were seen by some as something worth commemorating and coins indicate that *Víkingr* could be used as a personal name or nickname.[1] This may indicate that some warriors enjoyed being identified as 'Vikings' despite the fact that this placed them partly outside normal society, and there may have been a conscious element of social deviance among them. This can perhaps be seen in practices like the decorative filing of teeth, known from a number of examples of Scandinavian warrior burials (fig. 5). This would be both painful to have done and visually distinctive once complete, like modern piercings and tattoos.[2] Indeed, Arab writers comment on the fact that at least some Viking warriors decorated their bodies. Ibn Fadlān notes of Viking Rūs warriors on the Volga that 'from the tips of his toes to his neck, each man is tattoed in dark green with designs, and so forth', while al-Tartushi notes the use of eye make-up in Hedeby, which preserves and enhances the beauty of both men and women.[3] The attitude may also have been reflected in unusual clothing. This has parallels with modern groups such as punks and Hell's Angels, both of which combine a fierce visual image with a rejection of conventional social values. Archaeologist Neil Price has drawn comparisons with seventeenth- and eighteenth-century pirates, who favoured a flamboyant and socially deviant appearance, reflecting their outlaw status.[4] Following this interpretation it can be said that all 'Vikings' were warriors, but not all Scandinavian warriors of the eighth to eleventh centuries were 'Vikings'. However, to avoid confusion, the word Viking will be used in its more general sense (see p. 17) throughout this chapter, as well as in the rest of the book.

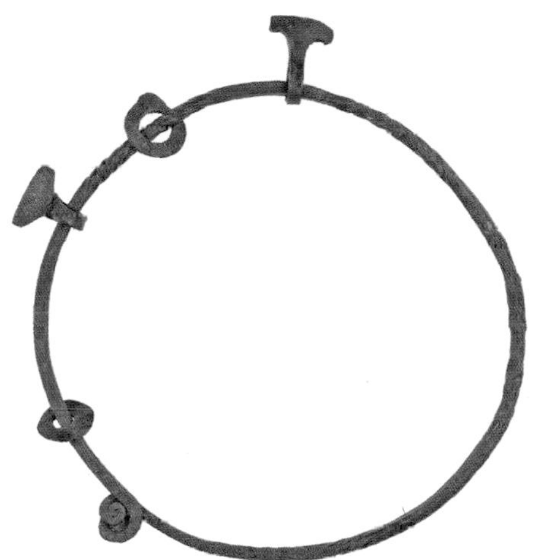

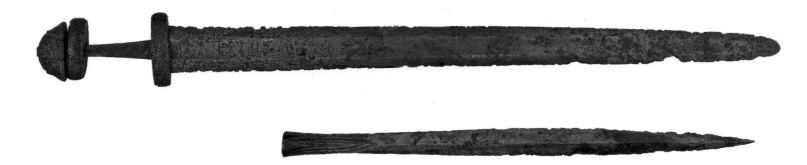

Expansion and warfare

Raiding and warfare certainly played an important part in the Viking expansion. This does not mean that Viking activity overseas was entirely driven by warfare. The settlement of the North Atlantic affected mostly unoccupied land and did not involve conquest, although there is plenty of conflict recorded in Iceland between different families of settlers and sometimes within individual families. This was driven by competition for land, wealth and power in much the same way as larger scale conflicts elsewhere, but on such a small scale that it cannot be considered warfare.

Similarly, much of the expansion to the east was driven by trade and was probably also mostly peaceful. Although the establishment of towns along the Russian river system may have taken place to facilitate long-distance trade, the introduction of a Scandinavian elite ruling over the mixed population is unlikely to have been completely peaceful, a view supported by the presence of a significant number of warrior graves in Russia and the Ukraine (figs 6–10). Conflict on a scale too small to be recorded in detail must have been relatively common, but there were also major clashes with all of the significant powers in the east. These are attributed to the Rūs, and sometimes to specific leaders, but the term Rūs was not applied consistently to a single group, and was

9.
Axehead of eastern Baltic type, *c.* 950–1100. Viehhof, Kr. Labiau/Tjulenino, Kaliningradskaja Obl., Russia.
Iron. L 15.5 cm, W 5.5 cm
Museum für Vor- und Frühgeschichte, Staatliche Museen zu Berlin, Berlin

10.
Axehead, late 10th–early 11th century. Löbertshof, Kr. Labiau/region of Slavjanskoe, Kaliningradskaja Obl., Russia.
Iron. L 24 cm, W 19 cm
Museum für Vor- und Frühgeschichte, Staatliche Museen zu Berlin, Berlin

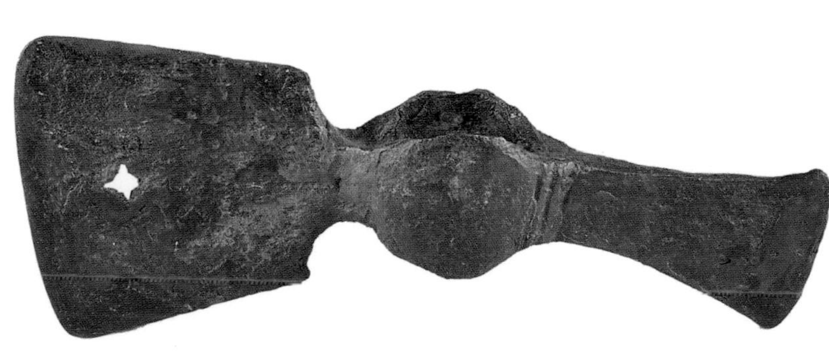

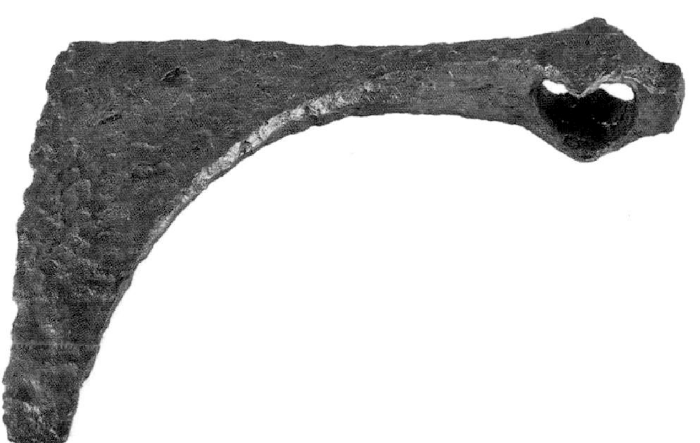

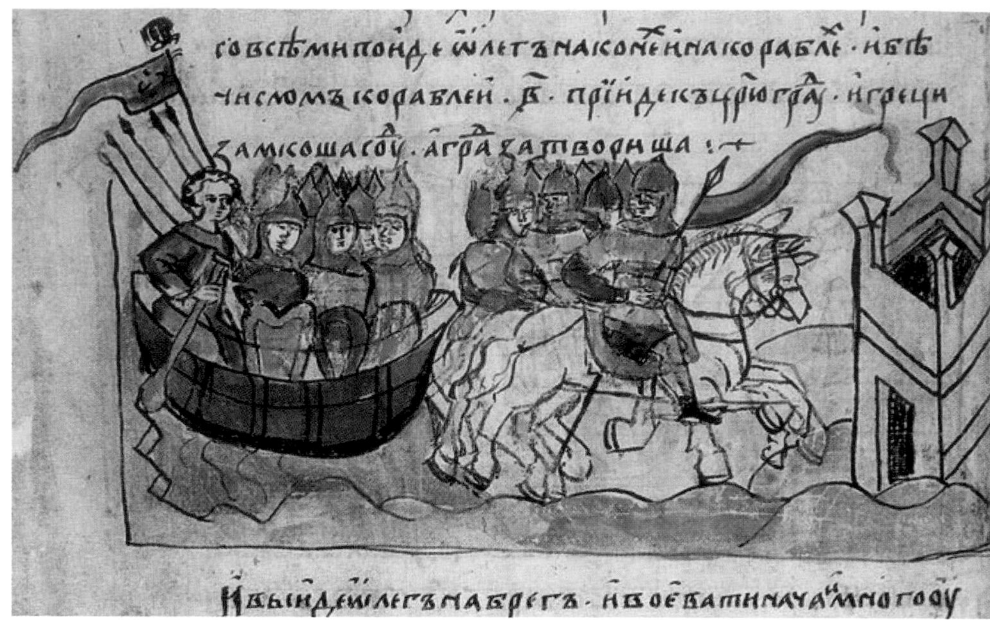

11.
Medieval depiction of the Rūs attack on Constantinople in 860.

***Radziwiłł Chronicle*, 15th-century copy of 13th-century original. Probably Russia.**
Paper. L 31.5 cm, W 21 cm
Library of the Russian Academy of Sciences

used both for the inhabitants of the emerging Russian towns and for Vikings more generally. Some accounts may also project back elements of the political situation of a later time (see p. 25). A Rūs fleet attacked Constantinople in 860, looting the surrounding territory and suburbs, but was unable to penetrate the city walls (fig. 11). The *Russian Primary Chronicle* records a second major Rūs attack on Constantinople in 907, but this is not mentioned in Byzantine sources; either it was on a smaller scale than Russian tradition suggests, or the date is mistaken, perhaps repeating the earlier one of 860. Both attacks were apparently followed by trading treaties establishing a more peaceful relationship, although the Rūs also served as mercenaries in the Byzantine army on a number of occasions in the late ninth and early tenth centuries.[5]

A further Rūs attack on Constantinople in 941 saw the Rūs fleet destroyed by the Byzantine use of Greek Fire, against which Viking ships had no defence.[6] According to Khazar sources (see pp. 48–9), this took place after the Rūs had undertaken an unsuccessful assault on the Khazars on behalf of Byzantium and in turn were forced by the Khazars to attack Constantinople. Once again, however, this was followed by a treaty redefining trade relationships and establishing terms for Rūs to serve in the Byzantine army.[7] With or without encouragement from Byzantium, the Rūs under Prince Sviatoslav of Kiev destroyed the Khazar khāqānate in 965, and in alliance with Byzantium Sviatoslav attacked and defeated the Bulgars (of Bulgaria, rather than the Volga Bulgars) in 968. Prince Sviatoslav was then killed by the Pechenegs (see p. 49) in 972 and his skull turned into a drinking cup (fig. 12).[8]

The Rūs also clashed with the Islamic world, despite the extensive trade between the two. A large raid south of the Caspian into modern Iran took place in 913, supposedly with the agreement of the Khazar khāqān, since this required travel through the Khazar khāqānate, and resulted in extensive plunder. However, the Rūs were then killed and plundered in turn on their homeward journey by Khazars and/or Volga Bulgars, again presumably with at least the tacit approval of the khāqān.[9]

A raid on Bardha'a in modern Azerbaijan in 943 was initially more successful. The Arab historian Miskawayh records that the Rūs held the city for several months, defeating repeated attempts by the Muslim governor first to hold them off, and subsequently to dislodge them. This was clearly a major expedition, and may have been aimed at establishing a permanent settlement. At first the Rūs sought only to install themselves as rulers, offering peace to the inhabitants if they accepted their authority: 'There is no dispute between us on the matter of religion; we only want to rule. It is our obligation to treat you well, and yours to be loyal to us.' While some of the city's population were willing to agree to this, others attacked the Rūs in support of the forces raised by the governor. Once these assaults had been defeated, the Rūs ordered the entire population to leave the city. Only those who had mounts to carry them did so, and 'on the fourth day, the Rūs put [the remainder] to the sword, killing a huge number beyond counting. After the massacre, they took captive over 10,000 men and boys with their womenfolk, their wives and their daughters.' The men were ransomed or killed, and the women and children kept as slaves. However, after a lengthy occupation of the city, Miskawayh records that the Rūs suffered from an epidemic (possibly dysentery), which he attributes to the eating of too much fruit, and eventually abandoned the city of their own accord, retreating with their ships and their loot.[10] A final expedition into *Serkland*, the Old Norse name for the Islamic world, took place around 1040.

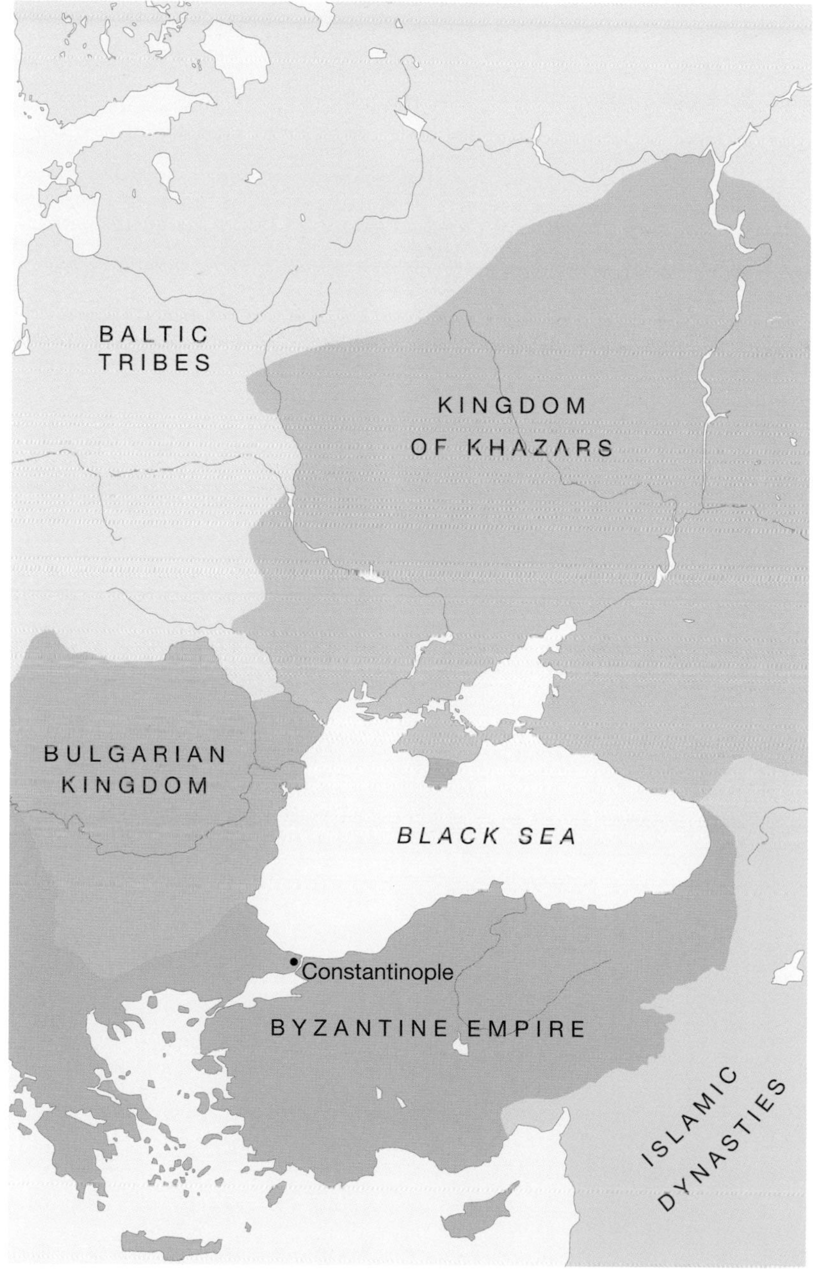

12.
The peoples of eastern Europe in the 10th century.

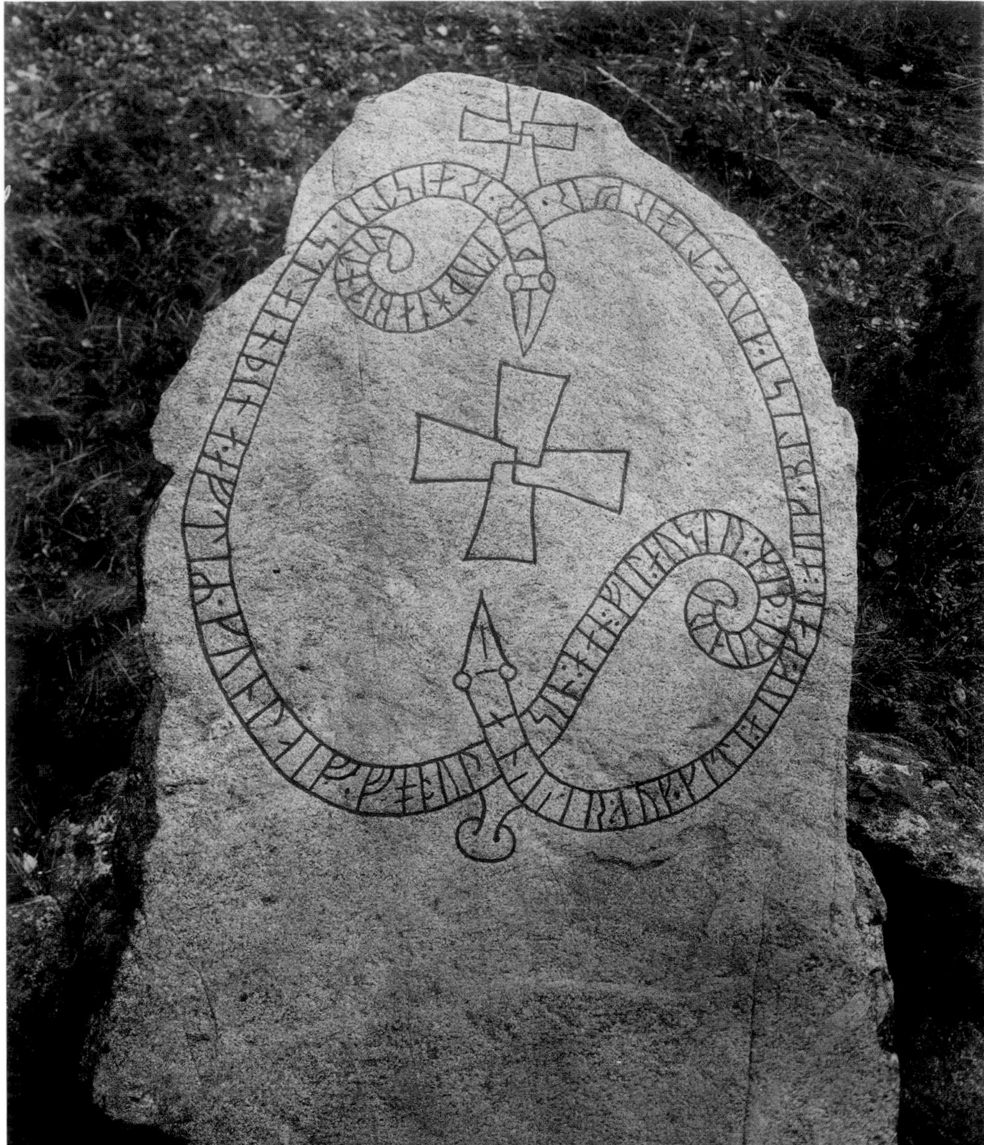

13.
This rune-stone (U 644), at Ekilla bro in Sweden, describes the death of a Viking called Gunnleifr, who died on Ingvar's expedition to the east. The runes can be translated as follows.

Old Norse transcription:
Andvettr ok <kiti> ok Karr ok Blesi ok DiarfR þæiR ræistu stæin þenna æftiR Gunnlæif, faður sinn. Hann fell austr með Ingvari. Guð hialpi andinni.

English translation:
Andvéttr and <kiti> and Kárr and Blesi and Djarfr erected this stone in memory of Gunnleifr, their father. He fell in the east with Ingvarr. May God help* [his] *spirit.

A Swedish chieftain named Ingvar led a large but spectacularly unsuccessful expedition to the east, although it is debatable exactly where he went, as the only substantial account is in the heavily fictionalized (and geographically muddled) *Saga of Yngvar the Far-travelled*. However, the fact that such an expedition took place is attested by no fewer than twenty-six rune-stones in eastern Sweden (fig. 13) commemorating those who fell with Ingvar.[11]

If such expeditions were not typical of Viking activity in the east, the same cannot be said for western Europe, where Viking raiding had a major impact in Britain, Ireland and on the Continent. Initial raiding was on a small scale, motivated by the acquisition of portable wealth that could be taken back to Scandinavia. Finds of Viking-Age metalwork from Britain and Ireland are known across Scandinavia (fig. 14), but especially from western Norway, suggesting that the main thrust of early raiding came from this area.[12]

In many ways, this small-scale raiding was typical of a slightly earlier age in western Europe. The violent acquisition of wealth was hardly unique to the Vikings, and the idea of young men 'proving' themselves by raiding neighbouring peoples has parallels in many early medieval societies, as well as in other periods and cultures. What set the Vikings apart to some extent was that by the late eighth century when Viking raids are first recorded, this sort of behaviour was increasingly seen as unacceptable. Under the influence of Christianity,

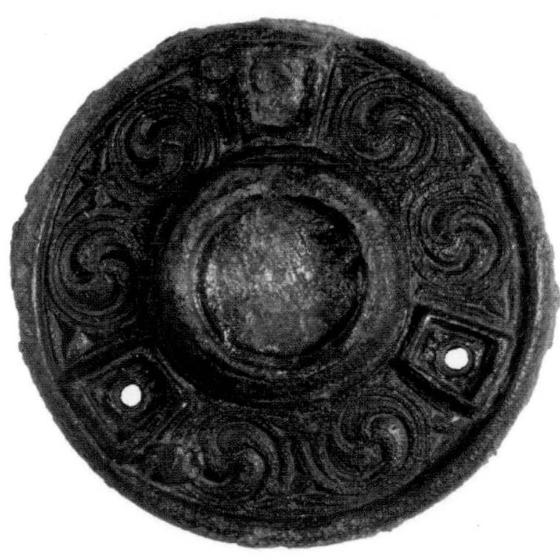

14.
Circular Anglo-Irish mount found in Denmark, 8th–9th century. Gamborg, Vindinge, Fyn, Denmark.
Gilt copper alloy. Diam. 3.25 cm
National Museum of Denmark, Copenhagen

violence was seen as the legitimate prerogative of kings, and warfare could be seen as morally acceptable under certain circumstances, but just robbing people (and especially robbing churches) was seen as both morally wrong and a challenge to legitimate authority.[13]

This view of violence explains the use of a term in Anglo-Saxon sources that has sometimes led to confusion over the scale of Viking warfare. Viking forces are often referred to as *here*, a word that is also used in the law code of Ine of Wessex (688–726). This indicates that when robbery with violence occurs, if it is undertaken by fewer than seven people, they are called 'thieves'. If there are between seven and thirty-five, they are called a 'band', and if there are over thirty-five, they are called a *here*. Since the term is used of Viking forces and is often translated as 'army', this led to the suggestion that anything above thirty-five people was large enough to constitute an army, and that Viking armies were really very small.[14] In fact, *here* is not the normal Old English word for an army: the more common term is *fyrd*. The use of *here* to describe the Vikings was instead intended to convey the fact that they were robbers on a large scale, rather than legitimate warriors, in the same way that they are also frequently referred to as 'pagans' or 'heathens', again emphasizing that they were outside the social norms of Christian Europe.[15]

As the Viking raids continued, the scale increased, with fleets of thirty or more ships recorded in the second quarter of the ninth century, and in the hundreds by the third quarter. Historians have debated the extent to which the size of these fleets has been exaggerated. The minimalist view that anything over thirty-five constituted an army has now largely been rejected, but warfare was still probably conducted on a moderately small scale, with forces rarely comprising more than a few hundred warriors. Occasionally, however, smaller groups might band together into a force numbering in the thousands, as seems to have been the case with the *micel here*, which raided in England between 865 and 878.[16] Here the size of the forces indicated by the historical accounts is reinforced by the large extent of some of their camps, as shown by recent archaeological investigations (see pp. 120–1). Some of the leaders of this force are said to have been the sons of Ragnar Hairy-Breeches, a semi-legendary king of the Danes, but composite groups of this sort were probably formed of smaller groups from many different petty kingdoms, each under their own leader. The same is probably true of some of the larger forces recorded in Frankish sources, such as the fleet active on the Seine in the 850s, which in 853 was commanded by *Sidricus* (Sigtryggr) and *Gotafridus* (Guðfriðr), while in 855 we are specifically told of a fleet under Sidricus being joined by another under *Bernus* (Björn).

The scale of Viking raiding is also indicated by the outcome (fig. 15). Raiding in the late ninth century turned to conquest, although it is not clear that this was necessarily the original intention. The *micel here* in England managed to conquer the kingdoms of East Anglia, Northumbria and Mercia, and came close to conquering Wessex, before a negotiated settlement in 878 left them in control of all of England apart from Wessex and the south-western part of Mercia.[17] A similar agreement in 911 led to the Viking leader Rollo and his descendants being formally recognized first as counts of Rouen and later as dukes of Normandy.[18] There were also short-lived grants of territory in Frisia (see p. 98) and attempts were made, although without lasting success, to establish Viking settlements in Brittany. Elsewhere in the Frankish kingdoms, large Viking fleets were able to overwinter on numerous occasions and to extort sizeable payments before leaving, but made no substantial settlements. While Vikings did not establish large territories in Ireland, they were able to found a number of coastal communities, with surrounding hinterlands, from which the native rulers were unable to dislodge them permanently, despite repeated attempts.[19] The conquest phase in Scotland is less reliably documented, since our evidence comes mainly from later sagas, but, left Viking rulers in control of large parts of northern and western Scotland, including the Northern and Western Isles.[20] In 1016 a Danish army

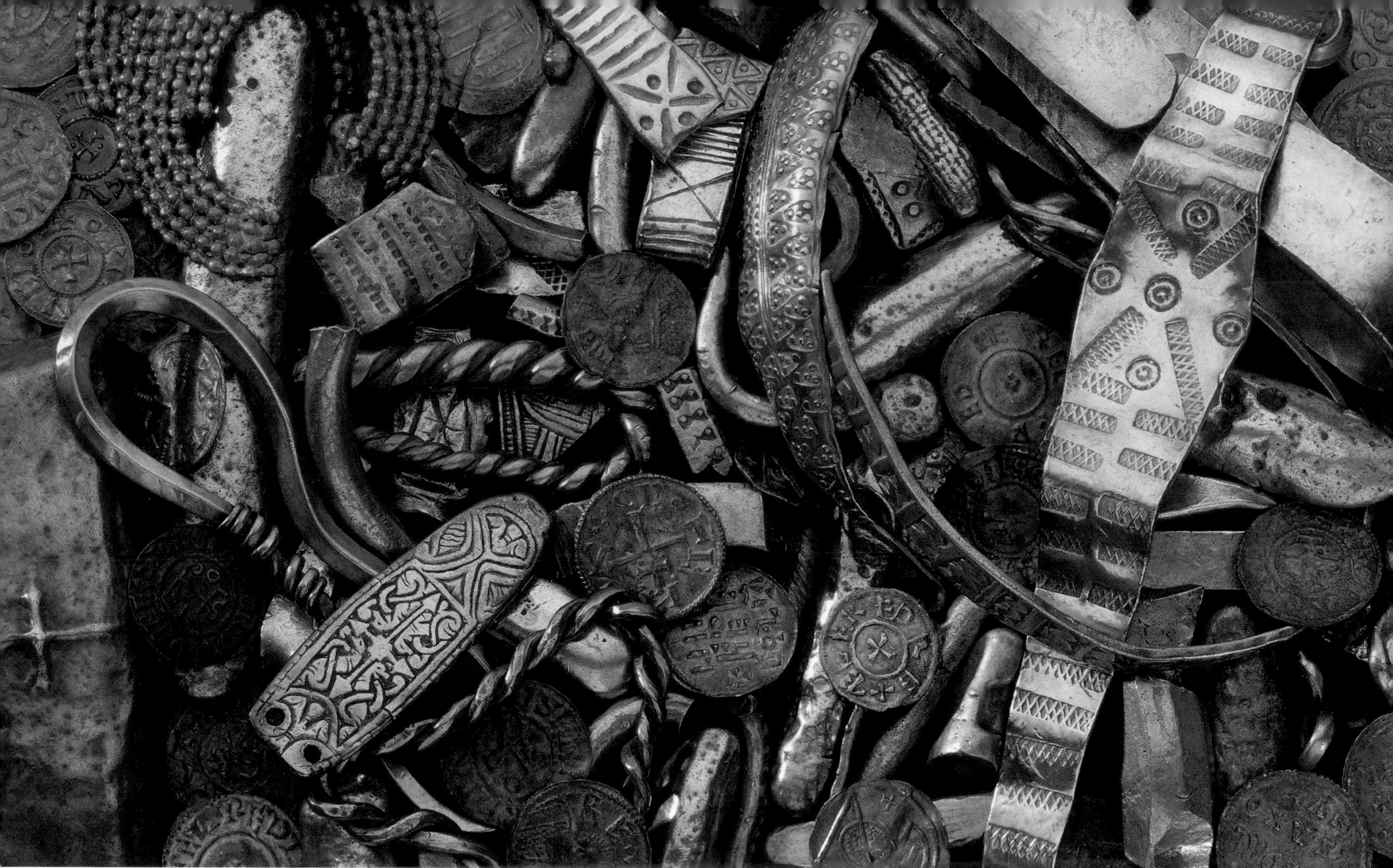

15.
Huge hoards of silver, like this one from Cuerdale in northern England, demonstrate the quantities of wealth that Viking raiders were able to accumulate.

Silver hoard, selection, *c.* 905–10. Cuerdale, Lancashire, England.
British Museum, London

was able to conquer England, while a Norwegian army came close to doing the same thing in 1066, but these need to be seen more in the context of national warfare than as Viking raids (see pp. 98–101).

Despite the large scale of some of these expeditions, raiding and warfare were activities undertaken by a small proportion of society. Although raiding was by no means limited to individuals of high social rank, such as kings and earls, it required a considerable financial investment and therefore the backing of wealthy individuals. Popular perceptions of the Vikings since the nineteenth century have tended to think in terms of a very flat social structure in which all free men were to some extent equals. In part this fits with a wider view at that time of free weapon-bearing peasant farmers among all the early Germanic peoples, including the Anglo-Saxons and the Franks.[21] It was also a view reinforced by the Icelandic sagas, which show a society without kings or even a formal aristocracy, and which could thus be seen as a society of free and equal farmers. However, much as ancient Greek democracy offered equality to everyone (except women, children, slaves, foreigners, etc.), some free men in Viking-Age Scandinavia were more equal than others. Even the relatively flat social hierarchy of Iceland had a limited number of people who held the position of *goði*, which until the conversion to Christianity combined the roles of priest and local chieftain. The Scandinavian homelands in the early Viking Age were still divided into many petty kingdoms, and although these gradually disappeared as the larger kingdoms of Denmark, Norway and Sweden emerged, local rulers and chieftains continued to hold important roles, as well as possessing more wealth than those around them.

16.
Wooden longbow.
Hedeby, Germany.
Yew. L 191 cm
Archäologisches Landesmuseum,
Schloss Gottorf, Schleswig

17.
Leaf-shaped arrowheads,
800–1050. Sørup,
Måløv, Zealand, Denmark.
Iron. L 9–12.5 cm
National Museum of Denmark,
Copenhagen

Ships were particularly expensive, requiring either the control of the substantial raw materials to create hull, sails and rigging, plus the manpower, both skilled and unskilled, needed to build a ship, or the wealth to buy one ready built (see chapter 5). Weapons and armour probably varied considerably in cost. Basic spears, axes and bows and arrows were relatively cheap, since they required little iron and were also to some extent multifunctional, since spears and bows could be used in hunting, while some types of axe could double as domestic tools (figs 16–21). Shields were comparatively inexpensive, since the iron boss could be reused, and either the whole of the rest of the shield or individual planks replaced at need (figs 22–23). However, the period also saw specialized forms of spear, axe and arrowhead that were designed only for warfare, and the existence of spearheads and axeheads with decorative inlays (figs 19–20) suggests that such weapons could be expensive indicators of personal status. Meanwhile, there was no such thing as a cheap sword, since even the most basic form involved a large amount of iron or steel, irrespective of the cost of the craftsmanship required to create a good blade and the ornate decoration (including use of gold and/or silver) found on many hilts. A large number of blades with inscriptions points to widespread trade in Frankish sword blades, while analysis of swords from across the Viking world also indicates the use of crucible steel, a high-quality steel probably imported from the Islamic world, as the techniques required to produce it are otherwise unrecorded in western Europe at the time.[22] Ibn Rusta notes that the Rus used 'Sulaymān swords', thought to be a reference to swords produced in Central Asia, although Miskawayh's account of the Rūs attack on Bardha'a in 943 describes the local population recovering Viking swords from burial mounds: 'After they left, the Muslims dug up the graves and found a number of swords, which are in great demand to this day for their sharpness and excellence'.[23] Armour was also highly expensive. Helmets required a quantity of iron or steel, although boiled leather may have produced a cheaper and lighter alternative, while mail shirts involved both metal and intensive labour. The technical skill needed to produce a mail shirt is limited, but with many thousands of rings making up each shirt, they were extremely time consuming to produce, especially if the rings were riveted to stop them springing apart (fig. 24).

The extent to which all Viking warriors were fully equipped with weapons and armour is debatable. Surviving examples of helmets and mail shirts are extremely rare, but this may say more about burial practice than about what was used in battle. Contemporary illustrations of warriors almost invariably show helmets and written accounts suggest that

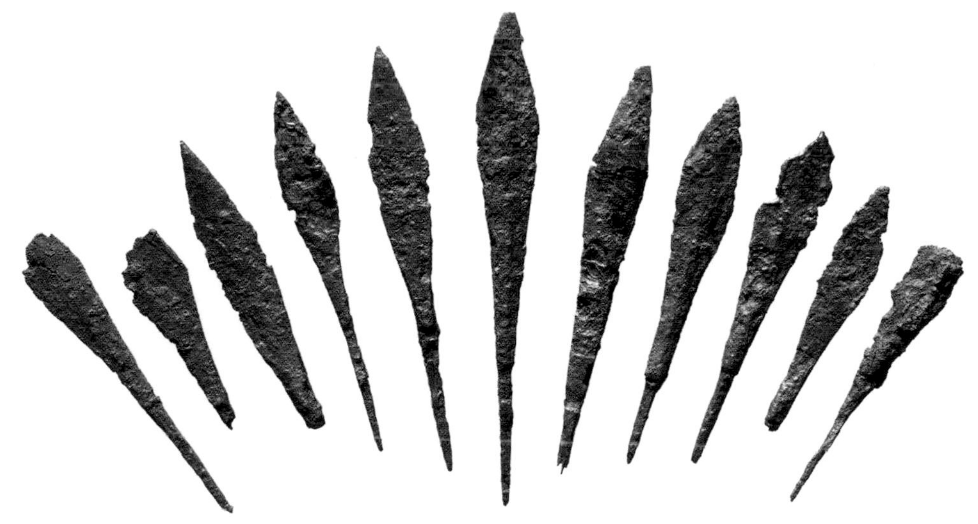

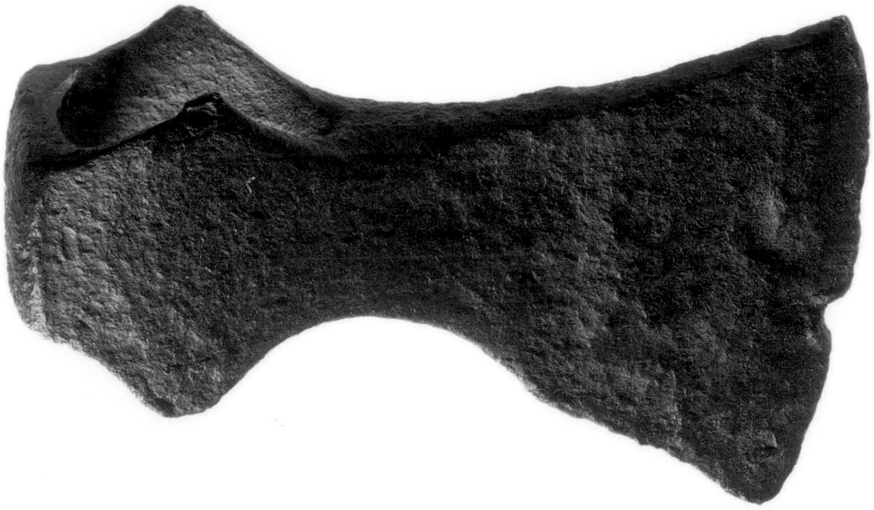

18.
Bearded axehead, 9th century. Øverli, Lom, Oppland, Norway.
Iron. H 16 cm
British Museum, London

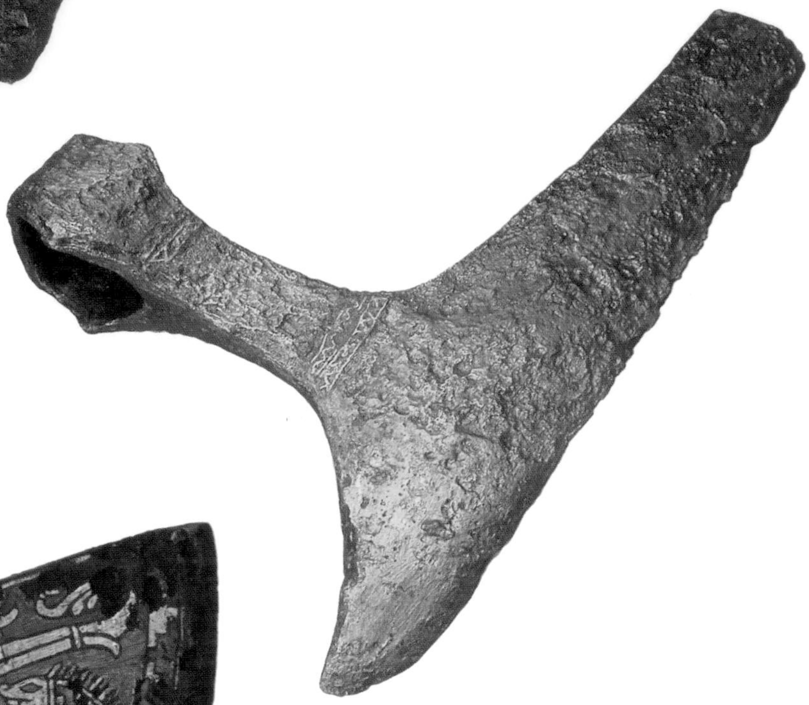

19.
Decorated iron axe, 11th–13th century. Teterow, Lkr. Ostvorpommern, Germany.
Iron, copper alloy. L 16 cm, W 15 cm
Landesamt für Kultur- und Denkmalpflege Mecklenburg-Vorpommern, Schwerin

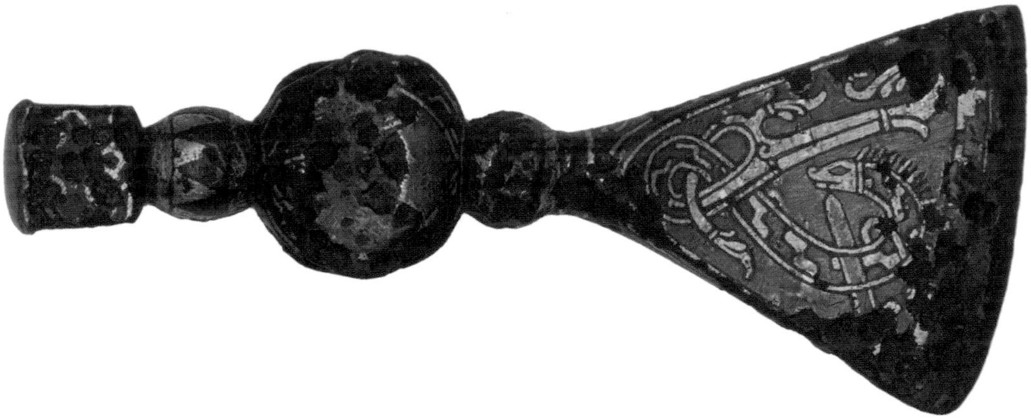

20.
Inlaid axehead, 1000–1050. Central Volga area (Kazan region), Russia.
Iron, gold, silver, niello. L 6 cm
State Historical Museum, Moscow

21.
Spearhead with inlaid socket. London, England.
Iron, silver. L 37.9 cm
British Museum, London

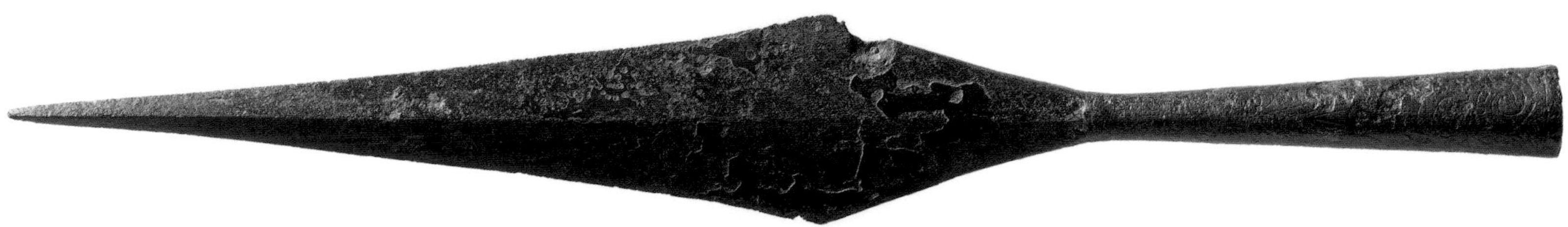

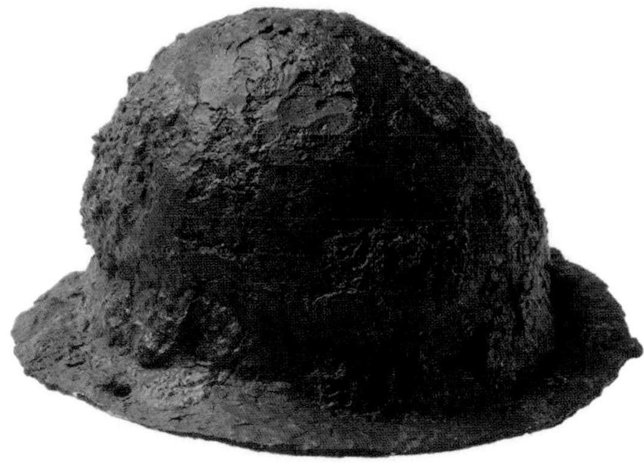

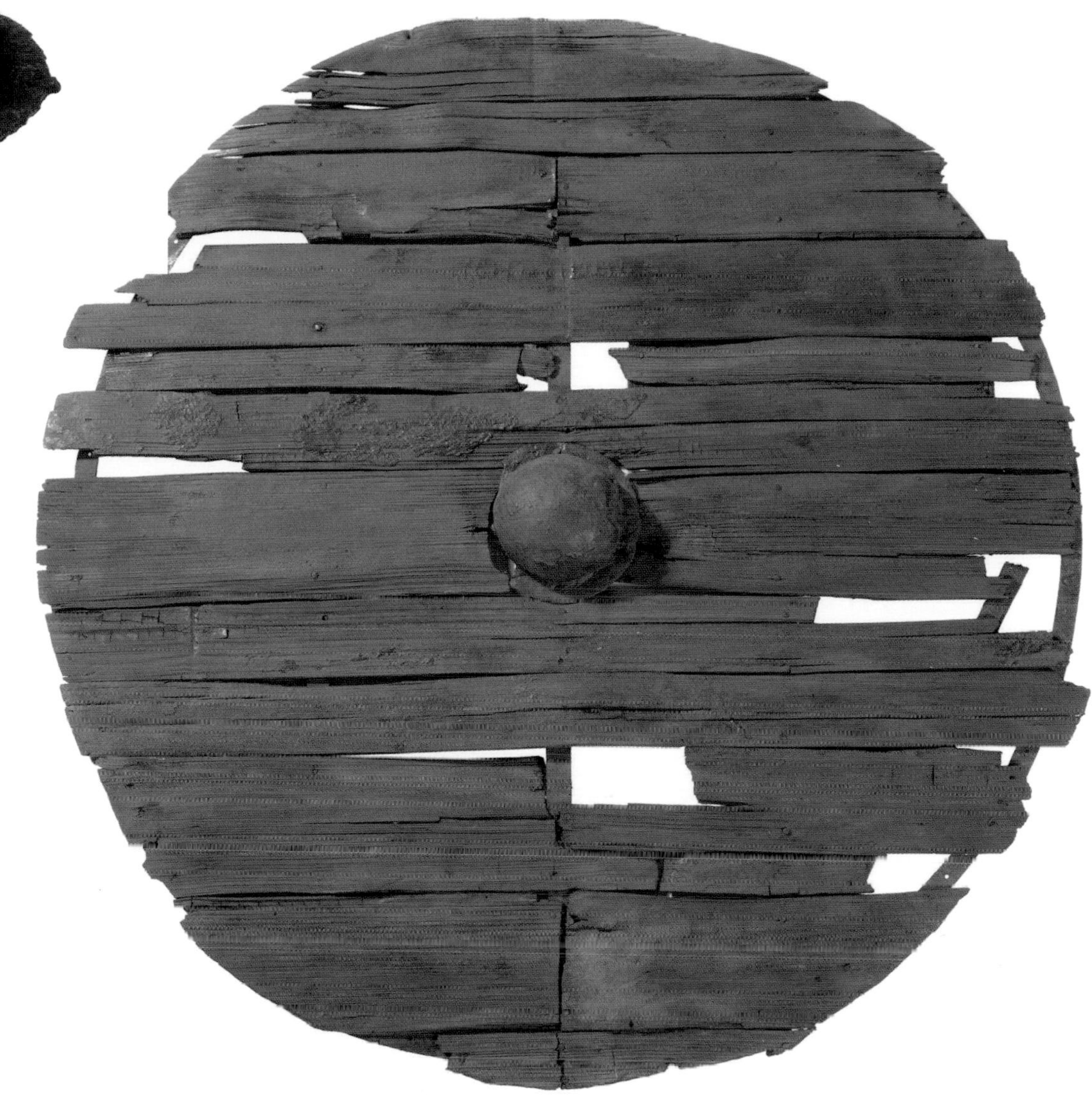

22.
Shield boss, 9th century. Bolstad, Sogn og Fjordane, Norway.
Iron. Diam. 14 cm
British Museum, London

23.
For shield timbers to survive in the archaeological record is extremely uncommon.

Wooden shield, late 9th century. Gokstad, Vestfold, Norway.
White pine, metal. Diam. 94 cm
Museum of Cultural History, University of Oslo, Oslo

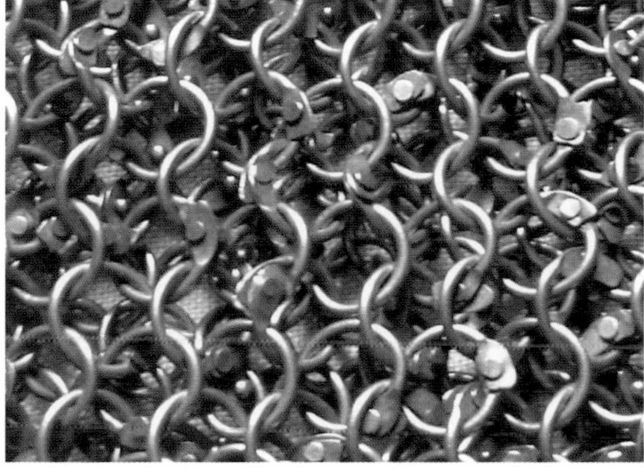

24.
This modern replica shows how each individual link in a mail shirt was closed with a rivet for added strength.
Private collection

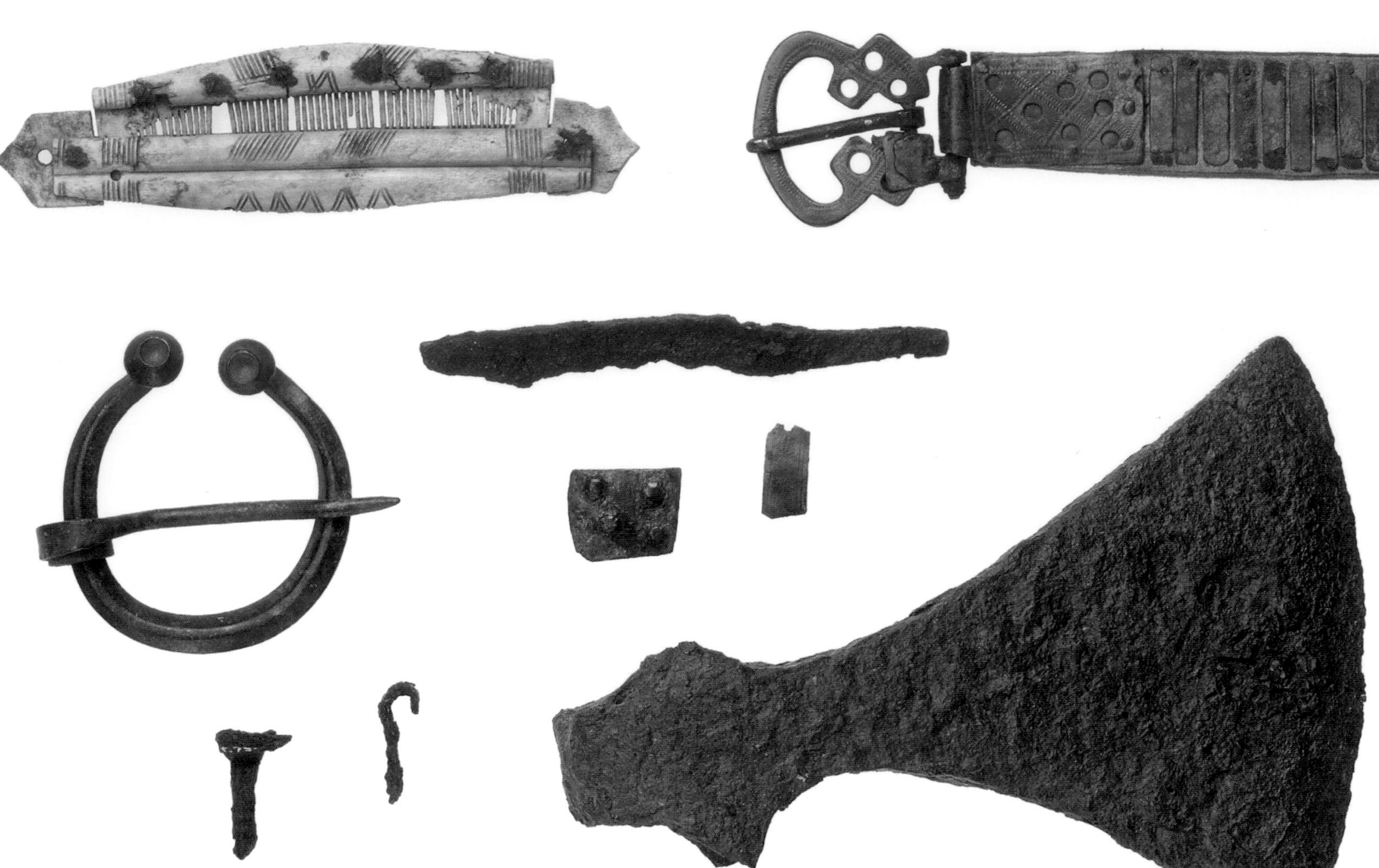

25.
While some graves contain the full range of weapons used by the Viking warriors, in others a single weapon was thought to be enough to show his warrior status.

Male weapon burial, including broad-bladed axe, late 10th–early 11th century. Grave 222B, Ire, Hellvi, Gotland.
Iron, copper alloy, bone. Axe L *c.* 16 cm
Gotlands Museum, Visby

26.
Middleton Cross B includes a rare Viking-Age depiction of a fully-equipped warrior, 10th century.
Stone. H 106 cm, W (head)
390 cm (shaft) 295 cm
St Andrew's Church, Middleton, North Yorkshire

mail was not unusual. The Anglo-Saxon king Æthelred II ordered that every man in the English *fyrd* should have both helmet and mail shirt, and judging from the success of the Vikings in his reign, they are likely to have been similarly well armoured. A fully-equipped warrior might thus have helmet, mail and shield for protection, plus spear, sword and/or axe and a *sax* or fighting knife (fig. 25). This is the combination of weapons attributed to the Rūs in Miskawayh's account of the attack on Bardha'a, which also corresponds to an image of a warrior on an Anglo-Scandinavian stone cross from Middleton, North Yorkshire (fig. 26).[24] This is not to say that all Viking raiders were so well equipped, and few warrior graves contain all these items, but possession of the majority of these items would imply significant personal wealth, or a wealthy lord who could afford to supply his followers, or perhaps a number of poorer people combining to equip one man between them. The last of these can perhaps be seen in the structured regional levies of the *leiðangr*, organized for mutual defence in the late Viking or post-Viking period (see p. 113), but is less likely in the early period. Early raiding was thus largely confined to those who could afford the investment in ships, weapons and armour, together with their followers, and perhaps some poorer and more lightly armed individuals brought along to make up the numbers required to row the ships.

In this respect, such raids were probably not fundamentally very far removed from more formal warfare in neighbouring kingdoms. Since the 1980s, interpretation of Anglo-Saxon and Frankish military organization at the beginning of the Viking Age has moved

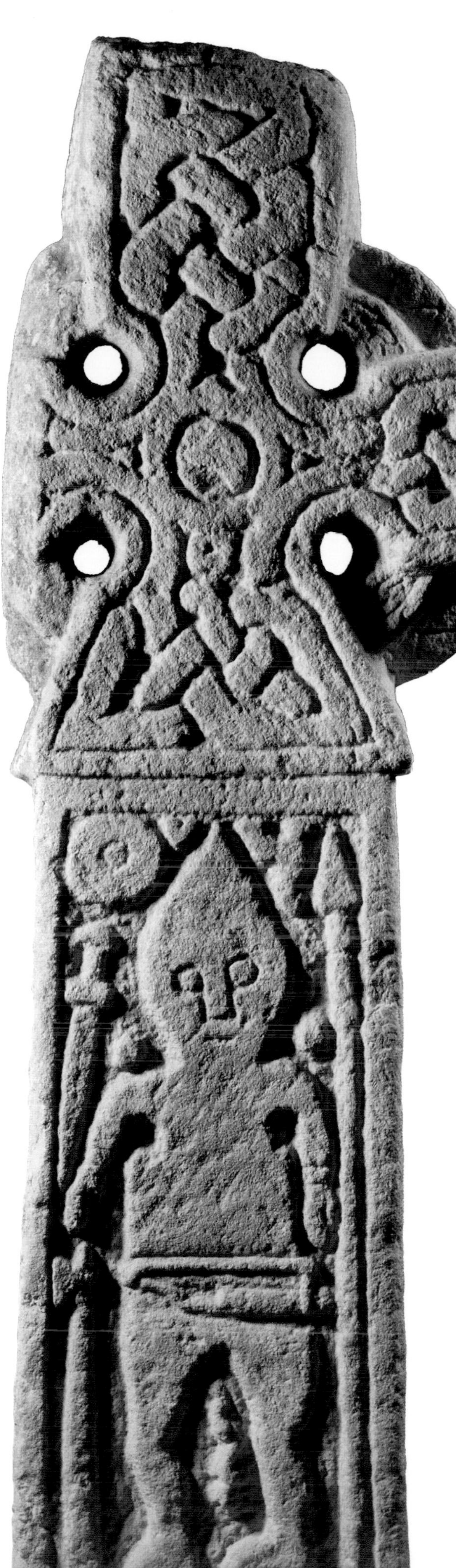

away from the idea of Germanic nations of free men sharing both a duty and a right to bear arms, to a view of warfare in this period as a more elite activity, pursued by the aristocracy and their households, together with whatever additional followers they could recruit from their own resources. Warfare was generally motivated by material gain as well as political advantage, and raiding was likely to involve either the submission of the invaded kingdom, in which case a tribute payment of precious metal, cattle, or other valuable goods was imposed as a sign of ongoing lordship, or straightforward plunder if such a tribute was not forthcoming. The proceeds would have been used by the successful leader to reward his followers, thereby giving them the wealth to equip themselves and their own followers for the following season. It has been argued that this approach may have been adopted by even the most powerful of rulers, such as the Frankish king Charlemagne, or Offa of Mercia, with more structured military organization introduced only through necessity as a response to external attacks from Vikings and others (see below).[25]

If this approach was good enough for Charlemagne and Offa, it was good enough for the Vikings too. The raiding and plunder of monasteries and trading centres have already been discussed, but Viking raids also on occasion involved the taking of tribute without having to fight for it. Anglo-Saxon accounts of the late ninth century talk of 'making peace' with the Vikings, but Frankish sources talk more bluntly of 'tribute', and payment that could be seen by one side as a gift in exchange for peace could easily be interpreted as tribute by the other. A gradual shift from plunder to regular tribute to total subjection probably also played a part in the way that the more powerful kingdoms within Scandinavia assimilated their neighbours to create the unified kingdoms of the later Viking Age.

In the raiding phase, warfare was thus apparently largely undertaken by, or sponsored by, those who were already wealthy, in the hope of gaining further wealth. Mention should perhaps be made, however, of one group of warriors notorious for not wearing much in the way of expensive armour. The *berserkir* (berserker), in later saga tradition, would fight naked, or at least without armour, going into a battle frenzy that enabled him to fight without feeling pain. The concept of warriors crazily chewing their shields, associated with the berserker, is also represented on a few of the famous Lewis chessmen (fig. 27; although these warriors are clothed and helmeted), but these date from the late twelfth century, the same period in which the sagas were beginning to be written down and, like the sagas, probably represent a post-Viking rationalization of something very different. A berserker with no need of armour might be seen as a less expensive alternative to the fully-equipped warrior, but the origins of the berserker, as discussed further on pages 116–17, seem to have more to do with a belief in warriors with beast-like strength and ferocity on the battlefield than with nudity.[26]

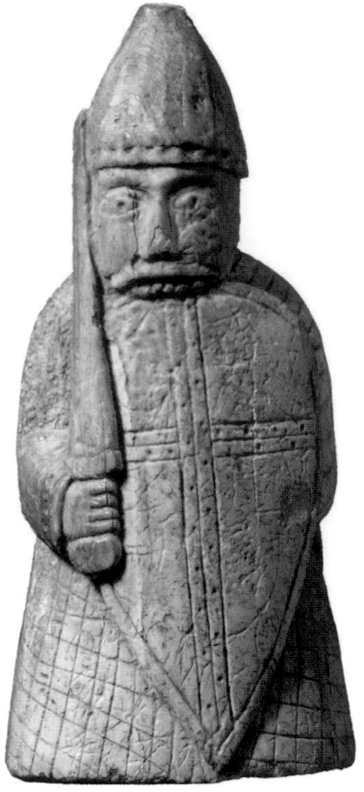
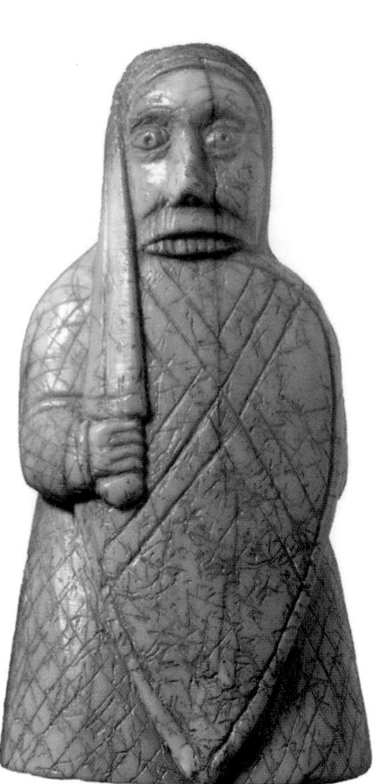

27.
These three chessmen are shown biting their shields. This behaviour was associated with 'berserkers' in the sagas but, like the chessmen, the sagas date from long after the Viking Age.

Chessmen, late 12th century, Uig, Lewis, Scotland
Walrus ivory. Central chessman H 9.2 cm
British Museum, London

Warriors and warships

One thing that did set the Vikings apart from others in the period was their strategic use of ships in warfare. Seaborne raiding was not new and neither was armed migration by sea. The Franks in particular seem to have been involved in maritime raiding during the Migration Age (fifth–sixth centuries), and a number of Germanic peoples, including the Franks, Anglo-Saxons and Danes, are recorded as engaging in coastal raiding and piracy in the centuries leading up to the Viking Age.[27] The Anglo-Saxon migration to England in the fifth and sixth centuries had been seaborne, and although the ship from the Sutton Hoo Mound 1 burial from the early seventh century represents an earlier stage in the development of north European shipbuilding, its relationship with the later Viking ships is immediately apparent (fig. 28).[28]

Developments in ship technology meant that the Vikings were able to use ships more effectively in warfare than their predecessors. They were not, however, primarily designed for battle at sea. The style of construction meant that they could not be used for ramming, and accounts of sea battles suggest that ships essentially provided platforms for a similar combination of missiles and hand-to-hand combat to that found in land battles, with the one distinctive feature that larger ships had an advantage of height over smaller ones.

Instead, the value of the ships themselves came from three factors. Firstly, they offered speed and mobility; secondly, their design allowed for flexibility of use both at sea and in shallower waters; and, thirdly, they could accommodate troops, their loot and supplies. The early Viking raids in particular seem to have been hit-and-run affairs, arriving, looting and withdrawing before a proper defence or counterattack could be mustered. From the tenth century onwards, there is clear evidence for specialization of shipbuilding, with distinct categories of ship for use as warships and as cargo vessels. Prior to this, to judge from the surviving archaeological evidence, ships had a more multipurpose design, with space for men and cargo (fig. 29). Therefore, it would not necessarily have been immediately apparent whether a ship was intending to raid or to trade until it landed. As discussed in chapter 1,

28.
The Sutton Hoo ship burial during excavation in 1939. The outline of the ship and the position of the timbers and boat rivets are clearly visible in the sand from which the burial was excavated. Sutton Hoo, Suffolk, England.

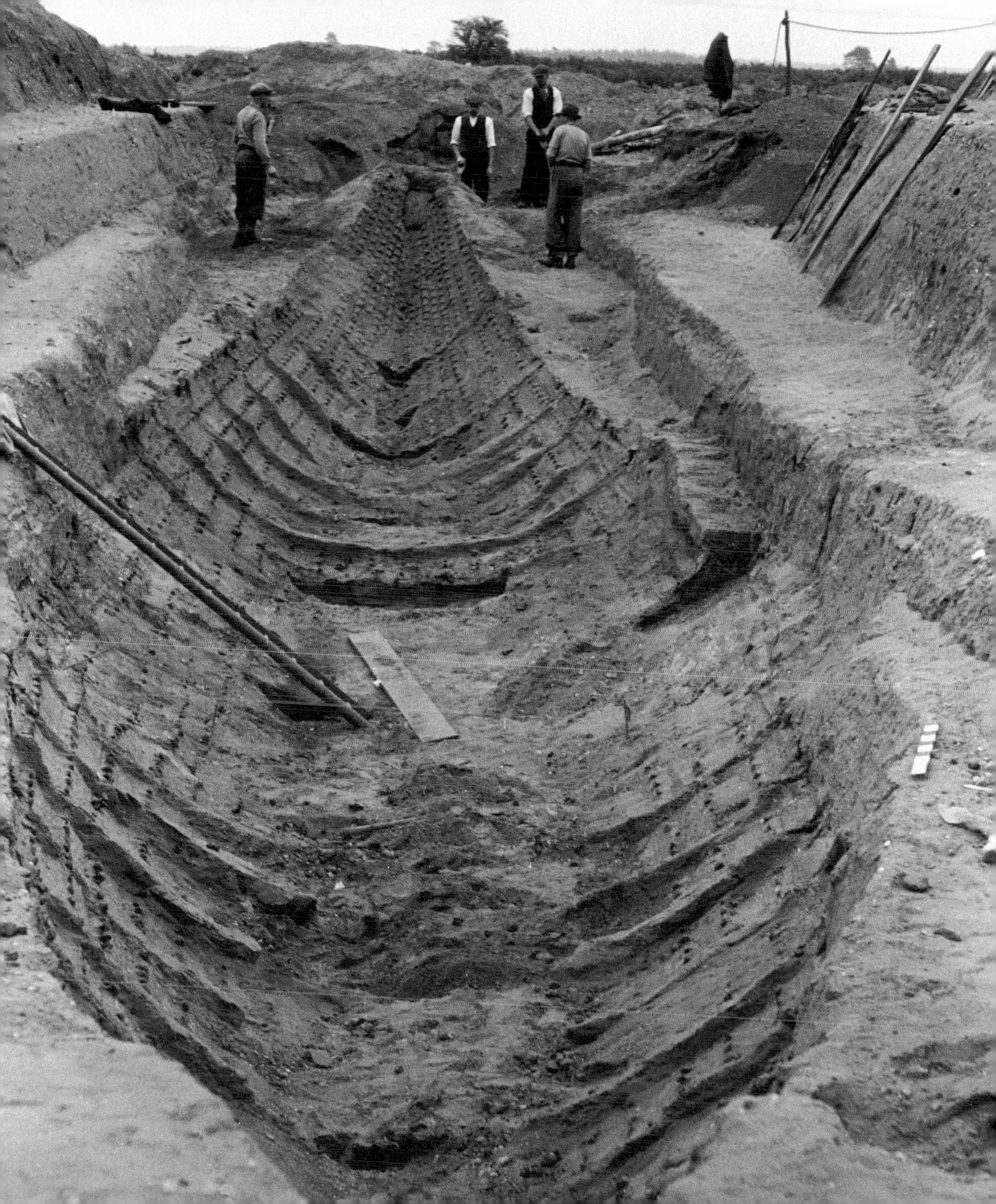

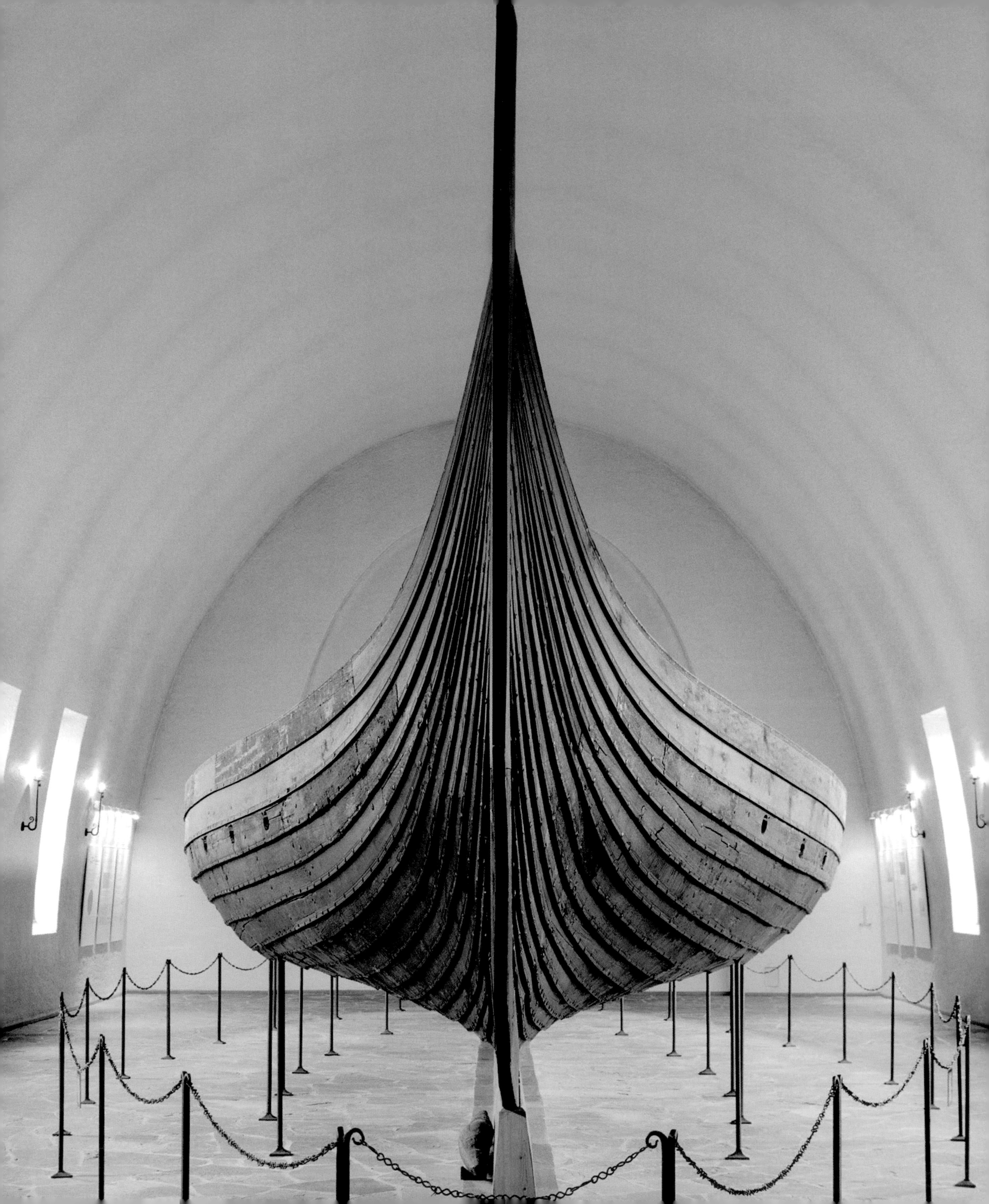

29.
The Gokstad ship dates from the late 890s and would have been suitable for warfare and trade.
Oak, iron. L 23.24 m
Museum of Cultural History, University of Oslo, Oslo

Scandinavia already had maritime trading contacts with neighbouring regions before the Viking Age began, and this trade seems to have continued alongside Viking warfare. Ships must have been a common sight in the coastal sea lanes and raising the alarm each time a sail, or even a small group of sails, was spotted risked frequent false alarms. Unless every trading centre, monastery and coastal settlement maintained a permanent garrison, or had some means of protecting or limiting access by water, preventing attack was almost impossible. Without ships of similar strength and speed to respond with, once the raiders were back on their ships they were likely to be able to retreat to safety.

This does not mean that it always worked so smoothly and such attacks could be countered to some extent by maintaining a defensive fleet to respond to news of raids. Einhard's *Life of Charlemagne* records that the Frankish ruler established coastguards, strongpoints and ships at all major ports and river mouths for this purpose.[29] The *Anglo-Saxon Chronicle* records in more detail how in 896 a group of six Viking ships raiding the south coast were surprised by a larger fleet of Anglo-Saxon ships while most of the crews were ashore. A battle ensued, partly on ships and partly on the beach, and the Vikings were defeated, with most of them either killed in battle or subsequently captured and executed. Only two ships escaped, one supposedly with just five survivors, and the men on the other 'very much wounded'.[30] Something similar may lie behind a mass grave found near Weymouth in Dorset in 2009 (fig. 30). The grave contained around fifty skeletons dating

30.
The mass grave from Weymouth, Dorset, England, early 11th century. The bodies were decapitated and the heads were piled separately at the edge of the grave.
Dorset County Council/ Oxford Archaeology

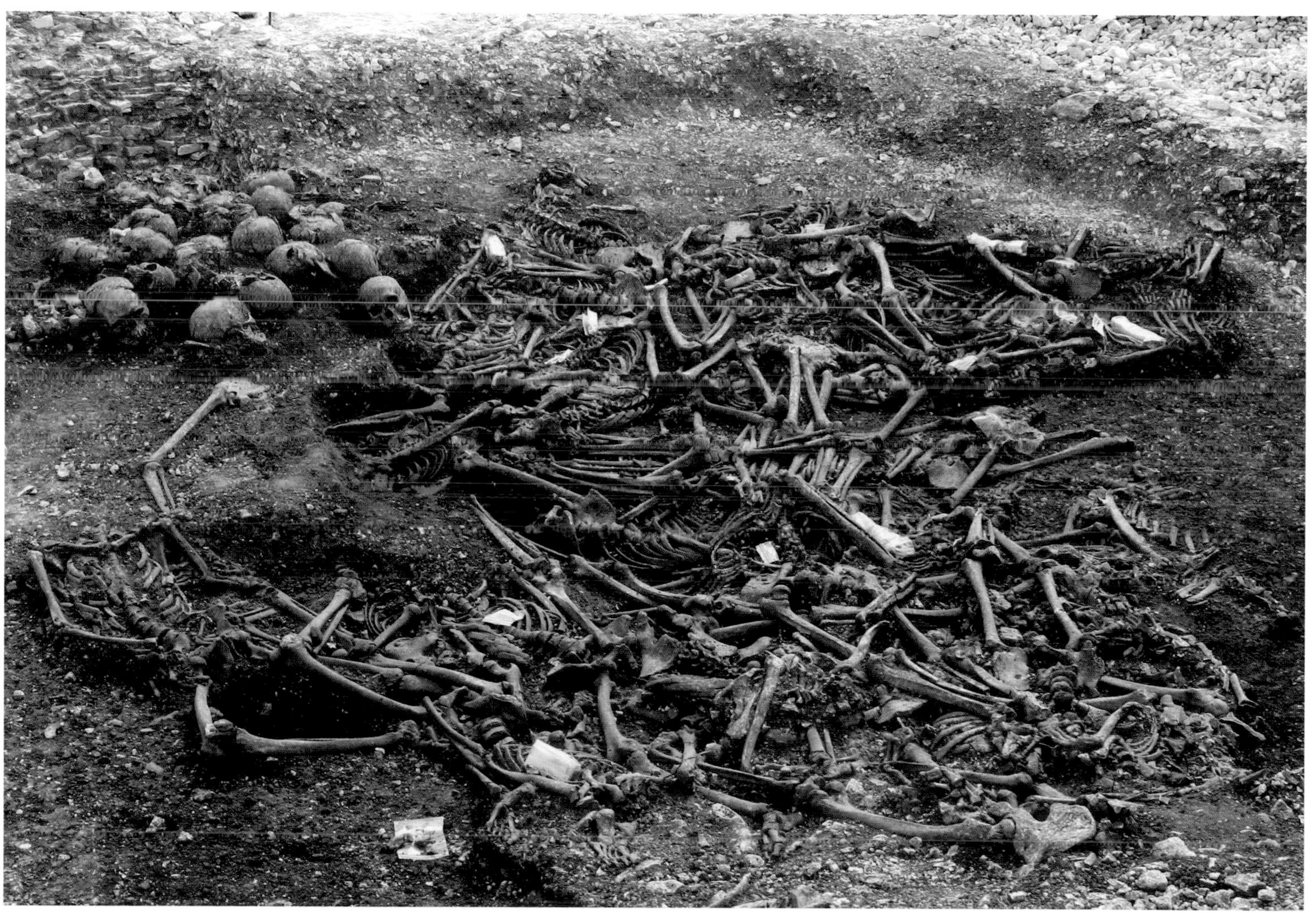

from the early eleventh century and isotope analysis indicates that all of those tested are likely to have originated in Scandinavia. All of them had been stripped of anything of value (there were no associated finds) and beheaded, so the grave clearly represents the aftermath of a mass execution.[31] While the exact circumstances are uncertain, fifty is a realistic number for the crew of a medium-sized warship and the date fits with a period of Viking raiding, so the capture and execution of an unsuccessful shipload of raiders is a likely explanation. However, such successful intervention seems to have been more the exception than the rule.

A second aspect of Viking ships was that their design offered considerable flexibility of use. Even relatively small ships were capable of crossing the open sea, while the more sizable ones had a shallow enough draft that they could easily be beached on the coast without being limited to deep-water harbours, and could also penetrate inland along larger rivers. The first point added to the value of ships for surprise attack. A fleet or ship sailing along the coast was more likely to be seen or intercepted than one arriving directly at its target from the open sea. The second point allowed Vikings to raid inland without abandoning their ships wherever there were navigable rivers, and this meant that even areas distant from the sea were vulnerable to attack. Thus it was possible for Viking fleets to raid sites like the monastery of Clonmacnoise (on the Shannon) in Ireland, Paris (on the Seine) and Orléans (on the Loire) in France, Cologne (on the Rhine) and Trier (on the Moselle) in Germany, and Nottingham and Repton (on the Trent) in England, despite the fact that a lengthy journey by river was required in each case.

This was important because of the third aspect of the use of Viking ships in war, which was that they offered considerable storage for troops, loot and supplies. Until the Industrial Revolution, ships and boats were always far more effective than any form of land transport for moving bulky or heavy loads.[32] The carrying capacity of their ships made it possible for Viking forces to transport provisions and any accumulated loot, without the necessity for slow and cumbersome baggage trains that would have been more vulnerable to attack. This allowed long raiding voyages by sea and also extended campaigns on land, as long as the raiders remained close to their ships.

One of the most remarkable features of Viking warfare was the ability to maintain forces in the field for years at a time. Warfare in this period was almost exclusively seasonal, in part because even the most powerful rulers could command only a finite length of military service from their followers, but more because of the logistical constraints of supplying armies on campaign in hostile territory over any length of time, especially over winter. Their ships allowed the Vikings to carry substantial supplies that could be replenished as they raided different areas, and thus to overwinter in hostile territory. If they targeted as winter camps wealthy monasteries and other major estate centres with an abundant food supply of their own and with good access to sea or river, they could also resupply from their ships.[33] The variety of types of Viking ship is discussed in more detail in chapter 5, but it is worth noting here that the earlier warships of the main raiding period were much broader in relation to their length than the later specialized warships like Roskilde 6, giving them more capacity for carrying supplies or plunder. Exactly when such ships developed is unclear, although this had certainly taken place by the late tenth century, by which time we have archaeological evidence of long, narrow warships – the archetypal 'longship' – designed to carry a large crew of warrior sailors, and of ships that were shorter but deeper and broader that could carry a maximum load of cargo, but which could be handled by a relatively small crew (see p. 209). However, even as early as the great raids of the late ninth century, small cargo ships with minimal crews would have been useful to support the warships on longer expeditions.

Slaughter to settlement

Many of the early Viking raids were on monasteries (fig. 31) and these continued to be a target throughout the ninth century. This has sometimes been seen as indicating a Scandinavian pagan reaction to the militant promotion of Christianity by the Frankish ruler Charlemagne.[34] However, it seems more likely that these attacks were motivated by the fact that pre-existing trading links meant that the Vikings were already aware that coastal monasteries such as Lindisfarne and Iona were both wealthy and almost undefended. Trading centres including Dorestad were also targeted, again pointing to familiarity, but it is possible to over-emphasize the impact of these assaults. Dorestad was able to recover economically from repeated attacks, and although it disappeared as a major trading centre in the course of the ninth century, this seems to have been the result of the silting up of that part of the Rhine estuary rather than Viking destruction.[35]

While the early raids were on only a small scale, the first half of the ninth century saw an escalation, with larger fleets involved. This was probably a response both to the success of the early raids and to the development of measures against them. Charlemagne's coastal defences are mentioned above, and a charter of Offa of Mercia describes the building of defences in Kent 'against the pagans' as early as the 790s.[36] A small raiding force could tackle undefended monasteries with little risk, but was in danger if even a relatively modest army could be summoned to oppose them. Once the raiding fleets began to number in tens of ships and the force they carried moved into the hundreds, it became harder for local rulers or royal officials to organize effective opposition, as it took longer to raise armies of equivalent size. With these larger forces the Vikings were also able to attack more significant targets, raiding trading centres and towns, and extracting ransoms and protection money as well as plunder.

The growth of substantial Viking forces increased their threat, but also their utility. Since the expeditions were undertaken for the primary purpose of generating wealth, it was possible for rulers elsewhere to buy the services of individual Viking leaders and their followers, and to use them as allies or mercenaries. Although the foundation of the famous Varangian Guard in Byzantium is normally dated to 988, when the emperor Basil II hired 6,000 Rūs as mercenaries for his wars against the Bulgars, trading agreements between Byzantium and the Rūs in the late ninth and tenth centuries routinely make provision for

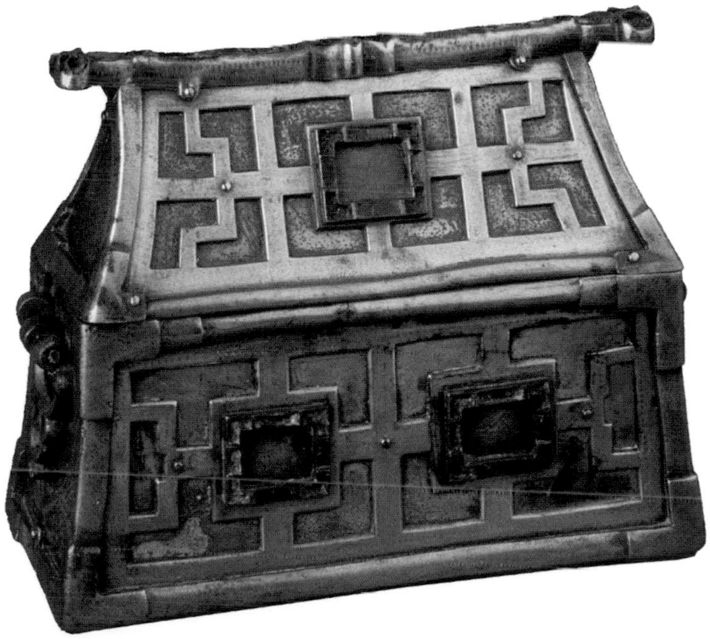

31.
Monasteries were a prime target for predatory raids and church treasures like this reliquary have been found in Scandinavia, providing evidence for this aspect of Viking activity.

Reliquary, Irish or Scottish, late 8th century. Unknown provenance, Norway.
Gilt copper alloy, yew wood.
H 10.3 cm, W 5.5 cm, L 13.5 cm
National Museum of Denmark, Copenhagen

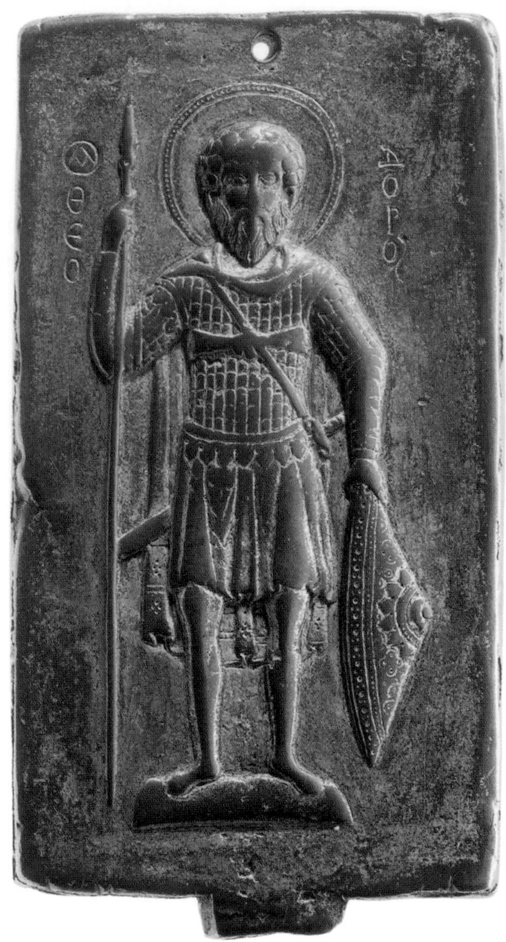

32.
Byzantine plaque of St Theodore depicted with military equipment of the eleventh century.

Byzantine plaque, 11th century. Constantinople (Istanbul), Turkey.
Gilt bronze. H 12.5 cm, W 6.7 cm
British Museum, London

the latter to serve in the Byzantine armies (fig. 32).[37] Local Frankish leaders sometimes hired Viking forces against their rivals, as in 862 when Salomon of Brittany and Robert of Anjou each procured a Viking fleet. In the same way, Irish kings took on Viking mercenaries or formed alliances with Viking rulers. The battle of Clontarf in 1014 is traditionally seen as one between the Irish and the Vikings, but in fact there were Irish kings, with Viking allies or mercenaries, on both sides.[38] As the Vikings were not a single unified people it meant that it was possible to hire Vikings to defend against other Vikings. This could be done with one-off payments, such as that made by the Frankish king Charles the Bald in 860 to the Viking leader Weland to attack a rival Viking fleet at Oissel on the Somme. Weland, however, subsequently accepted an even larger amount from these Vikings to break off his assault, and joined forces with them before again making his peace with Charles, only to be killed by his own men the following year. The story of Weland demonstrates the instability of a relationship based on one-off payments, but Vikings were also sometimes rewarded with grants of land in vulnerable coastal areas, thereby simultaneously giving them a permanent stake in the area and creating a useful buffer against further attacks. The best known and most successful of these was in Normandy – literally the land of the Northmen – where the Viking leader Rollo was granted the title of Count of Rouen in 911 and his descendants went on to become dukes of Normandy. There were also repeated grants of land in Frisia in the ninth century to Viking leaders from Denmark, but these were less successful. The grants recognized the fact that some of the attacks on the Franks were undertaken at least with the tacit approval of the king of the Danes, and sometimes with the king's active involvement. Godfred king of the Danes is said to have attacked Frisia with 200 ships in 810, a rare reference to such a large fleet so early in the ninth century, and Frankish rulers clearly held their Danish counterparts responsible for not preventing their subjects from raiding, although they may have overestimated the authority of Danish kings at this time. In any case, by granting estates in Frisia to Danish exiles, including rivals to the kingship, successive Frankish kings sought to create an effective barrier to Viking attacks and to win themselves important allies in the event that the exiles ever gained power in Denmark itself, although this policy met with only mixed success.[39]

The third quarter of the ninth century saw another major shift both in the scale and the nature of warfare, at least in western Europe. Forces continued to expand, with fleets now routinely numbering in the low hundreds, and in many cases this seems to represent temporary banding together by different Viking groups. At the battle of Ashdown in 870, the Viking army was said to be led by two kings and at least five earls.[40] There was also a move to longer and more complicated campaigns. Up until the mid-ninth century, attacks had generally taken the form of a straightforward raid – travel to the target, exact plunder or tribute, and return home. There might be multiple targets, and the raid might last for a few days, or for the whole summer sailing season, but the same principle applied, and the Vikings would return home, or at least to a safe haven for the winter to rest and resupply. On the one hand this limited the amount of supplies that they needed to carry with them, while on the other it meant that their activities were restricted by the weather: they needed to leave enough of a margin to ensure that they returned home before the seas became impassable as, for all their versatility, Viking ships were vulnerable to storms at sea.

Shorter raids no doubt continued, but from the mid-ninth century Viking raiders began to spend the winter months (to 'overwinter') in enemy territory. Viking forces did this in Ireland in 841 at Duiblinn (Dublin) and Linn Dúachaill (Annagassan, Co. Louth) and around the same time on an island off the mouth of the Loire in western France. In 850, Vikings overwintered in England for the first time, on the Isle of Thanet.[41] These raids seem to have been aimed primarily at plunder and extortion rather than conquest. With the exception of the short-lived grants in Frisia and later in Normandy, there was no lasting

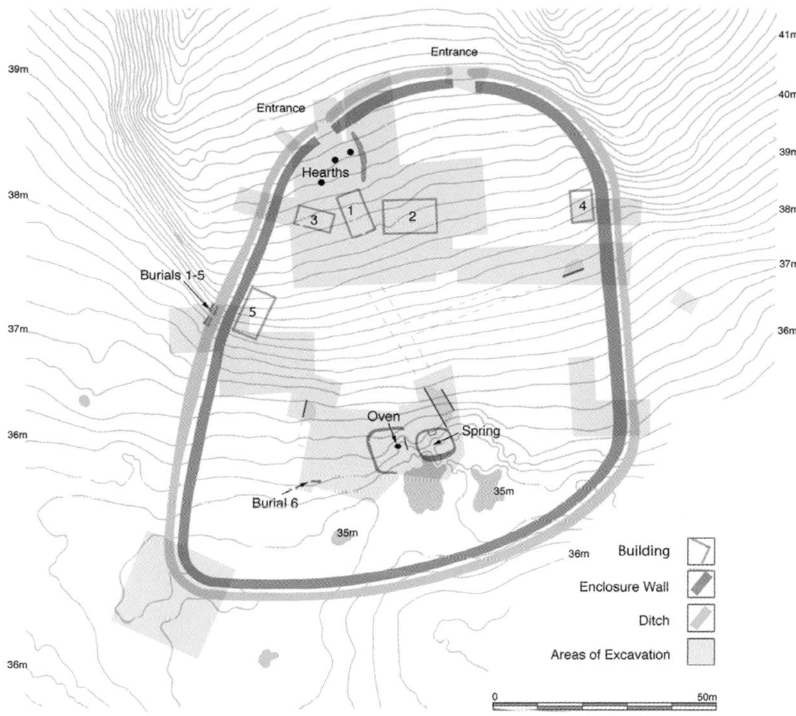

33.
The exact nature of the defended settlement at Llanbedrgoch, Anglesey remains debated. However, it shows clear evidence of Viking trade in the late 9th century, and has some similarities with Viking camps in England and Ireland.

Viking base in the Frankish kingdoms, and settlement in Ireland in the ninth century was extremely limited. Although temporary camps and overwintering became widespread, only Dublin remained more or less permanently occupied throughout the late ninth century, and it was not until the tenth century that other Viking towns emerged at Limerick, Cork, Waterford and Wexford. All of these towns had surrounding territories to support them, but the Vikings never conquered and settled large areas of Ireland as they did elsewhere.[42] Raiding is recorded in Wales around the same period, but actual settlement seems to have been limited, although a native site with some similarities to Viking camps in England and Ireland has been discovered at Llanbedrgoch on Anglesey (fig. 33). Anglesey is a Scandinavian placename and while there are a few other Scandinavian placenames around the Welsh coast, there are not enough to suggest extensive settlement.[43]

This is not the case in England. The *micel here* that arrived in England in 865 conquered Northumbria in 866, East Anglia in 870 and a large part of Mercia in 874, but they continued a pattern of moving on to new targets each year rather than exploiting their conquests directly, and it was not until 876 that they ceased campaigning and stayed put, suggesting that this was not part of their initial aim. Nevertheless, when they did, their settlements covered much of northern and eastern England and can be traced through a combination of placenames, sculpture, excavated sites, graves and widespread distribution of stray finds of both hoards and single objects. Although it has become customary for modern scholars to label the whole area of Viking settlement in England as the Danelaw, this is a later name and gives a false impression of unity, as the Viking territories in England, like the Scandinavian homelands, were politically fragmented. This allowed the West Saxons, who under Alfred the Great (871–99) had held out against the Viking attacks, to conquer the Vikings in turn, gradually extending their authority northwards to form a single kingdom of England in the mid-tenth century (fig. 34).[44]

There was another wave of activity in the late tenth century, probably stimulated by the collapse of the supply of silver dirhams from Central Asia, as relatively few dirhams seem to have entered Scandinavia after the 980s, and large-scale raiding on England resumed in the 990s.[45] Again the initial emphasis was on raiding rather than conquest, but one of the earliest assaults in this phase resulted in a major battle at Maldon in Essex in 991. It was commemorated in a poem a few years later, which provides one of the most detailed surviving accounts from this period:

Then Byrhtnoth set about drawing up the men there,
He rode and instructed, he told the soldiers,
How they should form up and hold the position,
And he asked that they should hold their shields properly,
Firmly with their fists, and not be at all afraid...

Then the wolves of slaughter rushed forward,
They cared nothing for the water,
The host of Vikings, west across the Blackwater,

34.
West Saxon conquests of Viking settlements in the 10th century contributed to the development of a unified English kingdom.

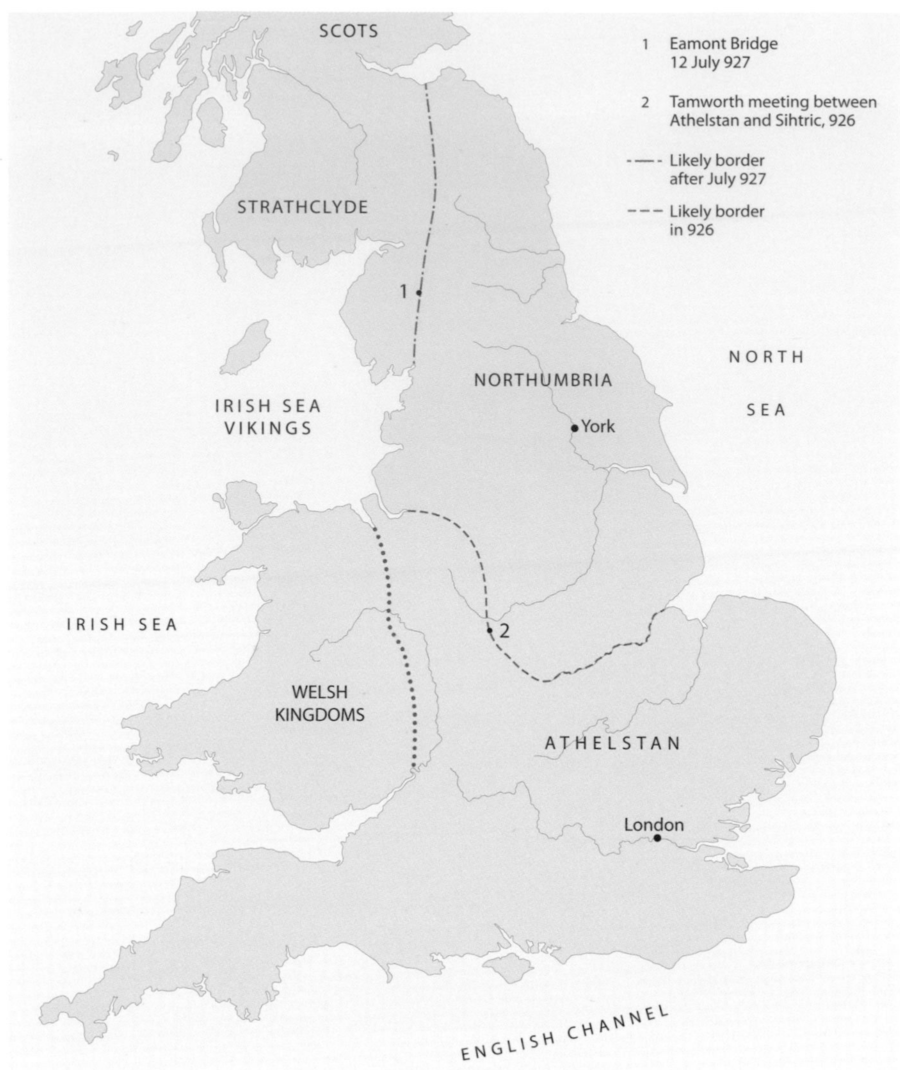

Across the shining stream, they carried their shields,
The sailors carried their lime-wood shields onto the land…
Then the fight was near,
Glory in battle: the time had come
When those fated to die must fall there.
The roar of battle was lifted up there; ravens circled,
the bird of prey eager for carrion; there was bedlam in the land.
They let the file-hard spears from their hands then,
Made fly the fiercely sharpened ones, the darts.
Bows were busy, shield absorbed spearhead.
The onslaught of battle was terrible; warriors fell
On either side, young men lay dead.[46]

The battle was a victory for the Vikings and following this the English adopted a policy of paying *gelds* (effectively tribute payments) in return for peace. This was unsuccessful, as it encouraged more raiders to try their luck, resulting in further payments. Hoards of coins of this period are widely known in Scandinavia and more late Anglo-Saxon coins have been found in Scandinavia than in England (fig. 35).[47] As in the late ninth century, raiding turned to conquest. England was not merely raided by fleets led by Viking chieftains such as Thorkell the Tall, but faced a full-scale invasion by the Danish king Svein Forkbeard. Svein's forces almost certainly included freebooters attracted by the prospect of loot (see below), but the invasion of England under Svein in many ways looks more like a national war of conquest. Svein succeeded in partially conquering England in 1013, and although Æthelred II and his son Edmund Ironside were able to muster some resistance, the process of conquest was completed in 1016 by Svein's son, Cnut the Great, following the death of all the other main parties. Cnut established himself as king of Denmark shortly afterwards and ruled both kingdoms until his death in 1035, adding Norway to his empire in 1028.[48] This last example is an important reminder that warfare within Scandinavia was common throughout the Viking Age and that not all of the expansion of the Viking kingdoms was outward-facing.

The ninth to tenth centuries saw extensive conquest and settlement in northern and western Scotland. Placenames and archaeological evidence suggest that the intensity of settlement varied, with the densest in Shetland, the closest part of Scotland to Scandinavia. There almost all the placenames are of Norse origin, but opinion remains divided on whether this merely represents political and cultural domination by Viking settlers and their descendants, or something more akin to genocide or enslavement of the native population.[49] Viking kingdoms were established in the Isle of Man and the Western Isles, while the Earldom of Orkney came to dominate both the Northern Isles and the northern part of mainland Scotland. Again, the late tenth and eleventh centuries seem to have been the high point of Norse power in the region.[50] These areas also seem to have fallen under the domination of Cnut the Great.[51] However, from the end of the tenth century they were intermittently under at least the nominal authority of the kings of Norway, and the two earls of Orkney, Paul and Erlend, accompanied Harald Hardruler of Norway on his unsuccessful invasion of England in 1066. Like the earlier conquests of Svein and Cnut, this should be seen in the context of national warfare rather than Viking raiding, as Harald was able to muster the resources of a whole kingdom in pursuit of a perceived claim to the English throne.[52] It is difficult to separate entirely the roles of 'king' and 'Viking leader' for figures such as Svein Forkbeard and Harald Hardruler, and Harald's death at Stamford Bridge in 1066 is often taken as a convenient endpoint to the Viking Age, although more traditional Viking raids undoubtedly continued both in Britain and elsewhere.

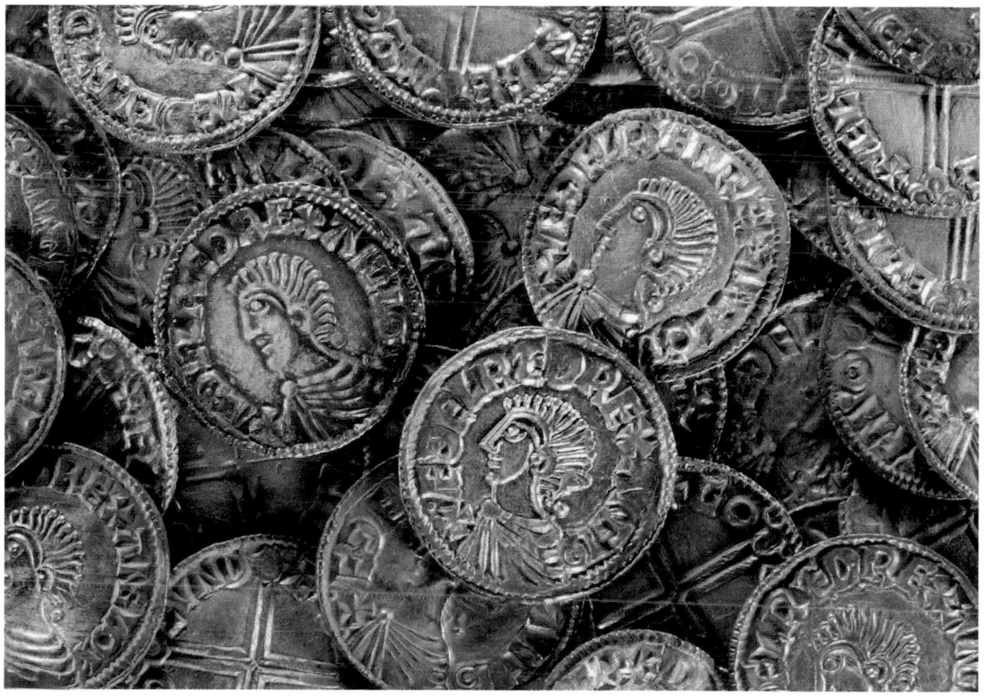

35.
Huge numbers of late Anglo-Saxon silver coins have been found in hoards in Scandinvia.

Hoard of Long Cross pennies from the reign of Æthelred II, *c.* 1000. Tyskegård, Bornholm, Denmark.
National Museum of Denmark, Copenhagen

Viking warfare in context

Successful conquests did not necessarily mean that the Vikings were inherently superior warriors, or that they were better equipped than others. Indeed, many of the best weapons seem to have been imported. Frankish laws of the early ninth century specifically forbid providing weapons or horses to the Vikings, either through sale or as ransom. This is mirrored in references in skaldic verse (see p. 25) to *vigra vestœnna ok valskra sverða* ('Western spears and Frankish swords').[53] These references are reflected in finds of weapons of Frankish type spread around the Viking world. In the case of swords, this applies to complete weapons and also to blades. Swords in this period came with hilt fittings in a variety of shapes and were often highly decorated. Both the shape of the hilt fittings and the

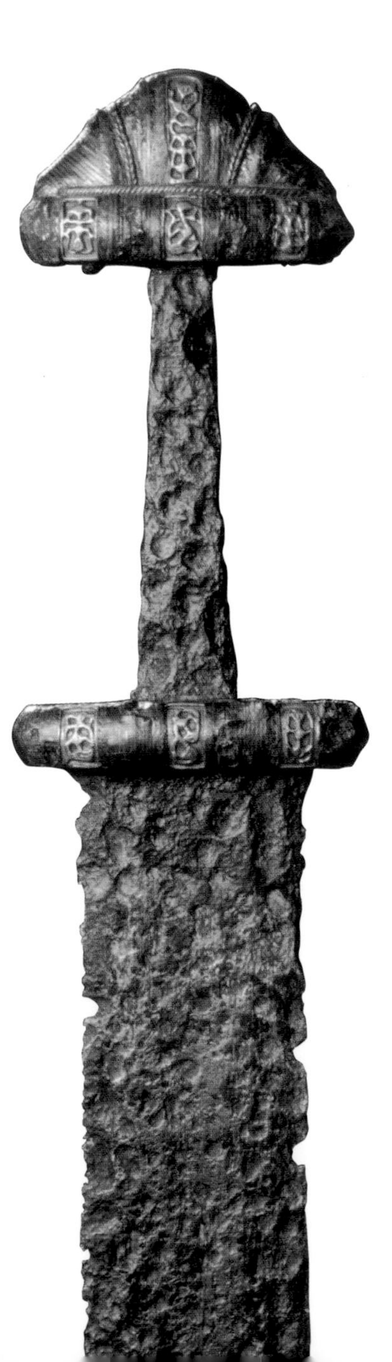

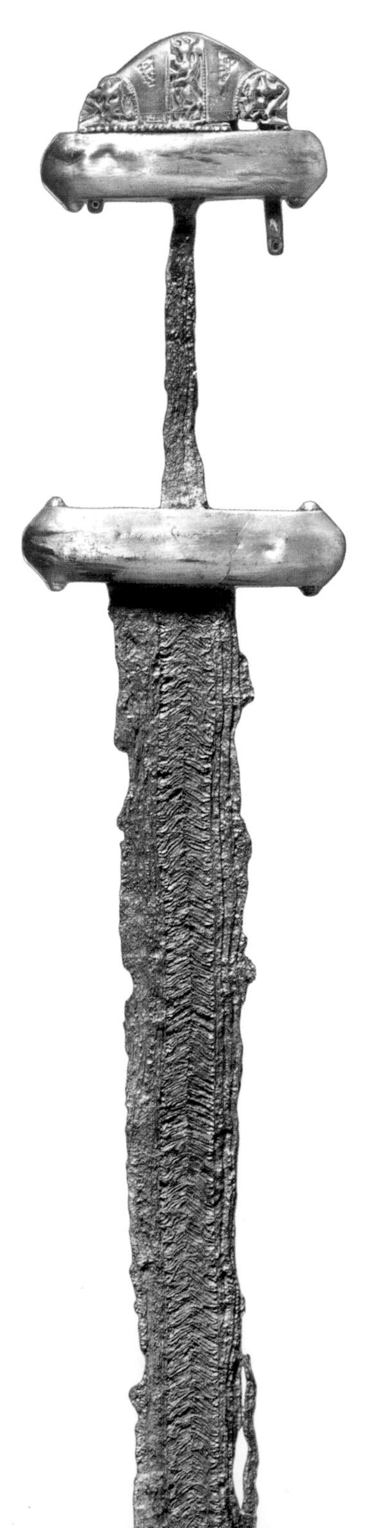

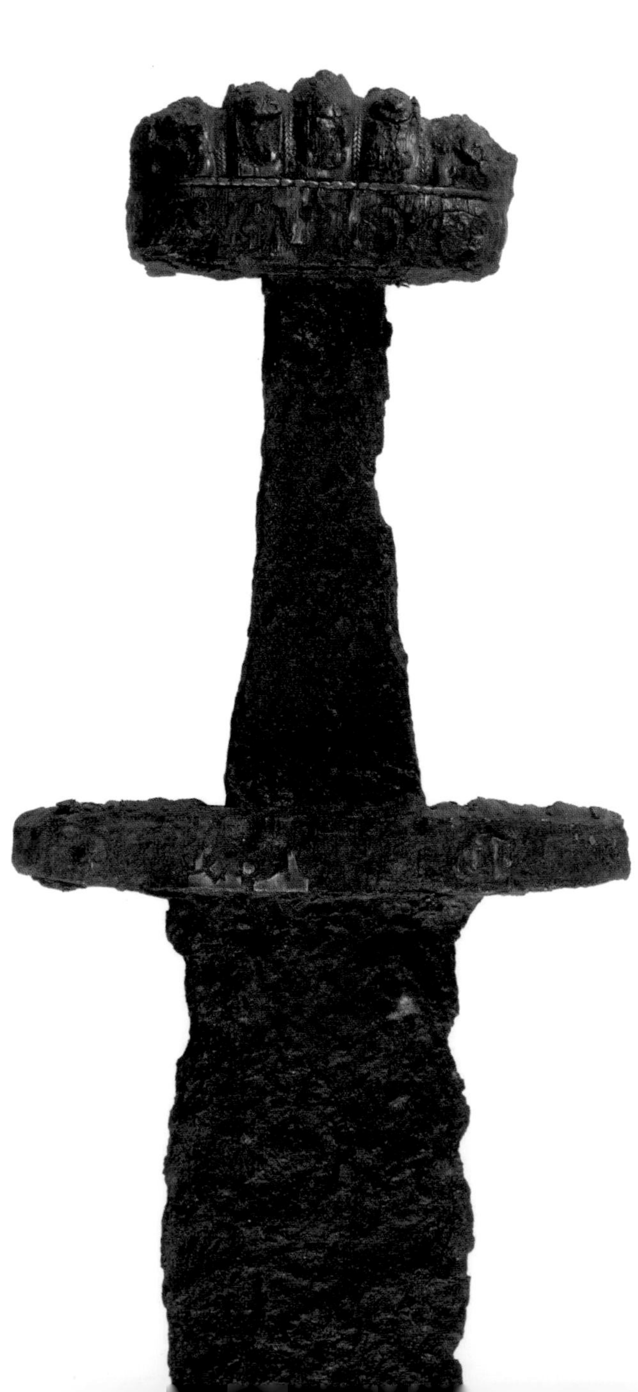

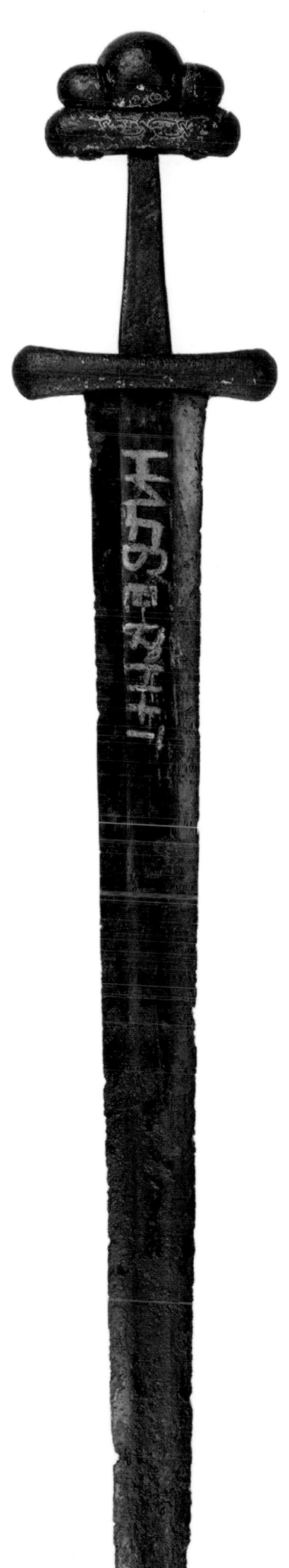

36.
Carolingian sword, 800–850. Steinsvik, Tjeldsund, Nordland, Norway.
Iron, copper alloy, silver. L 100.1 cm
Museum of Cultural History, University of Oslo, Oslo

37.
Sword, late 8th–early 9th century. Kalundborg or Holbæk, Zealand, Denmark.
Silver, iron. L 59.4 cm
National Museum of Denmark, Copenhagen

38.
Carolingian-type sword with silver-inlaid guards, 9th century. Near Kilmainham, Dublin, Ireland.
Iron, silver. L 56.8 cm, W 11.3 cm
National Museum of Ireland, Dublin

39.
Double-edged sword with VLFBERHT blade, Scandinavian-type hilt, 10th century. Schwedt, Brandenburg, Germany.
Iron, silver inlay. L 73.8 cm
Museum für Vor- und Frühgeschichte, Staatliche Museen zu Berlin, Berlin

40.
Double-edged sword with VLFBERHT blade, 800–950. Peltomaa, Hämeenlinna (Tavastehus), Häme, Finland.
Iron, copper, silver. L 91.6 cm
National Museum of Finland, Helsinki

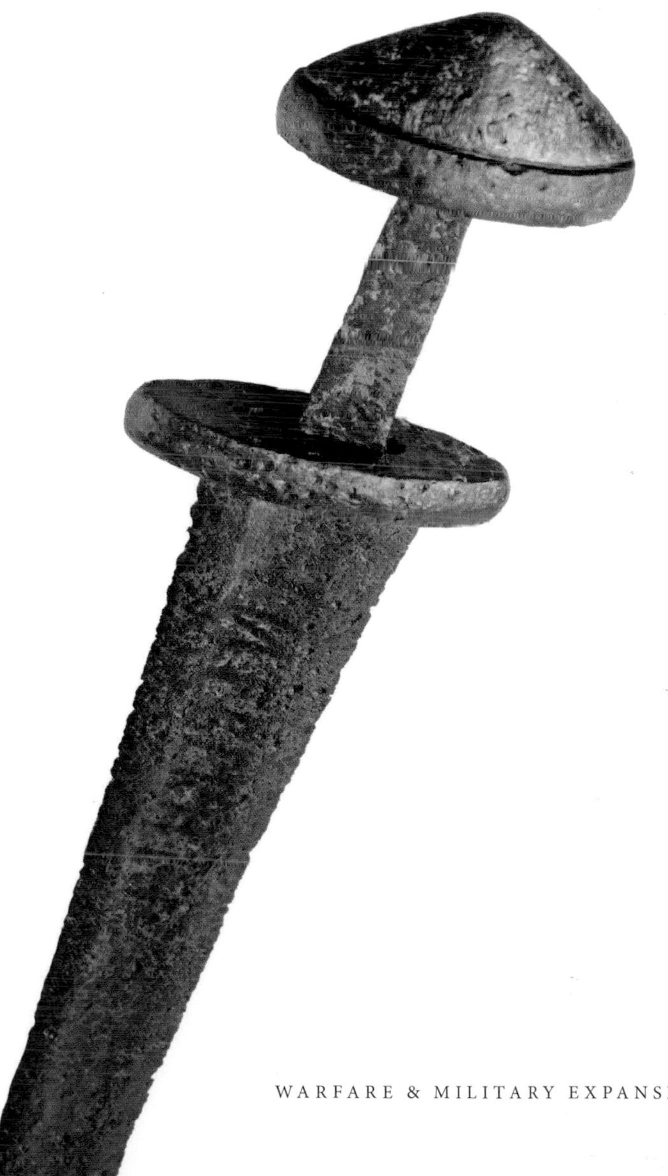

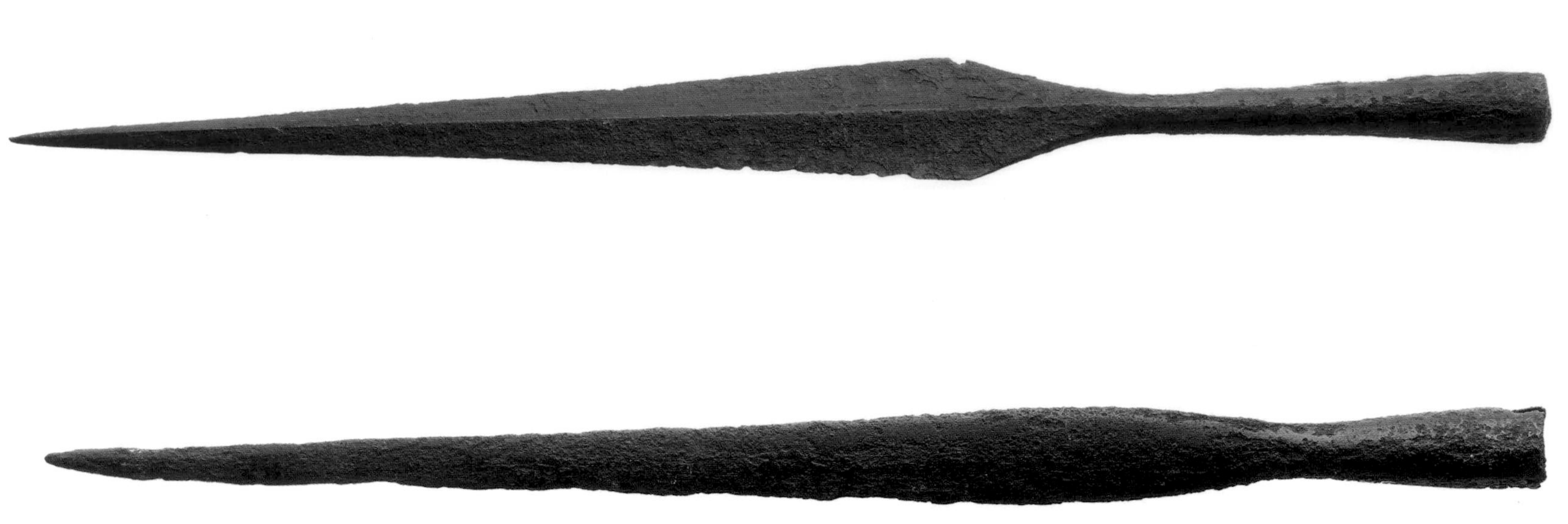

41.
Spearhead, 1000–1050.
London, England.
Iron. L 58 cm
British Museum, London

42.
Spearhead, 9th or 10th century.
London, England.
Iron. L 28.7 cm
British Museum, London

style of the ornamentation indicate the origins of individual sword hilts. Carolingian hilts are found all over the Viking world, from Russia to Ireland (figs 36–38).[54] In some cases similar fashions developed in different areas. Swords of Petersen type S, dating from the tenth century, with curved upper and lower guards and a distinctive pommel, have been found in significant numbers in both England and Scandinavia. Examples are known with clearly Anglo-Saxon or clearly Scandinavian decoration while others are more ambiguous, and it is uncertain where the type originated, and who copied whom.

There was also apparently a trade in Frankish blades, which are often found combined with Scandinavian hilt fittings. Blades inscribed with the Frankish names Ulfberht and Ingelrii probably originated somewhere in the Rhineland in the ninth century, but blades with the same names continued to be produced for at least two hundred years, and the details of the inscriptions and the way they were applied vary too (figs 39–40).[55] The continued use of the design may suggest production in the same workshops after the original makers were dead, but it probably also indicates that the designs were copied because these inscriptions were regarded as an indication of high quality, or even simply of fashionable desirability. Metallurgical analysis of some Ulfberht blades has revealed that they are actually of very poor quality. Since swords were symbols of warrior status as much as they were practical weapons, these poor-quality Ulfberht blades were perhaps the equivalent of modern cheap imitations of Rolex watches and Louis Vuitton handbags.

Swords were not the only military fashions to be adopted. Spearheads also came in a variety of shapes and sizes (figs 41–42). Those with projecting wings between the head and the socket seem to have come from the Franks, although not all surviving examples are necessarily of Frankish manufacture. Distinctive local styles could also develop, as in a type of shield boss that seems to have been unique to Viking Dublin and is neither typically Scandinavian nor Irish (fig. 43). Fashion seems to have been an element in helmet design. Contrary to the popular image of the Vikings established in the nineteenth century, there is no evidence that they wore horned or winged helmets. Pre-Viking helmets seem to have been highly individual, with a number of designs derived from late Roman cavalry helmets, incorporating various types of protection for the face and neck as well as the upper head. This probably continued into the early Viking Age, as a helmet from a tenth-century burial at Gjermundbu in Norway has a 'spectacle' face guard and mail aventail (neck-guard) in the

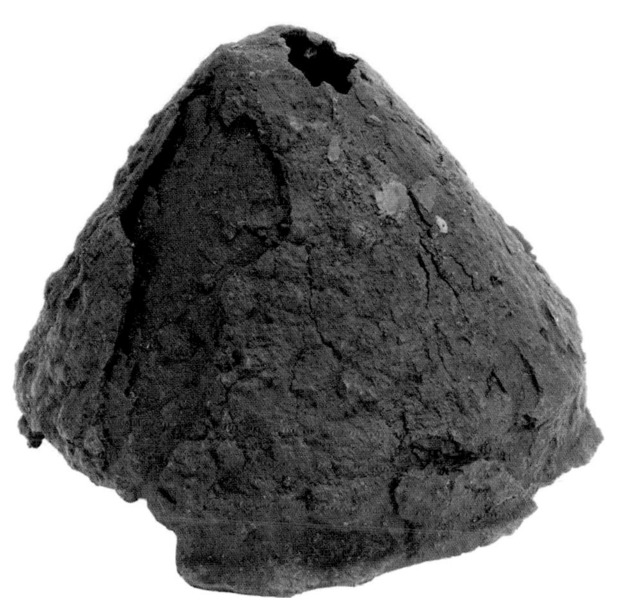

43.
Shield boss, Dublin type, 9th century. Near Kilmainham, Dublin, Ireland.
Iron. H 6.5 cm, Diam. 8.9 cm
National Museum of Ireland, Dublin

44.
Conical helmet. Černaya, Mogila, Černigov, Ukraine.
Iron, gilt copper alloy. H 25.0 cm, Diam. 25.0 cm
State Historical Museum, Moscow

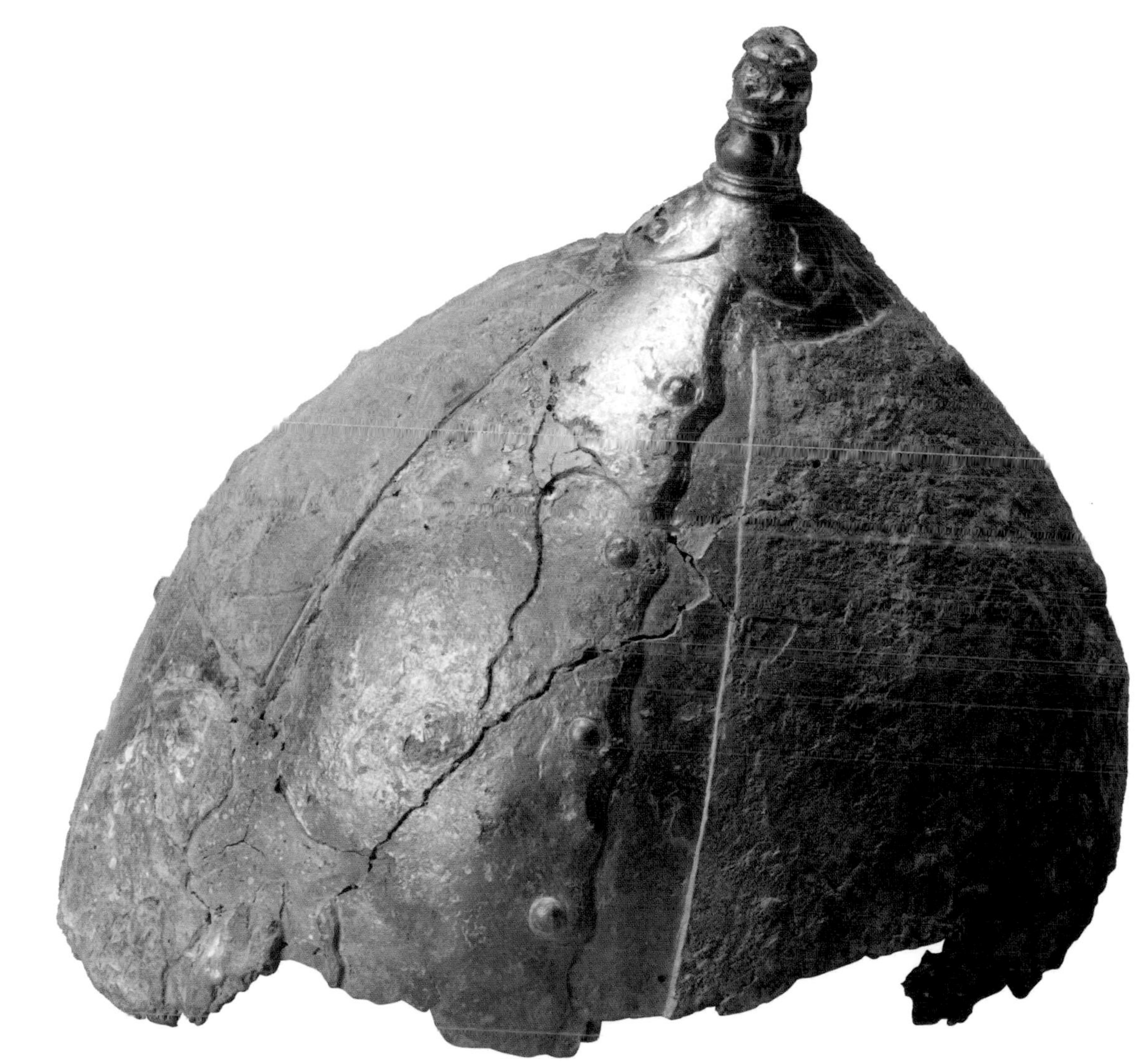

same tradition as the pre-Viking helemets from Vendel and Välsgärde.[56] By contrast, images of helmets suggest the widespread use of a conical helm with nasal (nosepiece). Although decoration may have varied, this basic type was shared with the Anglo-Saxons, Franks and Slavs, and probably again represents Frankish influence (fig. 44).

If the Vikings were no better equipped than many of their contemporaries, they were also not markedly more successful on the battlefield. They had some notable successes – victory in battle led directly to the conquest of Northumbria and East Anglia – as well as a number of major defeats. For example, their defeat by the West Saxons at Aclea in 851 was described as 'the greatest slaughter of a heathen *here* that we have ever heard tell of'.[57] If anything, the Viking strategy was to avoid pitched battle wherever possible. For all that a glorious death in battle might be seen as a fitting end in warrior culture, not to mention a passport to Valhöll, fighting against well-armed and well-organized opponents carried high risks in exchange for limited direct profit. Against such opponents the Vikings had no inherent advantage. Minor defeats were probably equally common, but more rarely recorded. For example it seems likely that the mass grave discovered in Weymouth discussed earlier (p. 95) represents the execution of a shipload of Vikings, even though this coincides with a period in which the written evidence largely records the success of Viking raids. Frankish annals, while they tend to provide more colourful accounts of Viking victories and supposed atrocities, also record numerous references to battles in which the Franks were victorious, including a major defeat of a large Viking fleet by the East Frankish King Arnulf on the River Dyle in 891.

Warriors to soldiers

One change that is visible in the course of the Viking Age is a shift from bands of individual warriors to something more akin to recognizable armies. In part this probably reflects the growth of centralized royal authority in the Scandinavian kingdoms (see pp. 150–5), but also the influence of the Vikings' external contacts. For example, the thousands of Vikings that served in the Byzantine army, initially as auxiliary troops under their own leaders, but from the late tenth century in the formally constituted Varangian Guard (see p. 97), may have transmitted some ideas of military organisation from Byzantium. Both the Franks and the Anglo-Saxons also provided models of structured military service, with requirements for landholders to supply a set number of men, with defined levels of military equipment, which led to a degree of standardization.[58]

Early Viking weapons and armour were highly individual (fig. 45), through the ornamentation of weapon and scabbard fittings and even visually distinctive blades for swords. Although many swords were made from a single piece of metal (fig. 46), some

45.
Some highly decorated weapons continued to be produced until the end of the Viking Age, despite a trend towards standardization.

Spearhead with silver-inlaid socket, 11th century. Vilusenharju, Tampere, Upper Satakunta, Finland.
Iron, silver.
National Museum of Finland, Helsinki

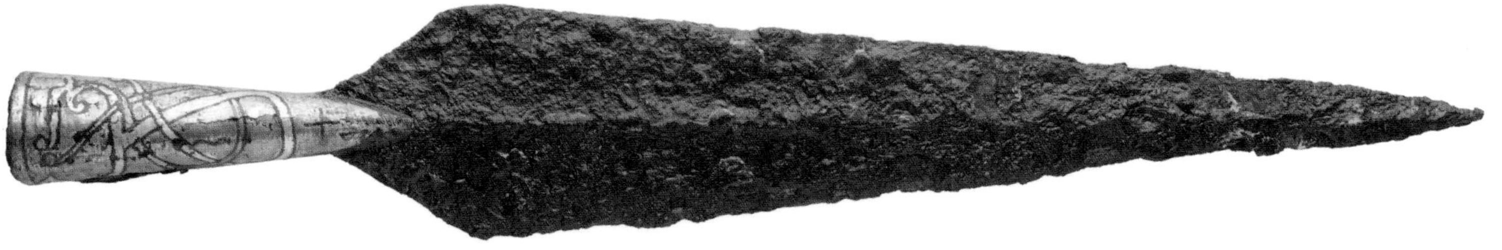

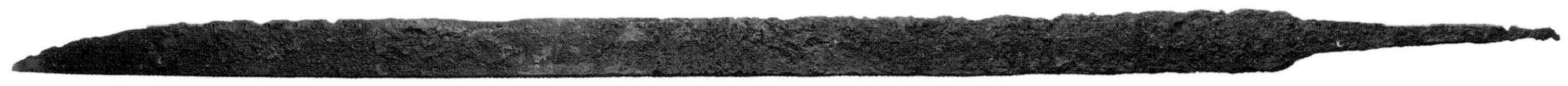

46.
Some weapons, like this one, were forged from a single piece of iron.

Single-edged sword, 700–900. Digeråkeren, Øverli, Lom, Oppland, Norway.
Iron. L 97 cm
British Museum, London

Chapes are metal fittings that attached to the tapered end of a sword scabbard. Decorative examples like these would have been on permanent display when the scabbard was worn, unlike the sword blade itself.

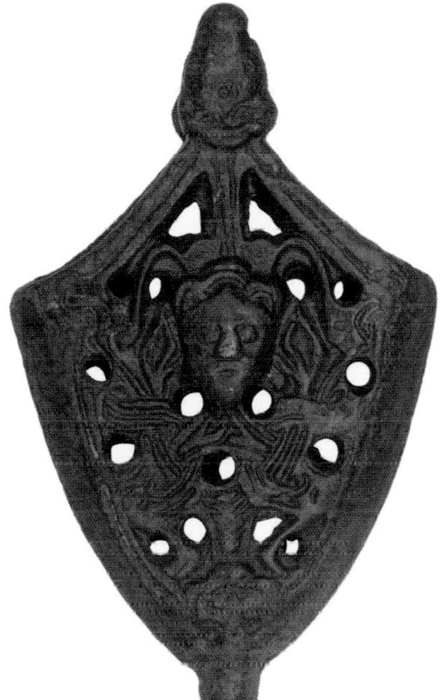

47.
Sword chape with Borre-style animal head, 10th century. Korosten, Obl. Žitomir, Ukraine.
Copper alloy. L 7.3 cm
State Historical Museum, Moscow

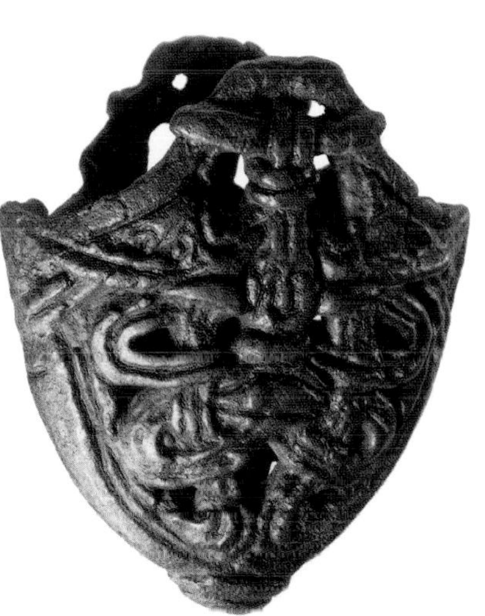

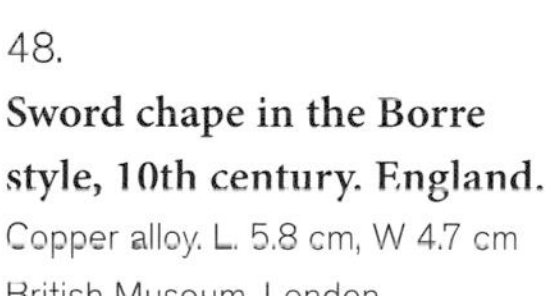

48.
Sword chape in the Borre style, 10th century. England.
Copper alloy. L 5.8 cm, W 4.7 cm
British Museum, London

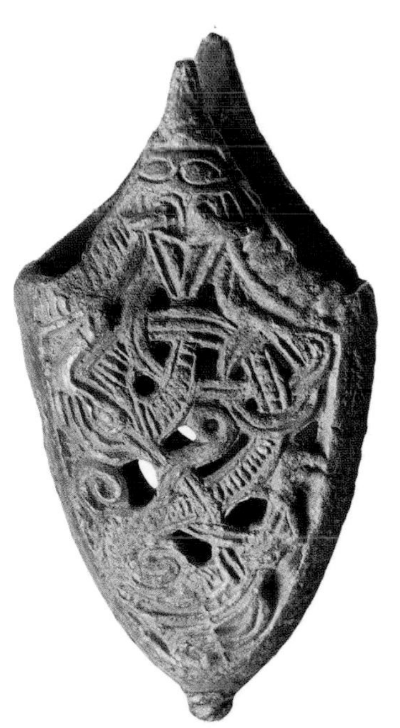

49.
Sword chape in the Jellinge style, 10th century. Selling Hedelod, Ødum, East Jutland, Denmark.
Copper alloy. L 9 cm, W 4.2 cm
National Museum of Denmark, Copenhagen

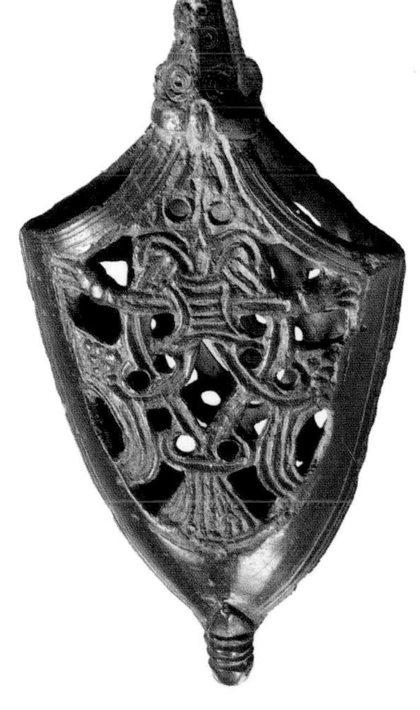

50.
Sword chape with bird motif, 10th century. Bjergene, Ballerup, Zealand, Denmark.
Copper alloy. L 9 cm, W 4.4 cm
National Museum of Denmark, Copenhagen

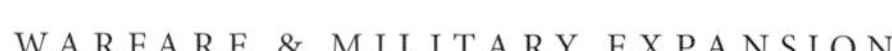

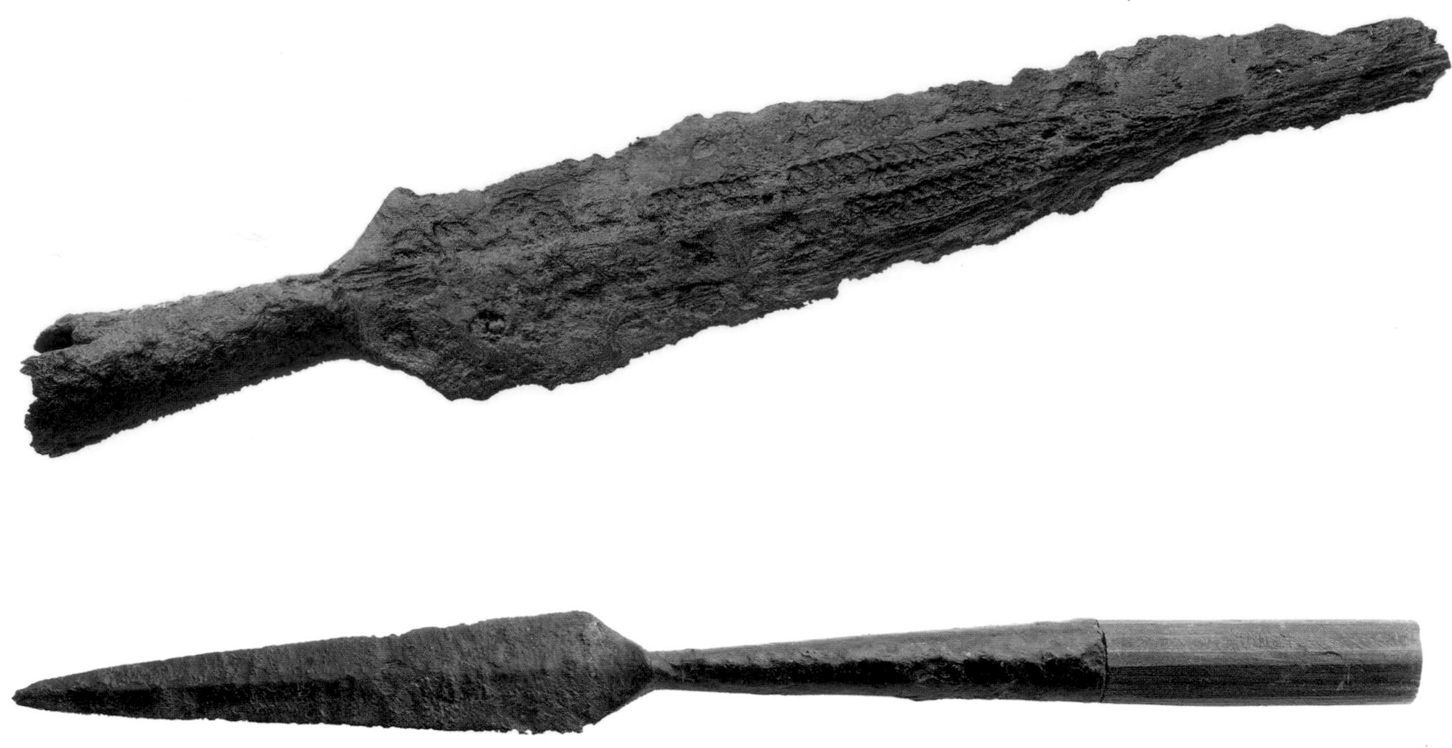

51.
Pattern-welded spearhead, 10th century. Near River Lodden/ Twyford, Berkshire, England.
Iron. L 34.7 cm
British Museum, London

52.
Pattern-welded spearhead, 9th–10th century. River Thames, England.
Iron. L 37 cm
British Museum, London

high-status blades were made by a process known as pattern welding, whereby multiple rods and bars were hammered and twisted together to provide a decorative core to the blade, with cutting edges welded to either side, a technique shared with the Franks and the Anglo-Saxons. Although some modern accounts suggest that this was a superior method of construction, combining the strength of iron with the flexibility of steel, more recent thinking (informed in part by experimentation) suggests that if anything this approach created a weaker weapon than a single piece of good steel, and that the process was likely to be intended more for decoration than function. Pattern welding became rarer after the ninth century, to be replaced with decorative inlay.[59]

The blades might be distinctive, but other than in combat the blade would rarely be seen by others, so the hilt fittings and scabbard fittings (figs 47–50) were important in giving each sword a clear identity, making them immediately recognizable both on and off the battlefield, and this could also apply to other types of weapon. Pattern welding could be applied to spearheads and knives as well as swords, and there are examples of both spearheads and axeheads with decorative inlay (figs 51–52). While no early Viking helmets survive, helmets from the pre-Viking Vendel and Välsgärde burials in eastern Sweden again indicate variety in shape and decoration (figs 53–54), so that the helmets were uniquely recognizable. These elaborate weapons and helmets have equivalents elsewhere and seem to represent development from the common origins of the Anglo-Saxons, the Franks and the various peoples who between them made up the Vikings. This emphasis on distinctiveness built on the sense of the status of the individual warrior.

Individual high-status weapons continued to be important throughout the Viking Age, but while specific decoration varied between weapons, the range of different types (defined in swords primarily by the shape of the guards and pommel) became more restricted, especially in Denmark. Danish weapon graves of the tenth century became increasingly standardized, typically containing a sword, spear and shield, with axes only rarely appearing in place of (and in the wealthiest examples, as well as) a sword. These graves also routinely

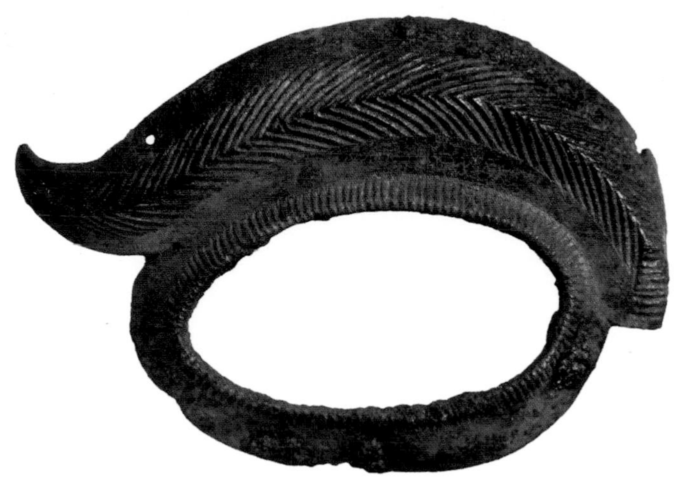

53.
This helmet eyepiece may date from the early Viking Age. It demonstrates striking similarities to pre-Viking helmets from burials at Vendel and Välsgärde (fig. 54).

Eyebrow ornament for a helmet, late Iron Age/Viking Age. Gevninge, Zealand, Denmark.
Copper alloy, partially gilt.
L 8 cm, W 5 cm
Roskilde Museum, Roskilde

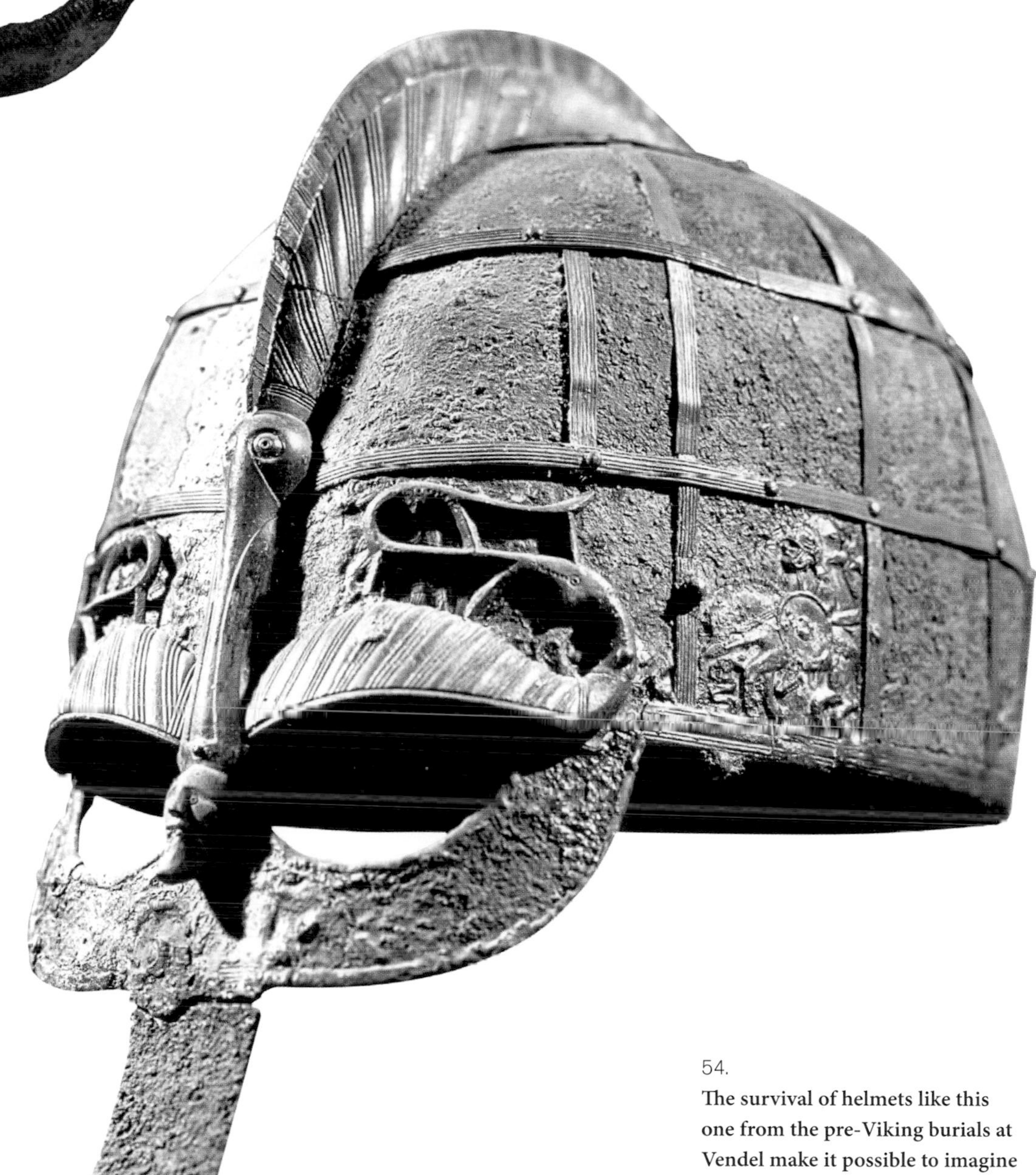

54.
The survival of helmets like this one from the pre-Viking burials at Vendel make it possible to imagine how the earliest Viking helmets might have looked.

Helmet, later 6th–8th century. Grave 1, Vendel cemetary, Uppland, Sweden.
Statens Historiska Museum, Stockholm

include horse fittings, most often stirrups, indicating the existence of a widespread elite of mounted warriors (fig. 55). Although mounted warfare is known in Scandinavia before the tenth century, this suggests the development of a mounted elite owing standardized military service to the king, an idea probably borrowed from the Carolingian or Ottonian Franks (figs 56–57).[60] Weapons and armour became increasingly similar across northern Europe in the late Viking Age, as seen in the adoption of plain conical helms in place of more complicated designs. However, some distinctly Scandinavian features remained and even developed, such as the large double-handed battle axe of the late tenth and eleventh centuries (fig. 58).[61]

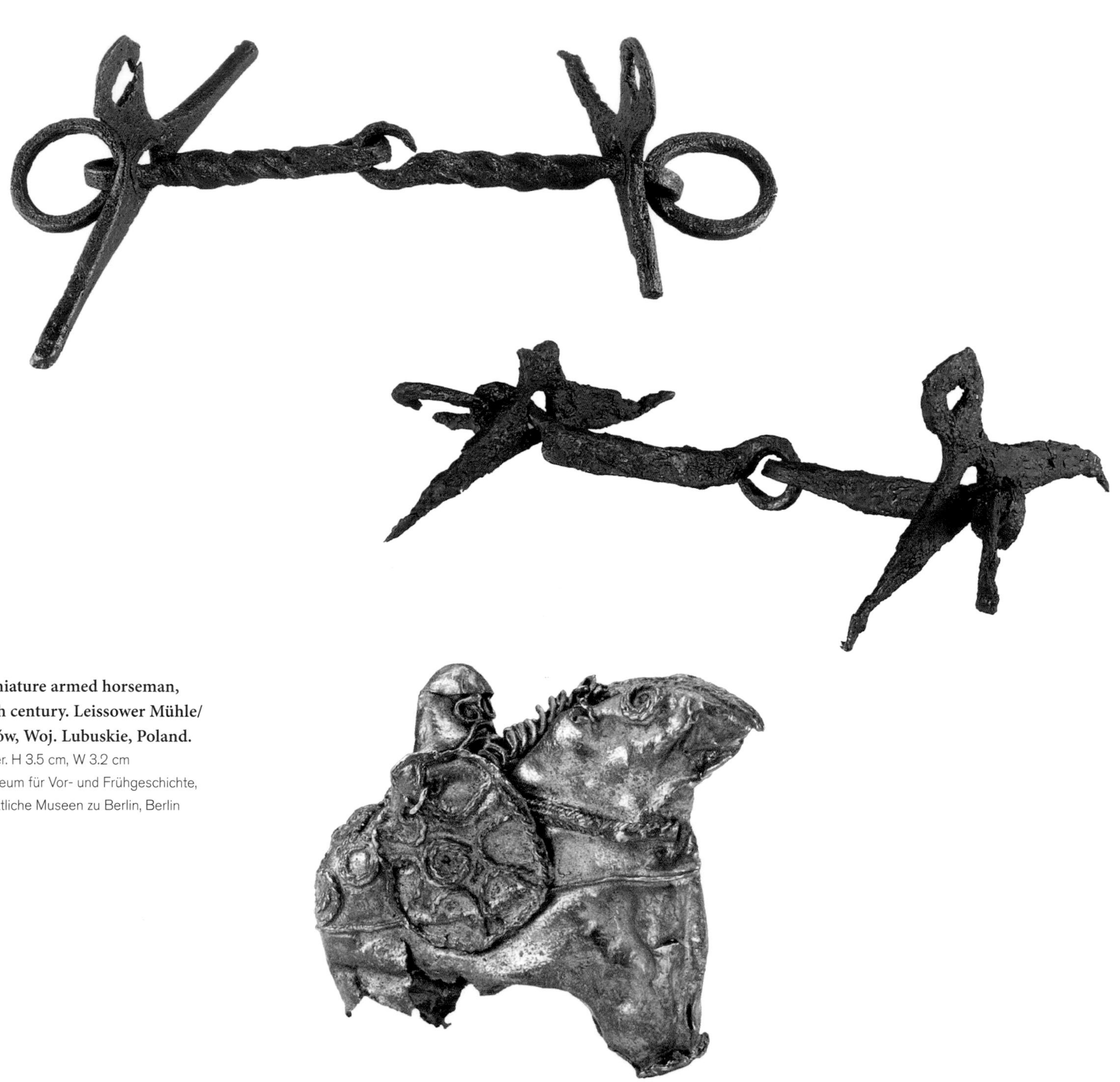

55.
Two bridles, 900–1100. Popelken, Kr. Wehlau/ Cholmy, Kaliningradskaja Obl., Russia.
Iron. L 22 cm, 22.7 cm
Museum für Vor- und Frühgeschichte, Staatliche Museen zu Berlin, Berlin

56.
Miniature armed horseman, 11th century. Leissower Mühle/ Lisów, Woj. Lubuskie, Poland.
Silver. H 3.5 cm, W 3.2 cm
Museum für Vor- und Frühgeschichte, Staatliche Museen zu Berlin, Berlin

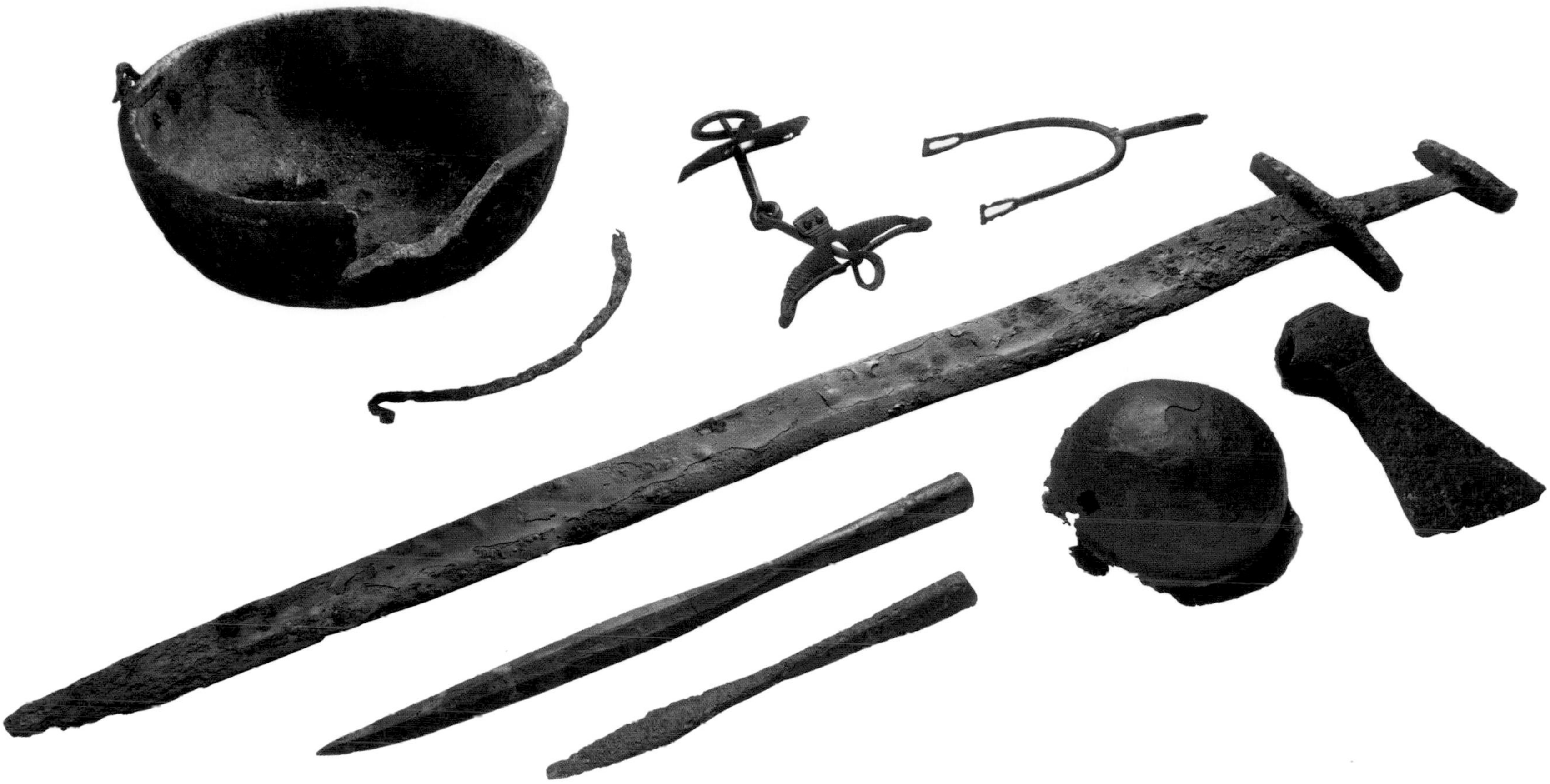

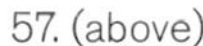

57. (above)

Male weapon burial with prominent equestrian elements: sword, shield boss, axe, spearheads, spurs, bridle, stirrups and soapstone vessel, 900–950. Asak, Skedsmo, Akershus, Norway

Iron, soapstone.

Museum of Cultural History, University of Oslo, Oslo

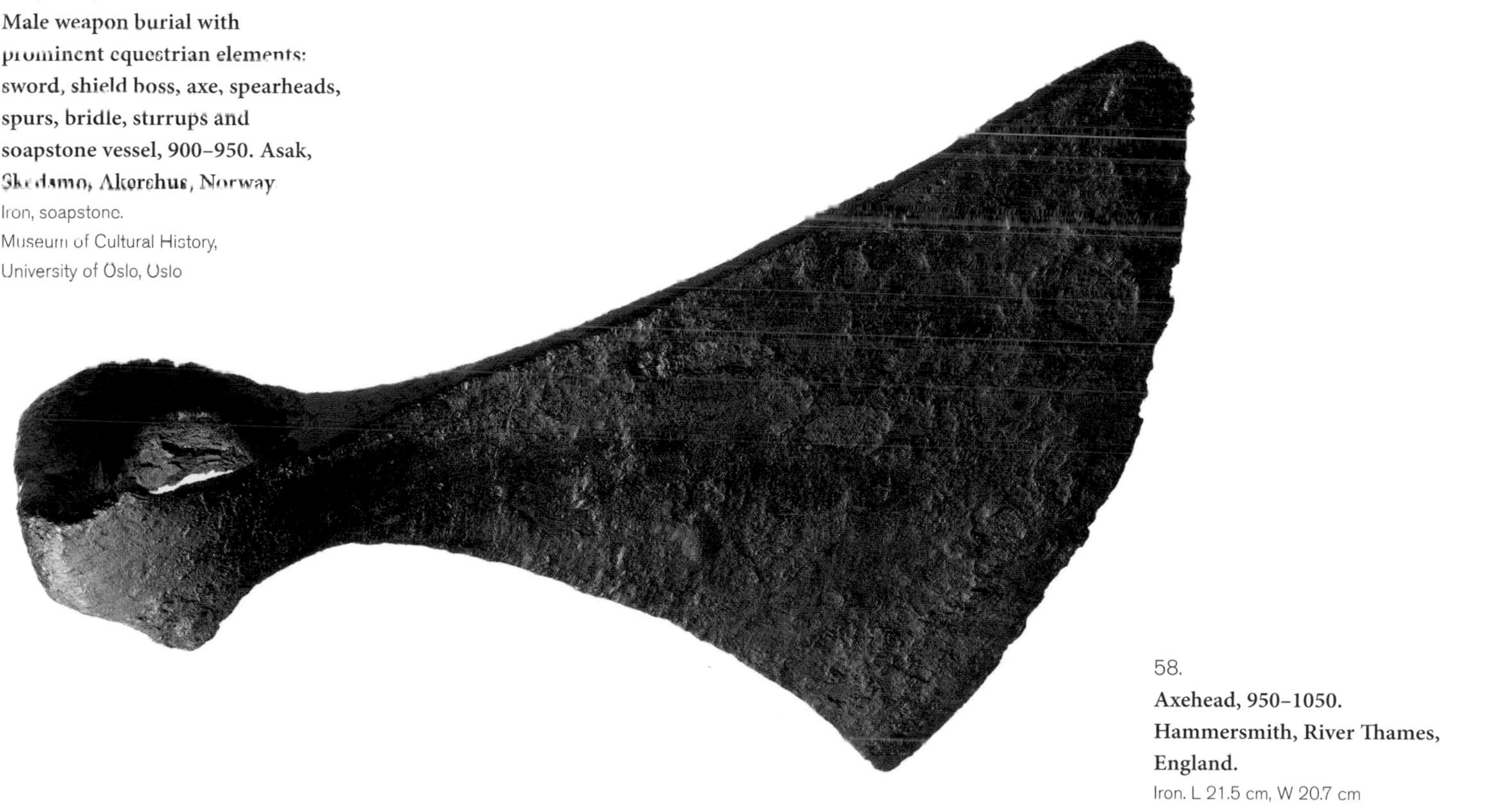

58.

Axehead, 950–1050. Hammersmith, River Thames, England.

Iron. L 21.5 cm, W 20.7 cm

British Museum, London

59.
The location of ring forts in Denmark.

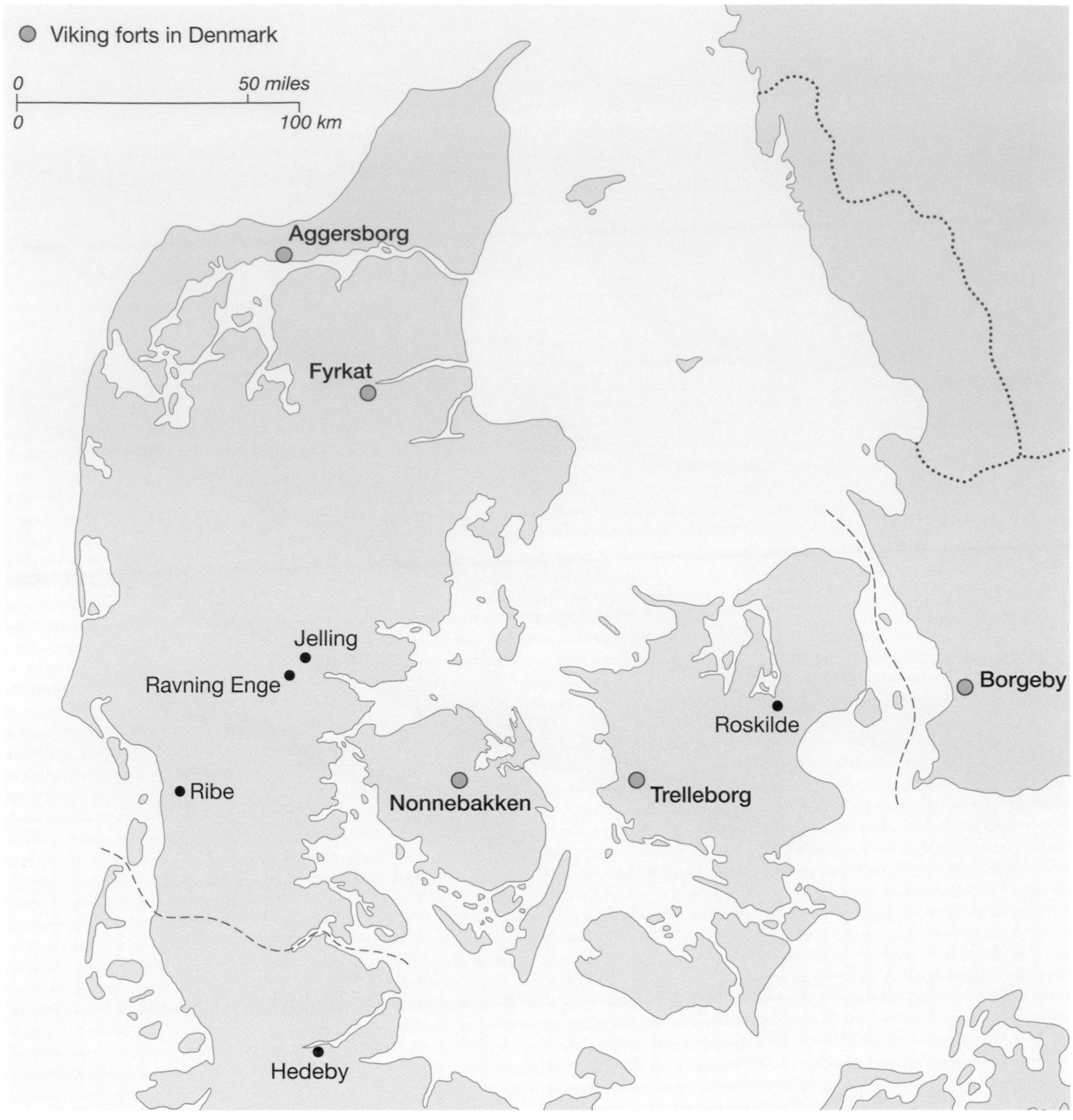

Standardization, organization and discipline are also implied in the development of the Danish ring forts built *c.* 980s (see pp. 151–2). Trelleborg (Zealand), Fyrkat and Aggersborg (both Jutland) were built according to common principles, although varying in size and in some details of construction. Further forts at Nonnebakken (Funen) and Borgeby (Skåne) appear to be related but were perhaps constructed on a less regular pattern. Trelleborg, Fyrkat and Aggersborg all have planned layouts with houses of standard size and shape, arranged in squares, surrounded by substantial earthworks that would originally have been topped with wooden palisades. Excavations suggest that not all of the houses were necessarily occupied, and that the populations included women and children as well as men, but it is hard to avoid the conclusion that these were designed at least in part to house garrisons. Taken together with the royal centre at Jelling (see p. 158), which has now revealed buildings of comparable type and date, these forts provide a network of royal centres controlling all of the regions of the expanding Danish kingdom (fig. 59).[62] This is reminiscent of the network of *burhs* in late Anglo-Saxon England that also combined military and non-military functions, but which originated as a planned response to Viking attacks in the late ninth and tenth centuries.[63] A combined military, economic and administrative role is also visible in Frankish towns throughout the Viking Age, and

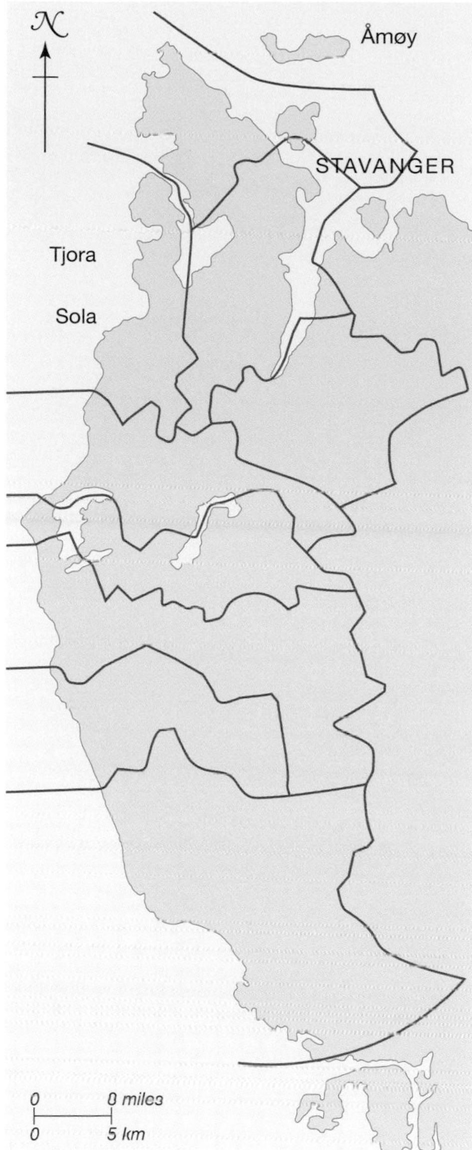

60.
Territorial units in Hordaland, south-west Norway that supported the raising of regional levies (*leiðangr*). Each unit of land was responsible for one fully equipped warship and crew.

especially in Ottonian Germany in the tenth century, and either Anglo-Saxon or Ottonian towns (or both) may be considered likely influences on the Danish ringforts. The shared design certainly indicates centralized planning, while the construction required resources in terms of timber and manpower on a national scale. However, there is no evidence to indicate the nature of the underlying organization of the construction, and these structures seem to have been a short-lived experiment rather than a typical feature of late Viking-Age Denmark.[64] Recent isotope analysis may suggest that the garrison of Trelleborg was in part composed of foreign mercenaries, rather than any sort of Danish national levy.[65]

Evidence of a greater degree of central organization and royal authority can be found in the systems of ship levies in Denmark, Norway and Sweden in the centuries following the Viking Age. The *leiðangr* (Danish *leding*, Norwegian *leidang*, Swedish *ledung*) functioned in similar ways in all three kingdoms, based on the principle that the king had the right to summon a fleet for the defence of the kingdom, and that the land was divided up into units that could furnish set numbers of ships and men, with appropriate standardized military equipment and provisions. The *leiðangr* could also be summoned by the king for offensive warfare, but then he was entitled to call out only a smaller levy. In years when neither an offensive nor defensive levy was required, the king had the right to demand the provisions, without the military service (fig. 60).[66]

Detailed descriptions of the different versions of the *leiðangr*, not only in the three kingdoms but in various regions within those kingdoms, are found in law codes of the twelfth and thirteenth centuries. Written law was introduced only towards the end of the Viking Age and the earliest do not survive, so it is not always clear which elements represent innovations at the time they were written, and what may have been retained from earlier written law, or even from customary law dating back still further. Since the 1980s the nature of *leiðangr* during the Viking Age has been questioned. Some continue to argue that the *leiðangr* can be projected back to the Viking Age, citing references in skaldic verse, and possible similarities between archaeological finds and the law codes. For example, the excavated Danish warship Skuldelev 5 has been interpreted as a *leiðangr* ship on the basis that it had been repeatedly repaired and had been kept afloat long after it was actually useful (fig. 61). According to this interpretation, the ship was much more likely to be a *leiðangr* ship than the personal vessel of a chieftain or other high-status individual.[67] At the opposite extreme, it has been argued that the law codes have no value as information for anything before the late twelfth or even the thirteenth century, and that no form of *leiðangr* existed before the late eleventh century at the earliest. According to this view, Viking raids were private ventures, led by individual war leaders and chieftains with their personal followers. Even when the leaders of documented raids were important Scandinavian kings, they supposedly attacked without recourse to anything recognizable as national armies.[68]

The truth probably lies somewhere between the two extremes. Later saga tradition attributes the introduction of the Norwegian *leiðangr* to Håkon the Good in the mid-tenth century. It is thought that Håkon was brought up at the court of Athelstan (924–39) in England, and learned English customs, and his approach to kingship generally appears more typically Anglo-Saxon than Norwegian.[69] This is significant because there are parallels for the *leiðangr* in late Anglo-Saxon England. Systematized military service and work on fortifications and bridges can be seen as early as the eighth century in some Anglo-Saxon kingdoms, but from the tenth century there are also references to ship-sokes, or units of land responsible for the provision of one ship to the levy, and the *Anglo-Saxon Chronicle* specifically mentions a ship levy in 1008.[70] The term *leiðangr* is also attested in skaldic verse from Norway in the late tenth century, although the contexts in which it appears could equally well apply specifically to a national levy or to a more general meaning of a war fleet. There is thus no doubt that something described as *leiðangr* existed as early as the tenth

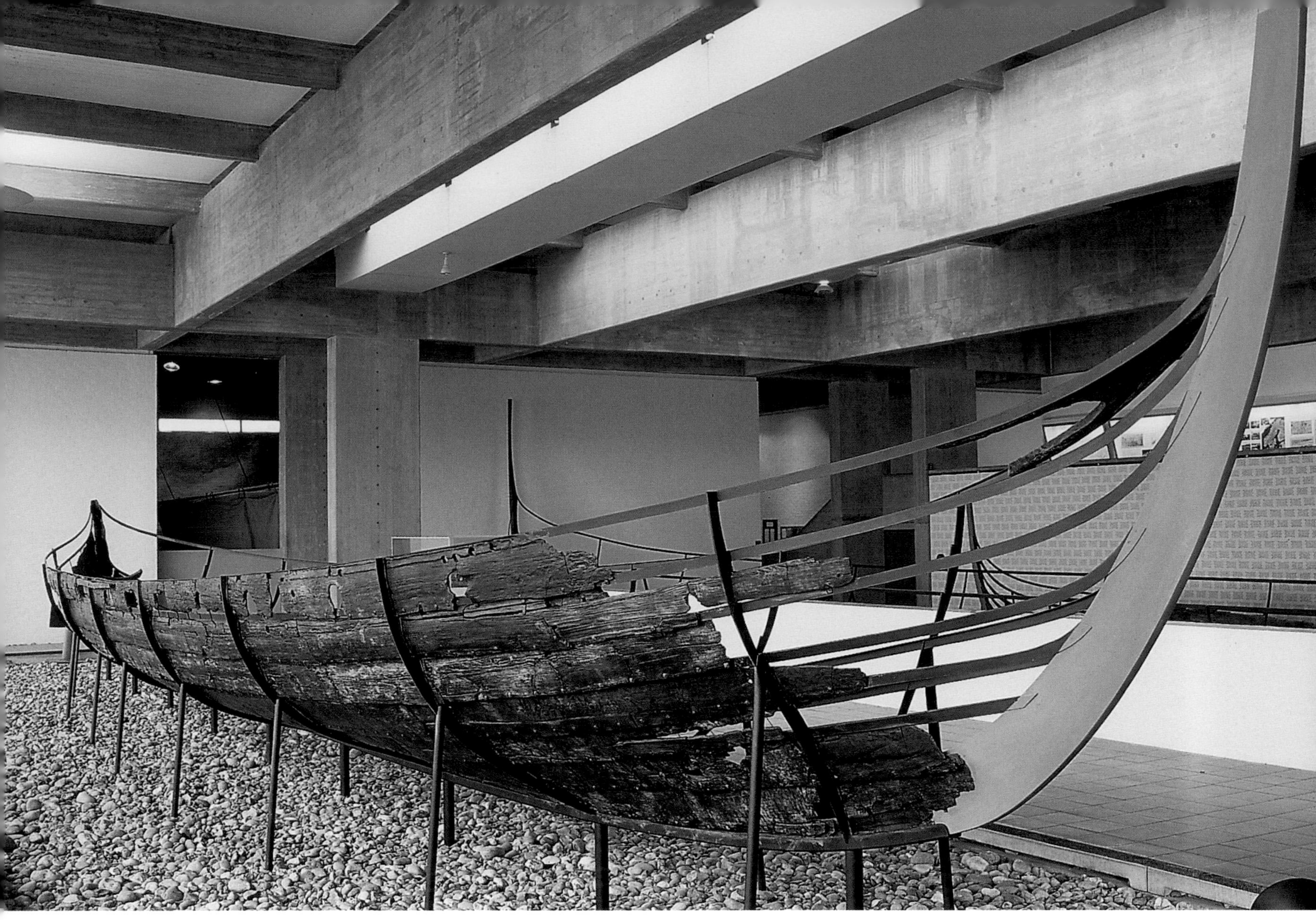

61.
Skuldelev 5 has been interpreted as a *leiðangr* ship – a warship called up for military service by royal command.
Oak, L. 17.3 m
Viking Ship Museum, Roskilde

century in parts of Norway, and while it certainly was not the fully developed system of the later law codes, a degree of standardization seems likely, if only along the western seaboard that formed the heartland of the emerging Norwegian kingdom.[71]

The existence of a ship levy system in later Anglo-Saxon England has important implications for the development of some form of *leiðangr* in Denmark. The first mention of *leiðangr* in Denmark comes in a charter of 1085. Since this is the earliest surviving Danish charter, the absence of any previous mention is hardly significant, and the lack of an explanation for the term in the charter suggests an institution already well established and understood. What does seem to be new at that time is the attempt to turn the levy into a tax, a demand that proved too much for the Danish people, and probably contributed to the murder of the Danish king Cnut the Holy the following year.[72] *Leiðangr* thus seems to have been introduced in Denmark some time before 1085, but while it is possible that Harald Bluetooth had some form of ship-levy system a century earlier, there is no direct evidence to support the suggestion, and historian Niels Lund has argued that even the armies of Svein Forkbeard and Cnut that conquered England in 1016 were simply old-style raiding armies on a large scale, rather than national levies.[73] That this is at least partly true is indicated by rune-stones from eastern Sweden commemorating men who 'took geld' in

England at this time (fig. 62), but it is possible that Svein's armies combined levy troops with more traditional raiders. Once Cnut became king of both England and Denmark, however, he governed his North Sea empire more as an Anglo-Saxon king than as a traditional Viking ruler. Other Anglo-Saxon influences are visible in Denmark in his reign, including developments in coinage, urbanization and the Church, and it would be surprising if he did not also learn from a system of military organization designed to strengthen the power of the king as well as to defend the kingdom.

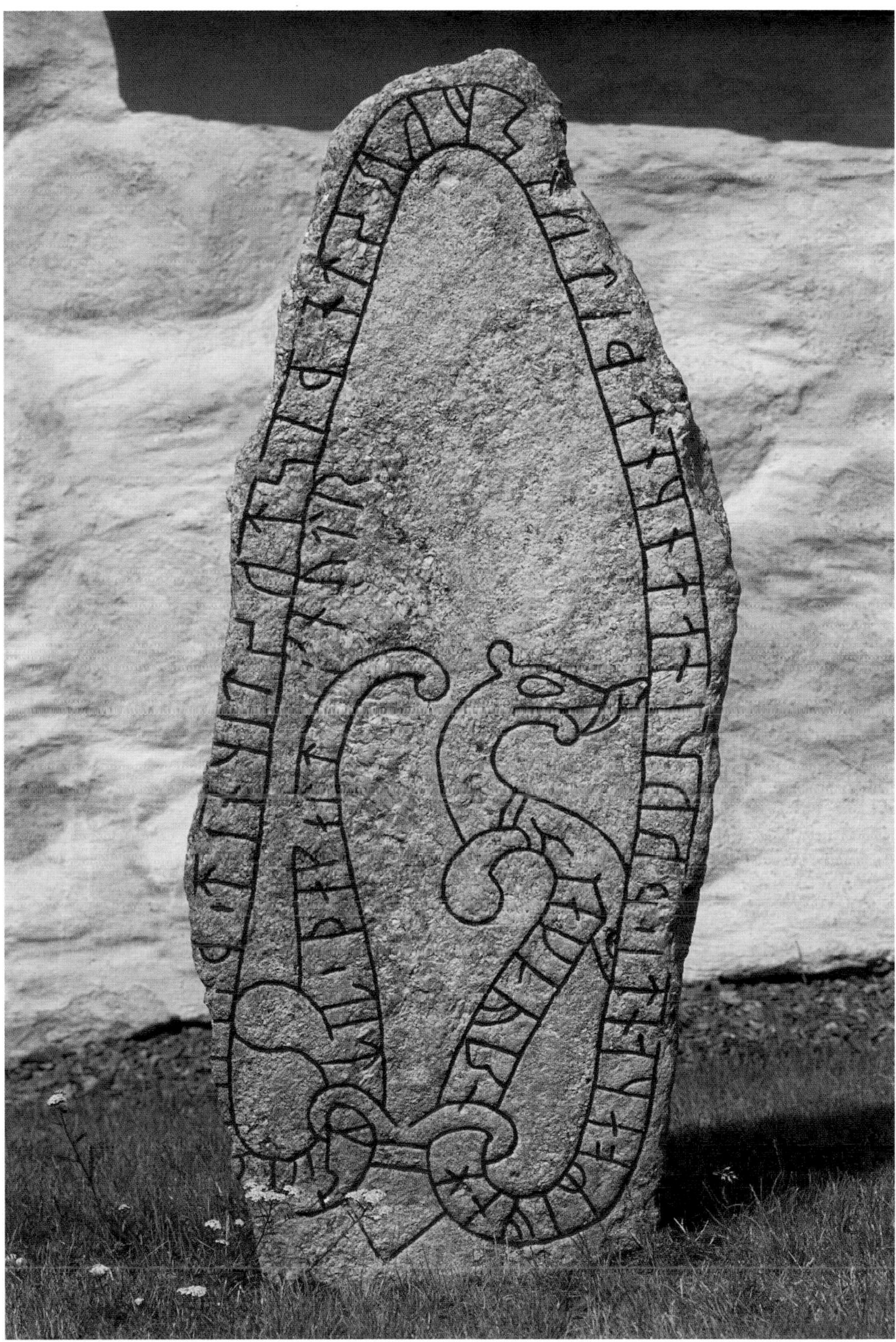

62.
This rune-stone (U 344) at Yttergärde, Uppland, Sweden describes the taking of tribute in England by a Viking called Ulfr.

Transcription in Old Norse:
En UlfR hafiR a Ænglandi þry giald takit. Þet vas fyrsta þet 's Tosti ga[l]t. Þa [galt] Þorkætill. Þa galt Knutr.

Translation in English:
Ulfr received three payments in England. That was the first that Tosti paid. Then Þorketill paid. Then Knútr paid.

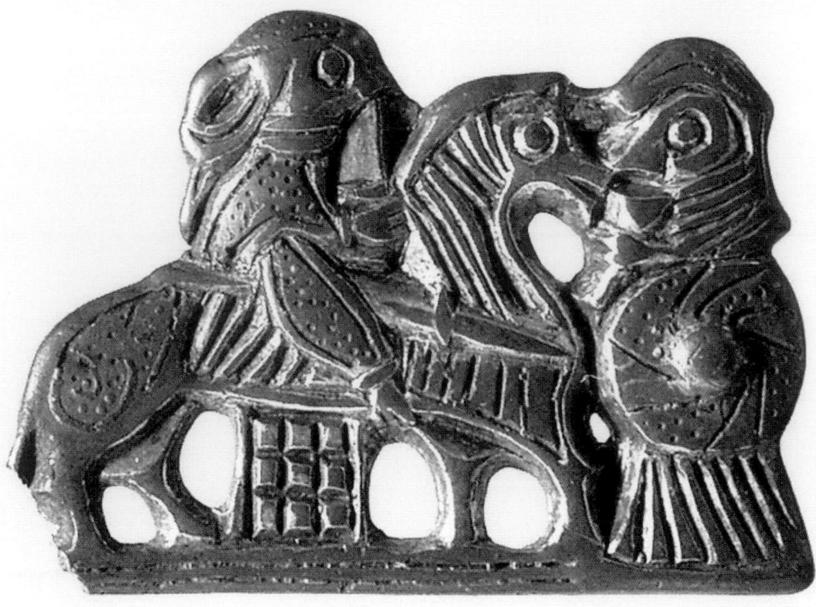

1.
Depictions of women with weapons have traditionally been interpreted as 'valkyries', but may simply represent female warriors.

'Valkyrie' pendant, 800–1050. Kalmergården, north-west Zealand, Denmark.
Silver with niello. H 2.7 cm, W 3.5 cm
National Museum of Denmark, Copenhagen

The way of the warrior

Neil Price

The warrior is one of the most enduring forms of the Viking stereotype, and has been current for centuries in both scholarship and the popular imagination. The material aspects of warfare, the toolkit of the Viking-Age fighter, are well known from excavations: all the varied knives and spears, shields, bows and arrows, swords for the wealthy, and the different types of protective clothing. A less explored topic, however, is the mindset of the Viking warrior and the ways in which the business of battle was embedded in the broader aspects of contemporary Scandinavian culture.

Perhaps the first assumption to be challenged is the idea that 'proper' Vikings were necessarily male. In general, this was almost certainly the case, as supported by both written sources and archaeological finds, but there are important exceptions. Weapons of various kinds, most often spears and arrows, are occasionally found in female graves. Their presence has often been explained away, in more or less convincing fashion, as representing gifts or marks of transferred status in the circumstantial absence of a man, or as symbols of some kind. However, there is no reason why they should not simply represent the possessions of the dead while they were alive: women with weapons (fig. 1). It is interesting that the majority of such items are projectile weapons, i.e. those that are less reliant on physical strength to wield effectively.

Warrior women were certainly part of the Norse imagination in the form of Valkyries and shield-maidens, and the possibility that a minority of real women may have fought on the battlefield is a serious one. An intriguing Byzantine source, documenting a campaign fought against the Scandinavian Rūs in 970, mentions the presence of armed and armoured women among their opponents' battlefield dead; the account seems reliable and is completely independent of Norse texts.[1]

Whether or not this was the case, there were also other senses in which women went to war. The Old Norse sagas and poems – difficult sources to negotiate – suggest the existence of specialized military sorceresses, casting spells of protective and offensive magic to aid men in battle (see pp. 175–7, 196–7).

This magical support system leads us to a wider perspective on Viking-Age combat: the ritual aspects of war. The Viking warrior entered into combat from within a thought-world that offered the protective though untrustworthy power of military deities of both sexes. Odin, Thor, Freyja and others were all gods of war, though in specific ways that suited their own character, whether concerned with the mental clarity needed for fighting, brute force or focused aggression. The battlefield was also the home of supernatural demons of carnage, the most prominent of which were the Valkyries. Far from Wagner's beautiful maidens longing romantically for dead heroes, the Valkyries of the Viking Age seem originally to have been terrifying spirits of war, unleashed into combat and literally personifying the essence of battle (alongside many anonymous ones,

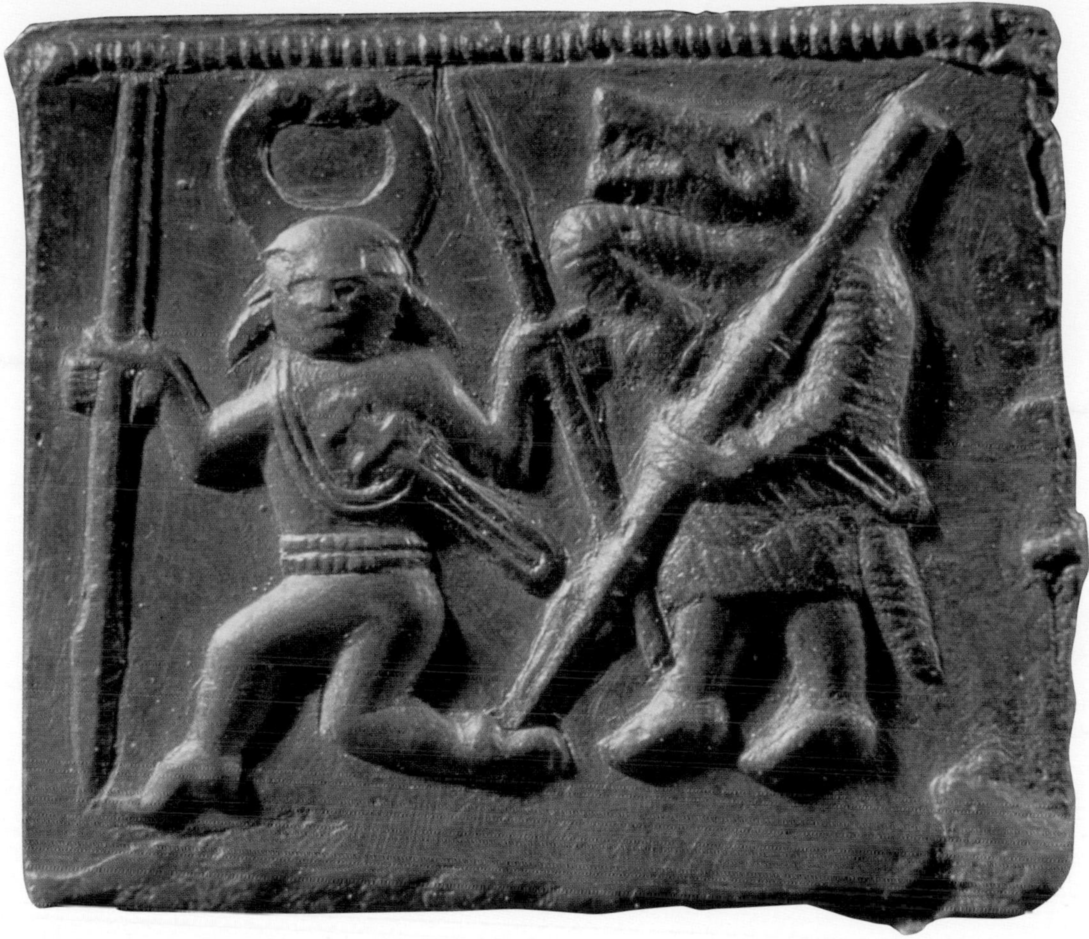

2.
A matrix is a die used to impress designs on sheet metal, in this case probably panels for a helmet. This matrix from Torslunda depicts a hybrid human-beast warrior. Matrix. Torslunda, Oland, Sweden.
Bronze.
Statens Historicka Museum, Stockholm

we know of fifty-one individual Valkyries, whose translated names embody what they really were: Sword-Noise, Battle-Weaver, Shield-Scraper, Teeth-Grinder, Killer, Silence and the rest).[2] The Old Norse prose texts speak of giant battle trolls, dog-like spirits of destruction and supernatural beasts roaming the battlefield.[3]

In addition to these shadowy figures, there are indications that at least some Viking warriors believed that they themselves could transform into creatures of power. Traditions concerning the famous berserkers – Old Norse *berserkir* – are well known and mostly post-date the Viking Age in problematic ways, but there is little doubt that the notion of men possessed by a consuming frenzy, a divinely inspired battle rage, was current at the time. Linked with shape-changing beliefs that were widespread in society, these bear and wolf warriors are apparently depicted on a range of metalwork and other media from the centuries around the Viking Age (fig. 2).[4]

This ritual violence also took physical form as amulets, charms and other symbols of what soldiers in every time and place have always called the luck of war. An example is the Viking warrior from Repton in Derbyshire, buried wearing a Thor's hammer around his neck – a direct reference to a god – and with 'charms' in the form of a boar's tusk and a jackdaw's leg. They did not help him, as he had been felled by two lethal spear-thrusts to the face and eye, disembowelled and possibly castrated: a grim reminder of what actually happened in combat.[5]

When all the above are combined, it can be seen that the way of the Viking warrior, male or (perhaps) female, was complex and multifaceted. In addition to the obvious martial skills that could mean life or death on the battlefield, it is clear that ritual of various kinds was thought to be as vital to the business of fighting as the sharpening of swords.

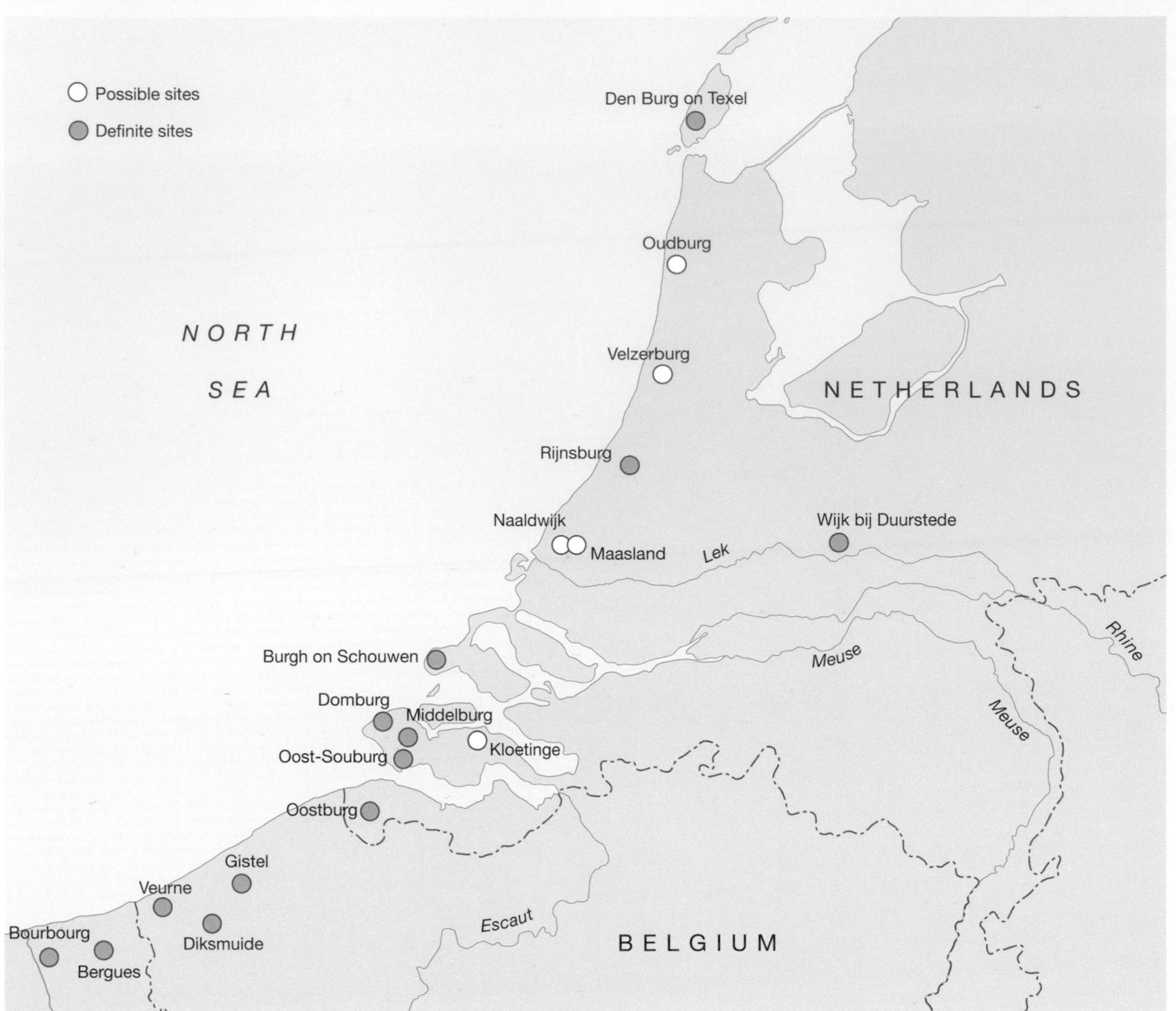

2
The location of defensive sites along the coastline of continental northern Europe.

Continental defences against the Vikings

Simon Coupland

The Viking invasions of the Continent have left few tangible or visible traces, but fortifications thrown up against the invaders, some of which can still be seen in the landscape, are the rare exception. In the Netherlands at Middelburg (fig. 1), at Oost-Souburg on Walcheren and Burgh on Schouwen, the ring fortresses that served as refuges for the local people can clearly be seen in the local topography. At Oost-Souburg the fort has been reconstructed following excavation of the site. Elsewhere there is less to see today, but archaeology has revealed a string of similar circular forts, from Flanders in Belgium to Texel in the Netherlands, which were built or rebuilt in the ninth century (fig. 2).[1]

As the reconstruction at Oost-Souburg shows, these forts consisted of earthen banks surrounded by a ditch and topped by a palisade (fence), as a ninth-century text describes. *The Miracles of St Bertin* refers to the fortification around the monastery of St Bertin as 'very skilfully and strongly built of stakes, soil and turves', and reports how it helped the locals to repel an attack by a band of 550 Vikings in April 891. It should be borne in mind that 'castles' or 'forts' referred to in contemporary texts were usually earth and wood constructions, not the stone keeps or strongholds familiar from the later Middle Ages (fig. 3). As a result they were significantly more vulnerable to both attack and fire: at St Vaast in Arras (France) in 892 'the stronghold accidentally caught fire, and the entire fortification was destroyed.'

However, many Frankish towns still retained their stone Roman walls, even if they had been allowed to fall into disrepair or used as quarries by local builders. As the Viking raids increased in number, scope and impact, some of these urban defences were restored or reinforced, including those at Angoulême, Tours, Le Mans and Orléans in the late 860s, Paris in the 870s, and Cologne, Langres, Mainz and Rheims in the 880s. Not that the Scandinavians were necessarily deterred by these stone ramparts: at Nantes in 843 they scaled the walls with ladders while battering down the gates that had been barred against them. Elsewhere, however, the ancient stone walls did enable several towns to withstand not only attack but also protracted sieges. The most celebrated was undoubtedly Paris, whose heroic resistance against an assault by the Great Army through the winter of 885–6 inspired the 600-line poem, *The Wars of the City of Paris*, by Abbo of St Germain.[2]

At the same time as urban defences were being strengthened a number of other sites were also fortified, including some high-status locations where stone was used as well as wood and turf. These included the monasteries of Arras, St Denis, St Quentin, Tournus and Vézélay, as well as the Frankish royal palaces at Compiègne and Quierzy. Excavation at the latter has revealed an earthen rampart surrounding the entire palace complex, with a water-filled moat encircling part, if not all, of this wall.

Given that the Viking attacks began in earnest in the 840s, why did the Franks not start building forts and reinforcing towns until the latter part of the ninth century? Only one fortification is known to have been constructed against the Scandinavians before 868: a rampart built in the 820s around the island monastery of Noirmoutier after it had been targeted repeatedly by raiders sailing across from the Irish Sea. Archaeology has revealed a similar fortification from the early ninth century around the Breton abbey of Landévennec, which may also be linked to these early incursions.[3]

There are three likely reasons for this lack of fortification construction before the late 860s. The first is that the early Viking raids tended to be hit-and-run affairs, costly and deadly, but not so much so as to justify the considerable effort and expense of constructing permanent fortifications. Another reason is that throughout the 840s and 850s there was tension and conflict between the Frankish kings, and it was only once Charles the Bald felt secure that he could turn his attention to a longer term solution to the Scandinavian problem. Around 870 the king fortified bridges across the key rivers Seine and Loire, constructing small stone forts on either bank to allow the river to be closed to Viking fleets and the bridge itself to be defended. Unfortunately the strategy did not prove effective, probably because of the unreliability of the troops guarding the bridges. Finally, in an era of political tensions and shifting allegiances, the Frankish monarchs may well have been unwilling to permit the construction of strongholds that could be used as power bases by local magnates. Consequently, as royal power declined in the late ninth century the ring forts in Flanders were built not by the king but by the local count, Baldwin II.

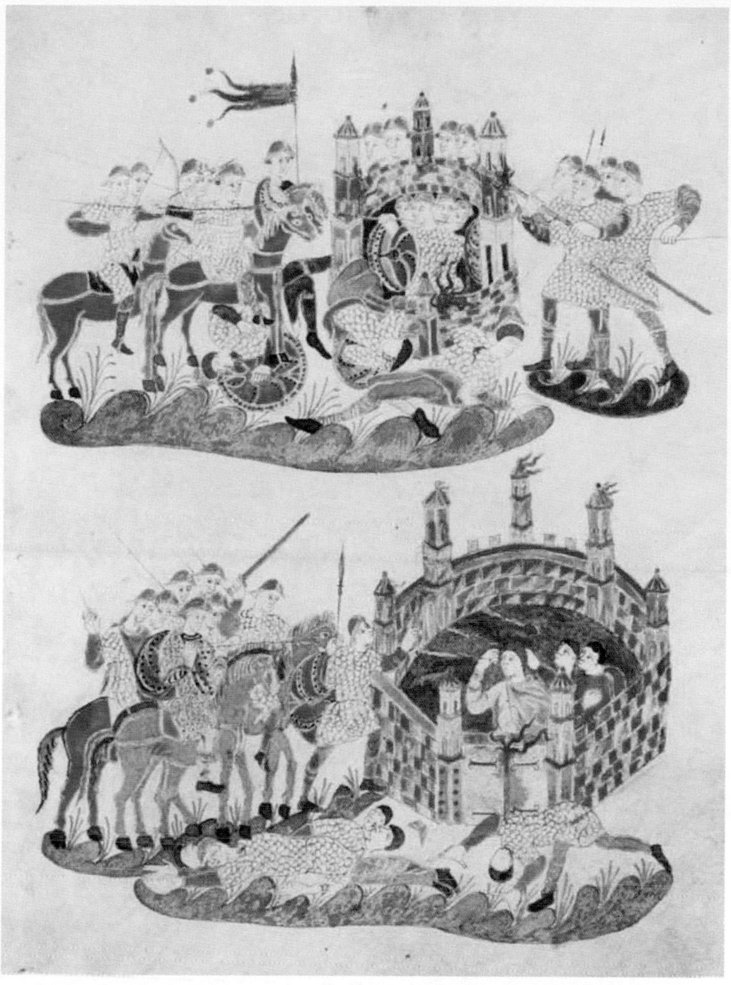

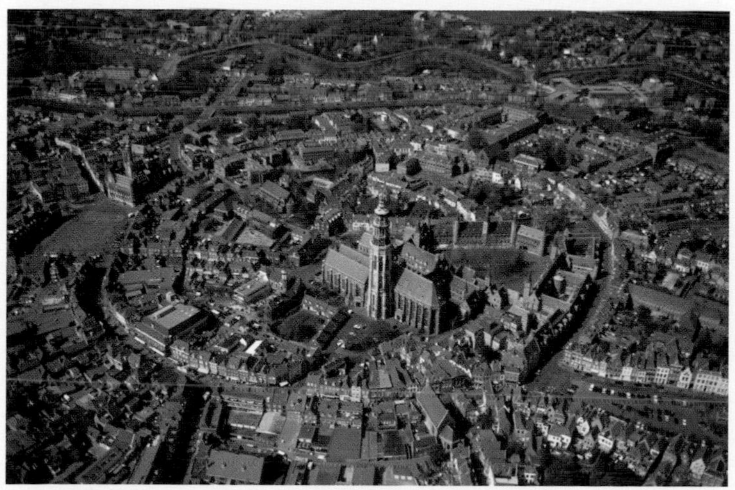

1. (left)
Middelburg, Netherlands seen from above. The outline of the Carolingian fort is still clear in the modern street layout.

3. (above)
Carolingian mounted warriors as depicted in the Golden Psalter of St Gallen, 9th century. St Gallen, Switzerland.
Parchment. L 19.2 cm, W 14.2 cm
Stiftsbibliothek, St Gallen

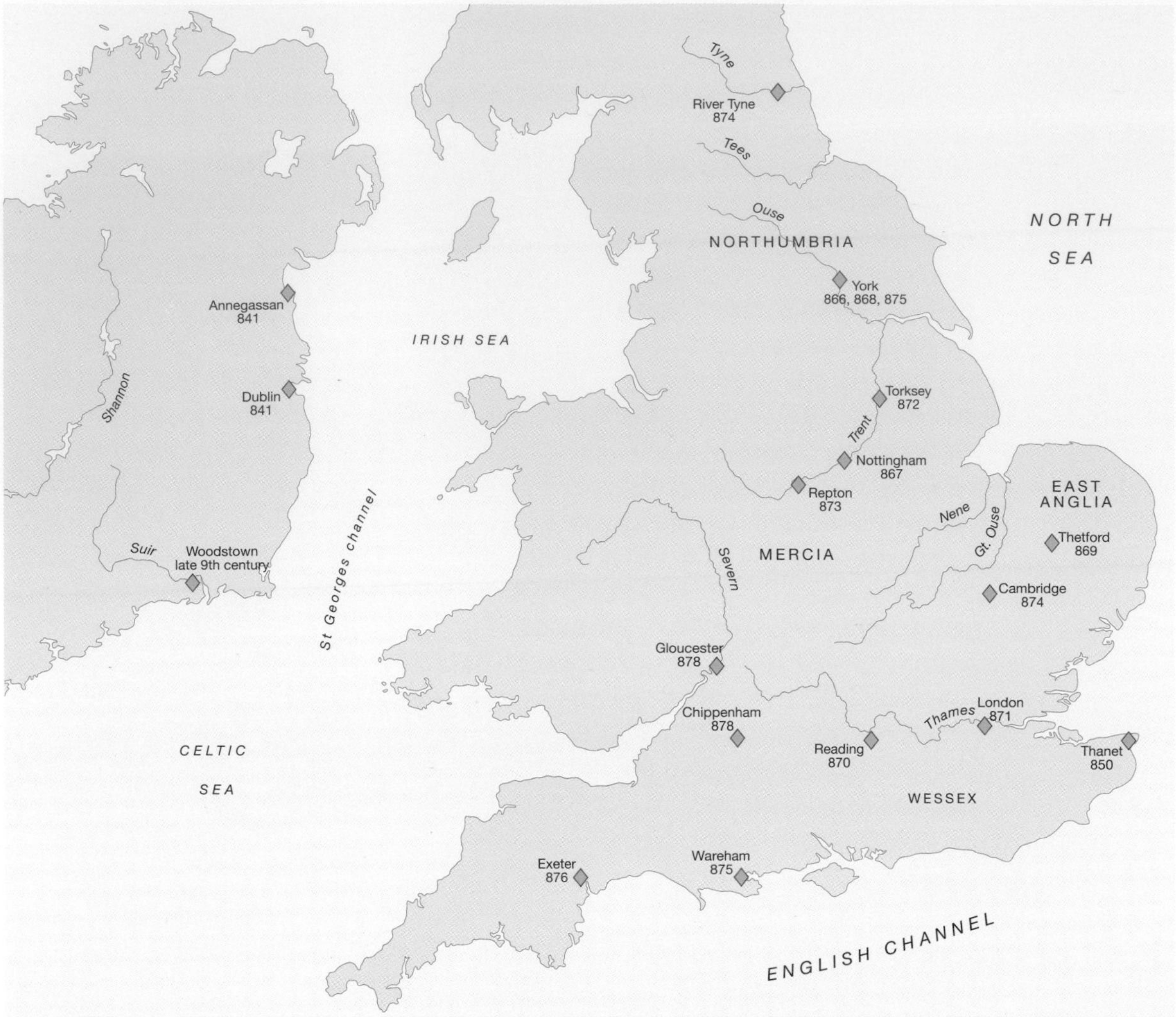

1.
The location of Viking camps in England and Ireland

Viking camps in England and Ireland

Gareth Williams

The early Viking raids were small-scale hit-and-run attacks on coastal targets, such as monasteries and trading centres, which contained valuable items that could be carried off as loot. Their ships allowed them to arrive without warning and to leave again before a proper defence could be organized. However, as the raids continued, coastal defences improved and fewer rich targets remained available to attack near the coast.

The Vikings responded by mounting larger expeditions. They also attacked further inland, taking their ships up the major rivers or leaving them under guard while they attacked overland on horseback or on foot. Either way involved spending time in hostile territory, which made it easier for local rulers to organize counter-attacks. At the same time, larger forces and longer raids meant that the Vikings needed more supplies to feed them.

Fortified camps provided both a defence against attackers and a secure place to store supplies and loot, as well as protecting the all-important ships (fig. 1). A camp of this sort was known in Ireland as a *longphort* (pl. *longphuirt*), which can be translated as 'ship-landing', 'ship-camp' or 'ship-fort'. The first *longphuirt* are recorded in 841 at Duiblinn (Dublin) and Linn Dúachaill (Annagassan, Co. Louth). Both probably reused existing monasteries, providing loot and supplies of food, and both were placed where major rivers met the sea. The rivers served as a route for further attacks inland, but also formed the borders between different local kingdoms.[1] By choosing bases on the fringes of the kingdoms, the Vikings reduced the chance of an instant response, since they posed a less urgent threat than if they were attacking the heart of the kingdom. Furthermore, these locations created potential diplomatic problems for local rulers to take decisive action against the Vikings in sensitive border areas.

At Dublin and Annagassan the Vikings stayed through the winter, which explains the importance of taking over existing estate centres. It meant that they could commandeer the food supplies that had already been gathered in to feed the occupants. Dublin was more or less permanently occupied until 902, and again from 917, and gradually developed into a fortified town and a major trading centre, with a permanent territory around it. Other camps lasted for a single winter, in which case the Vikings would strip the surrounding countryside for supplies and then move on in the spring. Others remained for much shorter periods, acting as temporary bases for a single raiding expedition. A *longphort* at Emly, Co. Tipperary is said to have been occupied for only two days.[2]

Although most camps were short-lived, overwintering became common from the mid-ninth century in England, Ireland and on the Continent. From staying over one winter, Vikings began to campaign for years on end, overwintering in a different place each time, and some contemporary accounts talk of them taking their women and children with them.[3] At the same time, their forces became larger than ever as they sought to match the kingdoms they attacked. This meant that they needed even more substantial camps as their bases.

In 865 a 'great raiding army' landed in East Anglia, and for the next ten years this force moved around between the different Anglo-Saxon kingdoms, establishing a winter camp in a different place each year. Only one such camp, at Repton in Derbyshire, has so far been excavated on any scale. The Vikings were here in 873–4, taking over one of the wealthiest monasteries in the area. Excavations show that they used the church as part of their defences, including it as a gatehouse through an earth rampart that defended an enclosure backing on to the River Trent.[4]

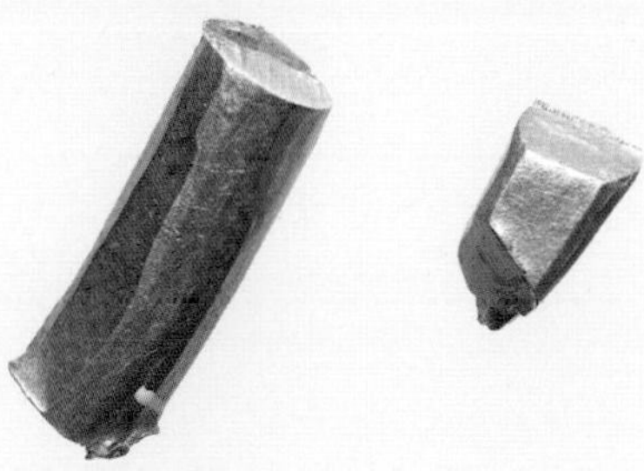

Two other camps in England have recently been investigated through a combination of metal detecting and limited archaeological fieldwork. One at Torksey in Lincolnshire was recorded as a winter camp in 872–3, the other in North Yorkshire was apparently occupied a few years later (figs 2–3). At around 26 hectares/65 acres and 31 hectares/76 acres respectively, both sites were substantial (much larger than the 1.46 hectares/3.65 acres suggested for Repton), a reminder of the size of the 'great raiding army' that came close to conquering the whole of England. There has also been excavation of some of the Irish *longphuirt,* most notably at Woodstown, near Waterford and at Annagassan, Co. Louth.[5]

The finds from these sites cast new light on the activity in Viking camps. As one might expect, there is evidence of both weapons and defences. However, large numbers of weights, coins and pieces of bullion point to extensive trading, while gaming pieces suggest how the Vikings spent their leisure time over the winter. The camps also show evidence of metal-working and, interestingly, textile production, reinforcing the historical accounts of women travelling with the Vikings. In their size and their variety these were not simply temporary military camps: they were the forerunners of the towns that would become central to Viking settlements in both England and Ireland.[6]

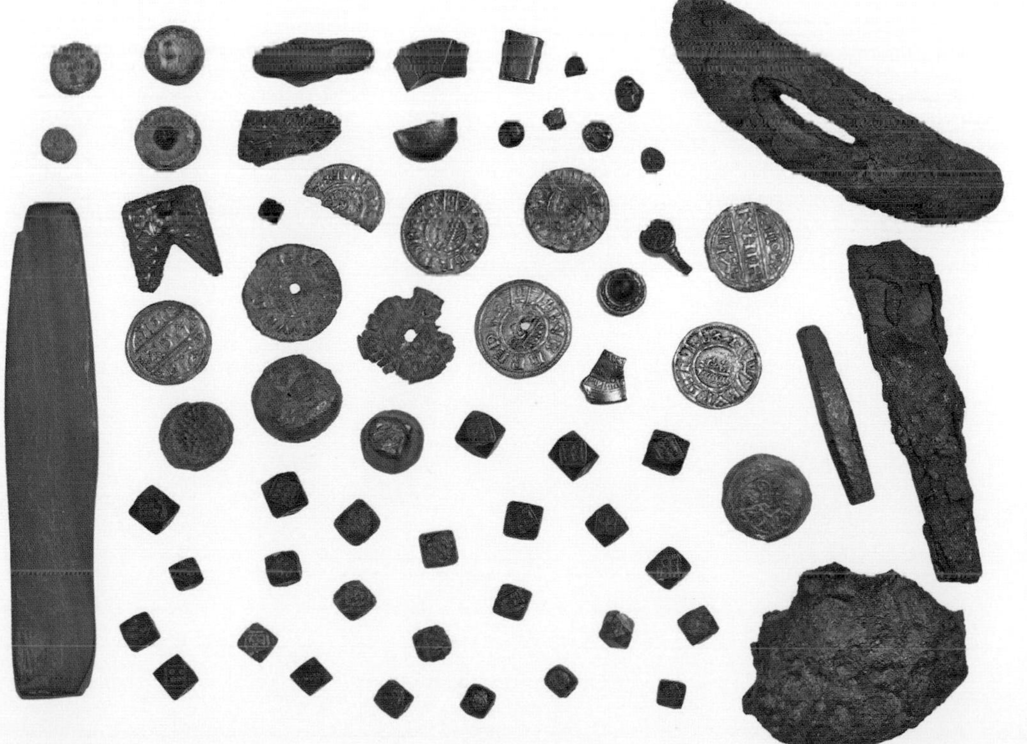

2–3

Finds from a Viking Camp in North Yorkshire include weights, coins, fragments of weapons and evidence of metalworking.

Hack-silver, hack-gold, coins, weights, ingots, whetstone, remains of sword hilt, late 9th century. North Yorkshire, England.

Gold, silver, copper alloy, iron, lead, stone
British Museum, London

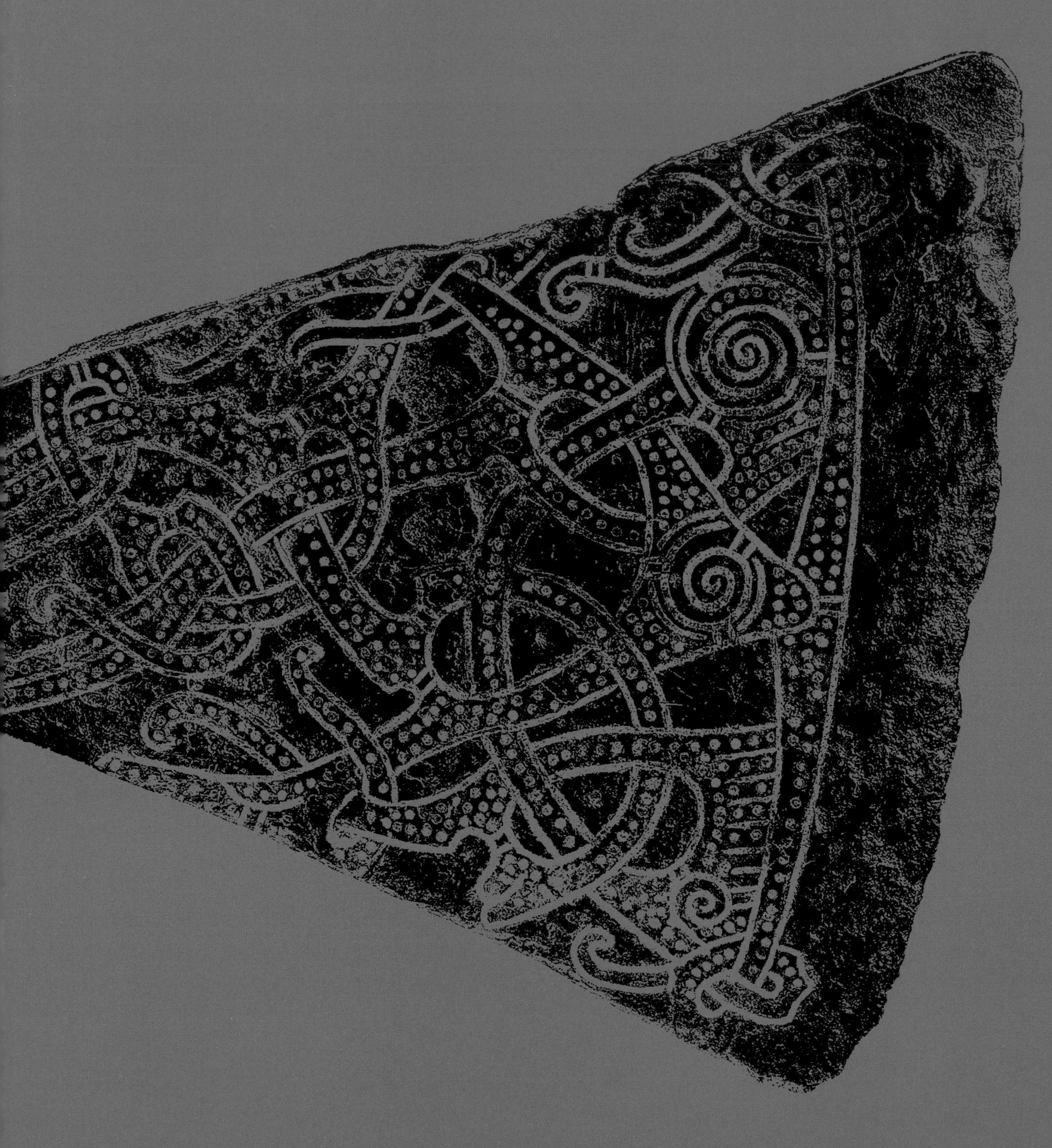

3
POWER & ARISTOCRACY

Anne Pedersen

On Saturday the fleet-lord throws off
the long tarpaulin, where splendid widows
gaze on the planking of the dragon [ship]
from the town. The young ruler steered
the brand-new warship west out of the
Nið, and the oars of the warriors fall
into the sea.

ÞJÓÐÓLFR ARNÓRSSON, IV, 19 (11th century)

POWER & ARISTOCRACY

THE VIKING AGE SAW THE DEVELOPMENT of the three Scandinavian kingdoms, Norway, Denmark and Sweden, which despite numerous political and territorial disputes through the centuries still exist today. At the close of the period a new form of kingship had developed, with kings claiming authority over far greater territories than before and exerting a far more decisive influence over the lives of their subjects. There were no central capitals or institutions of government and administration as we know them. Instead, Viking-Age kings and their successors travelled between residences, enforcing their authority by their presence and the monuments they commissioned. A few sites – Jelling in Denmark, Gamla Uppsala in Sweden and Avaldsnes in Norway – were not only significant in the Viking Age but have also since then attained iconic status in the historical narratives as core sites from which the Scandinavian kingdoms developed. The equivalent in Iceland – which was never a kingdom – is Thingvellir, an assembly site defined by the impressive landscape of a natural fault line. Here the annual Althing (general assembly) was held from *c.* 930 until 1798.

Rivalry between rulers and powerful families led to military conflicts and was visually expressed in monuments and objects, personal appearance and behaviour. The elegant ships preserved in the burials of the elite and as wrecks hidden under water are but one example. Monumental architecture and the deliberate use of landscape were part of the 'language of power' of Scandinavian royalty and their contemporaries at home and abroad. While the sagas and skaldic poetry tell of ceremonies and significant events that took place in the great halls, archaeology has shed light on their physical setting in the remains of impressive farmsteads and large-scale building works that demonstrate both extensive technical knowledge and control over human and natural resources.

Places of power

Over the past few decades archaeological traces of numerous settlements of the Iron Age and Viking Age have come to light across Scandinavia; they suggest a far more complex social hierarchy and arrangement of settlements than previously perceived.[1] Among the many ordinary rural settlements that were focused economically on local resources, a number of centres and aristocratic sites stand out, distinguished by a greater density of occupation, a broad variety of activities and extensive consumption. Discarded and lost objects show that the inhabitants of these sites not only had access to local products but also participated directly or indirectly in far-reaching social and economic networks that enabled them to acquire foreign and exotic goods – unusual brooches, fragile glassware, semi-precious cornelian and rock crystal beads, not to mention silver and gold.

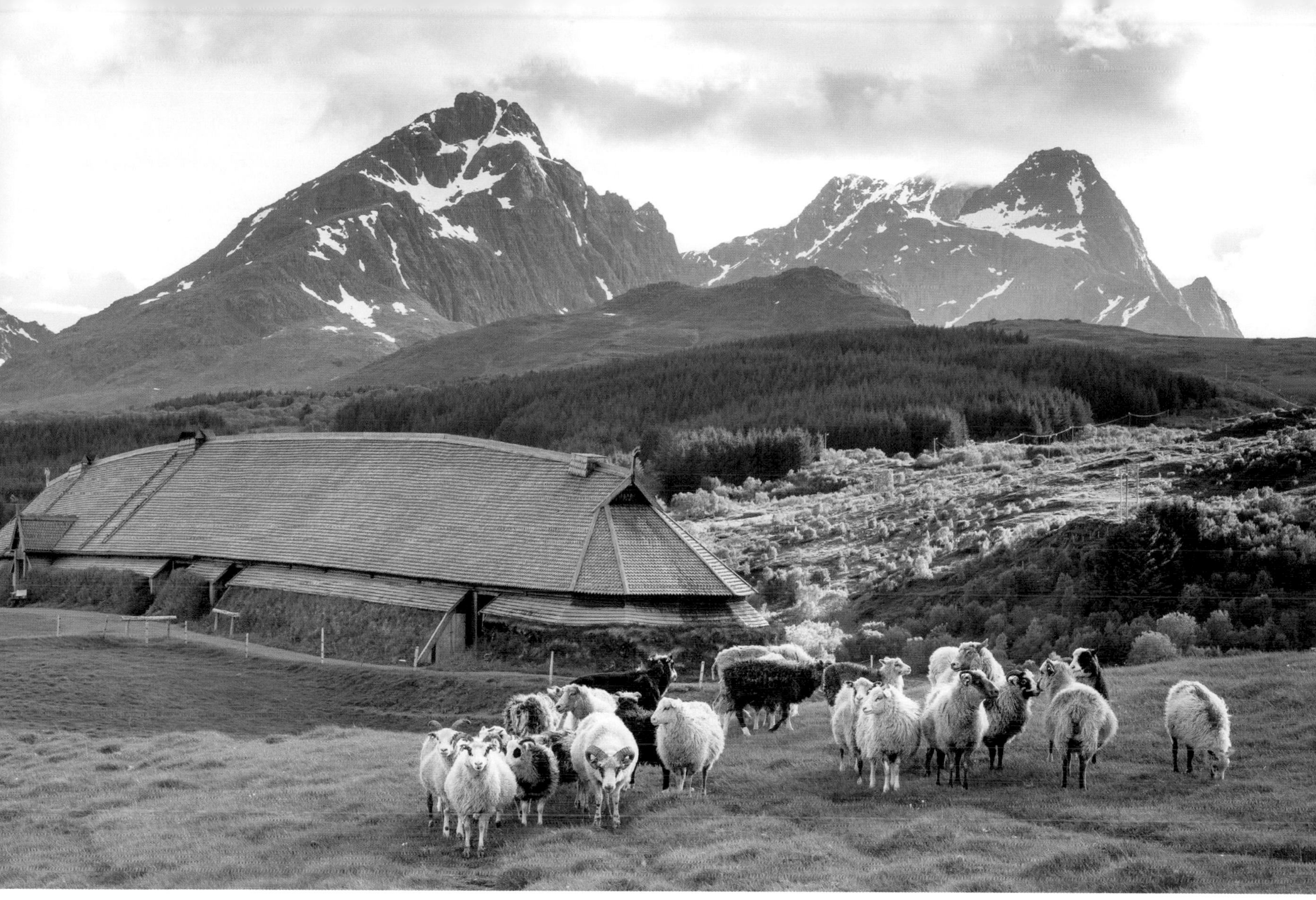

1.
Reconstruction based on the excavated remains of the main building of the chieftain's farm at Borg on Vestvågøy in northern Norway. The roof is shingled and an external sod wall protects the inner wooden wall against the weather.

The merchant Ohthere, one of the long-distance travellers of the Viking Age, journeyed from Hålogaland in northern Norway to Hedeby at the southern Danish border in the late ninth century, eventually giving an account of his travels to Alfred, king of the West Saxons, around 890. Ohthere is described as a very prosperous man and one of the foremost people of the land, his wealth based not on agriculture and cattle breeding as in the south but on reindeer and the natural resources of the north (see pp. 26, 34).[2]

Exactly where Ohthere lived, apart from Hålogaland, we cannot know, but his home may have resembled the chieftain's residence at Borg on the island of Vestvågøy in Lofoten, north of the Arctic Circle in Norway (fig. 1). This was no ordinary farm and clearly reflects both the wealth and elite status of its owners. With a length of about 80 metres, the main building exceeds all other known contemporary longhouses. The roof, covering 600 square metres, was supported by nineteen pairs of posts and an additional pair in each gable. This building had replaced an earlier, 64-metre-long structure on the site, probably some time in the eighth century, and it appears to have been demolished again by the second half of the tenth century.[3] Living quarters were located in one section of the building, economic functions including a byre in the other. An entrance room separated two sectors in the living quarters. The sector at the very highest point, interpreted as the hall (*c.* 120 square metres) with a central fireplace and traces of low benches along the walls, was dominated by

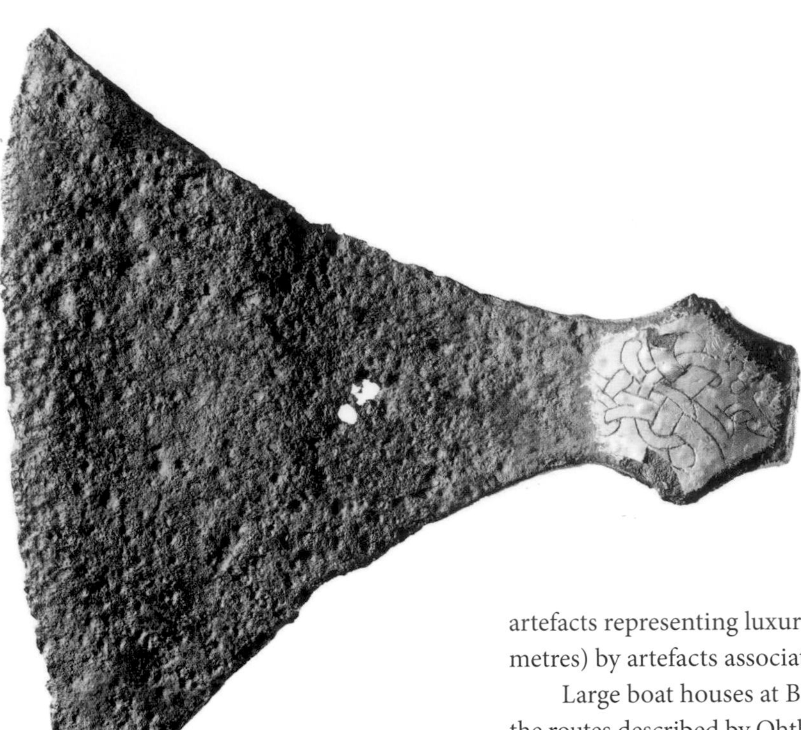

2.
Broad-bladed axe with gold inlay in the Ringerike style, 1000–1050. Botnhamn, Lenvik, Troms, Norway.
Iron, gold. L 14.1 cm, H 14 cm
Tromsø University Museum, Tromsø

3.
Silver neck-ring with runic inscription (see illustration), 11th century. Botnhamn, Lenvik, Troms, Norway.
Silver. Diam. 18 cm
Tromsø University Museum, Tromsø

artefacts representing luxury and crafts including textile-working, the other (*c.* 160 square metres) by artefacts associated with daily life and heavier production.[4]

Large boat houses at Borg indicate that the chieftain possessed ships capable of sailing the routes described by Ohthere, and like Ohthere he probably depended on the exchange of dried fish and other local natural resources such as furs, walrus tusk and strong rope of walrus hide in return for cereals and other basic commodities. In addition, evidence of luxury items such as Tating-ware pitchers and glass vessels can be seen in pottery and glass sherds, among them extremely rare examples of glass decorated with applied gold foil, possibly from one or two small funnel beakers. The pitchers and probably also the decorated glass were produced in the Rhine region, between *c.* 750 and 850.[5] Peaceful exchange was not the only way to access foreign luxuries – violence was also an option. The runic inscription on a silver neck-ring from Botnhamn, some 200 kilometres north of Borg, reads, 'We fared out to the men of Friesland, changing combat clothes with them', a metaphor for battle (figs 2–3).[6] The nature of the campaign cannot be determined but the strategy may well have included looting.

The farm at Borg was situated high in the farmland, in an impressive although not necessarily practical location considering the weather conditions of the region, and it commanded a wide view of the surroundings while being visible at a distance. Other magnate farms boasted a similarly prominent position, one of them being the complex immediately west of Lake Tissø in Zealand, Denmark (see pp. 198–9). Before the low-lying fields were drained and the water table of the lake lowered, the landscape was very different, with water and wetlands enclosing the higher ground of the farm and workshop area.

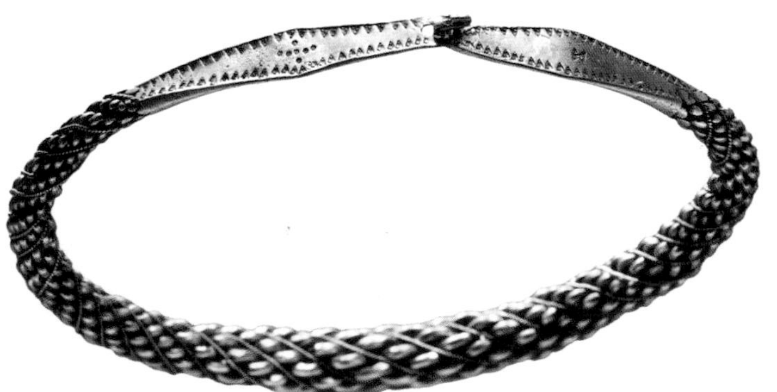

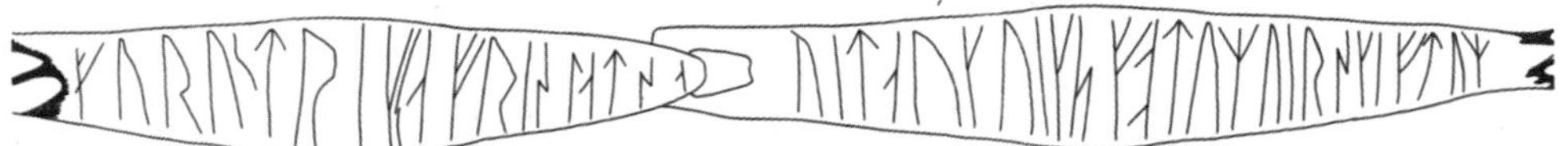

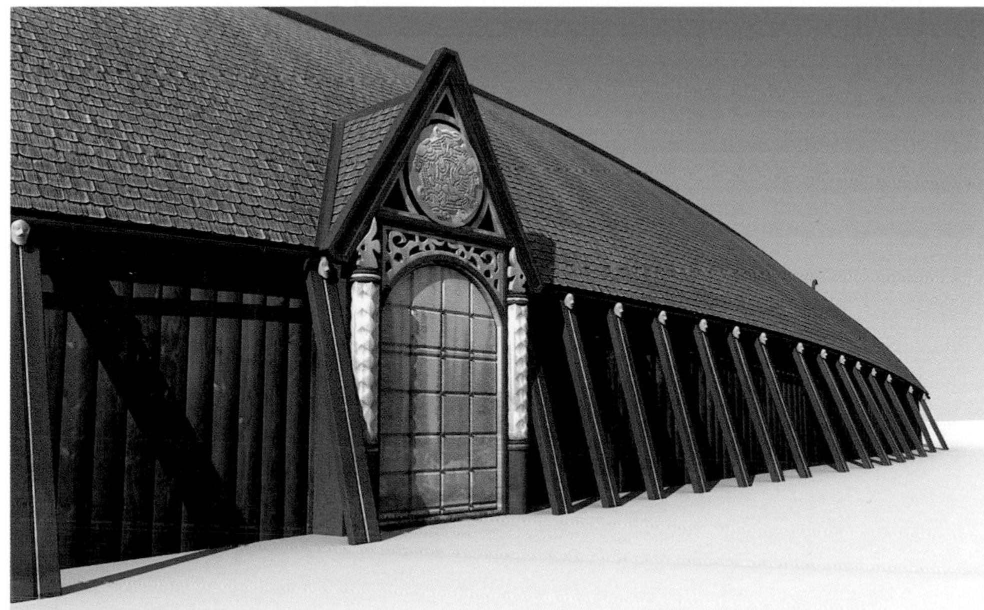

4.
Reconstruction of a hall excavated at Lejre in Zealand, Denmark.

5.
Replica of a decorated bed made of beech from the ship burial excavated at Oseberg, Vestfold in Norway, early 9th century.
Beech. L 2.2 m, W 1.9 m, H 1.59 m
Museum of Cultural History, University of Oslo, Oslo

Excavations at Tissø and Lejre further to the east in Zealand have revealed impressive central halls that were replaced on the same site over several generations, emphasizing a strong continuity in the status of these places and the families who controlled them. As found at Borg, the hall as a social and ritual space was often located under the same roof as the stable, but, particularly in eastern Scandinavia, separate halls were also built, some on artificial platforms, which created a powerful visual effect.[7] The grandeur of the building was probably enhanced by colour (fig. 4) and carvings like those surviving from the early wooden churches, and they would have been equipped with textiles and decorated furniture like the beds from the Norwegian ship burials at Oseberg and Gokstad (fig. 5).

The magnate farms in Viking-Age Scandinavia differed from the stone-built residential palaces and Pfalzes in neighbouring countries, but were no doubt in many ways inspired by

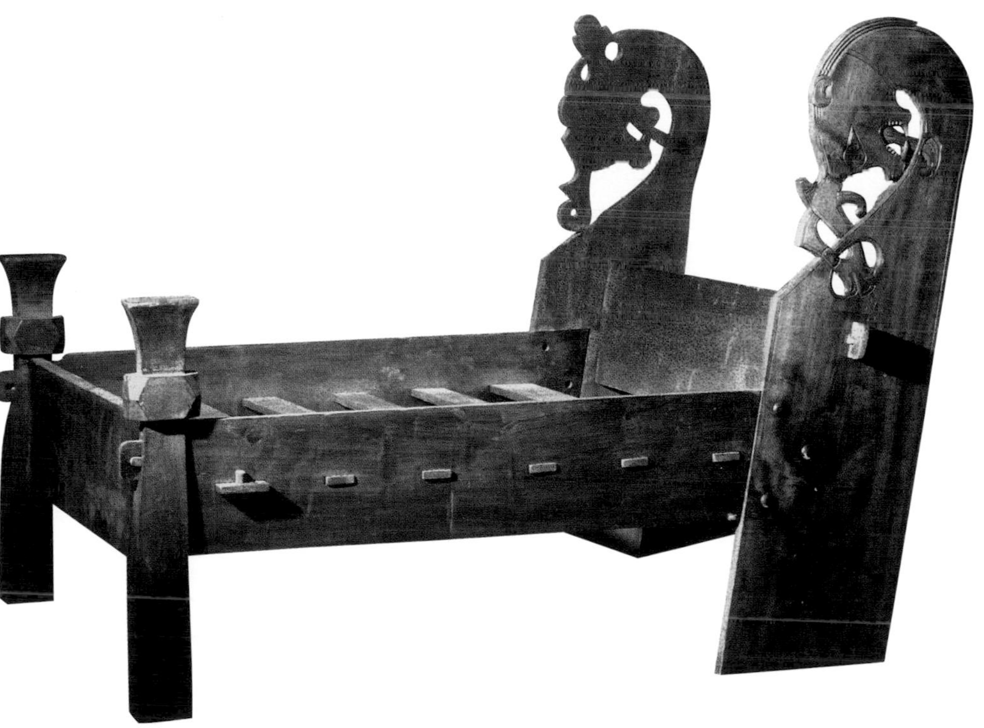

them and probably served similar functions (see p. 156). The architecture was adapted to the local environment and thus to the intended recipients of the statement implied by the buildings. The hall, whether separate or integrated with the main building of the farm, was a well-defined roofed space through which the owners could enforce their authority and position in society. Charlemagne's church in Aachen in Germany, commenced around the year 800, was considered a marvel. Contemporaries used the words *opere mirabili constructa* (a building of amazing workmanship), *mirae magnitudinis* (of admirable size) and *plurimae pulchritudinis* (remarkable beauty).[8] The same could no doubt be said of monuments and manors in Scandinavia, particularly the royal complex built in Jelling during the reign of King Harald Bluetooth. Here traditional architecture and monument types were developed and modified to create something amazing and impressive on a hitherto unseen scale, to which was added the memorial, of remarkable beauty and workmanship, to King Gorm and Queen Thyre.

Friends and allies

The maintenance of power and social bonds between equals or between lords and their retainers required access to resources, local and foreign. Generosity was a mark of the worthy ruler, and personal relations were both confirmed and visually demonstrated in the exchange and presentation of gifts – jewellery (figs 6–9), weapons, clothing or exotica of distant origin. Loyalty was rewarded and the gifts served as a constant reminder to all of the donor's wealth and status.

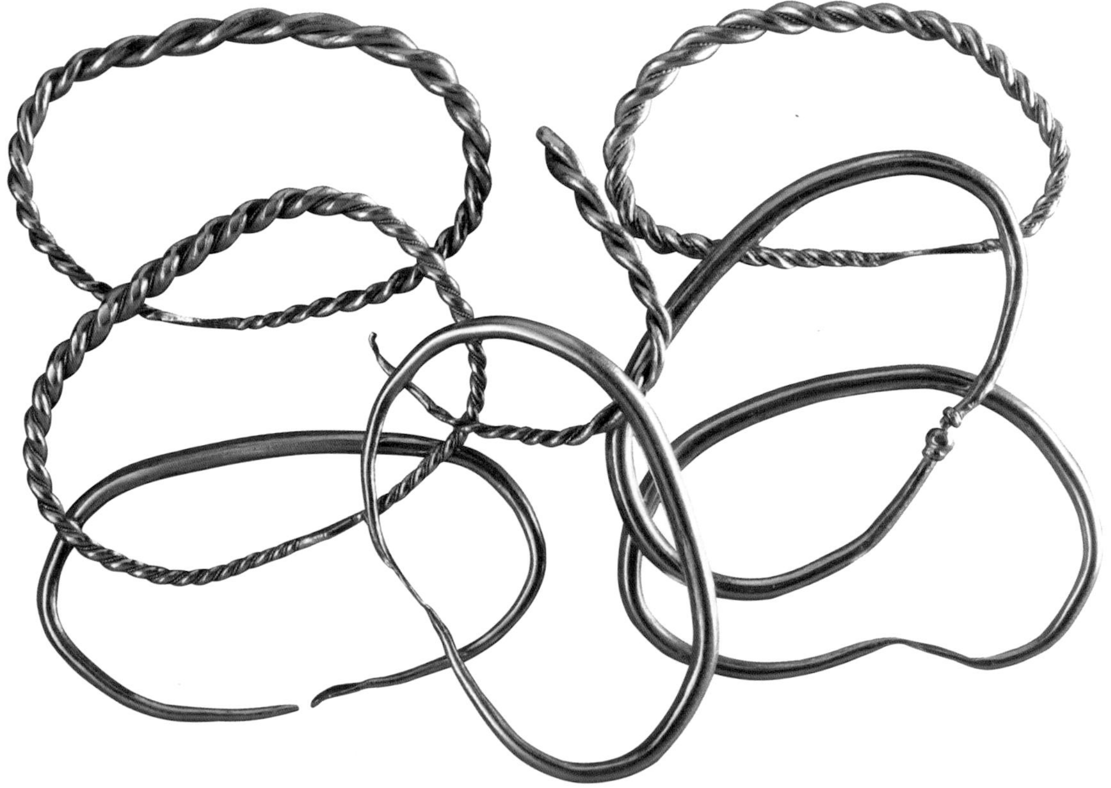

6.
Hoard of seven Scandinavian arm-rings and one fragment, 11th century. Peenemünde, Germany.
Gold.
Kulturhistorisches Museum der Hansestadt Stralsund, Stralsund

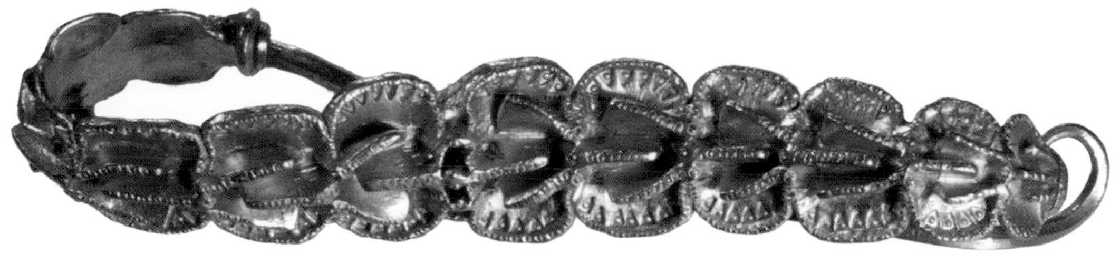

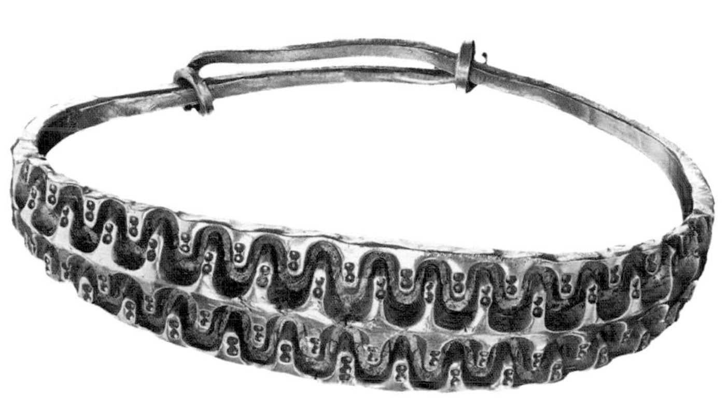

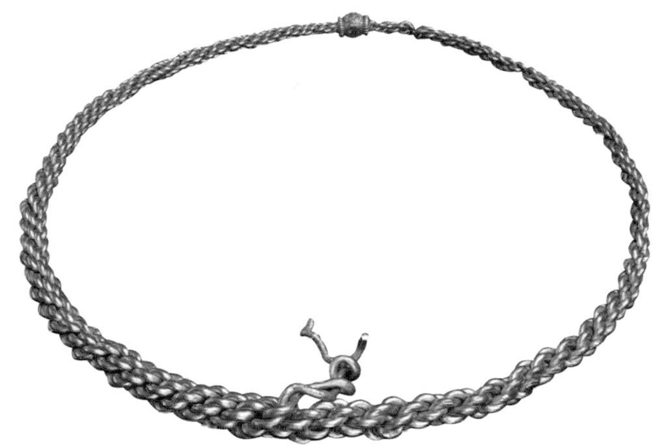

7. (top)
Arm-ring, 800–1050. Gevninge, Zealand, Denmark.
Gold. L 15 cm
National Museum of Denmark, Copenhagen

8. (above left)
Arm-ring, 800–850. Halleby, north-west Zealand, Denmark.
Gold. W 2 cm
National Museum of Denmark, Copenhagen

9. (above right)
Neck-ring, 10th century. Kalmergården, Tissø, Zealand, Denmark.
Gold. Diam. 35 cm
National Museum of Denmark, Copenhagen

By their clothing, their gold armlets
You see they are the king's friends.
They bear red cloaks, stained shields,
Silver-clad swords, ringed mailcoats,
Gilded sword-belts, engraved helmets,
Rings on their arms, as Harald gave them.
Haraldskvæði[9]

This praise poem to King Harald Finehair, who is said to have ruled all of Norway in the late ninth and early tenth centuries, records the regal generosity of the king and the magnificence of his retinue and royal court. King Harald counted other rulers among his friends and had spent time at their courts learning the manners and strategies of a king.

In his homage to the Carolingian emperor Louis the Pious, another poet, Ermoldus Nigellus, gives an account of the ritual proceedings and the gifts exchanged at the baptism of the Danish king Harald Klak in 826 at the court of Ingelheim (Mainz) in Germany (see p. 156).[10] The account begins with the arrival of the Danish king: 'Behold! A hundred ships came sailing down the Rhine, their fixed sails tied and gleaming; they were full of Danes, and of gifts too'. On his baptism King Harald received not only a magnificent sword and golden spurs but also a crown and costly robes including golden bands (*vincla*) for his arms. Harald's son and the rest of his retinue were given similar dress in Frankish style. No onlooker would have been in doubt of Harald's new status and the close relationship of his family to the emperor who (along with his own family) had stood sponsors at their baptism. Harald returned to his kingdom accompanied by priests and monks and with further gifts, including liturgical vessels and vestments.

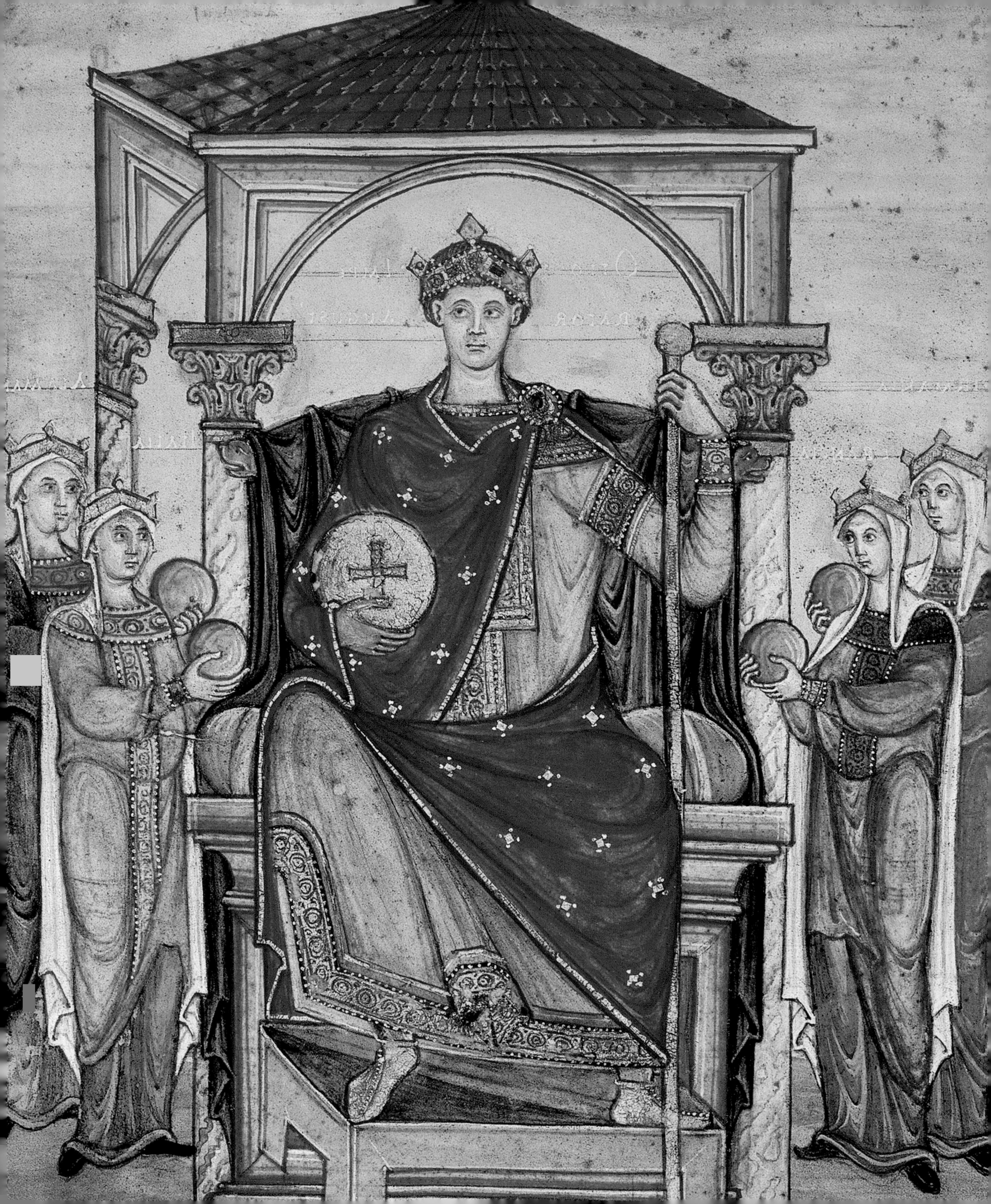

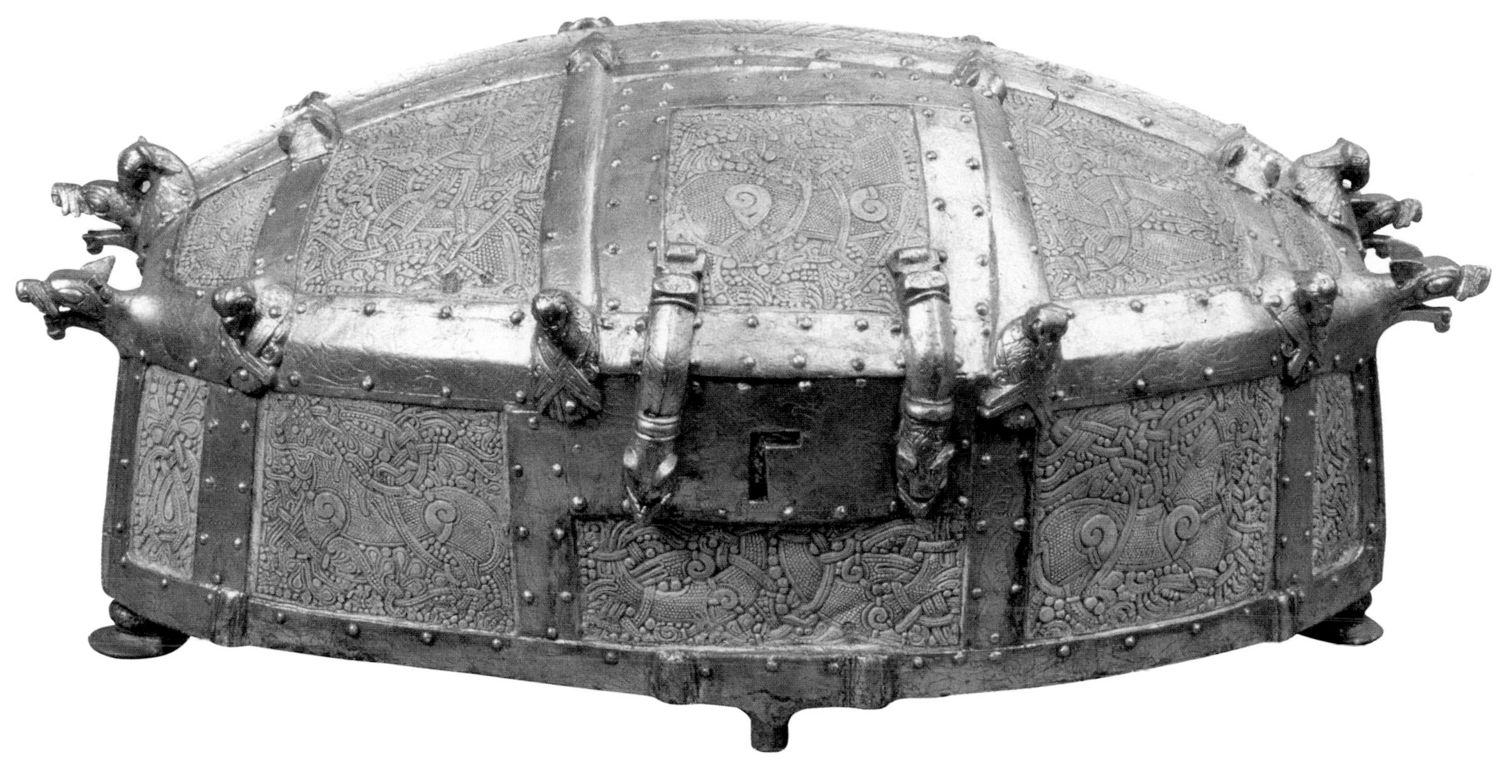

10.
The Holy Roman Emperor Otto II ruled over the area south of Denmark, including modern Germany and large parts of Italy, France and the Netherlands.

***Registrum Gregorii*, Trier, *c.* 983.**
Musée Condé, Chantilly, France

11.
Cammin casket, *c.* 1000 (replica; the original object, produced in Scandinavia, was destroyed during the Second World War). Kamień (Pomorski) Cathedral, Poland.
L 56.12 cm, W 35.24 cm
National Museum of Denmark, Copenhagen

King Harald's baptism may very well have been a political move. Ermoldus Nigellus describes him as someone who had already accepted Christianity, whereas Rimbert, the biographer of the missionary St Ansgar, says that the king had turned to Louis the Pious for help to regain his kingdom. The emperor persuaded Harald to undergo baptism to strengthen their mutual bond: if both sides worshipped the same God, one would more willingly help the other.[11]

The reception of political envoys and delegations from foreign powers formed a significant part of court life. Such delegations brought with them gifts (or tribute) and, to ensure their safe passage, personal credentials from their lord as recommendation and legitimation, while they in turn would receive gifts from their hosts. When the missionary Ansgar departed from Hedeby for the trading site of Birka in Sweden, the Danish king Horik gave him an escort and a hand sign.[12] It is not known what this sign was. However, three lead seals from Hedeby, Ribe and Tissø in Denmark shed light on the credentials used in the Byzantine empire in the early ninth century.[13] The inscriptions are identical and read, 'Mother of God, assist thy servant Theodosios *patrikios*, *basilikos protospatharios* and *chartoularios* of the *vestiarion*.' Theodosios was a high-ranking official in the Byzantine empire, responsible for weapons and supplies for the Byzantine armed forces. The seals (attached to official documents) may have been brought to Denmark by Theodosius himself or his delegates, and the trading sites of Hedeby and Ribe and the wealthy manor at Tissø would be obvious destinations where treaties for the supply of raw materials might be negotiated and possibly men recruited for the empire. One Theodosios Babutzicus is known to have travelled to Venice and as far north as the court of Lothar I in Trier between 840 and 842. Another Theodosios was in 839 a member of a delegation to the court of Louis the Pious in Ingelheim, his purpose to confirm a treaty of peace and perpetual friendship between Louis and the Byzantine emperor Theophilus, and to seek assistance for a group of 'Rhos', identified as people of the Swedes (Suconi), on their way home.[14]

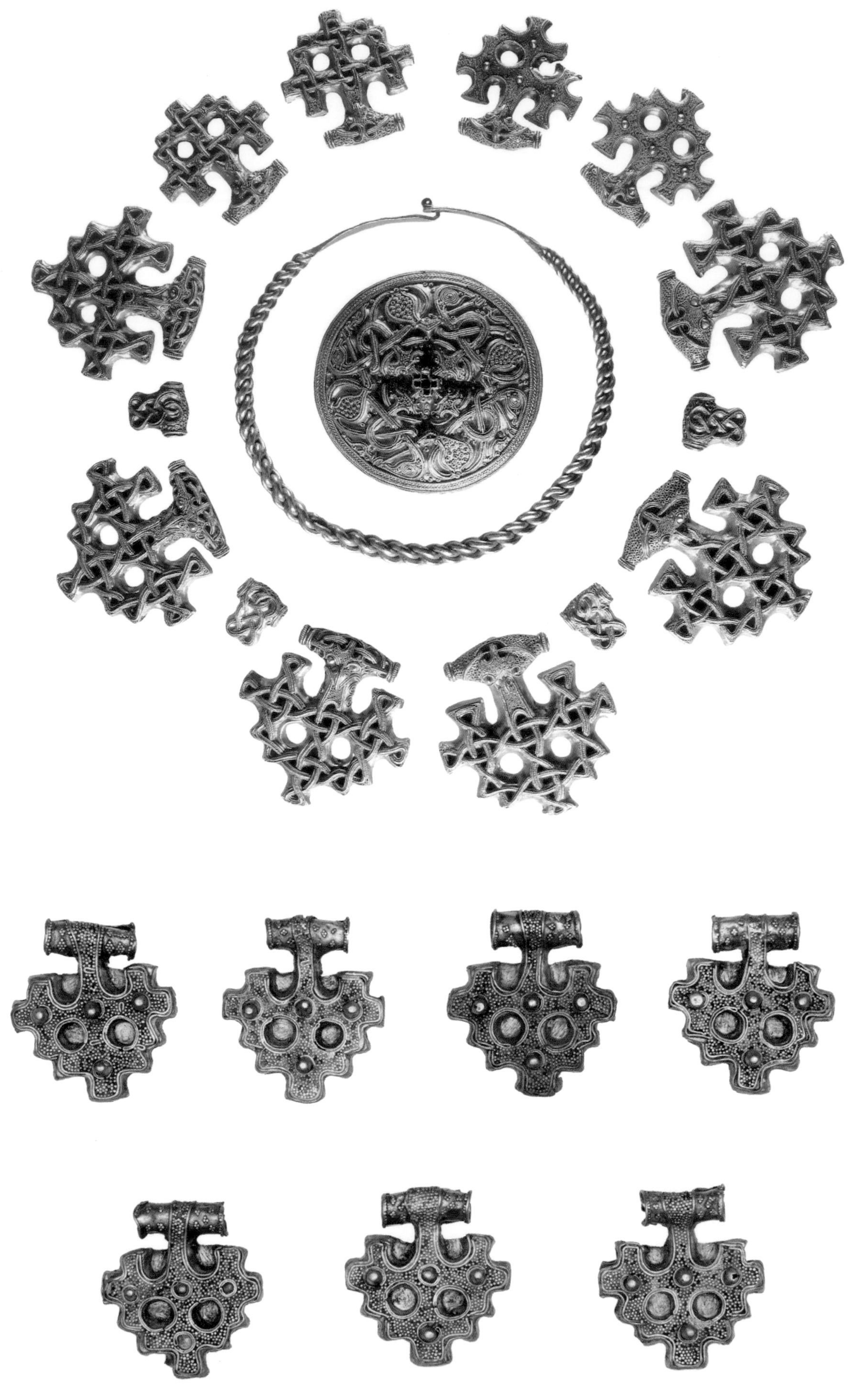

Later delegations from Scandinavia to western Europe and beyond are recorded in the chronicles of the royal courts and the Church. Among the guests noted by the chronicler Thietmar of Merseburg at the Easter celebration of the emperor Otto the Great (Otto I) (fig. 10) in March 973 in Quedlinburg, Germany are the dukes Mieszko I of Poland and Boleslaus II of Bohemia and delegates from the Greeks, Beneventans, Hungarians, Bulgarians, Danes and Slavs. The meeting was an opportunity to establish personal alliances that may have involved more or less directly formulated conditions and mutual obligations. Thietmar records that 'when all matters had been settled peacefully and gifts had been distributed, they went home satisfied.'[15] The nature of the gifts is not specified, but at a meeting in Gnesen in 1000, Otto III presented Bolesław I Chroby (the Brave, 967–1025), the first king of Poland, with a replica of the *sancta lancea* – a 51-centimetre-long Carolingian spearhead with an inserted iron point said to be a nail from the Cross of Christ. As a replica of the imperial relic, the gift was a powerful symbol and it was probably used as a royal insignia by the first rulers of the Piast dynasty in Poland.[16]

A number of high-quality works of art that have survived in European churches are examples of what the Scandinavian elite might have brought with them as gifts. Two magnificent caskets with carved panels of elk antler and walrus ivory were incorporated into the treasuries of Kamień Cathedral in Poland (fig. 11) and St Stephen's Church in Bamberg in Bavaria; a sword with guards of carved walrus ivory is kept in the St Vitus Cathedral in Prague, and a small antler reliquary with a lid of gilt copper alloy is in the church of San Isodoro in Léon, Spain.[17] The style of the carvings dates these objects to the second half of the tenth century, and they may have been commissioned by King Harald Bluetooth or his son Svein Forkbeard as part of their attempts to establish relationships and alliances with ruling powers, particularly in the periphery of the German empire.

According to a rune-stone at Sønder Vissing in east Jutland, Tove, the wife of King Harald, was the daughter of Mistivoi, prince of the Slavic Obodrites.[18] The connections of the royal family south of the Baltic were maintained by the next generation. Thietmar of Merseburg records that the first wife of Svein Forkbead was the daughter of Duke Mieszko I and sister to Mieszko's son and successor Bolesław I Chrobry;[19] one of Svein's daughters was married to a Slavic prince, possibly a grandson of Mistivoi. The royal family's connections may even have extended further east. More than a century ago, a set of gold ornaments was recovered on the island of Hiddensee, near Rügen off the northern coast of Germany (fig. 12). The ornaments – a neck-ring, a brooch, four small and six larger pendants, and four spacers – were probably made in Denmark in a royal workshop.[20] Seven identical cross pendants of the same type as those from Hiddensee but made of silver were found at the Mikhailovski monastery in Kiev as part of a large hoard of jewellery from the twelfth and thirteenth centuries (fig. 13).[21] The pendants may have been treasured by generations of a Kievan family, possibly as a memory of Scandinavian ancestors in their long-distant past.

The Danish ruling family was not alone in creating dynastic ties by means of marriage. This was common practice in both Scandinavia and the rest of Europe, and the status and aspirations of the elite and ruling families are reflected in the alliances they achieved. By the end of the Viking Age marriage ties extended across most of Europe. Like Harald Bluetooth and his son, the Swedish king Olof Skötkonung (995–1022) looked to the Slav region south of the Baltic for a wife while one of his daughters, Ingegerd, married Jaroslav I of Kiev, and the other, Astrid, married King Olaf II Haraldsson of Norway. The contemporary Ottonian emperors in Germany aimed higher. The first wife of Otto I (936–73) was Eadgyth (Edith) of England, daughter of Edward the Elder and granddaughter of Alfred the Great, and his second wife was Adelheid (Adelaide) of Italy; Otto II (974–83) married Theophanu, a Byzantine princess related to Emperor John I Tzimiskes (969–76), and Princess Zoe, second daughter of Emperor Constantine VIII (1025–8), was on her way to marry Otto III when he died in 1002.

12.
Hoard of fourteen filigree pendants, spacers, brooch and neck-ring, probably made in Denmark, late 10th century. Neuendorf/Hiddensee, Rügen, Germany.
Gold.
Kulturhistorisches Museum der Hansestadt Stralsund, Stralsund

13.
Seven filigree cross pendants of Scandinavian style, 10th century, part of a hoard dating from the 12th or 13th century. Mikhailovski monastery, Kiev, Ukraine.
Silver. H 4.0, W 3.6 cm
State Historical Museum, Moscow

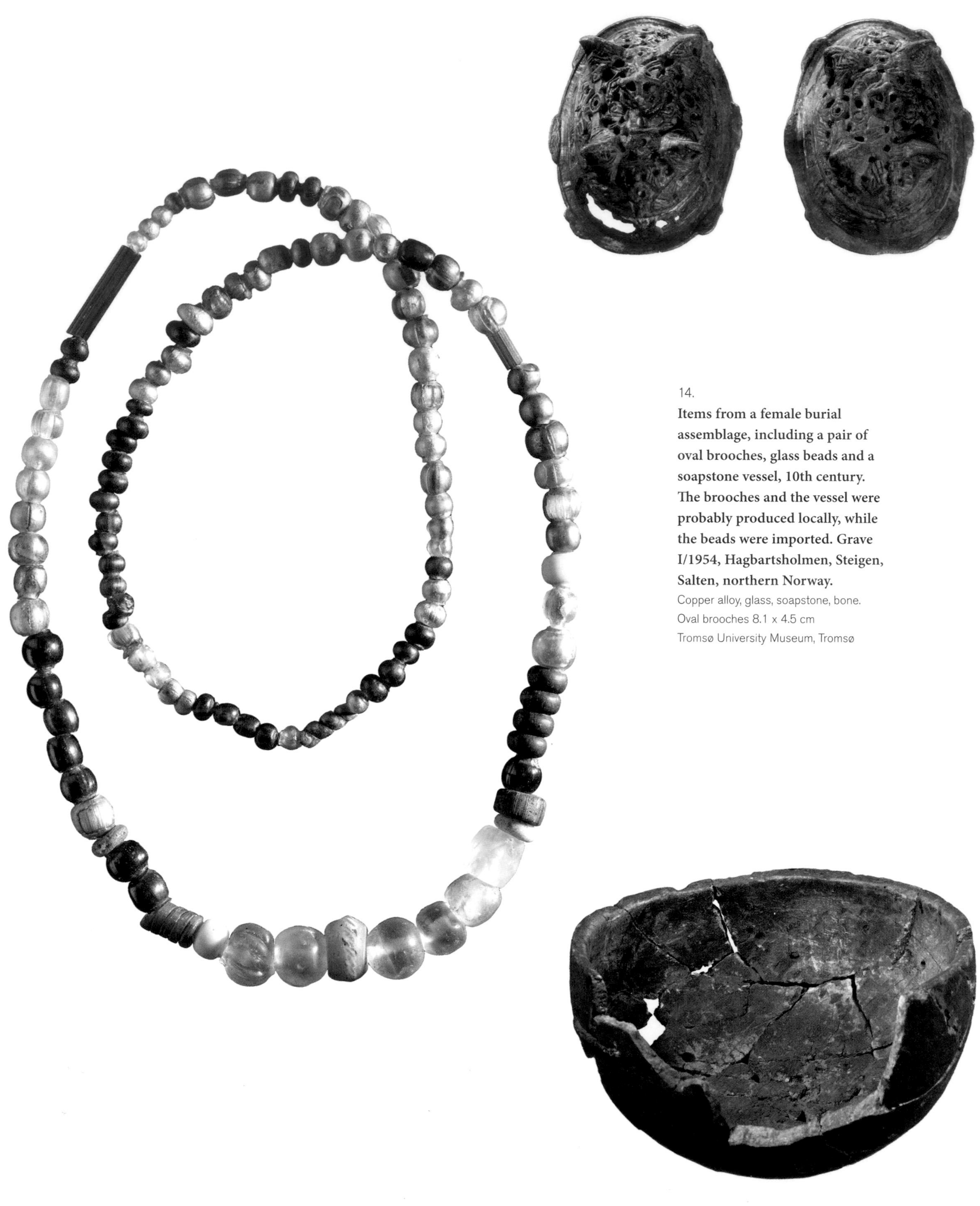

14.

Items from a female burial assemblage, including a pair of oval brooches, glass beads and a soapstone vessel, 10th century. The brooches and the vessel were probably produced locally, while the beads were imported. Grave I/1954, Hagbartsholmen, Steigen, Salten, northern Norway.

Copper alloy, glass, soapstone, bone.
Oval brooches 8.1 x 4.5 cm
Tromsø University Museum, Tromsø

Fostering was another means of acquiring allies and ensuring peaceful relations. When King Harald Klak left the court of Louis the Pious, his son and a nephew remained to serve Louis and to learn to observe Frankish laws.[22] It is said that as part of a peace agreement, the Norwegian king Håkon (934–61) was brought up as a Christian at the court of King Athelstan of England, earning him the nickname *Aðalsteins fóstri* (Athelstan's foster-son).[23] A later king of Norway, Magnus the Good (1035–47), had been forced with his father Olaf II and English mother Alfhild to flee in exile to *Garðariki* (the land of the Kievan Rūs), from where he was brought back and proclaimed king at the age of eleven.[24] Far from home, these young boys and men would have learned the customs and languages of other people in preparation for their own future.

Communicating power

Magnificent ships and great halls promised fame and prestige while illustrating the power of those who built them. No less impressive statements of power and wealth are the monuments raised for the dead. The North Mound in Jelling, measuring more than 60 metres in diameter, is among the largest from the Viking Age, built at a time when Christianity was gaining ground and simple burial was gradually becoming common practice. Numerous mounds and rich burials are known elsewhere in Scandinavia, among

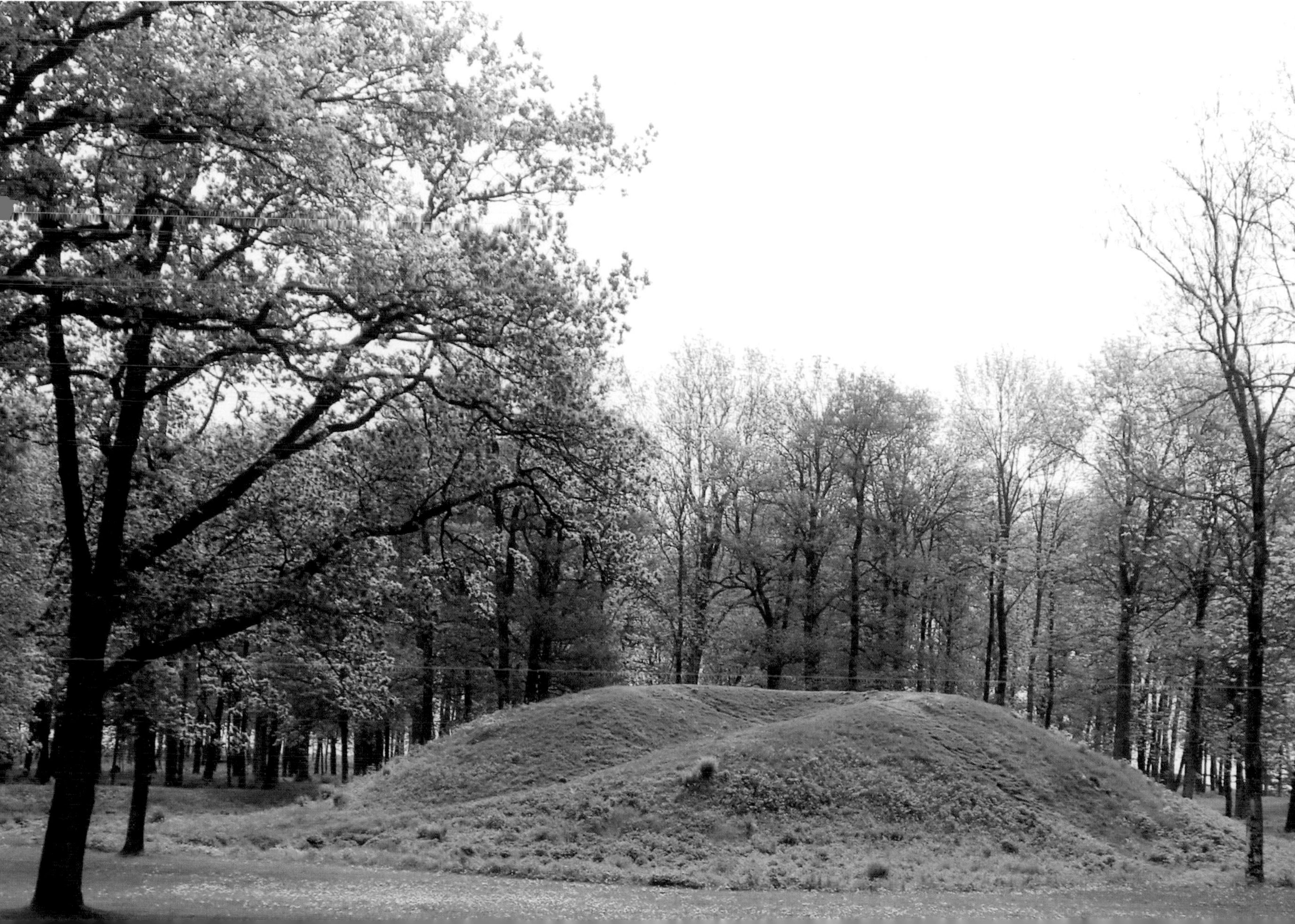

15.
Burial mound at Borre in Vestfold, Norway. The depression in the large mound is evidence of an early break-in.

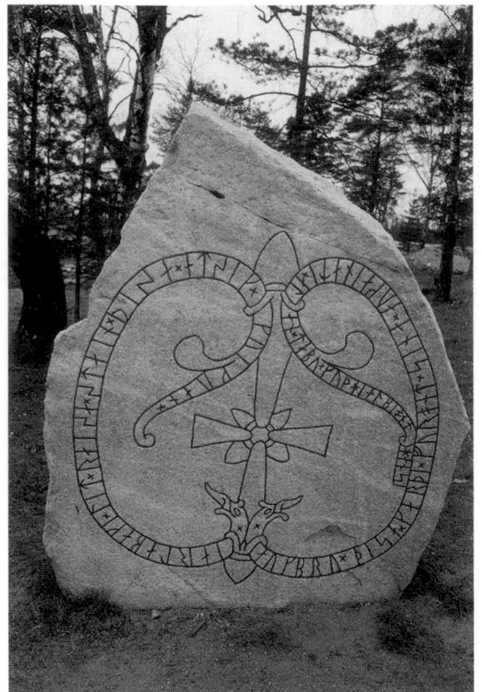

16.
One of Jarlabanke's four rune-stones raised at the end of a 150-metre-long causeway at Täby, Uppland in Sweden.

them the ship burials of Oseberg and Gokstad in Norway, Ladby in Denmark, the boat chamber grave at Hedeby in Germany, and the boat burials at Vendel and Välsgärde in Uppland, Sweden, all containing a wealth of furnishings, which offer a glimpse of the material culture available to these families (fig. 14)

After a mound was closed the contents could no longer be seen, but the funeral as an event could be recalled for years thereafter, and the monument remained as a visual testimony of what had taken place.[25] This, however, did not protect a burial from intrusion. Depressions at the top of numerous burial mounds bear witness to later plundering, sometimes only a few years or decades after the funeral (fig. 15). When the break-in took place at Ladby, the burial area was probably still free of earth. Many of the contents of the grave were removed while other objects were deliberately destroyed before being put back into the ship.[26] Rather than a random act of treasure hunting, this and other robberies give the impression of being dramatic, staged events carried out in full daylight. Dendrochronological dating[27] of wooden spades and stretchers left by the intruders at Oseberg and Gokstad has established that the two ship burials, although about seventy years apart (from 834 and *c.* 900–905), were most likely both broken into in the second half of the tenth century, at a time when political opponents, among them the Danish king Harald Bluetooth, all sought to gain control over Norway.[28] In this context, the destruction of the monuments may be viewed as a planned political act intended to weaken the opponent while demonstrating the power and authority of the one responsible.

Rune-stones commemorate both the dead and the living, many stressing the heroic deeds of the deceased and not least their travels to distant places. Most rune-stones were raised in Sweden, particularly in the eleventh century, and the name England occurs almost as often as that of Greece. Gudmar in Spånga, Södermanland had travelled west, his memorial stating that 'He stood like a man in the stem of the ship. He lies in the west ... '.[29] An additional (if indirectly voiced) purpose of many rune-stones appears to have been to

Arm-ring and finger rings of Scandinavian design from Britain.

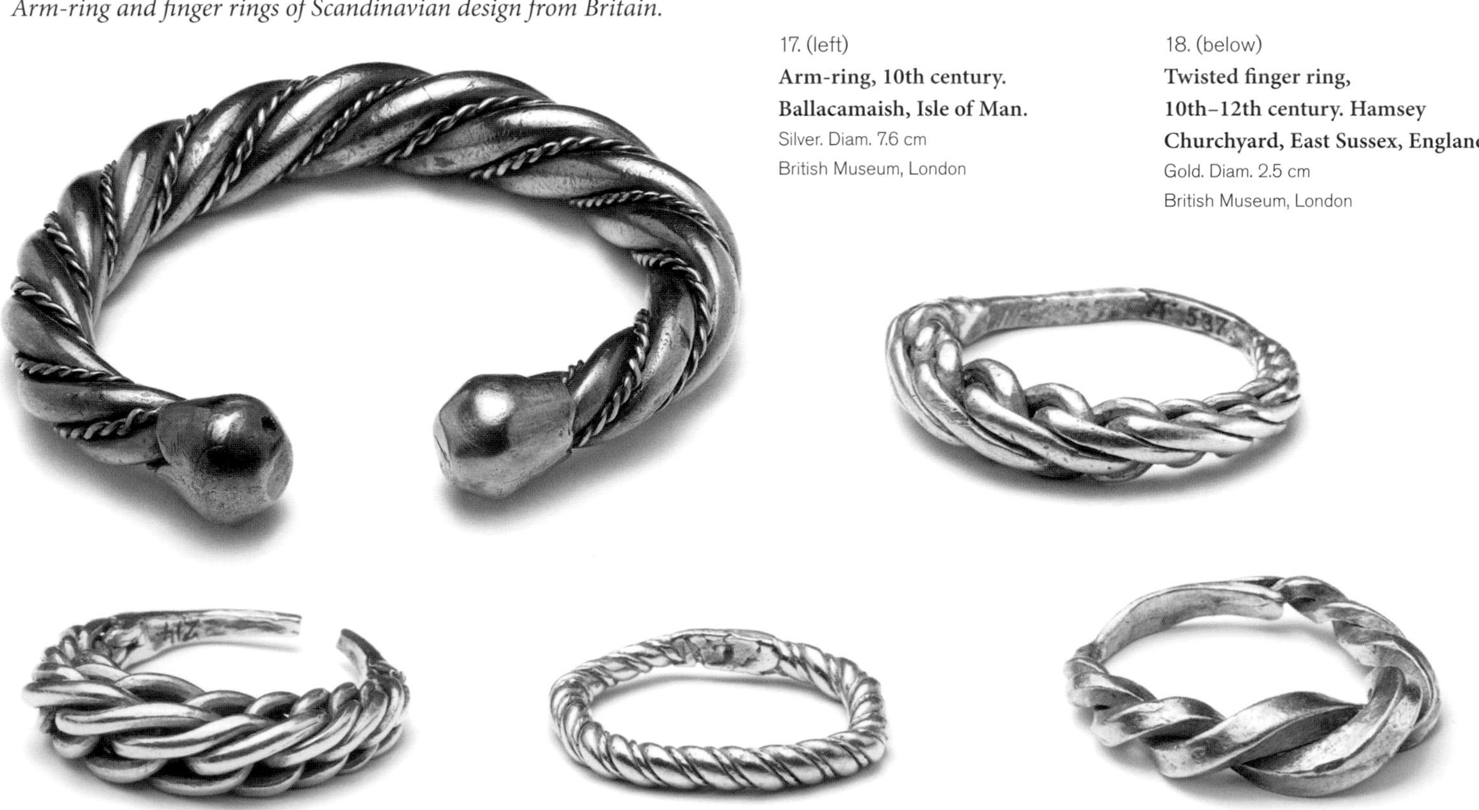

17. (left)
Arm-ring, 10th century. Ballacamaish, Isle of Man.
Silver. Diam. 7.6 cm
British Museum, London

18. (below)
Twisted finger ring, 10th–12th century. Hamsey Churchyard, East Sussex, England.
Gold. Diam. 2.5 cm
British Museum, London

Decorated axeheads in contrasting Danish and eastern Baltic styles.

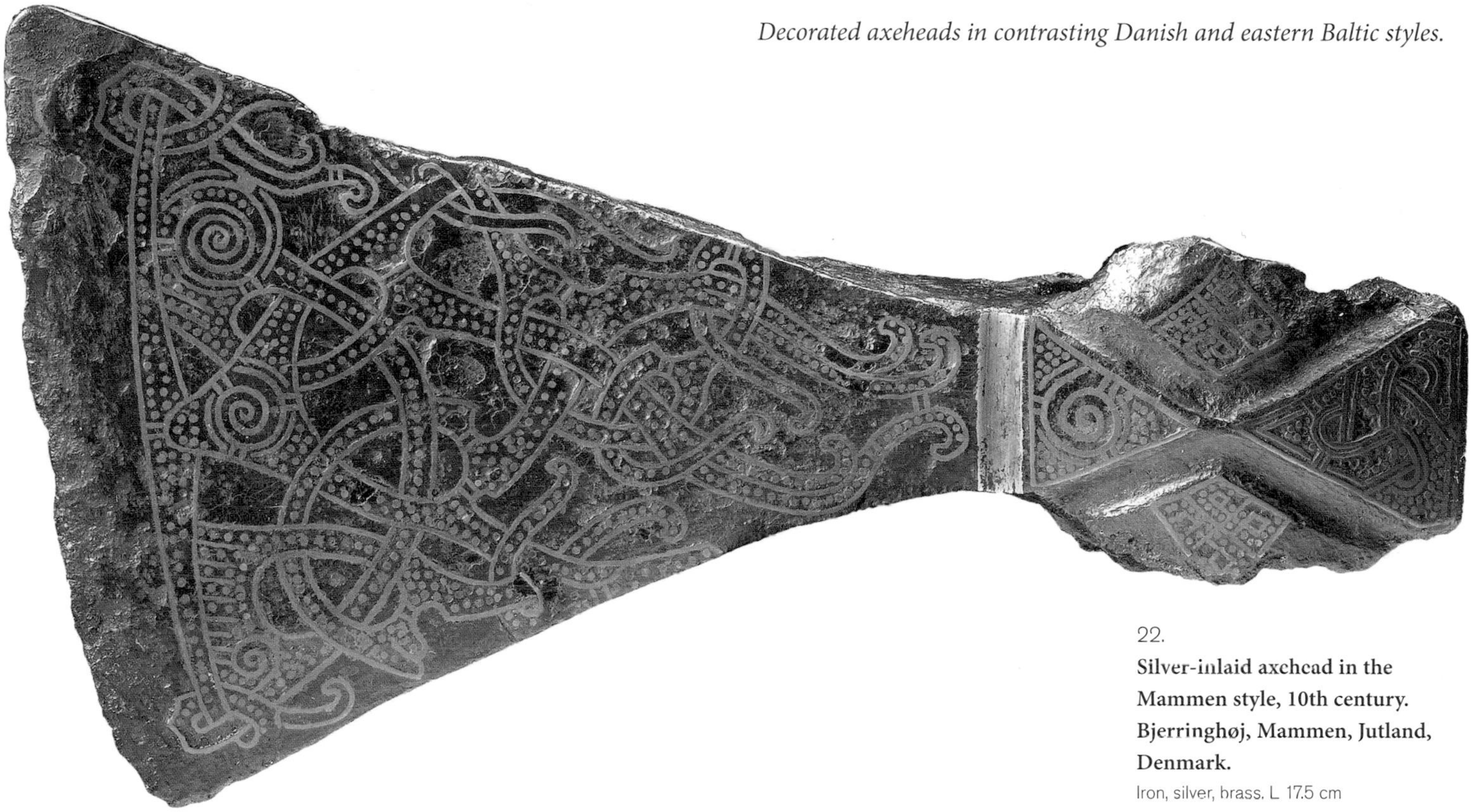

22.
Silver-inlaid axehead in the Mammen style, 10th century. Bjerringhøj, Mammen, Jutland, Denmark.
Iron, silver, brass. L 17.5 cm
National Museum of Denmark, Copenhagen

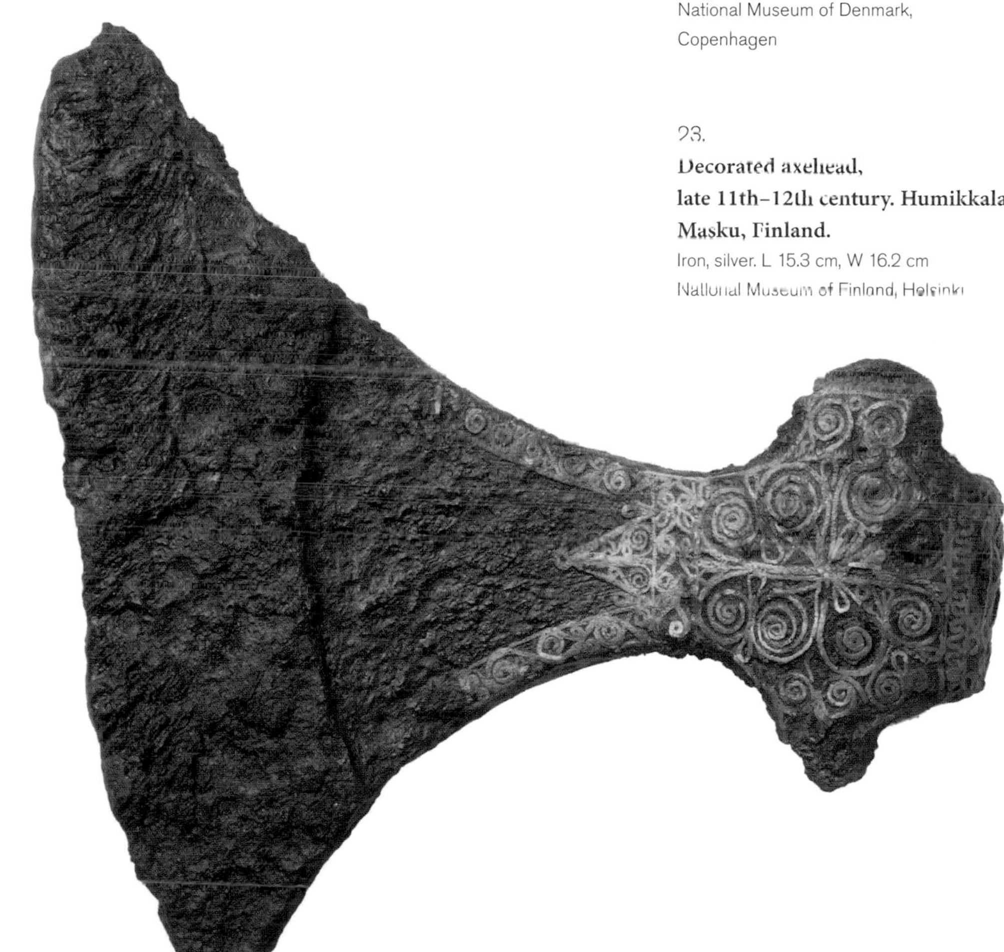

23.
Decorated axehead, late 11th–12th century. Humikkala, Masku, Finland.
Iron, silver. L 15.3 cm, W 16.2 cm
National Museum of Finland, Helsinki

19. (opposite, bottom left)
Plaited finger ring, 10th–12th century. St Aldates Church, Oxford, Oxfordshire, England.
Gold. Diam. 2.6 cm
British Museum, London

20. (opposite, bottom middle)
Twisted finger ring, 10th–12th century. Weston Turville, Buckinghamshire, England.
Gold. Diam. 2.0 cm
British Museum, London

21. (opposite, bottom right)
Twisted, square-section finger ring, 10th–12th century. East Sussex, England.
Gold. Diam. 3 cm
British Museum, London

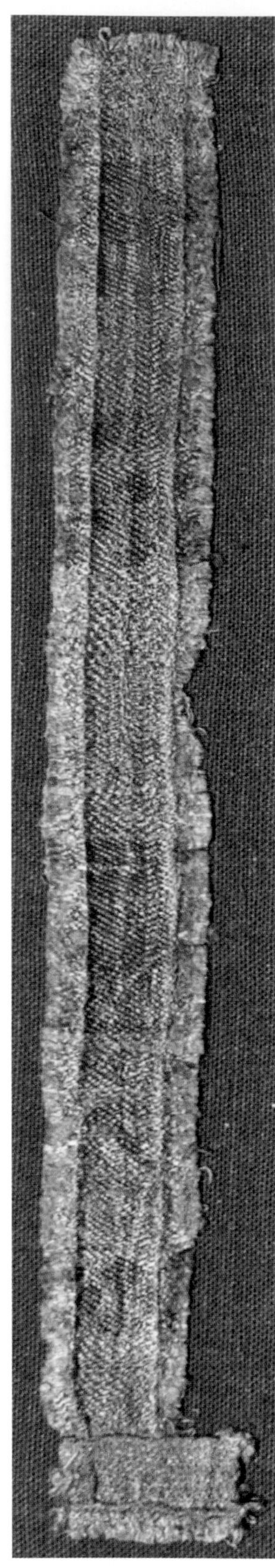

25.
Fragment of Persian silk, early 9th century. Oseberg, Vestfold, Norway.
Museum of Cultural History, University of Oslo, Oslo

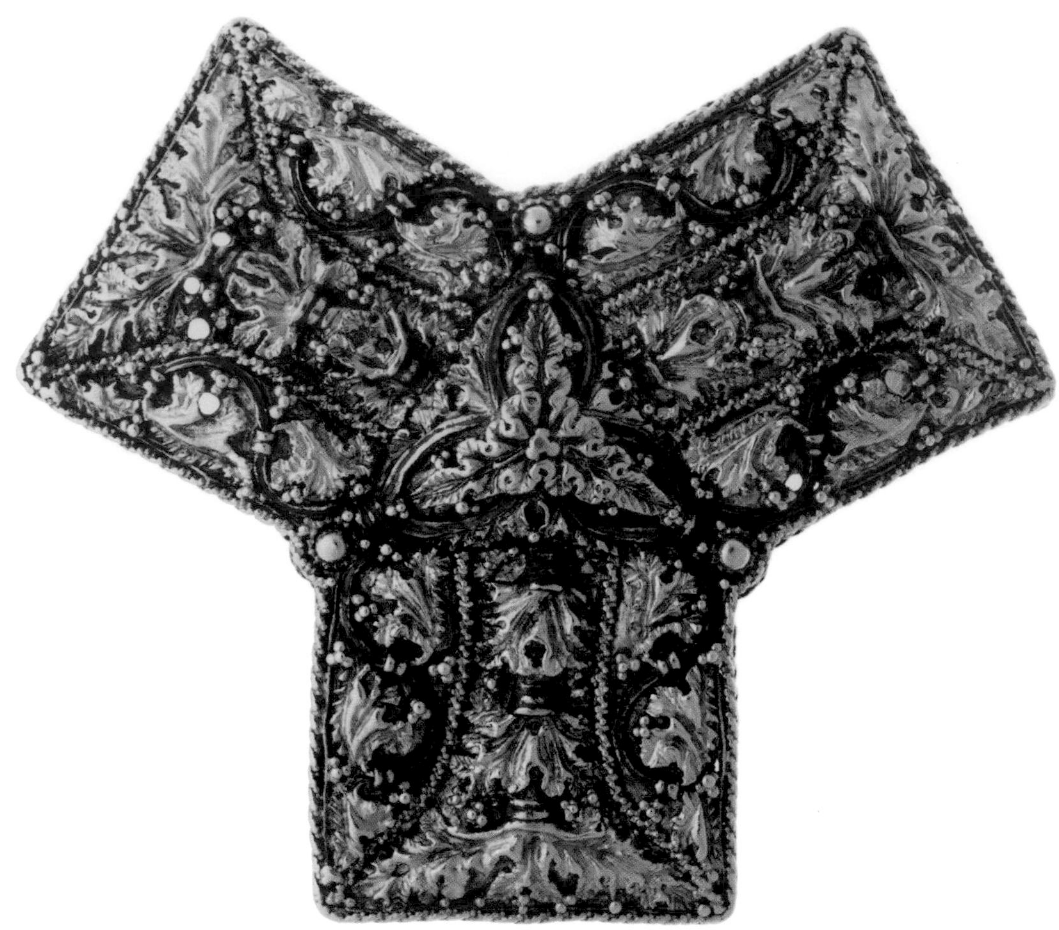

secure the inheritance and the rights to succession of the person who commissioned them. A rune-stone raised by Kår and Kabbe at Ulunda in Sweden honours the deceased with the words: 'He went boldly, wealth he won, out in Greece for his heir.'[30]

As a rule the runic inscriptions follow a fixed pattern in naming the person who commissioned the stone first, just as King Harald Bluetooth did on the large rune-stone in Jelling. Although on a smaller scale, the monument set up by Jarlabanke of Täby in southern Uppland, Sweden, is equally impressive as an unusual testimony to the status of a living man (fig. 16). The inscriptions of four almost identical rune-stones boast that 'Jarlabanke had these stones raised in memory of himself in his lifetime. And he made this bridge for his soul. And alone he owned the whole of Täby. God help his soul.' Jarlabanke's ancestors and his two sons are known from other rune-stones, which leave no doubt that this was a family of substance and high self-esteem.[31]

The status that an individual might achieve through personal qualities, social position and wealth, whether inherited or acquired through their own efforts, was enhanced by valuable clothing, finely worked jewellery made of precious metals (figs 17–21), and weapons (figs 22–23) and horse furnishings of exceptional quality, all of which are known from a multitude of archaeological finds. Families and individuals visually expressed the elements of other societies and cultures that they thought were desirable through the deliberate use of foreign and exotic objects (fig. 24).

Among the most highly valued luxury goods were costly textiles, either traded or obtained by other means. Exclusive items of clothing might be given in payment for services

24. (opposite)
Trefoil strap-distributors were an element of Carolingian military equipment. Their fine workmanship and cultural associations made them desirable objects, and they were often adapted or their style copied.

Frankish trefoil strap-distributor adapted for use as a brooch, 9th century. Hon, Buskerud, Norway.
Gold, silver. Max. W 9.7–11.0 cm; pin L 8.5 cm
Museum of Cultural History, University of Oslo, Oslo

26. (top left)
Ball-penannular brooch, 900–950. Flusco Pike, near Penrith, Cumbria, England.
Silver. L 26 cm, Diam. 7.4 cm
British Museum, London

27. (top right)
Ball-penannular brooch, 10th century. Gorodilovo, Vitebskaya Obl., Russia.
Silver, gold. L 12.9 cm, Diam. 11.1 cm
State Historical Museum, Moscow

28. (centre)
Ball-penannular brooch, 10th century. Rønvika, Bodin, Salten, Norway.
Silver. L 46 cm, Diam. 19.5 cm
Tromsø University Museum, Tromsø.

29. (bottom left)
Ball-penannular brooch with engraved terminals and pinhead, 10th century. Skaill, Sandwick, Orkney.
Silver. L 36 cm, Diam. 20 cm
National Museums Scotland, Edinburgh

30. (bottom right)
Bossed penannular brooch, late 9th–early 10th century. Near Virginia, Co. Cavan, Ireland.
Silver. L 20.3 cm, W 11.5 cm
National Museum of Ireland, Dublin

Large penannular brooches of types originally developed by Vikings in the Irish Sea area were adopted in Scandinavia and further east.

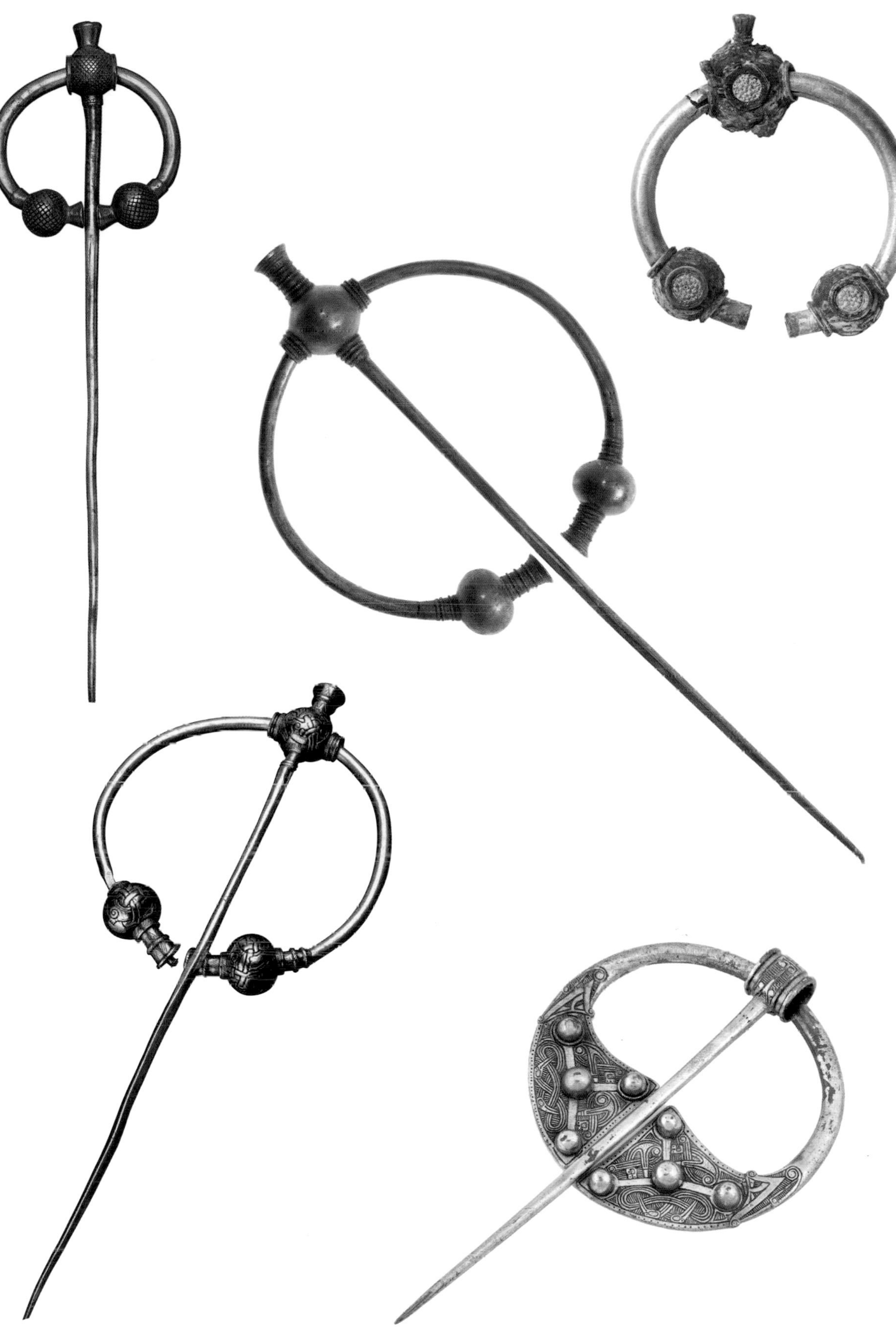

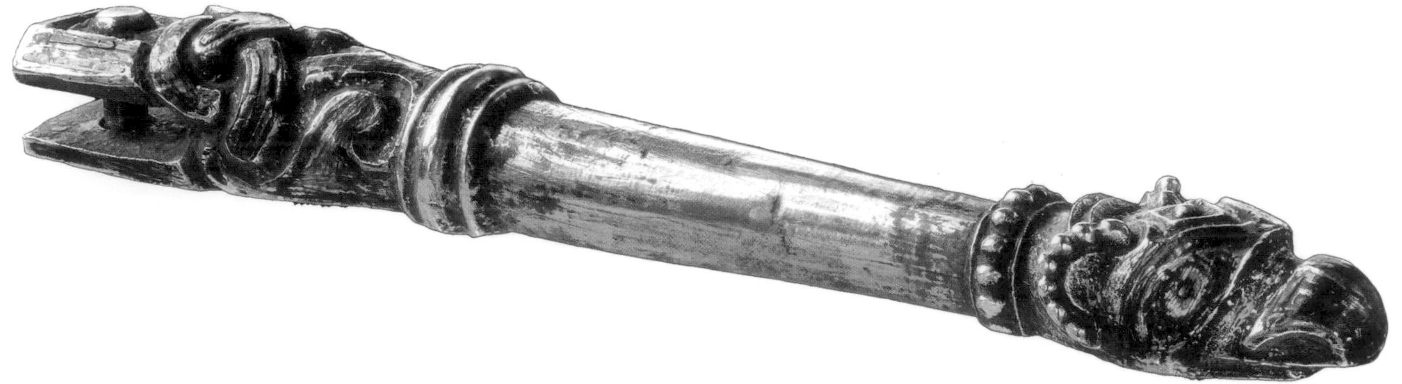

31.
Strap-end in the Jellinge style, 10th century. Anneksgården, Lille Fuglede, Zealand, Denmark.
Silver with niello. L 6.44 cm
National Museum of Denmark, Copenhagen

or donated as gifts on special occasions. According to Egil's saga, Egil Skalla-Grimsson received two gold rings and a mantle during his stay at the court of the English king Athelstan, in payment for his services to the king as a poet.[32] Additional honour is implied by the fact that the king himself had worn the mantle. When later visiting Arinbjörn, Egil received new clothing of English cloth in many colours and a cloak of silk with gold edgings and gold buttons, this time made to measure.[33] Like other organic material, textiles rarely survive in the ground for long. However, fragments of wool and silk have been recovered from water-logged layers in settlements, and a number of burials contain remains of high-quality woollen weaves, tablet-woven bands with silver and gold thread, and imported silk (fig. 25) and fur. The textiles have lost most of their original colour but in reconstruction they are bright and colourful, attesting to the wealth and status of the owner.[34]

A variety of dress accessories added to the visual impression given by textiles and furs. Men's cloaks were fastened on the shoulder with large brooches. Fashions merged and hybrid forms were introduced as a result of interaction between cultures. Long-pinned brooches typical of Irish and English dress fashion (figs 26–30) were copied and adapted, especially in Norway and Denmark, while other types with shorter pins but equally large rings were more popular further east in Scandinavia. In addition to cloak fasteners, men might also wear belts with metal buckles decorated in the prevailing style of the day (figs 31–32).

Scandinavian women wore dresses fastened with sets of identical brooches of copper alloy, the most common being oval in shape. Finds from the areas visited and settled by Scandinavians show that travelling women brought the fashion with them, the distinctive dress forming a link to their homelands and origins. The twin brooches were combined with a third brooch for the cloak and with other personal ornaments, such as necklaces with beads of glass, cornelian, rock crystal and silver. The status of the housewife was shown in the keys to storage rooms, chests and caskets that were suspended from her belt or a chatelaine (figs 33–35).

32.
Pair of Frankish knee-strap buckles and strap-ends, 900–950. Grave 1058, Lejre, Zealand, Denmark.
Gilt copper alloy. Buckles L 4.3 cm, 4.2 cm; strap-ends L 3.6 cm, 3.5 cm
National Museum of Denmark, Copenhagen

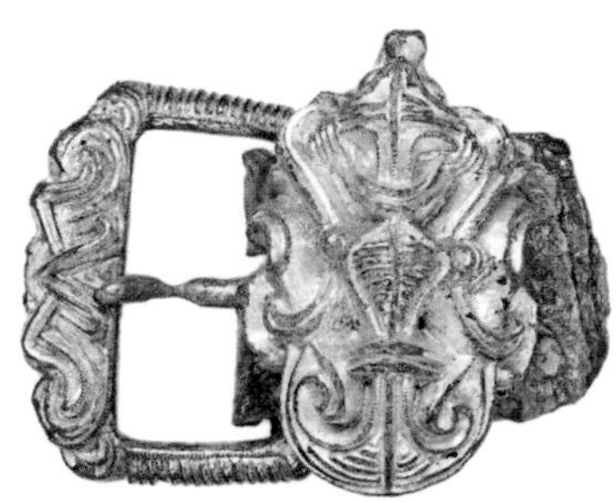

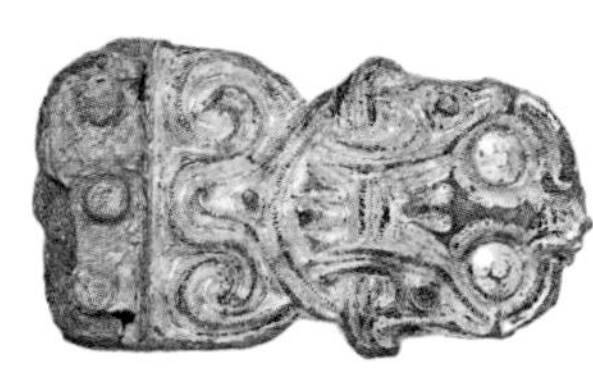

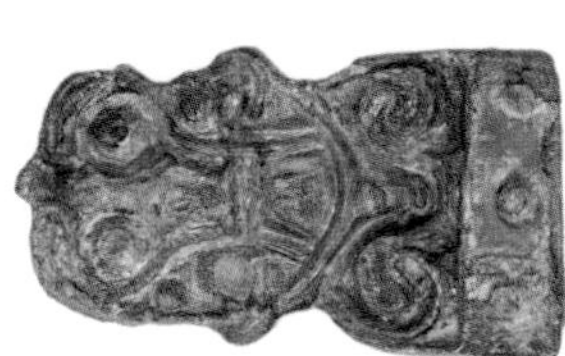

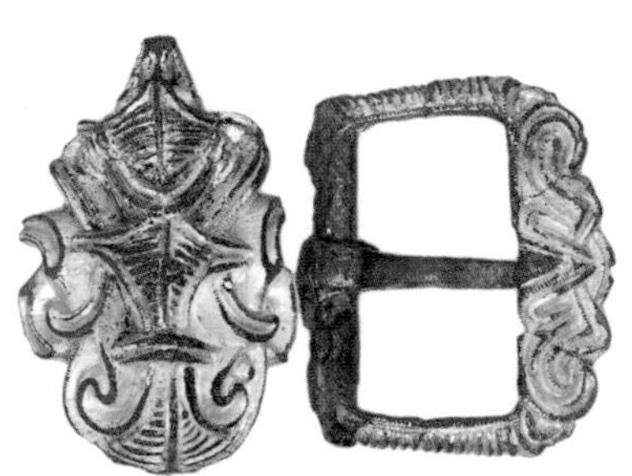

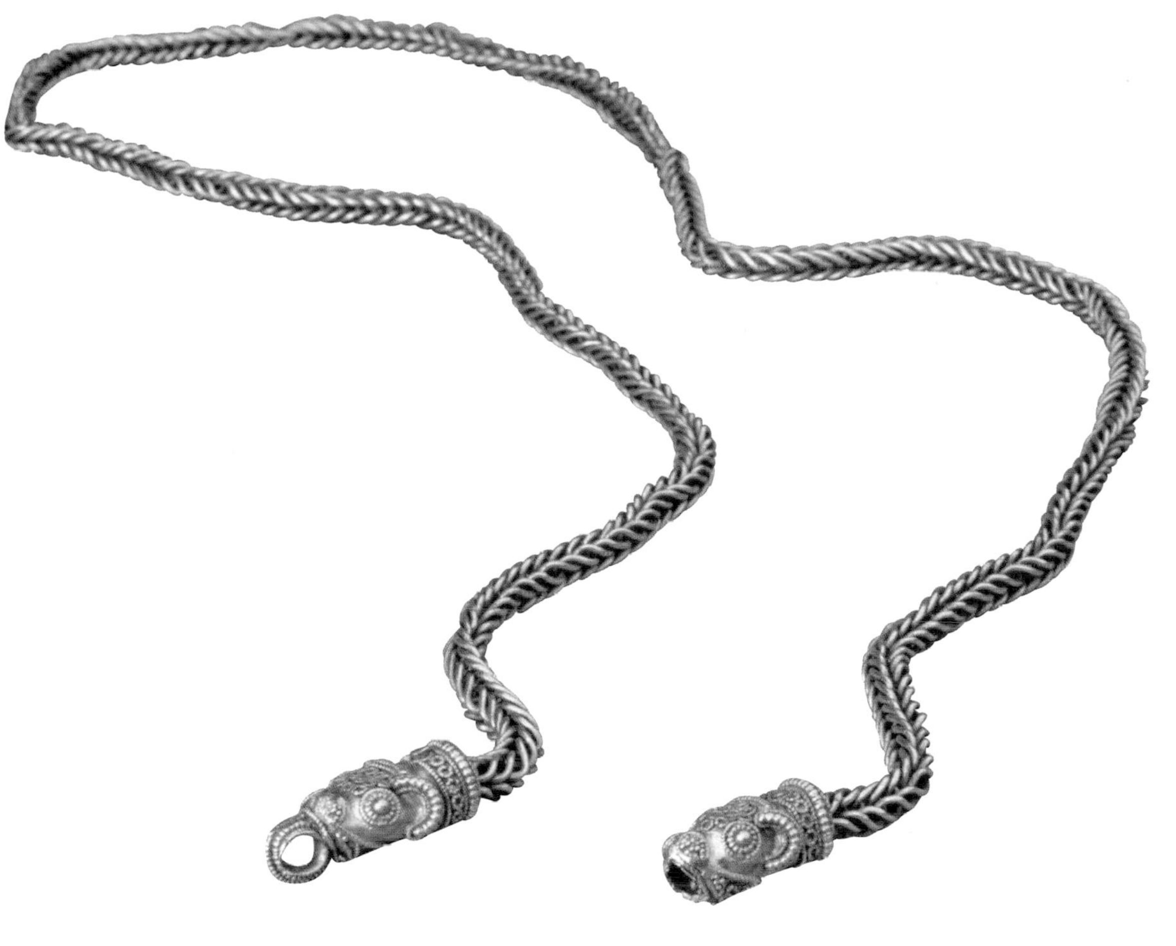

33. (left)
Women wore decorative chatelaines (belt fittings from which chains were attached) that could suspend keys and items used for personal grooming.

Chain with animal head terminals in the Jellinge style, 10th century. Fæsted, west Jutland, Denmark.
Gold. L 62 cm
National Museum of Denmark, Copenhagen

36. (below)
Filigree – a metalwork technique that involves the use of small beads and twisted wire threads – became popular in Scandinavia as a result of influence from the Carolingian and Ottonian empires.

Brooch with attached wire ring, 950–1000. Sperrestrup, Zealand, Denmark.
Gold. Diam. 4.57 cm
National Museum of Denmark, Copenhagen

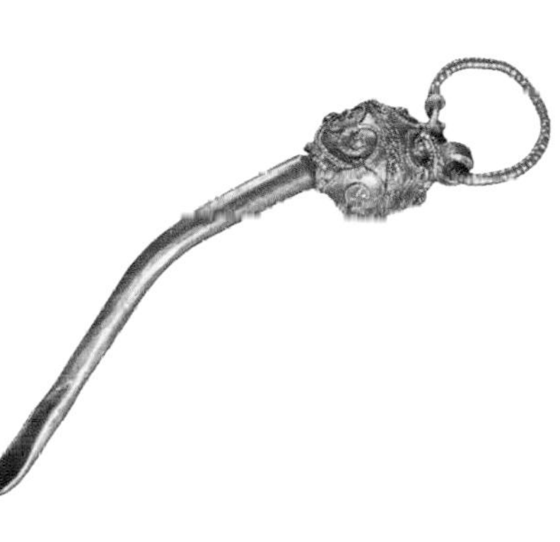

34.
Objects such as this gold ear spoon would have been worn on a belt or chatelaine.

Ear spoon with filigree terminal and suspension ring, 10th century. Gedehaven, south-west Zealand, Denmark.
Gold. L 5.4 cm
National Museum of Denmark, Copenhagen

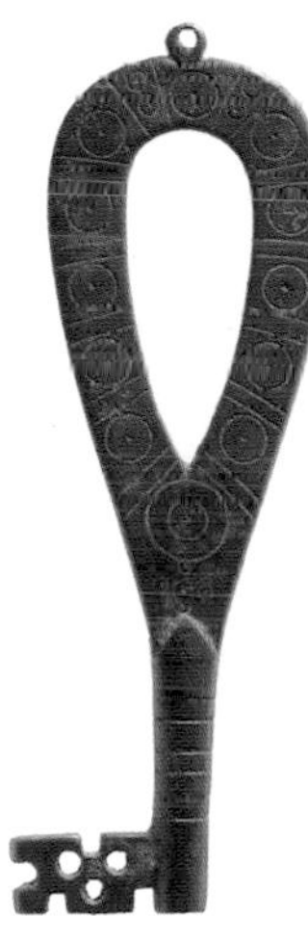

35.
This key would have been suspended from a belt or chatelaine, 800–1050.
Bronze. L 15 cm
British Museum, London

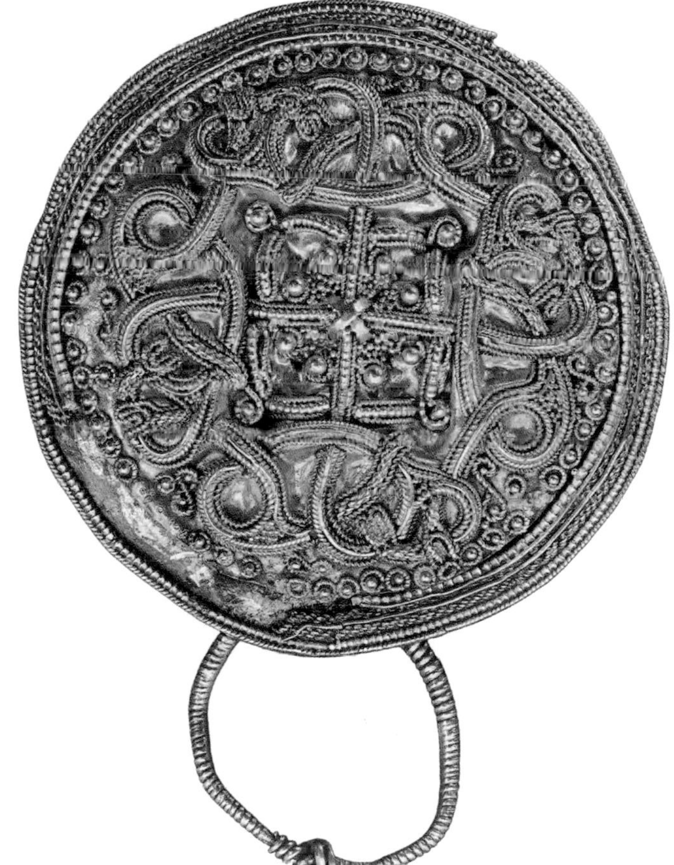

In the course of the tenth century, high-status women gradually abandoned their traditional costume in favour of western European dress after the fashion of the Carolingian and later Ottonian courts, a development parallel to that seen in the Saxon area of Germany in the ninth century after the conquest by Charlemagne (fig. 36).[35] Like their men, these women presumably took over many of the norms and values of their foreign counterparts, probably including the Christian religion as suggested by silver pendant crosses recovered from a few burials of the tenth century. The dress of men and women might also include rings of precious metal, but these are rarely found in burials. Presumably they belonged to the family wealth, to be melted down if need be or handed down and reused from generation to generation.

The good life

The grand halls of the elite and wealthy formed a setting for important events accompanied by music and speeches, recitations of poems composed in honour of the host and guests, board games and other amusements. Such banquets and feasts often entailed far more than just serving food and drink to friends and honoured guests; they were filled with subtle meaning and assumed the nature of a ritual or ceremony in which friendships were confirmed, whether real or assumed for the occasion, and former enemies might be reconciled, if only for a short while, in the sharing of food and drink.[36]

Great care was taken in the staging of a banquet, apparently no less so in the afterlife than in the world of the living. *Eíriksmál*, the funeral ode composed for King Erik Bloodaxe (d. 954) of Norway and Northumbria, describes the preparations necessary to receive a king who is called to take his place upon death in battle among Odin's warriors in Valhöll.

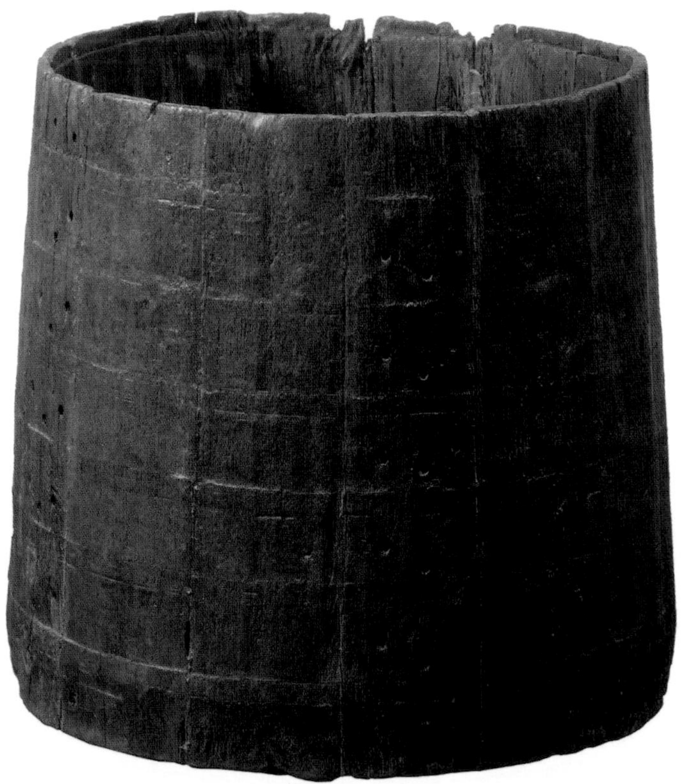

37.
Bucket, probably used for communal drinking at feasts, 10th century. Bjerringhøj, Mammen, Jutland, Denmark.
Oak. H 29.5 cm, Diam. 29 cm
National Museum of Denmark, Copenhagen

38.
Decorative mounts would have surrounded the outer rim of a drinking horn.

Mounts for a drinking horn, 10th century. Unknown provenance, Denmark.
Silver. Max. W 3.3 cm
National Museum of Denmark, Copenhagen

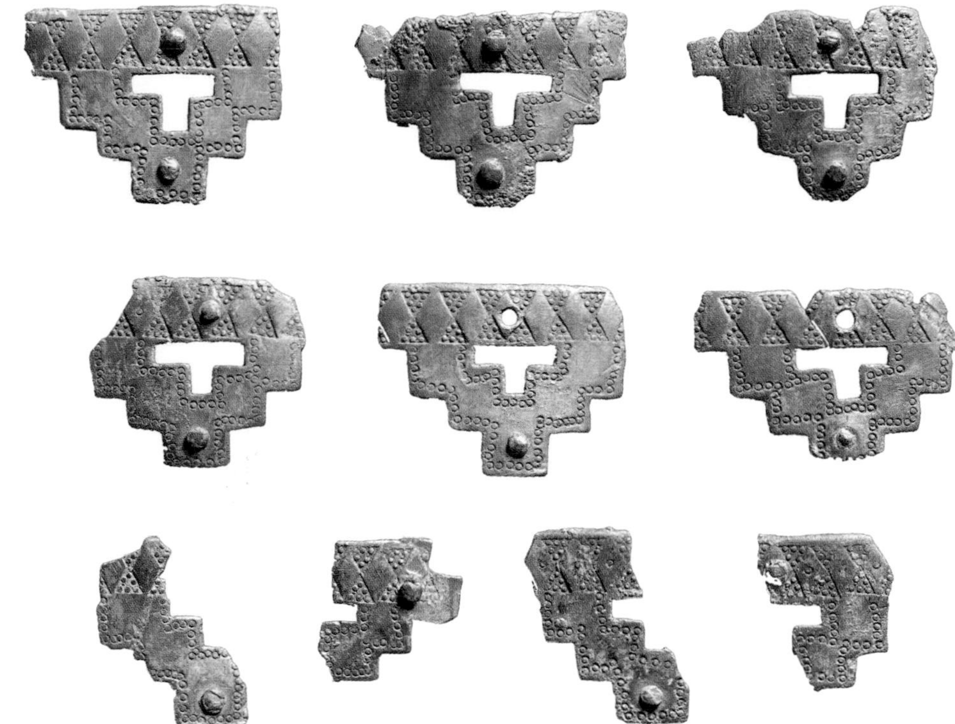

39.
The Bayeux tapestry shows a servant providing a basin and towel for assembled guests, a custom also practiced among Scandinavians in the Viking Age, 1070s. Probably Kent, England.
Embroidery (wool on linen). L *c.* 70 m
Musée de la Tapisserie de Bayeux, Bayeux

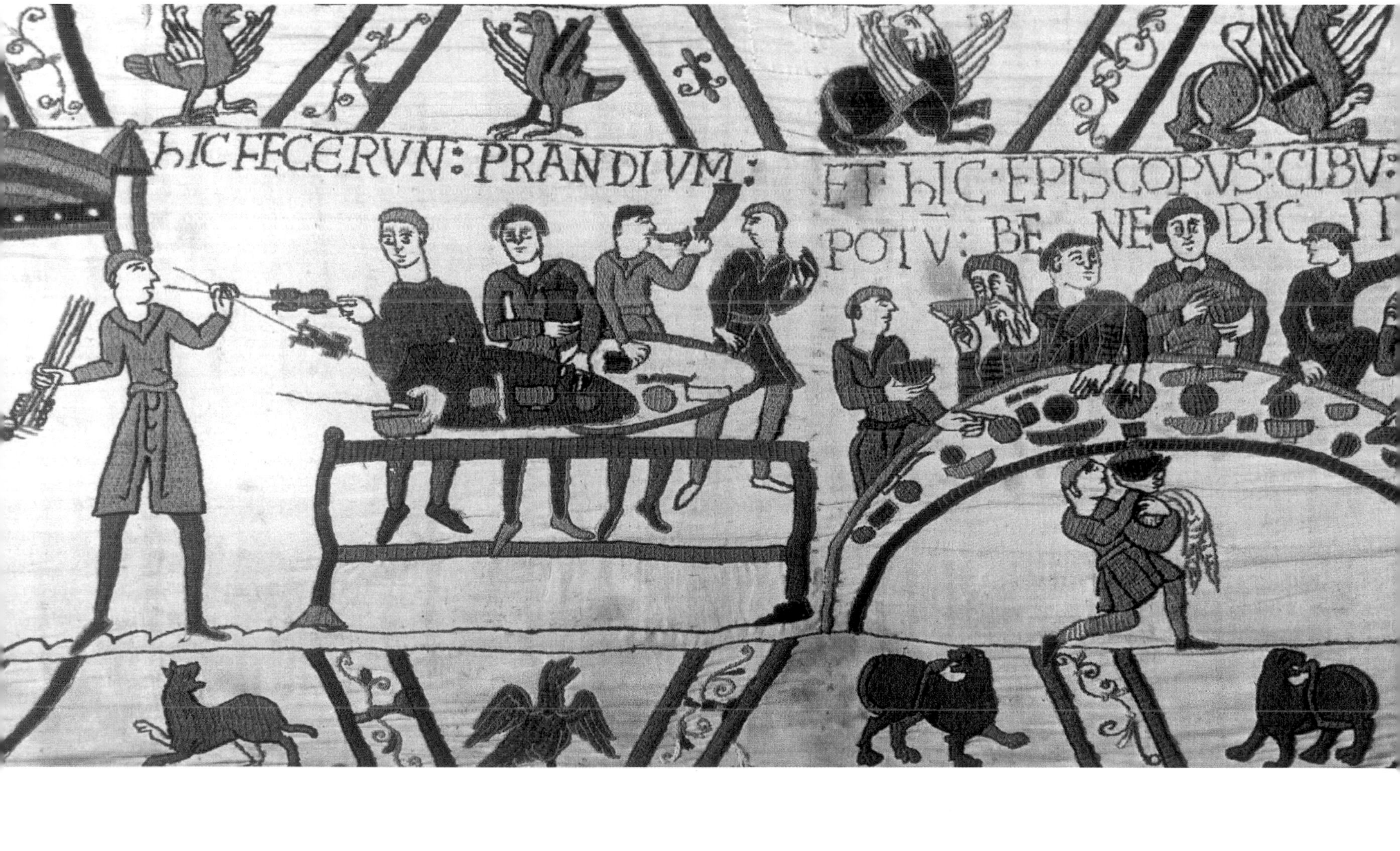

40.
The presence of a Bulgarian vessel in a wealthy grave from the Viking town of Hedeby may reflect diplomatic links with south-eastern Europe.

Bowl with old Bulgarian inscription, 800–850. Chamber grave 1, South Cemetery East, Hedeby, modern Germany.
Copper alloy. L 21.3 cm, W 22.2 cm, H 6 cm
Archäologisches Landesmuseum, Schloss Gottorf, Schleswig

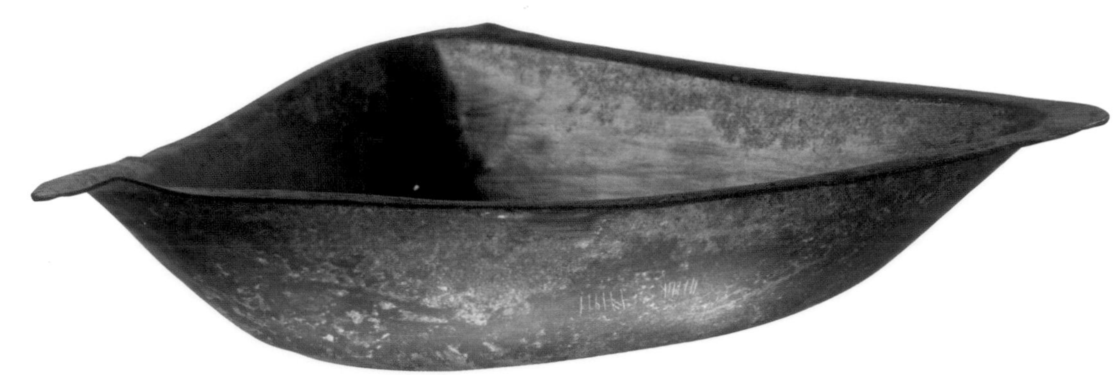

41.
Wooden tray or platter with Scandinavian decoration, 10th century. Berlin-Spandau, Berlin, Germany.
Beech. L 47 cm, W 34 cm
Museum für Vor- und Frühgeschichte, Staatliche Museen zu Berlin, Berlin

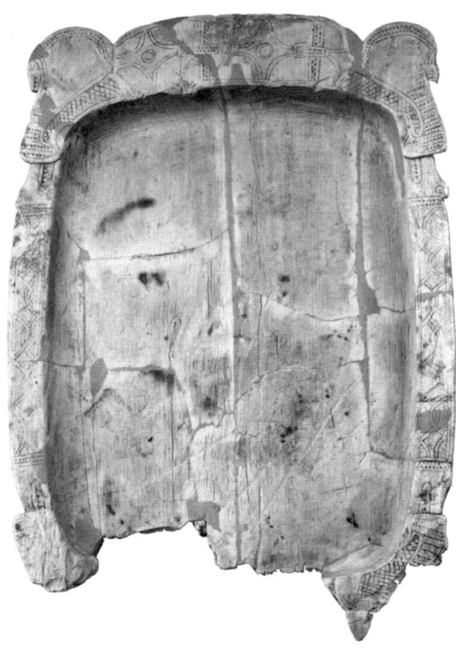

42.
In this allegorical representation of Luxury overthrowing Sobriety, Luxury is attended by two men offering filled funnel beakers. Prudentius, Physchomachie, Frankish, late 9th century.
Bibliotheque Nationale, Paris

'*What dream was that*', said Odin, '*when I thought before dawn*
I was clearing Valhalla for a slaughtered army?
I roused my great champions, bade the valkyries wake,
Strew the benches, wash out the beer-mugs,
Bring out the wine for a prince who was coming.
From the world I await such noble fighting-men
As will make my heart rejoice.'[37]

Any omissions from accepted manners might lead to unfortunate results, even death, as recorded in the saga of Egil Skalla-Grimsson; although not written down before the thirteenth century, events from Egil's life place him in the tenth century.[38] When at first Egil and his men arrived unannounced at the home of the wealthy farmer Armod Skæg in Värmland, they received a very disappointing reception bordering on an insult. The farmer's small daughter whispered a message to Egil from her mother not to eat too much as better food would arrive, and was hit by her father. Tables were then set out in the hall and a sumptuous meal with large amounts of strong beer was set before Egil and his men. A man was ordered to serve them, Armod deviously goading them to drink, which was seen as another insult. The next morning Egil confronted his host intending to kill him, but for the sake of Armod's wife and daughter Egil instead cut off his beard and poked out one of his eyes.

On their travels abroad men and women witnessed the customs and manners of other cultures, and upon their return they brought back with them not only material objects but also values and fashions that might be adopted and later modified to conditions at home. Life at foreign courts would have served as an ideal model, to be imitated or even surpassed if possible. This is reflected in a variety of objects and in the behaviour, ceremonies and rituals that emerge from archaeological contexts.

Nordic banqueting customs are evident in the tableware recovered from wealthy burials. Large wooden pails holding around 15 litres or more (fig. 37) probably contained beer, which was ladled into smaller vessels and drinking horns (fig. 38) at a table just as the one described for the meal in the home of Armod Skæg. Apart from their practical use, drinking horns appear to have had a ceremonial function. Gotlandic picture stones dating from the eighth to the eleventh centuries show women believed to represent Valkyries offering drinking horns to men on horseback, presumably dead warriors arriving in Valhöll (see pp. 116–7).[39] These scenes mirror the responsibility of the housewife to receive prominent guests and make them welcome (fig. 39). Advice on the needs of a visiting traveller but also a reminder of what the guest must contribute in return is offered by the Eddic poem *Hávamál*, 'The words of the High One'.

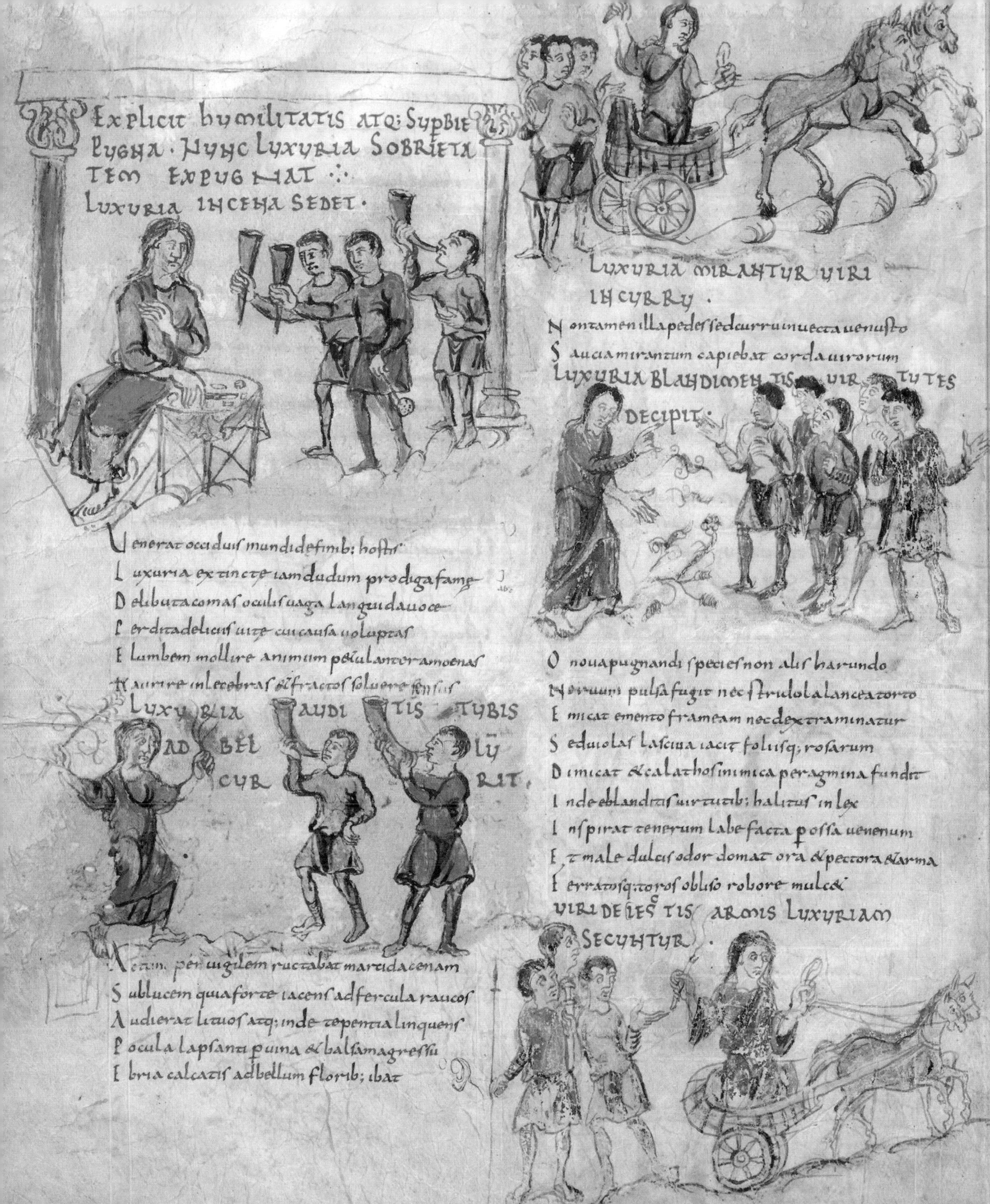

EXPLICIT HUMILITATIS ATQ; SUPBIE PUGNA. NUNC LUXURIA SOBRIETATEM EXPUGNAT.

LUXURIA IN CENA SEDET.

Venerat occiduis mundi de finib; hostis
Luxuria extinctę iamdudum prodiga famę
Delibuta comas oculis uaga languida uoce
Perdita deliciis uitę cui causa uoluptas
Elumbem mollire animum petulanter amoenas
Haurire inlecebras & fractos soluere sensus

LUXURIA AUDITIS TUBIS AD BELLUM CUCURRIT.

Et tum peruigilem ructabat marcida cenam
Sub lucem quia forte iacens ad fercula raucos
Audierat lituos atq; inde tepentia linquens
Pocula lapsanti p uina & balsama gressu
Ebria calcatis ad bellum florib; ibat

LUXURIA MIRANTUR VIRI IN CURRU.

Non tamen illa pedes sed curru inuecta uenusto
Saucia mirantum capiebat corda uirorum

LUXURIA BLANDIMENTIS UIRTUTES DECIPIT.

O noua pugnandi species non alis harundo
Neruum pulsa fugit nec stridula lancea torto
Emicat emento frameam nec dextra minatur
Sed uiolas lasciua iacit foliisq; rosarum
Dimicat & calathos inimica p agmina fundit
Inde eblanditis uirtutib; halitus inlex
Inspirat tenerum labefacta p ossa uenenum
Et male dulcis odor domat ora & pectora & arma
Ferratosq; toros obliso robore mulcet

VIRI DESERTIS ARMIS LUXURIAM SECUNTUR.

A wash he needs when he sits to eat,
A towel, and a hearty welcome.
Good humour, if he can manage it,
Converse and time to respond.[40]

In wealthy households, buckets, drinking horns and wooden cups might be supplemented by copper-alloy basins, imported glass funnel beakers, pitchers and silver vessels, among them Carolingian silver-gilt *pyxis* originally produced in the late eighth and ninth centuries for liturgical use in Christian western Europe,[41] but put to new uses in a possibly profane and yet also formal context (figs 40–42). Whether looted from Frankish churches or acquired by more peaceful means, the elaborately decorated cups were doubtless treasured items; several, like the silver cups from the Vale of York in England (see pp. 68–9) and Fejø in Denmark (fig. 43), survived into the tenth century before being hidden away together with other valuables.

The formal events of King Harald Klak's baptism in 826 were followed by a hunting party, which, alongside other amusements such as board games, offered an opportunity for mutual rivalry. Gaming pieces made of bone, or more exclusive materials including walrus ivory, amber and coloured glass, have been found in well-equipped burials. One of the most complete sets is from a man's grave from Oldenburg/Starigard in East Holstein (fig. 44). He had been buried with a fine sword and a filigree gold bead, and his dress was decorated with gold thread, all evidence of his high status. The Oldenburg pieces were most likely used in the popular game of *hnefatafl*, but further games were introduced as a result of contact with other cultures, among them chess.[42]

Living in style also implies travelling in style. Most people no doubt walked about their business in the Viking Age. Expensive riding equipment and valuable horses were a symbol of rank and authority, and were significant features in the *adventus*, a ceremony going back to classical times to mark the arrival of an important ruler. King Harald Klak no doubt appreciated the honour shown him when he and his followers, upon their arrival in Ingelheim in 826, were greeted by the emperor's men who brought magnificent horses for them to ride the few kilometres from the beach to the royal palace.[43]

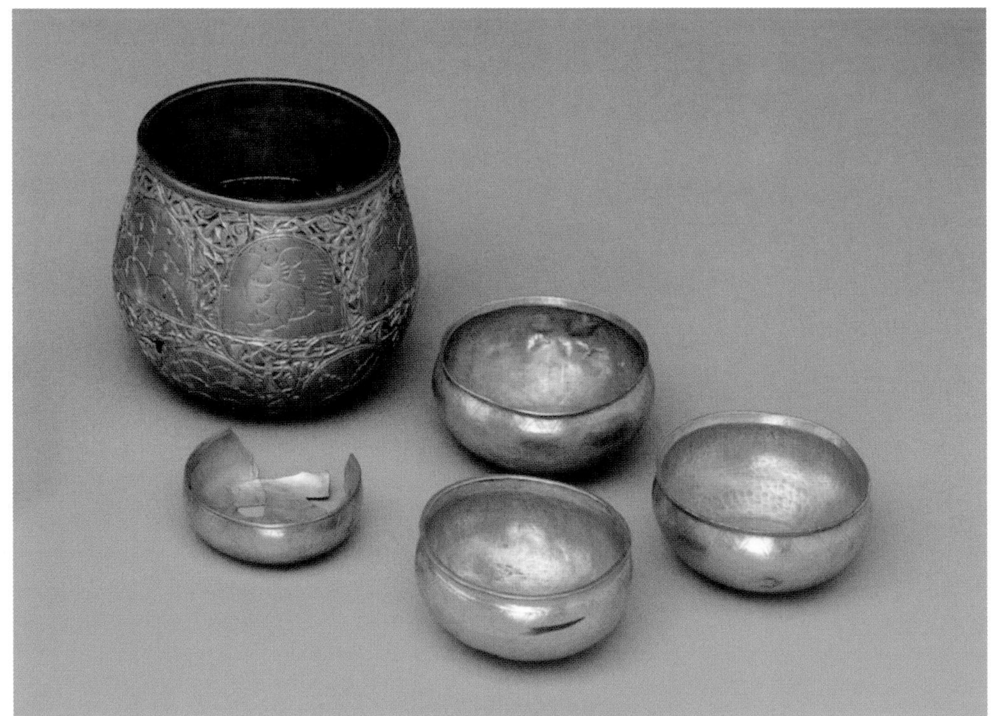

43.
Carolingian cup, 8th century, and set of small drinking vessels, 10th century. Østerby, Fejø (north of Lolland), Denmark.
Silver. Large cup H 9.6 cm, Diam. 9.6 cm; small cups Diam. up to 7.4 cm
National Museum of Denmark, Copenhagen

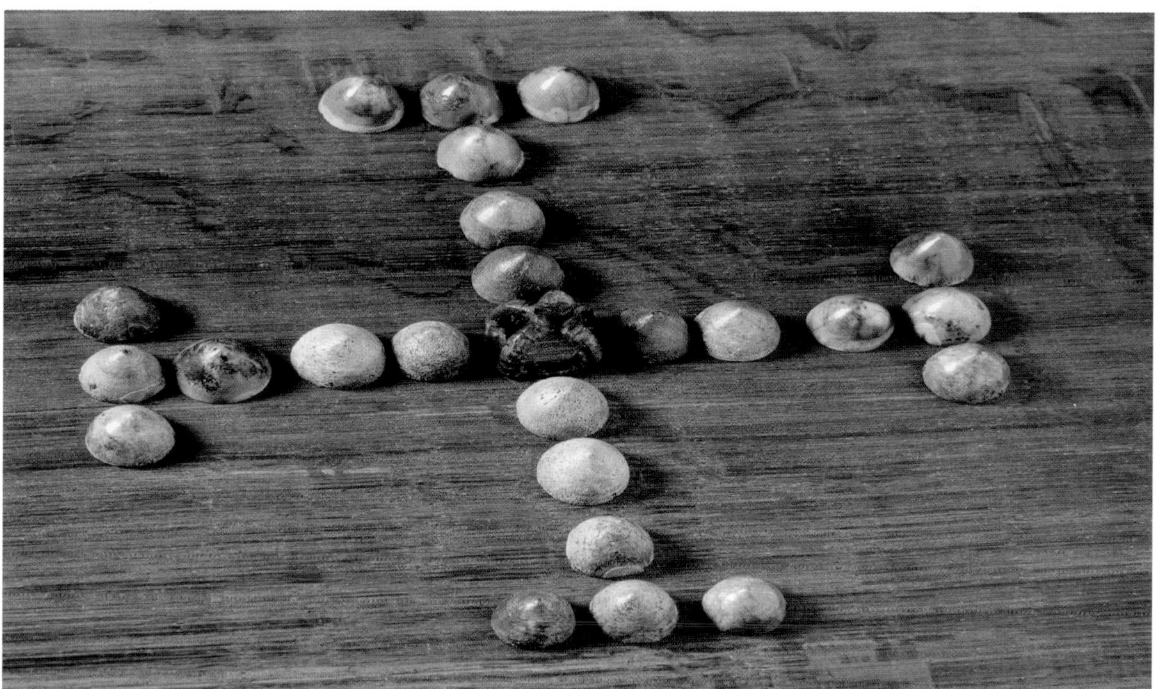

44.
Set of gaming pieces, 10th century. Grave 74, Starigard/Oldenburg, East Holstein, Germany.
Copper alloy with silver, whale and walrus ivory, walrus bone. King's piece
H 2.4 cm, D 3 cm
Archäologisches Landesmuseum, Schloss Gottorf, Schleswig

Saddles with stirrups were adopted from the Carolingians and from peoples further east. Some of the earliest burials in Scandinavia with full equipment for the horse are roughly contemporary with the attempts of King Henry I the Fowler (919–36) to improve his military forces, after the attacks of the Hungarians in the early tenth century, by training the Saxon warriors in the use of horses.[44] Few images and written sources give a clear impression of the warriors of his successor Otto I. However, finds of both weapons and horse furnishings have been recovered from settlements and burials in the areas east of the Ottonian empire (figs 45–46).[45] The care and expense invested in horse furnishings in Scandinavia confirms their significance not just as practical aids to riding but as demonstrations of the wealth and status of the owner. Like the weapons of the time, stirrups, bridles and spurs were made of iron, but often decorated with elaborate copper and silver inlay or, particularly in the eleventh century, with cast copper-alloy fittings, all serving to enhance the visual appearance of the warrior.

Some of the horse furnishings show close similarities that suggest that the owners had access to the same workshops or had received the harness and saddle, and possibly the trained horse, as a gift from the same source. This may be what lies behind an impressive hoard recovered in 1969 at Supruty, in the Upper Oka area in Russia. A copper vessel, identical to one used as an urn in the Skopintull mound at the royal site of Adelsö near Birka in Sweden, contained strap mounts and a richly decorated snaffle bit, thought to have been made on Gotland (fig. 47).[46]

Saddle and bridle are directly linked to the animal and were often buried next to it. Spurs, on the other hand, were worn by the rider and were buried with him whether or not he was accompanied by a horse. The gold spurs presented to King Harald Klak in 826 were of immense value, a fitting gift for the newly baptized king from his sponsor the emperor. Only a single equivalent is known from the Viking Age, a gold spur from Værne Kloster in Norway (fig. 48).[47] Spurs were otherwise made of iron, with silver or copper inlay or with decorative mouldings. They were doubtless highly valued by the owner as a symbol of his skill as a horseman, his economic means and, if received as a gift from his lord, also evidence of his rank and social affiliation.

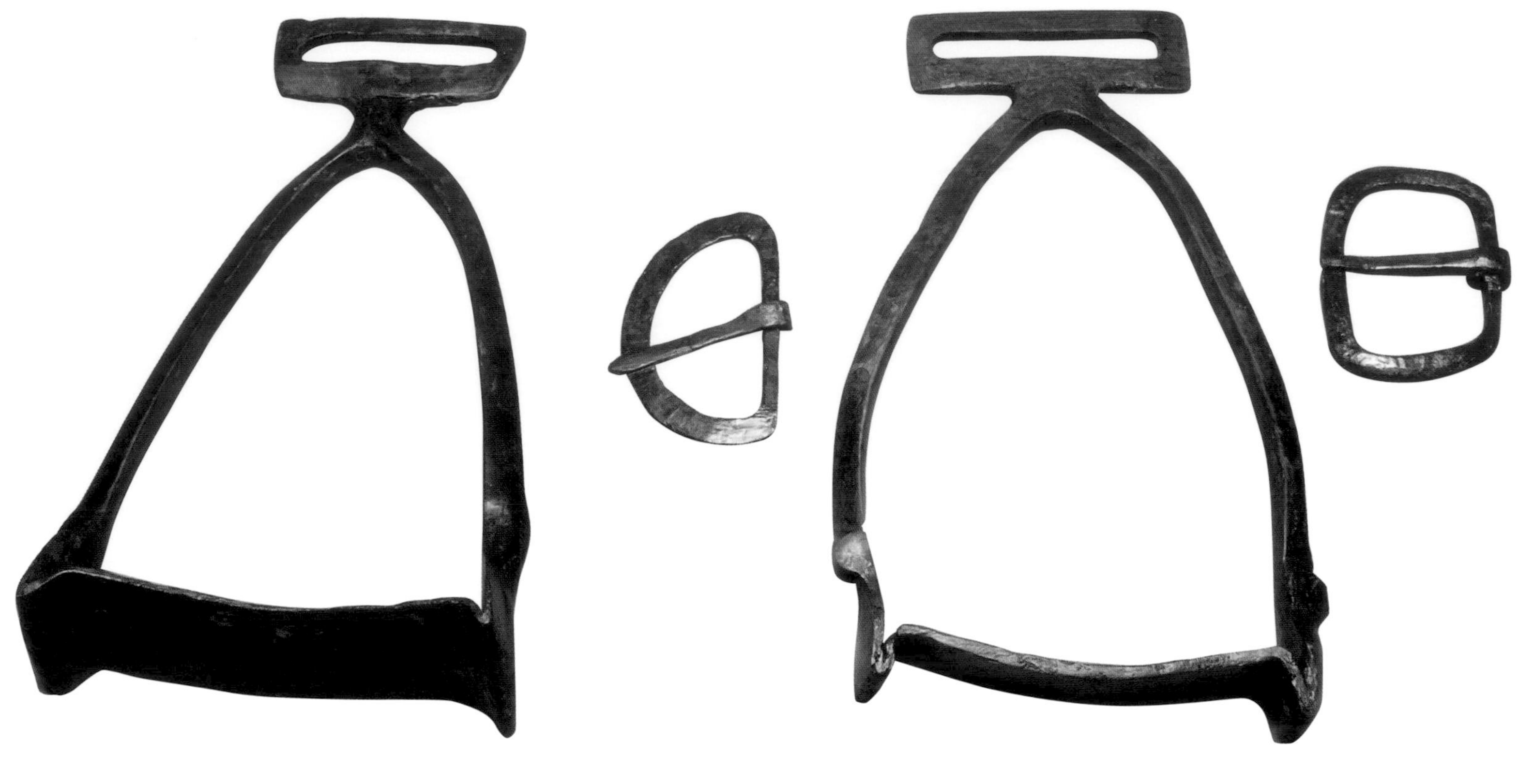

45.
Pair of stirrups, 10th century. Starigard/Oldenburg, East Holstein, Germany.
Iron, tin. Stirrup H 22.5 cm, W 12.5 cm
Archäologisches Landesmuseum, Schloss Gottorf, Schleswig

46.
Pair of spurs with strap fittings, 900–950. Grave 21, Starigard/ Oldenburg, East Holstein, Germany.
Copper alloy. Spurs L 14.5 cm, W 7.5 cm; goad L 3.2 cm
Archäologisches Landesmuseum, Schloss Gottorf, Schleswig

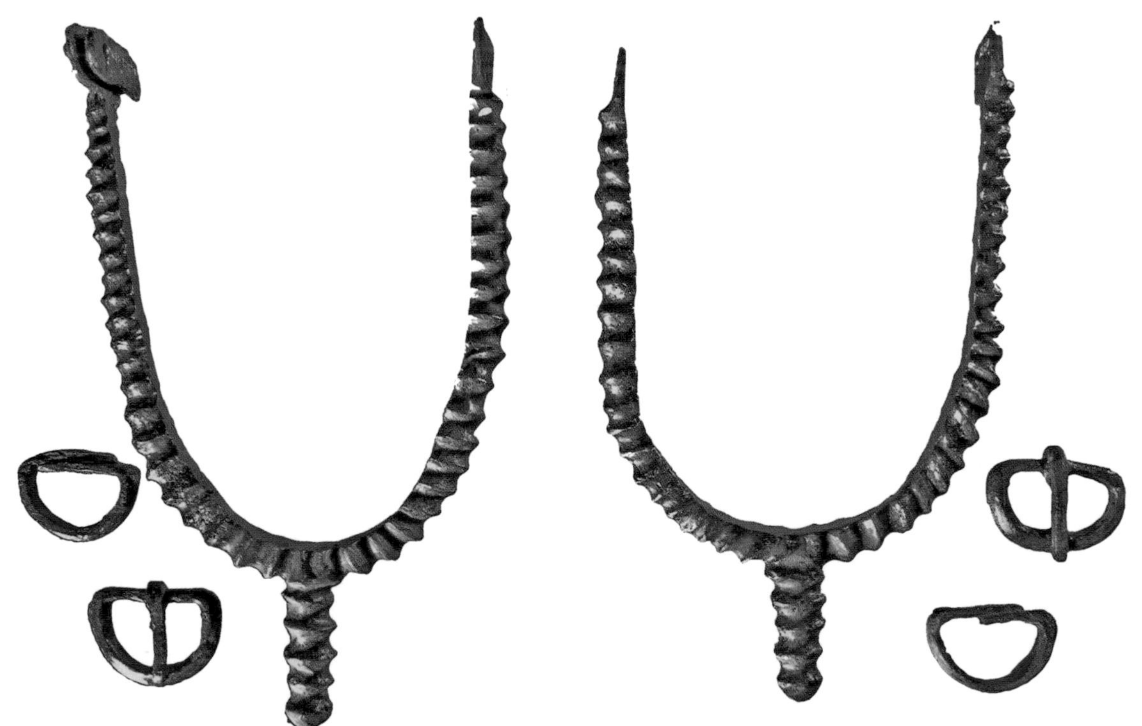

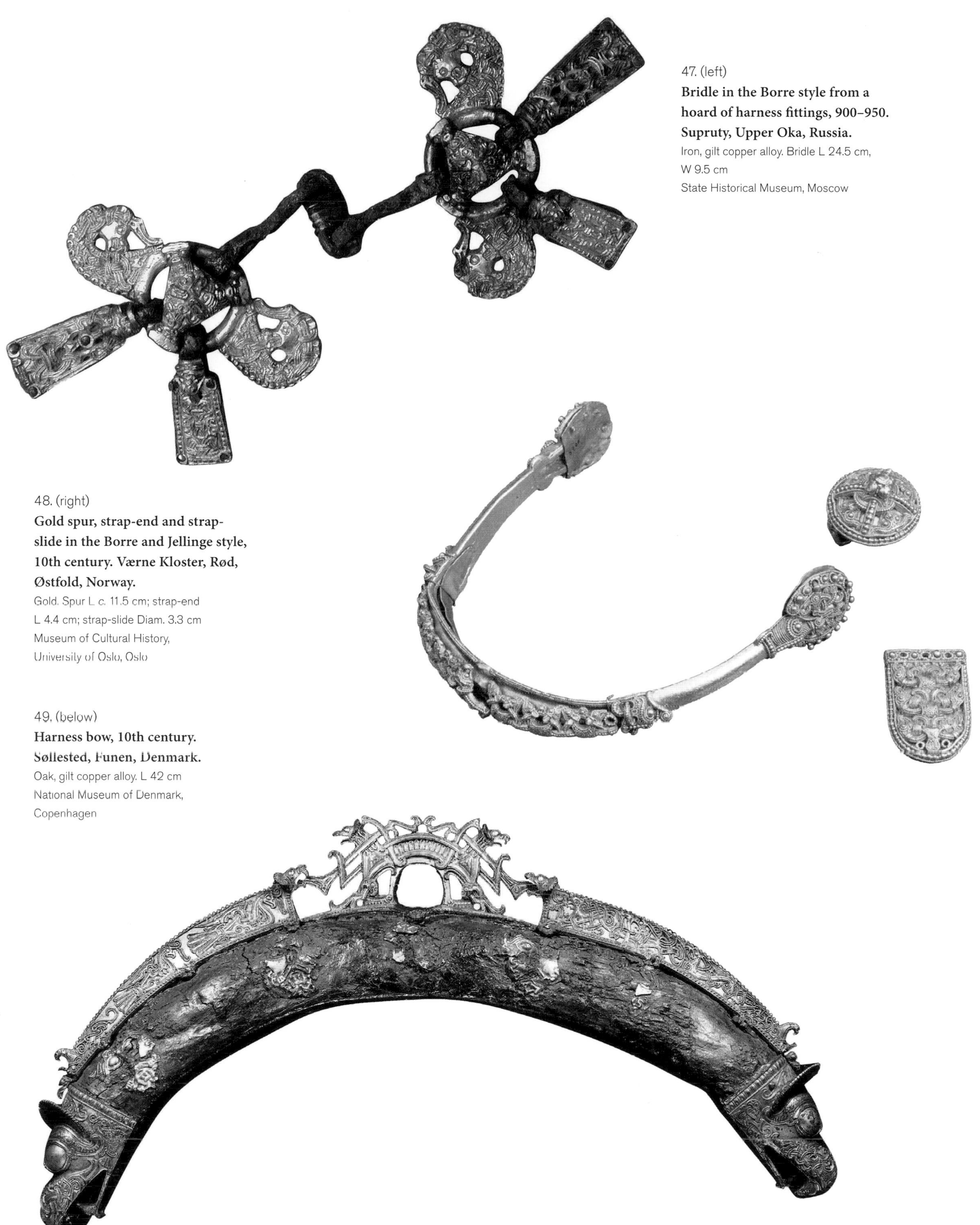

47. (left)
Bridle in the Borre style from a hoard of harness fittings, 900–950. Supruty, Upper Oka, Russia.
Iron, gilt copper alloy. Bridle L 24.5 cm, W 9.5 cm
State Historical Museum, Moscow

48. (right)
Gold spur, strap-end and strap-slide in the Borre and Jellinge style, 10th century. Værne Kloster, Rød, Østfold, Norway.
Gold. Spur L c. 11.5 cm; strap-end L 4.4 cm; strap-slide Diam. 3.3 cm
Museum of Cultural History, University of Oslo, Oslo

49. (below)
Harness bow, 10th century. Søllested, Funen, Denmark.
Oak, gilt copper alloy. L 42 cm
National Museum of Denmark, Copenhagen

While stirrups and spurs are associated with riding, decorated harness bows (fig. 49), iron traces and bridles suggest draught horses and wagons. Although men also had need of wheeled transport, wagon furnishings are generally associated with high-status women, not least the separate wagon body that was introduced as a coffin and most often used for women in the tenth century.[48] Burial with a wagon body appears almost exclusively to have been practised in southern Scandinavia. A few burials from Oldenburg and Ralswiek south of the Baltic offer further testimony of close relations between elite families in this area and Scandinavia.

The emergence of kingdoms

By the late Viking Age, after the year 1000, Scandinavia was vastly different from how it had been centuries before, when violent raids and attacks caused shock and despair in

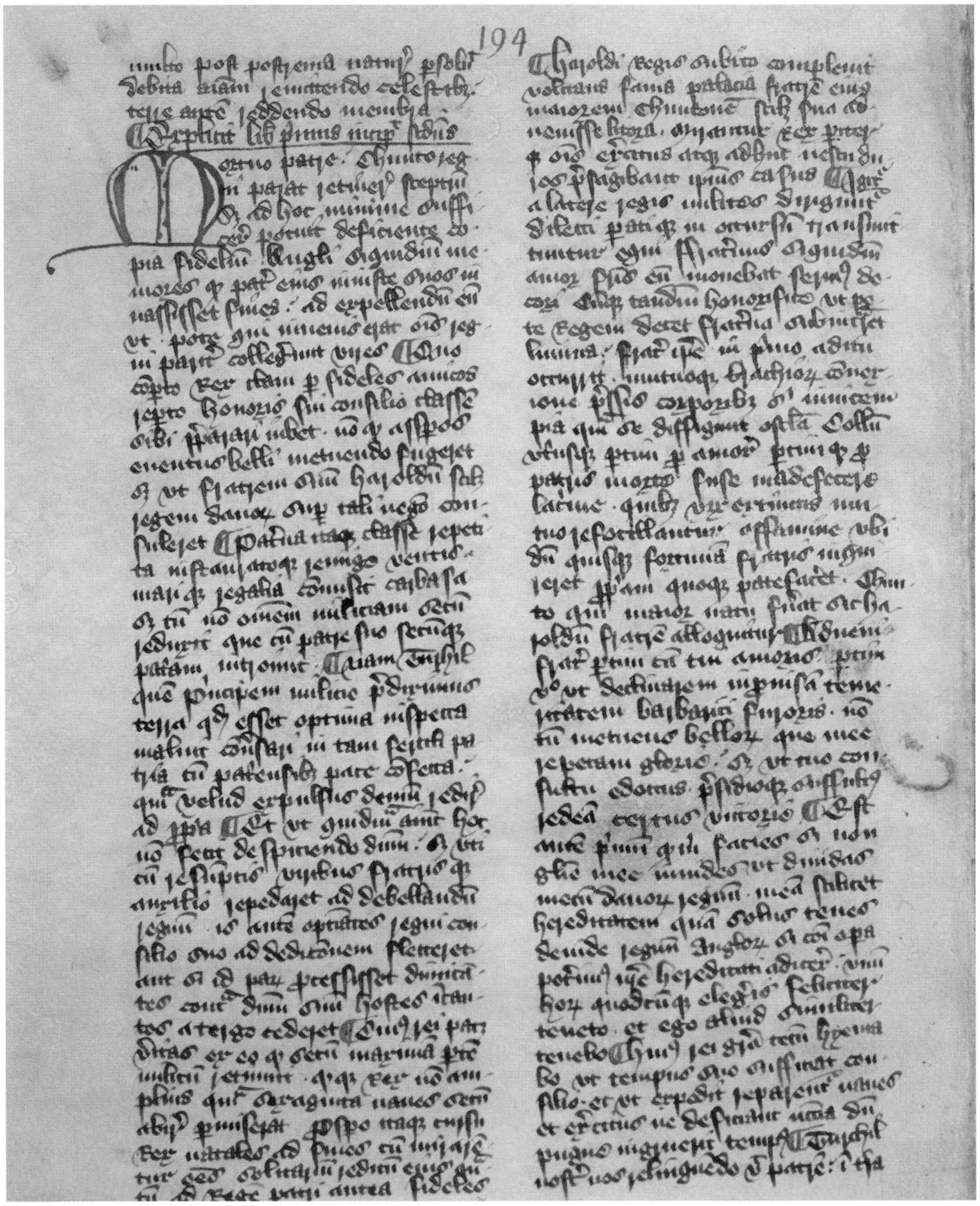

50.
A page from *Gesta Cnutonis regis* (the Deeds of King Cnut), written in 1042 or shortly after. The manuscript reproduced here is part of The Courtenay Compendium.
Parchment, leather.
Det Kongelige Bibliotek, Copenhagen

communities along the coasts and rivers of north-western Europe. Raiders and traders had been followed by settlers who adapted to life in their new homelands. Extensive journeys brought farmers into the far reaches of the North Atlantic and armed mercenaries southwards to join the imperial guard in Byzantium. One of these was Harald Hardruler, who returned a wealthy man after several years of service to become sole king of Norway in 1046. To the west the Danish king Svein Forkbeard embarked on a systematic conquest of England that was continued by his son Cnut the Great, who ruled England, Denmark and Norway until his death in 1035 (fig. 50); to the east, people of Scandinavian descent became prominent members of the elite of ancient Rūs, their heritage reflected in both archaeological and written sources.[49] Political units in Scandinavia had grown and new forms of lordship, influenced by images of royalty in the well-established kingdoms and empires of Europe, had emerged. The elusive political units of the Viking Age were gradually consolidated and transformed into the early medieval kingdoms that found their place within the cultural and political community of western Christianity,[50] a process mirrored in neighbouring countries such as Poland under the dynasty of the Piasts.

The process of unification differed from region to region and is most strongly demonstrated in Denmark during the reign of King Harald Bluetooth in the second half of the tenth century. King Harald had succeeded his father Gorm the Old shortly after the middle of the century, at a time when traditional values were under pressure from the cultural influence of Europe and the Ottonian empire was making its presence felt as a formidable political and military power immediately south of the Danish border. King Harald proved to be both an ambitious and innovative ruler. Among the most impressive of his building works are the unique circular fortresses built around 980 at Aggersborg and Fyrkat in Jutland, Nonnebakken in Funen, Trelleborg in Zealand, and possibly Borgeby in Scania (see pp. 112–13).

The fortresses differ in size and detail but show striking similarities in their strict geometric layout.[51] Common features include a precise if not perfectly circular rampart surrounded by a concentric V-shaped ditch, four gates oriented at the four points of the compass, straight streets crossing at right angles, and large timber buildings laid out in square courts aligned with the main streets (fig. 51). The engineering skills applied to set out the fortresses are mirrored in the royal complex at Jelling and in the Ravning Enge Bridge across the Vejle River valley, both built within the same short time frame from *c.* 960 to 985. The layout and construction of the fortresses have no known predecessors, nor were they maintained or repeated. Instead, the builders of King Harald may have looked to slightly older fortresses along the coasts of northern France and the Netherlands for inspiration, drawing additional details from Carolingian and Ottonian architecture, possibly even the fortified residences of Slavic princes south of the Baltic. Materials and building types, on the other hand, relied on traditional magnate or royal complexes.

The fortresses are situated near major land routes and rivers, but only Aggersborg on the Lim Fjord is directly accessible from the sea. Although military in nature, the fortresses no doubt served a variety of functions as centres of royal power from which the king could control the provinces of his kingdom while also responding to the strained relations with the German empire. As a consequence of the German expansion eastwards, many fortifications also sprang up in the Slav and German regions to the east.[52] Authority was possibly maintained with the aid of foreigners. Strontium isotope analysis of burials at Trelleborg has revealed that young men were recruited outside Denmark, perhaps from Norway or the Slavic regions.[53] Even three women in the analysis proved to be foreign, suggesting that the men who entered the service of the king were accompanied by their families. Living outside their original homeland, these men and women may have had few social ties to the local population; instead their identity and loyalty would be focused upon

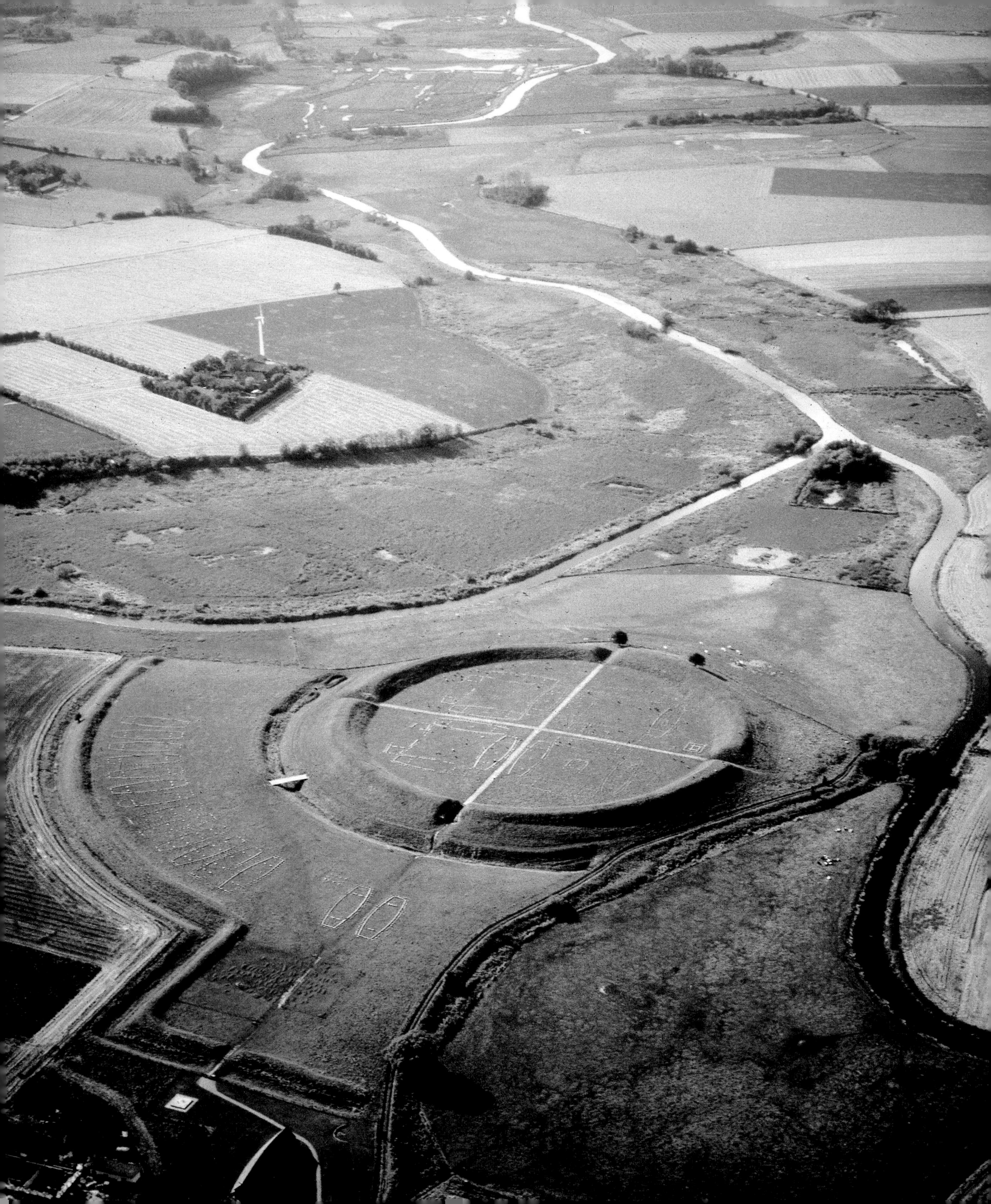

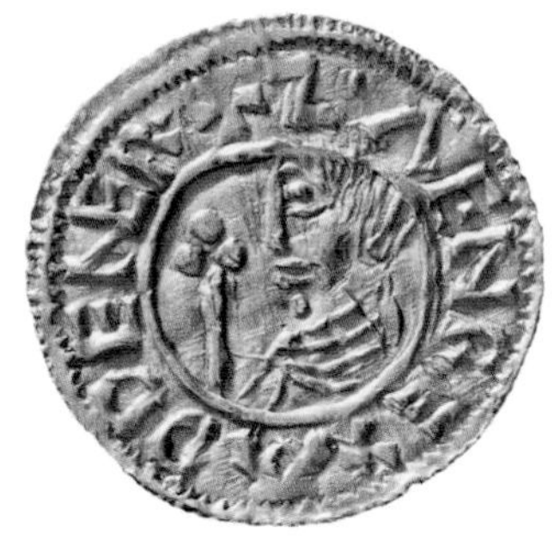

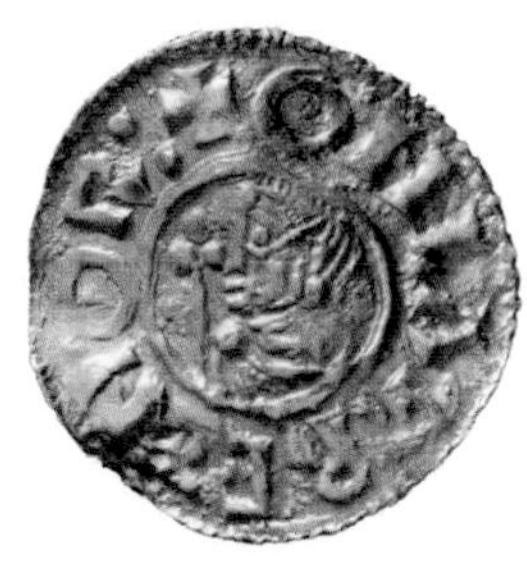

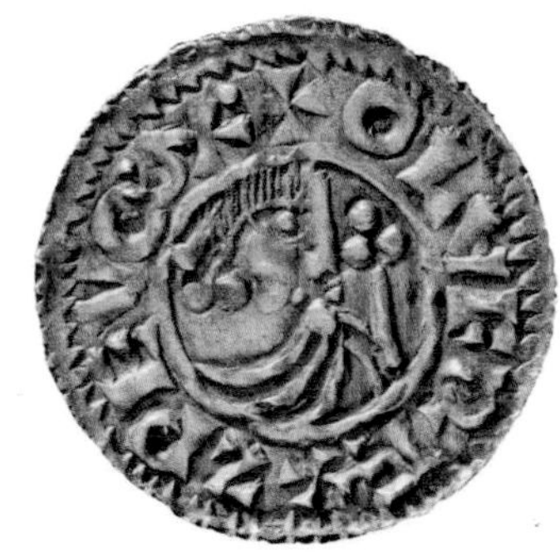

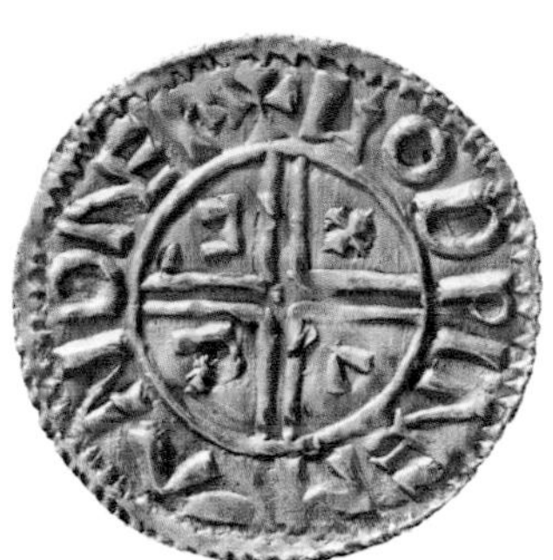

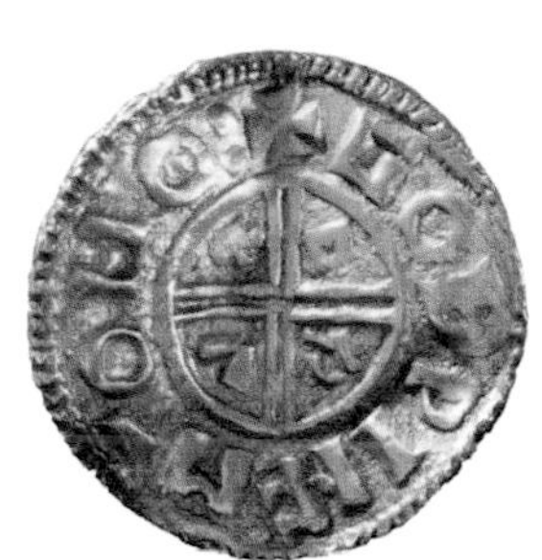

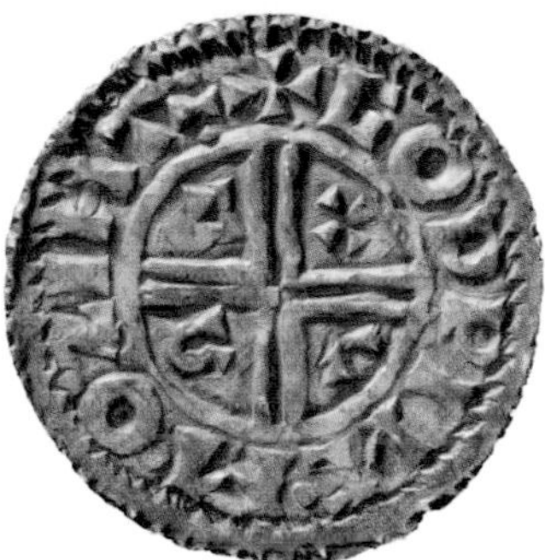

52.
Penny of Svein Forkbeard of Denmark (987–1014), *c.* 995. Unknown provenance
Silver. 1.29 g
National Museum of Denmark, Copenhagen

53.
Penny of Olaf Tryggvason of Norway (995–1000), *c.* 995. Iholm Island, Denmark.
Silver. 1.07 g
National Museum of Denmark, Copenhagen

54.
Penny of Olof Skötkonung of Sweden (995–1022), *c.* 995. Unknown provenance.
Silver. Diam. 2.0 cm
National Museum of Denmark, Copenhagen

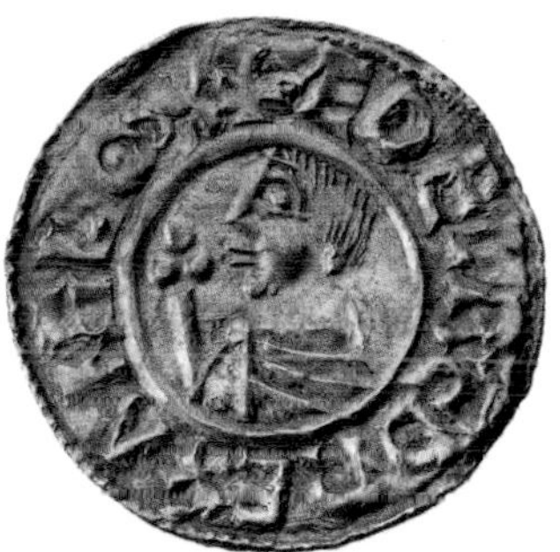

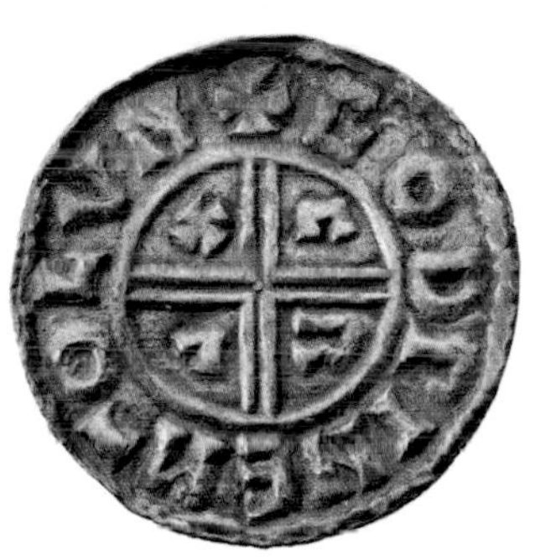

55.
Penny of Æthelred II of England (978–1016), minted *c.* 991–*c.* 997. Kelstup, Zealand, Denmark.
Silver. Diam. 2.0 cm, 1.28 g
National Museum of Denmark, Copenhagen

51.
Aerial view of the ring fortress at Trelleborg, Denmark.

the king. Along with alliances and marriages, the employment of foreigners was probably part of the political strategy of King Harald and his contemporaries.[51]

The ambition of the Danish king is evident on a far smaller scale in the coinage of the second half of the tenth century. The Viking Age has been termed an 'age of silver'. Silver was used in personal ornaments, to store wealth and as a means of payment. Much of the silver was acquired as coins, which were cut or melted down and reused. Foreign coinage dominated circulation, but coins were minted in Scandinavia, copying popular types from the Carolingian empire and later Anglo-Saxon England and Byzantium. In a bullion economy the silver content was more significant than the origin of the coinage and local minting fluctuated. A small silver hoard deposited in the final years of King Harald Bluetooth's reign at Pilhus in Jutland follows the general pattern of hoards in containing cut ingots, hacked jewellery and coins from many different countries, but by far the largest number of coins is Danish. Some are imitations of Charlemagne's Dorestad coinage minted in Hedeby at the southern Danish border, while others belong to a new coinage introduced around 975, most likely on behalf of King Harald (see p. 189, fig. 40). With their distinct cross motifs, the purpose of these coins may have been to promote the king's status as a Christian ruler. Whether his aim was to establish a coin monopoly, or the coins were special issues mainly intended as payment for loyal retainers, is not known.[55] Either way they represent a significant step towards regal coinage in Scandinavia.

Around 995, less than a decade after the death of King Harald, the three Scandinavian rulers Olaf Tryggvason of Norway (995–1000), Olof Skötkonung of Sweden (995–1022) and Svein Forkbeard of Denmark (987–1014) all issued new coins modelled on the silver CRVX pennies of King Æthelred II of England (978–1016) in the 990s (figs 52–55). The choice of pattern was probably no coincidence. In an attempt to ward off attacks from Denmark and Norway, King Æthelred paid enormous sums of silver as Danegeld. Thousands of his coins are known from Scandinavia, northern Germany and the Baltic. The three Scandinavian kings may have been political rivals but they appear to have been united in their wish to appear as Christian rulers, and their coins, naming both the king and his people, are classic

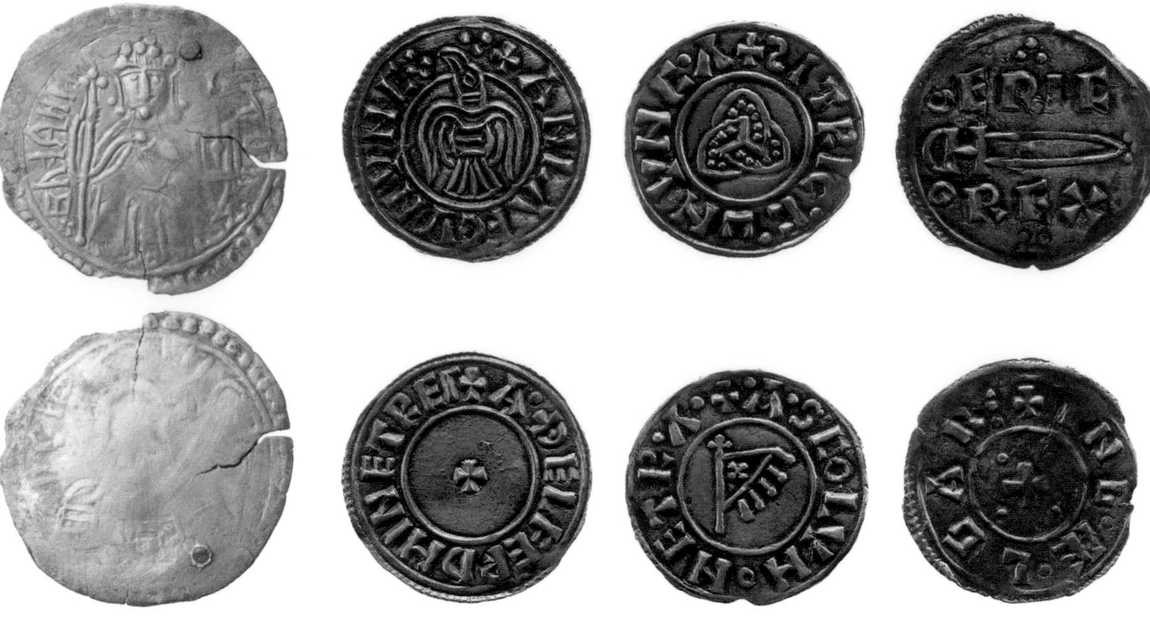

57. (left)
Coins issued by Viking rulers in Britain and Ireland displayed a range of traditional Scandinavian and Christian iconographic motifs.

Penny of Anlaf Guthfrithsson of Northumbria (939–41). England.
Silver. Diam. 2 cm
British Museum, London

Penny of Sihtric II of Northumbria (mid-940s). England.
Silver. Diam. 1.95 cm
British Museum, London

Penny of Eric Bloodaxe of Northumbria (*c.* 952–4). England.
Silver. Diam. 2.1 cm
British Museum, London

56. (above)
Silver coin of Prince Vladimir Sviatoslavovich (980–1015). Mogilevskaya, Votnya, Russia.
Silver. Diam. 2.6 cm
State Historical Museum, Moscow

examples of a form of mass media or propaganda intended to be seen and used by many (figs 56–57). In Ireland, silver pennies of King Æthelred II also served as patterns for the first coins struck by the Viking rulers of Dublin in the last decade of the tenth century. The earliest of these coins were anonymous but soon coins were struck in the name of Sihtric III Silkbeard (989/995–1036) (fig. 58).[56]

The following century saw many new coinages drawing on inspiration from Anglo-Saxon and Byzantine coins, suggesting that the development of kingship was accompanied by new economic structures. Some coins ended up far from their place of origin. Thus, a silver coin minted under King Cnut the Great at Ørbæk in northern Jutland in Denmark was recovered from beneath the floor in the church of St Peter in Rome. As a personal sacrifice the coin was of little value, but it is meaningful as a symbol of pilgrimage.[57] King Cnut was already a Christian when he became king, and when he died he was buried in Old Minster at Winchester in England. The king had himself journeyed to Rome in March 1027 for the coronation of Conrad II as emperor. Other members of the Scandinavian royalty and elite had now, long after the first ventures of the Vikings into the Mediterranean, added pilgrimage to their travels.

Despite the many crucial changes that took place in the Viking Age, the past was not fully forgotten and played an active role in the political and dynastic strategies of the rulers. In this they were no different from their contemporaries, particularly Charlemagne and Otto the Great, who had antique columns transported from Italy to decorate their great churches in Aachen and Magdeburg. The antique spoils were a physical manifestation of the might of the empire and its ability to compete with the architectural monuments south of the Alps. Rulers across northern Europe may well have followed similar lines of thought, referring to ancient traditions as a means to demonstrate their ancestral roots and thus legitimize their power and authority while at the same time seeking to adapt existing structures to new cultural concepts and new forms of kingship and governance (figs 59–60).

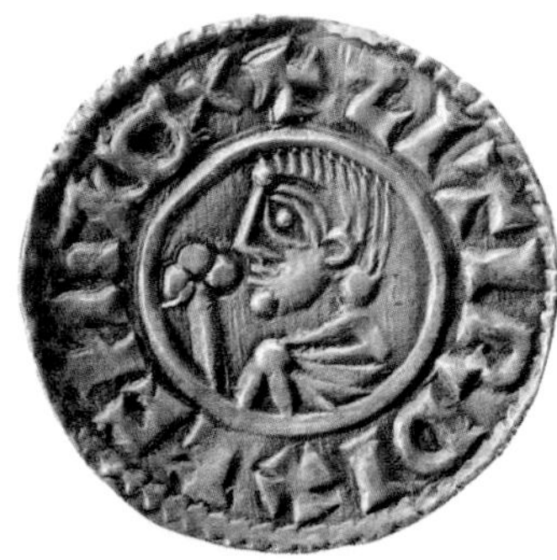

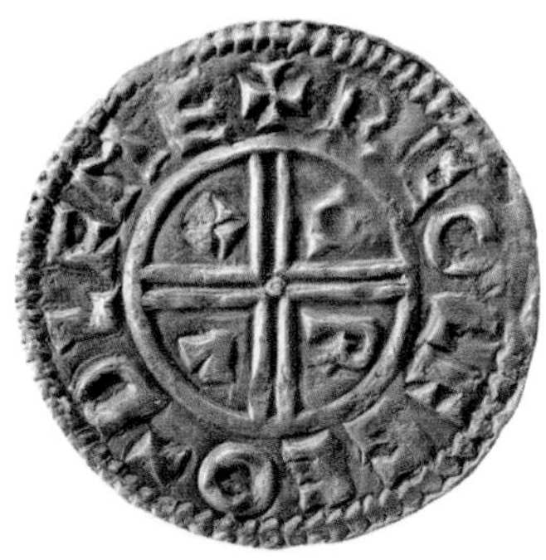

58. (above)
Penny of Sihtric Silkbeard of Dublin (AD 989–1036). *c.* 995. Ireland.
Silver. Diam. 2.15 cm
British Museum, London

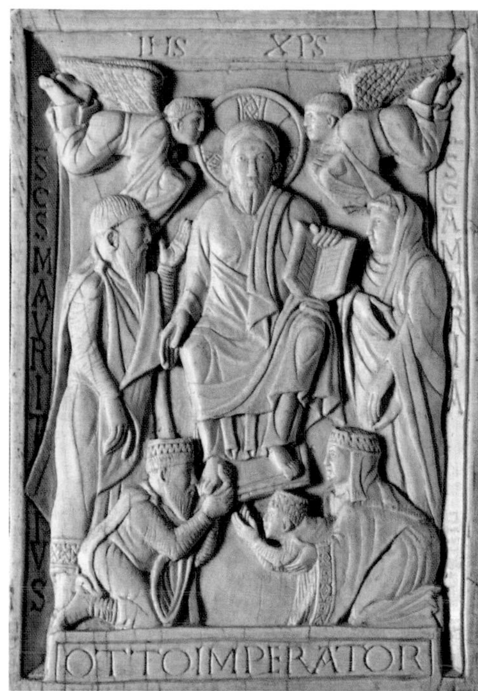

59.
Ivory plaque showing an image of Christ flanked by Mary and Mauritius. The three people are probably Otto II with the Empress Theophanu and their son Otto III, who was crowned in May AD 983. The plaque may have been commissioned by Theophanu after the death of Otto II to enforce the claims of her son to the throne. Milan, 983–4.
Ivory. H 14 cm, W 9.5 cm
Castello Sforzesco, Civiche Raccolte D'Arte, Museo D'Arte Antica, Milan

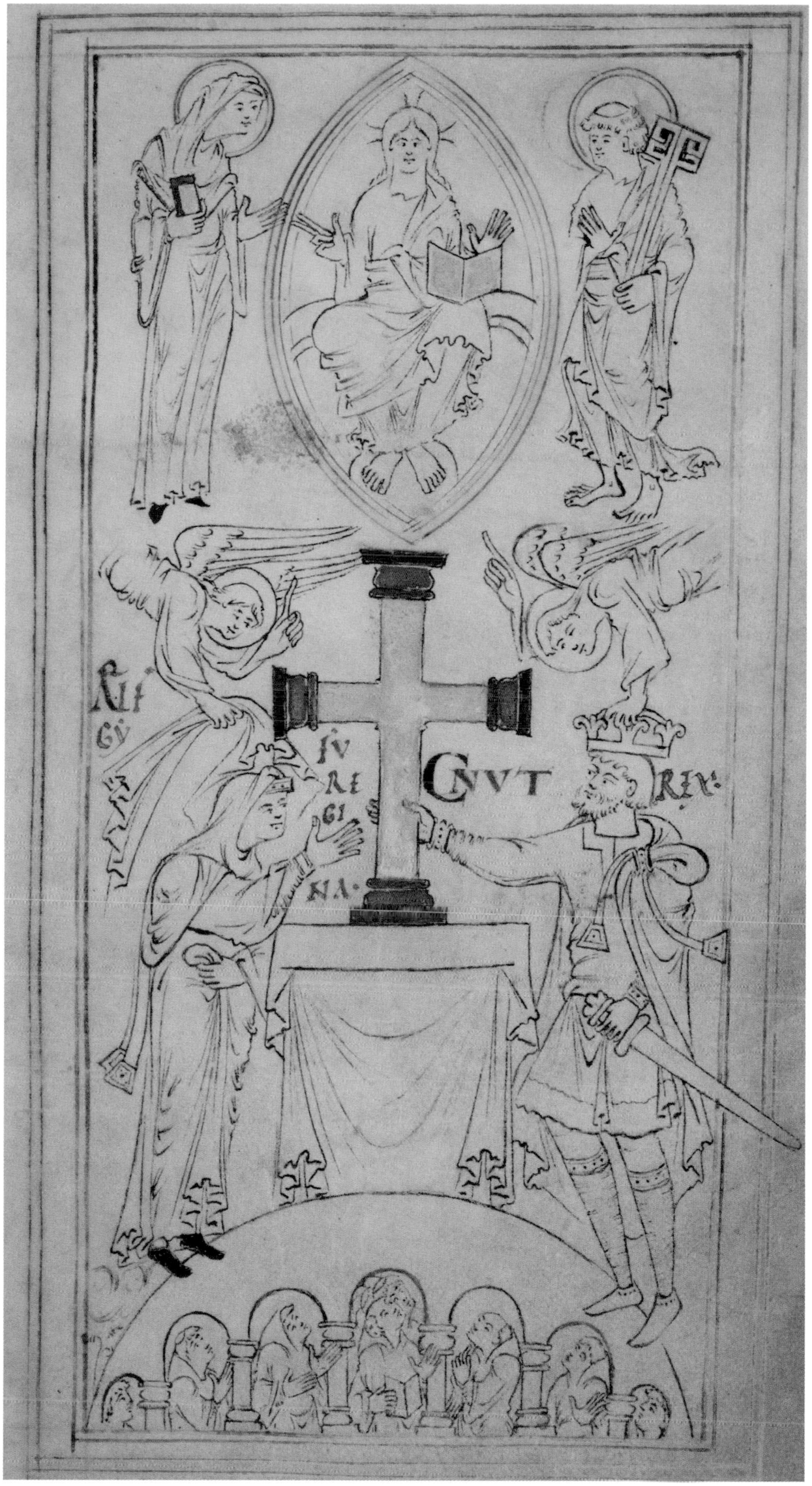

60.
Cnut the Great and his Queen Emma (Ælfgyfu) present an altar cross to the church. Apart from images on coins, the drawing from the *Liber Vitae* of New Minster, Winchester, is the only known portrait of the king.

***Liber Vitae*, 1031. New Minster, Winchester, England.**
Parchment. L 26 cm, W 15 cm
British Library, London

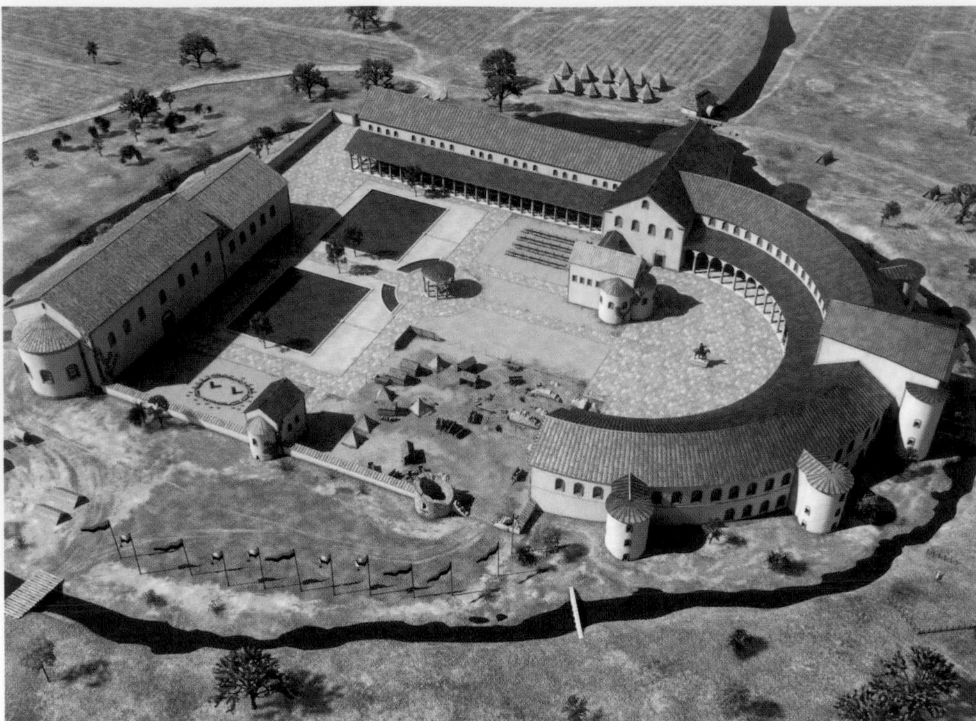

1.
Digital reconstruction of the exterior view of the Carolingian palace hall (the Aula Regia) at Ingelheim, west of Mainz, Germany

2.
Digital reconstruction of the interior view of the Carolingian palace hall (the Aula Regia) at Ingelheim, west of Mainz, Germany

Great halls and palaces

Matthias Wemhoff

In the year 826, the feast of St John the Baptist (24 June) offered the perfect setting for a highly symbolic event. In the presence of the Carolingian emperor Louis the Pious and the entire imperial family and household, the Danish king Harald Klak was baptized in Ingelheim.[1] Although this baptism was not the cause of the Vikings' later conversion to Christianity, it provides impressive evidence of Viking-Age rulers' participation in and awareness of the ceremonial occasions that were part of Carolingian culture (see pp. 129–30).

Louis the Pious had chosen the palace of Ingelheim with forethought. Nowhere else could he display his empire as so deeply rooted in ancient tradition. When the magnificent procession after the baptism in the Abbey of St Alban in Mainz approached the palace at Ingelheim, the participants would already have seen the palace complex standing in splendour on the slope above the Rhine (fig. 1). The semicircular building with its detached towers, an unusual feature of palace architecture, was the first to catch the eye. Afterwards the feast was celebrated in the great hall (fig. 2). A large part of the apse is still standing today: the four windows are discernible and their position is reminiscent of the model for the architecture of this hall, the Aula Palatina (also known as Constantine's Basilica) in Trier. In a poem in praise of Louis the Pious, Ermoldus Nigellus gives an account of the event and describes magnificent scenes depicting great victories over the heathens from Constantine to Charlemagne, relating them to accounts from classical antiquity.[2] Though archaeological investigations have found evidence of a painted background from numerous plaster fragments, there are no indications of figurative painting.[3] Perhaps the possibility of transportable woven tapestries depicting appropriate scenes should be considered. This would correspond to the account given of one of the great events of the reign of Charlemagne, the reception of Pope Leo III in Paderborn in 799. After the service in the nearby 'church of wondrous size',[4]

> *Charlemagne invites Pope Leo to dine with him in his lofty palace. The halls within shine magnificently with woven tapestries, everywhere the seats are richly decorated with gold and purple. They sit at table with cheerful hearts, enjoy many delicious delicacies; thus they celebrate the banquet in the palace and on the tables the golden pitchers are brimming with Falernian wine.*

It is clear that the high point of this kind of ceremonial occasion was the large, opulent meal. The hall was essentially created for this purpose. Tapestries, seat cushions and golden pitchers provided an

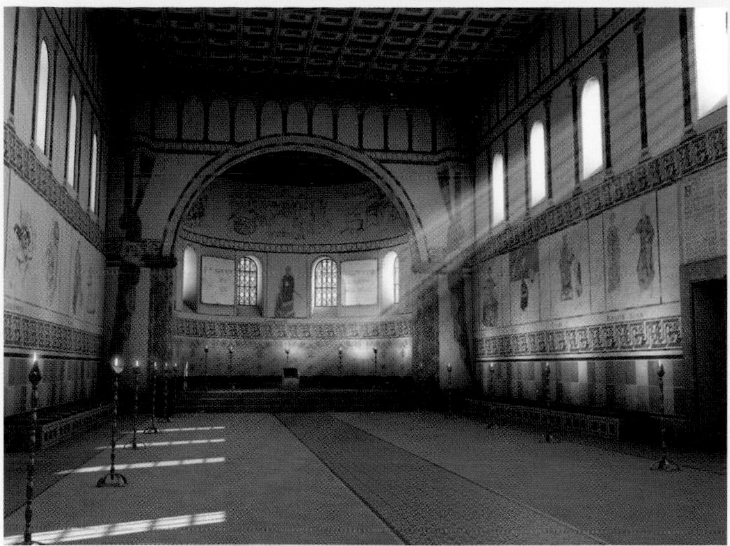

imposing background. Despite the status associated with the Paderborn palace after the victory over the Saxons, the exterior shows no sign of classical architectural features. It is a two-storey hall of large dimensions (approximately 31 x 10 metres), but still considerably smaller than the hall at Ingelheim, which is an enormous 14.5 metres wide.[6] A glassblower's workshop was discovered during the excavation. This would have produced drinking glasses to meet the evidently high demands of the imperial table (fig. 3).[7] The sherds of Tating-ware jugs must also be a direct result of the banquets.[8]

When Harald Klak was baptized in Ingelheim, the nearby palace in Frankfurt had just been newly founded and also incorporated a two-storey great hall. Measuring 26.5 x 12.6 metres, it was somewhat more compact than the building in Paderborn.[9] This makes it clear that the two-storey palace with adjoining rooms for residential purposes was the building of the future, whereas the antique-style building in Ingelheim remained the exception.

When Harald Bluetooth 'won all of Denmark and Norway and made the Danes Christian' (see pp. 158–9),[10] the Saxon royal house had emerged as the dominant ruling power in the east Frankish kingdom. Palace complexes in what was then the Saxon heartland in the area around the Harz Mountains give a clear idea of the great variety of ceremonial buildings of that time and also show that their dimensions and construction are not comparable with the buildings of Charlemagne. The halls were mostly 20–25 metres long and only 8–9 metres wide, which made them easy to roof with wooden ceilings.[11] The hall stood in relative isolation by a large courtyard. Groups of residential buildings or the site of a church are separated by a space. Particularly striking is the great wooden hall of the palace in Tilleda, to the south of the Harz, which has been dated to around the turn of the first millennium.[12] Surrounded by lower porches stood what might have been a two-storey hall building with large posts 1.2–1.5 metres wide. Building in wood, which seems so strange after the Carolingian examples, evidently still continued, even for large official buildings.[13] This is where comparison with ceremonial sites in Denmark can begin. The location and size of halls in Denmark, the arrangement of the overall use of the sites and the relationship to cult sites and churches should be seen in the light of developments in the Frankish-German kingdom. The building of temporary residences for emperors and kings, also known as 'Pfalz', increased after the beginning of the eleventh century, culminating in the great 'Palas' of the High Middle Ages. The functions of ceremonial halls, chapels and residences were combined into a single building with different wings and two storeys, as can already be seen in buildings from the time of the emperor Henry II – the palace of Bishop Meinwerk in Paderborn,[14] Goslar.[15]

This implies that the hall is of the greatest, possibly even spiritual, importance in both cultures:

More fair than the sun a hall I see,
Roofed with gold, on Gimle it stands.
There shall the righteous rulers dwell
And happiness ever they shall have.[16]

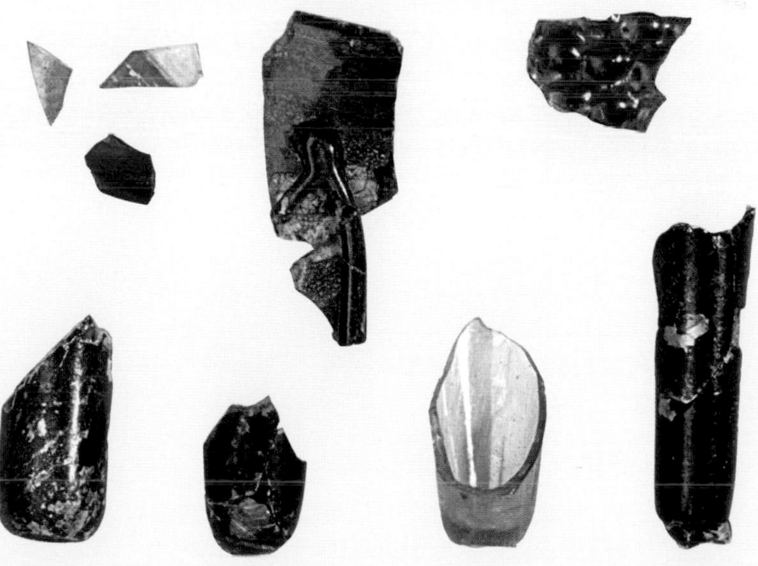

3.
Fragments of glass vessels and funnel beakers, 9th century. Carolingian palace site at Paderborn, Germany.
Glass. Bottom right fragment H c. 5 cm
Museum in der Kaiserpfalz, Paderborn

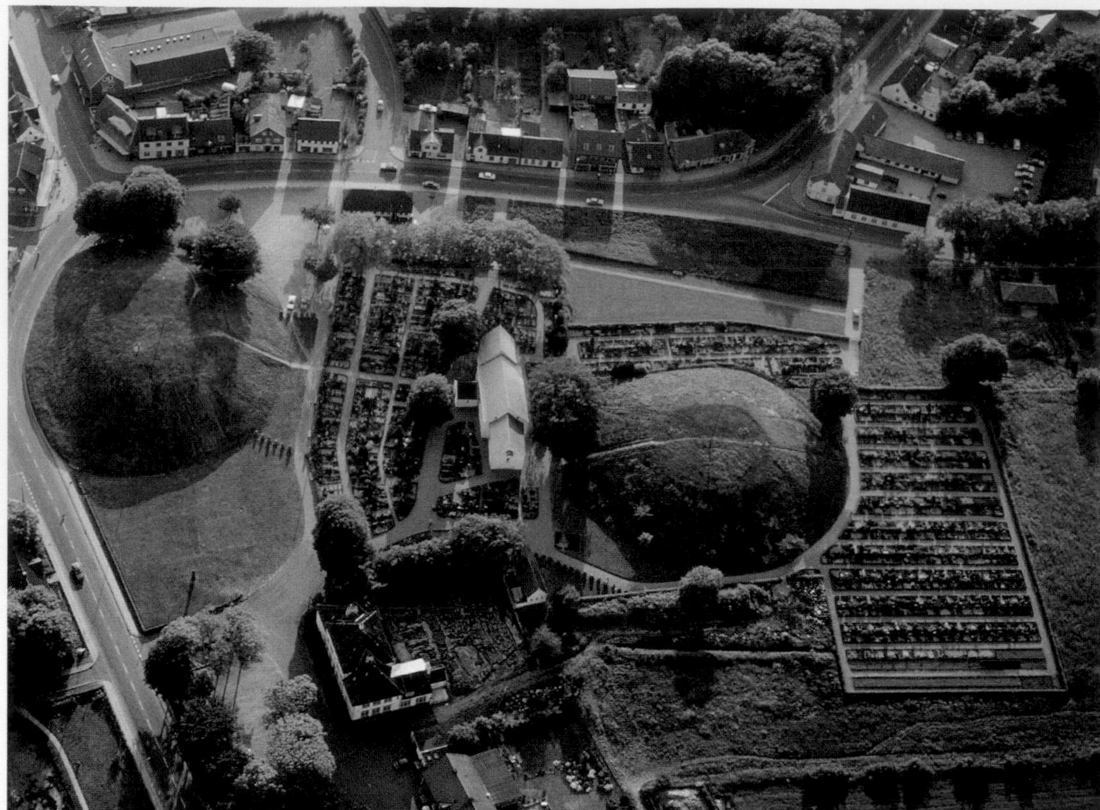

1.
Aerial view of the monuments at Jelling, Denmark.

The royal monuments of Jelling

Anne Pedersen

The royal complex at Jelling in central Jutland (fig. 1) is one of the most evocative sites of the Viking Age. The standing monuments consist of two huge grass-covered mounds and between them two rune-stones in front of a Romanesque stone church built around 1100 (fig. 2).

The large rune-stone, commonly known as the 'birth certificate of Denmark', was raised by King Harald Bluetooth, an ambitious and innovative ruler, probably around 965. The inscription records that

> King Harald commanded this monument to be made in memory of Gorm, his father, and in memory of Thorvi [Thyre], his mother – that Harald who won the whole of Denmark for himself, and Norway, and made the Danes Christian.

These claims are reinforced by images of a powerful beast fighting a snake and the figure of Christ Triumphant. The language and runic script are in Nordic tradition, intended for the king's subjects, but the lines are written horizontally and the two images unfold like pages in a Latin manuscript. The magnificent effect was almost certainly inspired by books of the Christian church[1] and, although no traces of paint are preserved, the images and inscription probably stood out in bright colours.

The inscription on the small rune-stone, from around the middle of the tenth century, reads: 'King Gorm made this monument in memory of Thorvi [Thyre], his wife – Denmark's adornment'. Exactly where the stone was raised for Thyre remains unknown. It had been used as a bench in front of the church door before it was moved beside King Harald's rune-stone around 1630. It may have been part of the first Jelling monument, an enormous stone ship setting built before the mid-tenth century.

The earliest archaeological finds came to light in 1820 when local farmers digging in the North Mound encountered large stones and the roof of an unusually spacious burial chamber. Unfortunately, it had already been robbed in antiquity. Apart from a small silver cup decorated with animal figures in a style now known as the Jellinge style, a few metal objects and wooden fragments, very little remained of the furnishings.[2] The mound was

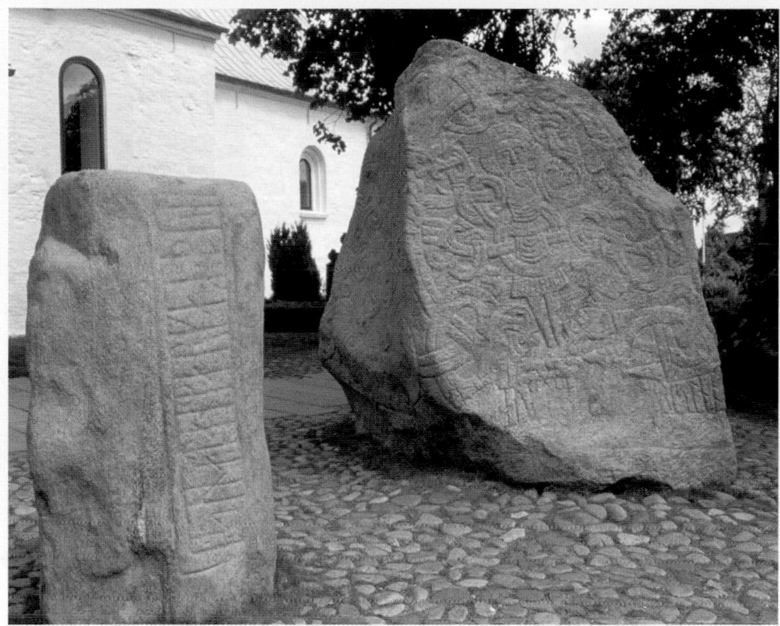

in Sweden, and supports the story recorded by the Danish historian Sven Aggesen around 1185 that the parents of Harald Bluetooth were buried according to pagan custom in two mounds, close to the royal estate in Jelling. Jelling is the largest known royal site from the Viking Age, comparable in its scale and geometrical layout to contemporary courts and royal residences in Ottonian Germany. It is a complex worthy of King Harald's rune-stone: perhaps the realities behind Harald's political and religious claims were negotiated and communicated to his contemporaries and subjects here. Like the other building works ascribed to Harald – the Trelleborg fortresses and a 760-metre-long bridge across the Vejle river valley only 10 kilometres south of Jelling – the Jelling enclosure was quickly abandoned. King Harald's successors had no need for such monuments to enforce their power and authority but could achieve their aims with other means. England rather than Germany was the focus of political attention and the centre of power moved eastwards in Denmark.[6]

interpreted as the burial of King Harald's mother Queen Thyre. Excavations in 1861 failed to locate a similar burial for King Gorm in the South Mound. Re-excavation of the mound in 1941 revealed only two rows of monoliths, the remains of the earlier stone setting.

Further excavations in the church in the 1970s revealed traces of earlier wooden buildings and a second burial chamber containing the remains of a middle-aged man interred with a set of silver-gilt belt fittings in the Jellinge style. The proximity of the two chamber graves, one in the North Mound and the other beneath the church, and the stylistic similarity of their contents suggested that the deceased had been transferred from his original burial mound to a new resting place beneath the first church on the site. This interpretation has since been challenged by new discoveries and renewed study of the North Mound.[3] The damage to the North Mound may have been a deliberate act linked to the opening of other prominent burials in the second half of the tenth century,[4] and the chamber beneath the church is possibly independent of the earliest wooden building on the site.

A magnetic survey in 2006 led to the discovery of large monoliths north of the North Mound, and renewed excavations over the past few years have added new structural elements to the complex.[5] The North Mound lies at the centre of a huge enclosure. The sides, each measuring around 360 metres in length, were constructed of closely set vertical planks and supporting posts at intervals of on average 1.25 metres (fig. 3). This impressive wall defined an area of 12.5 hectares – far larger than any known Viking-Age 'manor' – and so far only one entrance has been identified, a 2-metre-wide gateway to the north. Three virtually identical buildings in the north-east sector appear to have been located according to an overall master plan. The complex can be dated to Harald Bluetooth's reign.

Jelling has similarities with ancient royal centres in Scandinavia, like Lejre in Zealand, Denmark, and Gamla Uppsala

2.
The Jelling rune-stones raised by King Gorm and his son Harald Bluetooth, with the church in the background.

3.
Remains of the north-east corner of the palisade at Jelling. The North Mound and Jelling church can be seen in the distance; they lie at the centre of a large area once enclosed by the palisade.

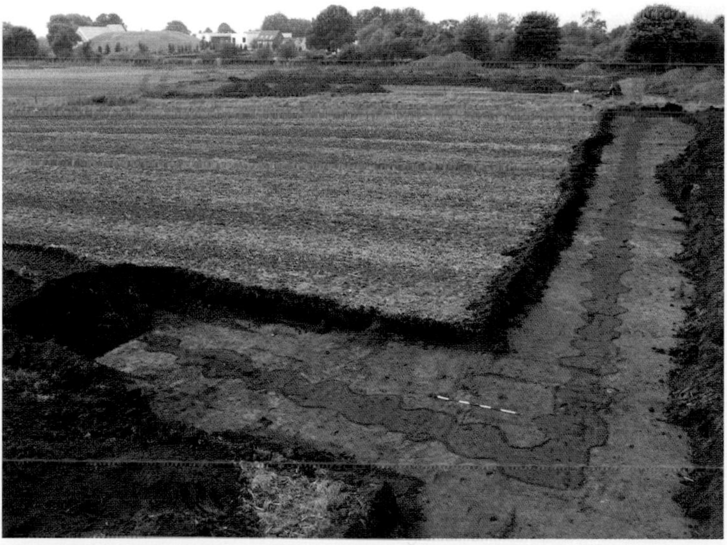

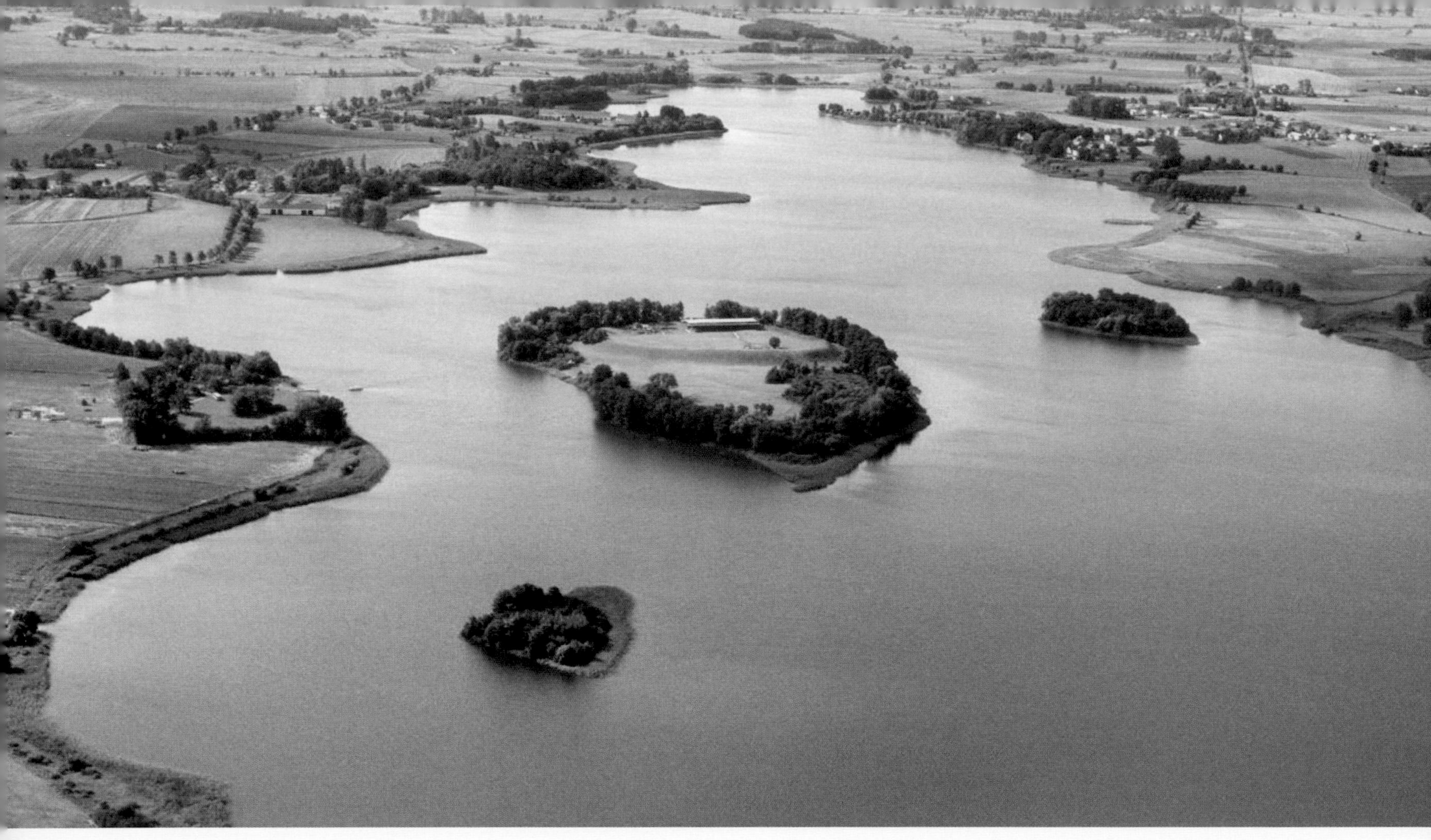

1.
Aerial view of Ostrów Lednicki, situated on an island in Lake Lednica, Poland.

Neighbours along the southern Baltic coast

Sunhild Kleingärtner

In the Viking Age, dominion and power were partly based on access to resources, which were mainly concentrated in sites along the Baltic and North Sea coasts. Merchants were the economic driving force behind these maritime trading centres. An entry in the Royal Frankish Annals for the year 808 underlines the importance of these emporia in terms of political power. It describes how the Danish king Godfred first demanded taxes from the inhabitants of Reric and eventually forced them to move to Hedeby. The deliberate destruction of Reric would have played a key role in the rising importance of Hedeby (see pp. 50–1).[1]

Based on extensive evidence of settlement, the location of Reric has been identified as the town of Gross Strömkendorf close to the Bay of Wismar in Germany.[2] During the first half of the eighth century, this area of Slavonic settlement appears to have been used as a seasonal meeting place for traders, whose visits were not at first coordinated.[3] The increasingly structured settlement pattern, with Grubenhäuser (houses with sunken floors) standing close together and systematically laid out, suggests that a higher authority was imposed only at a later stage.[4]

Reric is the furthest west and most extensively investigated of the maritime trading centres on the southern Baltic coast. Three centres located further to the east – Rostock-Dierkow, Menzlin and Truso – are notable for a similar range of finds relating to the working of glass, bone, antler and amber (fig. 2). The Rostock-Dierkow hoard, consisting of sword parts of Scandinavian origin, beads and metalworking tools (fig. 3), can be interpreted as a set of

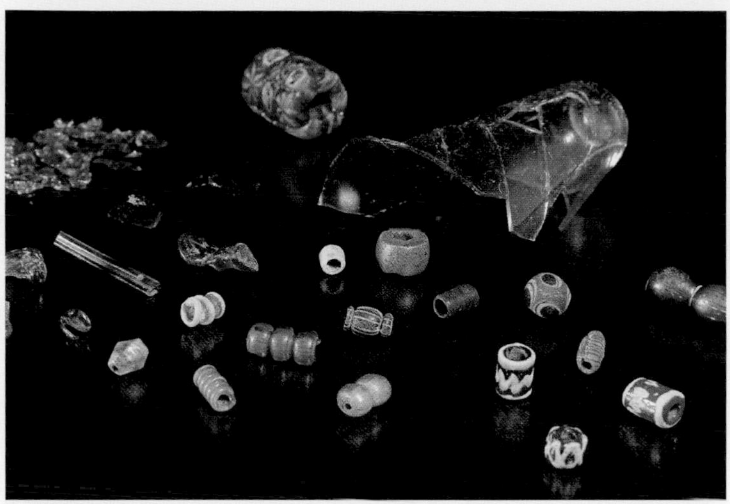

tools for the local production of jewellery and weapons,[5] or, according to the most recent conjecture, as a collection of valuable objects preserved in the ground.[6]

Of the many people who must have stayed in these trading centres, only one is known to us by name. That man is Wulfstan who, according to the description of his travels in King Alfred's Old English translation in Orosius' history of the world (*Historiarum Libri Septem Adversus Paganos*) sailed from Hedeby to Truso.[7] Finds from Truso, the easternmost of the centres, located close to the present-day Polish village of Janów Pomorski, suggest that locally available resources were of particular importance – after all, the placename Truso comes from the Old Prussian word *Drusa*, meaning 'salt works, source of salt or salt water'.[8]

King Godfred's political intervention in events in the Baltic area can be seen as a reaction to structural changes along the southern Baltic coast.[9] As the maritime trading centres were abandoned, the concentration of economic power along the coast came to a complete standstill during the ninth century. The increase in the building of defensive ramparts resulted for a time in decentralized development inland. It can be seen from the archaeological evidence that this led to the emergence of local elites, particularly in the tenth century.[10]

Ostrów Lednicki (fig. 1) in present-day Poland provides examples of structures and elements that were used by the social elite at the time of the rise of the Piast dynasty under Mieszko I, Bolesław I the Brave and Mieszko II in the second half of the tenth and first half of the eleventh century as a way of displaying their social status. During this time, the inland routes gained considerably in importance over the sea routes. This can most obviously be seen from the widespread finds of hoards, scales and weights away from coastal areas.[11] Graves containing military and horse equipment have been found around ramparts erected in Poland in the tenth century.[12] The similarities between these and weapons from Scandinavia have been evaluated in different ways, depending on the contemporary political situation. They have, for instance, been interpreted as trade goods or as signs of foreign influence,[13] although there is no archaeological evidence to back up the latter hypothesis. It is not currently possible to determine whether the specific recruitment of foreigners by a local elite occurred in the Piast empire as seems to have happened elsewhere (see pp. 152–3).

Objects of foreign origin indicating social status – notably including some of a Christian nature – have been found at Ostrów Lednicki. This centre is particularly notable for its stone buildings, both secular (palace/*palatium*) and sacred (chapel, baptistry, stone church),[14] and for precious jewellery[15] found within a fortification erected in several stages.[16] The unique nature of this settlement is emphasized by its location, on an island in Lake Lednicka in modern Poland that is accessible by two bridges, and its consequent rise to power. The bridges were part of the military and trade route running from Posen to Gnesen.[17] Almost 300 objects, some of Scandinavian origin, have been found in the area of the lake and the island – the biggest collection of weapon finds from Piast Poland.[18]

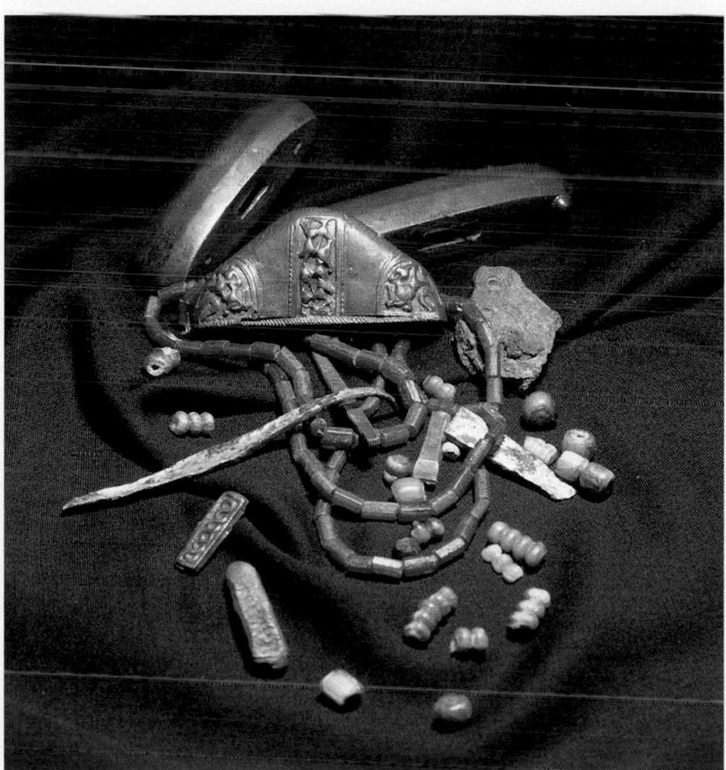

2. (above)
Among the many objects exchanged in Reric/Groß Strömkendorf and other sea trading sites were glass beads.
Landesamt für Kultur- und Denkmalpflege Mecklenburg-Vorpommern, Schwerin

3. (right)
Hoard including decorated Carolingian hilt mounts, 800–850. Rostock-Dierkow, Germany.
Silver, partially gilt, glass, brass, tin, lead.
Landesamt für Kultur- und Denkmalpflege Mecklenburg-Vorpommern, Schwerin

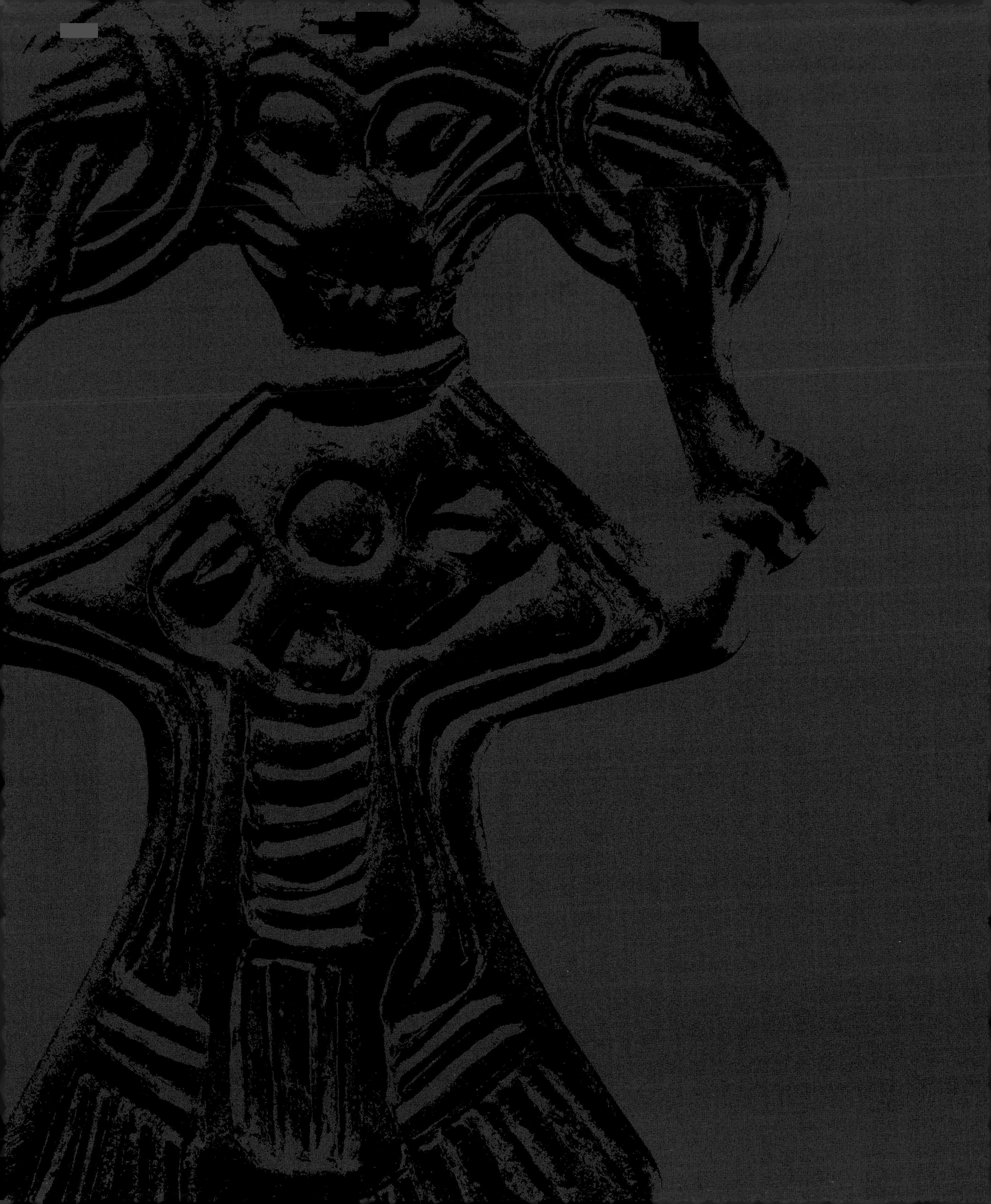

4 BELIEF & RITUAL

Neil Price

The Æsir took the body of Baldr and brought it to the sea. Hringhorni is the name of Baldr's ship: it was greatest of all ships; the gods would have launched it and made Baldr's pyre thereon ... Then was the body of Baldr borne out on shipboard; and when his wife Nanna saw that, straightway her heart burst with grief, and she died; she was borne to the pyre, and fire was kindled.

GYLFAGINNING XLIX (SNORRI STURLUSSON, *c.* 1220)

BELIEF & RITUAL

IN THE VIKING ENCOUNTERS with their nearest neighbours in north-western Europe, one aspect of their culture seems to have struck contemporary observers more than any other: their paganism. Again and again in the monastic texts that record the first raids by Scandinavians, we see them labelled with the Latin *pagani* or its Germanic counterpart *hæðena*, 'heathen'. However, both then and now these definitions are based upon what the Vikings were not – i.e. Christians – and tell us very little about what they actually believed.[1] Any discussion of the spiritual beliefs and rituals of the Vikings must therefore begin with a brief analysis of what 'religion' may really have meant in the context of their society.

The Vikings themselves had no word for 'religion', the closest equivalent being a much broader terminology of 'customs' in the sense of traditional practices that it was considered appropriate to follow. Crucially, these embraced many more facets of social behaviour than the human relationship with the divine that lies at the centre of today's world faiths. The

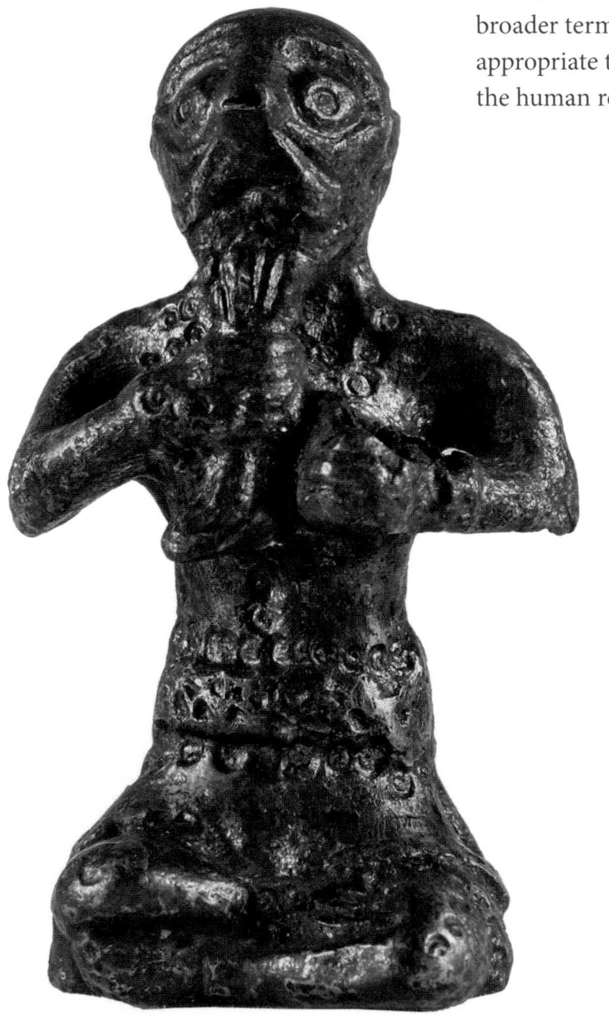

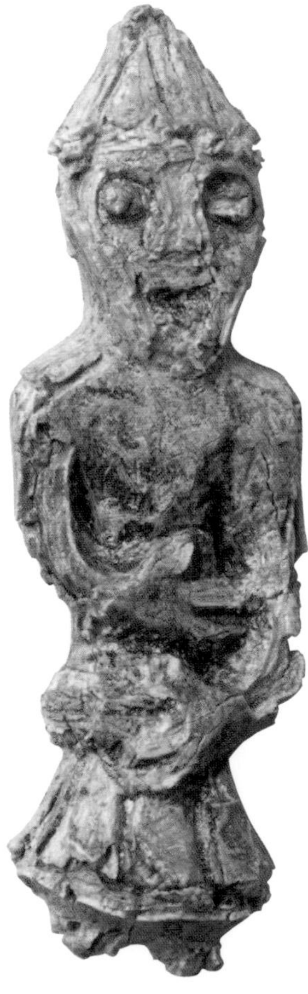

1.
Seated male figure, possibly the god Thor, Scandinavian, 10th century. Černaya Mogila, Černigov, Ukraine.
Copper alloy, gilt. L 4.7 cm, W 2.2 cm
State Historical Museum, Moscow

2.
Figure possibly of Scandinavian origin. Gnezdovo, Obl. Smolensk, Russia.
Lead. H 2.9 cm
State Historical Museum, Moscow

spiritual beliefs of the Vikings instead placed a great emphasis on interaction with the natural world, and the understanding that what we might term supernatural powers – whether gods, spirits or other creatures – were all an immutable part of that whole. These beings were spread across several different worlds or realms of existence, but all were interconnected and mutually accessible under the right circumstances (figs 1–5).

In exploring the Viking relationship with these other worlds, it is also critical to dispense with many aspects of orthodox religion that might be familiar to us today. The traditional customs of the Norse included no moral codes laid down by divine law, indeed no divine authority at all. The human relationship with the gods involved no element of worship, obedience or even unreserved approval. The gods were powerful beings with whom it was necessary to come to an accommodation in order to survive and prosper, but one did not have to like them in the process. Beyond the gods and goddesses, the human world was also shared with a myriad of other beings with whom one needed to remain on good terms and, at times, one might need to placate. It may be readily understood why the Christian peoples with whom the Vikings came into contact interpreted their world-view so critically.

That so many people today speak of 'Norse religion' may in fact be a legacy of the Christian missionaries who were responsible for the gradual decline of these practices. An ordered, structured 'religion' presents a concentrated target and is relatively easier to destroy and replace with something different. By contrast, a loosely held and largely unformulated set of beliefs, customs and traditional knowledge is much more difficult to eradicate, being more localized and subject to fluid interpretation. Strange though it may sound, it is thus possible that an early part of the Christian strategy for conversion included the effective construction of a non-Christian 'religion'.

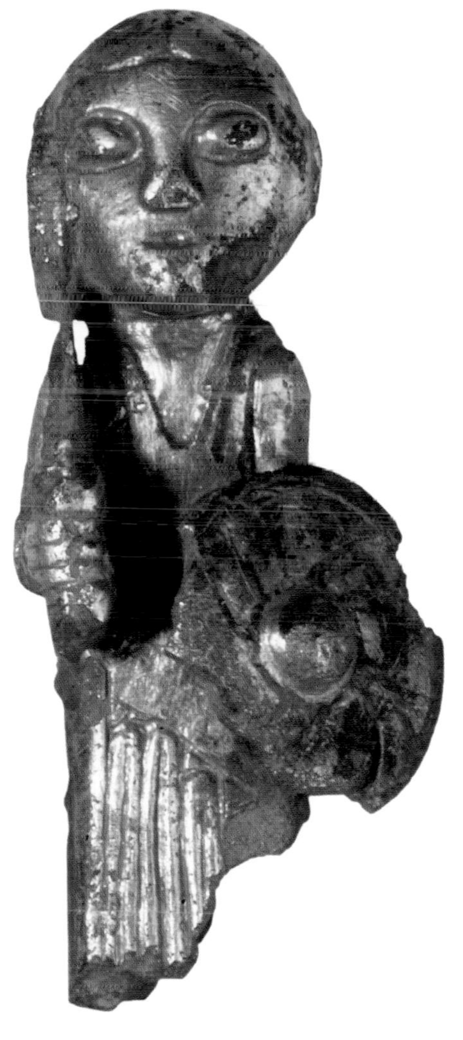

3.
Figurine, possibly a Valkyrie, *c.* 800. Hårby, Funen, Denmark.
Gilded silver with black niello inlay.
H 3.4 cm
National Museum of Denmark, Copenhagen

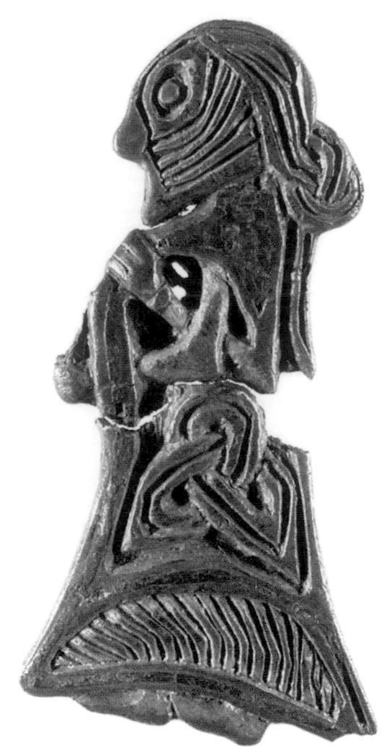

This is not to say that the Christians actually invented the Norse supernatural world – there is no evidence of this – but rather that they gradually codified it into a form that was suitable for displacement (and, to some extent, absorption) en masse. An alternative view would be that they simply misunderstood it. Whichever was the case, this process has been perpetuated in later centuries as scholars have assembled the disparate written sources into an illusory codex of 'Norse myths', bringing them together in a structured fashion that does not reflect Viking-Age reality. In fact, there is little evidence that Norse spiritual practices were ever strictly organized, or even necessarily consistently understood by those who followed them. They varied greatly across the Viking world and also changed over time.

This chapter explores this spiritual world, looking at the evidence for the ideas that shaped the Vikings' outlook on life and the rituals through which they articulated it.[2]

Landscapes of belief, landscapes of knowledge

The stories that relate the Norse cosmogony are fragmented, difficult to date and, not least, mutually contradictory. It is clear, however, that the Viking understanding of the universe was intensely spatial, involving a complex series of intersecting worlds and landscapes that gave a home not only to humanity but to all the other powers, living and dead. In rejecting 'religion' as a suitable framework within which to place these ideas, some scholars have opted instead for the notion of a 'belief system', but this is similarly unsatisfactory in that it implies a coherence where none may have existed. Indeed, belief itself is perhaps an anachronistic concept in this context: a Viking-Age person would no more claim to 'believe in' the Norse gods and other similar beings than they would 'believe in' a mountain or the sea. These things were self-evident, a matter rather of knowledge, with no distinction between the physical and the spiritual.

Representations of female figures can be understood in a number of different ways, and may represent a range of supernatural forces including goddesses, valkyries, norns and dísir. Alternatively, images such as these might represent a völva, *a human sorceress.*

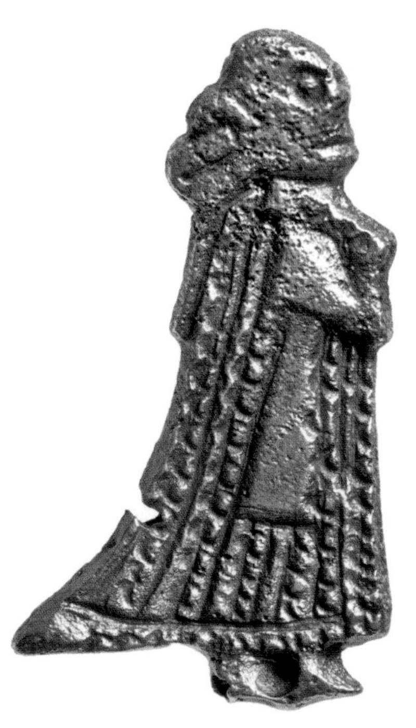

The cosmos was thought to have formed from the great void, *Ginnungagap*, with a complex series of tales relating how the gods and giants emerged as the primal beings in an environment of fire, ice, mist and cold. Murderous disputes arose from the very beginning and the worlds were eventually created from the body parts of a slain giant. Human beings – the first couple, called Askr and Embla – were created by the gods from the stumps of trees, washed up on the original shore. Other narratives provide origins for the dwarves, dwelling in the mountains and under rock, and the elves, spirits of woodland and the countryside.

The gods lived in Asgard in two families, the *Æsir* and the *Vanir*, paralleled by Midgard, the 'Middle Place' (and inspiration for Tolkien's Middle Earth), where humans dwelled. Asgard was essentially a divine-scale replica of the human world, an open landscape dotted with halls and ancillary buildings, each the home of a god or goddess and their retainers. Some have become famous, such as Odin's residence Valhöll, but there are in fact around fourteen named homes for the individual gods, and some have more than one house. Asgard even had temples and cult buildings: one of the deeply strange aspects of Norse belief is that the Viking gods were among the very few pantheons in world culture who themselves also worshipped something, though we do not know exactly who or what it was.[3]

The giants lived in Jötunheim ('Giant World'), with other, more nameless and demonic powers consigned to Utgard, the 'Outer Place'. There was also an underworld – or perhaps nine gradations of it – called Hel, with much argument as to a possible relationship to its Christian near-namesake. This was certainly one of the many destinations for the dead – the gods' halls were another, and there are still more, such as an enigmatic water-world – but the notions of specific afterlives for good and bad people should be discarded for the

4. (opposite, top)
Female figure pendant, 800–1050. Fugledegård, north-west Zealand, Denmark.
Silver with niello, partially gilt, and silver. H 4 cm
National Museum of Denmark, Copenhagen

5. (opposite, bottom)
Female figure pendant of Scandinavian style, 9th–10th century. Janów Pomorski/Truso, Poland.
Silver. H 2.7 cm
Museum of Archaeology and History in Elblag

6. (below)
Female figure, 800–1050. Fugledegård, north-west Zealand, Denmark.
Silver. H 4.5 cm
National Museum of Denmark, Copenhagen

7. (below right)
This silver cup is decorated with a representation of a female form that echoes the design in fig. 6.

Cup depicting female figures, 10th century. Lejre, Zealand, Denmark.
Silver. H 4.4 cm, Diam. 6 cm
National Museum of Denmark, Copenhagen

Viking Age. The simple fact is that we do not know exactly where Norse people were believed to go after death, or for what reasons, and there remain some significant gaps in our understanding (the afterlife of women is almost entirely unknown, for example).

We do know that this cosmos was held together by Yggdrasil, the great ash that echoes the 'World Tree' motif found in many cultures. There is disagreement as to the relative location of the worlds – some researchers seeing them as successive discs on the vertical spindle of the tree (like old-fashioned vinyl singles on a turntable), while others view them as concentric horizontal circles like an archery target lying flat, enclosing each other with the tree standing at the centre. The ambiguity may in fact be original – how many modern believers have a precise idea of the geography of their respective afterlives?

The worlds were connected in several ways, equally contradictory and confusing: travellers could move between them along the roots of the World Tree, via sacred rivers and lakes, and across Bifröst, the 'Rainbow Bridge' (of all these routes, the one with obvious visibility in the material world). The sea played a critical role, not least as the home of the Midgard Serpent, a dragon-like creature that encircled the world(s).

These landscapes of supernatural knowledge also had their guardians, beings of power, who performed specific functions. Three otherworldly women, called Norns, controlled the past, present and future; there may have been other norns for the elves, dwarves and so on.[4] Special animals moved about the tree – an eagle, a dragon, a squirrel – with others such as cockerels that heralded major events in the cosmos. The gods possessed their own individual steeds and beasts of burden. The worlds were populated still further by dozens of supernatural creatures: trolls, ogres, spirits, *dísir* (perhaps some kind of ancestral being), terrible wolves and hounds, and many others (figs 6–7). There were also the powers of the earth itself (land spirits) and the elemental dwellers in streams and stones, in the air and the fog. The Vikings thus lived in the midst of a vast, invisible population. These beings were not 'supernatural' in our sense of the word, but as much a part of nature as humans themselves, and – to their understanding – just as real.

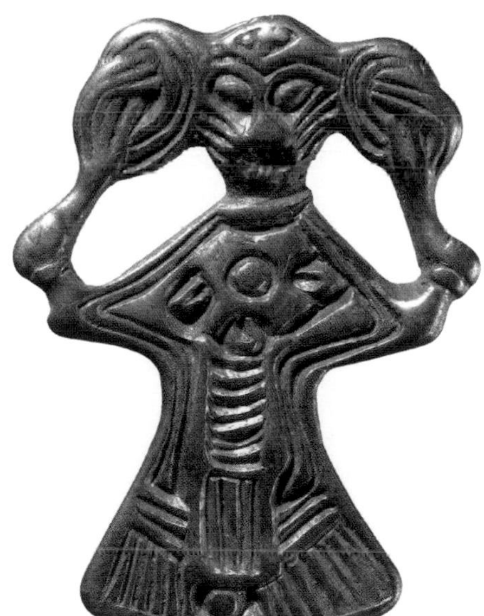

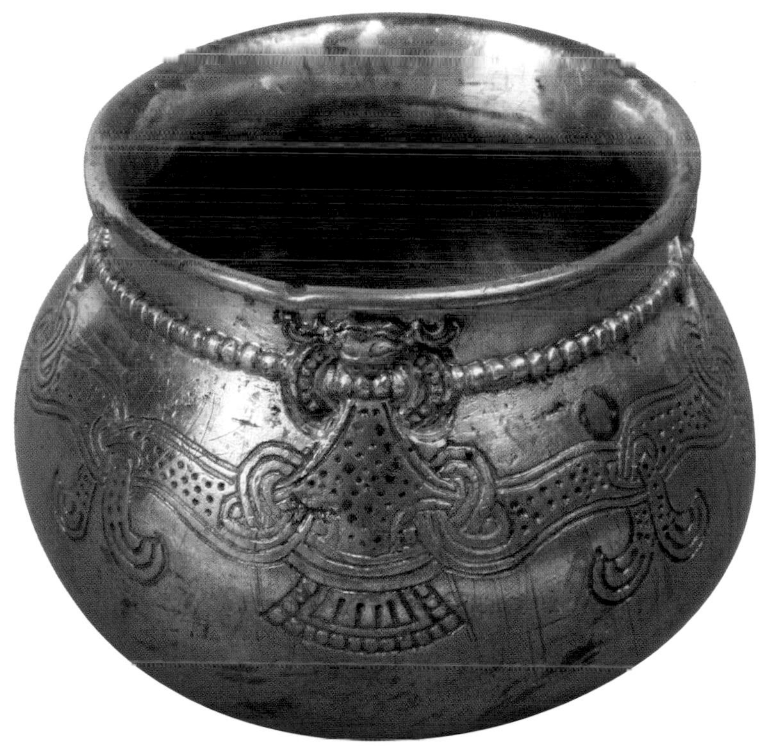

Humans and the supernatural

The popular perception of Norse 'religion' has always focused above all on the higher powers of the Viking thought-world, the gods, goddesses and occasionally their more prominent servants. However, there is little evidence that the ordinary people of the Viking world regularly communed with these deities, in the sense that people 'go to church' or participate in the formal services of other faiths today. Archaeology has shown that there were special buildings during the Viking Age, which are believed to have been set aside for 'cultic' functions (for want of a better term), and there are also indications of sacred sites in the open air. The gods may have been approached or placated at these places, but there is also literary evidence for the appeasement of other spirit-like beings too, and perhaps a kind of ancestor veneration.

The later written sources mention ritual sites called *hörgr*, which are implied to have been small buildings or enclosed spaces where rites were performed, perhaps linked to another kind of holy sanctuary called a *vé* (also found in placenames, as *vi*). Debate on the true nature, or even existence, of Norse cult buildings continues,[5] but archaeologists have found intriguing evidence that supports the texts.

A number of square wooden structures have been found that seem to have had no domestic or manufacturing function, but were instead reserved for ceremonies involving sacrifice of various kinds. Often enclosed within fences that set them spatially apart, these buildings have been found next to feasting halls at sites such as Tissø in Denmark (see p. 198), on smaller settlements such as Borg in Östergötland and in cemeteries such as Valsta in Uppland – both in Sweden – and under churches as at Mære in Trøndelag, Norway.[6] A definite identification is impossible, but a link with the *hörgr* of the sagas seems likely. An earlier building of a similar kind has been found at the high-status settlement of Uppåkra in southern Sweden, which had been maintained on the same spot for centuries and went out of use only at the very start of the Viking Age.[7] At least in some places, where they are located in direct association with halls, these structures may have functioned as something resembling 'private chapels' for the upper classes of the later Iron Age.

The *vé* sanctuaries have also left archaeological traces, especially at two recently excavated sites in Sweden where the placenames themselves preserve such a connection. At Lilla Ullevi (the 'Little *vé* of Ull') in Uppland, a square, curbed packing of stones has been found with two linear stone projections that appear to form a kind of forecourt, the whole situated at the edge of a prominent hill. There is evidence for post-built features around it – platforms and standing pillars perhaps – as well as considerable deposits of weapons, fire-steels and more than sixty amulet rings. These offerings appear to have been made at the beginning of the Viking period, with activities on the site stretching back at least a century.[8]

A comparable site has been excavated at Götavi (the 'Gods' *vé*') in Närke, with even more remarkable features.[9] Here, in the middle of an open and apparently unoccupied plain, nine parallel lines of stone packings had been laid out and then buried beneath a layer of clay (fig. 8).[10] The resulting rectangular feature appears to have had a slightly bowl-shaped depression at the centre and been bounded by a fence. Chemical analyses show that a great deal of blood had been spilled within the enclosure, especially near one end where huge posts had been erected. A connection to animal (and perhaps human) sacrifice seems clear and that this too was some kind of ritual site. Many fires had been lit around the outside of the clay area and it appears that whatever happened within would have been shielded by screens of smoke. Unlike Lilla Ullevi, the sanctuary at Götavi is astonishingly late in date, with indications that it was still in use during the eleventh century. This would seem to bear out the many literary traditions that depict Sweden as especially resistant to Christian influence for much longer than the rest of Scandinavia.

Some more ordinary buildings also seem to have had multiple purposes, especially the great halls of the leading families. There is now a growing consensus that major landowners and local chieftains may themselves have played a role in cultic ritual, and that the feasting halls of their estates could on occasion host sacrifices and other ceremonies. This may explain why, in his celebrated description of the alleged 'temple' at Gamla Uppsala in Sweden, the cleric Adam of Bremen says that the main rituals took place in the *triclinium*, the Latin word for the dining room of a house.[11] The idea of the 'temple-hall' as a category of building higher up the social scale than regular longhouses has been supported by excavations at sites such as Hofstaðir in Iceland, where evidence was found for animal offerings.[12] This interpretation is reinforced by the placename element *hof* itself, which is found in the Old Norse textual sources as a term for a ritual site in a permanent building.

We know relatively little of what went on inside these buildings, though what is loosely called 'sacrifice' – the Viking term was *blót* – seems central. Animals were certainly killed in these rites, often using a greater amount of violence than necessary simply to dispatch them. Even large creatures such as oxen and horses were decapitated, in a manner calculated to produce an impressive spray of arterial blood; this gruesome display seems to have been intentional. Oaths could be sworn on rings, ceremonies hallowed by hammer-form motions in the air (perhaps a late addition responding to the Christian *signum crucis*), and sealed by scattering sacrificial blood from twigs.[13]

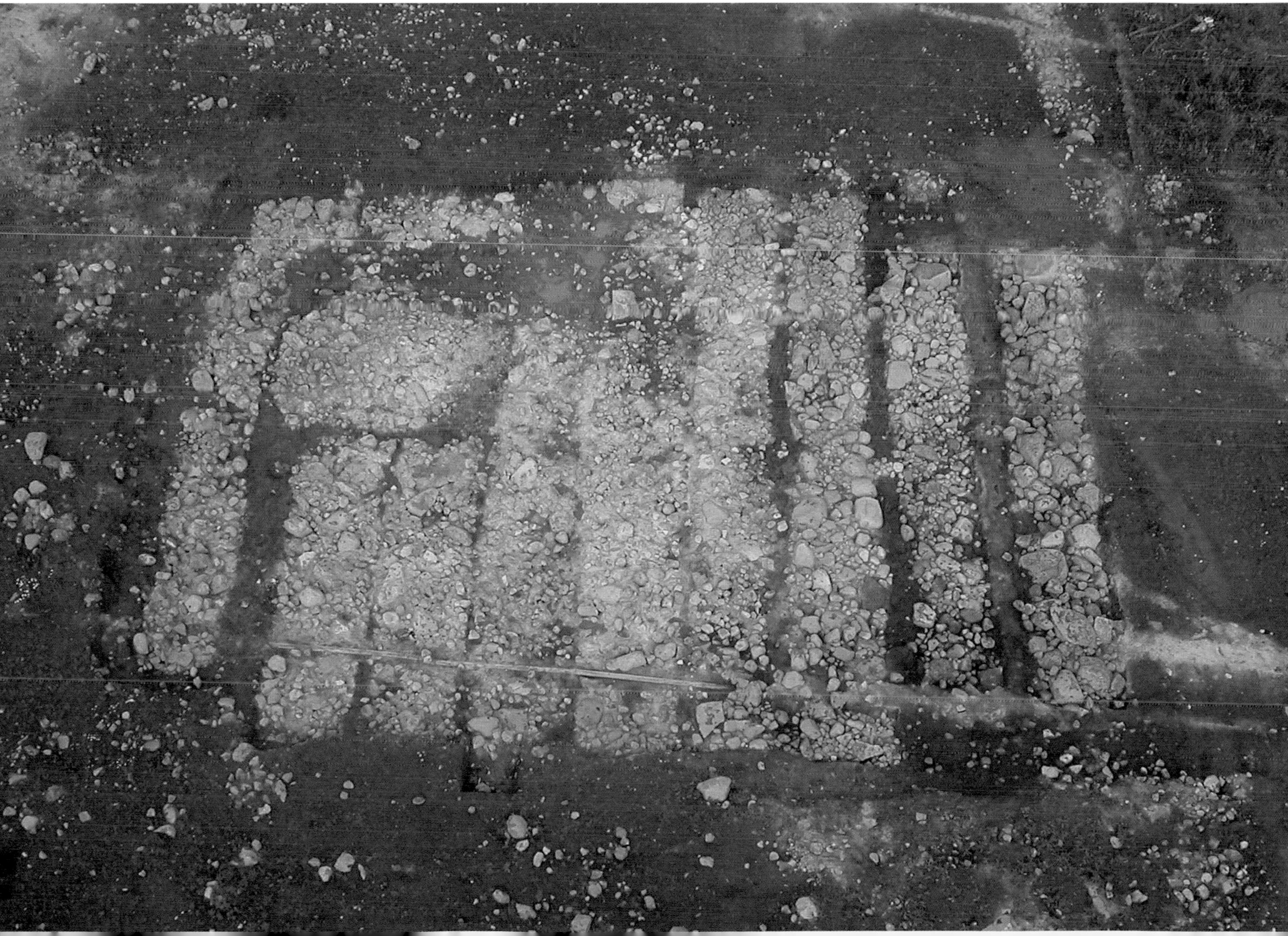

8.
The nine rectangular packings of stone that lay beneath the clay surface used for animal sacrifices in the 11th century at Götavi in Närke, Sweden. The number nine had a mystical power in the Norse thought-world.

At other sites, deposits of material have been found that built up over time as people repeatedly scattered or buried objects in and around the cultic structures. Examples include not only the weapons and amulet rings mentioned above, but also other, less intelligible objects, such as crampons, spreads of broken beads and metalworking slag. It is also clear that food was consumed at these ceremonies – presumably in ritual feasts – and the debris was sometimes thrown about. Some of the buildings show evidence for great bonfires being lit around them over long periods, perhaps suggesting that some of the rituals may have taken place at night.[14]

Beyond these structures, there is ample evidence for rituals conducted in the open air and at natural places of sacred significance. Offerings were made in bogs and other watery areas such as marshes, streams and tide zones. Finds of weapons and other metalwork are particularly common in these contexts and have been recovered even from the Vikings' overseas colonies.[15]

Most dramatic, perhaps, is the evidence for sacred groves (fig. 9). The idea of holy trees in the Germanic north, with an obvious link to Yggdrasil, is found in many ancient writers dating back to Classical times and beyond, but groves are mentioned as places of sacrifice in specific connection with Viking ritual. Adam of Bremen's description of the rites at Gamla Uppsala in Sweden, dating to around 1070 and thus very late, includes a grove of trees in which the bodies of male animals – and humans – were strung up.[16] Hanging people are shown on several picture stones from the island of Gotland, and a tree full of hanging

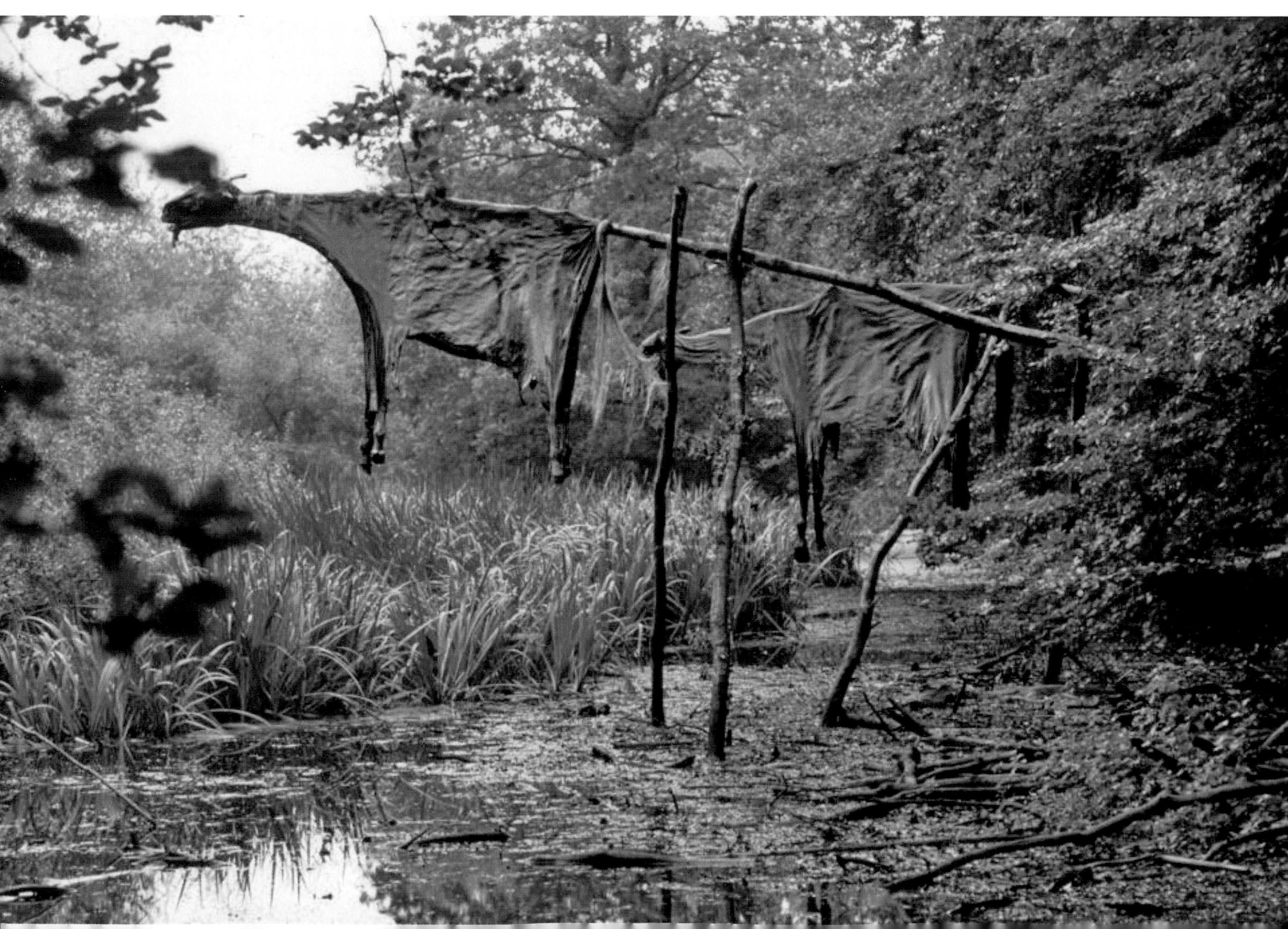

9.

A reconstructed sacrificial scaffold of late Iron Age type, with the skin, head and hooves of a horse. This form of offering is encountered around bogs and wetlands, and may also resemble the finds around the tree at Frösö.

Lejre Experimental Research Centre, Denmark

human bodies is also depicted on one of the tapestries from the Oseberg ship burial in Norway (see p. 200). It may not be coincidental that several of Odin's names refer to him as the god of the gallows, and some of the myths relate how he could wake the hanging dead and interrogate them about the future. We know that divination played a major part in Viking ritual and this too may be connected with the sacrificial groves.

Such sites are of course very hard to trace through archaeology, but something of this kind has remarkably survived at the site of Frösö (the name interestingly means 'Frey's Island') in Jämtland province, Sweden.[17] In the 1980s, alterations were carried out inside the medieval church, requiring the removal of the floor. Underneath the altar was found the well-preserved stump of a birch tree, surrounded by hundreds of bone fragments. Radiocarbon analysis has shown that the tree was cut down in the late eleventh century, in other words just about the time that the first wooden church was erected (and close to the date of Adam of Bremen's tale of the Uppsala grove). The deposits surrounding the trunk and in which the bones are preserved can be dated to the tenth century, suggesting that the Frösö site was in use then. Animals had clearly been offered there and perhaps even hung in the branches. The bones represent the heads and hooves (maybe attached to the skin) of eleven pigs, two cows and five sheep or goats, together with the heads of six elks and two stags. In addition it seems that five whole bears had once either lain by or been strung from the tree. Bones of squirrel, reindeer, horse and dog were found in addition, and the assemblage also includes human remains, implying that people too may have been sacrificed at the tree. The location of the site is telling: at the highest point of the island, the tree would have been visible from a great distance. It can be no accident that this holy place was so directly appropriated by the Christians when they built the altar of the church over exactly this spot. It is also unlikely to be a coincidence that the placename of the church site is Hov, i.e. *hof*.

These kinds of natural holy sites within the landscape may be what lies behind the distribution of theophoric placenames, i.e. those that incorporate the name of a Norse god or goddess.[18] These dot the Scandinavian countryside today and are also found more sparsely in the British Isles and the north European continent. Odin, Frey, Thor and Ull are the most commonly represented gods, though others are known. The divine name is often combined with elements that reference natural features with presumably sacred overtones; some Swedish examples include Odenslunda ('Odin's Grove'), Torsåker ('Thor's Field') and so on. Others link the god's name with that of a specific type of ritual sanctuary or cultic place, such as Ullevi, 'Ull's *vi*'. The various gods' names group geographically in Scandinavia, with different divinities being apparently more popular in some regions than others.

In summary, we see therefore an intricate landscape of supernatural power, with different kinds of activities taking place at radically varying types of site – the small *hörgr* enclosures and buildings, the sacrifices and ritual depositions at the stone and clay platforms, the rites of the 'temple-halls', and the sanctuaries in the open air, the holy trees, groves, fields and watercourses, including the bogs where offerings continued to be made as they had been for millennia. Each of these sites may have served different constituencies or may equally have met the varying needs of the same communities.

In considering the interaction of Viking-Age people and the supernatural, one can lastly explore the most personal level of all, the human body itself. From the written sources we know a considerable amount about Viking beliefs in what we might loosely call the soul.[19] Each person consisted of an outer form, the *hamr* meaning 'shape' or 'shell', containing the *hugr* – their 'essence' or mind. The latter represented their true character: thus the Hun warlord Attila was described in the sagas as having an *úlfshugr*, in the sense that he may have appeared as a man but in reality had the nature of a wolf. There was a widespread belief in shape-shifting, the ability to change form from human to animal, often to bears or wolves for men, and to sea creatures or birds for women. Each person had

10.
Thor's hammer pendant, 900–950.
Vålse, Falster, Denmark.
Silver. L 2.8 cm
National Museum of Denmark, Copenhagen

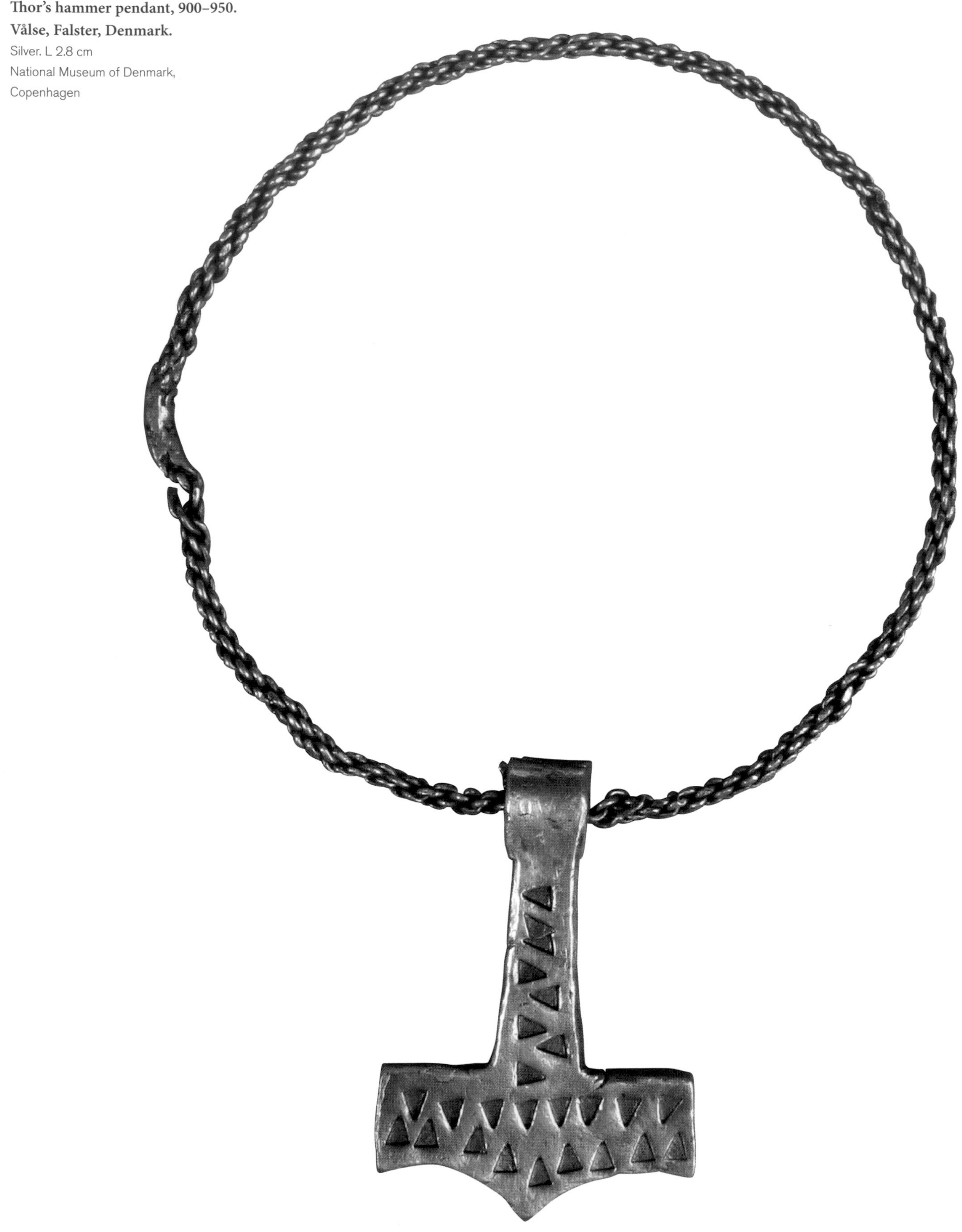

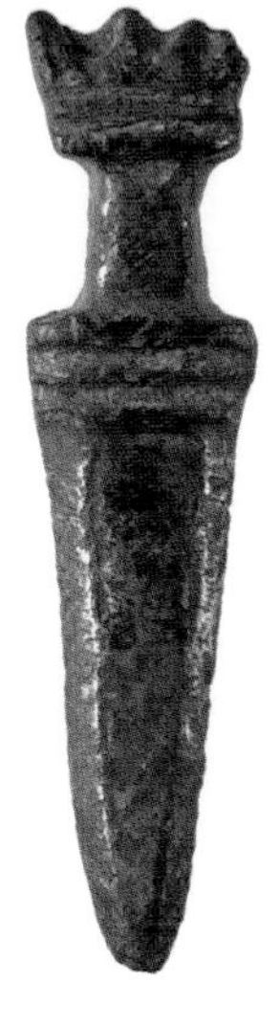

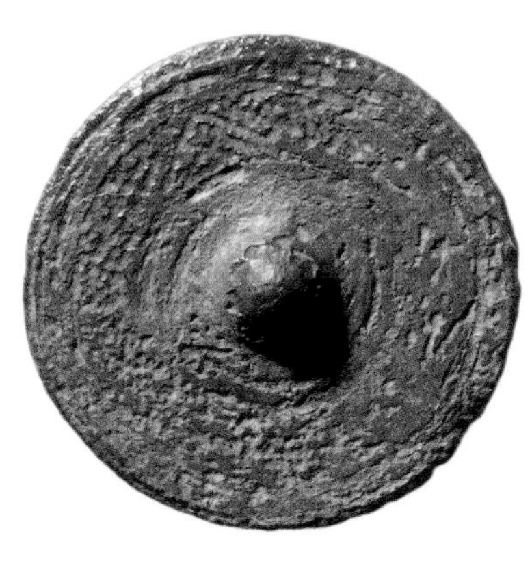

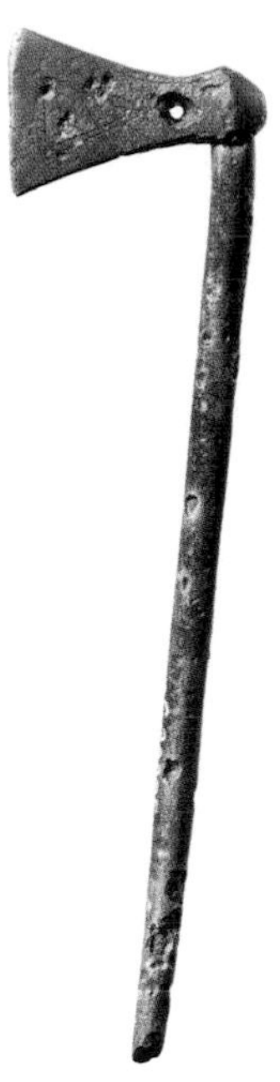

11. (above left)
Miniature pendant sword, 800–1050. Kalmergården, north-west Zealand, Denmark.
Copper alloy. L 3.3 cm
National Museum of Denmark, Copenhagen

12. (above centre)
Shield-shaped pendant, 800–1050. Nørholm, northern Jutland, Denmark.
Copper alloy. Diam. 2.12 cm
National Museum of Denmark, Copenhagen

13. (above right)
Miniature hafted axe, 800–1050. Avnsøgård, Avnsø, north-west Zealand, Denmark.
Tinned copper alloy. L 10.3 cm
National Museum of Denmark, Copenhagen

a *hamingja*, a kind of spirit that was contained within the body but which could also move independently. The *hamingja* was literally the personification of an individual's luck – a very important concept in Viking society – and could desert its host in extreme circumstances. The notion of one's luck having 'run out' is related to this, in a literal sense. Everyone had a *fylgja*, often translated as 'fetch' but literally meaning 'follower'. These were also spirits, but with a protective function, appearing in dreams to warn of impending danger or to give advice. *Fylgjur* were always female, even for a man, and were inherited within families. Many people in Iceland today still hold very strong beliefs in these beings and they are among the longest-lived aspects of Viking-Age spirituality.

People signalled their supernatural allegiances, to others or just to themselves, with a variety of personal amulets. Often found in graves but also in settlements, these took a wide range of forms of which only a few can be securely linked to named deities or beings, the most obvious example being pendants in the form of Thor's hammer (fig. 10). Other amulets were made as rings of fire-steels (for lighting fires), or miniature items such as spears, sickles, arrows, staves and shields (figs 11–13). Several finds have been made of tiny silver chairs with or without occupants. There are pendant heads, small silver depictions of women in various postures (routinely labelled as 'Valkyries' but equally likely to be *dísir* or other female beings; see pp. 165–6, figs 3–7), three-dimensional figurines and many others that resist easy categorization as idols of the gods and the like (see figs 1–2, p. 164).[20] In this as in every other aspect of the Vikings' ritual life, the variety of expression – and presumably of the underlying beliefs – was immense.

Magic and sorcery

When considering the interaction of Viking-Age people with their supernatural worlds, we have seen how the traditional focus on the gods and goddesses has been over-emphasized at the expense of connections with the more 'everyday' realm of local powers and spirits. The practical link with these beings was not cult, but magic.[21] It is relatively useless to attempt a firm definition of practices that were probably never rigidly understood at the time, but in essence magic and sorcery can be described as the mechanisms by which people tried to influence or compel supernatural powers to do their bidding. In the Viking Age, this was a field of behaviour that lay very much within the realm of ordinary communities rather than any kind of priestly or royal officialdom.

The hard evidence for sorcery in the Viking Age is difficult to evaluate, as it comes overwhelmingly from the sagas and poems preserved in medieval Icelandic manuscripts produced at least 200 years after the events they claim to describe. It is fair to say, however, that these tales are utterly saturated in magic, which appears to a greater or lesser degree in almost every story. But how far can we trust this as a reflection of the Viking Age itself? Is it effectively a kind of medieval historical fiction? It is most unlikely that any of the texts preserve exact, eye-witness descriptions of real Viking-Age practices and practitioners, but it is striking how generally consistent the image of sorcery is over many different, unrelated manuscripts that range across several centuries. One can also observe how the overall world of Norse magic is not a replica of medieval European witchcraft as it was perceived at the time of the saga-writers. In fact, the material culture depicted in the sagas is generally consistent with the Viking-Age world that they describe, not the medieval one of their paper production, arguing strongly for at least a basis in historical circumstances and oral memory. The saga descriptions of magic also have specific echoes in the archaeology of the Viking period, as we shall see below.

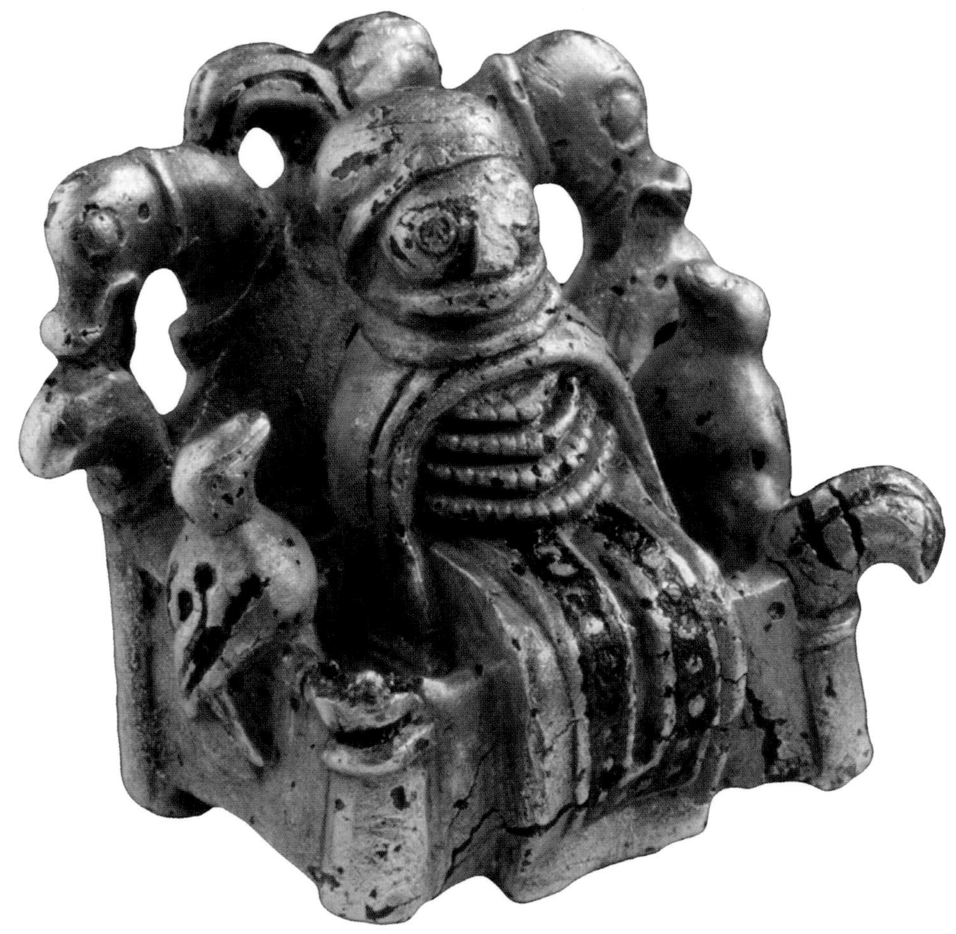

14.
This small silver figurine may represent Odin, flanked by his pet ravens Huginn and Muninn. The association of Odin with feminine magic may explain his appearance in apparently female clothing. Alternatively, the figure might depict a *völva*.

Odin or *völva* figure, 800–1050. Lejre, Zealand, Denmark.
Silver with niello. H 1.75 cm, W 1.98 cm
Roskilde Museum, Roskilde

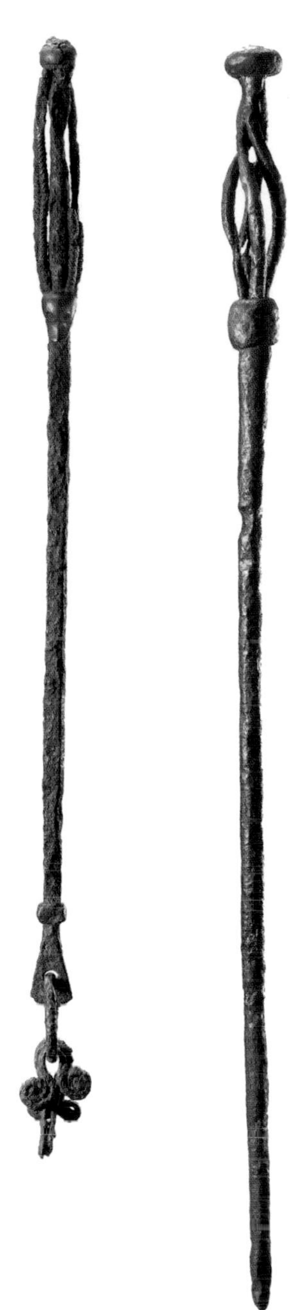

15.
Objects of this type have been interpreted as staffs used by Viking sorceresses.
(left) **Gävle, Sweden.**
Iron. L 44.37 cm
(right) **10th century. Fuldby, Zealand, Denmark.**
Iron. L 56.12 cm
National Museum of Denmark, Copenhagen

The most obvious aspect of Viking-Age sorcery as viewed through the obscure lens of the textual sources is its immense variety. There appear to have been different kinds of magic, used by different people for different purposes. The most frequently mentioned, and most feared, was called *seiðr*. Alongside this were *galdr* (magic based on a high-pitched singing), *gandr* and several others. Their functions were distinctive but also partly overlapped, and their various spells could be combined; it is perhaps most helpful to think of them all as tools in the larger toolkit of magic, selected in various combinations to achieve particular outcomes.

As the practice of magic was intensely diverse, so too was the range of its practitioners. We have nearly forty different terms for sorcerers of both sexes from the sagas and poetry, some with specific roles and others with more generalized meanings akin to the modern sense of 'witch'. Broadly speaking, Viking-Age magic was overwhelmingly the province of women. Men who performed it were stigmatized by life-threatening connotations of effeminacy, cowardice and a suggestion of passive homosexuality.[22] Faced with such consequences one might reasonably ask why men performed magic at all, but the answer seems to be that male magic conveyed the greatest potential, perhaps precisely for its transgressive qualities. *Seiðr* was taught to the gods by Freyja, but its master was Odin. The contradiction of this female magic's embodiment by the highest male god lies at the root of Viking sorcery's terrible power (fig. 14).

The textual sources contain dozens of detailed descriptions of sorcery, but in the corpus of magical descriptions as a whole, two themes emerge as steady constants: the use of sorcery for aggressive ends (ranging from neighbourly disputes to full-scale war) and a strong element of sexuality. The latter appears both in the objectives of magic (love charms and the like) and in the ritual practices themselves, which often have clearly carnal overtones and perhaps actually involved a degree of sexual performance. In this, too, we see reflections of Freyja's and Odin's personalities.

It is impossible to correlate exactly the archaeological material with the terminology of the medieval sources, but we can examine categories of excavated data that fit well with this general picture. Over fifty female graves have been recorded that contain metal staffs closely resembling the saga descriptions of a sorceress's main attribute, enshrined even in the name of the most common kind of magic-using woman, the *völva* or 'staff-bearer' (fig. 15). Graves of this type sometimes also contain bags of charms, amulets and even narcotics. Such women dressed distinctively (see p. 197). We certainly cannot say for sure that the grave of a *völva* or any other specific type of magic-worker has been identified, but we can be reasonably secure in asserting that the sorcerous practices of the medieval written sources have a genuine support in the Viking-Age excavated data (figs 16–20).

One interpretation of magical practices such as *seiðr* has been current for over 150 years, namely the idea that they represent some kind of Norse equivalent to what has elsewhere been called shamanism.[23] In general it seems advisable to use the original terminologies rather than an external one that is, in addition, an invention of anthropology, but the comparison bears discussion. Both in the variety of the magical toolkit and its technicians, and especially in the specific purposes to which sorcery was put, it must be said that there are exact parallels across the circumpolar sphere usually held to be the so-called 'cradle of shamanism'; the complex gender identities with which Norse magic was encoded also find close parallels there. The similarities are so great that some scholars have argued the saga descriptions are in fact a medieval transference of Sámi ritual practices on to the ancient Norse. Academic debate continues on the subject, but the entire complex of Norse sorcery does seem to find a natural place as an independent cultural tradition within the larger pattern of northern spirituality.

16. (right)
Miniature coiled snake pendant, 9th century. Hon, Norway.
Gold. L 3 cm, W 1.95 cm
Museum of Cultural History, University of Oslo, Oslo

17. (below left)
Miniature coiled snake, 800–1050. Denmark.
Copper alloy, L 4.8 cm, W 2.9 cm
National Museum of Denmark, Copenhagen

18. (below right)
Miniature coiled snake, 800–1050. Menzlin 5, Germany.
Copper alloy. L 2.5 cm, W 1.5 cm
Landesamt für Kultur- und Denkmalpflege Mecklenburg-Vorpommern, Schwerin

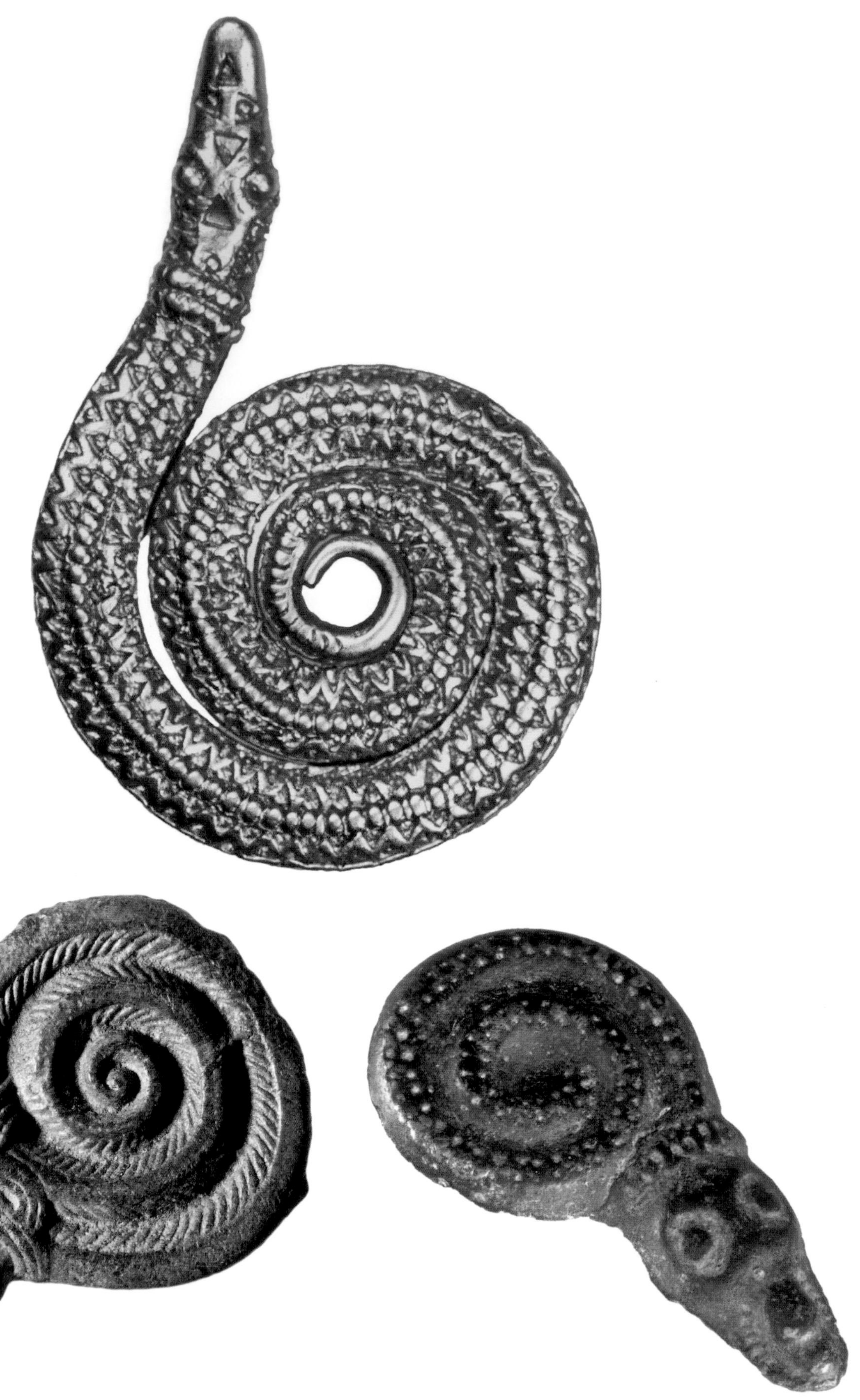

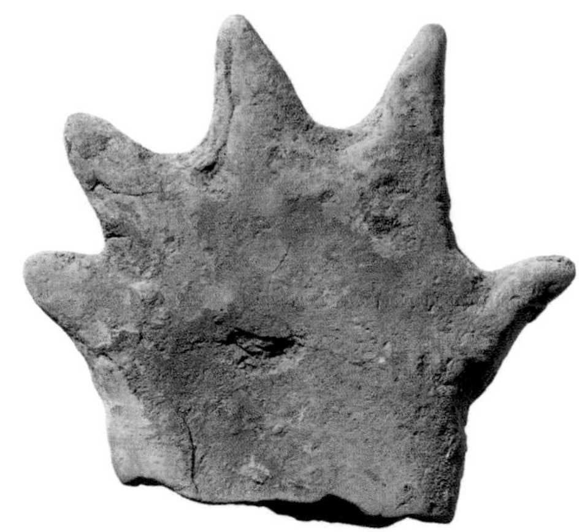

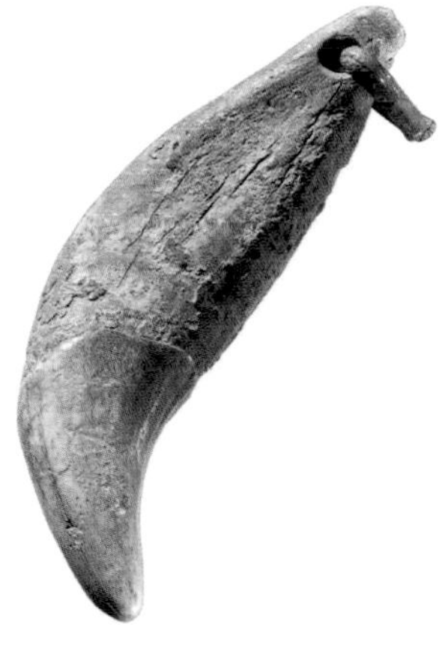

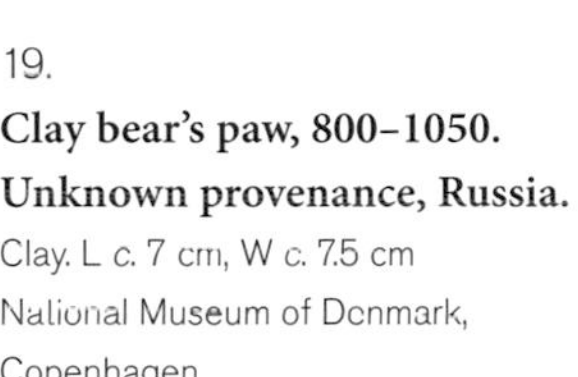

19.
Clay bear's paw, 800–1050. Unknown provenance, Russia.
Clay. L *c.* 7 cm, W *c.* 7.5 cm
National Museum of Denmark, Copenhagen

20.
Bear's tooth, 800–1050. Unknown provenance, Russia.
Tooth. L 8.5 cm
National Museum of Denmark, Copenhagen

Dealing with the dead

The most long-lasting signals of Viking spiritual beliefs can be found in the many thousands of funerary monuments that cover Scandinavia and the territories in which the Norse settled. The Vikings lived in a veritable necropolis of the visible dead, their tombs dotting the landscape as an ever-present reminder of the ancestors. Each of these memorials is encoded with meaning, a material record of ideas about mortality and what lay beyond.[24]

Before considering these death rituals in more detail, it should first be noted that not everyone seems to have received a burial monument. There are too few graves in the archaeological record to represent the entire population and at least some of the dead must have been disposed of in a manner that left no physical trace. They may have been deposited in waterways, or had their cremated ashes scattered, or perhaps been exposed to the elements in a fashion similar to some Native American scaffold burials. Estimates of what percentage of the Viking-Age population is represented by these 'missing' dead vary widely, from a small proportion to more than half: we simply do not know and nor is it clear who these people were. Perhaps the most obvious suggestion is that the unburied dead made up the slave population of Viking-Age Scandinavia (it is often forgotten that this was at least partly a slave-based economy). They may also, or alternatively, have been the poor, or people of low status. Equally, it may be that there is no consistent pattern to find and that other, less predictable, factors played a role.

One social group that is certainly under-represented among the excavated dead is that of children.[25] Infant mortality was probably as high as in other societies of the time and yet comparatively few burials of children have been found. This may have to do with notions of status and what was thought appropriate in relation to the age of the dead, and it might reflect the fluid definition of what actually constituted childhood. In those graves that have been identified, some children are laid to rest with the most minimal of artefactual accompaniment, while others are effectively buried as scaled-down adults even extending to child-size weapons and armour. In this as in most other aspects of Viking society there was little consistency, and nor should we expect it.

At the most basic level, the Scandinavians of the later Iron Age either burned or buried their dead, with cremation being overwhelmingly more common. Burials could take a number of different forms – about ten or so types can be distinguished – and up to a point it is likely that the same categories into which archaeologists divide them today would also have been intelligible to the people of the time. However, beyond this broad repertoire of external forms, there is an almost infinite variety in the detail of what people actually did with the dead, as discussed below.

The majority of recorded graves take the form of an earthen mound, though some were flush with the ground. Barrows are found in various sizes ranging from a couple of metres to several times the size of a house. They are encountered singly, in small groups and in cemeteries numbering thousands of mounds. Occasional finds of postholes and other structural indicators suggest that either wooden burial markers or perhaps even small buildings stood over some graves. Many of them were marked by settings of standing stones erected either in patterns (with many permutations of form) or alone. Sometimes stone settings are present without a mound, with the ashes of the dead buried within or around them.

When cremation was chosen, the actual burning of the body was occasionally carried out at a designated area within a cemetery, with the ashes then transported to the grave site, but more often the finished monument would be constructed over the remains of the pyre itself. Interestingly, it is comparatively rare for the ashes of a whole body to be found in Viking-Age cremation burials. At the very least, the remains were sifted, the larger fragments cleaned, washed and sometimes crushed to a finer powder. More often, however, parts – and sometimes the majority – of the cremated remains were removed before the grave was sealed.

When the dead were buried unburnt, they could be laid to rest in coffins, in boxes, in shrouds or simply lowered into the grave; other containers are also known. In rare cases, which sometimes occur together in clusters at particular cemeteries, the bodies were buried in underground wooden rooms known as 'chamber graves'. Up to 8 square metres in size or even bigger, these graves could be furnished with objects, chairs, even wall hangings and a variety of other material including animals and food. The dead were laid down inside the chambers, or occasionally buried seated, in rituals that suggest this grave type was for the wealthier or more important members of society.[26]

In the popular image of the Vikings, one burial form above all others has come to symbolize their time: the great ship graves of Scandinavia. Like other aspects of Viking funerals, these have antecedents in a continuous tradition stretching back centuries earlier than the Viking Age. Although it is the burials of entire ocean-going vessels that have become famous, we also find individuals interred in rowing boats, coastal craft and similar smaller vessels. At some sites, only parts of boats – a few clinker-built timbers – are placed in a grave, perhaps an aspiration or another kind of connection to a full ship. In still other cases, graves have been shaped like boats, or outlined that way in stone. The archaeological record of ship burial is dominated by the finds from Norwegian Vestfold, at the sites of Oseberg and Gokstad, and Tune in Østfold, though the ritual is known from other parts of Norway, Sweden and Denmark, and even from the Scandinavian colonies in the British Isles and Brittany.

In most cases, the ship has been dragged up from the shore and partly buried in a stabilizing trench. Often a wooden structure with a sloping roof like a tent was constructed near the mast and furnished much like the chamber graves found elsewhere. The dead are found inside, either laid on the deck, tucked into beds, or sometimes seated. These burials – especially at Oseberg – have provided the richest assemblages of artefacts from any Viking graves so far known, including literally thousands of objects. The ships were usually buried,

21.
A wide variety of items could be interred with the dead. The objects contained in this grave from Gotland included scales, weights and a padlock, leading to the suggestion that this was the grave of a 'merchant'.

Male burial assemblage with folding scales, weights and a padlock, late 9th–10th century. Grave 50, Kopparsvik, Visby, Gotland.
Iron, copper alloy.
Gotlands Museum, Visby

sometimes in stages that left part of the vessel open and accessible for an unknown period of time. They could also be burned before being covered with a mound.

Most graves of all kinds contain one individual, though multiple burials of up to four or more people are found. A recent ship grave excavated in Estonia and dating to about a century before the Viking Age contained an astonishing thirty-six men, all of whom appear to have died in battle and perhaps represent the fallen members of a Scandinavian raiding party. Other mass graves have been discovered, notably at Repton in Derbyshire, England, where a charnel deposit contained what are believed to have been disease victims from the 'Great Army' of Danes who overwintered there in the 870s.[27]

There is also a largely unacknowledged problem with the sex determination of the excavated dead, which is not always unequivocally clear even where skeletal material survives.[28] Poor bone preservation has often meant that burials are labelled as 'male' or 'female' solely on the basis of their artefactual content. This in turn links to possibly unwise assumptions about what kinds of things are 'typical' for men and women to use, with the vital caveat of alternative gender constructions that may have been socially signalled very differently. These uncertainties may potentially have skewed our overall perception of the funerary data in radical ways.

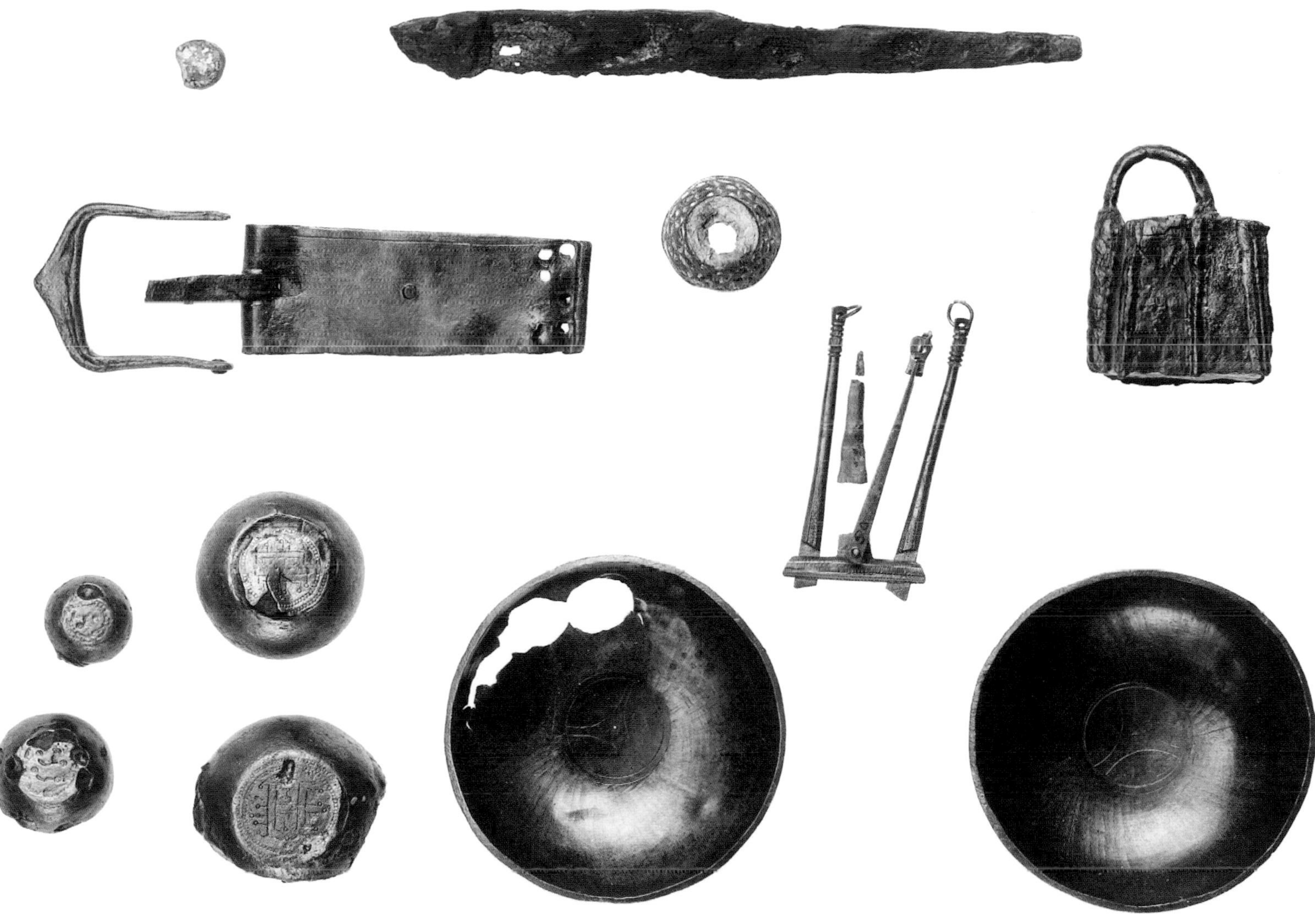

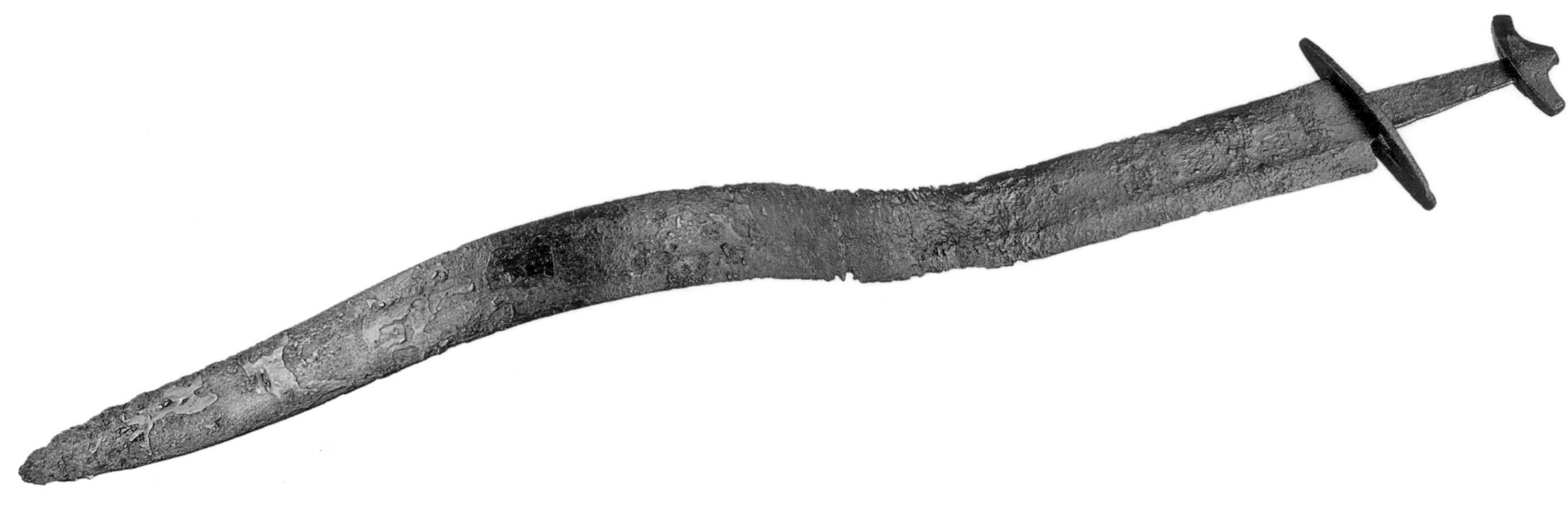

22.
Sword with bent blade, 900–1050. Löbertshof, Kr. Labiau/region of Slavjanskoe, Kaliningradskaja Obl., Russia.
Iron. L 84 cm, W 12.8 cm, H 13 cm
Museum für Vor- und Frühgeschichte, Staatliche Museen zu Berlin, Berlin

Animals are a very frequent presence in Viking graves. These predominantly include domestic species such as cattle, pigs, sheep, goats and poultry. Horses are also known, singly and in pairs, often bridled for riding or harnessed as if for drawing a wagon; in some of the great ship burials, up to twenty or more horses may be found, an enormous expenditure in terms of wealth. Birds of prey, probably used for hunting, are occasionally found in high-status burials. Dogs (though almost never cats) are not uncommon, alongside occasional finds of more unusual creatures such as owls and peacocks.

As we have seen above, in association with 'cultic buildings' there is archaeological and textual evidence to suggest that animals were killed in very specific ways, and this is also found in the graves. There is the same emphasis on blood and violence, and even birds seem to have been physically ripped apart. In some instances, dogs and horses were actually bisected. Sometimes the flesh has been crudely slashed from the bones. Another common feature of both inhumations and cremations is that only parts of the animals are present, often but not always representing the conventional cuts of meat. These creatures were clearly not 'food' alone.

When the burials are considered together and their individual details are examined, a great many variables come into play: the numerous body positions of the deceased reflect all the flexible possibilities of the human form; animals may or may not be present in widely ranging numbers and species; objects are found buried with the dead in a profusion that essentially reflects everything Viking technology could produce (fig. 21), including clothing and dress accessories, weapons, tools for all kinds of household and farmyard activity, kitchen ware and domestic items, riding gear, agricultural equipment, furniture and even vehicles such as sleds, wagons and ships. On occasion, even other humans seem to have been killed as part of the funeral rites and deposited with the dead. Above all this, each human or animal corpse, each object, could be treated in a range of ways. Bodies are sometimes found dismembered, with the parts either reassembled in roughly anatomical

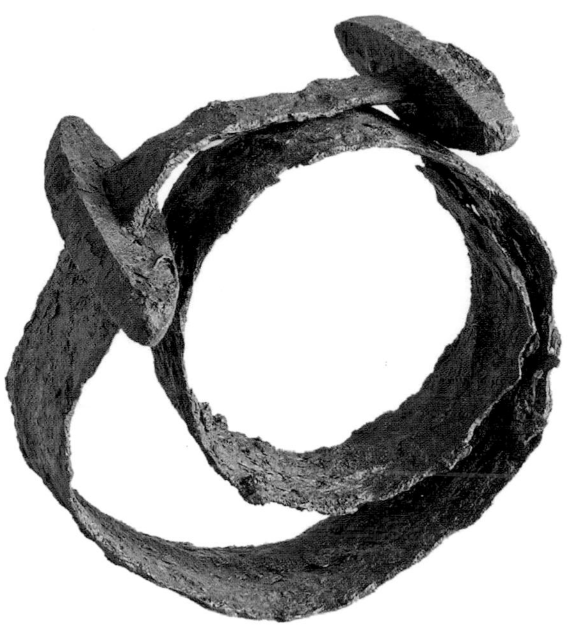

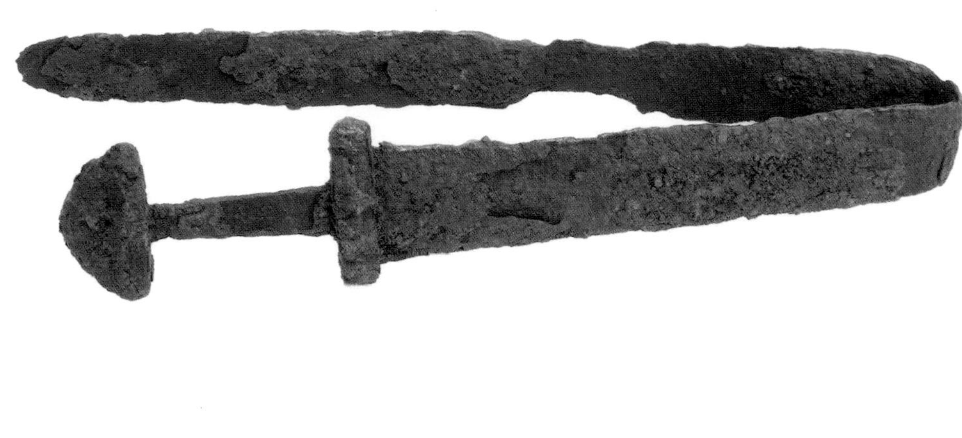

23.
Sword with rolled-up blade, 800–1100. Grave 126 B, Linkuhnen, Kr. Niederung/ Ržcvskoe, Kaliningradskaja Obl., Russia.
Iron. L 15.5 cm, (folded), W 17 cm, H 11 cm
Museum für Vor- und Frühgeschichte, Staatliche Museen zu Berlin, Berlin

24.
Ritually 'killed' sword, 800–1100. Near Kilmainham, Dublin, Ireland.
Iron. L 47.5 cm (folded)
National Museum of Ireland, Dublin

position, placed in different sections of the grave, or entirely missing. Artefacts, especially weapons, were sometimes deliberately broken before burial (figs 22–24), or may have been made for the funeral. Again, each grave is also different in the precise location and positioning of its contents. Sometimes graves reference others nearby, and occasionally parts of the same dead person, or the smashed remains of individual objects, are distributed between two or more burial monuments. Other burials are added to over time, with further people being interred in an earlier mound, for example. Some graves have clearly been opened, sometimes repeatedly, and the objects (sometimes bodies too) either taken away or moved around.[79]

This extraordinary variety, with almost every grave having its distinctive features, but nonetheless expressed within a relatively limited number of outer burial forms, is a central problem in understanding Viking burial practices. In these circumstances, more questions naturally follow: how do we define a 'grave' or a 'funeral' at all?

The combination of Viking burials raises many fascinating questions, not least because the material in graves often inescapably implies activities that must have been carried out somewhere else. When cremations are not found on the site of the pyre, where were the dead burned? In the case of animals, where were they killed? Where only some body parts of animals or humans are present, what happened to the rest? Although the objects buried with the dead are often assumed to be their possessions, we do not know this; they may have belonged to a variety of people, and by their presence signalled different meanings accordingly.

It is clear that the funeral rituals were complex affairs and took a considerable period of time, sometimes so long that the body was placed in a temporary grave while the primary site was being prepared (an example of this has been excavated in northern Iceland). A unique eye-witness description of a ship cremation in Russia has been left to us by an Arab diplomat, ibn Fadlān, who travelled the Volga in 921–2 (see p. 71), which can be precisely correlated with many of the discoveries of boat graves made elsewhere.[30] He notes that there the funeral rites took ten days of continuous activity, which may not be untypical.

One obvious factor in understanding Viking burials is the question of where the individual dead were thought to be destined. As we have seen, we know relatively little of specific afterlife beliefs and what we do know contains many contradictions. The graves give us small clues, though these are hard to interpret. The buried dead, and even the accompanying horses, sometimes wear crampons on their feet – does this imply that the funeral took place in winter, or are the dead travelling to somewhere cold? The written sources mention special 'Hel-shoes' to speed the dead on their way: is this something similar? When vehicles are involved, especially ships, it is often assumed that death was therefore a journey, and that the deceased would travel by boat, wagon or sled into the next world (fig. 25). This may be true, but there is no reason why these might not just represent exceptionally expensive possessions of the dead (or their living relatives) alongside all the other artefacts. In the greatest ship burial of all, Oseberg, the vessel was actually moored in the grave by a hawser tied to a massive boulder; apparently the intention was that it should not 'travel' anywhere at all (see p. 200).

Explaining this immense range of funerary ritual is not easy. Some scholars have suggested that it represents a variety of local and regional customs, from community tradition to family practice.[31] Others argue for more complex readings, for example that the detail of ritual activity suggests a literally dramatic element to the funerals, perhaps involving some kind of narrative or story acted out as part of the ceremonies and adapted for each dead person.[32] At present we simply cannot be sure, other than that the Viking way of death was diverse indeed.

25.
Wagon from the Oseberg ship burial, early 9th century. Oseberg, Sem, Vestfold, Norway.
Museum of Cultural History, University of Oslo, Oslo

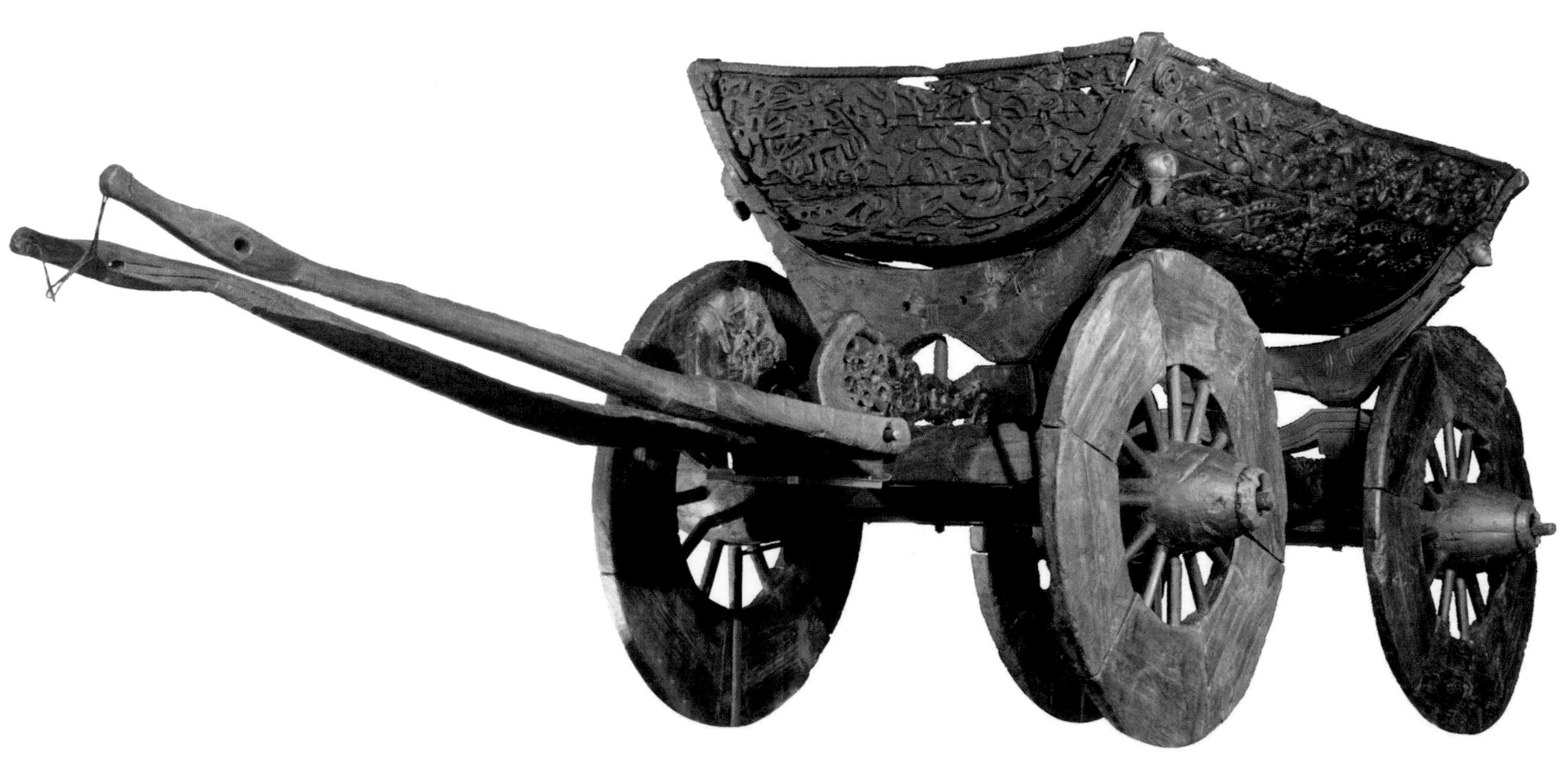

A change of faith

One of the most profound transformations that took place in Scandinavia during the Viking Age – indeed, one of the factors that justifies the notion of a discrete historical period at all – was the erosion of traditional spiritual beliefs by the social and political structures of Christianity. This process used to be conceptualized as one of 'conversion', effectively the replacement of one set of ideas with another, but it is clear that what happened was in fact much more nuanced and prolonged. In one sense, there is no doubt that Scandinavia in the eighth century was a mass of tribal territories and astonishingly varied traditional beliefs, and yet only 350 years later took its place on the European political stage as the three Christian nation states of Norway, Sweden and Denmark. However, the degree to which this outward transformation reflects deep social change and actual spiritual practice is less clear.

In their European travels of the seventh and eighth centuries, the Scandinavians certainly encountered Christians and their beliefs, and would also have seen their material expression in the form of churches and the culture of monasteries. We do not know how much of this detailed theology was understood by the Vikings, but the basic ideas were probably familiar at least to those making regular journeys abroad. As these people returned home, Christian concepts – and perhaps those of other faiths, such as Islam (see p. 70) – thus seeped into Scandinavia for centuries before the nominal conversion. When ecclesiastical treasures such as book mounts and church plate entered the north as loot, it is also inevitable that people would have had some idea of their function.

We know from Continental written sources that Christian missions had been active in Scandinavia from at least the ninth century (fig. 26), most of them originating in Germany, and there may have been earlier efforts that have left little textual trace.[33] Consisting initially of a handful of missionaries, most of these projects focused on larger settlements such as trading sites and early towns. Their leaders also made efforts to acquire a measure of protection from the local authorities, royal or otherwise. A few local converts were made and permission was sought to build churches (or to consecrate existing buildings), but with little long-term result until the tenth century. Successive missions to the Swedish lake-town of Birka did not establish a firm foothold, though others met with greater success in Denmark. Due to its geographical location, contacts with the surrounding Christian cultures had naturally been more intensive here over a longer period.

26.
Objects like this pendant, incorporating a Carolingian Christian coin, perhaps provide evidence of early contact with Christian missions.

Pendant made from *Christiana Religio* denier, Louis the Pious, (814–40). Janów Pomorski/Truso, Poland.
Silver. Diam. 2.1 cm
Museum of Archaeology and History in Elblag

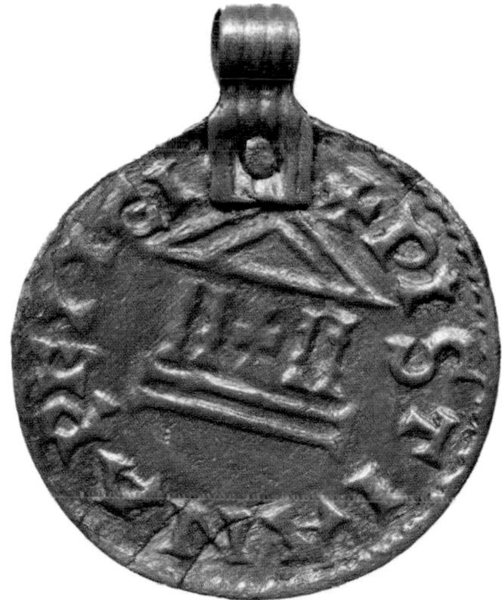

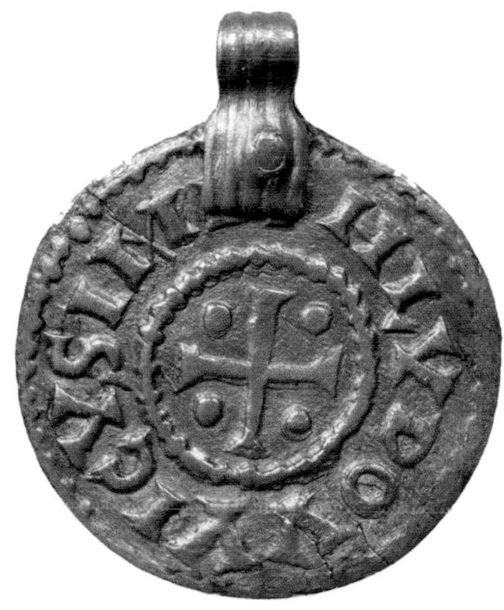

It is also important to note that the tone of these first missions emphasized an outward conversion to the liturgy and practices of Christianity, but placed much less stress on what people actually believed. Several early law codes leave space for private ritual of a decidedly non-Christian nature, so long as this took place behind closed doors and proper respect was publicly shown to the Church.[34] A genuine shift of faith was a development of the early Middle Ages and this should be remembered in the context of Viking-Age spiritual ideas.

Formal conversion followed very much a top-down model, as the papacy sought to bring Scandinavian kings into line with the 'true' faith and therefore integrate the emerging Viking kingdoms into Christian Europe. The link between church and state, and the centralization of both secular and religious power, was crucial (fig. 27). King Harald Bluetooth of Denmark proclaimed the conversion of Denmark on his monumental rune-stone at Jelling in the late tenth century, and set this in the context of an equally ambitious programme of infrastructure investment and royal display; even the bones of his father, Gorm, were translated from a burial mound to the new church founded beside it (see pp. 158–9). From the contemporary archaeological record, however, it is clear that the traditional forms of burial continued elsewhere in the country and the practical observance of indigenous spiritual beliefs was maintained for some time alongside increasing Christian influence. Not least, Harald himself was deposed in a popular uprising that may have been at least partly connected with his religious convictions, or more particularly their expense. The same process was even more drawn out in Norway, where a series of civil wars was nominally fought on grounds of religious conscience as well as power (figs 28–29). Formal Christian governance was not fully established in Sweden until the twelfth century,

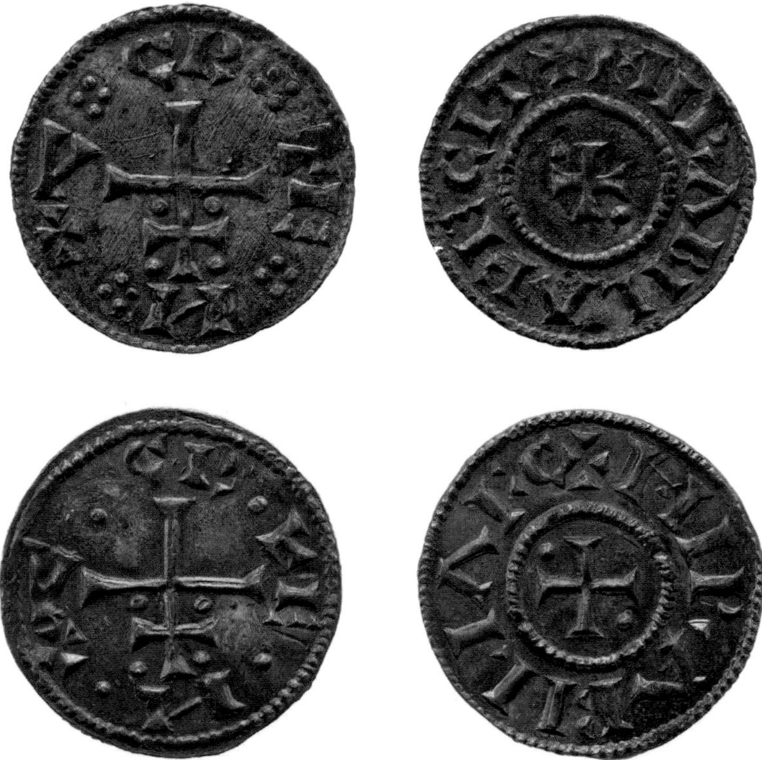

27.
These silver coins of a Viking king of Northumbria, Cnut (*c.* 900–905), spell out the king's name in the sign of the cross (i.e. from top to bottom and then left to right). The reverse of the coin bears the biblical quotation MIRABILIA FECIT ('[he] has done marvelous things'). They make a clear association between royal and heavenly power.

Two pennies of Cnut of Northumbria, Mirabilia fecit type, *c.* 900–905. Cuerdale, Lancashire, England.
Silver. Left Diam. 1.9 cm; right Diam. 2.0 cm
British Museum, London

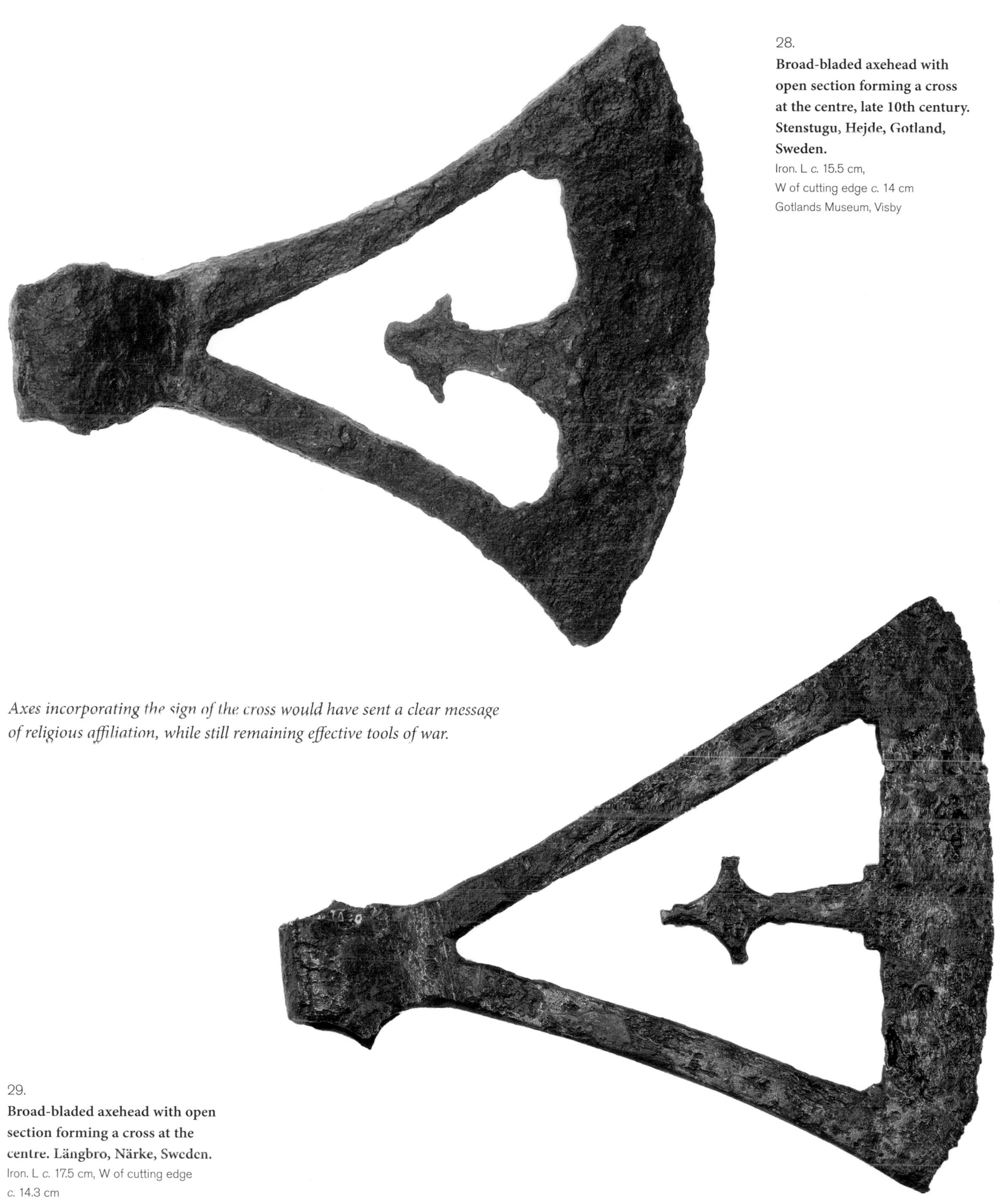

28.
Broad-bladed axehead with open section forming a cross at the centre, late 10th century. Stenstugu, Hejde, Gotland, Sweden.
Iron. L *c.* 15.5 cm,
W of cutting edge *c.* 14 cm
Gotlands Museum, Visby

Axes incorporating the sign of the cross would have sent a clear message of religious affiliation, while still remaining effective tools of war.

29.
Broad-bladed axehead with open section forming a cross at the centre. Längbro, Närke, Sweden.
Iron. L *c.* 17.5 cm, W of cutting edge *c.* 14.3 cm
Statens Historiska Museum, Stockholm

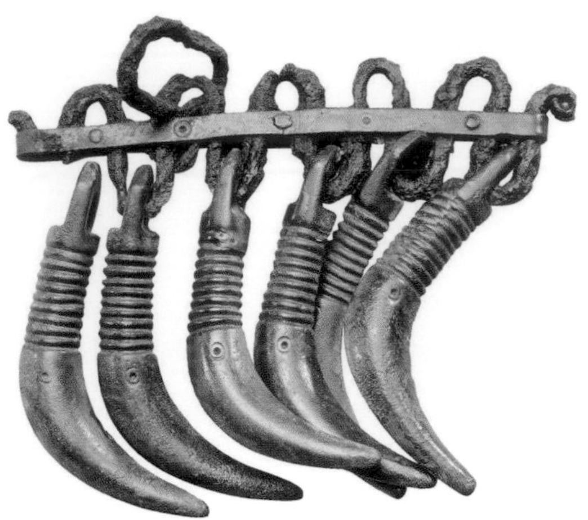
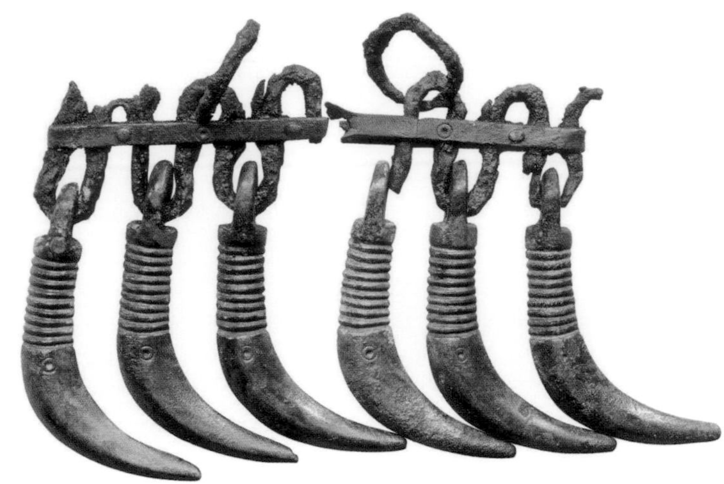

30.
Finnish ornaments of non-Christian magical significance.

Bear's tooth pendants, early 1000s. Lehtimäki, Kalanti, Varsinais-Suomi, Finland.
Copper alloy, iron.
National Museum of Finland, Helsinki

although centres of the new faith had flourished earlier in places such as Sigtuna. Even as late as the fourteenth century, law codes were still being written forbidding pagan practices, and it is clear that the gap between the public and private spheres of belief was long-lasting.[35]

The material culture of Christianity is equally ambiguous, despite its outward signals. Overtly Christian objects, such as cross pendants, first occur in graves alongside other amulets that undoubtedly relate to non-Christian beliefs (fig. 30). The new symbols are being added to an existing set, rather than replacing them, and we may gather that the 'new' god – the White Christ, as he was known at times in the north – first sat beside the existing Norse pantheon (figs 31–2). This essential pragmatism is revealed in other aspects of material culture, as in a soapstone mould found in Trendgården, Denmark (fig. 33), designed for making cheap pendants for the mass market. The mould contains spaces for casting three separate pieces simultaneously: one Thor's hammer and two Christian crosses, perhaps an indication of relative supply and demand. There is also space on the end of the mould for an additional Thor's hammer. It is worth considering that the first definite Christian crosses appear in Scandinavia in the ninth century, the first crucifix is known from around 900, while the last Thor's hammers are from the early twelfth century (figs 34–41).

This relationship between coexisting cultures was also evident in the monuments of ritual, especially graves. Just as the process of increasing Christian influence was gradual, the nature of the traditional customs also changed over the same period. If non-Christian ritual practice can perhaps be seen to become more dramatic in the late Viking Age, this may be a deliberate reaction to the growing power of the missions. There is certainly a sense in which these spiritual beliefs were more monumentally expressed – for example, in massive burial mounds of increasing elaboration – and this too might be a conscious harking back to the prehistoric barrows of earlier times, a demonstrative link to the ancestors and the 'old ways'.

Some aspects of pre-Christian Viking culture, such as the erection of rune-stones, were appropriated and expanded as the new faith became more embedded among the populace. Clear regional patterns emerge and the Mälar Valley of central Sweden formed the core of

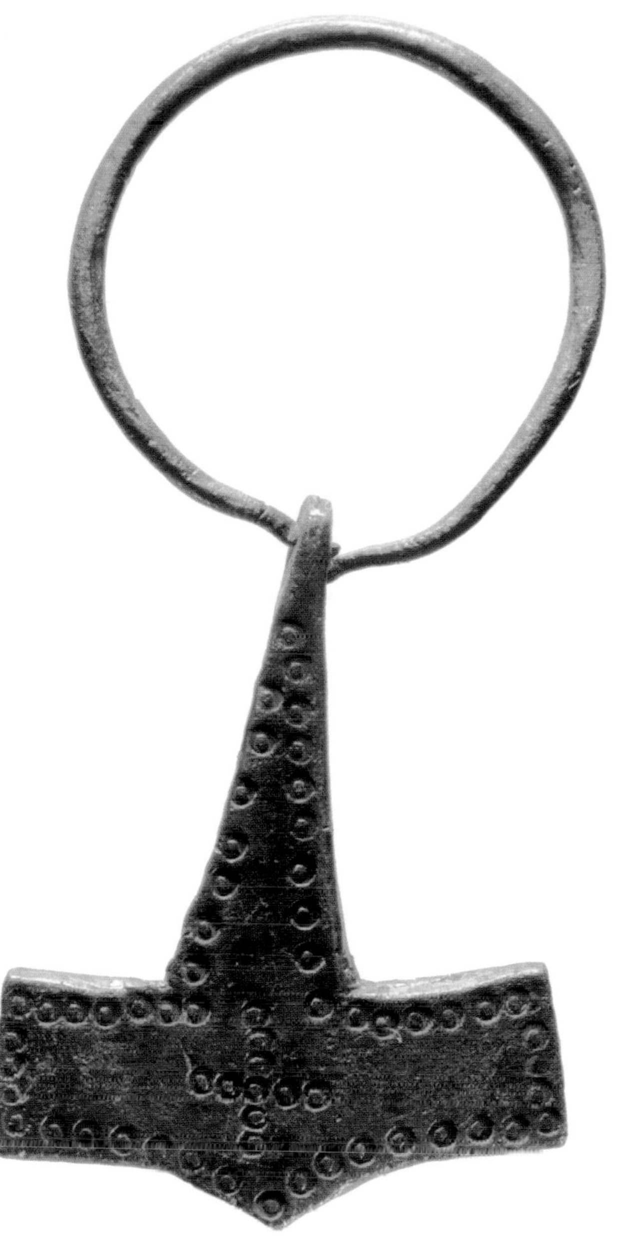

31. (left)
This Thor's hammer pendant has been decorated with a Christian cross at the centre, suggesting that belief in Christ did not necessarily mean that the old gods were immediately abandoned.

Thor's hammer with punched cross ornament, 10th century. Hedeby, Germany.
Silver. L 8.2 cm, W 3.9 cm
Archäologisches Landesmuseum, Schloss Gottorf, Schleswig

32. (below left)
On this coin from Viking York, Thor's hammer forms part of the name of St Peter. The point may have been to link the saint with Thor to aid in the conversion of the non-Christian Scandinavian population.

St Peter coin with Thor's hammer, *c.* 921–7. York, England.
Silver. Diam. 1.9 cm
British Museum, London

33. (below)
Mould for crosses and Thor's hammers, 950–1000. Trendgården, northern Jutland. Denmark.
Soapstone. L 9.7 cm, W 3.7 cm, H 3.3 cm
National Museum of Denmark, Copenhagen

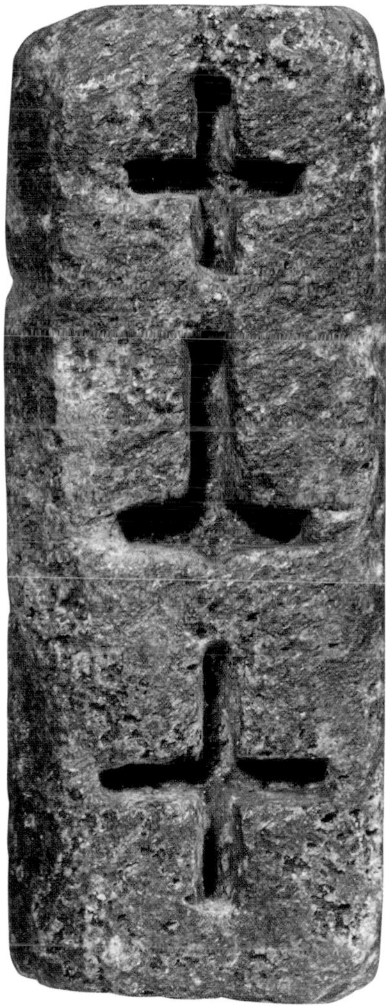

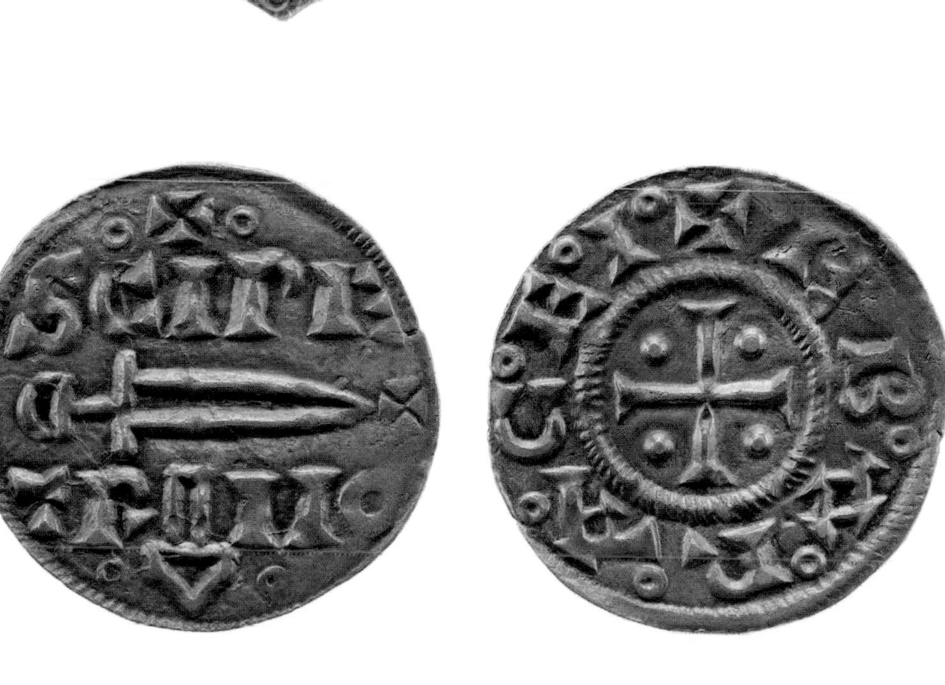

34. (below)

Selection of Thor's hammers, 10th century. Tissø, Zealand, Denmark.

Iron, silver and silver gilt, L 3–5 cm
National Museum of Denmark,
Copenhagen

35. (right)

Thor's hammer, 800–1050. Blåvand/Skallingen, south-west Jutland, Denmark.

Amber. L 2.3 cm, W 1.6 cm
National Museum of Denmark,
Copenhagen

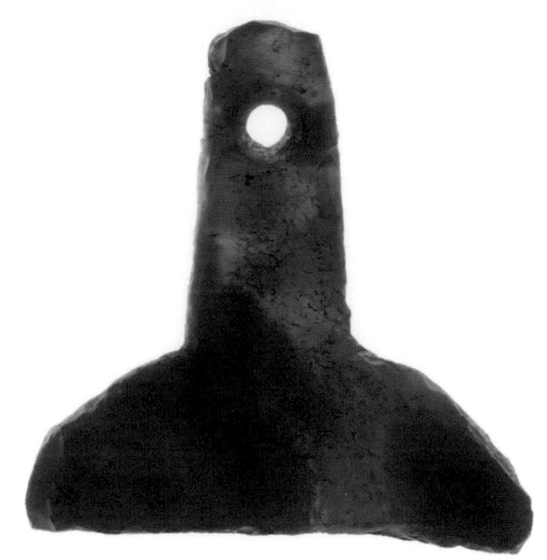

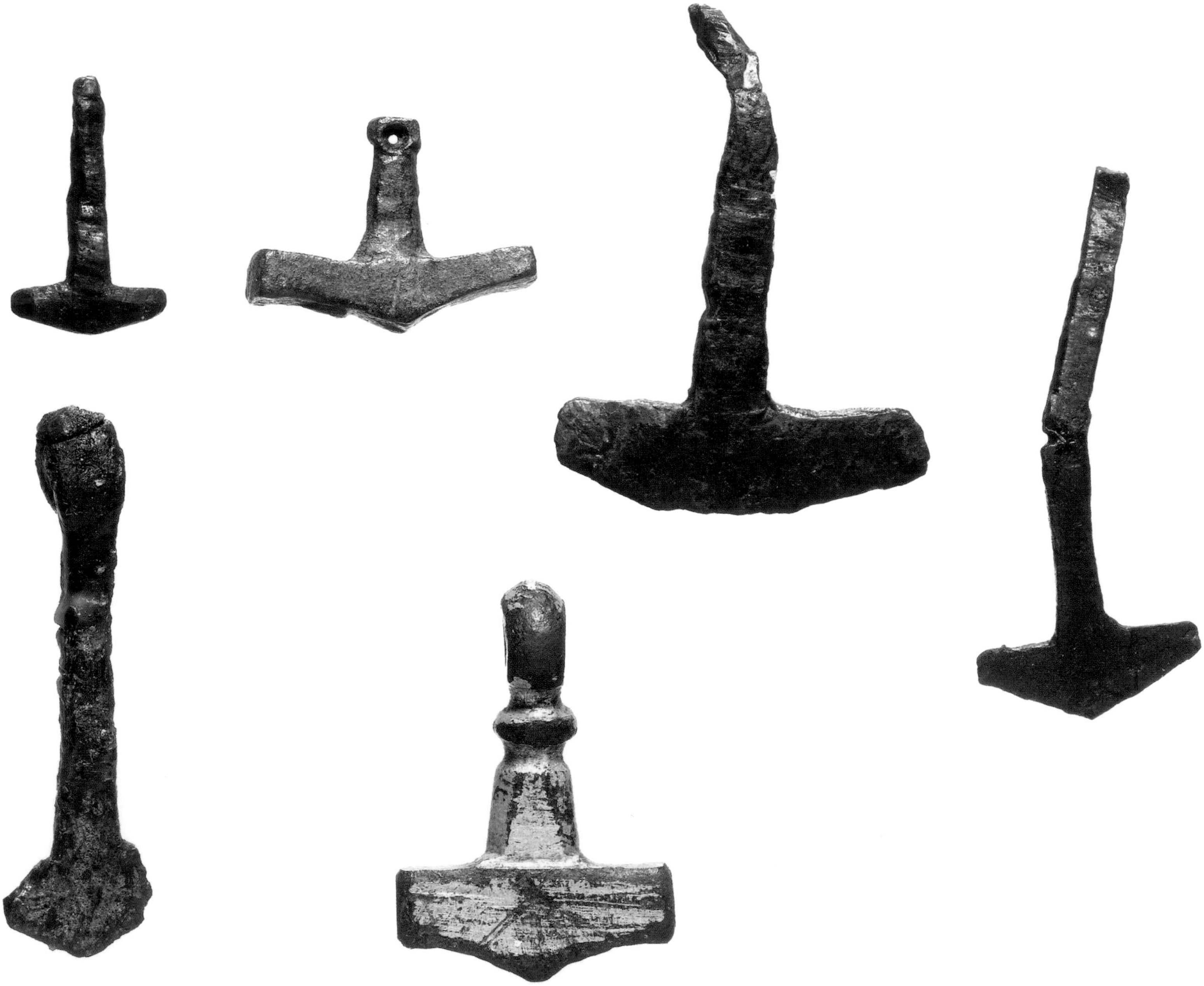

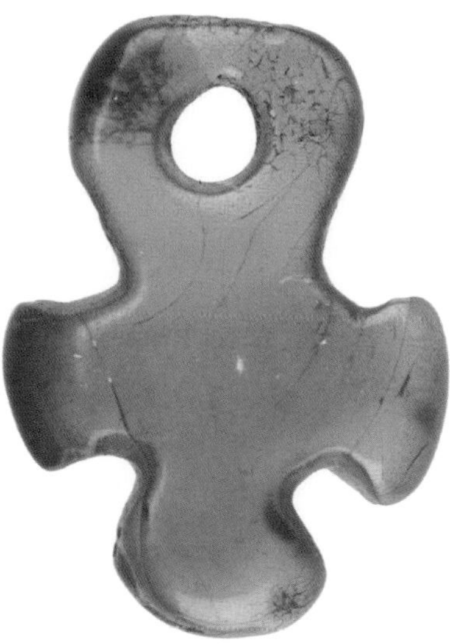

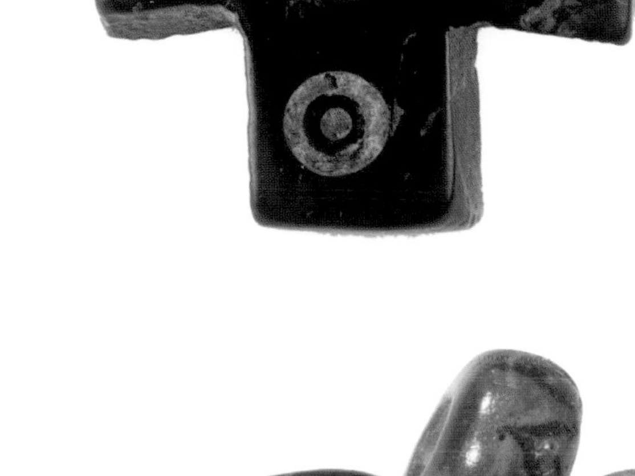

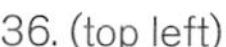

36. (top left)
Cruciform pendant, 10th–11th century. Fishamble Street, Dublin, Ireland.
Amber. L 2.49 cm, W 1.6 cm
National Museum of Ireland, Dublin

37. (top right)
Cruciform pendant, 10th–11th century. High Street, Dublin, Ireland.
Jet. L 1.57 cm, W 1.62 cm
National Museum of Ireland, Dublin

38. (right)
Pendant cross and beads, 10th century. Female grave K/1954 V, Kaupang, Vestfold, Norway.
Silver, glass. Cross L 3.1 cm; beads Diam. 0.9–2.1 cm
Museum of Cultural History, University of Oslo, Oslo

39. (bottom left)
Arm-ring depicting stylized mounds, trees and crosses, symbolic renderings of the triple crucifixion at Golgotha, 9th–early 10th century. Råbylille, Elmelunde, Møn, Denmark.
Gold. L 7.7 cm
National Museum of Denmark, Copenhagen

40. (bottom centre)
Penny with stylized representation of the Golgotha triple crucifixion, 950–1000. Pilhus, Denmark.
Silver.
National Museum of Denmark, Copenhagen

41. (bottom right)
Cross pendant adapted from a coin of Otto Adelheid coin, c. 1000. Øster Vandet, Thy, Denmark.
Silver. Diam. c. 2.0 cm
National Museum of Denmark, Copenhagen

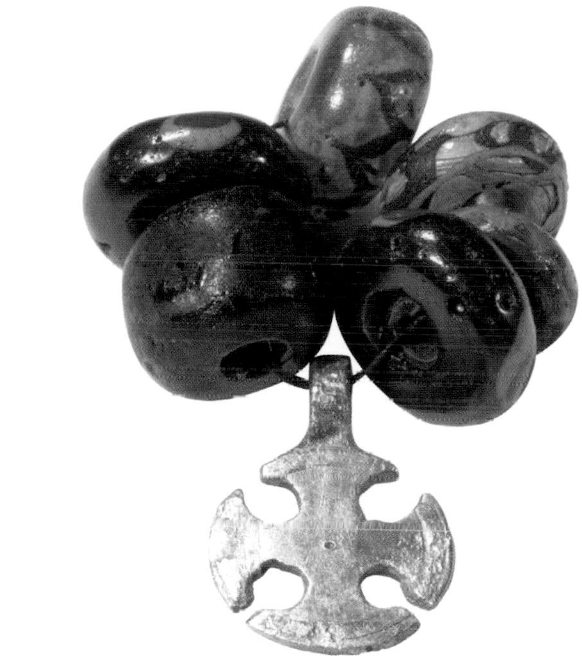

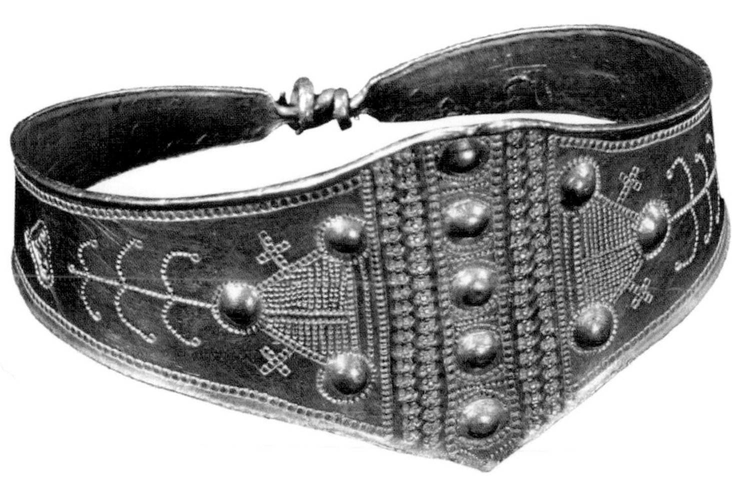

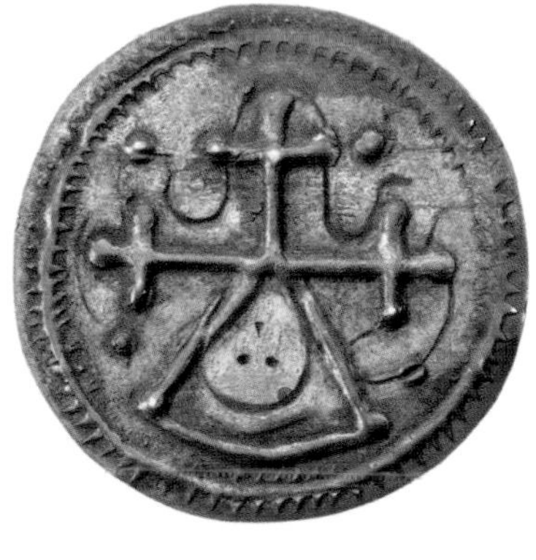

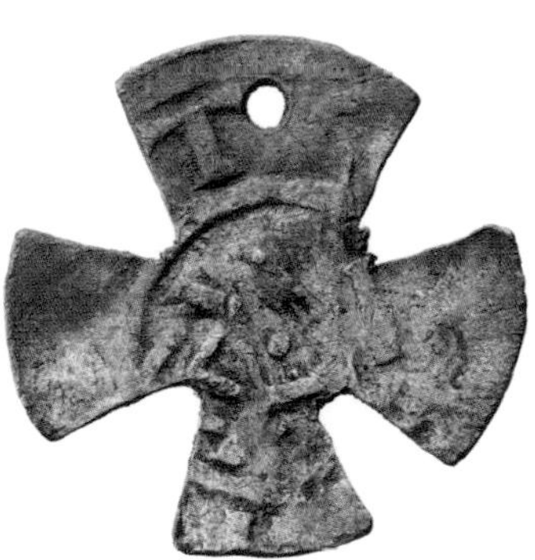

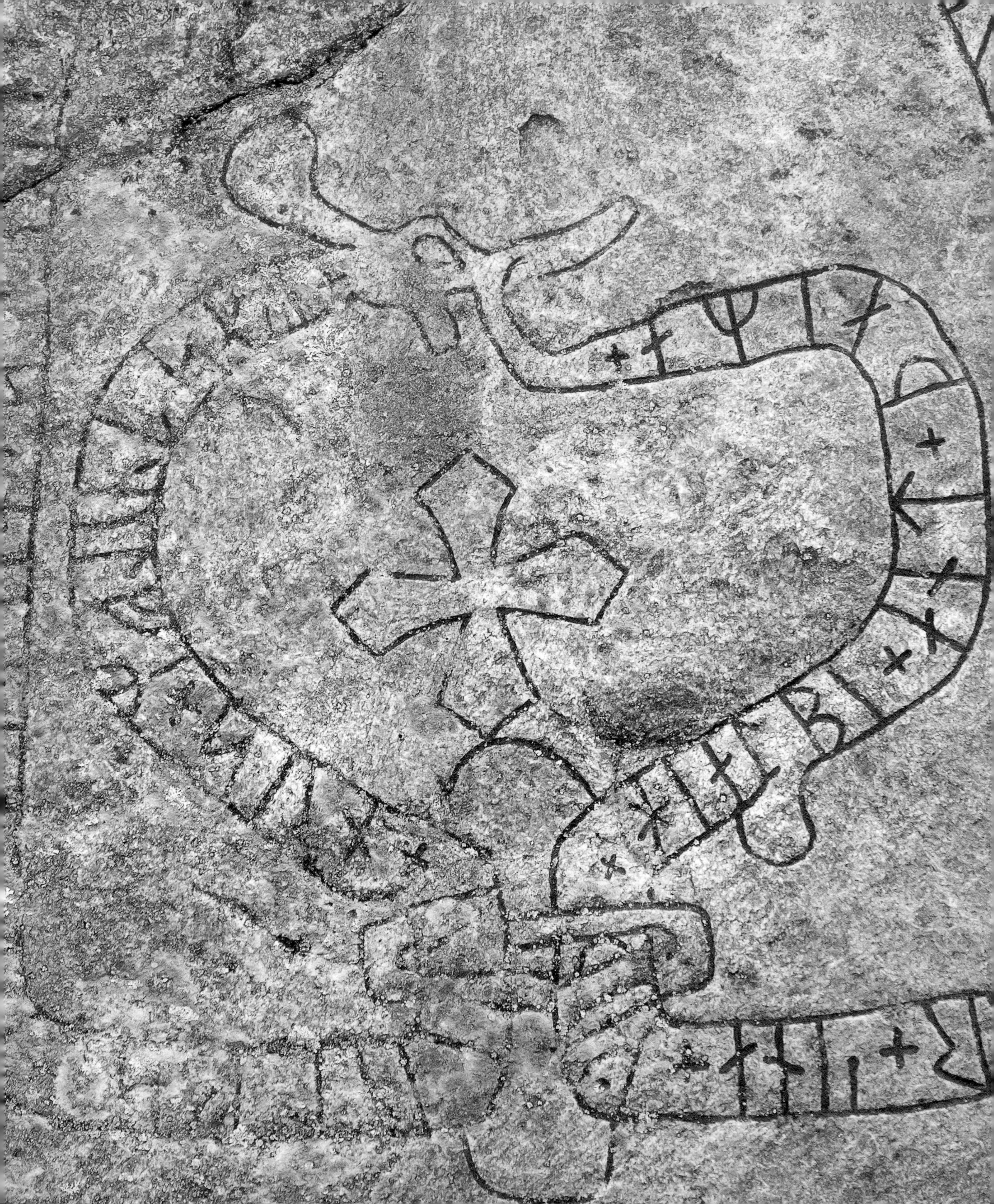

43.
Not all Christian symbols related to the cross. The pelican was believed to pierce its own breast to provide nourishment for its young; this was used to symbolize the self-sacrifice of Christ.

Bird-shaped brooch, probably a pelican, 11th century. Toftegård Syd, south-east Funen, Denmark.
Silver. H 3.8 cm, W 4.7 cm
National Museum of Denmark, Copenhagen

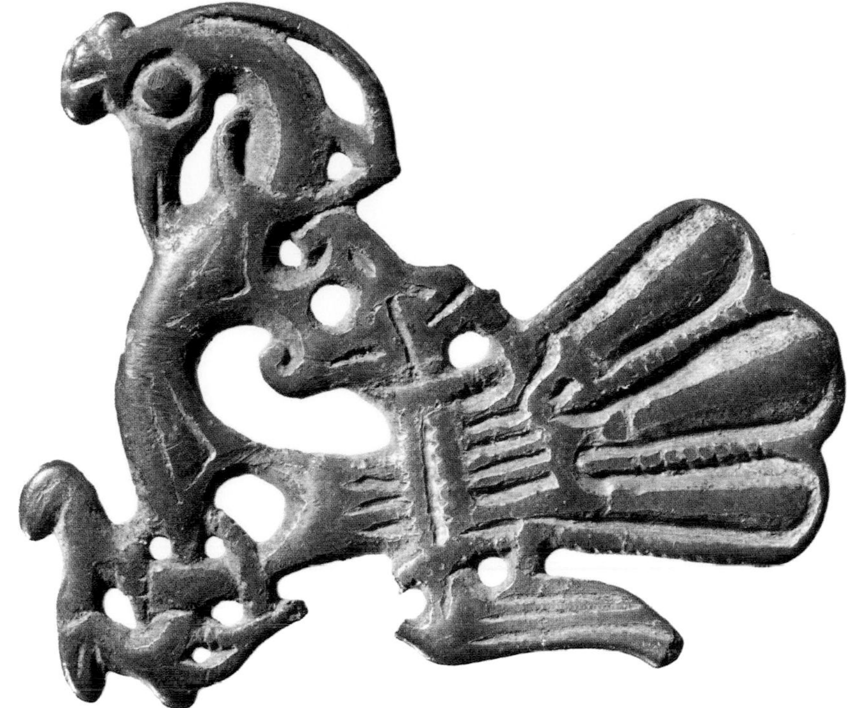

this tradition: several thousand rune-stones were raised in this area alone in the course of the eleventh century and on into the early twelfth (fig. 42). Standard formulae begin to appear in the inscriptions, asking divine help for the soul of the deceased, but as in pre-Christian times the stones also demonstrate as much if not more effort to emphasize who is doing the commemorating. These were very much monuments for the living as well as the dead; in some instances, prominent landowners erected rune-stones to themselves in their own lifetimes. These new Christians were actively signalling their allegiance not only to the one God, but also to the whole social and political package within which these beliefs were set (fig. 43). The concentrations of rune-stones may represent the primary foothold of Christianity, but it is possible that they instead reflect the area where these ideas were most resisted, thus requiring such visible signals of belief.[36]

It is important to understand that the practical changes brought by the new faith, especially modes of burial and 'worship' (even the concept was probably alien, as we have seen above), overturned not just the customs of the Viking Age but of centuries further back into the past. At first, Christian burials took place in the existing grave fields, presumably on ground hallowed for the purpose, but in the late tenth century we begin to see permanent churches and churchyards appearing.

The first Christian services would have been held in existing buildings or even in the open air, spaces temporarily consecrated with portable altars and crosses (figs 44–45). When proper structures were erected for the purpose, they would have been relatively small, one-room affairs. At their simplest, like the tiny church probably built for Erik the Red's wife at Brattahlið in Greenland, they were made of turf and scarcely large enough to accommodate more than a handful of people. The more costly examples were of wooden, stave-built construction, using the techniques familiar from contemporary hall buildings, though still very small (fig. 46). Into the twelfth century, these wooden churches began to be replaced in stone or expanded into much larger timber structures as we see in the magnificent surviving stave churches of Norway (fig. 47).[37]

42.
One of the many rune-stones from the Mälar Valley.

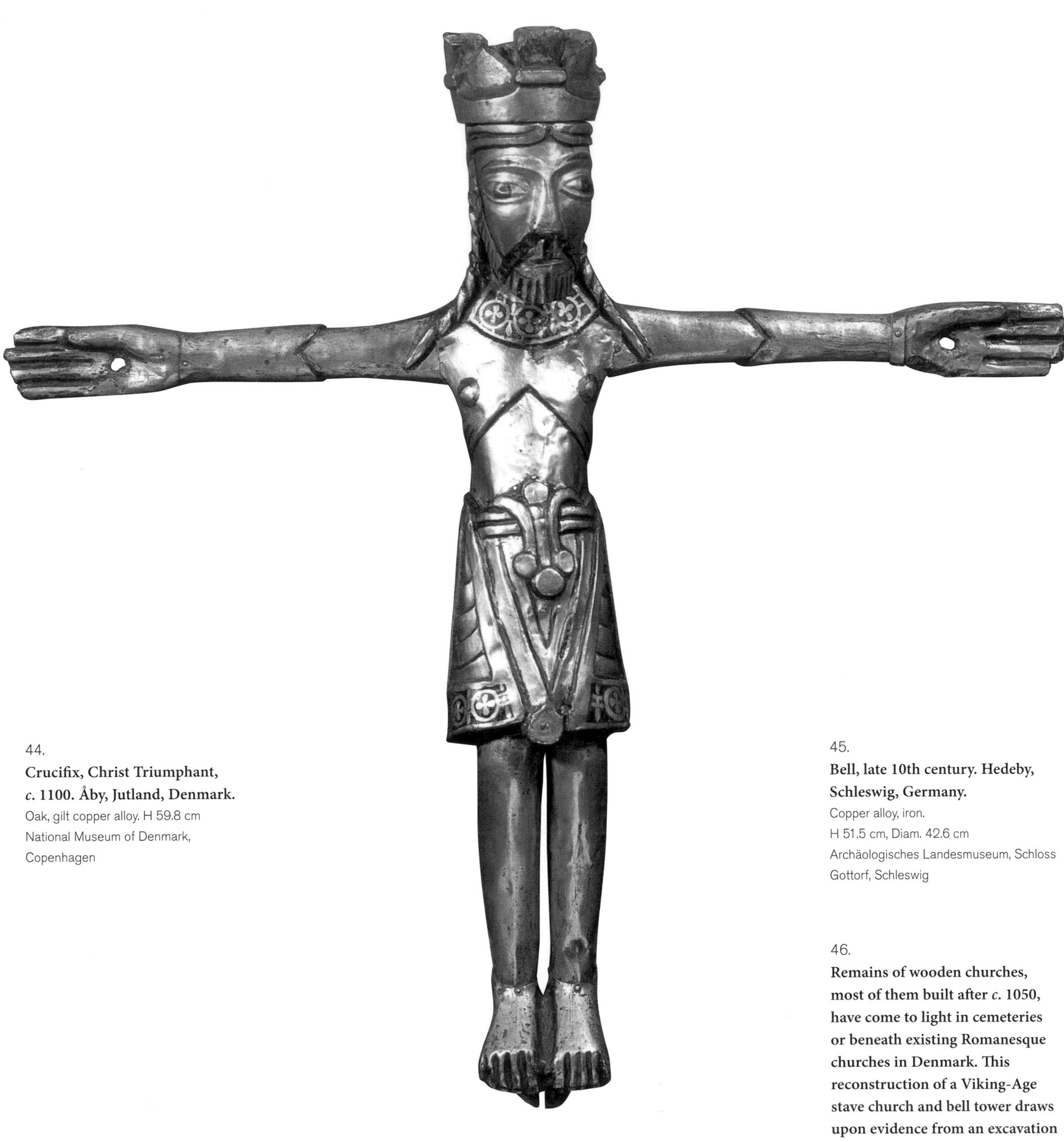

44.
Crucifix, Christ Triumphant, *c.* 1100. Åby, Jutland, Denmark.
Oak, gilt copper alloy. H 59.8 cm
National Museum of Denmark, Copenhagen

45.
Bell, late 10th century. Hedeby, Schleswig, Germany.
Copper alloy, iron.
H 51.5 cm, Diam. 42.6 cm
Archäologisches Landesmuseum, Schloss Gottorf, Schleswig

46.
Remains of wooden churches, most of them built after *c.* 1050, have come to light in cemeteries or beneath existing Romanesque churches in Denmark. This reconstruction of a Viking-Age stave church and bell tower draws upon evidence from an excavation at Hørning in Jutland.
Moesgaard Museum, Århus

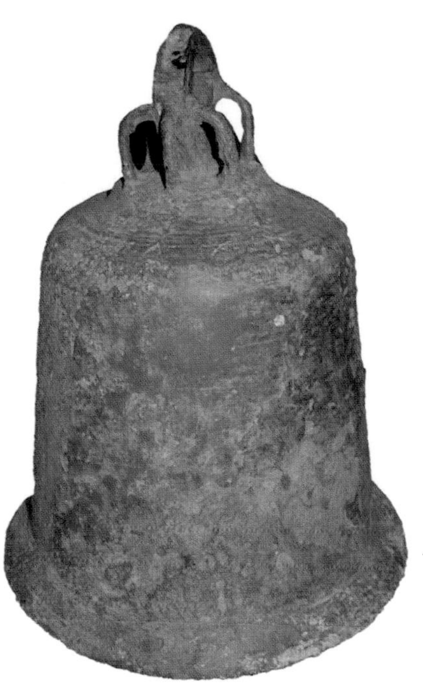

The question of cult continuity, the development of hybrid religion and the reuse of existing sacred sites, have long been topics of dispute in Viking studies. At some sites, such as Frösö, it is clear that a direct relationship can be seen between material manifestations of different beliefs, while elsewhere the pattern differs widely. One must also consider the diversity of the traditional ritual landscape and the question of which specific part(s) of it the new churches might physically reference.

Other material factors are also relevant in this context of conversion, such as the ecclesiastical introduction of Latin and the culture of book-learning. The pre-Christian Vikings did not use books, parchment or ink-based writing at all, having their own centuries-old traditions of runic scripts that were adapted for carving on wood or stone. However, it is equally obvious that they were well aware of these things, understood them and rejected them. With the political adoption of Christianity, holy texts not only became an integral part of Scandinavian culture, but so did the restriction of access to them – and to literacy itself – through their monopoly by the Church and the developing royal state. A new dimension of social power had been introduced to the north. In time, Christianity would also come to morally regulate the total sphere of domestic life, dictating what people ate, when and how they worked and the relative social standing of the sexes, and exercising control over their most intimate habits.

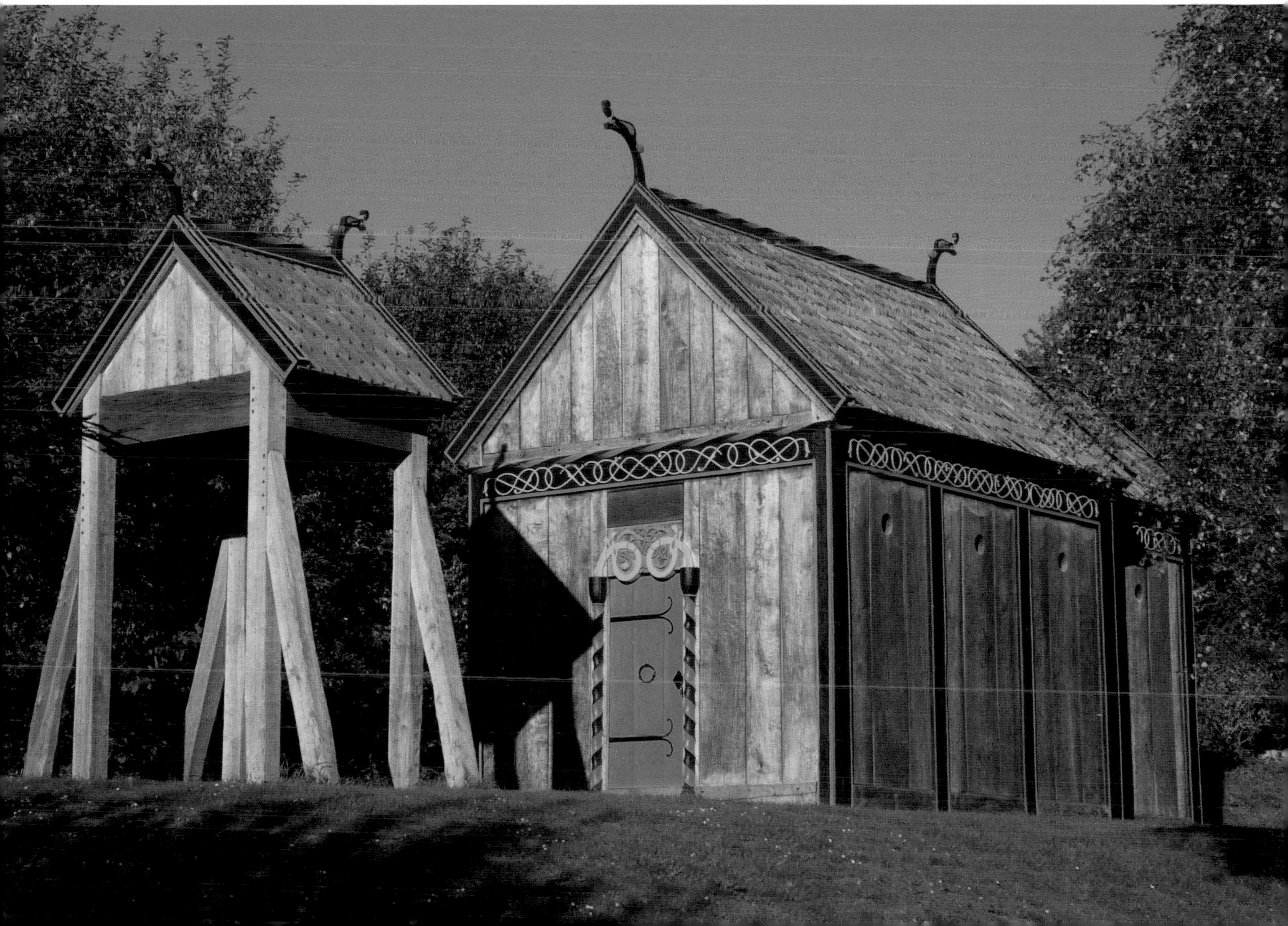

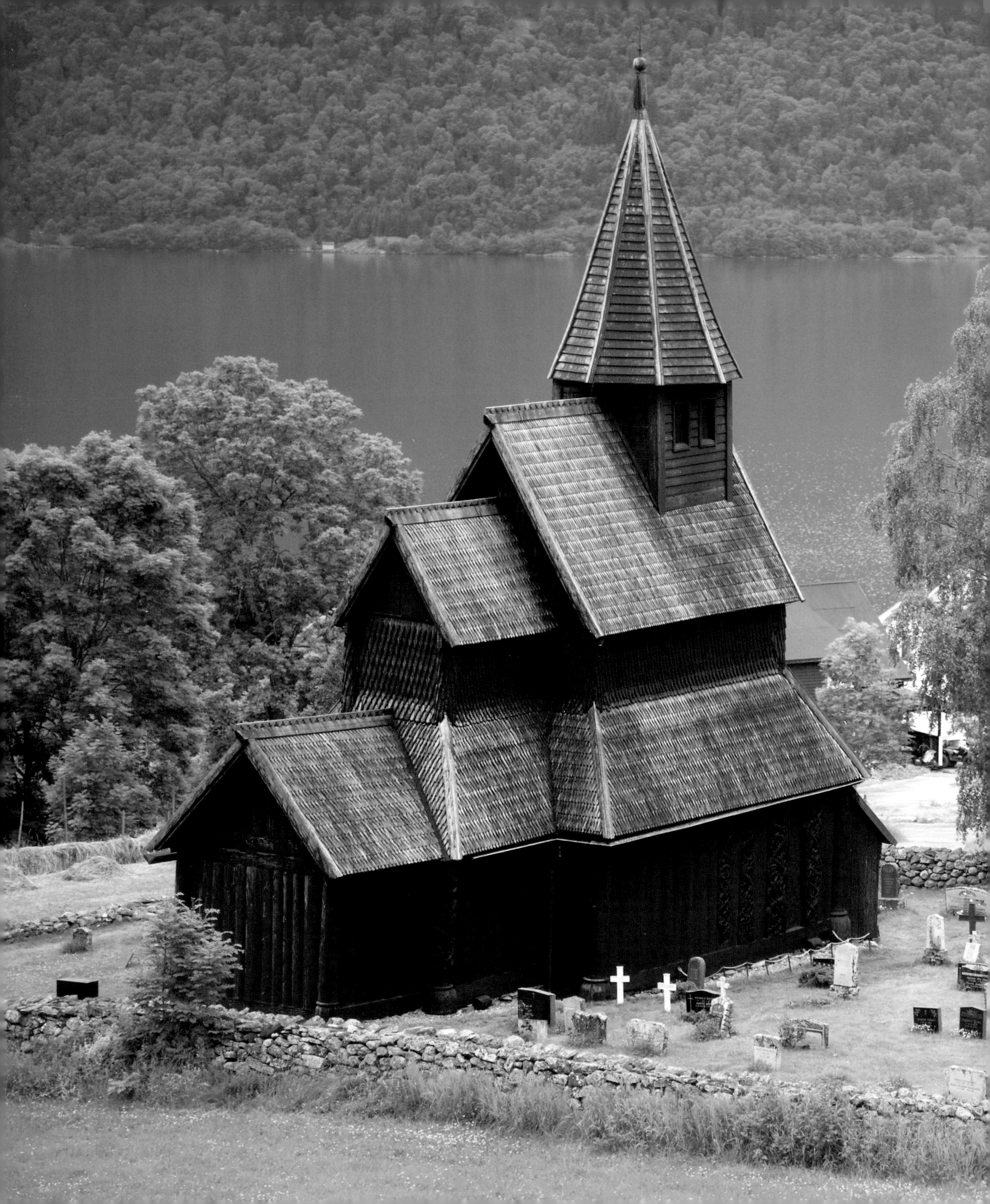

47.
The Urnes stave church dates from the 1130s and is one of the oldest and finest examples of early Scandinavian church architecture. Urnes, Sogn og Fjordane, Norway.

48.
Two birds – whose bodies form two halves of a ring – meet beak-to-beak above an elongated face. This may be a representation of Odin and his ravens.

Dress pin with Odin mask, 800–1050. Kalmergården, north-west Zealand, Denmark.
Bronze. L 4.5 cm
National Museum of Denmark, Copenhagen

Alongside such enduring structures of Christianity, which with our knowledge of medieval and later European history we cannot help but view with hindsight, there are other possibilities to consider what-might-have-been. By way of example we can take the controversial speculation concerning possible Islamic missions to Scandinavia.[38] Could it be that the numerous objects from the Muslim world found in Scandinavia (not least the tens of thousands of silver coins, all with pious inscriptions) may have had a symbolic religious significance as well as commodity value? Even if this was the case, the effort clearly failed, though northerners would have come into frequent contact with Islamic culture on their journeys east and in Iberia.

The legacy of the traditional beliefs of the north is still with us today: literally so in English, since the very days of the week are named after Germanic religious models (Sunday, Moonday, Tyr's Day, Woden's/Odin's Day (fig. 48), Thor's Day and Frey's Day; only Saturday derives from Latin and the god Saturnus, but in the Scandinavian languages it still retains an echo of the Old Norse for 'bath day', which might also have ritual overtones in the sense of a cleansing practice). The Norse gods reappear as comic books and movies, everyday brands and computer software, and they can also be found in placenames around north-western Europe. Similarly, it is impossible to travel the Scandinavian landscape without moving through the pre-Christian world of burial mounds and other monuments that one encounters by the thousand. That these often survive so close to the medieval churches, which are also one of the north's great architectural treasures, in communities still rich in semi-pagan folklore, is testament to the unique patterns of belief and spiritual practice that made the Scandinavians who they are today.

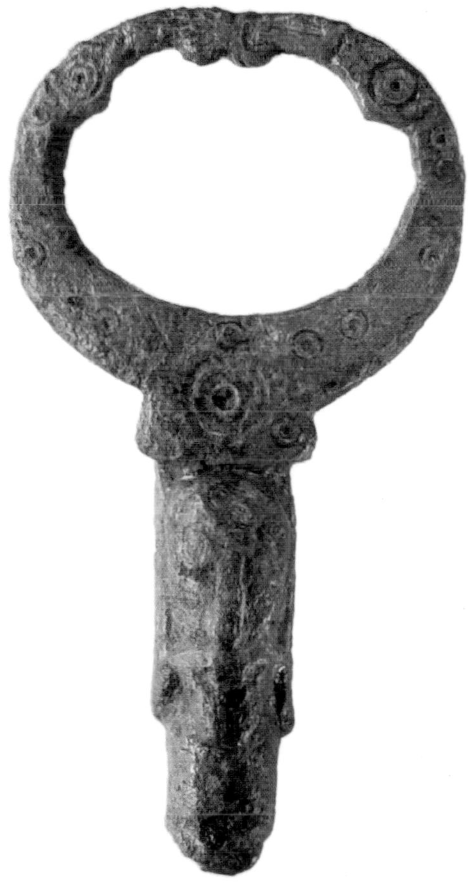

The Fyrkat woman

Peter Pentz and Neil Price

Fyrkat lies in the northern half of Denmark's Jutland peninsula. In the period after 980, during the turbulent reign of King Harald Bluetooth, it was the site of a great circular fortress, one of several that were constructed in Denmark at this time. These enclosures are discussed more fully in chapter 3, but they seem to have combined the functions of military camp, high-status manufacturing centre and administrative base. Outside the rampart at Fyrkat, on a promontory spur of land with views over the surrounding country, is the small fortress cemetery.[1]

Excavated in the 1950s, the grave field is laid out on an unusual east-west alignment, following a similar focus on the cardinal points in the design of the fortress. The cemetery is bisected by a unique wooden platform or raised walkway, elevated above the ground on vertical posts, with burials clearly clustering to the north and south of this strange structure. On the north side, in a prominent position and a little isolated from its neighbours, is Grave 4 – the spectacular burial of a woman that is in fact the wealthiest and largest in the entire Fyrkat cemetery.

Probably about 170 cm tall, she had been laid on her back in the detachable wooden cargo body of a wagon, a type of receptacle occasionally found reused as coffins for women of high status. A number of enigmatic structural elements also hint at a more three-dimensional grave than was the norm, including two posts that inclined over the burial at an angle of about 45 degrees. Did these support a platform or roof of some kind, perhaps flags, or something else?

Even when first excavated, it was evident that in life the Fyrkat woman had been an unusual person. Clearly wealthy, she was either well-travelled herself or had close connections who were. Most significant, however, were a number of objects that together implied she had been skilled in the working of magic.[2] These included 'charms' made from the body parts of animals, a bag full of henbane seed – a powerful hallucinogen – and a fragmentary iron staff of a kind that has been identified elsewhere as the main tool of a *völva*, a term meaning 'staff-bearer' and used for a sorceress in the Old Norse sources (see pp. 175–7).

Recent laboratory work at the National Museum of Denmark has subjected the grave contents and environmental samples to intensive scientific analysis, and enables us to reconstruct the clothing and appearance of a Viking-Age sorceress in vivid and

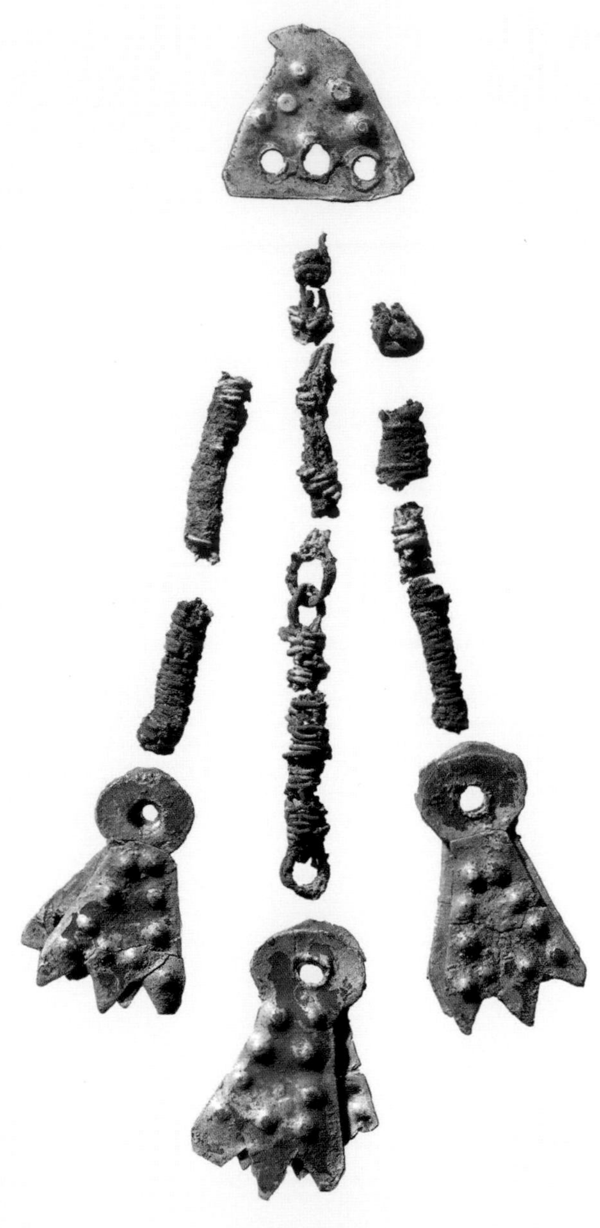

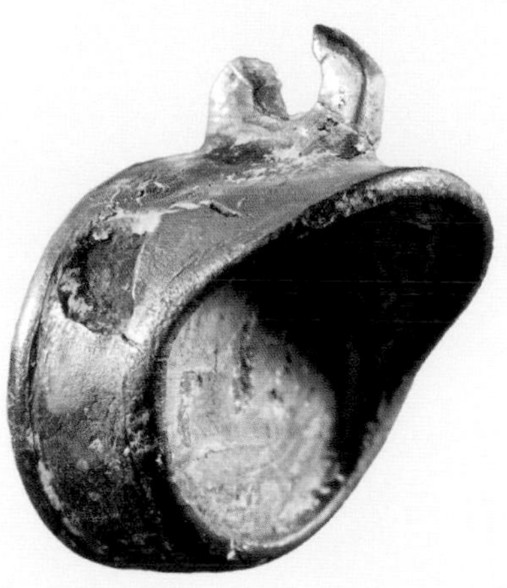

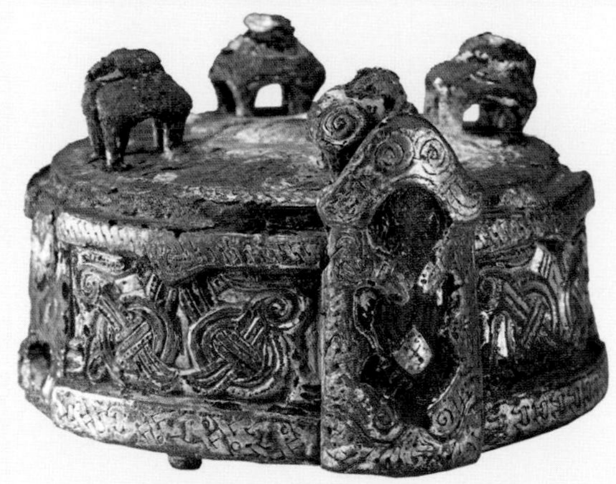

unprecedented detail. When buried the woman was wearing a blue costume, surprisingly fashionable for the time, with red details. She wore a kind of veil, ornamented in gold thread. Her jewellery consisted of amulets and silver pendants decorated with 'swan's feet' designs (figs 1–2).

Equally unexpected were her belongings. A Gotlandic so-called box brooch (fig. 3), rarely found outside the island of Gotland, contained white lead, which can be used as make-up or ointment. A small thin-walled glass could be a mirror, but contained a substance made of phosphorus, lead and calcium. A round-bottomed vessel of copper alloy, possibly of eastern origin, was covered by a grass lid or 'sieve' (fig. 4). It contained traces from a fatty material, which when combined with the henbane seeds would have produced a hallucinatory substance known from medieval sources as 'witch ointment'. Giving a powerful sense of flight when smeared on the body, it could have been used by the Fyrkat woman for rituals or 'consciousness-expanding' seances.[3]

Overall, the grave reveals a person of substantial sophistication, giving an appearance of power and recognition as a sorceress through her tokens and remedies. These artefacts served an important function by promoting the image of the woman as a *völva*, or something similar, capable of manipulating nature's forces and gaining mastery over the physical world. As such, she may have been one of the most formidable individuals in King Harald's army.

1-4.
Objects from the grave at Fyrkat, late 10th century. Grave 4, Fyrkat, east Jutland, Denmark.
(left) **Swan's feet pendants.**
(top left) **'Throne' amulet.**
Diam. 1.3 cm
(top right) **Box brooch.**
Diam 6 cm
(right) **Copper alloy container**
H 6 cm
Gold, silver, copper alloy, niello, brass, iron.
National Museum of Denmark, Copenhagen

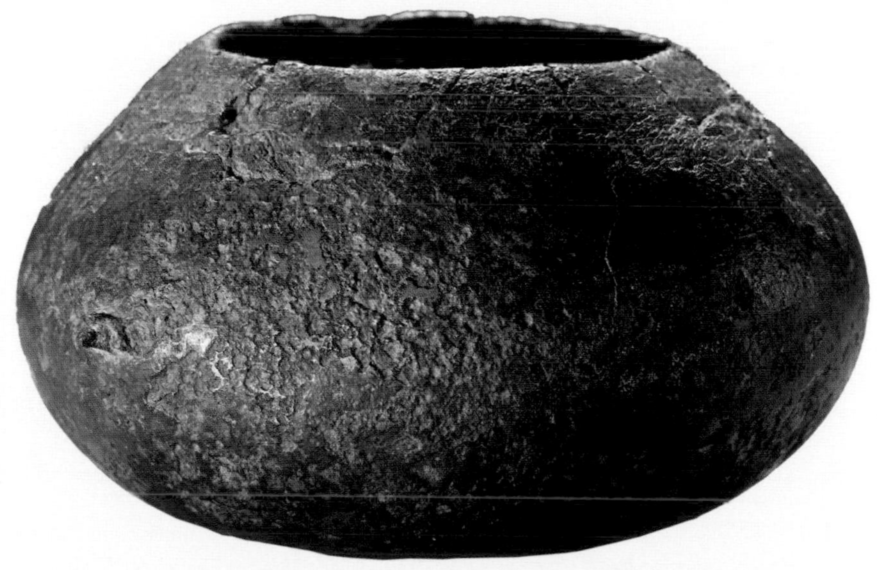

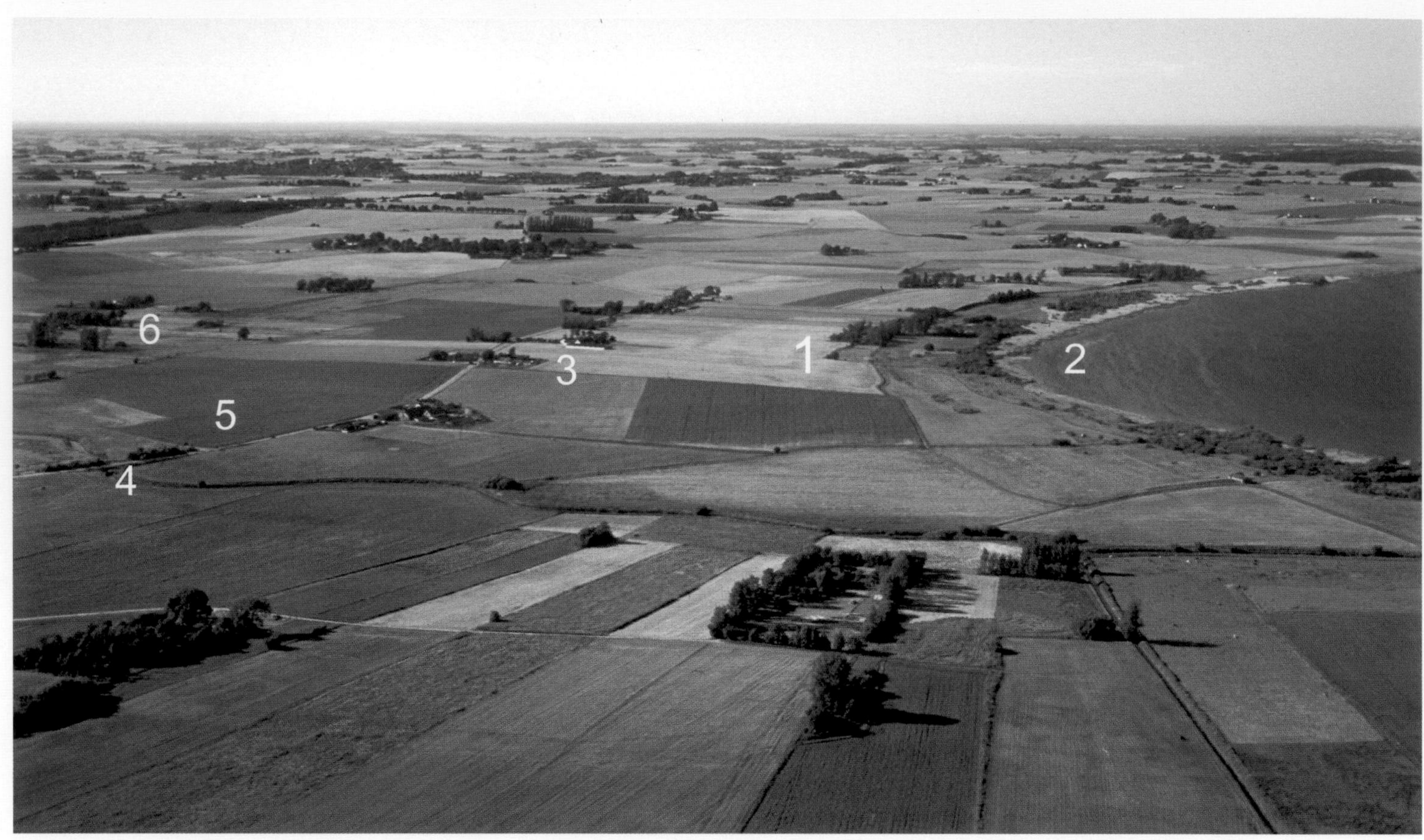

Ritual sites at Lake Tissø

Lars Jørgensen

Archaeological finds from the Viking Age can often enable us to catch a glimpse of the cosmological world of their time. Of course these are only fragments, but the constant stream of new archaeological finds increases our knowledge of how the Vikings organized and perceived the landscapes surrounding them.

The excavation of what was possibly a royal residential complex on the western shore of Lake Tissø in Zealand, Denmark, has provided evidence for the existence of a ritual landscape surrounding the actual residence (fig. 1). Within a distance of approximately 1 kilometre, six sites have so far been found at significant points in the landscape, all of which served various ritual purposes during the Viking Age.[1] Throughout the nineteenth and twentieth centuries, swords, spears, axes and jewellery, mainly from the Viking Age, were found in the lake, which takes its name from the god Tir/Tyr. The sporadic appearance of such finds right under the residential area suggests that these objects were sacrificed individually. A tool chest containing, among other items, a tenth-century template for metal box fittings and a few swords was discovered in the River Halleby, which forms the southern boundary of the 50-hectare built area.

On the western side the built area is bordered by the marshy Maderne, where a large number of horse bones have been unearthed that may be the remains of sacrifices. A system of clay pits was discovered on a hilltop a few hundred metres to the west of the residence, from which the clay used in the construction of the monumental buildings on the site was extracted. In the same area were found obvious remains of ritual meals together with sacrificed objects – silver jewellery, glass beads and even a few human bones – indicating that the great building works were accompanied by a series of rituals. In the residence itself, deposits of objects and the remains of meals also suggest the presence of several cult buildings and ritual areas. Lastly, a number of wells have been found in the adjacent marketplace area to the north of the River Halleby (fig. 2). Their contents, particularly the skulls and limb bones of various animals such as horses, bulls, cows, pigs, dogs and goats, may indicate that the wells were used as a site of sacrifice in connection

1.
Sites of ritual activity during the Viking Age in the area around the aristocratic residence at Lake Tissø, Zealand, Denmark.

1 residence with cult buildings and ritual sites

2 weapons and jewellery sacrificed in Lake Tissø

3 objects and remains of meals deposited in the clay pit area

4 tool chest/box and sword deposited in the River Halleby

5 well in the market place area with deposits of animal parts

6 possible horse sacrifices in the marshland area

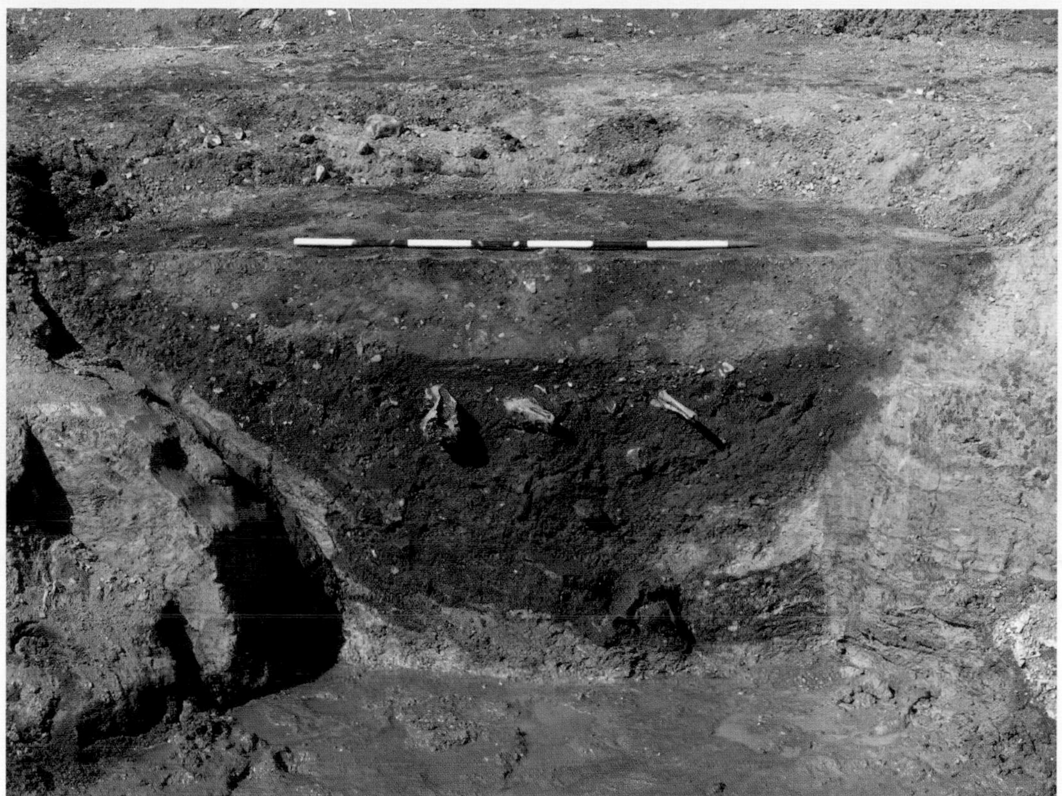

2.
Excavation of a well in the market place area at Lake Tissø used for ritual deposits, mainly of skulls and limb bones of various animals.

with ritual meals in the ninth and tenth centuries. The clear sequence of layers in the wells shows that the sacrifices were made over a relatively long period.

Probably only parts of the original ritual landscape have been uncovered in connection with the great building complex at Lake Tissø. Scattered finds suggest that more sites of the same character may be discovered. The ritual sites at Lake Tissø are almost all nameless – only the lake still bears its theophoric name, which clearly refers to the pre-Christian religion. However, similar ritual sites, and also a number of placenames in the rest of Scandinavia, show that these pre-Christian sites still bear sacred, descriptive names relating to their function in the Viking Age.[2]

The ritual sites at Lake Tissø indicate a conscious organization of the landscape and their varied character suggests that they had a range of functions: religious sacrifices to different gods, rituals for different times, rituals of a more social nature, etc. The fascinating picture from Tissø shows us how the ritual landscape in the neighbourhood of a great residence might have been arranged in the Viking Age immediately before the arrival of Christianity. Several sites apparently held a particular significance and consequently special rituals were associated with them. The closeness of the sites to one another suggests that the Vikings may have imposed their cosmological perceptions on the local environment. Viking-Age people organized these 'psychological' landscapes to give concrete, physical expression to their religious world. Tissø gives us an insight into the complexity of these landscapes at a local level. We know of the existence of similar organized landscapes, but on a much larger geographical scale, through the images that emerge from placenames such as Vi/Væ (pagan religious site), Ullevi (pagan site dedicated to Ull), Torslunda (Thor's grove), Fröslunda (Frey's grove) etc., especially in the Swedish countryside.[3]

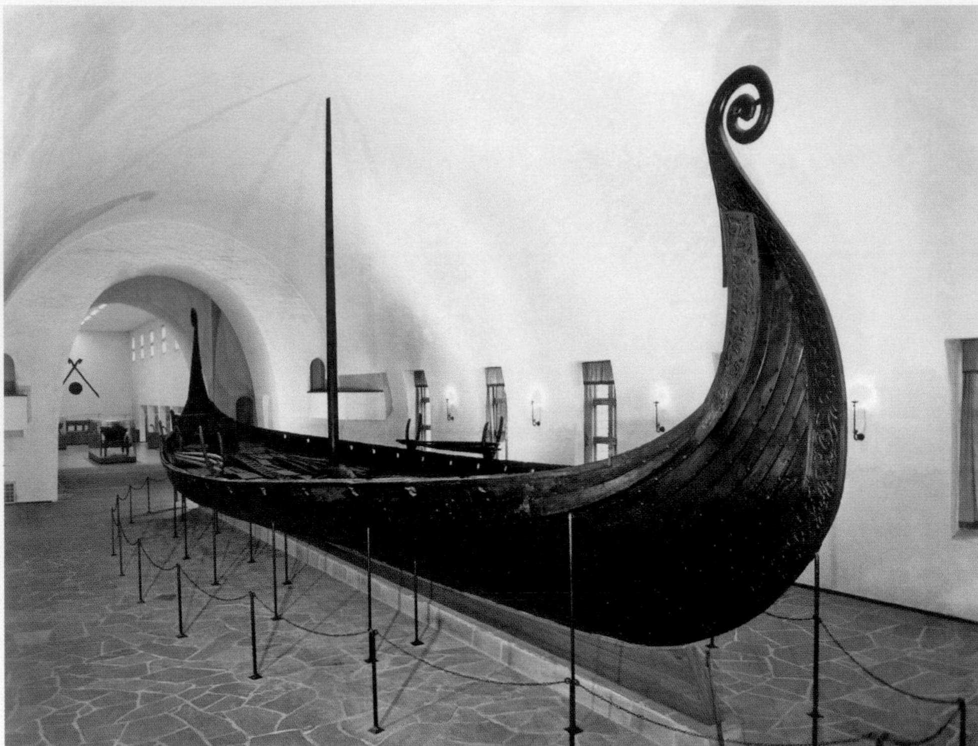

1.
The Oseberg ship, on display in the Viking Ship Museum on Bygdøy, Oslo, Norway.

The Oseberg ship and ritual burial

Jan Bill

The most startling example of a ritual burial from the Viking Age is that from Oseberg, dated to 834 (fig. 1).[1] Situated in the county of Vestfold in eastern Norway, it is an extreme example of the boat burial tradition, which existed in Scandinavia from before the beginning of the first century AD and spread with the Vikings far into Russia, to the British Isles and the North Atlantic, and to Brittany in France.[2]

The Oseberg mound was excavated in 1904 and revealed an almost intact, completely equipped Viking ship of 21.5 metres in length, built in 820 in western Norway and presenting elaborate wood carvings on its stem and stern (fig. 2).[3] Behind the mast of the ship a tent-shaped wooden burial chamber had been constructed in which the corpses of two women were placed, along with a wide range of personal belongings and other objects. Among these were four animal postheads with associated ropes and rattles, probably devised for magical protection of the burial. Along with many other items placed in the foreship, a wagon (see p. 182, fig. 25) and three sledges, all splendidly decorated, provided the deceased with additional means of travel, as did fifteen sacrificed horses, with a saddle placed in the burial chamber. Many of the objects found in the chamber and the foreship were related to textile production, and a tapestry with scenes of processions, ships and warriors is one of the highlights of the find (fig. 3).[4]

Who was buried in the Oseberg ship?

The best preserved of the two skeletons represents a female who had died from cancer at the age of eighty or more. In spite of the excellent preservation conditions in the burial, only a few bones were found of the second individual, but these were unusually delicate for a Scandinavian, and the teeth showed furrows from the use of a metal toothpick – an indication of high social status. This woman appears to have died in her fifties.[5]

The dating of the burial and the ages of the deceased make it unlikely that they were any of the few named women known from documentary sources.[6] A religious role, as sorceresses or priestesses, has been suggested by several researchers, but it may have been their political importance, as part of a ruling or high-status family, that necessitated their unusual burial ritual.[7] The mound was broken into in ancient times through an extensive ditch more than 20 metres long, and during the robbery the skeletons as well as

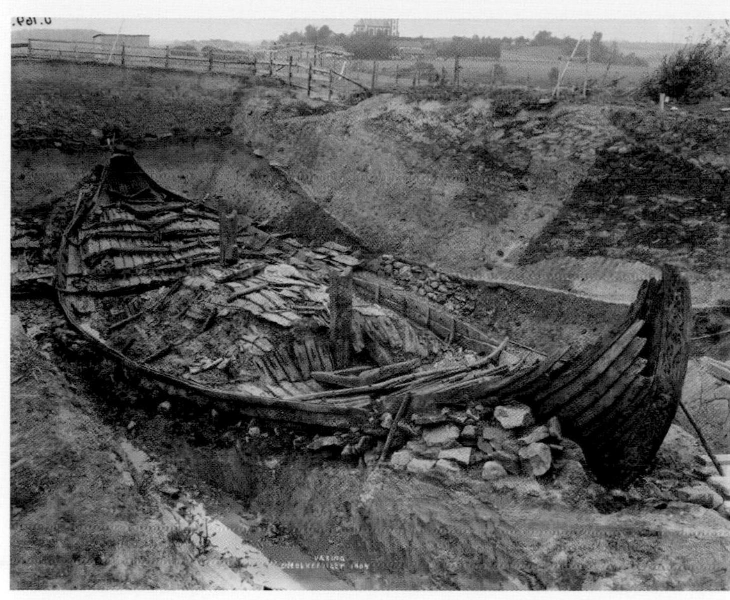

2.
The Oseberg ship burial after excavation in 1904.

3.
Reconstruction of the Oseberg tapestry. The tapestry was recovered from the ship. It depicts a procession, presumably of a religious nature.

many of the grave goods and the stem of the ship were purposely destroyed. Recently this defacing of the monument has been dated to between 953 and 975 and linked to a similar, contemporary event at the nearby Gokstad ship burial, erected around 900.[8] Chronologically this coincides with the fighting over the region between the Danish king Harald Bluetooth and the two major competing dynasties in Norway, the Finehair dynasty and the Earls of Lade. It has been suggested that the destruction of the Oseberg burial, at that time over 120 years old, indicates that it attested hereditary rights in the area.

Ship burials and central places

Ship burials like Oseberg and Gokstad are few, but they are often located close to important seats of power. Near the royal site of Avaldsnes, on Karmøy in western Norway, two ship burials from the late eighth century have been excavated, and at Hedeby one was erected in the first part of the ninth century.[9] The three ship burials known in Vestfold (Oseberg, Gokstad and Borre) were located between the royal site at Borre in the north and Sandefjord, north of the oldest Norwegian town Kaupang, 44 kilometres to the south.[10] It appears that the ship burials, with their extensive rituals and overt sacrifices, were used to mark out rights and positions of power in especially important territories. Ongoing excavations at Gokstad add an important facet to this picture – only 500 metres from the burial mound a market site, in terms of richness and international connections almost on a par with Kaupang, has recently been found. The site can preliminarily be dated to the century around 900 and is a strong indication that an important centre of power must have existed in the vicinity of the Gokstad burial – perhaps this was also the case at Oseberg and Borre. If so, it may appear that the ship burials are not only some of the most impressive archaeological monuments from the Viking Age, but also some of the most important testimonies to Scandinavian political development in this period.

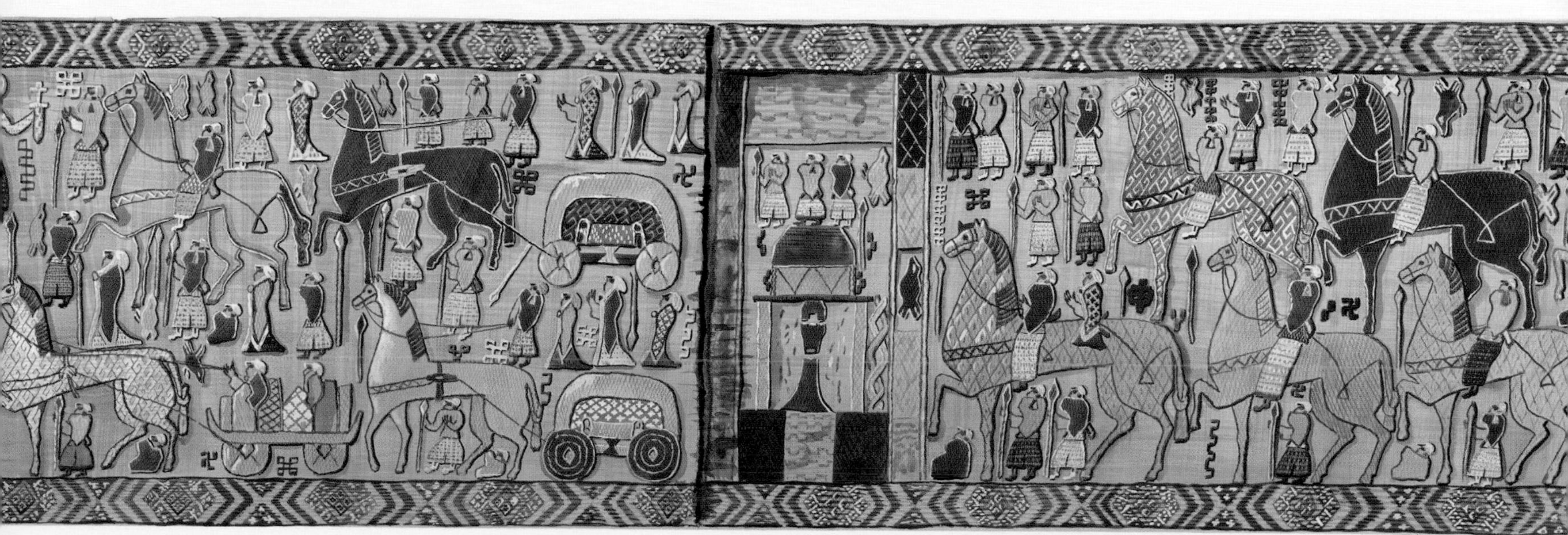

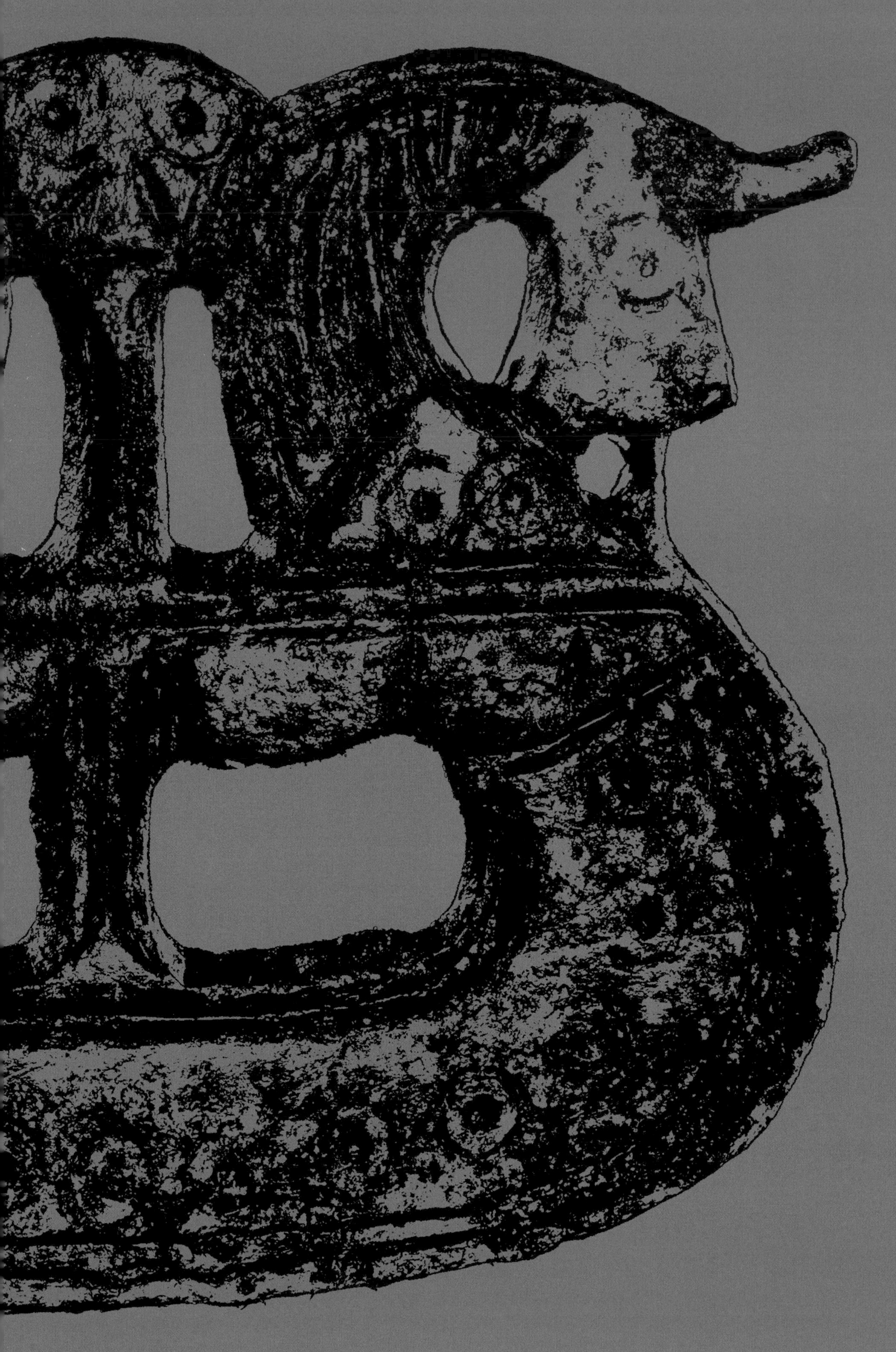

5
SHIPS & THE VIKINGS

Peter Pentz

On one side lions moulded of gold were to be seen on the ships, on the other birds on the tops of the masts indicated by their movements the winds as they blew, or dragons of various kinds poured fire from their nostrils ... The royal vessel excelled the others in beauty as much as the king preceded the soldiers in the honour of his proper dignity.

ENCOMIUM EMMAE REGINAE, BOOK 1.4 (1040–2)

SHIPS & THE VIKINGS

MORE THAN ANYTHING ELSE, THE SHIP is the symbol of the Viking Age. Viking ships conjure up images of savage warriors surging over the gunwales of a longship or a sea-going ship on a long voyage towards distant shores and wonderful adventures. But if we think of the Viking ship as no more than a means of transport, we have understood only a small part of its significance for its time.

The Viking ship is a concept that covers several types of ship and its roots reach much further back than the start of the Viking Age. The geographical position of the Scandinavian countries, with their long coastlines, lakes and watercourses, has made travelling by water essential for thousands of years. Prehistoric boats and ships are known both from archaeological finds and from pictures, but it is not until the first few centuries after Christ that we can begin to recognize features that appear on Viking-Age ships (figs 1–2).

The most obvious ancestor of the Viking ship is the Nydam boat, which was found in 1863 in Nydam in southern Jutland (figs 3–4). The Nydam boat is 24 metres long, built from an oak tree felled in 310–20.[1] Each side is made from five broad, overlapping strakes, rising from a broad bottom plank. The boat was steered with a large oar at one side. At the top of the sides, lashed to the gunwales, had been twenty-eight thole pins that would have guided

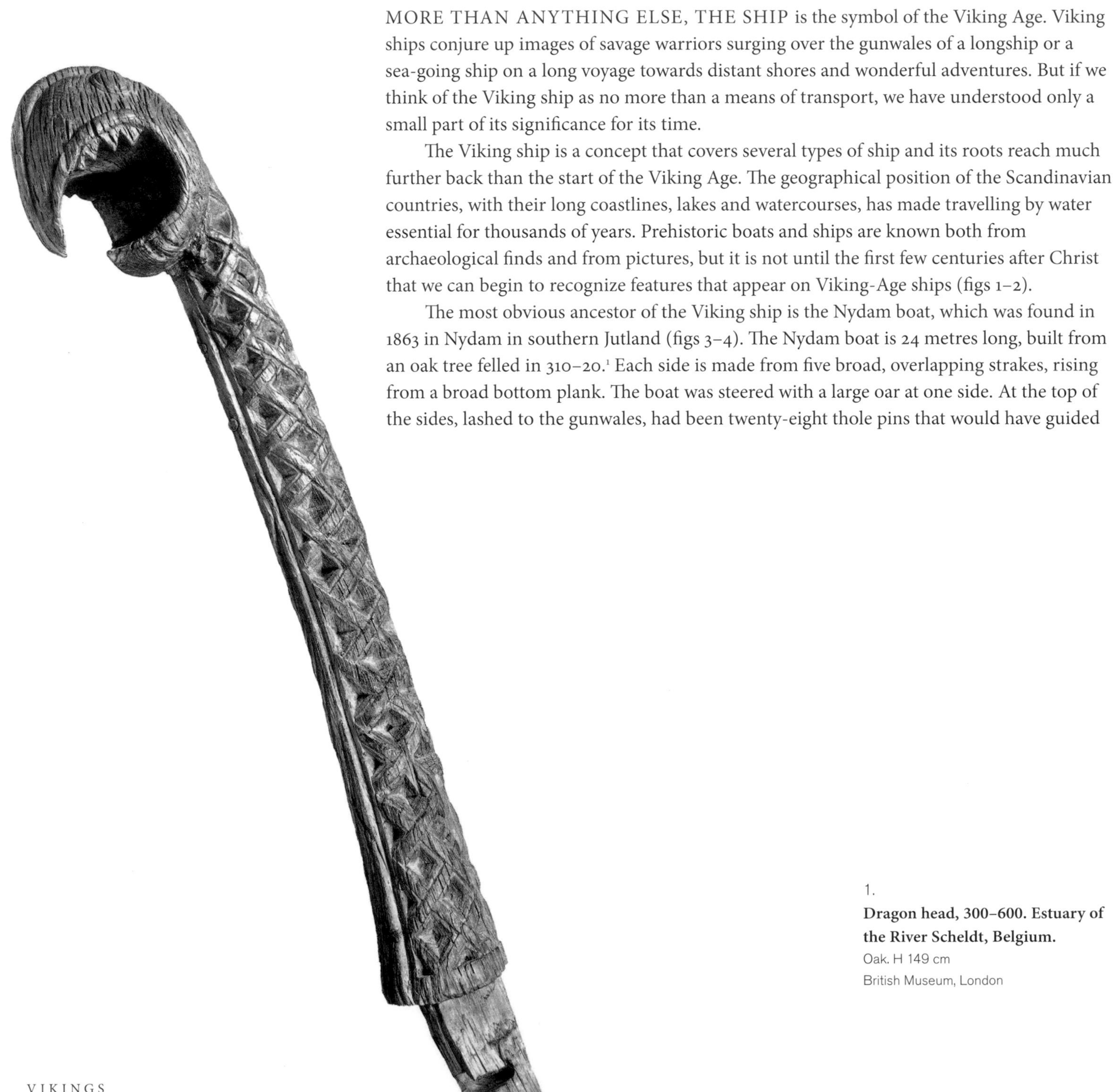

1.
Dragon head, 300–600. Estuary of the River Scheldt, Belgium.
Oak. H 149 cm
British Museum, London

The image of the dragon-headed Viking longship is ingrained in the popular imagination. No dragon prows from the Viking Age survive to compare against written sources or artistic depictions (such as the Bayeaux tapestry), but fragments from earlier boats give an indication of the possible appearance of Viking ships.

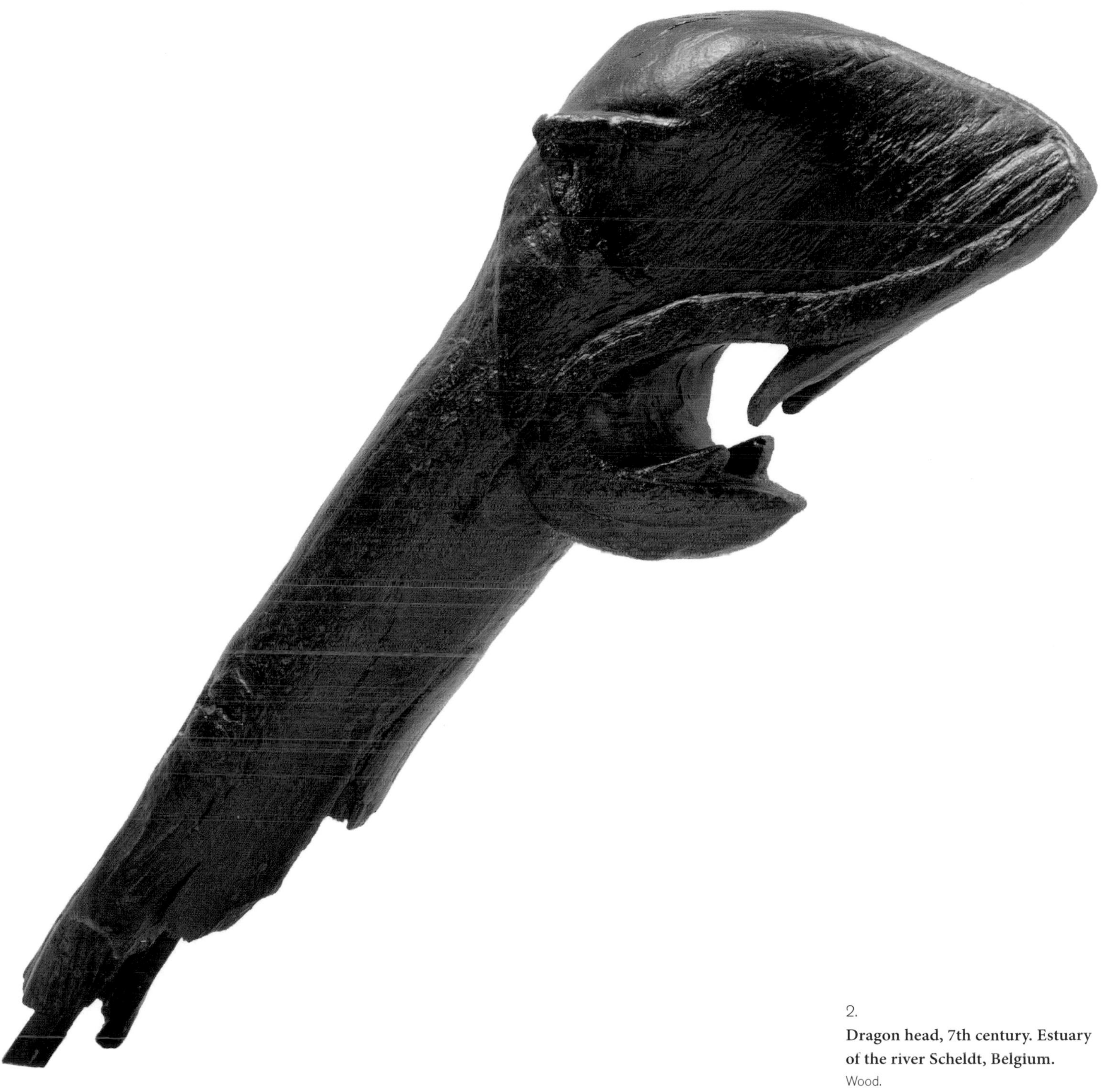

2.
Dragon head, 7th century. Estuary of the river Scheldt, Belgium.
Wood.
Museum Aan de Stroom, Antwerp

the oar. The Nydam boat had no mast and therefore did not carry a sail. It was probably by using vessels like this that the Angles, Saxons and Jutes terrorized the English coast in the fifth century. They may have made the actual crossing from Calais or the Rhine estuary. It was probably also from this kind of ship that, according to Gregory of Tours, the Danish king Hugleik attacked the Frankish coasts in around 520.[2]

Scandinavian ships developed quickly over the three centuries from 500 to 800. The stem and stern of the Nydam boat, the overlapping strakes and the steering oar are all elements that lived on in the Viking ship. However, the most important development was from rowing to sailing ships, which could of course still be propelled by oars alone. This transformation required certain changes to the construction of the ships, including giving them a proper keel. Historical sources from the eighth and ninth centuries leave us in no doubt that at that time the Vikings had mastered the art of shipbuilding by making the ship's hull, mast and rigging function as a single unit. They could now sail by day and night, wind permitting, and the sail provided the perfect basis for the kind of surprise attack suffered by the monastery of Lindisfarne in 793. Wind was so important that, one stormy evening in the ninth century, an Irish monk happily wrote a little poem in the margin of his manuscript:

Bitter is the wind tonight
It tosses the white-waved sea
I do not fear the coursing of the great sea
By the fierce warriors of Lochlin[3]

3.
Reconstruction drawing of the boat from Nydam, Denmark.

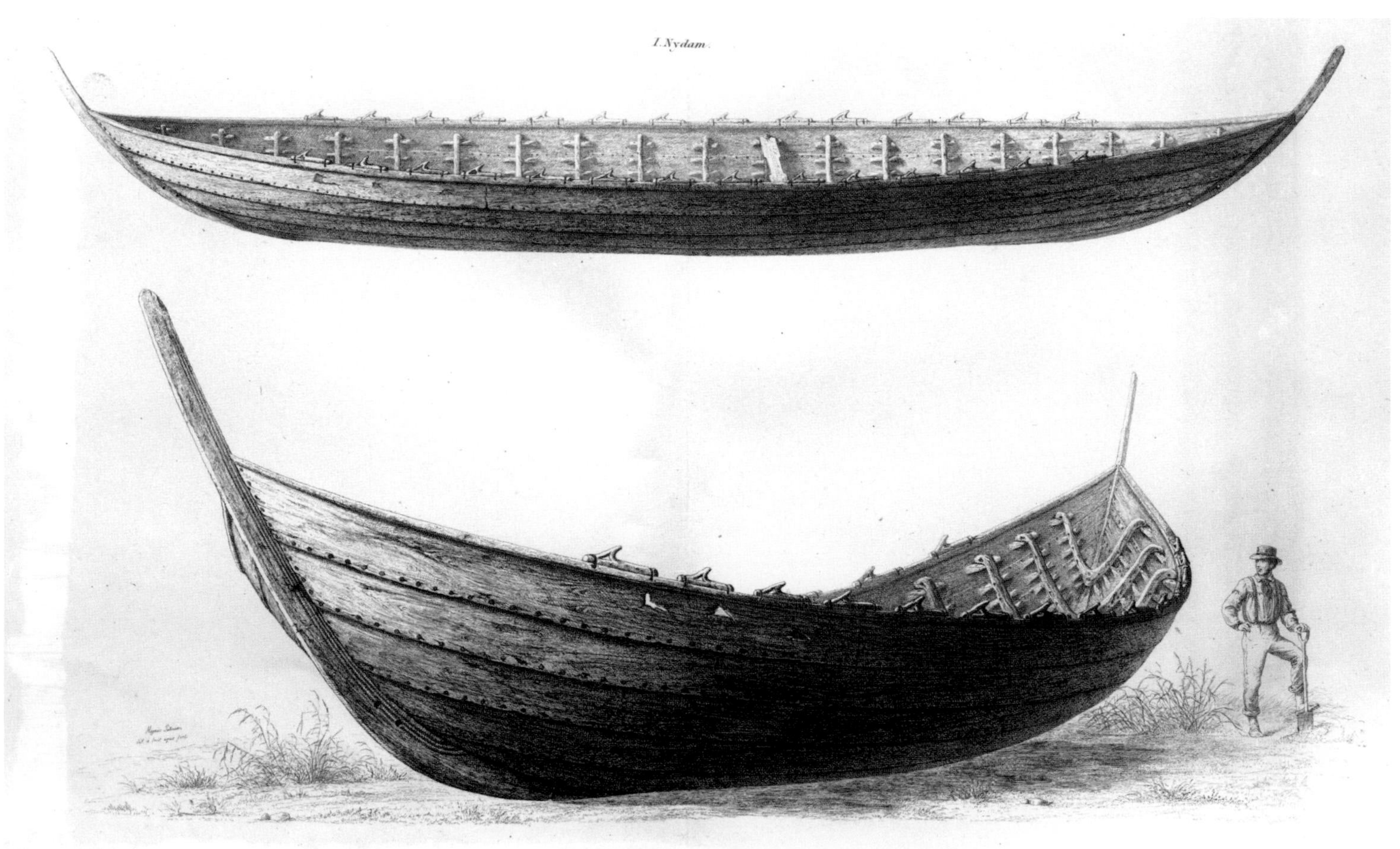

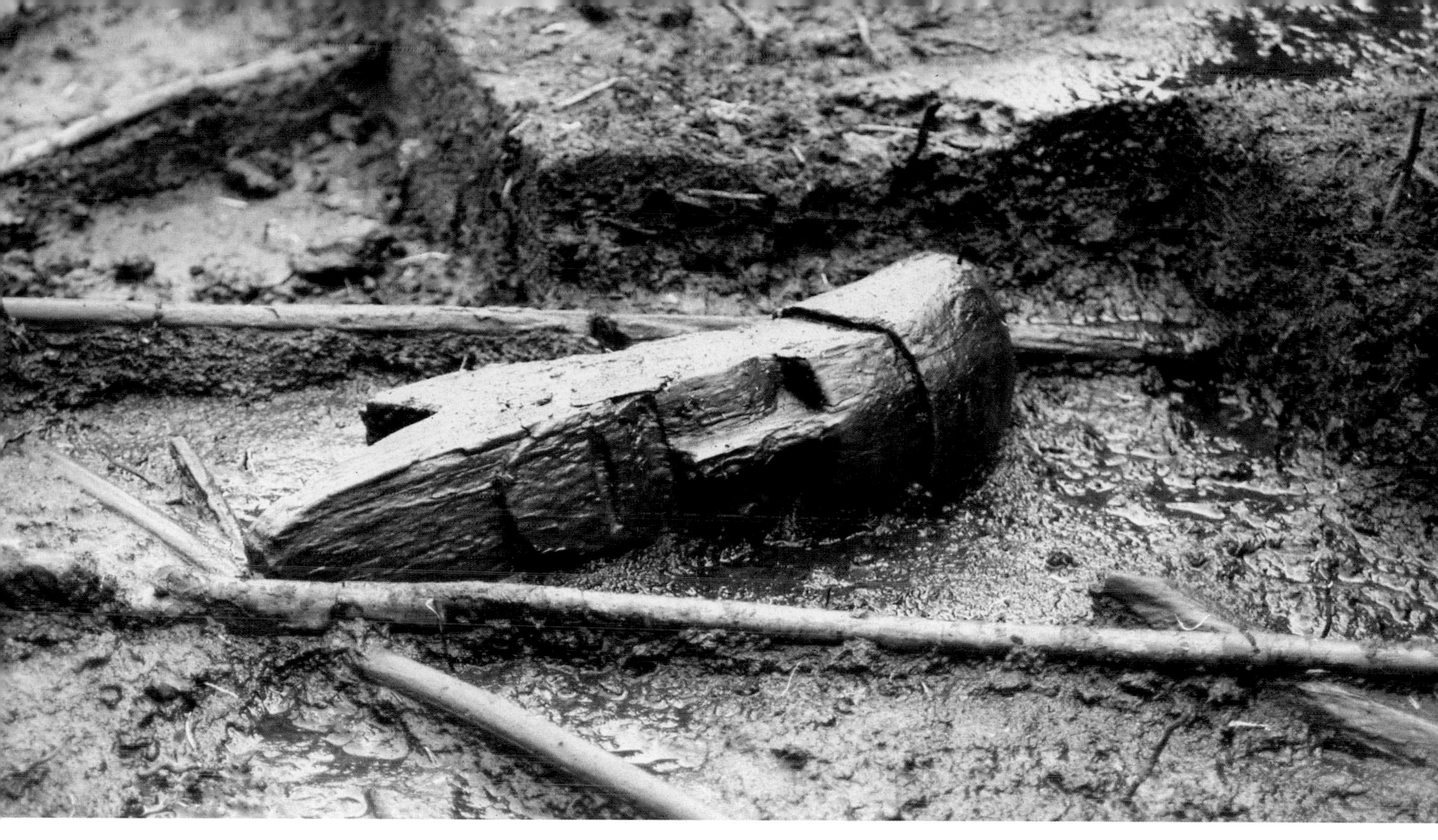

4.
Carved head associated with the Nydam boat.

Ships for travel and trade

Our impression of Viking-Age ships is influenced by the well-preserved, famous ships such as those from the Oseberg and Gokstad burials (see pp. 200–1). The low freeboard, the side of the ship between the waterline and the deck, of longships meant that they were light and could sail close in to the shore. However, the bigger ships like Havhingsten fra Glendalough (The Sea Stallion from Glendalough) – a reconstruction of the great warship Skuldelev 2 (see below) – were also capable of sailing on rough, open seas. The seaworthiness of this warship was demonstrated when it sailed across the North Sea to England, Scotland and Ireland in 2007 and back again in 2008.

But there were far greater numbers of smaller, lightweight ships that needed less water to float. These vessels, with a very shallow draft, served different purposes, such as fishing, hunting, minor trade and exchange, and transport. Faster ships made it possible to make longer journeys in shorter times. Late in the eleventh century, Adam of Bremen compared the overland journey from Scania, which was then part of Denmark, to Sigtuna in Sweden with the corresponding sea voyage. Travelling overland would have taken a month, whereas by sea it took only five days.

These smaller ships were of much greater importance for the infrastructure of the Scandinavian countries than the big Viking ships. Sheltered landing places and modest harbours with relatively shallow water were established, and the number of marketplaces and quays along the coasts – temporary or more permanent – increased. There is archaeological evidence for significant numbers of this kind of maritime trading site.

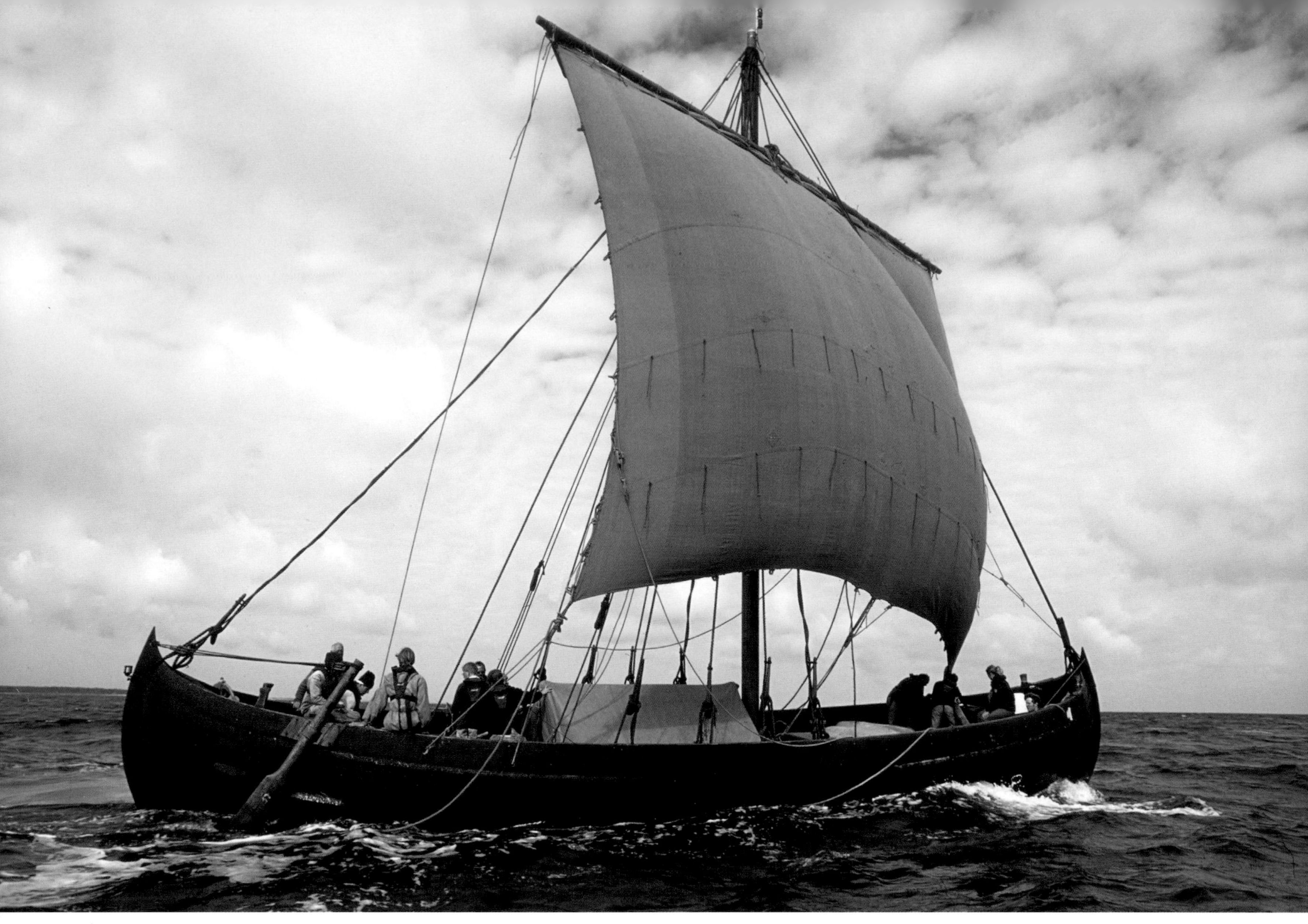

5.
Ottar, a reconstruction of the Viking ship Skuldelev 1.

Enormous quantities of small finds have been made at these sites, where large-scale production must have been taking place.[4] Such sites functioned as 'gateway' settlements, through which goods and people were funnelled in both directions.[5]

Proper quays were better for bigger ships with greater draught. It was during the Viking Age that harbours in the modern sense appeared in Scandinavia. At the same time the first Scandinavian towns developed – with connections to the long-distance trade routes. However, extended journeys such as the voyage to Greenland were probably most often made in another kind of Viking ship, the knarr. The name *knarr* or *knörr* is known from both skaldic poetry and rune-stones, and it is assumed that the term refers to trading ships. In the sagas, the knarr is sometimes called *hafskip*, meaning 'sea-ship', i.e. a sea-going vessel. While the longship was primarily propelled by oarsmen, the main means of power for the trading ship was the sail. Those Viking ships that are interpreted as being trading ships are characterized by a heavier construction: they are broad in the beam, with high gunwales and only a few oars.

The best example we have of such a ship is Skuldelev 1, one of the wrecks from the Skuldelev blockade (see p. 214).[6] It is contemporary with the great 37-metre-long warship Roskilde 6 and was also built in present-day Norway, in the Sognefjord or not far from there.

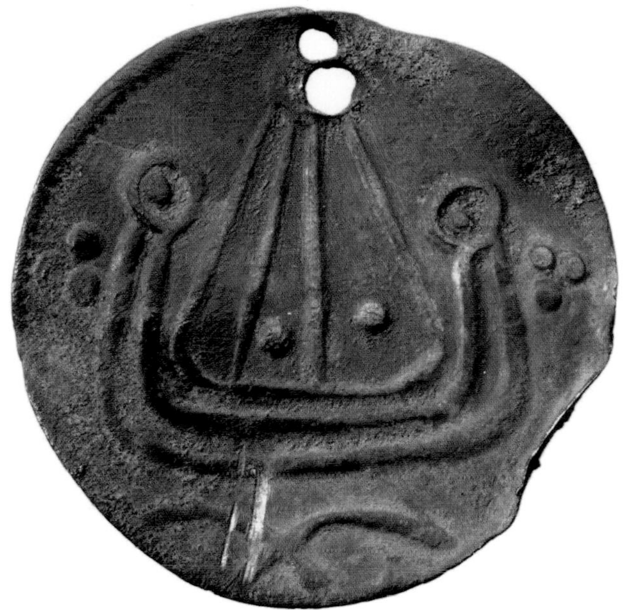

6.
Coins with images of ships minted at Hedeby emphasized the maritime connections of the settlement.

Hedeby coin with ship image, *c*. 825–850. Hollenæs, Lolland, Denmark.
Silver, 0.85 g
National Museum of Denmark, Copenhagen

The timber used is mostly slow-growing pine, but the keel is of oak. The ship must have been just over 16 metres long and could have carried about 24 metric tons, but it was by no means one of the largest trading ships of the time. One of the ships found in Hedeby harbour had a hull that could carry more than twice that of Skuldelev 1, as much as 50–60 tons.[7]

Like other traditional Scandinavian clinker-built ships, Skuldelev 1 was rigged with a single square sail. The sail was probably of considerable size, with an area of 80 to 90 square metres, making it bigger than the sail carried by the reconstructed warship Havningsten of Glendalough, though the latter was almost twice as long. In 1983 a reconstruction of the trading ship Saga Siglar from the Skuldelev blockade was built, and its qualities were demonstrated when it sailed round the world in 1984–6, although it later sank in the Mediterranean. Another reconstruction of Skuldelev 1, named Ottar, was built in 1999–2000 in Roskilde, confirming its seaworthy qualities (fig. 5).

A ship like Skuldelev 1 could be sailed by just five to eight men. The development of trading ships with ever greater cargo-carrying capacity in relation to the size of the crew is closely linked to a marked increase in trade during the Viking Age. However, it also indicates that the balance had shifted from smaller, valuable items to goods of lower value in relation to their volume. An increasingly stratified society may have resulted in a greater demand for the exchange of goods for the lowest possible cost.[8]

The building of the big trading ships was accompanied by the development of larger towns, and particularly the extension of harbour quays. At Hedeby (fig. 6) a landing and marketplace developed into a harbour, first through the building of a structure that would have acted as a breakwater or pier and then into a U-shaped wooden platform covering a total of at least 1,500 square metres. This platform functioned as a trading place in itself, a market that may have relieved the pressure on the original market on the shore. The extension of the harbour quays took place from some time in the ninth century until 1010.[9]

Ships like the knarr Skuldelev 1 were probably also used on occasion for military action.[10] Their great carrying capacity meant that they could transport many men and other materials for use in warfare. In the Viking Age seas, such as the Baltic were plagued by pirates and a few men on a cargo ship laden with goods must have been easy prey. If they

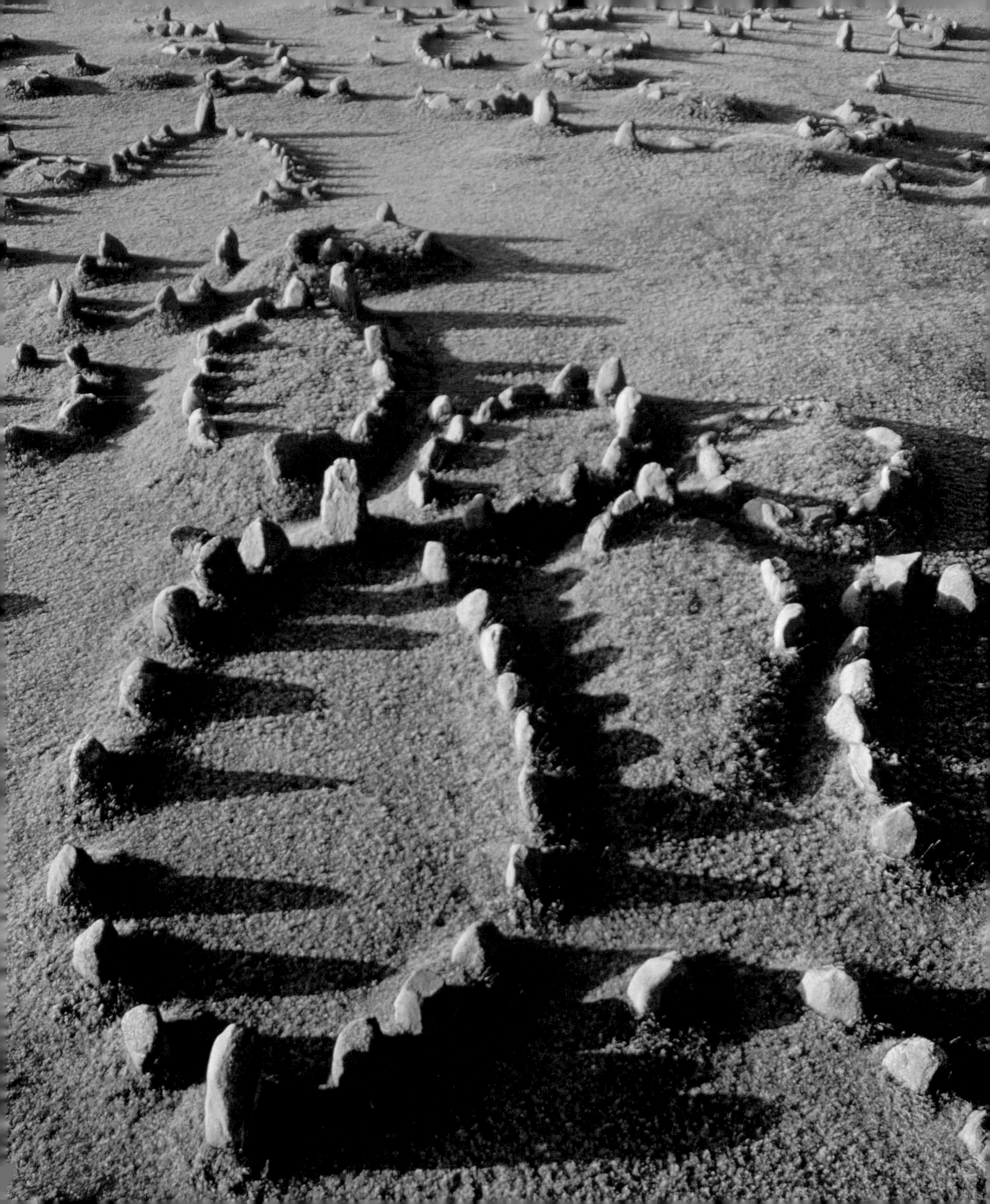

did not actually have other ships escorting them, they would probably have needed a larger crew than was necessary just to sail the ship.

Both the great warship Roskilde 6 and the trade ship Skuldelev 1 had a limited lifetime. A number of repairs, carried out in places other than where they were built, tell us that they had sailed for some considerable time. Both ships ended their days in Roskilde Fjord and they may well have been sailing there at the same time.

The great majority of Viking navigation was up rivers, in fjords or along the coast. They probably navigated by landmarks and by sounding the depth with a lead line. Lead weights have been found in harbours of the Viking Age, but it is probable that simple sticks were often used. Today it seems incomprehensible that they could have sailed and navigated on the open sea. They might have developed a feeling for direction and position by observing the sun and the stars. Their use of actual navigational instruments is hotly disputed but no conclusive evidence has been found for the use of, for example, a sun compass or a sun stone, which only allows the sun's rays to pass through it in a specific direction. It has been suggested that the Vikings knew about Arab navigation, which made extensive use of astronomical observations,[11] but the connection has never been proved.

We do not know much about how the Vikings thought of the sea. A late Viking-Age rune-stone from Södermanland in Sweden says that a man called Óleifr 'ploughed his barð to the east and died in the land of the Lombards'. 'Barð' is taken to refer to a warship with a prow of a particular shape. On this stone, the sea is conceived of as a field that can be ploughed and cultivated – and from which one can then reap a harvest.[12] The sea could also be seen as threatening, a powerful force of nature to be subdued, or the home of monsters. In skaldic poetry there are various descriptions of the ship's struggle against the waves, where the boat is the best weapon known to man in his battle with the elements. In Norse mythology the sea is also the abode of the terrible Midgard Serpent; cast there by Odin, the monster will not rise from the sea until Ragnarök – the end of the world.[13]

Sailing across the open sea was always difficult. The emotion men must have felt on returning home after a dangerous voyage is described in a poem, *Háttatal*, quoted by Snorri Sturluson:

> *The wave beats the high benches; the keel cleaves the wave, the ugly sea will break the beautiful ship … the cold wave makes the weak keel strong; the ship rushes ahead, the year goes by. The stroke of the oars lacks hands of the king*['s men] *… the long ships rest after the voyage by Liste's sea; the good ale dulls the men's senses; the empty hall is easily filled; but the full golden bowl glides pleasantly as a drink …*

We know about the Vikings' long journeys – to Greenland and America in the west and along the rivers of Russia in the east. But we do not know how many ships did not reach their goal. An eleventh-century rune-stone from Nylars on Bornholm tells in its own simple, sober language of the fate that was undoubtedly met by many: 'Sasser erected this stone in memory of his father Halvard; he drowned at sea with all his crew'.[14]

Ships left their mark on the land in many ways, not just along the coasts but also in the hinterland. Many placenames bear witness to the significance of ships in the landscape. They may start with words for ship, such as *skib-*, *skep-* or *snekke-*, or end with *-drag* or *-dræt*, which refer to places where vessels were hauled across the land. Of course, it can be difficult to determine whether the names originate from the Viking Age. The word *snekke* – *snäck/snekk* – is a name for a smaller vessel, a kind of warship. It most often appears in connection with a feature of the landscape, such as *Snekke-vik* or *Snäck-sund* (Warship Bay or Warship Sound). Most of these names are found in Norway, Sweden, Denmark and Finland, but significantly they also appear outside Scandinavia on the islands of Orkney and

7.
Viking burial site with graves marked by stone settings in the shape of ships, 800–1050. Lindolm Høje, north of Ålborg, Denmark.

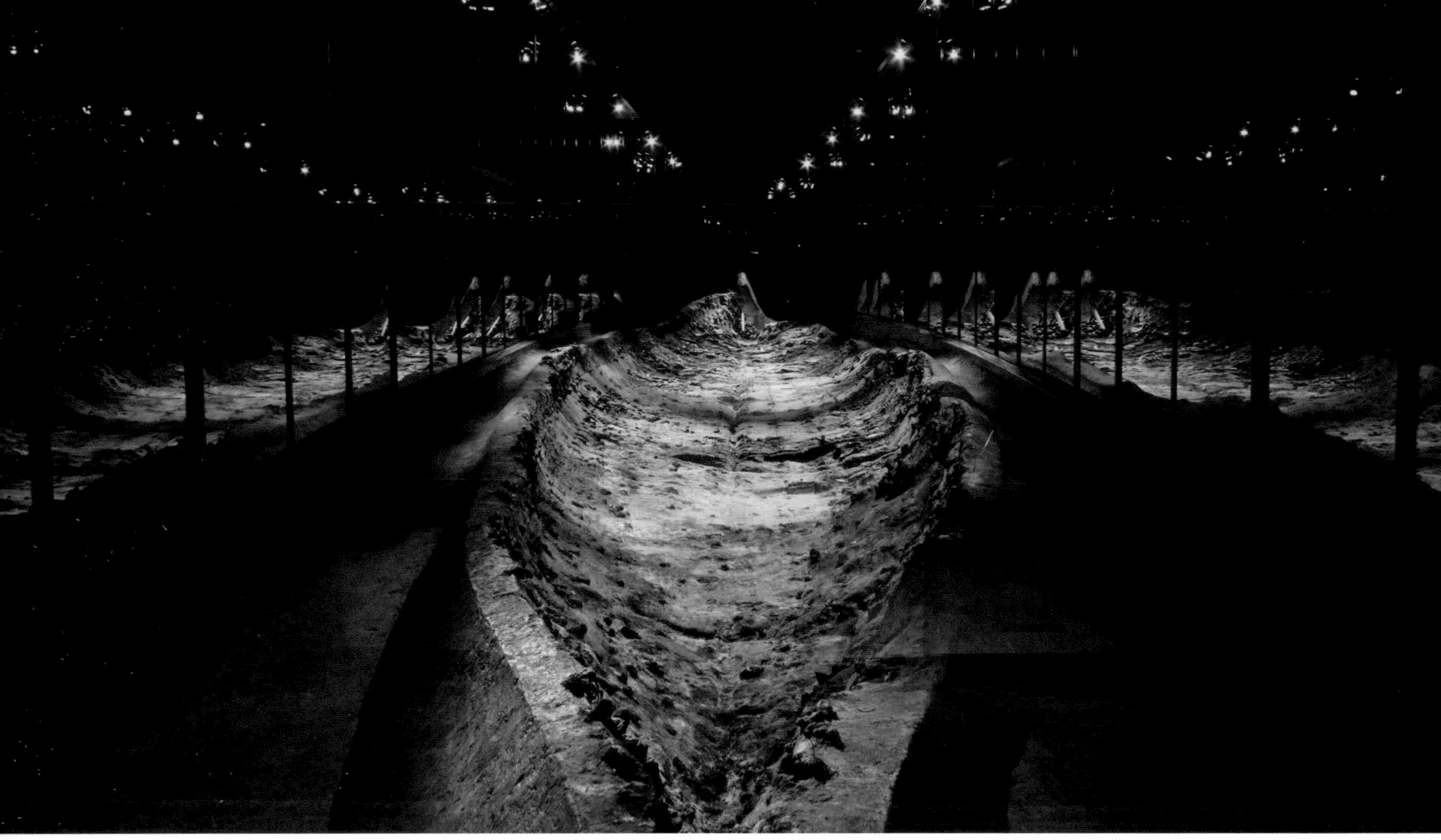

8.
The Ladby ship, built around 900 and buried around 925.
Vikingemuseet, Ladby

Shetland.[15] However, it is quite possible that the names occasionally referred to natural phenomena in the landscape that resembled ships or to one of the countless stone ships erected as burial monuments that have been an everlasting reminder in the landscape of the importance of seafaring. In many places, these stone ships were erected close to the shore, so the 'ship' created a visual unity with the sea (fig. 7). But stone ships were also built further inland; for instance, the largest of all the known ship settings can be seen in Jelling (see p. 158).

The Viking ship was a rapid attack weapon and was not only used for expeditions outside Scandinavia. A rune-stone in Uppland was set up in memory of a man called Asser, who had been a great 'protector against the Vikings'. In a number of places, underwater blockades have been found, which were intended to prevent attacking ships from coming in to shore or entering harbours and trading places. Blockades of this type, which are known from far back in the Iron Age, could be very complex constructions of posts and horizontal underwater piles, or they might simply consist of old, worn-out ships that were filled with stones and then sunk. At various places along the coast there were undoubtedly sites from which warning could be given of the arrival of enemy ships. A system of this kind may have included hills, from which messages could be relayed by means of beacons. Surviving placenames that include the elements *bavn*, *böte*, *warth* or *varð* may have been sites that were parts of such a system.[16]

The area surrounding the site where the Ladby ship was found – a beautiful, elegant, 22-metre-long Viking ship, which was hauled ashore sometime around 925 and used for a

Viking's burial – is a good example of a Viking-Age maritime landscape (fig. 9). The site, Kertinge Nor, lies at the head of Kertinge Fjord in the north-east of the Danish island of Funen and was accessible from the east (via the fjord) as well as from the west, where it might have been possible to haul smaller ships across from the nearby Odense Fjord – hence the placename Dræby, meaning the town or hamlet where ships were hauled or dragged. The inlet was protected by a blockade dating from the tenth century, which would have been impassable by ships manned by people unacquainted with local conditions. Close by is the village of Snekkeled (see p. 211). Even the name Ladby may be understood as the place where goods were trans-shipped or landed. The nearby placename Kølby may also be associated with the Viking-Age landscape and the area has a significantly higher number of names including the element *bavn-* than the rest of Funen. The Ladby burial ship was a light construction whose thirty to thirty-two rowers could have manoeuvred rapidly in fjords and along the coasts. The ship may have been secured by an iron anchor and chain when it lay close to the shore.[17]

Another such maritime landscape is Roskilde Fjord, a part of the Isefjord complex of inlets, which penetrates from the north deep into central Sjælland (Zealand), ending at the southernmost tributaries at Roskilde and Lejre Vig (fig. 10). Not much is known about Roskilde before the eleventh century, but the town must have had some importance if Adam of Bremen is right in claiming that Roskilde was chosen as the location for the burial of King Harald Bluetooth (who died within the period 980–5). The early medieval town of Roskilde consisted of an upper and lower part, the lower town concentrated around the churches of St James and St Clement, close to the shores of the fjord. Lejre is assumed to have been the location of Heorot, the royal hall mentioned in the Beowulf poem, and the twelfth-century Danish cleric Saxo Grammaticus (*c.* 1200) held Lejre to be the legendary homeland of the Danish royal house of Skjoldungerne, the Scyldings. Ongoing excavations in Lejre seem to verify the importance of the site in the early Viking period (see p. 127).

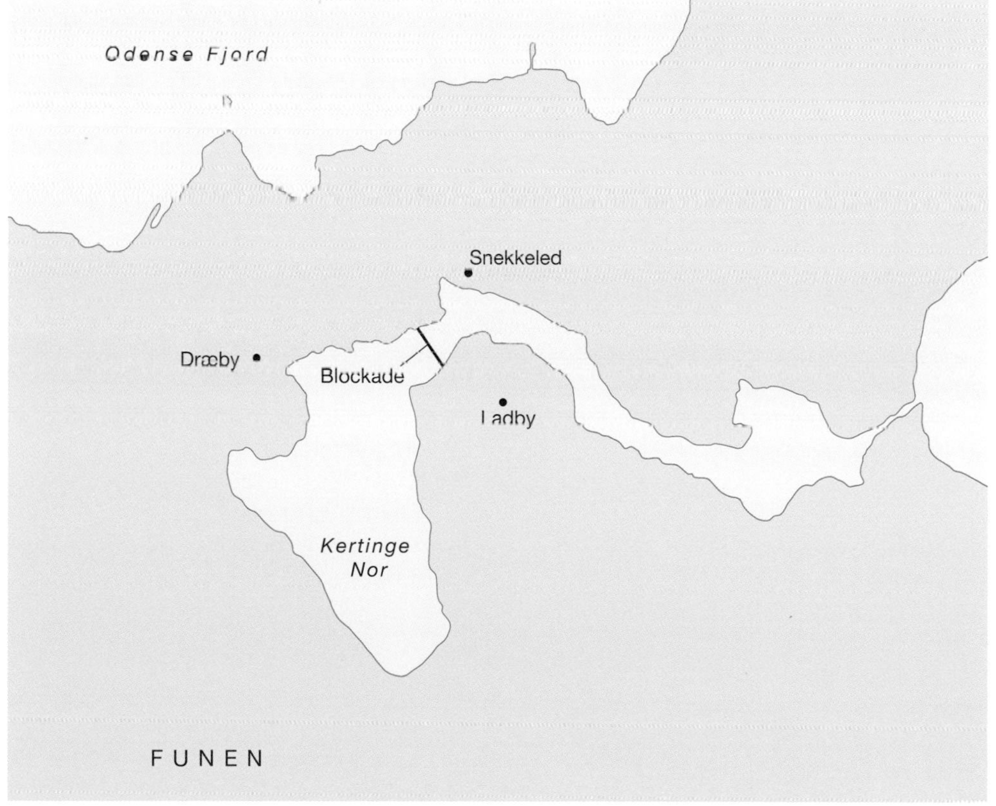

9.
Kertinge Nor on the Danish island of Funen is a natural harbour, and was defended in the Viking Age with a blockade across the entrance constructed from timber stakes driven into the sea bed, as indicated here. Similar defences have been located in many Scandinavian bays and rivers.

10.
Map showing the position of the Roskilde Fjord in Denmark in relation to other places mentioned in this chapter.

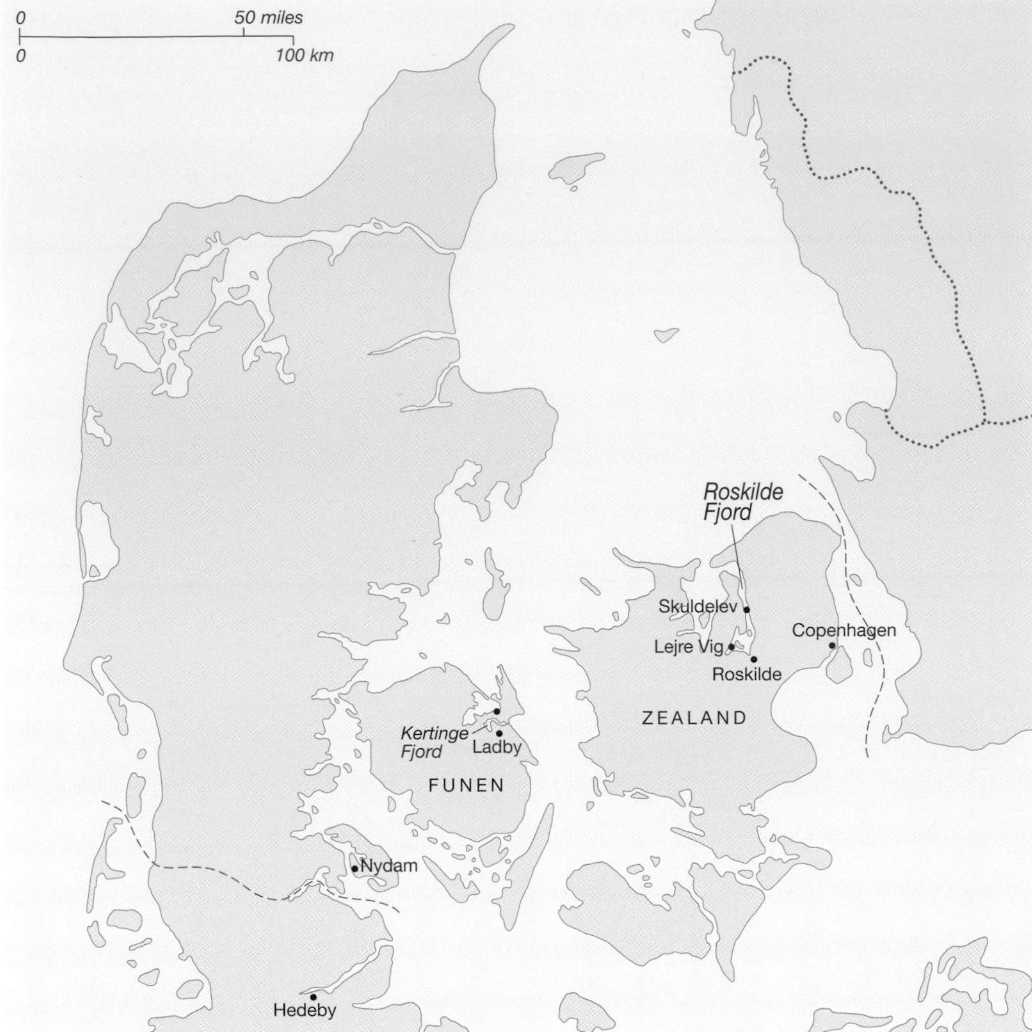

Roskilde Fjord has yielded more Viking and early medieval shipwrecks than any other area. In a narrow current-induced channel at Skuldelev, north of Roskilde, a blockade of deliberately sunk ships was examined underwater in the years 1957–9. Five ships were excavated in 1962, dating from the eleventh century.[18] Through analysis of the timber used for these ships, their origins could be determined. Two were built of Danish wood, two were built in present-day Norway and one ship was built in Ireland. The 'nationality' of the Skuldelev ships mirrors the middle-range circle of late Viking Age Denmark and also the political reach of King Cnut's North Sea empire (see pp. 16–17).

Ships at war

11.
This brooch in the shape of a stylized ship incorporates a representation of a reefed sail.

Brooch shaped like a ship, 800–1050. Tjørnehøj II, Fyn, Denmark.
Copper alloy. L 5.5 cm
National Museum of Denmark, Copenhagen

The Irish-built ship from the Skuldelev blockade – the so-called Skuldelev 2 – was a warship, almost 30 metres long, dating from *c.* 1040–45. A reconstruction of this longship, named 'The Sea Stallion of Glendalough', was built between 2000 and 2004 at the Viking Ship Museum's boatyard using copies of Viking-Age tools, identical building material and techniques according to the original principles. For the construction of the hull alone 27,000 effective working-hours were estimated, and tar, ropes, nails, rivets and sail etc. had to be made at the same time. The building of the ship required fourteen oak trees, of a thickness of 1 metre each.

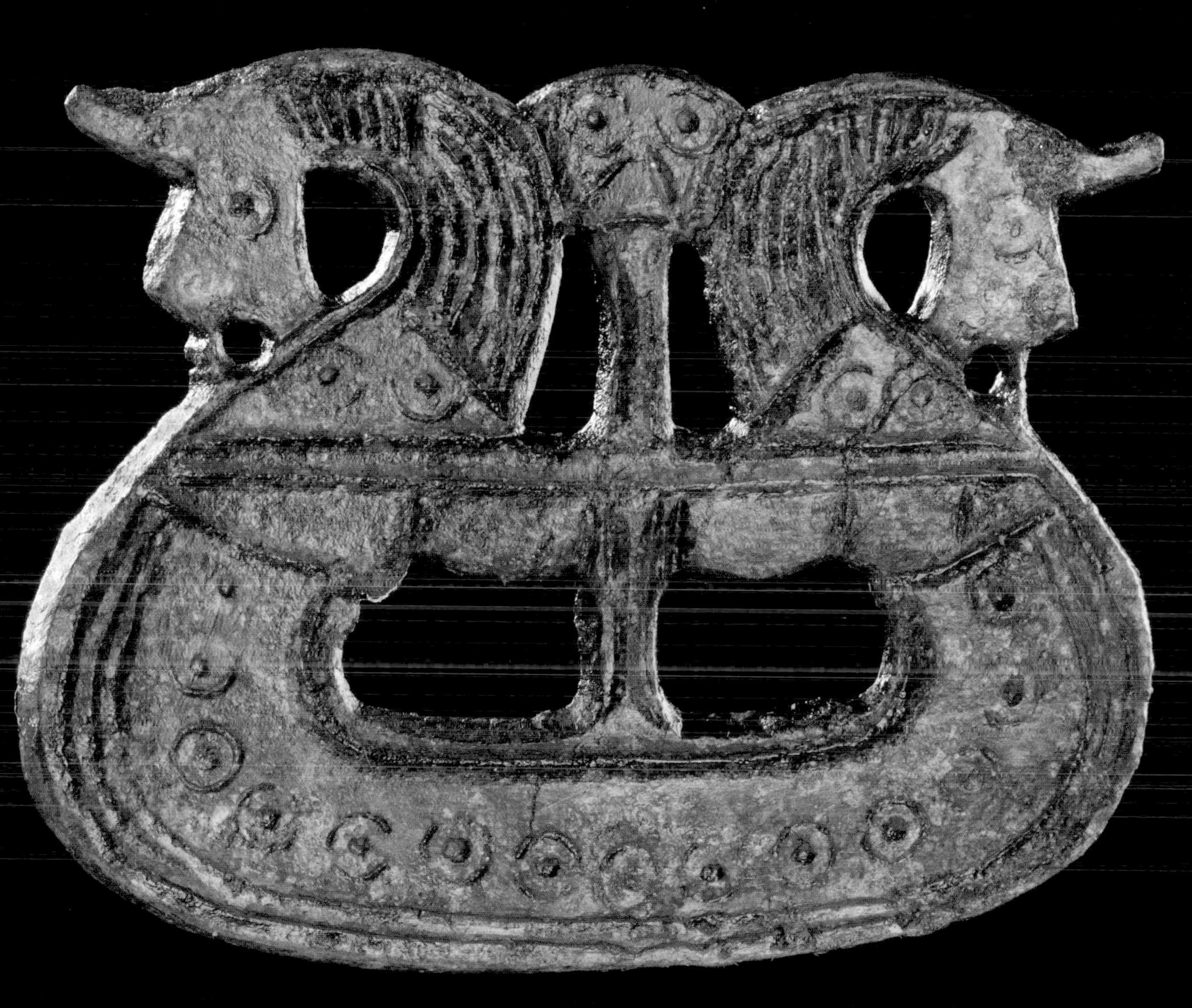

The Skuldelev 2 warship probably had a square, or rectangular or trapezoid, sail of wool or flax of around 112 square metres (fig. 11). Even more sensitive than timber to the ravages of time, no complete sails from the Viking period are preserved. Only a few fragments provide us with information about this crucial part of the Viking ship. The resources needed for sailmaking were extensive, even rivalling those of producing the hull. The collection of flax or wool, sorting and preparing, making it ready for spinning fibres, spinning thread and weaving of canvas must have represented tremendous effort and required specialized knowledge of the properties of materials for processing and utilization. Not all of the wool from the sheep was suitable for sails. Sources from early modern Iceland and the Faroe Islands show that the woollen thread for sails was spun by means of the spindle whorl, while the fabric was woven on a vertical loom. The work was probably carried out on farms within a large catchment area, from which the finished cloth was supplied to the sailmaker, who then sewed and shaped the sail. The edges were probably lined by horse-hair rope.[19] In skaldic poetry and sagas dyed sails are mentioned[20] – dark blue, red and purple – and well-produced sails were highly esteemed, even serving as royal gifts.

The Skuldelev blockade and other barriers in Roskilde Fjord served as efficient means of controlling navigation in the fjord. They did not, however, prevent all ships from coming to Roskilde. This was conspicuously demonstrated in 1996–7 when the new museum island of the Viking Ship Museum in Roskilde was constructed. Nine ships, ranging in date from the eleventh to the fourteenth century, were found in the harbour basin, wrecked in the bottom of the fjord, perhaps by northerly winds. One of the wrecks seemed to have been a surprisingly huge vessel. Attempts had been made to pull this ship up on to the land, but these were apparently unsuccessful. Instead the ship was stripped and eventually left in the shallow waters of the harbour of the young town of Roskilde.[21]

Roskilde 6, the great wreck from Roskilde harbour, was a warship, the longest so far known. The length of the keel is 32 metres and including the stem and stern the ship was around 37 metres long. Obviously the building of such a large ship involved many people. For the construction of the hull of a traditional Viking ship, the first critical phase was the selection of suitable timbers. Having chosen the trees, parts of them had to be cut down before felling in order to avoid undesired splitting. Curved branches were important for some parts of the ship, as such branches are much stronger than pieces cut out of a larger piece of wood.

After felling the trees, the treatment of the wood followed. In this process lies one of the reasons behind the success of the ships. Instead of sawing, the technique used from the Middle Ages, the Vikings split the trees with axes. This is why Viking ships were both strong and flexible, because splitting, in contrast to sawing, maintains the fibres of the wood. Then the hull itself was built, the planks overlapping each other in 'clinker' technique. Clinker building combined with the strength of the radially split planks explains why the Viking ships were stronger and lighter than ships built later in history (fig. 12). We do not know the number of people involved in the building of the hull. It takes time to split wood instead of just sawing, and cutting the planks with axes is time-consuming as well. Teams of men were probably involved, with those in the forest occupied by felling and splitting while boatbuilders constructed the general outline and laid the keel. Smiths produced nails, rivets, shroud rings (for fastening the shroud, a part of the rigging, to the hull) and other metal fittings.[22]

Writing in around 1230, Snorri Sturluson describes in *Heimskringla* how in around the year 1000 King Olaf Trygvasson ordered the building of a huge longship Ormen den Lange (the long serpent). A man called Thorberg Skafhug was to set up the stem and stern, and others were to carry timber, assemble the ship and tar it. When it was time to fit the final topmost strakes, Thorberg unfortunately had to leave the shipyard and travel home on an

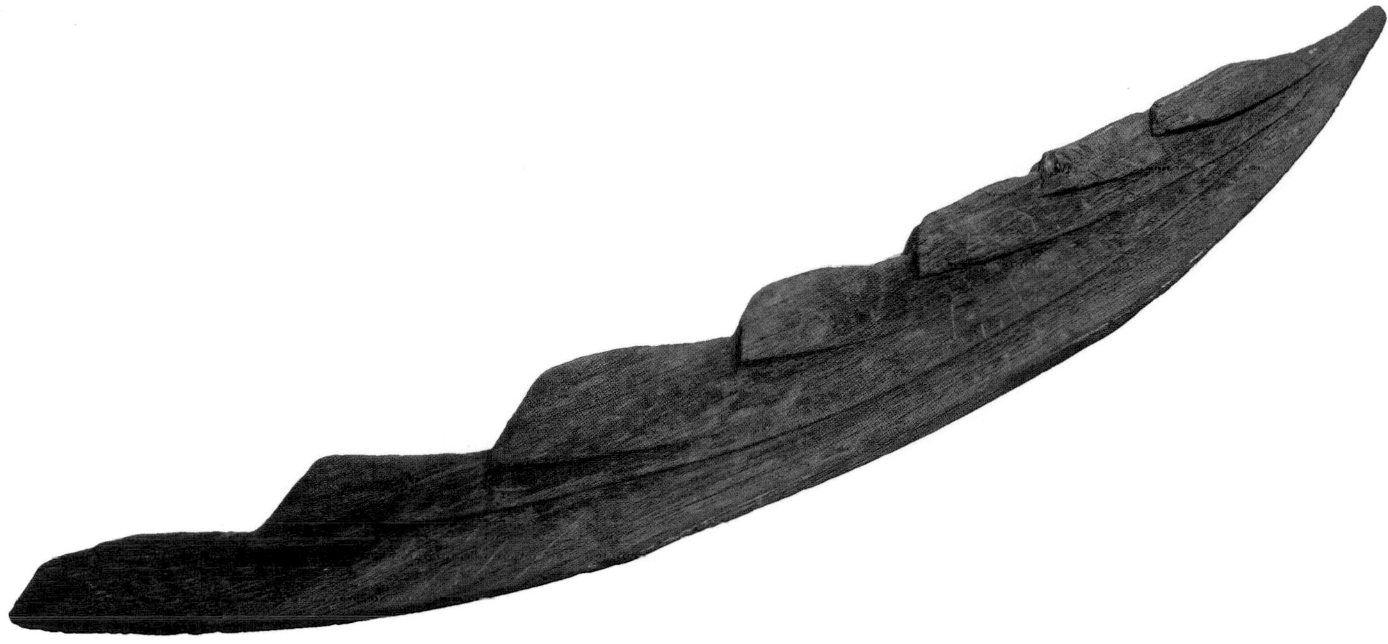

12.
Stepped stem post for a boat of Scandinavian type, 885–1035. Laig, Isle of Eigg, Inverness-shire, Scotland.
Oak. L 193 cm, H 30 cm
National Museums Scotland, Edinburgh

13.
Strake with oar port, late 12th century. Wood Quay, Dublin, Ireland.
Wood. L 170 cm, W 29 cm
National Museum of Ireland, Dublin

important errand. When the ship was finally ready the king came to inspect it along with his retinue and Thorberg, and everyone said they had never seen such a big, beautiful ship. But early the next morning it was discovered that the strakes on one side of the ship had been hacked to pieces during the night. The king flew into a rage and promised to reward anyone who could expose the vandal. Thorberg confessed that he was the culprit and the king ordered him to make good the damage. Thorberg did so, and when the damaged side was complete again, everyone could see that his work was much finer, and the king asked him to replace the strakes on the other side of the ship as well.[73]

Snorri's account was not written down until sometime in the early thirteenth century. However, the traditional ways of shipbuilding probably did not change radically during those two centuries and the account of the division of responsibility, with the king himself commissioning the building and the various crews of workers, is the most detailed we have. At the heart of the story is Thorberg's destruction of the strakes he had not been involved in making, thus demonstrating a shipbuilder's envy but also his pride in his work, which is ultimately rewarded when King Olaf also orders him to replace the side of the ship that had not been destroyed.

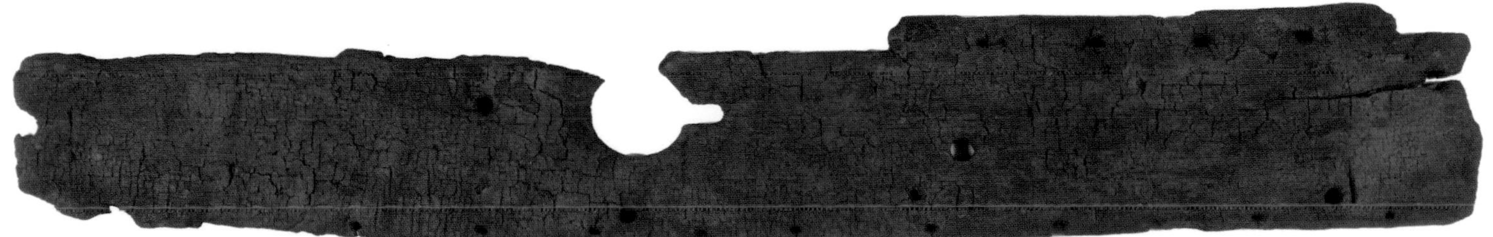

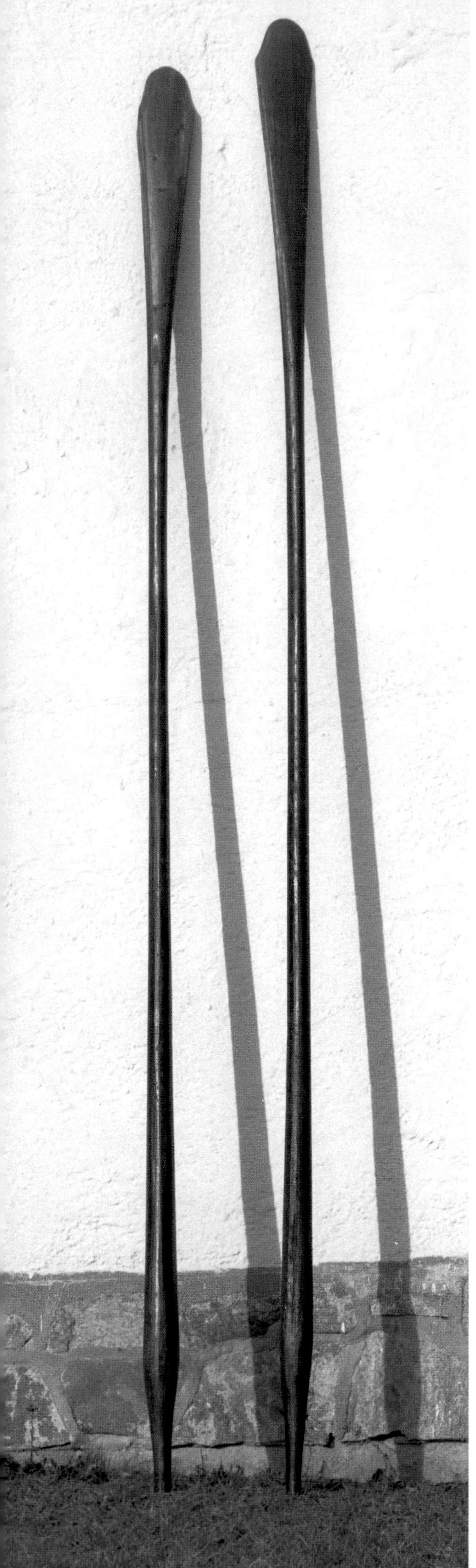

The strong feelings Thorberg has for the ship can be compared with the imagery relating to ships, especially warships, in skaldic poetry. Here we find countless poetic kennings[24] and similes for ships, which are often compared to birds and animals such as falcons, swans, dogs, wolves and horses.[25] The way the ships were decorated with ornate wind vanes, dragons' heads and carvings – as seen on the Oseberg ship – also bears witness to the great care their builders took.

Although longships carried sail, it was mainly the oarsmen who propelled them (figs 13–14). During swift attacks on foreign shores and in sea battles – as mentioned in the sagas and in poetry[26] – rapid manoeuvring without dependence on the wind was absolutely crucial. The many oarsmen were also employed as warriors. The great warships belong to the late Viking Age. The development of the longship may reflect similar advances in methods of warfare and it is probably not by chance that the very large ships appear at the same time as Anglo-Saxon and Frankish sources report great Viking fleets, where the number of ships frequently exceeds fifty. What the Vikings themselves called their longships is somewhat uncertain; particular attention has been drawn to the name *snekke*, but the word *drage* is also used.[27] Rune-stones are the best source of information and there longships most often appear under the name of *skeið*.

Taking its size and hence the resources needed for building it into account, Roskilde 6 is most likely a royal enterprise. As seen now, a wreck, fragmented and only dark brown and black in colour, it can be difficult to imagine its original appearance and glory. However, a written source, less than two decades later than the building of the ship, might give us a hint of its former splendour.

The *Encomium Emmae Reginae*, or *Gesta Cnutonis Regis*, is a book in honour of Queen Emma, the wife of King Cnut and previously of King Æthelred (the Unready), probably written about 1040 at the court of her and Cnut's son, Harthacnut.[28] The fleets assembled by the kings Svein Forkbeard and Cnut in 1013 and 1016 respectively, for the conquest of England, are vividly described in this manuscript. Of King Svein's fleet it is said that:

> on one side lions moulded of gold were to be seen on the ships, on the other birds on the tops of the masts indicated by their movements the winds as they blew, or dragons of various kinds poured fire from their nostrils ... The royal vessel excelled the others in beauty as much as the king preceded the soldiers in the honour of his proper dignity.

The ships of King Cnut were no less lavishly decorated:

> So great, also, was the ornamentation of the ships, that the eyes of the beholders were dazzled ... the flashing of arms shone in one place, in another the flame of suspended shields. Gold shone from the prows, silver also flashed ... So great, in fact, was the magnificence of the fleet, that if its lord had desired to conquer any people, the ships alone would have terrified the enemy, before the warriors whom they carried joined battle at all.

How far these colourful descriptions are rooted in reality is much debated, but the overall language in the manuscript is Scandinavian maritime.[29] Elements such as the gilded weathervane (figs 15–16) and the suspended shields on the gunwales are recognizable from depictions of ships and finds, as are the monstrous or zoomorphic moulded figures.

According to the *Anglo-Saxon Chronicle*, in September 994 London was attacked by ninety-four ships under the command of Olaf and Svein. The indication of the number of ships is just one of several appearing in the chronicle and other written sources, where large

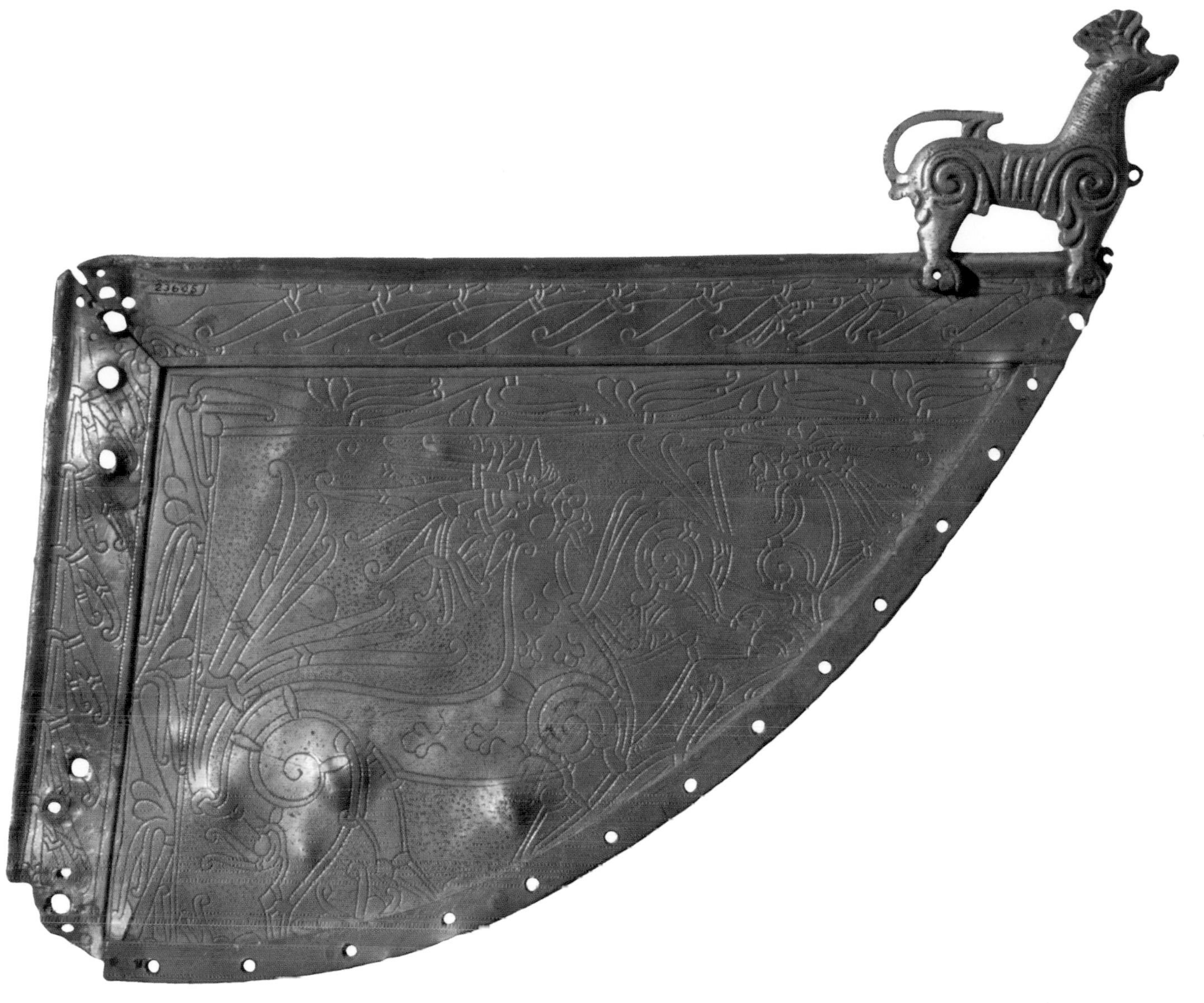

14. (opposite)
Oars, 9th century. Oseberg, Sem, Vestfold, Norway.
Fir. L 400 cm
Museum of Cultural History, University of Oslo, Oslo

15. (above)
Weather vane. 1000–1050. Heggen Church, Buskerund, Norway.
Gilt copper, brass. L 28 cm, H 29 cm
Museum of Cultural History, University of Oslo, Oslo

numbers indeed are given. There may be a certain amount of exaggeration, but there is no doubt that huge fleets of Viking ships appear in the later part of the Viking Age. These great fleets reflect an enormous investment of resources in the areas from where the ships came, not only in manpower, timber and iron, but also in sheep and wool or flax for caulking and sails. Added to this are materials for the rigging, ropes and pitch.

A high degree of organization was therefore required at all levels of society, from the individual household right up to the king. This system of organization must have been similar to the regional levies (*leiðangr*, see pp. 113–5) that are known from the time immediately following the Viking Age in Denmark, Norway and Sweden. In fact, the system in Norway is mentioned in skaldic poems as early as the tenth century.[30] The basis of the *leiðangr* was a duty to make a military contribution, mainly by building, equipping and manning the ships of the fleet.

In order for the *leiðangr* system to function, the Scandinavian countries had to be divided into units. In Sweden, the country is thought to have been divided into districts

16.
Metal animals such as this horse figurine were mounted on top of elaborate ornamental weather vanes. Complete weathervanes have been found, such as the famous example from Söderala in Sweden, and are depicted on the Bryggen ship stick (see p. 7).

Animal figure for a weathervane. Lolland, Denmark.
Gilt copper alloy. L 9.7 cm
National Museum of Denmark, Copenhagen

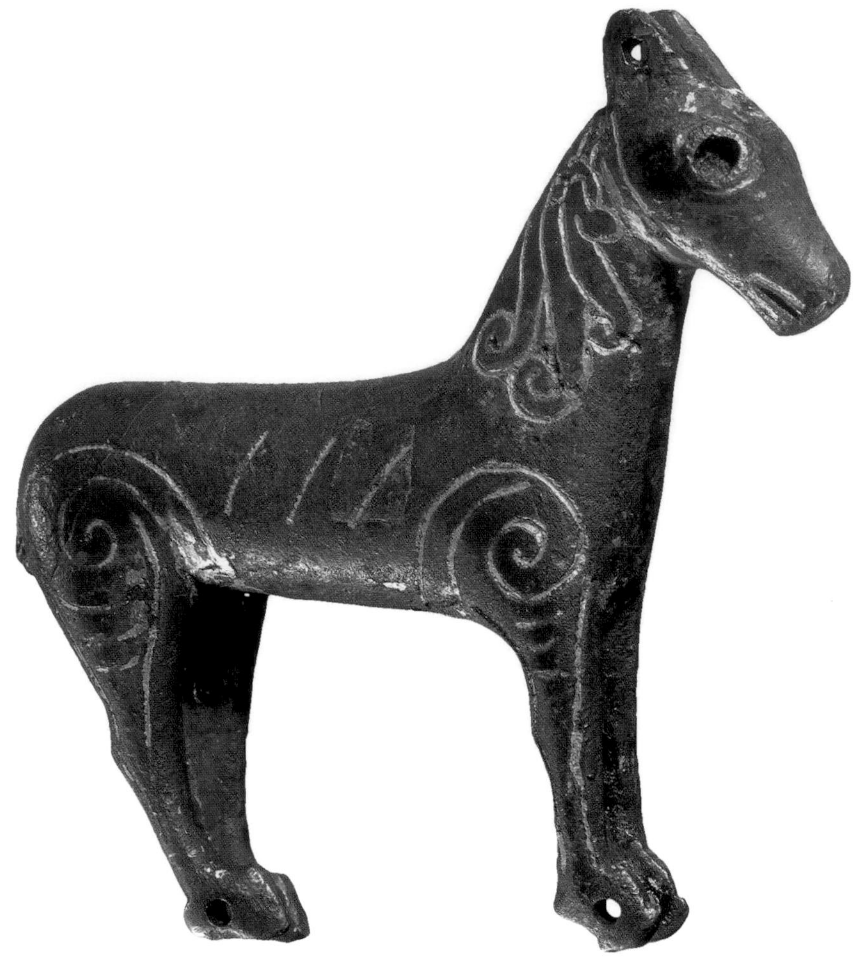

known as *hundare*, which were made up of several *skepslag*. In medieval Denmark it was the *herred*, which was divided into one to four *skipæn*, each of which had to provide a ship with a captain.[31] This captain may have been a local aristocrat, like the captain Erik, mentioned on a rune-stone from Hedeby:

Torulv, Svein's retainer
erected this stone in memory of his partner Erik
who met his death
when brave men besieged Hedeby
and he was a captain
a very high-born warrior

So in this way the ship formed the basis for administrative unity throughout the country, just as the churches did later through the creation of parishes.

Even if a ship was part of a larger fleet, it was probably owned by an individual. Various rune-stones mention people who owned longships.[32] They also tell of a division of labour when the ship was at sea. The captain was in command of the ship, at least when it was *i leding* (on military service). An inscription on a rune-stone from Esta names a man called Sigvið as *skeiðar vísi*, i.e. commander of the warship. Under the orders of the commander or captain were the oarsmen, the actual crew, known as *skiparar*. The raids were led by a commander, a king or a nobleman, who controlled the entire fleet and to whom the individual ships' captains had a duty of loyalty. It is likely that the Erik named on the Hedeby stone, who was a captain and fell at the side of King Svein Forkbeard in the battles at Hedeby around 980, was not only in command while his ship was at sea, but also led his crew on the battlefield.

The last raids on England took place under the kings Svein Estridsen (1047–74) and Cnut the Holy (1080–86). Although the Danes had been Christian for almost a century by then, they did not stop plundering churches and monasteries, if the English sources are to be believed. When Cnut was murdered in Odense in 1086 by angry yeomen, it may have been due to their dissatisfaction with the king for levying a kind of military service tax. The literature produced in connection with Cnut's subsequent canonization states that the purpose of his expedition to England – which was acceptable to God – was to reawaken the old warrior ideals of the Danes.

Ships, status and power

In the Edda poem *Rigsþula*, the god Heimdall is the ancestor of all the social classes of the Viking Age: thralls, yeomen and warriors. Warriors, says the poem, '... have costly halls, better land than your lands, they know how to captain snekker, test swords and slash open wounds'.[33] These few words encapsulate the ideals of the seafaring warrior, for whom the hall, wealth, the ship and the sword were of the highest value.

The improvements in communications and infrastructure that ships brought with them created a useful network for the exercise of power. It may have happened at the local level, but the developments in shipbuilding technology have also been mentioned as an important requirement for the empire-building that took place in Scandinavia in the Viking Age.[34]

Various rune stones, mainly in Sweden and most often from the last part of the Viking Age, praise people who travelled far. One such stone from Uppland tells of a man named Asgautr, who travelled 'both to the east and to the west'.[35] Voyaging and seafaring were exploits, and long-distance travel was a deed for which great men might be remembered. Other stones honour men who died far from home. To 'find death', as those who carved the rune-stones often expressed it, in distant lands was evidently proof of strength and courage. This was true of Gudbjørn from Södermanland in Sweden, who 'stood bravely at the prow of the ship, and now lies buried in the west', probably in England.

However, people could also be remembered for the wealth they acquired while they were *a-viking*, i.e. on Viking raids. A rune-stone in Uppland commemorates a man named Ulf, who 'took three [Dane]gelds', one together with Toste, one with Thorkil and lastly one with Cnut. Another stone, also from Uppland, pays tribute to a man called Harald, who 'bravely travelled far in search of gold' – so he grew rich, but it is specifically stated that he had to travel a long way to gain his wealth. The inscription also says that Harald 'fed the eagle' in the east, which means that he fought and left a trail of bodies behind him, but he himself died in the south, in Serkland, i.e. the land of the Saracens (see p. 24). The many rune-stones that name particular foreign destinations all mention places very far away. It was journeying over great distances that conferred status and was worthy of commemoration on rune-stones.

The notion that long-distance travel, fighting and the acquisition of wealth were the noblemen's ideals also found expression in the 'good life' of the aristocracy. The sagas report that King Olaf Tryggvasson excelled at all kinds of sport. Among others he mastered one associated with longships and sailing: he could walk on the oars over the entire length of the

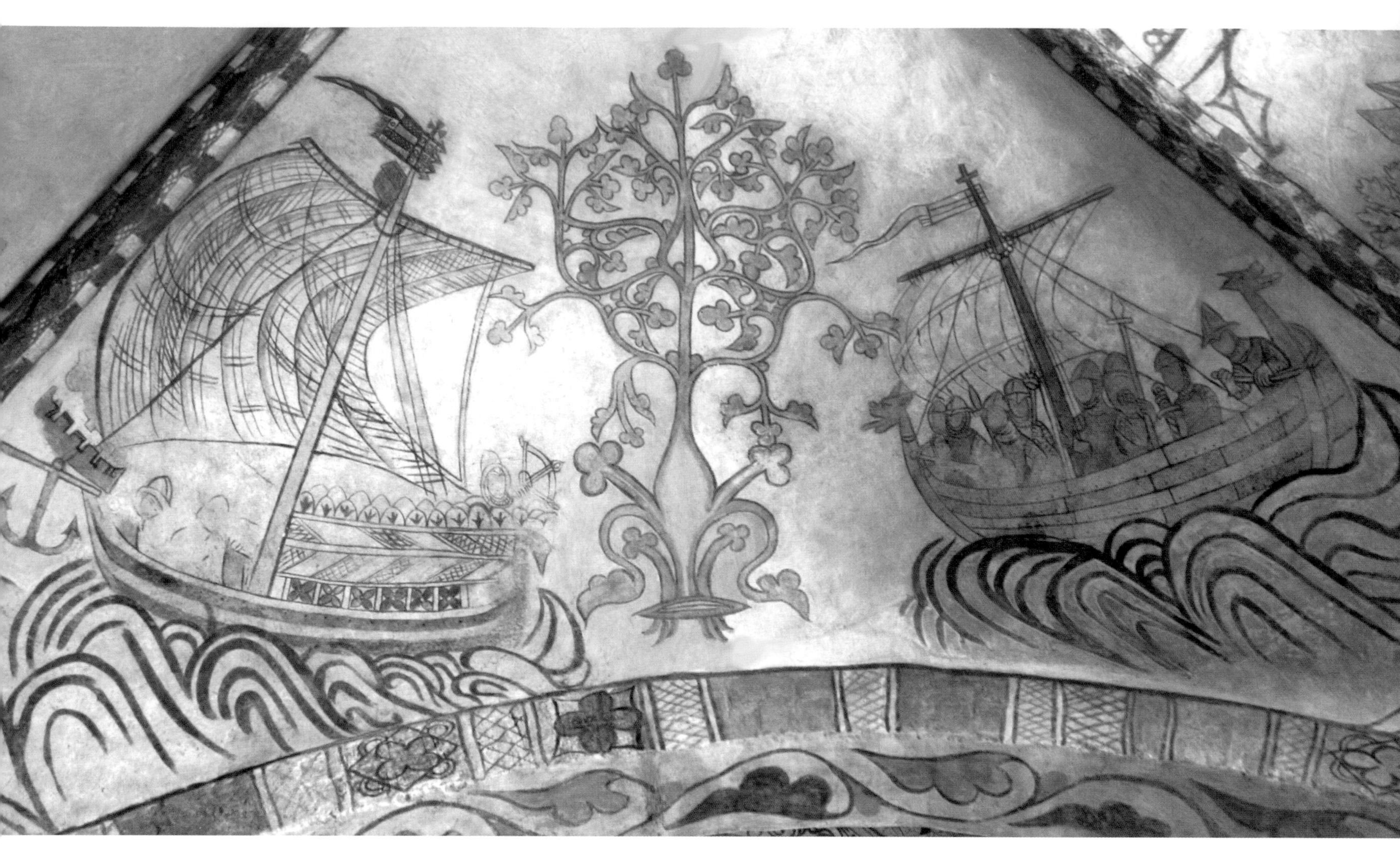

17.
St Olaf's sailing race, as depicted in a 14th-century wall painting in the parish church at Skamstrup, Denmark.

longship on one side and back along the other, and what is more while the ship was being rowed at speed, without getting his feet wet, and juggling three swords at the same time.[36] Less tricky than Olaf's walking on the oars, perhaps, Earl Rognvald I of Orkney boasted of his skill at rowing among other things: 'I am quick at playing chess, I have nine skills, I hardly forget runes, I'm often at either a book or craftsmanship. I am able to glide on skis, I shoot and row so it makes a difference, I understand both the playing of the harp and poetry.'[37]

Earl Rognvald I of Orkney lived in the first half of the twelfth century, and his poem must date from this time, but he had retained the classic Nordic virtues. As a Christian nobleman, he too went on long journeys like his forefathers but as a pilgrim or a crusader, and his characteristic reaction when he approached the River Jordan was to leap in and swim across. Long-distance travel still conferred status, even if it had acquired Christian clothing, and swimming was still a nobleman's sport.

A legend of uncertain date tells that Olaf Haraldsson ('St Olaf') and his brother, Harald Hardruler, raced their ships to Trondheim to win the crown of Norway. Even though Olaf took the time to take part in a church service, he sailed faster than Harald. It was said that his ship sailed so amazingly fast that it reached the destination before the arrow he shot from his bow during the voyage (fig. 17).[38]

The ship – belief and magic

It is not clear what rituals may have accompanied the building and naming of Viking ships, although there have been a number of finds from the latter part of the Viking Age of carpentry and metalworking tools that appear to have been sacrificed. These can be entire tool chests with their contents or just individual tools. They are typically found along coasts, on lake shores and on river banks.[39] Among them are tools associated with shipbuilding.

The names the Vikings gave their ships are known only from skaldic poetry and the sagas. These are mostly bird or animal names, such as the Serpent, the Bison and the Crane. For some time after the beginning of the Christian period a ship could still be given an animal name, such as Renen (the Reindeer), built in the early twelfth century by King Inge of Norway.

In the poem *Beowulf*, King Skjold, the mythical ancestor of the kings of Lejre (otherwise known as the Skjoldungs), arrives in Denmark as a naked child on board a ship. According to one of the sagas, Skjold was the son of Odin. Several versions of the story are known. In some he is alone on the ship, in others he is surrounded by weapons, and in yet others he is accompanied by the fertility symbol of a sheaf of corn. The royal house of Sweden, the Yngling dynasty, also invoked their kinship with the gods, with the fertility god Frey, whose most important symbol was the ship. So the great royal houses claimed to descend from the gods and the ship may have been the medium linking the world of the gods to the human world, carrying members of these families from one to the other.[40]

It has also been suggested that fertility rituals took place in connection with ship burials.[41] In ibn Fadlān's well-known account of the burial of a Viking prince in a ship by the River Volga, the men have intercourse with the woman who is to be sacrificed. This could be interpreted as a fertility ritual. In the Norse mythology of the sagas the ship of the god Frey is a magic vessel named Skíðblaðnir. When empty, it was just a little piece of cloth and weighed no more than that. It could be unfolded in no time and, wherever it sailed, it always had the wind behind it.

Just as Skjold came to Denmark in a ship, after his death he was returned in the same way to the world from which he had come. According to the *Beowulf* poem, he was laid in a ship with many weapons and great wealth. It is these ship burials that are the clearest link between belief, ritual and ships. Burials in ships – burned, partly burned and unburned – are mainly known from the Viking Age, although there are other, older examples. The custom was most widespread in western Norway and parts of Sweden, but it is found over the entire area settled by the Vikings, from Russia and across the Baltic lands to the British Isles.

Saxo's account of the exploits of the Danes, written around 1200, tells how King Frode made a law about the burial of warriors. The head of a family should be buried with his horse and weapons. The bodies of ten captains could be burned in one ship, but the body of a commander must be burned on a pyre set up on his own ship.[42] A king or an earl who had fallen in battle should be burned in his own ship. Although the value of Saxo's legendary history of Denmark as a source is limited, King Frode's law on the burial of warriors agrees astonishingly well with the archaeological finds. Warriors are found in horse and ship burials. Further confirmation that the size of the ship reflects the status of the person buried in it can be found in the introduction to ibn Fadlān's account of the burial of the Viking prince, where the Arab author explicitly states that the poorer Vikings are buried in a small boat.[43]

Even if the best-known ship burials such as Oseberg and Gokstad contain big ships, the great majority of ship burials are in small boats, most often in clinker built rowing boats. On the other hand, burials in large trading ships are completely unknown. The small boats were not owned by the poor, if we are to believe ibn Fadlān's account. These are not small fishing boats or punts for hunting but well-built, usually slender vessels made of oak. They are reminiscent of those found in the Gokstad burial, known as 'færinger', and could be interpreted as boats intended for the swift transport of a nobleman and his closest kin.[44]

The inscription on a rune-stone from Tryggevælde at Stevns on Zealand confirms that stone ships really were considered ships. The 3-metre-high stone, with its inscription dating from the first half of the tenth century, says that the woman Ragnhild made a grave mound and *skæið* in memory of her husband, Gunnulf. *Skæið* means stone ship and the rune-stone was undoubtedly part of a monument of this kind, probably the stone at the prow.

The connection between the stone ships and graves is not clear, but they must be some kind of burial monument. The size of the stone ships, like that of the actual ship burials, may have reflected the status of the dead man. At any rate, the biggest known stone ship, the 300-metre-long stone ship at the Jelling complex (see pp. 158–9), has been interpreted as a royal monument. Unlike the 'real' ship burials, which were covered with soil, the ship monuments were visible as ships in the landscape.

Side by side with the ship graves have been found other types of grave for Viking-Age aristocrats: wagons (see p. 182), chamber or horse graves and, more rarely, sledges. Perhaps it is not by chance that all these elements are associated with transport in one way or another. It has been pointed out that the Gotland picture stones are also burial monuments, almost ship graves without ships (fig. 18). The pictorial world that appears on stones of the late Viking Age includes enormous numbers of ships, horses and wagons and the occasional sledge. When ships are shown, prominence is often given to a particular person on board, perhaps the dead man in whose memory the stone was erected. As a rule he sits in the bows of the ship and may be holding a weapon or a triangular symbol in his hand. In a few cases, there is even a runic inscription on the stem of the boat.[45] One cannot help but think of the text on a rune-stone from Spånga in Södermanland, where the dead man is remembered as: 'he who stood boldly in the bows of the ship now lies buried in the west'.

A society formed of ships

The ship left its mark on all levels of Viking society: as a means of transport, a weapon, a burial ship – the ship of death. The ship is the motif most often used in graffiti in Scandinavian contexts in the Viking Age and the early Middle Ages. It is also found as a children's toy (figs 19–20).

Landscapes were formed by ships through the building of harbours, blockades and defences against attack from the sea. Viking settlement shows a pattern in which coastal areas or major waterways were preferred. Perhaps even the land was divided into administrative units directed by a basically maritime levy system.

Viking houses looked like ships. Among the types of wooden buildings for which archaeological evidence has been found is the so-called 'Trelleborg house', the main house, the hall. The curve of its long walls is reminiscent of the shape of a ship. In the ring forts (see pp. 151–3) these stand side by side and have given rise to suggestions that the buildings housed a ship's crew – oarsmen and captain – and that *skibsfreden*, the special law applying to ships in time of war and on long voyages, also prevailed in these halls.[46] The Norse clinker-built ship, whether warship, cargo ship or smaller boat, was the basic mode for all movements of goods and people in the Viking world. Gold, silver and jewellery are the physical remains of these movements. But the artefacts we find are only a minor part of the bulk of goods transported. Archaeology favours 'glitter', as metals are better preserved than organic materials. Traded or taken 'items' such as slaves, fur, cattle and cereals can be

18.
Picture stone depicting a ship under sail.

Picture stone, 8th century. Broa, Halla parish, Gotland, Sweden.
Limestone. H 74 cm, W 48 cm
Gotlands Museum, Visby

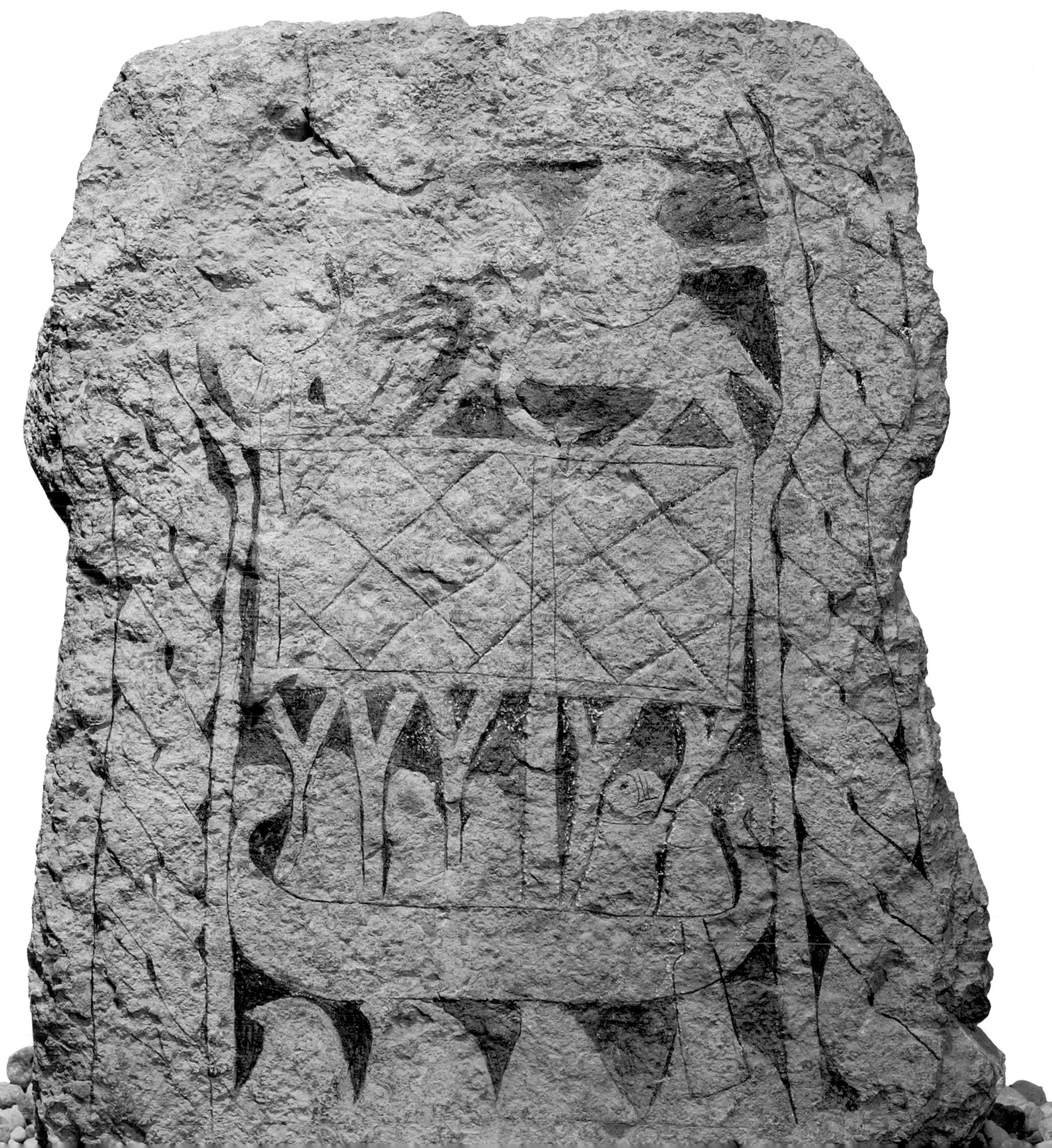

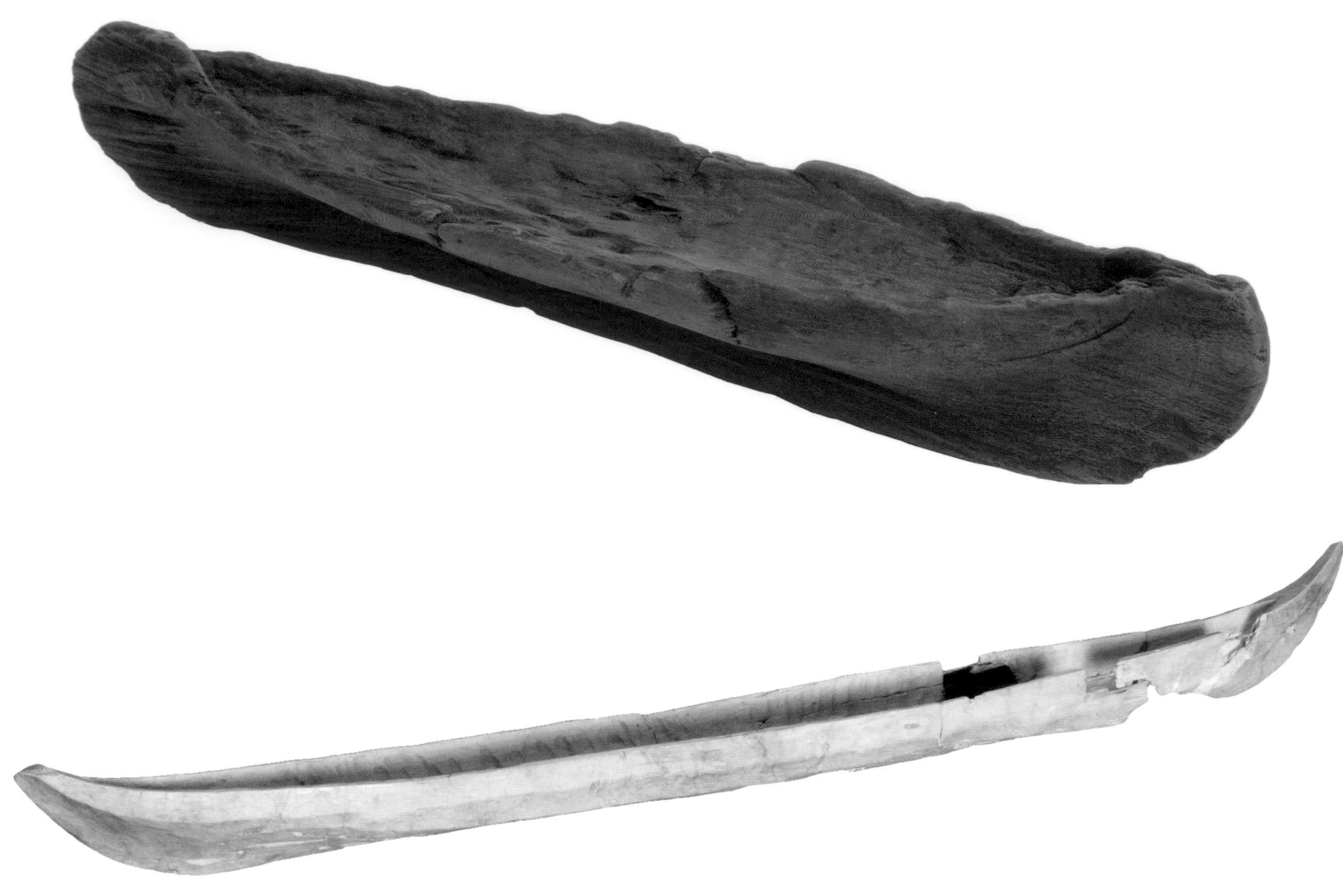

19.
Model or toy boat, probably 10th–11th century. Fishamble Street, Dublin, Ireland.
Wood. L 31.5 cm, W 9 cm
National Museum of Ireland, Dublin

20.
Model or toy boat, 800–1050. Hedeby, Germany.
Alder wood. L 58 cm, W 7 cm
Archäologisches Landesmuseum, Schloss Gottorf, Schleswig

archaeologically invisible. Just as the Viking warship has dominated our notion of the Viking ship, the 'glitter' has biased our view of the contents of trade and exchange, favouring long-distance traffic, transporting valuable and attractive commodities. In the general picture of the Viking economy, the importance and volume of low-value goods, transported either by larger cargo ships or by minor boats for local transfer, should not be underestimated. The latter, the small boats, were the medium by which more distant water-borne contacts were extended into the land by navigable rivers.

Gifts and plunder took their place beside barter and purchase. Regulated commerce, as reflected in the many finds of weights and balances, had a reverse side, incorporating piracy, violence and eventually taking of land. Some of these weights are in themselves symbols of this mutuality – fragments of gilded shrines, probably spoils from plunder – filled in with lead and serving as weights in legalized commerce (see pp. 57–60).

Improved skills in boatbuilding enabled the Vikings to exchange ideas rapidly and more effectively with the people around them, from mode and manners to ideas of kingship (see pp. 62–8) and even religion. The interplay of status and the movements of people, deliberate as well as irregular, are as important to the Viking network as the exchange and trade of goods.

More than most of its neighbours, Scandinavia in the Viking period must be understood as a vast conglomerate of smaller sub-regions and larger groups of sub-regions. Their connectivity depended on infrastructure, which relied on ships. When King Harald Bluetooth in *c.* 965 had his famous stone raised, boasting of having won for himself 'all of Denmark and Norway and having made the Danes Christians', his achievements were dependent on and facilitated by seafaring and ships – both directly and practically as well as in a wider perspective through ideas of kingship and belief developed through interaction with neighbours.

Whether from burial mounds (Oseberg, Gokstad, Ladby) or dredged out of barriers and harbours (Skuldelev, Roskilde, Hedeby), finds of whole or partial ships rank among the most spectacular Viking artefacts. But even less conspicuous finds – a rusty axehead, a simple clay loom weight or a small spindle whorl – are the remains of shipbuilding and sailmaking in a society based on maritime activity.

In the late summer of 2010, a little lead spindle whorl was found in Saltfleetby St Clement in Lincolnshire (fig. 21). Saltfleetby lies on the east coast of England, an area that was strongly influenced by harrowing and later settlement by the Vikings; the name is partly Scandinavian.[47] St Clement's Church itself was built in the early thirteenth century, but in both Scandinavia and England there are churches dedicated to St Clement, typically associated with old maritime communities.[48] The spindle whorl bears a runic inscription from the beginning of the eleventh century or perhaps a little earlier, part of which is legible: 'may Óðinn and Heimdallr and Þjálfa help you, Úlfljótr'. This allows us to imagine an anxious woman in a small, Anglo-Scandinavian community by the North Sea, with the spindle whorl in her hand invoking the pagan Norse gods Odin and Heimdal to help Ulfjot out at sea.

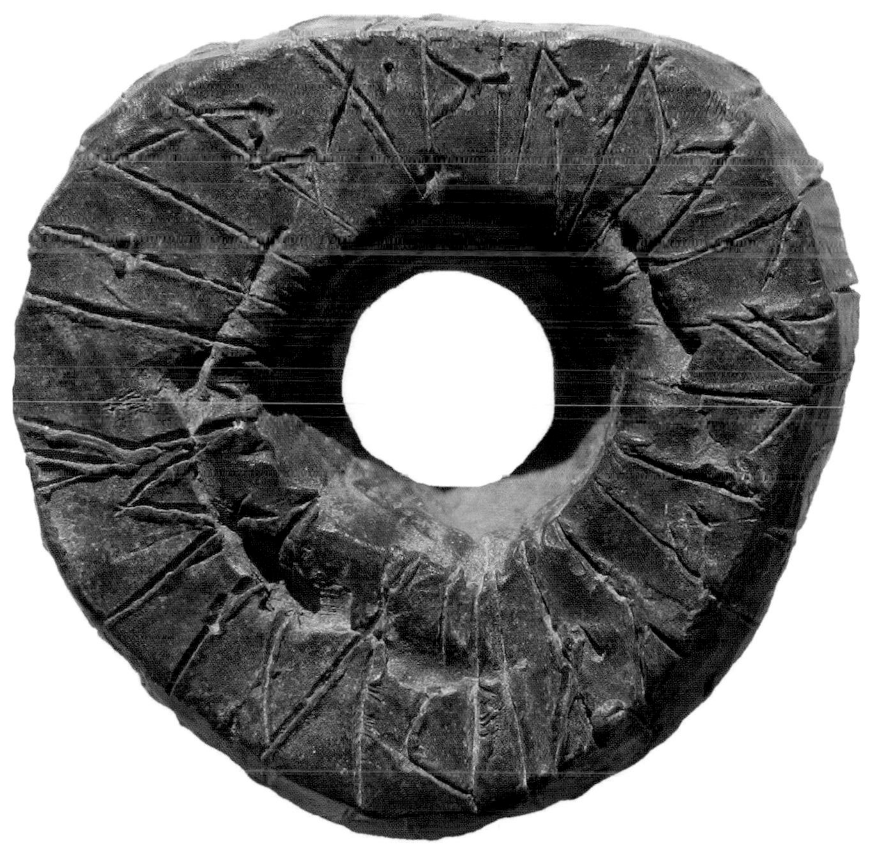

21.
This spindle whorl bears a Norse runic inscription, which has been tentatively translated as 'may Óðinn and Heimdallr and Þjálfa help you, Úlfljótr'.

Spindle whorl with runic inscription, early eleventh century. Saltfleetby, Lincolnshire, England.
Lead. Diam. 2.6 cm
Private collection

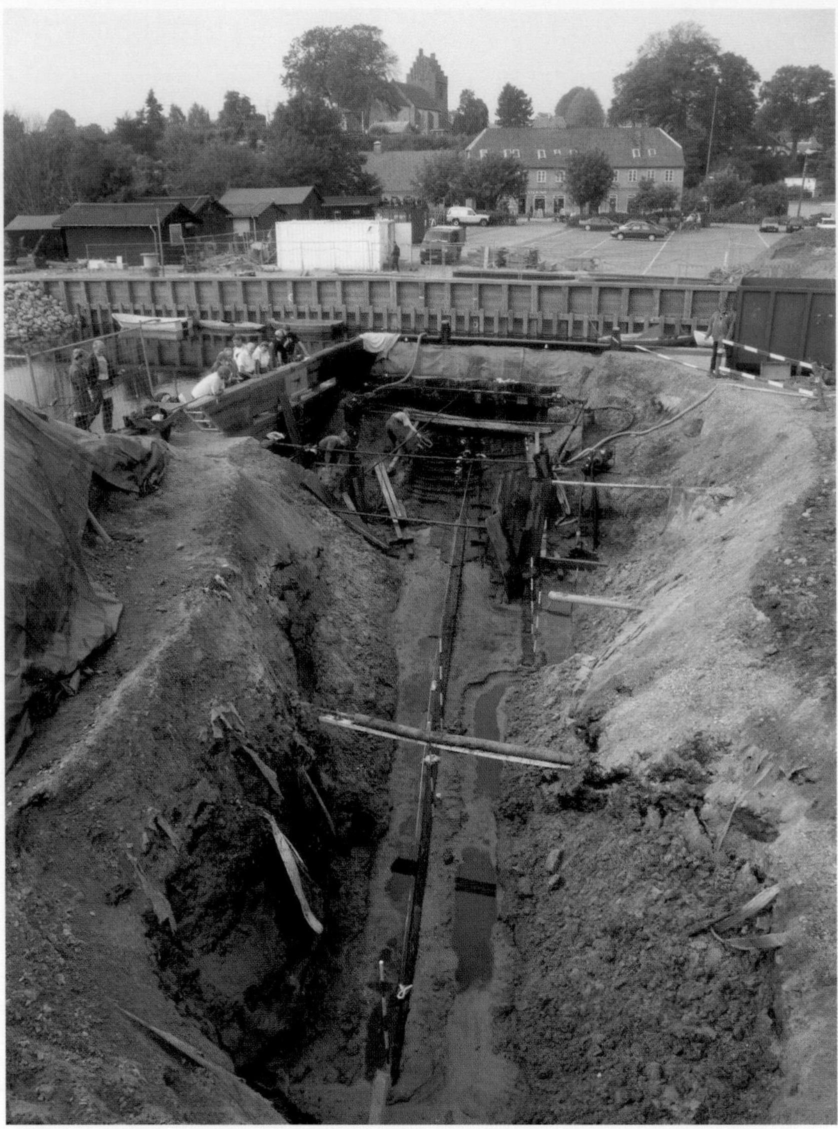

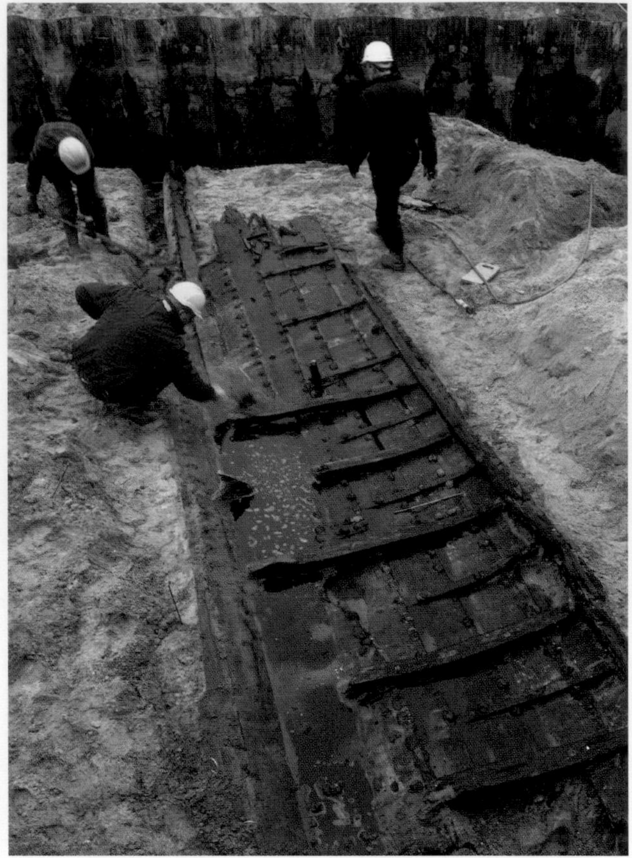

1–2.
The excavation of the ship at Roskilde in 1997.

3. (opposite)
A section of the bottom of the ship during excavation.

Roskilde 6

Jan Bill

With a reconstructed length of more than 37 metres, Roskilde 6 is the longest ship preserved from the Viking Age. It was discovered and excavated in 1996–7 in the harbour area of one of the earliest cities in Denmark, the royal cathedral city of Roskilde (figs 1–2).[1] It is the oldest of some ten or so wrecks found here and came to light when work began on the extension of the Viking Ship Museum. Since then, the ship has been painstakingly documented, analysed and conserved.

Today the ship consists of a well-preserved section of the bottom and almost all of the 32-metre-long keel. The wreck shows clear traces of the building work that led to its discovery. Just aft of amidships, 2 metres of the hull fell victim to the excavators before it was discovered. Nevertheless, the find is sufficiently well-preserved to make it possible to reconstruct the main features, particularly as it is contemporary with and similar in construction to the five Viking ships from nearby Skuldelev, now in the Viking Ship Museum, Roskilde.

How old is Roskilde 6 and where did it come from?

Roskilde 6 has been dated using dendrochronology, a method by which measuring and comparing the distances between the annual

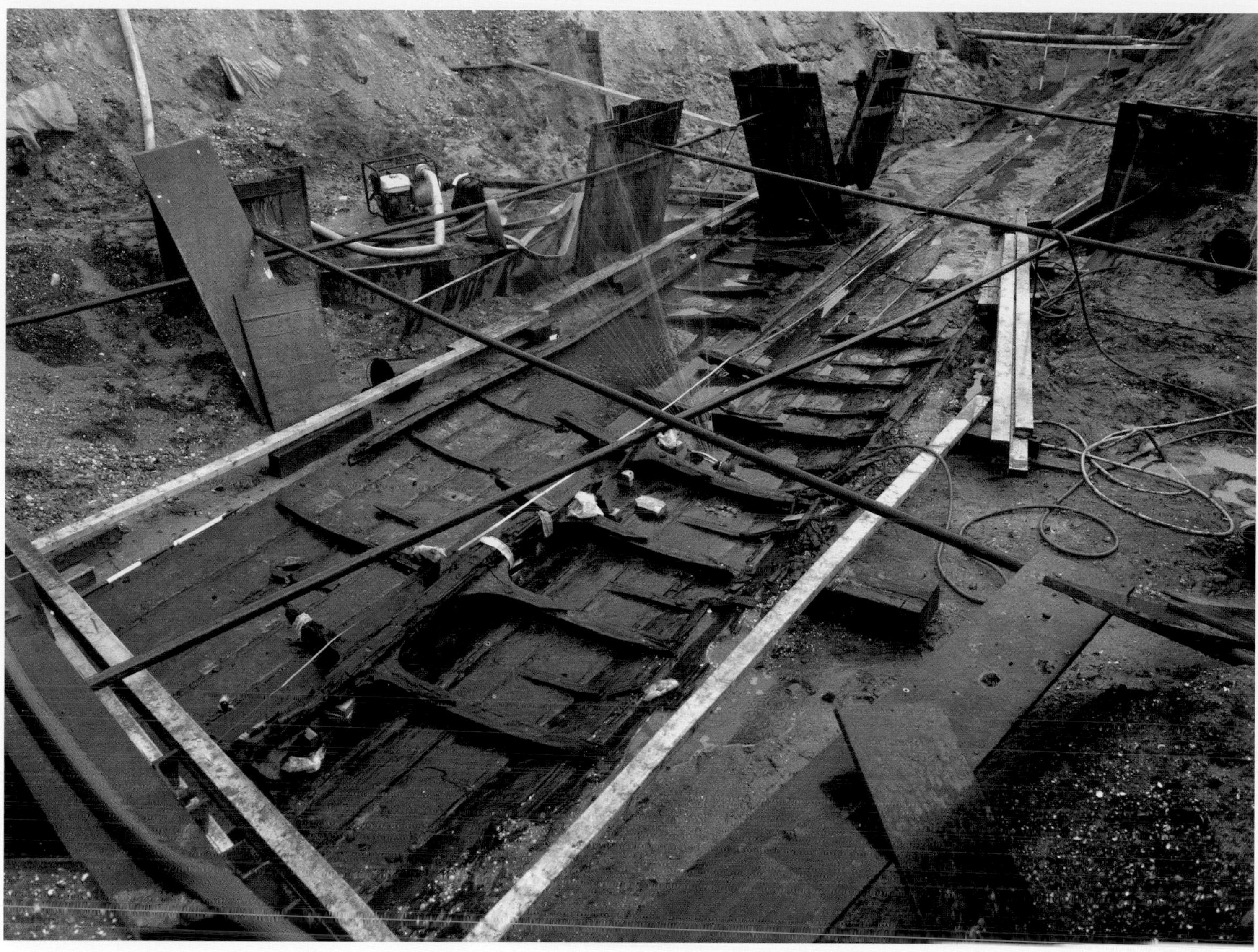

growth rings in timber from archaeological sites makes it possible to determine when – and often also where – the tree was felled. In the case of Roskilde 6, it showed that the trees used in the building of the ship were cut down during the period 1018–32, most probably towards the middle of this period – i.e. around 1025. The timber for the ship must have been felled in the area around the Oslo Fjord in south-eastern Norway, as its annual growth ring pattern coincides with that of the timbers of the famous ship burials from Oseberg and Gokstad.[2] In the Viking Age, timber for shipbuilding was not dried or transported over long distances before use, so it may be assumed that this was also where the ship was built. Measurements of the growth rings in a plank used to repair the hull offer a tiny glimpse of its history, as they show that at some point after the year 1039 the ship was repaired at an unknown site in the Baltic area, far away from where it was built.

What kind of ship was Roskilde 6?

Only about a fifth of the original hull has survived and nothing remains of the mast, rigging or sail (fig. 3). Nevertheless it is possible to form a clear picture of the kind of ship that Roskilde 6 once was. Length and beam have been reconstructed to 37.27 metres and 3.99 metres respectively, while the draught has been calculated to only 83.5 centimetres. All the parts of the ship are made with great expertise and of the best raw materials. Only oak, the strongest and most durable of the woods used in the building of Viking-Age ships, was used for the keel, the surviving planks from the bottom and sides of the ship and the carefully shaped frames. The floor timbers – which are the bottom part of the frames – have been cut from cautiously selected timber, which had fibres growing in the exact shape needed for the frame. This meant that it was possible to make them very thin and thus save weight. The distance between the floor timbers is relatively small, a mere 78 centimetres. In many Viking ships it is up to a metre. On top of the floor timbers

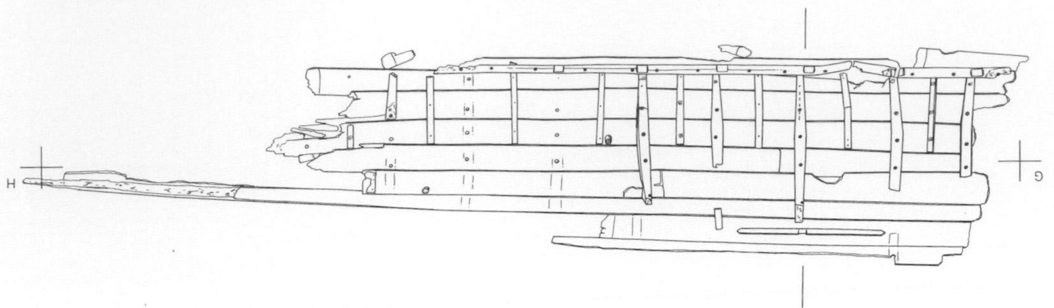

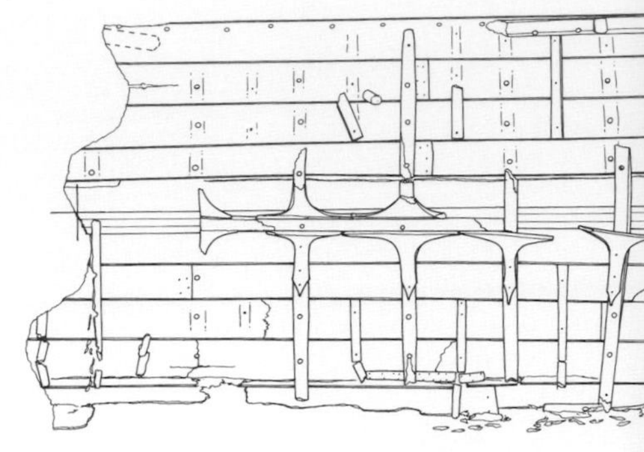

would have been the bites, thin beams that were fastened at each end to the side of the ship with knees (angled pieces supporting the ship's beam) made of timber that had grown in the right shape and, higher up, the thwarts on which the oarsmen sat: all of this has been lost. On the other hand, lying along a short section of the middle of the ship is a surviving piece of timber, which was jammed between the floor timbers and the bites, above and along the keel. This is all that remains of the keelson, a special structural member that extended over most of the length of the ship and served both to hold the mast foot and to strengthen the long keel. The keelson was fastened with elaborately carved knees, which held it firmly in place (fig. 4).[4]

Many of the features of Roskilde 6 can also be found in two other remarkable ship finds, namely the great longships Skuldelev 2 and Hedeby 1.[5] Skuldelev 2 was built in 1042 in the Dublin area in Ireland, while Hedeby 1 dates from around 985 and was built in or near Hedeby, the big international trading centre of the Viking Age on the border between what was then the south of Denmark and the Holy Roman Empire. The most striking characteristics of these vessels are their great length, narrow beam and shallow draught. Hedeby 1 and Skuldelev 2 are both about 30 metres long. As previously mentioned, Roskilde 6 is over 37 metres in length, and none of the vessels are more than 3.7 metres wide or have a draught of much more than a metre (fig. 5). This means that they were all about ten times longer than they were wide and could have sailed close enough in to the coast for the crew to be able to jump out of the ship and wade ashore. These are characteristics associated with the Vikings' amphibious warfare methods and this is precisely what these ships were built for – the rapid transport of large forces, the ability to penetrate far up rivers and into fjords, and instant landing on any shore. Other special features of longships, including the small distances between the frames and the extremely light construction of the hulls, also served this purpose. The short distance between the thwarts meant that there was room for more men on board, and higher speeds and greater manoeuvrability could be achieved when the oars were being used. While Hedeby 1 and Skuldelev 2 each had thirty pairs of oars, Roskilde 6 had as many as thirty-nine – maybe even forty – pairs. Using high-quality materials and reducing the weight of individual parts as far as possible made the ship lighter, which in turn made it faster and more manoeuvrable. There is no doubt that Roskilde 6 can be classified as a specialized Viking-Age warship and, moreover, the biggest we know.

4.
Illustration of the surviving timbers from the ship. The missing section indicates where part of the ship was destroyed during the work that led to its recovery.

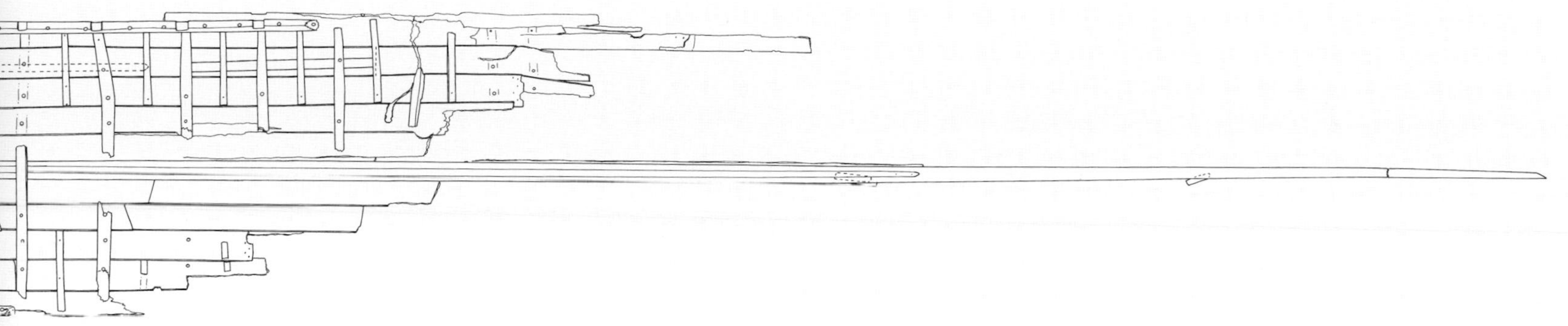

Why and for whom was Roskilde 6 built?

Late Viking-Age sources hardly ever give the size of the different types of ship, but it appears that the most common name for a large warship is *skeið*, a word of uncertain etymological origin.[6] The slightly more recent sagas of the kings, written by Snorri Sturluson, provide us with information on *skeið* that belonged to eleventh-century earls and kings and are said to have had anywhere from thirty to as many as a formidable sixty pairs of oars.[7] At the time when Snorri was writing the sagas of the kings in the first half of the thirteenth century, warships had long since become considerably larger than they were in the Viking Age and possibly Snorri exaggerates a bit – but the picture he conveys of the biggest warships being owned by kings and earls tallies with reports in earlier sources. The man for whom Roskilde 6 was built must have been in the very highest rank of the elite in Norway or Denmark around 1025. Many of the kings and earls of that time are known to us by name from written sources. The reason it is nevertheless difficult to suggest who is most likely to have been the owner is to do with the many events involving this elite that occurred around this time, particularly in 1025.[8]

At that time, Denmark and southern Sweden were ruled from England by Cnut the Great, while up until 1028 Norway was led by Olaf II Haraldsson, later canonized as St Olaf.[9] Olaf was born and raised among the local aristocracy in Østlandet, the eastern part of Norway. He had fought in England for several years, first on the Danish side and then with the English. He had returned to Norway in 1015 and been crowned king, and he was the first Norwegian king to succeed in joining eastern Norway to what was otherwise a mainly west Norwegian kingdom. However, in 1025 Cnut claimed that he should become king of Norway with the result that Olaf, in alliance with the Swedish king Anund Jakob, started waging war against Denmark. The final clash between Cnut and Olaf took place at the River Helgeå in eastern Scania in 1025 or 1026. The battle, which was fought on both land and sea, crucially weakened Olaf's position. Cnut was able to form an alliance with the west Norwegian earls and in 1028 Olaf was forced to flee to the east to his brother-in-law, Prince Jaroslav of Kiev-Novgorod, whence he returned in 1030 in an unsuccessful – and, for him, fatal – attempt to regain the throne of Norway.

Because we cannot say precisely in which year of the period 1018–32 Roskilde 6 was built, it is not possible to determine for

5.
Reconstructed section amidships through the four known great longships: Roskilde 6, Skuldelev 2, Hedeby 1 and Skuldelev 5.

6.
View from Roskilde Fjord towards the cathedral. The cathedral, which was built over a long period from the late 12th century onwards, occupies the former site of a Viking-Age church and royal residence.

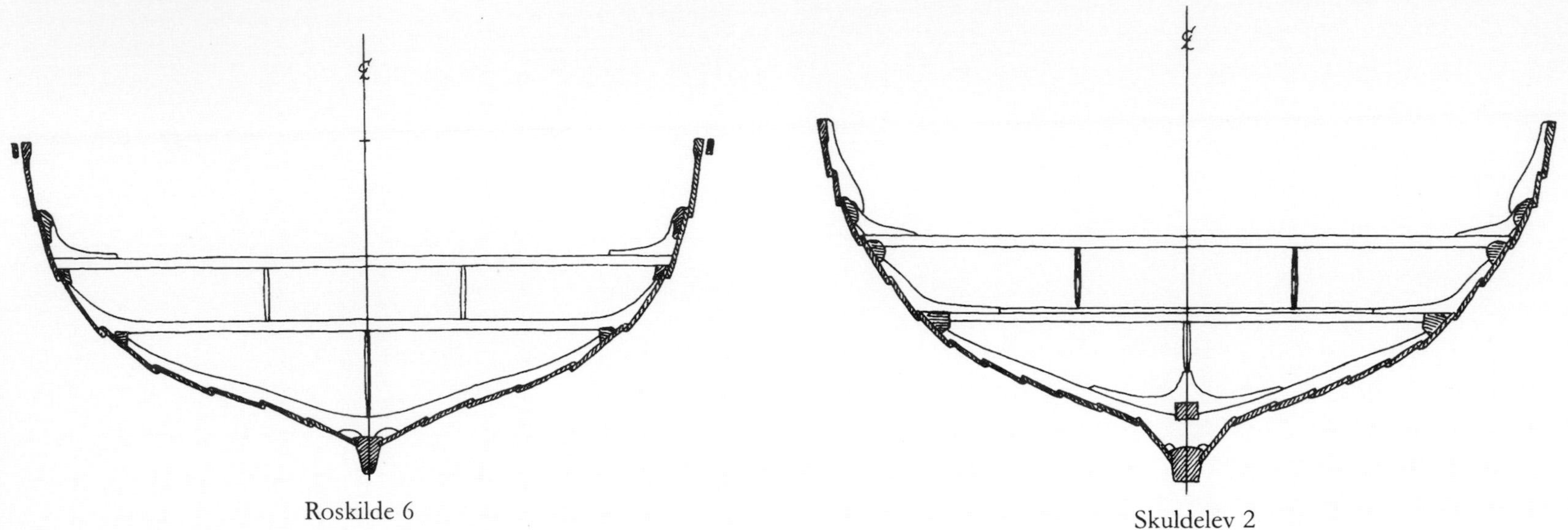

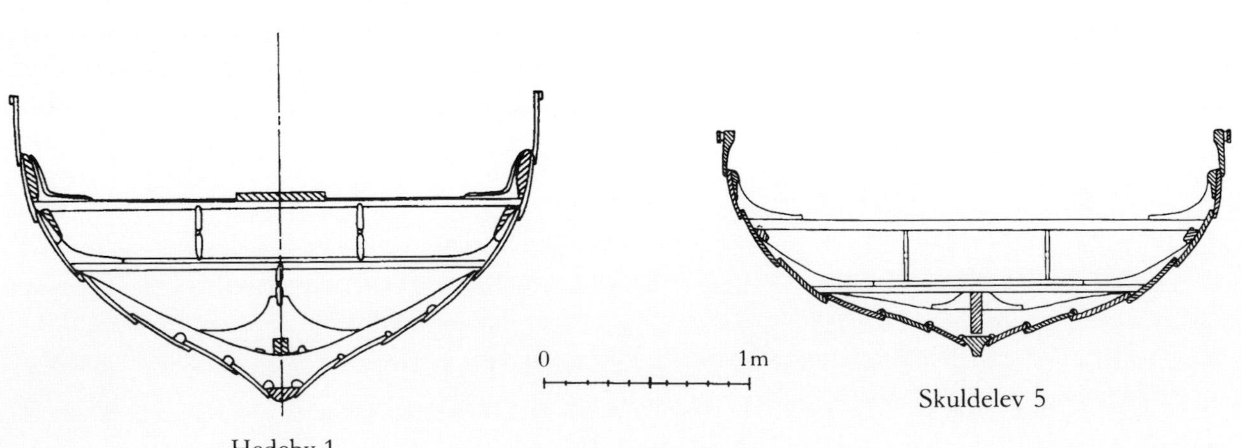

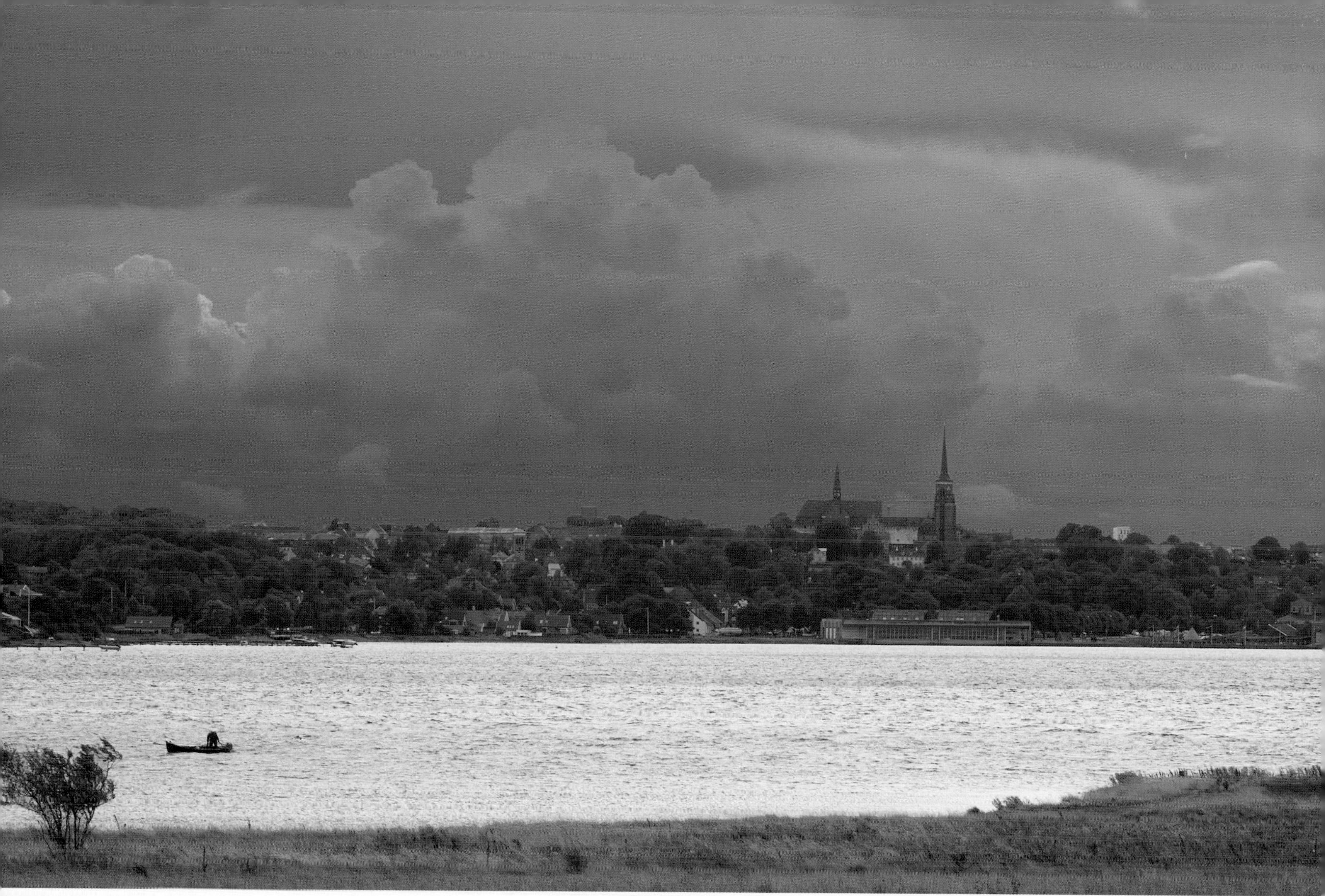

certain whether the man for whom the ship was built was on one side or the other of the dividing line in this conflict. The reaction of Olaf and Anund to Cnut's claim to the Norwegian throne was to conduct amphibious warfare against Denmark, which could have been more than sufficient reason to build a ship of this kind, in which case it would certainly have been Olaf or a powerful ally in eastern Norway who was responsible for its construction. On the other hand, if the ship was not built until after the battle of Helgeå, and perhaps even after Olaf's flight in 1028, it could just as easily have been one of Cnut's allies or Cnut himself who had the ship built. Using the conquered king's forests to build a magnificent warship would have sent a message whose significance would certainly not have been lost on the elite of the time, for whom honour and seafaring were so important.

We will probably never have a precise answer to this question, and the information about the ship's stay and repair in the Baltic area in 1039 does not get us much further. Nor do we know when and how the ship came into Roskilde on its final voyage – only that it met its end there in a way that contrasted sharply with the brilliant, heroic role for which it was originally built. Filled with water, perhaps old and decaying as well, it was dragged as far out of the shallow water as the strength of those present would allow and then the axes began their sad task of breaking up as much as possible of the great ship. Perhaps history had turned full circle: the two Danish kings who most probably occupied the throne at that particular time were Cnut the Great's son Harthacnut (1035–42) and St Olaf's son Magnus the Good (King of Denmark 1042–7).[10] The cathedral and the royal residence look down on the harbour from the hill above (fig. 6). If either king happened to be in Roskilde on those days, he would certainly have known exactly what kind of ship was being broken up at the water's edge.

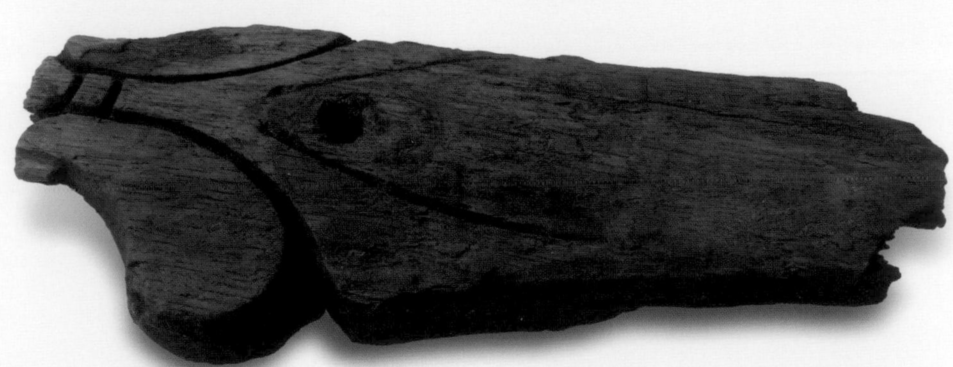

1.
A fragment from Roskilde 6, recovered during the excavation, which displays decorative carving.
Oak, L 19.8 cm, H 2.8 cm
Roskilde Museum, Roskilde

Conservation of Roskilde 6

Kristiane Strætkvern

In 1997, during the construction of a new museum island of the Viking Ship Museum in Roskilde, Denmark, nine ship-finds were discovered and excavated. Among these ships was the longest Viking ship ever found, Roskilde 6. The preserved keel had a length of 32 metres giving a total length for the ship of over 37 metres after reconstruction. Approximately 25 per cent of the ship was preserved – mainly the bottom and aft sections of the ship.

After the ship had been documented in situ and all the parts numbered, it was carefully taken apart and the planks, keel sections, frames, intermediate frames and other pieces were taken up from the harbour bed one by one. Even though the timber looked quite intact when it was first exposed, the material was very degraded and required support during the recovery. As many of the ships found during the excavations in Roskilde Harbour required conservation, Roskilde 6 was first kept in long tanks in which the timber could be kept wet. The initial stages of the conservation process, cleaning and documentation, were carried out in Roskilde, where a finds reception centre had recently been set up. Over several months, in parallel with the documentation work, the ship timbers were cleaned using water and paint brushes. During the cleaning process, such surface traces as tool marks and carvings became very clear and easier to register on photographs and in drawings (fig. 1). Cleaning while the timber is still wet is the gentlest way of dealing with the wood, and this first stage also provides an opportunity to fit in fragments and put loose parts in place. Cleaning also contributes to improved conservation and a better-looking final result as the preserving agents can penetrate and are more evenly distributed in the wood. A clean surface without deposits of clay, silt or mud ensures that the outer layers dry uniformly and that the need for later treatment of the wood is reduced to a minimum. The documentation phase was carried out partly through 1:1 scale drawings on plastic film and partly through digital measurement. The tool marks from the axes and the carvings along some of the interior timbers were recorded during this phase, but even more important was the documentation of the original contours of the individual timbers giving their dimensions and shapes. The drawings of these features were crucial for the reconstruction of the ship (fig. 2).

In order to bring the archaeological wet ship timbers into a stable condition and enable them to be displayed to the public, the timber needed to be preserved and dried out in a lengthy, technically demanding and controlled process. Following the initial cleaning and documentation, the wood was transported to the National Museum of Denmark's conservation laboratories in Brede, north of Copenhagen. Here the wood was placed in a watery solution of polyethylene glycol (PEG) 2000. PEG is a type of water-soluble wax, the purpose of which is to soak into the timber and gradually replace the water in the wood. Over several years, the concentration in the tanks is raised from 10 per cent to 40 per cent PEG 2000, until the wood is ready for drying.

Wood that has lain in a low-oxygen or oxygen-free environment below the surface of the water for almost a thousand years may look intact, but in reality it is badly degraded. Many of its natural components, such as cellulose and hemicellulose, have entirely or partly disappeared and the cells of the wood are full of water. If the timber dries out in an uncontrolled way, it will collapse

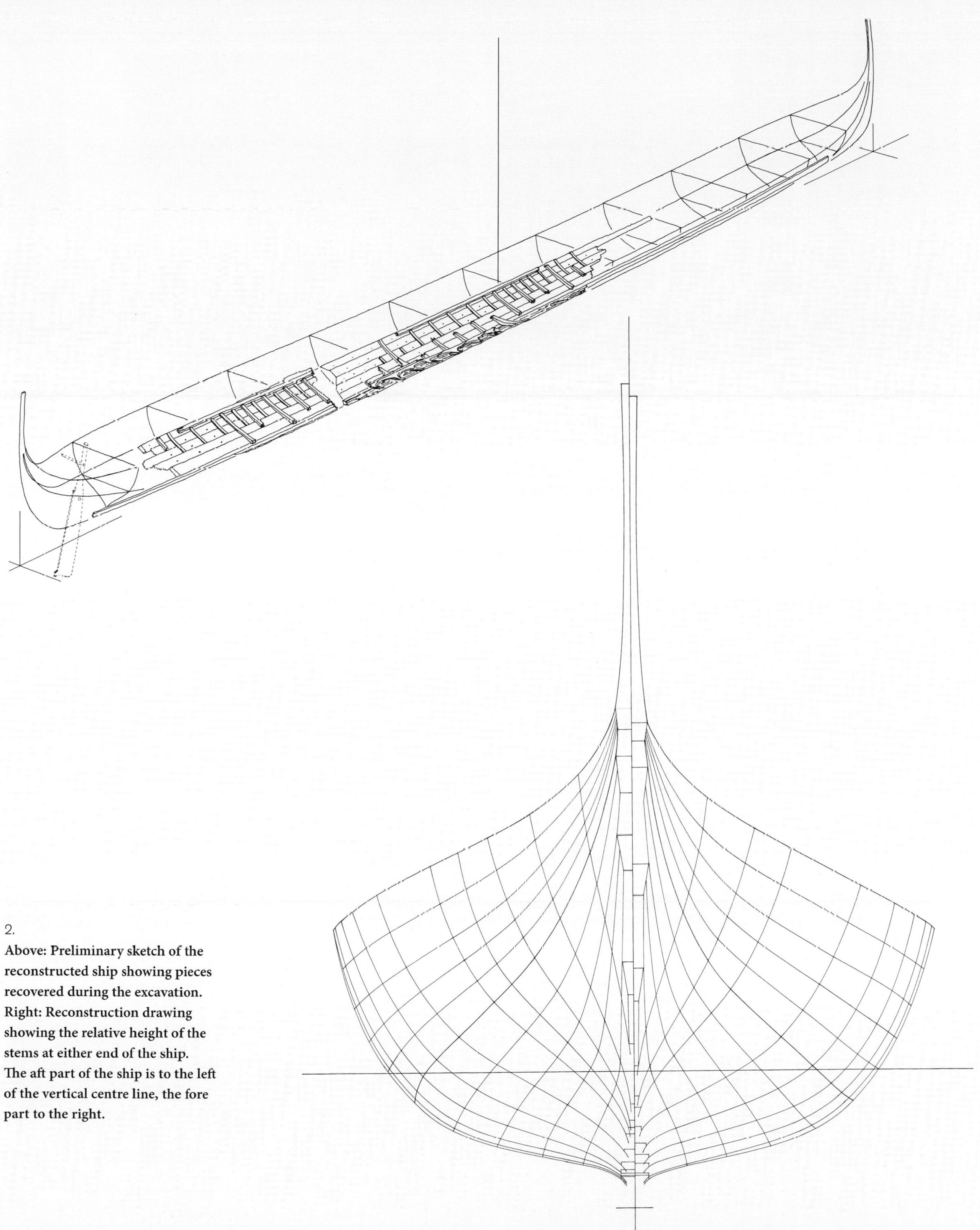

2.
Above: Preliminary sketch of the reconstructed ship showing pieces recovered during the excavation. Right: Reconstruction drawing showing the relative height of the stems at either end of the ship. The aft part of the ship is to the left of the vertical centre line, the fore part to the right.

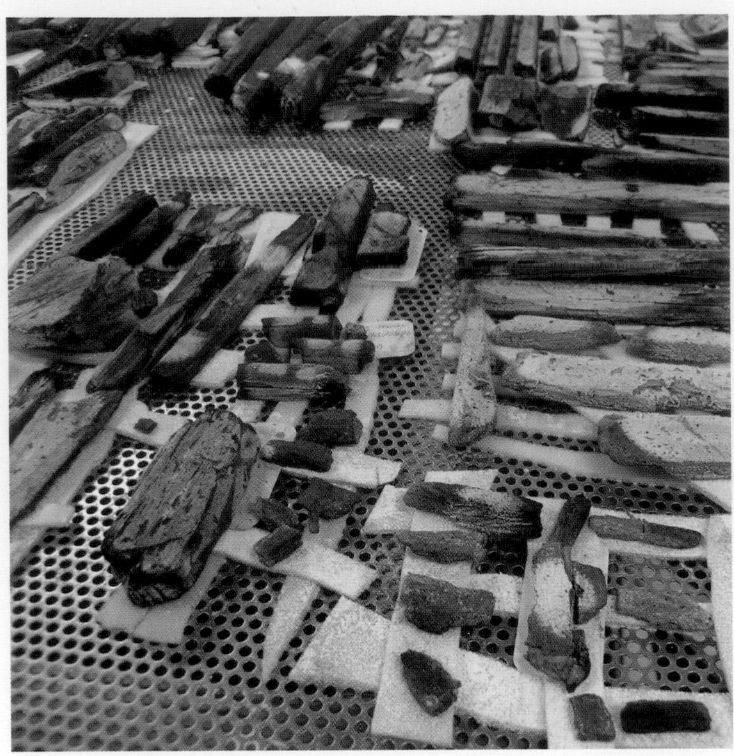

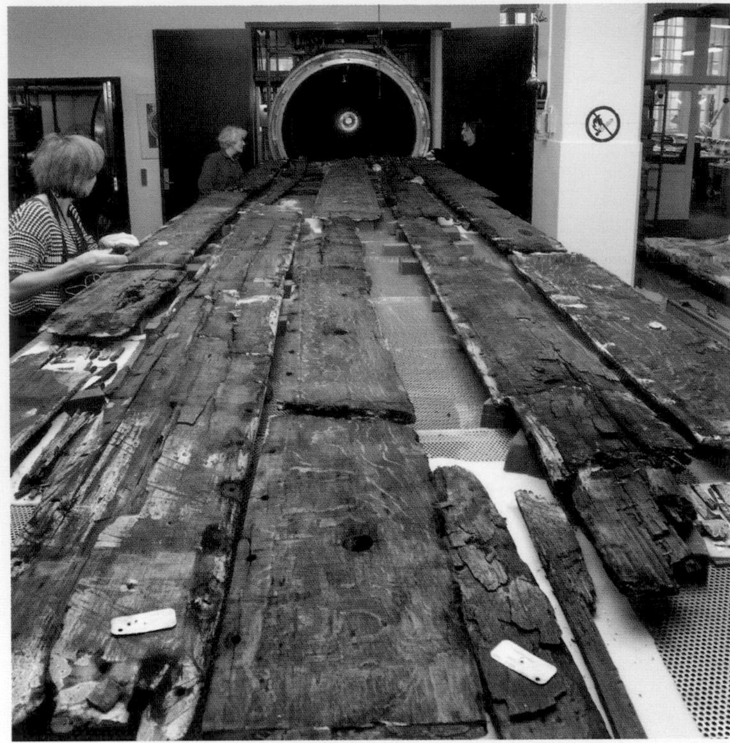

3–4.
Fragments and planks of wood immediately after vacuum freeze-drying. Fig. 4 shows the 8-metre-long freeze-drying plant in the background. The white deposit on the surface of the wood is dry (surplus) Polyethylene glycol (PEG) 2000.

and split. In order to prevent this happening, the water was removed from the impregnated wood by vacuum freeze-drying. The PEG-impregnated wood is frozen in a large vacuum tank, the temperature is reduced to -27 degrees Celsius and a vacuum is created in the tank at a pressure of 0.2 mbar. Under these conditions, the water in the wood will first freeze to form ice and then, when the vacuum has been created, the ice will turn to vapour and be removed from the tank (figs 3–4). Using this process means that the wood will not collapse and will retain a shape close to its original. The process takes five to six months, and with a tank 8 metres long and 1.8 metres wide, the effective drying surface per process is about 14.5 square metres. The first of a total of nine freeze-drying processes was begun in 2009 and the last in July 2012.[1]

The surviving parts of the wreck consisted of around 200 pieces and most of them were broken in many places. As the components had to be reassembled after impregnation and freeze-drying, the parts needed to be held in the right shape throughout the entire freeze-drying process. For this reason the ship was first reconstructed on the drawing board as a 1:10 model, using 1:10 down-scaled drawings from the initial documentation of the timbers. This was an exciting phase as it revealed the original length, breadth, height and shape of the ship.[2] The detailed knowledge gained from this process about the shape of the individual parts was transferred to the wet, impregnated wood, which was held in the correct shape by wedges, sandbags and steel braces during the drying process.

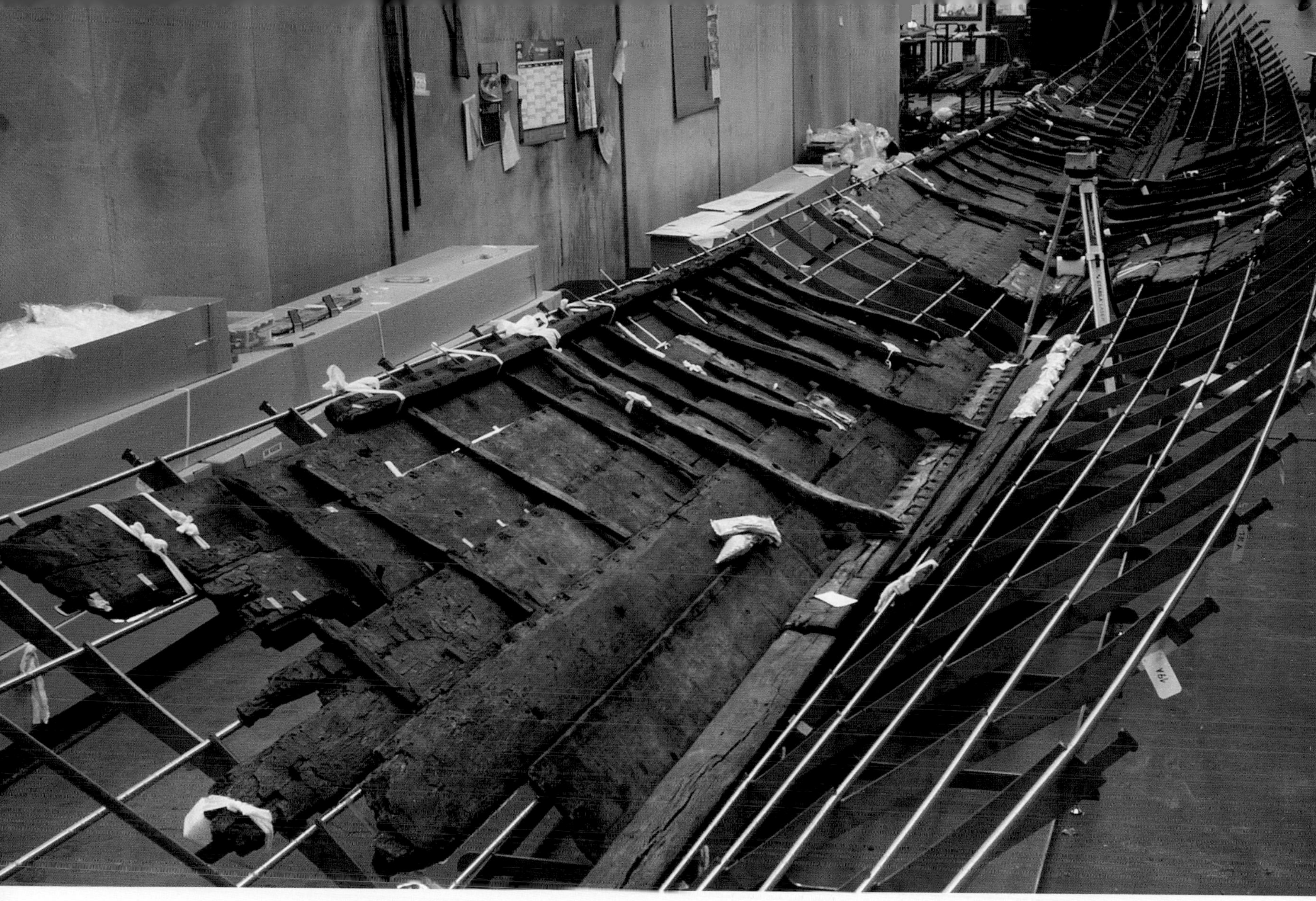

The final part of the conservation process was to glue the broken pieces together, collect the fragments and remove surplus impregnation agent from the surfaces of the planks, frames and sections of the keel. In order to ensure safe transport and exhibition of the ship all the planks were provided with individual stainless steel supports. To ensure a safe move from one exhibition to the next, the timbers are packed in thirty-five boxes with individually designed crates.

The reconstruction of the ship, which was carried out by the architect Morten Gøthche from the Viking Ship Museum in Roskilde, was also used in the design and production of the stand on which the conserved parts are exhibited and supported (fig. 5). All the reconstructed lines of the ship – the gunwales, planks, stem and stern, thwarts and floor – have been created in steel, and the positioning of the original frames is reproduced in the stand that holds the original planks. This ensures that the conserved parts fit into the purpose-built stand giving the best possible idea of what the ship would have looked like.

5.
The scale of the vessel became evident when the conserved timbers were mounted on the specially made steel frame at the workshop in Denmark.

The stand itself can be dismantled and consists of parts that can be snapped together. The stand and supports are the result of a development project between Herfølge Kleinsmedie and the National Museum of Denmark and are the first of their kind.[3] After fifteen years of conservation treatment, including forty-eight months of vacuum freeze-drying in nine processes and more than 8,000 working hours in the conservation laboratory, we can finally display Roskilde 6 in a meaningful context.

Notes

Introduction

1 K. Lawson, *Cnut: The Danes in England in the Early Eleventh Century* (London and New York 1993); T. Bolton, *The Empire of Cnut the Great: Conquest and the Consolidation of Power in Northern Europe in the Early Eleventh Century* (Leiden and Boston 2009).

2 Indeed, the distribution of finds of metalwork from Britain and Ireland suggests that the early raids came more from western and south-western Norway. E. Wamers, *Insularer Metallschmuck in wikingerzeitlichen Gräbern Nordeuropas. Untersuchungen zur skandinavischen Westexpansion* (Offa-Bücher 56, Neumünster 1985); E. Wamers, 'Insular finds in Viking Age Scandinavia and the state formation of Norway', in H.B. Clarke, M. Ní Mhaonaigh and R.Ó Floinn (eds), *Ireland and Scandinavia in the Early Viking Age* (Dublin 1998), 37–72.

3 R. Hodges, *Dark Age Economics: The Origins of Towns and Trade A.D. 600–1000* (London 1982); M. Anderton (ed.), *Anglo-Saxon Trading Centres: Beyond the Emporia*, (Glasgow 1999); T. Pestell, 'Markets, emporia, wics, and productive sites: pre-Viking trade centres in Anglo-Saxon England', in D. Hamerow, D.A. Hinton and S. Crawford (eds), *The Oxford Handbook of Anglo-Saxon Archaeology* (Oxford 2011), 556–79.

4 S. Coupland, 'The Vikings in Francia and Anglo-Saxon England to 911', in *The New Cambridge Mediaeval History* (Cambridge 1995), 190–201; S. Coupland, 'Trading places: Quentovic and Dorestad reassessed', in *Early Medieval Europe* 11(3) (2002), 209–32.

5 C. Etchingham, 'Laithlinn, "Fair foreigners" and "dark foreigners": the identity and provenance of Vikings in ninth-century Ireland', in J. Sheehan and D. Ó Corráin (eds), *The Viking Age: Ireland and the West. Proceedings of the Fifteenth Viking Congress* (Dublin 2010), 80–9.

6 S. Brink, 'People and land in early Scandinavia', in I. Garipzanov, P. Geary and P. Urbańczyk (eds), *Franks, Northmen and Slavs: Identities and State Formation in Early Medieval Europe* (Turnhout 2008), 87–112; C.E. Downham, '"Hiberno-Norwegians" and "Anglo-Danes": anachronistic ethnicities and Viking-Age England', *Mediaeval Scandinavia* 19 (2009), 139–69.

7 I. Garipzanov, 'Frontier identities: Carolingian frontier and the Gens Danorum', in Garipzanov *et al.* (eds) (2008), 113–44.

8 P.B. Golden, 'Rus', in C.E. Bosworth, E. van Donzell, W.P. Heinrichs and G. Lecomte (eds), *The Encyclopedia of Islam, New Edition* VIII, NED-SAM, (Leiden 1995), 618–29; J. Montgomery, 'Ibn Fadlān and the Rūssiyah', *Journal of Arabic and Islamic Studies* 3 (2000), 1–25.

9 The term *Westfaldingi* appears in Frankish sources. See E. Wamers, 'The 9th century Danish Norwegian conflict: maritime warfare and state formation', in A. Nørgård Jørgensen, J. Pind, L. Jørgensen and B. L. Clausen (eds), *Maritime Warfare in Northern Europe: Technology, Organisation, Logistics and Administration 500 BC–1500 AD* (Copenhagen 2002), 237–48.

10 L. Lönnroth, 'The Vikings in history and legend', in P. Sawyer (ed.), *The Oxford Illustrated History of the Vikings* (Oxford 1997), 225–49.

11 W. Duczko, *Viking Rus. Studies on the Presence of Scandinavians in Eastern Europe* (Leiden and Boston 2004), 3–7; F. Androshchuk, 'The Vikings in the East', in S. Brink with N. Price (eds), *The Viking World* (Abingdon 2008), 517–42, at 529–34; O.P. Tolochko, 'The *Primary Chronicle*'s "ethnography" revisited: Slavs and Varangians in the Middle Dnieper region and the origin of the Rus "State"', in Garipzanov *et al.* (eds) (2008), 169–88, 183–7.

12 The value of DNA in identifying the genetic heritage of specific individuals is often exaggerated, since techniques of DNA analysis focus on one line of ancestry out of millions. However, DNA becomes more useful when looking at trends within a wider population, as it is possible to establish broad patterns of similarities between the populations of areas of Viking settlement and the areas from which they were settled.

13 E. Moltke, *Runes and their Origin, Denmark and Elsewhere* (Copenhagen 1985); S.B.F. Jansson, *Runes in Sweden* (trans. P. Foote) (Stockholm 1987); R.I. Page, *Runes and Runic Inscriptions* (Woodbridge 1995); J. Jesch, *Ships and Men in the Late Viking Age: The Vocabulary of Runic Inscriptions and Skaldic Verse* (Woodbridge 2001); T. Spurkland, *Norwegian Runes and Runic Inscriptions* (trans. B. van der Hoek) (Woodbridge 2005).

14 Spurkland (2005).

15 M. Clunies Ross, *The Cambridge Introduction to the Old Norse-Icelandic Saga* (Cambridge 2010).

16 Jesch (2001).

17 J. Bateley and A. Englert (eds), *Ohthere's Voyages*, Maritime Cultures of the North 1 (Roskilde 2007); A. Englert and A. Trakadas (eds), *Wulfstan's Voyage*, Maritime Cultures of the North 2 (Roskilde 2009).

18 G. Williams, 'Hoards from the northern Danelaw from Cuerdale to the Vale of York', in J. Graham-Campbell and R. Philpott (eds), *The Huxley Viking Hoard: Scandinavian Settlement in the North West* (Liverpool 2009), 73–83; J. Kershaw, *Viking Identities: Scandinavian Jewellery in England* (Oxford 2013).

19 G. Fellows-Jensen, 'Scandinavian place-names in the British Isles', in Brink with Price (eds) (2008), 391–400; Jean Renaud, *Vikings et noms de lieux de Normandie* (Bayeux 2009); H.R. Ellis Davidson, *The Viking Road to Byzantium* (London 1976), 83–6.

1. Contacts & Exchange

1. S.M. Sindbæk, 'Silver economies and social ties: long-distance interaction, long-term investments – and why the Viking age happened', in J. Graham-Campbell, S. Sindbæk and G. Williams (eds), *Silver Economies, Monetisation and Society in Scandinavia AD 800–1100* (Aarhus 2011), 41–66.

2 U. Sporrong, 'The Scandinavian landscape and its resources', in K. Helle (ed.), *The Cambridge History of Scandinavia. I: Prehistory to 1520* (Cambridge 2003), 15–42; C. Krag, 'The creation of Norway', in S. Brink with N. Price (eds), *The Viking World* (Abingdon 2008), 645–51; S. Brink, 'People and land in early Scandinavia', in I. Garipzanov, P. Geary and P. Urbańczyk (eds), *Franks, Northmen and Slavs: Identities and State Formation in Early Medieval Europe* (Turnhout 2008), 87–112.

3 J. Bateley 'Wulfstan's voyage and his description of Estland: the text and the language of the text', in A. Englert and A. Trakadas (eds), *Wulfstan's Voyage. The Baltic Sea Region in the Early Viking Age as Seen from Shipboard* (Roskilde 2009), 15, 17–18; A. Nørgård Jørgensen, 'Harbours and trading centres on Bornholm, Öland and Gotland in the late 9th century', in Englert and Trakadas (eds) (2009), 145–50.

4 M. Barnes, 'Language and ethnic groups', in Helle (2003), 94–102; S. Brink, 'People and land in early Scandinavia', in I. Garipzanov, P. Geary and P. Urbańczyk (eds), (2008), 87– 112.

5 J. Bately, 'Text and translation', in J. Bateley and A. Englert (eds), *Ohthere's Voyages. A Late 9th-Century Account of Voyages Along the Coasts of Norway and Denmark and its Cultural Context* (Roskilde 2007), 41–50, 45.

6 I. Valonen, '"Who were the Finnas?" and "Who were the Cwenas?"', in Bateley and Englert (eds) (2007), 106–7, 108–11; N.A. Makarov, 'The land of the Beormas', in Bateley and Englert (eds) (2007), 140–9.

7 C. Stiegemann and M. Wemhoff (eds), *799 – Kunst und Kultur der Karolingerzeit 1–2. Karl der Große und Papst Leo III in Paderborn. Katalog der Ausstellung* (Mainz 1999).

8 See contribution by Matthias Wemhoff in this volume, pp. 156–7.

9 R. Hodges, *Dark Age Economics. The Origins of Towns and Trade AD 600–1000* (London 1982); M. McCormick, *Origins of the European Economy. Communications and Commerce AD 300–900* (Cambridge 2001), especially 573–613, 639–73; A. Willemsen and H. Kik, *Dorestad in an International Framework: New Research on Centres of Trade and Coinage in Carolingian Times. Proceedings of the First 'Dorestad Congress' Held at the National Museum of Antiquities in Leiden 2009* (Turnhout 2010).

10 The relative lack of settlement in marginal areas is visible across distribution maps based on various types of evidence throughout D. Hill, *An Atlas of Anglo-Saxon England* (Oxford 1981).

11 B. Yorke, *Kings and Kingdoms of Early Anglo-Saxon England* (London 1990).

12 J. Blair, *The Church in Anglo-Saxon Society* (Oxford 2005), 246–90; T. Pestell, 'Markets, *emporia, wics*, and "productive" sites: pre-Viking trade centres in Anglo-Saxon England', in D. Hamerow, D.A. Hinton and S. Crawford (eds), *The Oxford Handbook of Anglo-Saxon Archaeology* (Oxford 2011), 556–79.

13 M. Townend, *Language and History in Viking Age England* (Turnhout 2002).

14 W. Davies, *Wales in the Early Middle Ages* (Leicester 1982); T.M. Charles-Edwards, *Wales and the Britons, 350–1064* (Oxford 2013); D. Ó Cróinín, *Early Medieval Ireland, 400–1200* (London and New York 1995); K. Jankulak and J. Wooding (eds), *Ireland and Wales in the Middle Ages* (Dublin 2007); A. Woolf, *From Pictland to Alba, 789–1070* (Edinburgh 2007).

15 For an overview of the Celtic boatbuilding tradition, see G.J. Marcus, *The Conquest of the North Atlantic* (Woodbridge 1980), 3–32, although this offers a more positive interpretation of the scale of Celtic seafaring and exploration.

16 S. Brather, *Archäologie der westlichen Slawen. Siedlung, Wirtschaft und Gesellschaft im früh- und hochmittelalterlichen Ostmitteleuropa*. Ergänzungsbände zum Reallexikon der Germanischen Altertumskunde 61 (Berlin 2008).

17 T.S. Noonan, 'The Vikings in the east. Coin and commerce', in B. Ambrosiani (ed.), *Development Around the Baltic and the North Sea in the Viking Age*, Viking Congress 12, Birka Studies 3 (Stockholm 1994), 215–36.

18 P.M. Barford, 'Silent centuries. The society and economy of the northwestern Slavs', in F. Curta (ed.), *East Central & Eastern Europe in the Early Middle Ages* (Ann Arbor 2005), 60–102.

19 C. von Carnap-Bornheim, V. Hilberg, A. Radiņs and F. Schopper (eds), *Lettlands viele Völker. Archäologie der Eisenzeit von Christi Geburt bis zum Jahr 1200* (Zossen 2009), 32.

20 J. Peets, 'Salme Ship Burials', *Current World Archaeology* 58, April/May 2013, 18–24.

21 T. Edgren, 'The Viking age in Finland', in Brink with Price (eds) (2008), 470–84.

22 P.C. Buckland, 'The North Atlantic environment', in W. Fitzhugh and E.I. Ward, *Vikings: The North Atlantic Saga* (Washington and London 2000), 146–53.

23 J. Byock, *Viking Age Iceland* (Harmondsworth 2001); Gísli Sigurðsson, 'The North Atlantic expansion', in Brink with Price (eds) (2008), 562–70.

24 P. Schledermann, 'East meets West', in Fitzhugh and Ward (2000), 189–92; D. Odess, S. Loring and W.W. Fitzhugh, '*Skræling*: first peoples of Helluland, Markland and Vinland', in Fitzhugh and Ward (2000), 193–206; P.D. Sutherland, 'The Norse and Native Americans', in Fitzhugh and Ward (2000), 238–47; P.D. Sutherland, 'Norse and natives in the eastern Arctic', in Brink with Price (eds) (2008), 613–17.

25 As note 24; H.C. Gulløv, 'Natives and Norse in Greenland', in Fitzhugh and Ward (2000), 318–26.

26 J. Shepard, 'The Viking Rus and Byzantium', in Brink with Price (eds) (2008), 496–516.

27 C. Mango, *The Oxford History of Byzantium* (Oxford 2002); T.E. Gregory, *A History of Byzantium*, 2nd edn (Oxford 2009).

28 H. Kennedy, *The Prophet and the Age of the Caliphates: The Islamic Near East from the 6th to the 11th Century (A History of the Near East)* (London 2004); J. Montgomery, 'Arabic sources on the Vikings', in Brink with Price (eds) (2008), 550–61; P. Lunde and C. Stone, *Ibn Fadlān and the Land of Darkness. Arab Travelers in the Far North* (Harmondsworth 2012).

29 R. Frye, *Ibn Fadlan's Journey to Russia: A Tenth-Century Traveler from Baghdad to the Volga River* (Princeton 2005), 109–11; K.A. Brook, *The Jews of Khazaria*, 2nd edn (Lanham 2006); P.B. Golden, H. Ben-Shammai and A. Róna-Tas, *The World of the Khazars: New Perspectives* (Leiden and Boston 2007); F. Curta and R. Kovalev, *The Other Europe in the Middle Ages. Avars, Bulgars, Khazars, and Cumans* (Leiden and Boston 2008).

30 Frye (2005), 97–103; A. Róna-Tas, *Hungarians and Europe in the Early Middle Ages: An Introduction to Early Hungarian History* (Budapest 1999), 220–7; Curta and Kovalev (2008).

31 P.B. Golden, 'Pečenegs', in C.E. Bosworth, E. van Donzell, W.P. Heinrichs and G. Lecomte (eds), *The Encyclopedia of Islam, New Edition* VIII, NED-SAM, (Leiden 1995), 289–91.

32 W. Duczko, *Viking Rus. Studies on the Presence of Scandinavians in Eastern Europe* (Leiden and Boston 2004), 60–95.

33 C. Feveile, 'Ribe', in Brink with Price (eds) (2008), 126–30.

34 *Anglo-Saxon Chronicle* (A, E & F), *sub.* 787[789]

35 Bately (2007)

36 D.M. Metcalf, 'Inflows of Anglo-Saxon and German coins into the northern lands, *c.* 997–1024', in B. Cook and G. Williams (eds), *Coinage and History in the North Sea World, c. 500–1250. Essays in Honour of Marion Archibald* (Leiden and Boston 2006), 349–88; J.C. Moesgaard, 'The import of English coins to the northern lands: some remarks on coin circulation in the Viking Age based on new evidence from Denmark', in Cook and Williams (eds) (2006), 389–434.

37 Agnar Helgason, E. Hickey, S. Goodacre, Vidar Bosnes, Kári Stefánsson, R.Ward, and B.Sykes, 'mtDNA and the islands of the North Atlantic: estimating the proportions of Norse and Gaelic ancestry', *American Journal of Human Genetics* 68 (2001), 723–37.

38 B.W. Scholz, *Carolingian Chronicles* (Ann Arbor 1972), *Royal Frankish Annals, sub.* 809.

39 F. Curta, 'Introduction', in Curta (ed.) (2005), 14, n. 82.

40 S.M. Sindbæk, 'Close ties and long-range relations: the emporia network in early Viking-Age exchange', in J. Sheehan and D. Ó Corráin (eds), *Ireland in the Viking Age* (Dublin 2010), 430–40; S.M. Sindbæk, 'Silver economies and social ties: long-distance interaction, long-term investments – and why the Viking age happened', in J. Graham-Campbell and G. Williams (eds), *Silver Economy in the Viking Age* (Walnut Creek 2007), 41–66.

41 Ibid.; H.B. Clarke, 'Proto-towns and towns in Ireland and Britain', in H.B. Clarke, M. Ní Mhaonaigh and R.Ó Floinn (eds), *Ireland and Scandinavia in the Early Viking Age* (Dublin 1998), 331–80; H. Andersson, 'Urbanisation', in Helle (ed.), (2003), 312–42; R.A. Hall, 'Burhs and boroughs: defended places, trade and towns. Plans defences, civic features', in Hamerow, Hinton and Crawford (eds), (2011), 600–21.

42 G. Williams, 'Towns and minting in northern Europe in the early Middle Ages', in F. Lopez Sanchez (ed.), *The City and the Coin in the Ancient and Early Medieval Worlds* (BAR International Series 2402, 2012), 149–60. G. Williams, 'Towns and identities in Viking England', in D.M. Hadley and L. Ten Harkel *Everyday life in Viking Towns: Social Approaches to Viking Age Towns in Ireland and England, c. 850–1100* (Oxford 2013), 14–34; W.I. Miller, *Bloodtaking and Peacemaking. Feud, Law and Society in Saga Iceland* (Chicago and London 1990), 77–108.

43 C. Feveile, 'Series X and coin circulation in Ribe', in T. Abramson (ed.), *Two Decades of Discovery. Studies in Early Medieval Coinage 1* (Woodbridge 2008), 53–67; B. Malmer, 'South Scandinavian coinage in the ninth century', in Graham-Campbell and Williams (eds), (2007), 13–27; V. Hilberg, 'Silver economies of the ninth and tenth centuries AD in Hedeby', in Graham-Campbell, Sindbæk and Williams (eds) (2011), 203–2; G. Williams, 'Silver economies, monetisation and society: an overview', in Graham-Campbell, Sindbæk and Williams (eds) (2011), 337–72.

44 Lunde and Stone (2012), 46, 121; D. Skre, 'Commodity money, silver and coinage in Scandinavia', in Graham-Campbell, Sindbæk and Williams (eds) (2011), 67–92; S.H. Gullbekk, 'Norway: commodity money, silver and coins', in Graham-Campbell, Sindbæk and Williams (eds) (2011), 93–112.

45 Williams, 'Silver economies, monetisation and society: an overview', in Graham-Campbell, Sindbæk and Williams (eds) (2011), 337–72.

46 Ibid.; B. Hårdh, 'Hacksilver and ingots', in D. Skre (ed.), *Means of Exchange: Dealing with Silver in the Viking Age* (Oslo 2008), 95–118; B. Hårdh, 'Viking-Age silver from hoards and cultural layers', in Graham-Campbell, Sindbæk and Williams (eds) (2011), 281–96; M.M. Archibald, 'Testing', in J.A. Graham-Campbell, *The Cuerdale Hoard and Related Viking-Age Silver and Gold, from Britain and Ireland, in The British Museum*, British Museum Research Publication 185 (London 2012), 51–64; G. Williams, 'Hack-silver and precious metal economies: a view from the Viking Age', in F. Hunter and K. Painter (eds), *Late Roman Silver: The Traprain Law Hoard in Context* (Edinburgh 2013), 381–94.

47 U. Pedersen, 'Weights and balances', in Skre (ed.) (2008), 119–95; H. Steuer, 'Principles of trade and exchange: trade goods and merchants', in Englert and Trakadas (eds) (2009), 294–308; Williams, 'Silver economies, monetisation and society: an overview', in Graham-Campbell, Sindbæk and Williams (eds) (2011), 337–72.

48 Lunde and Stone (2012), 46.

49 B. Hårdh, 'Oriental-Scandinavian contacts on the Volga, as manifested by silver rings and weight systems', in Graham-Campbell and Williams (eds) (2007), 135–48; G. Williams, 'Kingship, Christianity and coinage: monetary and political perspectives on silver economy in the Viking Age', in Graham-Campbell and Williams (eds) (2007), 177–214.

50 M.A.S. Blackburn, 'Coinage and contacts in the North Atlantic during the seventh to mid-tenth centuries', in A. Mortensen and S.V. Arge (eds), *Viking and Norse in the North Atlantic* (Tórshavn 2005), 141–51; M.A.S. Blackburn, *Viking Coinage and Currency in the British Isles* (London 2011).

51 G. Williams, 'Kingship, Christianity and Coinage, in Graham-Campbell and Williams (eds) (2007), 177–214.

52 *Anglo-Saxon Chronicle* (E and F), *sub.* 793.

53 Sindbæk, 'Silver economies and social ties', in Graham-Campbell, Sindbæk and Williams (eds) (2011) 41–66.

54 D. Whitelock (ed. and trans.), *English Historical Documents I, c. 500–1042* (London 1955), 775–7.

55 C.H. Robinson (ed. and trans.), *Rimbert: Life of Anskar, the Apostle of the North, 801–865* (London 1925); H. Birkeland, *Nordens historie i middelalderen etter arabiske kilder*, Skrifter udgiven av Det Norske Videnskaps Akademi i Oslo. Hist.-filos. klasse, 2 (Oslo 1954), 103–5; E. Roesdahl, *Viking Age Denmark* (London 1982), 28.

56 P. Bauduin, *Les fondations scandinaves en Occident et les débuts du duché de Normandie.* Colloque de Cheisy-la-Salle 2002 (Caen 2005), 80.

57 See Anne Pedersen's contribution on power and aristocracy in this volume, pp. 158–9.

58 M. Panum Baastrup, 'Carolingian-Ottonian disc brooches – early Christian symbols in Viking age Denmark', in U. von Freeden, H. Friesinger and E. Wamers (eds), *Glaube, Kult und Herrschaft. Phänomene des Religiösen im 1. Jahrtausend n. Chr. in Mittel- und Nordeuropa* (Bonn 2009), 517–28.

59 C. Capelli *et al.*, 'A Y chromosome census of the British Isles', *Current Biology* 13 (27 May 2003), 979–84.

60 B. Solberg, 'Weapon export from the Continent to the Nordic countries in the Carolingian period', *Studien zur Sachsenforschung* 7 (1991), 241–59.

61 Graham-Campbell (2012).

62 J. Kershaw (2013).

63 S. Youngs, *"The Work of Angels", Masterpieces of Celtic Metalwork, 6th–9th Centuries AD* (London 1989), 90–2.

64 B. Sawyer (2000), *The Viking-Age Rune-Stones: Custom and Commemoration in Early Medieval Scandinavia*, new edn (Oxford 2003); Jesch (2001); G. Larsson, *Ship and Society. Maritime Ideology in Late Iron Age Sweden* (Uppsala 2007).

65 E. Mikkelsen, 'Islam and Scandinavia during the Viking Age', in E. Piltz (ed.), *Byzantium and Islam in Scandinavia. Acts of a Symposium at Uppsala University*, 15–16 June, 1996. Studies in Mediterranean Archaeology, 126 (1998), 48–50.

66 S. Toropov, 'Hoards of the Viking Age and chance finds of Scandinavian artefacts in Novgorod Land: the topography and composition', lecture at *Eastward and Westward: Inter-ethnic Contacts at the Time of the Formation of Rus'* [*sic*] *of Novgorod. Culture, Memory and Identity*, St Petersburg and Novgorod, Russia, 21–24 July 2009.

67 B. Ager and G. Williams, *The Vale of York Hoard* (London 2010).

Vikings in Arabic sources

1 H. Birkeland, *Nordens historie i middelalderen etter arabiske kilder*, Skrifter udgiven av Det Norske Videnskaps Akademi i Oslo. Hist.-filos. klasse, 2 (Oslo 1954); R. Frye, *Ibn Fadlan's Journey to Russia: A Tenth-Century Traveler from Baghdad to the Volga River* (Princeton 2005); J. Montgomery, 'Arabic sources on the Vikings', in S. Brink with N. Price (eds), *The Viking World* (Abingdon 2008), 550–61; P. Lunde and C. Stone, *Ibn Fadlān and the Land of Darkness. Arab Travelers in the Far North* (Harmondsworth 2012).

2 Lunde and Stone (2012), 204.

3 Ibid., 105–9, 147–52.

4 P.B. Golden, '"Rus" and "Al-Sakāliba"', in C.E. Bosworth, E. van Donzell, W.P. Heinrichs and G. Lecomte (eds), *The Encyclopedia of Islam, New Edition* VIII, NED-SAM (Leiden 1995), 618–29, 872–81; J. Montgomery, 'Ibn Fadlān and the Rūssiyah', *Journal of Arabic and Islamic Studies* 3 (2000), 1–25.

5 S. Pons-Sanz, 'Whom did al-Ghazāl meet? An exchange of embassies between the Arabs from al-Andalus and the Vikings', *Saga Book* 28 (2004), 5–28.

6 Lunde and Stone (2012), 127, 151.

7 Frye (2005), 67–70; Lunde and Stone (2012), 50–4.

8 Birkeland (1954), 103–5; E. Roesdahl, *Viking Age Denmark* (London 1982), 28.

Wiskiauten: a trading site on the southern coast of the Baltic?

1 See, for example, Wulff [first name unknown], 'Bericht über die Aufdeckung altpreußischer Begräbnisstätten bei dem zum Gute Bledau gehörigen Vorwerke Wiskiauten', *Altpreußische Monatsschrift*, 2 (1865), 641–6; B. von zur Mühlen, 'Die Kultur der Wikinger in Ostpreußen', *Bonner Hefte für Vorgeschichte* 9 (Bonn 1975).

2 Von zur Mühlen (1975), 56.

3 T. Ibsen, 'Wiskiauten – Bernstein aus dem Samland', *Archäologie in Deutschland* 5(2007), 34–5.

4 www.wiskiauten.eu

5 J. Frenzel and T. Ibsen, 'In search of the early medieval settlement of Wiskiauten/Mohovoe in the Kaliningrad Region', *Lietuvos Archeologija* 36 (2010), 51.

Reuse of foreign objects

1 B. Maixner, *Haithabu. Fernhandelszentrum zwischen den Welten* (Schleswig 2010), 22, fig. 8.

2 E. Wamers, 'Insignien der Macht. Das Schwert', in E. Wamers and M. Brandt, *Die Macht des Silbers. Karolingische Schätze im Norden* (Regensburg 2005), 54.

3 C. Hedenstierna-Jonsson and L. Holmquist Olausson, *The Oriental Mounts from Birka's Garrison. An Expression of Warrior Rank and Status*, Antiquarian Archive 81 (Stockholm 2008).

4 A, Pedersen, 'Schwert', sect. 7, 'Carolingian and Viking Age', in J. Hoops, *Reallexikon der Germanischen Altertumskunde* 27, 2nd edn (Berlin and New York 2004), 593; 'Gürtel' [belti], sect. 3, *Reallexikon der Germanischen Altertumskunde* 12, 2nd edn (Berlin and New York 1999), 176.

5 Maixner (2010), 145, fig. 166.

6 R. Frye, *Ibn Fadlan's Journey to Russia: A Tenth-Century Traveler from Baghdad to the Volga River* (Princeton 2005).

7 Historisches Museum der Pfalz Speyer (ed.), *Die Wikinger* (Munich 2008), 151.

8 A. Wendt, 'Viking age gold rings and the question of "Gefolgschaft"', *Lund Archaeological Review* 13–14 (2007/2008), 75–89.

9 A. Carlsson, *Vikingatida ringspännen från Gotland*, Stockholm Studies in Archaeology 8 (Stockholm 1988), 19–22; H. Steuer, 'Scales and weights', sect. 5, 'Carolingian and Viking Age', in J. Hoops, *Reallexikon der Germanischen Altertumskunde* 35, 2nd edn (Berlin and New York 2007), 571, fig. 77.

10 See, for example, H. Schilling, 'Duesminderskatter', *Skalk* 6 (2003), 5–12.

11 E. Wamers, 'Pyxides imaginatae. Zur Ikonographie und Funktion karolingische Silberbecher', *Germania* 69(1) (1991), 142.

12 See also J. Graham-Campbell, S.M. Sindbæk and G. Williams (eds), *Silver Economies, Monetisation and Society in Scandinavia AD 800–1100* (Aarhus 2011).

2. *Expansion & Warfare*

1 J. Jesch, *Ships and Men in the Late Viking Age: The Vocabulary of Runic Inscriptions and Skaldic Verse* (Woodbridge 2001), 44–56.

2 C. Arcini, 'The Vikings bare their filed teeth', *American Journal of Physical Anthropology*, 128(4) (December 2005), 727–33.

3 P. Lunde and C. Stone, *Ibn Fadlān and the Land of Darkness. Arab Travelers in the Far North* (Harmondsworth 2012), 46; H. Birkeland, *Nordens historie i middelalderen etter arabiske kilder*, Skrifter utgivet av Det Norske Videnskaps Akademi i Oslo. Hist.-filos. klasse 2 (Oslo 1954), 103–5.

4 N. Price, 'Ship-men and slaughter-wolves: pirate polities in the Viking Age', in L. Müller and S. Amirell (eds), *Persistent Piracy: Historical Perspectives on Maritime Violence and State Formation* (Basingstoke, in press).

5 S. Blöndal and B.S. Benedikz, *The Varangians of Byzantium* (Cambridge 1978); R. D'Amato, *The Varangian Guard 988–1453* (Oxford 2012).

6 A. Roland, 'Secrecy, technology, and war: Greek fire and the defense of Byzantium, 678–1204', *Technology and Culture* 33(4) (1992), 655–79.

7 J. Shepard, 'The Viking Rus and Byzantium', in S. Brink with N. Price (eds), *The Viking World* (Abingdon 2008), 496–516, at 501.

8 Shepard, 'The Viking Rus and Byzantium', in Brink with Price (eds) (2008), 503–4; Lunde and Stone (2012), 175, 178.

9 Lunde and Stone (2012), 144–6; P.B. Golden, 'Rus', in C.E. Bosworth, E. van Donzell, W.P. Heinrichs and G. Lecomte (eds), *The Encyclopedia of Islam, New Edition* VIII, NED-SAM (Leiden 1995), 618–29, at 625.

10 Lunde and Stone (2012), 147–52.

11 H. Palsson and P. Edwards, *Vikings in Russia: Yngvar's Saga and Eymund's Saga* (Edinburgh 1989); Jesch (2001), 104–5.

12 E. Wamers, *Insularer Metallschmuck in wikingerzeitlichen Gräbern Nordeuropas. Undersuchungen zur skandinavischen Westexpansion* (Offa-Bücher 56, Neumünster 1985); E. Wamers., 'Insular finds in Viking Age Scandinavia and the state formation of Norway', in H.B. Clarke, M. Ní Mhaonaigh and R. Ó Floinn (eds), *Ireland and Scandinavia in the Early Viking Age* (Dublin 1998), 37–72.

13 G. Halsall, *Warfare and Society in the Barbarian West, 450–900* (London 2003), 14–19.

14 P.H. Sawyer, *The Age of the Vikings*, 2nd edn (London 1971), 120–31.

15 Halsall (2003), 15–16; R.P. Abels, 'Alfred the Great, the *micel hæden here* and the Viking threat', in *Alfred the Great: Papers from the Eleventh-Centenary Conferences*, ed. by T. Reuter (Aldershot 2003), 265–80.

16 N.P. Brooks, 'England in the ninth century: the crucible of defeat', *Transactions of the Royal Historical Society*, 5th series, 29 (1979), 1–20; R. Lavelle, *Alfred's Wars: Sources and Interpretations of Anglo-Saxon Warfare in the Viking Age* (Woodbridge 2010), 41–2.

17 J.D. Richards,'Viking settlement in England', in Brink with Price (eds) (2008), 368–75; K. Holman, 'Defining the Danelaw', in J. Graham-Campbell *et al.* (eds), *Vikings and the Danelaw: Papers from the Proceedings of the Thirteenth Viking Congress* (Oxford 1997), 1–11.

18 J. Renaud (2008) 'The Duchy of Normandy', in Brink with Price (eds) (2008), 453–7; P. Bauduin, *Les fondations scandinaves en Occident et les débuts du duché de Normandie*, Colloque de Cheisy-la-Salle 2002 (Caen 2005).

19 J. Bradley, 'The interpretation of Scandinavian settlement in Ireland', in J. Bradley (ed.), *Settlement and Society in Medieval Ireland* (Kilkenny 1988), 49–78; R. Ó Floinn, 'The archaeology of the early Viking Age in Ireland', in H.B. Clarke, M. Ní Mhaonaigh and R. Ó Floinn (eds), *Ireland and Scandinavia in the Early Viking Age* (Dublin 1998), 131–65; P.F. Wallace, 'Archaeological evidence for the different expressions of Scandinavian settlement in Ireland', in Brink with Price (eds) (2008), 434–8; J. Bradley, 'Some reflections on the problem of Scandinavian settlement in the hinterland of Dublin in the ninth century', in J. Bradley, A.J. Fletcher and A. Simms (eds), *Dublin in the Medieval World. Studies in Honour of Howard B. Clarke* (Dublin 2009), 39–62.

20 J.H. Barrett, 'The Norse in Scotland', in Brink with Price (eds) (2008), 411–27.

21 T. Reuter, 'The recruitment of armies in the early Middle Ages: what can we know?', in A. Nørgård Jørgensen and B.L. Clausen (eds), *Military Aspects of Scandinavian Society in a European Perspective AD 1–1300* (Copenhagen 1997), 32–7.

22 A. Williams, 'A metallurgical study of some Viking swords', *Gladius* 29 (2009), 121–84.

23 Lunde and Stone (2012), 151.

24 Ibid., 147.

25 T. Reuter, 'Plunder and tribute in the Carolingian empire', *Transactions of the Royal Historical Society*, 5th series 35 (1985), 75–94; T. Reuter , 'The end of Carolingian military expansion', in P. Godman and R. Collins (eds), *Charlemagne's Heir: New Perspectives on the Reign of Louis the Pious (814–40)* (Oxford 1990), 391–405; G. Williams, 'Military institutions and royal power', in M.P. Brown and C.A. Farr (eds), *Mercia: an Anglo-Saxon Kingdom in Europe,* (Leicester 2001), 295–309; G. Williams, 'Military obligations and Mercian supremacy in the eighth century', in D. Hill and M. Worthington (eds), *Æthelbald, Offa and Beonna*, BAR British Series 283 (Oxford 2005), 101–10.

26 N. Price, *The Viking Way: Religion and War in Late Iron Age Scandinavia* (Uppsala 2002).

27 J. Haywood, *Dark Age Naval Power: A Reassessment of Frankish and Anglo-Saxon Seafaring Activity* (Abingdon 1991).

28 A.W. Brøgger and H. Shetelig, *The Viking Ships* (Oslo 1953), 52–5; G. Williams, *Treasures from Sutton Hoo* (London 2011), 20–1.

29 Einhard, 'The Life of Charlemagne', Chapter 17 in L. Thorpe (ed. and trans.), *Einhard and Notker the Stammerer: Two Lives of Charlemagne* (Harmondsworth 2008).

30 *Anglo-Saxon Chronicle* [A] sub. AD 897, M. Swanton (ed. and trans.), *The Anglo-Saxon Chronicle* (London 1996).

31 L. Loe, A. Boyle, H. Webb and D. Score, 'Given to the Ground': A Viking Age Mass Grave on Ridgeway Hill, Weymouth. DNHAS Monograph 22 (Oxford 2014).

32 J. Blair (ed.), *Waterways and Canal-Building in Medieval England* (Oxford 2008).

33 G. Williams, 'Raiding and warfare', in Brink with Price (eds), (2008), 193–204.

34 B. Myhre, 'The archaeology of the early Viking Age in Norway', in Clarke, Ní Mhaonaigh and Ó Floinn (eds) (1998), 3–36.

35 S. Coupland, 'Dorestad in the ninth century: the numismatic evidence', *Jaarboek voor Munt – en Peningkunde* 75 (1988), 5–25.

36 Brooks (1979), 1–20.

37 S. Blöndal and B.S. Benedikz (1978), 32–53.

38 C. Downham, *Viking Kings of Britain and Ireland. The Dynasty of Ivarr to AD 1014* (Edinburgh 2007).

39 S. Coupland, 'The Frankish tribute payments to the Vikings and their consequences', *Frankia* 26(1) (1999), 57–75; S. Coupland, 'From Poachers to Gamekeepers: Scandinavian war lords and Carolingian kings', *Early Medieval Europe* 7(1) (1998), 84–114.

40 *Anglo-Saxon Chronicle* [A, E], *sub.* AD 871; Asser, 'Life of King Alfred', I, 37–39, S. Keynes and M. Lapidge (ed. and trans.), *Alfred the Great* (Harmondsworth 1983).

41 See p. 120–21 in this catalogue.

42 See note 19.

43 M. Redknap, *Vikings in Wales. An Archaeological Quest* (Cardiff 2000).

44 K. Holman, 'Defining the Danelaw', in J. Graham-Campbell *et al.* (eds), *Vikings and the Danelaw: Papers from the Proceedings of the Thirteenth Viking Congress* (Oxford 1997), 1–11; L. Abrams, 'Edward the Elder's Danelaw', in N.J. Higham and D. H. Hill (eds), *Edward the Elder, 899–924* (London 2001), 128–43; G. Williams, 'Towns and identitites in Viking England', in D.M. Hadley and L. Ten Harkel, *Everyday Life in Viking Towns: Social Approaches to Viking Age Towns in Ireland and England, c. 850–1100* (Oxford 2013), 14–34.

45 G. Williams, 'Silver economies, monetisation and society: an overview', in J. Graham-Campbell, S.M. Sindbæk and G. Williams (eds), *Silver Economies, Monetisation and Society in Scandinavia AD 800–1100* (Aarhus 2011), 337–72; T.S. Noonan, 'Scandinvians in European Russia', in P. Sawyer, *The Oxford Illustrated History of the Vikings* (Oxford 1997), 134–55.

46 D. Scragg, 'The battle of Maldon', in D. Scragg (ed.), *The Battle of Maldon, AD 991* (Oxford 1991), 1–37, at 19–23.

47 D.M. Metcalf, 'Inflows of Anglo-Saxon and German coins into the northern lands, *c.* 997–1024', in B. Cook and G. Williams (eds), *Coinage and History in the North Sea World, c. 500–1250. Essays in Honour of Marion Archibald* (Leiden and Boston 2006), 349–88; J.C. Moesgaard, 'The import of English coins to the northern lands: some remarks on coin circulation in the Viking Age based on new evidence from Denmark', in Cook and Williams (eds) (2006), 389–434.

48 K. Lawson, *Cnut: The Danes in England in the Early Eleventh Century* (London and New York 1993); T. Bolton, *The Empire of Cnut the Great: Conquest and the Consolidation of Power in Northern Europe in the Early Eleventh Century* (Leiden and Boston 2009).

49 B. Smith, 'The Picts and the martyrs, or did Vikings kill the native population of Orkney and Shetland', *Northern Studies* 36 (2001), 7–32; J. Bäcklund, 'War or peace? The relations between the Picts and the Norse in Orkney', *Northern Studies* 36 (2001), 33–48.

50 B. Crawford, *Scandinavian Scotland* (Leicester 2007), 63–91.

51 B. Hudson, 'Cnut and the Scottish kings,' *English Historical Review* 107 (1992), 350–60.

52 N. Lund, *Lið, leding og landeværn. Hær og samfund i Danmark i ældre middelalde* (Roskilde 1996); G. Williams. 'Ship-levies in the Viking Age: the methodology of studying military institutions in a semi-historical society', in A. Nørgård Jørgensen, J. Lind, L. Jørgensen and B. Clausen (eds), *Maritime Warfare in Northern Europe. Technology, Organisation, Logistics and Administration 500 BC–1500 AD* (Copenhagen 2002), 293–308.

53 P.G. Foote and D.M. Wilson, *The Viking Achievement: The Society and Culture of Early Medieval Scandinavia* (London 1970), 273, 323.

54 B. Solberg, 'Weapon export from the Continent to the Nordic countries in the Carolingian period', *Studien zur Sachsenforschung* 7 (1991), 241–59.

55 Ibid.

56 S. Norr, 'Old gold – the helmet in *Hákonarmál* as a sign of its time', in S. Norr (ed.), *Valsgärde Studies: the Place and People, Past and Present* (Uppsala 2008), 83–114.

57 *Anglo-Saxon Chronicle* [A, E], *sub.* AD 851

58 T. Reuter, 'Plunder and tribute in the Carolingian empire', *Transactions of the Royal Historical Society*, 5th series 35 (1985), 75–94; T. Reuter, 'The end of Carolingian military expansion', in P. Godman and R. Collins (eds), *Charlemagne's Heir: New Perspectives on the Reign of Louis the Pious (814–40)* (Oxford 1990), 391–405; R.P. Abels, *Lordship and Military Obligation in Anglo-Saxon England* (London 1988).

59 B. Solberg, 'Weapon export from the Continent to the Nordic countries in the Carolingian period', *Studien zur Sachsenforschung* 7 (1991), 241–59.

60 A. Pedersen, 'Weapons and riding gear in burials – evidence of military and social rank in 10th century Denmark', in Nørgård Jørgensen and Clausen (eds) (1997), 123–36.

61 A. Pedersen, 'Viking weaponry', in Brink with Price (eds), (2008), 204–11.

62 P. Nørlund, *Trelleborg*, Nordiske Fortidsminder, Bind 4, Hefte 1(København 1948); O. Olsen, E. Roesdahl and H. Schmidt, *Fyrkat. En jysk vikingeborg* (2 vols), Nordiske Fortidsminder, Serie B, Bind 3 (København 1977); F. Nørgaard, E. Roesdahl and R. Skovmand (eds), *Aggersborg gennem 1000 år* (Herning 1986); E. Roesdahl, 'Viking Age Denmark', 147–55, and B. Jacobsson, 'Utgrävningen av Borgen i Trelleborg, Skåne', in G. Fellows-Jensen and N. Lund (eds), *Fjortende Tværfaglige Vikingesymposium*, (Copenhagen 1995), 12–22; S.W. Andersen, *The Viking Fortress of Trelleborg* (Slagelse 1996).

63 D. Hill and A.R. Rumble (eds), *The Defence of Wessex: The Burghal Hidage and Anglo-Saxon fortifications* (Manchester 1996); Lavelle, (2010), 209–63; J. Baker, S. Brookes and A. Reynolds (eds), *Landscapes of Defence in Early Medieval Europe* (Turnhout 2013).

64 Lund (1996), 112–13; G. Williams. 'Ship-levies in the Viking Age: the methodology of studying military institutions in a semi-historical society', in Nørgård Jørgensen, Lind, Jørgensen and Clausen (eds) (2002), 293–308.

65 T.D. Price, K.M. Frei, A.S. Dobat, N. Lynnerup and P. Bennike, 'Who was in Harold Bluetooth's army? Strontium isotope investigation of the cemetery at the Viking Age fortress at Trelleborg, Denmark', *Antiquity* 85(328) (2011), 476–89.

66 Lund (1996), 187–208; T. Lindkvist, *Plundring, skatter och den feodala statens framväxt: organisatoriska tendenser i Sverige under övergången från vikingatid till tidig medeltid* (Uppsala, 1988); B. Varenius, 'Maritime warfare as an organising principle in Scandinvian society 1000–1300 AD', in Nørgård Jørgensen and Clausen (eds) (1997), 249–256; B. Varenius, *Han ägde bo och skeppslid : om rumslighet och relationer i vikingatid och medeltid* (Umeå 1988); G. Williams. 'Ship-levies in the Viking Age: the methodology of studying military institutions in a semi-historical society', and G. Williams, 'Raiding and warfare', 199, in Nørgård Jørgensen, Lind, Jørgensen and Clausen (eds) (2002), 293–308.

67 On *leiðangr* in skaldic verse, see R. Malmros, *Vikingernes syn på militær og samfund: Belyst gennem skjaldenes fyrstedigtning* (Aarhus 2010); on Skuldelev 5 as a *leiðangr* ship, see O. Crumlin-Pedersen, 'Splendour versus duty – 11th century warships in the light of history and archaeology', in A. Nørgård Jørgensen, J. Lind, L. Jørgensen and B. Clausen (eds) (2002), 257–70.

68 N. Lund, 'The armies of Svein Forkbeard and Cnut: *leding* or *lið*?', *Anglo-Saxon England* 15 (1985), 105–18; N. Lund, 'If the Vikings knew a *Leding* – what was it like?', in B. Ambrosiani and H. Clarke (eds), *Developments Around the Baltic and the North Sea in the Viking Age*, Proceedings of the Twelfth Viking Congress (Stockholm 1994), 98–105; N. Lund, *Lið, leding og landeværn* (1996); N. Lund, 'Is *leidang* a Nordic or a European phenomenon', in Nørgård Jørgensen and Clausen (eds) (1997), 195–9; M.H. Gelting 'Det comparative perspektiv i dansk højmiddelalderforskning. Om familia og familie, lið, leding og landeværn', *Dansk Historisk Tidsskrift* 99(1) (1999), 146–88.

69 G. Williams, 'Hákon *Aðelsteins fostri*: aspects of Anglo-Saxon kingship in tenth-century Norway', in L.E.M. Walker and T.R. Liszka (eds), *The North Sea World: Saints, Seamen and Soldiers* (Dublin 2001), 108–26.

70 Brooks (1979), 1–20; Abels (1988), 109–11; G. Williams (2001), 295–309; G. Williams (2005), 101–10; Lavelle (2010), 47–176; J. Pullen-Appleby, *English Sea Power, c 871 to 1100* (Hockwold-cum-Wilton 2008).

71 G. Williams. 'Ship-levies in the Viking Age: the methodology of studying military institutions in a semi-historical society', in Nørgård Jørgensen, Lind, Jørgensen and Clausen (eds) (2002), 293–308.

72 Ibid.

73 N. Lund (1985), 105–18.

The way of the warrior

1 The account is by Johannes Skylitzes; see H. Ellis Davidson, *The Battle God of the Vikings* (York 1972), 26 and N. Price, *The Viking Way: Religion and War in Late Iron Age Scandinavia* (Uppsala 2002), 332.

2 Price (2002), 331–46.

3 Ibid., 347–50.

4 Ibid., 366–78.

5 M. Biddle and B. Kjølbye-Biddle, 'Repton and the Vikings', *Antiquity* 66 (1992), 36–51.

Continental defences against the Vikings

1 R.M. van Heeringen, P.A. Henderikx and A. Mars (eds), *Vroeg-Middeleeuwse ringwalburgen in Zeeland* (Goes and Amersfoort 1995).

2 N. Dass (ed. and trans.), *Viking Attacks on Paris – The 'Bella Parisiace Urbis'* (Louvain 2007).

3 *Les Vikings en France, Dossiers d'Archéologie* 277 (October 2002), 54.

Viking camps in Britain and Ireland

1 R. Ó Floinn, 'The archaeology of the early Viking Age in Ireland', in H.B. Clarke, M. Ní Mhaonaigh, and R. Ó Floinn (eds), *Ireland and Scandinavia in the Early Viking Age* (Dublin 1998), 131–65, at 162; J. Sheehan, 'The longphort in Viking age Ireland', *Acta Archaeologica* 79 (2008), 282–95.

2 R. Ó Floinn 'The archaeology of the early Viking Age in Ireland', in Clarke, Ní Mhaonaigh, and Ó Floinn (eds) (1998), 161.

3 M.A.S. Blackburn, 'The Viking winter camp at Torksey, 872–3', in M.A.S. Blackburn, *Viking Coinage and Currency in the British Isles* (London 2011), 221–64, at 246.

4 M. Biddle and B. Kjølbye-Biddle, 'Repton and the "great heathen army", 873–4', in J. Graham-Campbell, R.A. Hall, J. Jesch and D.N. Parsons (eds), *Vikings and the Danelaw: Select Papers from the Proceedings of the Thirteenth Viking Congress, 21–30 August 1997* (Oxford 2001), 45–96.

5 Blackburn (2011), 221; G. Williams, 'Towns and Identitites in Viking England', in D.M. Hadley and L. Ten Harkel, *Everyday Life in Viking Towns: Social Approaches to Viking Age Towns in Ireland and England, c. 850–1100* (Oxford 2013), 14–34, p. 17.

6 G. Williams, 'Towns and Identitites in Viking England', in Hadley and Ten Harkel (2013), 17–19.

3. Power & Aristocracy

1 See, for instance, L. Jørgensen, 'Manor and market at Lake Tissø in the sixth to eleventh centuries: the Danish "productive" sites', in T. Pestell and K. Ulmschneider (eds), *Markets in Early Medieval Europe. Trading and 'Productive' Sites, 650–850* (Macclesfield 2003), 175–207.

2 J. Bately (ed.), 'The source. Text and translation', in J. Bately and A. Englert (eds), *Ohthere's Voyages. A Late 9th-Century Account of Voyages Along the Coasts of Norway and Denmark and its Cultural Context*, Maritime Culture of the North 1 (Roskilde 2007), 40–50.

3 G. Stamsø Munch, O. Sverre Johansen and E. Roesdahl (eds), *Borg in Lofoten. A Chieftain's Farm in North Norway*, Arkeologisk Skriftserie 1 (Trondheim 2003).

4 F. Herschend and D. Kaldal Mikkelsen, 'The main building at Borg', in Stamsø Munch, Sverre Johansen and Roesdahl (eds) (2003), 41–76, especially 62–6.

5 I. Holand, 'Pottery' and 'Glass vessels', in Stamsø Munch, Sverre Johansen and Roesdahl (eds) (2003), 199–229, especially 203–8, 216–21.

6 T. Sjøvold, *The Iron Age Settlement of Arctic Norway* (Tromsø 1974), 156.

7 M. Dengsø Jessen, 'The hall and the church during Christianization', in N. Johannsen *et al.* (eds), *Excavating the Mind. Cross-sections Through Culture, Cognition and Materiality* (Aarhus 2012), 133–60.

8 T. Meier, 'Magdeburg zwischen Aachen und Jelling: Repräsentationsarchitektur als semiotisches System', in J. Henning (ed.), *Europa im 10. Jahrhundert. Archäologie einer Aufbruchszeit. Internationale Tagung in Vorbereitung der Ausstellung 'Otto der Grosse, Magdeburg und Europe'* (Mainz am Rhein 2002), 311–22.

9 From *Haraldskvæði*, a poem of praise to the Norwegian King Harald Finehair, quoted in R.I. Page, *Chronicles of the Vikings* (London 1995).

10 E. Nigellus, lines 1882–2513; see 'Ermoldus Nigellus, in Honour of Louis', in T.F.X. Noble (trans.), *Charlemagne and Louis the Pious. The Lives by Einhard, Notker, Ermoldus, Thegan, and the Astronomer* (University Park, PA 2009), Book 4.

11 G. Waitz (ed.), *Vita Anskarii auctore Rimberto*, Monumenta Germaniae Historica, Scriptores Rerum Germanicarum. (Hannover 1884), chs 7–8.

12 Ibid., ch. 26.

13 V. Laurent, 'Ein byzantinisches Bleisiegel aus Haithabu', *Berichte über die Ausgrabungen in Haithabu* 12 (1978), 36–40; C. Feveile and S. Jensen, 'Ribe in the 8th and 9th century', in S. Stummann Hansen and K. Randsborg (eds), *Vikings in the West*, Acta Archaeologica 71/Acta Archaeologica Supplementa II (Copenhagen 2000), 9–24; L. Jørgensen, 'Manor and market at Lake Tissø in the sixth to eleventh centuries: the Danish "productive" sites', in Pestell and Ulmschneider (eds), (2003), 203.

14 J. Shepard, 'The Rhos guests of Louis the Pious: whence and wherefore?', *Early Medieval Europe* 4 (1995), 41–60.

15 Thietmar of Merseburg, *Chronicon*. See W. Trillmich (ed.), *Thietmar von Merseburg. Chronik*. Ausgewählte Quellen zur deutschen Geschichte des Mittelalters IX (Berlin 1957). See also D.A. Warner (trans.), *Ottonian Germany. The Chronicon of Thietmar of Merseburg* (Manchester 2001), Book 2.31.

16 A. Wieczorek and H.-M. Hinz (eds), *Europas Mitte um 1000. Katalog* (Stuttgart 2000), 532–3.

17 E. Roesdahl, 'Cammin – Bamberg – Prague – Léon. Four Scandinavian *Objects d'Art* in Europe', in A. Wesse (ed.), *Studien zur Archäologie des Ostseeraumes von der Eisenzeit zum Mittelalter. Festschrift Michael Müller-Wille* (Neumünster 1998), 547–54.

18 E. Moltke, *Runes and their Origin. Denmark and Elsewhere* (Copenhagen 1976), 203.

19 Thietmar of Merseburg, Book 7.39.

20 H. Eilbracht, 'Von kurzer Dauer: zur Biografie des Goldschmucks', in B. Armbruster and H. Eilbracht (eds), *Wikingergold auf Hiddensee* (Rostock 2010), 184–95.

21 W. Duczko, *Viking Rus. Studies on the Presence of Scandinavians in Eastern Europe. The Northern World. North Europe and the Baltic c. 400–1700 AD. Peoples, Economies and Cultures* 12 (Leiden and Boston 2004), 226–8.

22 See 'Ermoldus Nigellus, in Honour of Louis', in Noble (trans.) (2009), 183.

23 G. Williams, 'Hákon *Aðalsteins fóstri*: aspects of Anglo-Saxon kingship in tenth-century Norway', in T.R. Liszka and L.E.M. Walker (eds), *The North Sea World in the Middle Ages* (Dublin 2001), 108–26.

24 Snorri Sturluson, 'The Saga of Magnus the Good', in L.M. Hollander (trans.), *Heimskringla. History of the Kings of Norway* (Austin 1964), 538–76, especially 538–9 and the skaldic verse sections included here, which provide some authority for the saga account.

25 For a description of a cremation in a ship, see Snorri Sturluson (1964). Snorri notes that the burial was much talked about and that it gave the deceased great fame.

26 A.C. Sørensen, *Ladby. A Danish Ship-Grave from the Viking Age*, Ships and Boats of the North 3 (Roskilde 2001), 111–18.

27 A technique of dating based on investigating annual growth rings in trees.

28 J. Bill and A. Daly, 'The plundering of the ship graves from Oseberg and Gokstad: an example of power politics?', *Antiquity* 86 (2012), 808–24.

29 S.B.F. Jansson, *Runes in Sweden* (Värnamo 1987), 74–5.

30 Ibid., 43–4.

31 M. Olausson (ed.), *Hem til Jarlabanke. Jord, makt och evigt liv i östra Mälardalen under järnålder och medeltid* (Lund 2008).

32 H. Pálsson and P. Edwards (trans.) with an introduction, *Egil's Saga* (Harmondsworth 1976), ch. 55.

33 Ibid., ch. 70.

34 I. Hägg, 'Rangsymboliska element i vikingatida gravar. Hedeby – Birka – Mammen', in M. Iversen *et al.* (eds), *Mammen. Grav, kunst og samfund i vikingetid.* Jysk Arkæologisk Selskabs Skrifter 28 (Højbjerg 1991), 155–62; A. Hedeager Krag, 'Fränkisch-byzantinische Trachteinflüsse in drei dänischen Grabfunden des 10. Jahrhunderts', *Archäologisches Korrespondenzblatt* 29 (1999), 425–44.

35 H. Vierck, 'Mittel- und westeuropäische Einwirkungen auf die Sachkultur von Haithabu/Schleswig', in H. Jankuhn *et al.* (eds), *Archäologische und naturwissenschaftliche Untersuchungen an ländlichen und frühstädtischen Siedlungen im deutschen Küstengebiet vom 5. Jahrhundert v. Chr. bis zum 11. Jahrhundert n. Chr. Band 2. Handelsplätze des frühen und hohen Mittelalters* (Weinheim 1984), 366–422, at 405–6, Figs 193–4.

36 See, for instance, G. Althoff, 'Der friedens-, bündnis- und gemeinschaftsstiftende Charakter des Mahles im früheren Mittelalter', in I. Bitsch *et al.* (eds), *Essen und Trinken in Mittelalter und Neuzeit. Vorträge eines interdisziplinären Symposions vom 10.–13. Juni 1987 an der Justus-Liebig-Universität Giessen* (Sigmaringen 1987), 13–26; K. Leyser, 'Ritual, Zeremonie und Gestik: das ottonische Reich', *Frühmittelalterliche Studien* 27 (1993), 1–26.

37 Quoted in Page (1995), 110.

38 *Egil's Saga* (1976), chs 74–5.

39 E. Nylén and J.P. Lamm, *Bildstenar*, 3rd edn (Värnamo 2003).

40 Page (1995), 139–40. The dating of Hávamál is debated, but it is generally accepted that in part at least it illustrates aspects of the Viking Age.

41 E. Wamers, 'Pyxides imaginatae. Zur Ikonographie und Funktion karolingischer Silberbecher', *Germania* 69 (1991), 97–152.

42 For a discussion on the adoption of chess, see J. Robinson, *The Lewis Chessmen* (London 2004), 43–55.

43 See 'Ermoldus Nigellus, in Honour of Louis', in Noble (trans.) (2009).

44 See, for instance, Widukind of Corvey, Book I, chs 35, 38.

45 See, for instance, E. Szameit, 'Fränkische Reiter des 10. Jahrhunderts', in M. Puhle (ed.), *Otto der Grosse. Magdeburg und Europa* II, *Katalog* (Mainz am Rhein 2001), 254–6; M. Schulze-Dörrlamm, 'Die Ungarneinfälle des 10. Jahrhunderts im Spiegel archäologischer Funde', in Henning (ed.) (2002), 107–22; T. Kind, 'Archäologische Funde von Teilen der Reitausrüstung aus Europa und ihr Beitrag zur Kultur- und Sozialgeschichte der Ottonenzeit', in Henning (ed.) (2002), 283–99.

46 Duczko (2004), 109, 200–1.

47 B. Hougen, 'Studier i Gokstadfunnet', *UOÅrbok* (1931–1932) 5, 74–112, 94 ff.

48 See, for instance, E. Roesdahl, 'Review of M. Müller-Wille, Das wikingerzeitliche Gräberfeld von Thumby-Bienebek (Kreis Rendsburg-Eckernförde) I', *Zeitschrift für Archäologie des Mittelalters* 11/1983 (1985), 175–8; A. Pedersen, 'Søllested and Møllemosegaard – burial customs in 10th century Denmark', in M. Müller-Wille (ed.), *Rom und Byzanz im Norden. Mission und Glaubenswechsel im Ostseeraum während des 8.–14. Jahrhunderts* 1, Akademie der Wissenschaften und der Literatur, Abhandlungen der Geistes- und Sozialwissenschaften Klasse 1997, I(3) (Mainz 1997), 249–78.

49 F. Androshchuk, 'The Vikings in the east', in S. Brink with N. Price (eds), *The Viking World* (Abingdon and New York 2008), 517–42.

50 See S. Brink (Christianization), A.-S. Gräslund and L. Lager (rune-stones), C. Krag (for Norway), E. Roesdahl and N. Lund (for Denmark), and T. Lindkvist (for Sweden) in Part III, 'Scandinavia enters the European State', in Brink with Price (eds) (2008), 619–74.

51 P. Nørlund, *Trelleborg*. Nordiske Fortidsminder IV (Copenhagen 1948); O. Olsen and H. Schmidt, *Fyrkat. En jysk vikingeborg I. Borgen og bebyggelsen* (Copenhagen 1977); F. Nørgaard, E. Roesdahl and R. Skovmand (eds), *Aggersborg gennem 1000 år. Fra vikingeborg til slægtsgård* (Herning 1986); E. Roesdahl, 'Harald Blauzahn – ein dänischer Wikingerkönig aus archäologischer Sicht', in Henning (ed.) (2002), 95–108.

52 J. Henning, 'Der slawische Siedlungsraum und die ottonische Expansion östlich der Elbe: Ereignisgeschichte – Archäologie – Dendrochronologie', in Henning (ed.) (2002), 131–46; M. Dulinicz, 'Forschungen zu den Herrschaftszentren des 10. bis 11. Jahrhunderts in Polen', in Henning (ed.) (2002), 147–60.

53 T.D. Price *et al.*, 'Who was in Harold Bluetooth's army? Strontium isotope investigation of the cemetery at the Viking Age fortress at Trelleborg, Denmark', *Antiquity* 85 (2011), 476–89.

54 A.S. Dobat, 'The state and the strangers: the role of external forces in a process of state formation in Viking-Age South Scandinavia (*c.* AD 900–1050)', *Viking and Medieval Scandinavia* 5 (2009), 65–104.

55 J.C. Moesgaard, 'Skattefundene fra Grågård og Pilhus. Harald Blåtands møntreform', in M. Andersen and P.O. Nielsen (eds), *Danefæ. Skatte fra den danske muld* (Copenhagen 2010), 187–91.

56 J.S. Jensen (ed.), *Tusindtallets Danke Mønter fra Den kongelige Mønt- og Medaillesamling. Danish coins from the 11th century in The Royal Collection of Coins and Medals* (Copenhagen 1995), 22–4; G. Williams, 'Kingship, Christianity and coinage: monetary and political perspectives on silver economy in the Viking Age', in J. Graham-Campbell and G. Williams (eds), *Silver Economy in the Viking Age* (Walnut Creek 2007), 177–214.

57 See C. von Heijne, 'Danska mynt från tusentalet funna i St Peterskyrkan, Rom', *Nordisk Numismatisk Unions Medlemsblad* 2 (2012), 46–8.

Great halls and palaces

1 A. Angenendt, *Kaiserherrschaft und Königstaufe. Kaiser, Könige und Päpste als geistliche Patrone in der abendländischen Missionsgeschichte*, Arbeiten zur Frühmittelalterforschung 15 (Berlin and New York 1984), 215–17.

2 'Ermoldus Nigellus, in Honour of Louis', in T.F.X. Noble (trans.), *Charlemagne and Louis the Pious. The Lives by Einhard, Notker, Ermoldus, Thegan, and the Astronomer* (University Park, PA 2009), Book 4.

3 H. Grewe, 'Die Ausgrabungen in der Königspfalz Ingelheim am Rhein', in L. Fenske, J. Jarnut and M. Wemhoff (eds), *Splendor palatii. Neue Forschungen zu Paderborn und anderen Pfalzen der Karolingerzeit. Deutsche Königspfalzen. Beiträge zu ihrer historischen und archäologischen Erforschung* 5, *Veröffentlichungen des Max-Planck-Institutes für Geschichte* 5(11) (Göttingen 2001), 158.

4 G.H. Pertz (ed), *Annales et chronica aevi Carolini*, Monumenta Germaniae Historica, Scriptores 1, (Hannover 1826), 38; M. Balzer, *Paderborn als karolingischer Pfalzort*, in *Deutsche Königspfalzen. Beiträge zu ihrer historischen und archäologischen Erforschung* 3, *Veröffentlichungen des Max-Planck-Institutes für Geschichte* 3(11) (Göttingen 1979), 38ff., 9–85.

5 F. Brunhölz (ed. and trans.), *Karolus Magnus et Leo papa. Ein Paderborner Epos vom Jahre 799*, MGH Poetae 1 (Munich 1881) 367–79. J. Brockmann (ed.), *Studien und Quellen zur westfälischen Geschichte* 8 (1966), new, unchanged edition, *Studien und Quellen zur westfälischen Geschichte* 36 (Paderborn 1999), 47, l.24–9.

6 S. Gai, 'Die Baugeschichte des Pfalzkomplexes. Analyse und Deutung der stratigraphischen Befunde. Die Gründung der Paderborner Pfalz im Jahre 776', in S. Gai and B. Mecke, *Est locus insignis. Die Pfalz Karls des Großen und ihre bauliche Entwicklung bis zum Jahr 1002, Denkmalpflege und Forschung in Westfalen* 40 (Mainz 2004), 103–14.

7 S. Gai, 'Karolingische Glasfunde der Pfalz Paderborn', in C. Stiegemann and M. Wemhoff (eds), *799. Kunst und Kultur der Karolingerzeit. Karl der Große und Papst Leo III in Paderborn. Beiträge zum Katalog der Ausstellung* (Mainz 1999), accompanying book 212–17, catalogue 160–9.

8 A. Grothe, 'Zur karolingischen Keramik der Pfalz Paderborn', in Stiegemann and Wemhoff (eds) (1999), accompanying book 209–11, catalogue vol. 1, 144 ff.

9 M. Wintergerst, *Franconofurd, 1, Die Befunde der karolingisch-ottonischen Pfalz aus den Frankfurter Altstadtgrabungen 1953–1993. Schriften des Archäologischen Museums Frankfurt 22/1* (Frankfurt 2007), 46–60.

10 Part of the inscription of the large rune-stone in Jelling.

11 B. Ludowici, *Die Halle des Königs. Repräsentative Profanarchitektur der ottonischen Pfalzen im Harzraum*, in K. Gereon Beuckers, J. Cramer and M. Imhof (eds), *Die Ottonen, Kunst-Architektur-Geschichte* (Petersberg 2002), 259–65.

12 M. Dapper, *Die ottonische Pfalz Tilleda* in *Die Ottonen* (Petersberg 2002), 266; M. Dapper, *Die Neuinterpretation der Grabungsergebnisse der Pfalz Tilleda*, in C. Ehlers, J. Jarnut and M. Wemhoff (eds), *Zentren herrschaftlicher Repräsentation im Hochmittelalter. Geschichte, Architektur und Zeremoniell. Deutsche Königspfalzen. Beiträge zu ihrer historischen und archäologischen Erforschung 7, Veröffentlichungen des Max-Planck-Institutes für Geschichte* 7(11) (Göttingen 2007), 151–69.

13 Further examples are the great hall of Burg Elten on the Lower Rhine dating from the middle of the tenth century, or a wooden building at the monastical court and temporary royal residence of Gebesee in Thüringia.

14 S. Gai, 'Zur Rekonstruktion und Zeitstellung der spätottonischen Pfalz in Paderborn', in Ehlers, Jarnut and Wemhoff (eds) (2007), 121–50.

15 G. Binding, *Deutsche Königspfalzen von Karl dem Grossen bis Friedrich II. (765–1240)* (Darmstadt 1996), 223–34.

16 H.A. Bellows (trans.), *The Edda, Voluspa 64* (Princeton 1936).

The royal monuments of Jelling

1 E. Wamers, '... ok Dani gærði kristna ... Der große Jellingstein im Spiegel ottonischer Kunst', *Frühmittelalterliche Studien* 34 (2000), 132–58, Plates X–XVI.

2 K.J. Krogh, *Gåden om Kong Gorms Grav. Historien om Nordhøjen i Jelling. Vikingekongernes Monumenter i Jelling* 1 (Copenhagen 1993); K.J. Krogh and B. Leth-Larsen, *Hedensk og Kristent. Fundene fra den kongelige gravhøj i Jelling. Vikingekongernes monumenter i Jelling* 2 (Copenhagen 2007).

3 See H. Breuning-Madsen *et al.*, 'Brønden på toppen af Nordhøjen i Jelling', *Nationalmuseets Arbejdsmark* (Copenhagen 2010), 192–203; and H. Breuning-Madsen *et al.*, 'The hydrology in huge burial mounds built of loamy tills: a case study on the genesis of perched water tables and a well in a Viking Age burial mound in Jelling, Denmark', *Geografisk Tidsskrift-Danish Journal of Geography* 112(1) (2012), 40–51.

4 J. Bill and A. Daly, 'The plundering of the ship graves from Oseberg and Gokstad: an example of power politics?', *Antiquity* 86 (2012), 808–24.

5 M. Kähler Holst, M. Dengsø Jessen, S. Wulff Andersen and A. Pedersen, 'The late Viking-Age royal constructions at Jelling, central Jutland, Denmark. Recent investigations and a suggestion for an interpretative revision', *Praehistorische Zeitschrift* 87(2) (2012), 474–504.

6 See, for instance, E. Roesdahl, 'Scandinavia in the Melting-pot, 950–1000', in S. Sigmundsson (ed.), *Viking Settlements and Viking Society. Papers from the Proceedings of the Sixteenth Viking Congress, Reykjavík and Reykholt, 16th–23rd August 2009* (Reykjavík 2011), 347–74.

Neighbours along the southern Baltic coast

1 See summary in H. Jöns, 'Was the Emporium of Reric the forerunner of Hedeby?', *Bodendenkmalpflege Mecklenburg-Vorpommern, Jahrbuch* 47 (1999), 201–13.

2 Summary in M. Müller-Wille, 'Emporium Reric', in S. Brather, D. Geuenich and C. Huth (eds), *Historia Archaeologica. Festschrift für Heiko Steuer zum 70. Geburtstag.* Supplements to the Reallexikon der Germanischen Altertumskunde 70 (Berlin and New York 2009), 451–71.

3 S.M. Sindbæk, *Ruter og rutinisering. Fjernhandel i Nordeuropa* (Copenhagen 2005), 19.

4 A. Tummuscheit, *Die Baubefunde des frühmittelalterlichen Seehandelsplatzes von Groß Strömkendorf, Lkr. Nordwestmecklenburg.* Early Mediaeval Archaeology between the Baltic and the Mediterranean 2. Research on Gross Strömkendorf 4 (Wiesbaden 2011).

5 D. Warnke, 'Der Hort eines Edelmetallschmiedes aus der frühslawischen Siedlung Rostock-Dierkow', *Offa* 49/50 (1992/93), 197–206.

6 According to S.M. Sindbæk, 'Silver economies and social ties: long-distance interaction, long-term investments – and why the Viking Age happened', in J. Graham-Campbell, S.M. Sindbæk and G. Williams (eds), *Silver Economies, Monetisation & Society in Scandinavia, 800–1100* (Aarhus 2011), 51–2.

7 J. Bately, 'Wulfstan's voyage and his description of *Estland*: the text and the language of the text', in A. Englert and A. Trakadas (eds), *Wulfstan's Voyage. The Baltic Sea Region in the Early Viking Age as Seen from Shipboard.* Maritime Culture of the North 2 (Roskilde 2009), 15.

8 M. Jagodziński, *Truso. Między Weonodlandem a Witlandem. Between Weonodland and Witland* (Elbląg 2010), 162, n. 203.

9 S. Kleingärtner, *Die frühe Phase der Urbanisierung an der südlichen Ostseeküste im ersten nachchristlichen Jahrtausend.* Studien zur Siedlungsgeschichte und Archäologie der Ostseegebiete 13 (Neumünster 2013).

10 Kleingärtner (2013).

11 S. Brather, 'Polen sect. 3, Historisch-Archäologisches', in J. Hoops, *Reallexikon der Germanischen Altertumskunde* 23, 2nd edn (Berlin and New York 2001), 260.

12 Z. Kurnatowska, 'Herrschaftszentren und Herrschaftsorganisation', in A. Wieczorek and H. -M. Hinz (eds), *Europas Mitte um 1000.* Beiträge zur Geschichte, Kunst und Archäologie 1 (Stuttgart 2000), 459, fig. 306.

13 See summary in W. Rohrer, 'Wikinger oder Slawen? Die Interpretationsgeschichte frühpiastischer Bestattungen mit Waffenbeigabe', in A. Klammt and S. Rossignol (eds), *Mittelalterliche Eliten und Kulturtransfer östlich der Elbe. Interdisziplinäre Beiträge zu Archäologie und Geschichte im mittelalterlichen Ostmitteleuropa* (Göttingen 2009), 28–37.

14 D. Banaszak and A. Tabaka, 'Der Siedlungskomplex des mittelalterlichen Zentrums auf der Insel Ostrów Lednicki', in I. Boháčová and L. Poláček (eds), *Burg – Vorburg – Suburbium. Zur Problematik der Nebenareale frühmittelalterlicher Zentren.* International Conferences in Mikulčice 7. Spisy Archeologického Ústavu Av Čr, Brno, 35 (Brno 2008a), 81–2.

15 Banaszak and Tabaka (2008a), 80–1, fig. 5.

16 D. Banaszak and A. Tabaka, 'Relikte der Handwerkstätigkeit im Hinterland der frühpiastischen Burg auf der Insel Ostrów Lednicki', in L. Poláček (ed.), *Das wirtschaftliche Hinterland der frühmittelalterlichen Zentren.* International Conferences in Mikulčice 6. Spisy Archeologického Ústavu Av Čr, Brno 31 (Brno 2008b), 111–15.

17 A. Kola and G. Wilke, *Brücken vor 1000 Jahren. Unterwasserarchäologie bei der polnischen Herrscherpfalz Ostrów Lednicki* (Toruń 2000), 53.

18 J. Górecki, 'Die Burg in Ostrów Lednicki ein frühstaatliches Zentrum der Piastendynastie', in A. Wieczorek and H.-M. Hinz (eds), *Europas Mitte um 1000.* Beiträge zur Geschichte, Kunst und Archäologie 1 (Stuttgart 2000), 470; J. Górecki, 'Waffen und Reiterausrüstungen von Ostrów Lednicki. Zur Geschichte des frühen polnischen Staates und seines Heeres', *Zeitschrift für Archäologie des Mittelalters* 29 (2001), 42.

4. Belief & Ritual

1 P.B. Sturtevant, 'Contesting the semantics of Viking religion', *Viking and Medieval Scandinavia* 9 (2013) 8.

2 As background to this chapter, the Norse myths can principally be found in two medieval Icelandic texts, *The Poetic Edda* and Snorri Sturluson's *Prose Edda*; good recent translations can be found in C. Larrington (trans.), *The Poetic Edda* (Oxford 1996) and J. Byock (trans.), *Snorri Sturluson – The Prose Edda* (London 2005). There is a vast literature on their analysis, but well-referenced recent studies can be found in H. O'Donoghue, *From Asgard to Valhalla* (London 2010), C. Abram, *Myths of the Pagan North: the Gods of the Northmen* (London 2011) and L. Hedeager, *Iron Age Myth and Materiality: an Archaeology of Scandinavia AD 400–1000* (London 2011); R. Simek, *Dictionary of Northern Mythology* (Cambridge 1993) remains the standard dictionary of the tales. Research into Old Norse belief and ritual has a similarly impressive bibliography, but again recent overviews can be found in C. Raudvere and J-P. Schjødt (eds), *More Than Mythology: Narratives, Ritual Practices and Regional Distribution in Pre-Christian Scandinavian Religions* (Lund 2012) and the *Vägar till Midgård* series, A. Andrén, K. Jennbert and C. Raudvere (series eds),

Vägar till Midgård: Nordisk Hedendom i Långtidsperspektiv (14 vols) (Lund 2001–11). A series of useful essays and comprehensive references can also be found in S. Brink with N. Price (eds), *The Viking World* (Abingdon 2008).

3 K.C. Patton, *Religion of the Gods: Ritual, Paradox and Reflexivity* (Cambridge, Mass. 2009).

4 K. Bek-Pedersen, *The Norns in Old Norse Mythology* (Edinburgh 2011).

5 The range of discussion can be traced from O. Olsen, *Hov, hørg og kirke* (Copenhagen 1966) to O. Sundqvist, 'The question of ancient Scandinavian cultic buildings with particular reference to Old Norse *hof*', *Temenos* 1(45) (2009), 65–84.

6 See, for example, H.-E. Lidén, 'From pagan sanctuary to Christian church. The excavation of Mære church in Trøndelag', *Norwegian Archaeological Review* 2 (1969), 3–32 and A-L. Nielsen, 'Rituals and power: about a small building and animal bones from the late Iron Age', in A. Andrén, K. Jennbert and C. Raudvere (eds), *Old Norse Religion in Long-Term Perspectives* (Lund 2006), 243–7.

7 L. Larsson (ed.), *Continuity for Centuries: a Ceremonial Building and its Context at Uppåkra, Southern Sweden* (Lund 2004).

8 M. Bäck, A-M. Hållans Stenholm and J-Å. Ljung, *Lilla Ullevi – historien om det fridlysta rummet* (Stockholm 2008).

9 The Götavi excavations have not yet been published; I am grateful to site director Kenneth Svensson and Arkeologikonsult AB for information.

10 The number nine is of great significance in Norse mythology, occurring as a magical sign dozens of times in various contexts, including the number of the underworlds, the duration of rituals in days or nights, and so on. At the final battle of the Ragnarök, the god Thor takes nine steps as he falls and dies.

11 See M. Alkarp, *Det Gamla Uppsala: Berättelser och Metamorfoser* (Uppsala 2009) for an overview of Gamla Uppsala studies.

12 G. Lucas, *Hofstaðir: Excavations of a Viking Age Feasting Hall in North-Eastern Iceland* (Reykjavík 2009).

13 B.-M. Näsströrn, *Blot – Tro och Offer i Norden* (Stockholm 2002).

14 It has been conjectured that the prominent role played by fire in the Norse myths may reflect a bias towards Iceland, with its volcanic landscapes and lava. We know that much of our source material was composed on this North Atlantic island, and it may therefore reflect a local variant of beliefs. However, the excavated indications of burning at many of these sites imply that it was a more widespread component of Norse ritual.

15 J. Lund, *Åsted og vadested: deponeringer, genstandsbiografier og rumlig strukturering som kilde til vikingetidens kognitive landskaber* (Oslo 2009).

16 Adam of Bremen, *History of the Archbishops of Hamburg-Bremen* (New York 2002), 208 ff.

17 B-M. Näsström, 'Offerlunden under Frösö kyrka', in S. Brink (ed.), *Jämtlands Kristnande* (Uppsala 1996), 65–85.

18 P. Vikstrand, *Gudarnas platser. Förkristna sakrala ortnamn I Mälardalen* (Uppsala 2001); S. Brink, 'Mytologiska rum och eskatologiska föreställningar i det vikingatida Norden', in A. Andrén, K. Jennbert and C. Raudvere (eds), *Ordning mot Kaos. Studier av nordisk förkristen kosmologi* (Lund 2004), 291–316.

19 N. Price, *The Viking Way: Religion and War in Late Iron Age Scandinavia* (Uppsala 2002), 59–60.

20 N. Price, 'What's in a name? An identity crisis for the Norse gods (and some of their friends)', in Andrén, Jennbert and Raudvere (2006), 179–83.

21 For comprehensive overviews of magic in Viking society, see Price (2002), F-X. Dillmann, *Les magiciens dans l'Islande ancienne* (Uppsala 2006), E. Heide, *Gand, seid og åndevind* (Bergen 2006) and S.A. Mitchell, *Witchcraft and Magic in the Nordic Middle Ages* (Philadelphia 2011).

22 See P. Meulengracht Sørensen, *The Unmanly Man: Concepts of Sexual Defamation in Early Northern Society* (Odense 1983); Viking society was one of the most homophobic in history – an unfounded allegation of homosexual behaviour was an offence ranked with murder.

23 For a critical review of this topic, see C. Tolley, *Shamanism in Norse Myth and Magic* (2 vols) (Helsinki 2009).

24 See N. Price, 'Dying and the dead: Viking Age mortuary behaviour', in Brink with Price (eds) (2008), 257–73 for a more comprehensive, referenced overview of Viking burial practices.

25 For child burial in the Viking Age, see C. Mejsholm, *Gränsland: Konstruktion av tidig barndom och begravningsritual vid tiden för kristnandet i Skandinavien* (Uppsala 2009).

26 H. Robbins, *Seated Burials at Birka: a Select Study* (Uppsala 2004).

27 Peets (2013); M. Biddle and B. Kjølbye-Biddle, 'Repton and the Vikings', *Antiquity* 66 (1992), 36–51.

28 See I-M. Back Danielsson, *Masking Moments: the Transitions of Bodies and Beings in Late Iron Age Scandinavia* (Stockholm 2007) for an excellent critique of this problem.

29 See, for example, A. Klevnäs, 'Robbing the dead at Gamla Uppsala, Sweden', *Archaeological Review from Cambridge* 22(1) (2007), 24–42.

30 J. Montgomery, 'Ibn Fadlān and the Rūsiyyah', *Journal of Arabic and Islamic Studies* 3 (2000), 1–25.

31 F. Svanberg, *Decolonizing the Viking Age* (2 vols) (Stockholm 2003) has even suggested that the diversity of local identities this might represent would effectively render meaningless any notion of a coherent 'Viking-Age Scandinavian' culture at all.

32 N. Price, 'Bodylore and the archaeology of embedded religion: dramatic licence in the funerals of the Vikings', in D.M. Whitley and K. Hays-Gilpin (eds), *Belief in the Past: Theoretical Approaches to the Archaeology of Religion* (Walnut Creek 2008), 143–65; N. Price, 'Passing into poetry: Viking-Age mortuary drama and the origins of Norse mythology', *Medieval Archaeology* 54 (2010), 123–56; N. Price, 'Mythic acts: material narratives of the dead in Viking Age Scandinavia', in Raudvere and Schjødt (eds) (2012), 13–46.

33 For a range of studies on the Christian conversion, see B. Nilsson (series ed.), *Projektet Sveriges Kristnande* (5 vols) (Uppsala 1992–6); A. Sanmark, *Power and Conversion: a Comparative Study of Christianization of Scandinavia* (Uppsala 2004); Brink with Price (eds) (2008), Part III; A. Winroth, *The Conversion of Scandinavia: Vikings, Merchants and Missionaries in the Remaking of Northern Europe* (New Haven 2011).

34 See, for example, Jón Hnefill Aðalsteinsson, *Under the Cloak: the Acceptance of Christianity in Iceland with Particular Reference to the Religious Attitudes Prevailing at the Time* (Uppsala 1978).

35 See, for example, N. Price (2002), 74–5.

36 On rune-stones, see B. Sawyer, *The Viking Age Rune Stones* (Oxford 2000) and A.-S. Gräslund, *Runstensstudier* (Uppsala 2002).

37 See L. Anker, *The Norwegian Stave Churches* (Oslo 2012) for a recent guide to the twenty-nine surviving stave churches.

38 E. Mikkelsen, 'The Vikings and Islam', in Brink with Price (eds) (2008), 543–9.

The Fyrkat woman

1 E. Roesdahl, 'En gravplads fra tidlig kristen tid', in N. Lund (ed.), *Kristendommen i Danmark før 1050* (Roskilde 2004), 153–8; E. Roesdahl, *Fyrkat. En jysk vikingeborg*, II Oldsagerne og gravpladsen (Copenhagen 1977).

2 N. Price, *The Viking Way. Religion and War in Late Iron Age Scandinavia* (Uppsala 2002), 149–57; P. Pentz, M.B. Baastrup, S. Karg and U. Mannering, 'Kong Haralds vølve', Nationalmuseets Arbejdsmark (Copenhagen 2009) 215–32.

3 Pentz, Baastrup, Karg and Mannering (2009).

Ritual sites at Lake Tissø

1 L. Jørgensen, 'Pre-Christian cult at aristocratic residences and settlement complexes in southern Scandinavia in the 3rd–10th centuries AD', in U. von Freeden, H. Friesinger and E. Wamers (eds), *Glaube, Kult und Herrschaft. Phänomene des Religiösen im 1. Jahrtausend n. Chr. in Mittel- und Nordeuropa*, Kolloquien zur Vor- und Frühgeschichte 12 (Frankfurt 2009), 329–54.

2 P. Vikstrand, 'Berget, lunden och åkern. Om sakrala och kosmologiska landskab ur ortnamnens perspektiv', in A. Andrén *et al.* (eds), *Ordning mot kaos – studier av nordisk förkristen kosmologi* (Lund 2004), 317–41.

3 S. Brink, 'Naming the land', in S. Brink with N. Price (eds), *The Viking World* (Abingdon 2008), 57–66.

The Oseberg ship and ritual burial

1 N. Bonde, 'Dendrochronological dating of the Viking age ship burials at Oseberg, Gokstad and Tune, Norway', in A. Sinclair, E. Slater and J. Gowlett (eds), *Archaeological Sciences* (Oxford 1995), 195–200; A.W. Brøgger, H. Schetelig and J. Holmboe, *Osebergfunnet*, 1st edn (Kristiania 1917).

2 M. Müller-Wille, *Bestattung im Boot. Studien zu einer nord-europäischen Grabsitte* (Neumünster 1970).

3 N. Bonde and F-A. Stylegar, 'Fra Avaldsnes til Oseberg. Dendrokronologiske undersøkelser av skipsgravene fra Storhaug og Grønhaug på Karmøy', *Viking* LXXII (2009), 149–68.

4 A.E. Christensen and M. Nockert, *Osebergfunnet. Tekstilene* (Oslo 2006).

5 P. Holck, *Skjelettene fra Gokstad- og Osebergskipet*, Antropologiske skrifter 8 (Oslo 2009).

6 B. Myhre, 'Kronologispørsmålet og ynglingeættens gravplasser', in A.E. Christensen, A.S. Ingstad and B. Myhre (eds), *Osebergdronningens grav* (Oslo 1992), 272–8.

7 A.S. Ingstad, 'The interpretation of the Oseberg-find', in O. Crumlin-Pedersen and B. Munch Thye (eds), *The Ship as Symbol in Prehistoric and Medieval Scandinavia. Papers from an International Research Seminar at the Danish National Museum, Copenhagen, 5–7 May 1994* (Copenhagen 1995), 139–47; G. Røthe, *Osebergfunnet: en religionshistorisk tolkning* (Oslo 1994); B. Solli, *Seid. Myter, sjamanisme og kjønn i vikingenes tid* (Oslo 2002).

8 J. Bill and A. Daly, 'The plundering of the ship graves from Oseberg and Gokstad: an example of power politics?', *Antiquity* 86(333) (2012), 808–24.

9 U. Arents and S. Eisenschmidt, *Die Gräber von Haithabu* (Neumünster 2010); N. Bonde and F-A. Stylegar, 'Fra Avaldsnes til Oseberg. Dendrokronologiske undersøkelser av skipsgravene fra Storhaug og Grønhaug på Karmøy', *Viking* LXXII (2009), 149–68; M. Müller-Wille, *Das Bootkammergrab von Haithabu* (Schleswig-Holstein 1976).

10 Brøgger, Schetelig and Holmboe (1917); B. Myhre and T. Gansum, *Skibshaugen 900 e.Kr. Borrefunnet 1852–2002* (Vestfold 2003); N. Nicolaysen, *Langskibet fra Gokstad ved Sandefjord – The Viking-Ship Discovered at Gokstad in Norway* (Kristiania 1882); D. Skre (ed.), *Kaupang in Skiringssal. Kaupang Excavation Project Publications Series* 1 (Århus and Oslo 2007).

5 Ships & the Vikings

1 N. Bonde, 'Dendrokronologische Altersbestimmung des Schiffes von Nydam', *Offa* 47 (1990), 161; F. Rieck, 'Skibene fra Nydam mose', in L. Jørgensen, B. Storgård and L.G. Thomsen (eds), *Sejrens Triumf. Norden i skyggen af det romerske Imperium* (Copenhagen 2003), 304; F. Rieck, 'The Iron Age ships from Nydam. Age, equipment and capacity', in A. Nørgård Jørgensen, J. Pind, L. Jørgensen and B. Clausen (eds), *Maritime Warfare in Northern Europe. Technology, Organisation, Logistics and Administration 500 BC–1500 AD. Papers from an International Research Seminar at the Danish National Museum, Copenhagen, 3–5 May 2000* (Copenhagen 2002), 73–81.

2 In the third book of Gregory's 'Libri Historiarum' (*Gregorii episcopi Turonensis Libri Historiarum X. Editionem alteram cvravervnt Brvno Krvsch et Wilhelmvs Levison. Monumenta Germaniae Historica. Scriptores rervm Merovingicarvm Tom. I. Pars I.* (Hannover 1951)). The name of the Danish King is here Chlochilaichus, and the identification as Hygelac – also a Swedish king mentioned in the Beowulf poem – has been challenged by Arne Søby Christensen (Arne Søby Christensen, Beowulf, Hygelac og Chlochilaichus. Om beretningskronologien i Beowulf. *Historisk tidsskrift* (Denmark), 105:1 (2005), 40–79.

3 W. Stokes and J. Strachan (eds and trans.), *Thesaurus Palaeohibernicus: A Collection of Old Irish Glosses, Scholia, Prose, and Verse* (2 vols) (1901–3), repr. (Oxford 1975), vol. 2, 290, here quoted from M. Ní Mhaonaigh, 'Friend and foe: Vikings in ninth- and tenth-century Irish literature', in H.B. Clarke, M. Ní Mhaonaigh and R. Ó Floinn (eds), *Ireland and Scandinavia in the Early Viking Age* (Dublin 1998), 381.

4 J. Ulriksen, *Anløbspladser, besejling og bebyggelse i Danmark mellem 200 og 100 e. Kr.: en studie af søfartens pladser på baggrund af undersøgelser i Roskilde fjord* (Roskilde 1998), 9, 13.

5 R. Hodges, *Primitive and Peasant Markets* (Oxford 1988), 45–52; J. Korpela, *The World of Ladoga: Society, Trade, Transformation and State Building in the Eastern Fennoscandian Boreal Forest Zone, c. 1000–1555*. Nordische Geschichte 7 (Berlin 2008), 209–10.

6 O. Crumlin-Pedersen and O. Olsen (eds), *The Skuldelev Ships I. Topography, Archaeology, History, Conservation and Display.Ships and Boats of the North 4.1* (Roskilde 2002), 97–136; J. Bill, 'Viking ships and the sea', in S. Brink with N. Price (eds), *The Viking World* (London 2008), 176.

7 J. Bill, 'Viking ships and the sea', in Brink with Price (eds) (2008), 176; S. Kalmring, *Der Hafen von Haithabu* (Neumünster 2010), 124.

8 J. Bill, 'Viking ships and the sea', in Brink with Price (eds) (2008), 176.

9 Kalmring (2010), 453–6.

10 J. Jesch, *Ships and Men in the Late Viking Age: the Vocabulary of Runic Inscriptions and Skaldic Verse* (London 2001), 135; G. Larsson, *Ship and Society: Maritime Ideology in Late Iron Age Sweden* (Uppsala 2007), 66.

11 Larsson (2007), 177–8.

12 The Djulefors stone in Södermanland, see Jesch (2001), 148.

13 Snorri Sturluson, *Gylfaginning*, Kap 50, ch. 48 in Thøger Larsen (trans.) *Edda-myterne. Nordens Gudekvad & Snorris Eddasagn* (2004).

14 E. Moltke, *Runes and their Origins. Denmark and Elsewhere*. The National Museum of Denmark (Copenhagen 1985), 336.

15 The word 'snekke' and the place names it is part of are discussed by B. Holmberg and J. Skamby Madsen, 'Da kom en snekke. Havnepladser fra 1000- og 1100-tallet', *KUML* (1998) 1997–8, 197–225, and C. Westerdahl, 'The cognitive landscape of naval warfare and defence – Toponymic and archaeological aspects', in A. Nørgård Jørgensen, J. Pind, L. Jørgensen and B. Clausen (eds), *Maritime Warfare in Northern Europe. Technology, Organisation, Logistics and Administration 500 BC–1500 AD. Papers from an International Research Seminar at the Danish National Museum, Copenhagen, 3–5 May 2000* (Copenhagen 2002), 169–90. The term is also known from older German, Dutch and Russian sources, and as a loan-word in Norman French. In Old English, the word 'snacc' is known from the *Anglo-Saxon Chronicle*, where it means a ship that sails less swiftly: see Holmberg and Skamby Madsen (1998), 204.

16 See C. Westerdahl 'The cognitive landscape of naval warfare and defence – Toponymic and archaeological aspects', in Nørgård Jørgensen, Pind, Jørgensen and Clausen (eds) (2002), 179–80.

17 A.C. Sørensen, *Ladby, A Danish Ship-Grave from the Viking Age*. Ships and Boats of the North 3 (Roskilde 2001), 51, 56.

18 Crumlin-Petersen and Olsen (2002), 30–42.

19 E. Andersen, 'Square sails of wool', in O. Olsen, J. Skamby Madsen and F. Rieck (eds), *Shipshape – Essays for Ole Crumlin-Pedersen* (Roskilde 1995), 249–70.

20 Jesch (2001), 163–5.

21 J. Bill, M. Gøthche and H.M. Myrhøj, 'Nordeuropas største skibsfund', in *Ni vrag fra vikingetid og middelalder under museumsøen i Roskilde* (Arbejdsmark 1998), 151.

22 O. Crumlin-Pedersen, *Viking-Age Ships and Shipbuilding in Hedeby/Haithabu and Schleswig*. Ships and Boats of the North 2 (Schleswig/ Roskilde 1997), 177–88.

23 *Snorre Sturlason, Olav Tryggvessons Saga*, trans., revised by Alexander Bugge (Oslo 1929), 88.

24 A kenning is an ambiguous compound expression with metaphorical meaning, e.g. oar-steed means 'ship'.

25 Jesch (2001), 34.

26 J. Jesch, 'Sea-battles in skaldic poetry', in Nørgård Jørgensen, Pind, Jørgensen and Clausen (eds) (2002), 57–64.

27 Larsson (2007), 75–6.

28 E.M. Tyler, 'Talking about history in eleventh-century England: the *Encomium Emmae Reginae* and the Court of Harthacnut', *Early Medieval Europe* 13(4) (2005), 359–83.

29 E.M. Tyler, '"The eyes of the beholders were dazzled": treasure and artifice in *Encomium Emmae Reginae*', *Early Medieval Europe* 8(2) (1999), 265, for discussion see 257 ff.

30 The value of skaldic poetry as a source of information on the *leding* system age is hotly debated: see R. Malmros, 'Leiđangr in Old Norse court poetry', in Nørgård Jørgensen, Pind, Jørgensen and Clausen (eds) (2002), 277–86, R. Malmros, *Vikingernes syn på militær og samfund. Belyst genmem skjaldenes fyrstedigtning* [with English summaries] (Aarhus 2010), N. Lund, *Lið, leding og landeværn. Hær og samfund i Danmark i ældre middelalder* (Roskilde 1996), N. Lund, 'Leding, skjaldekvad og bønder', *Historisk Tidsskrift* 106 (Denmark 2006), 243–52, and also Larsson (2007), 299–303 with references. See also Jesch (2001), 197 on the appearance of the word in skaldic poetry of the tenth century, where it is stressed that, even though the word appears, the interpretation of its meaning is uncertain.

31 Larsson (2007), 307–10.

32 For example, a rune-stone from Uppland, where a man at Banke owned his own ship. A stone from Aarhus talks of a single ship being jointly owned by Asser Sakse and Arne.

33 *Den ældre Edda. Edda Sæmundar* [The Elder Edda], (Danish trans. Frederik Winkel Horn) (Copenhagen 1869).

34 O. Olsen, 'Royal power in Viking age Denmark', in H. Bekker-Nielsen and H. Frede Nielsen (eds), *Beretning fra Syvende Tværfaglige Vikingesymposium*, Odense Universitet 1988 (Århus 1989).

35 Larsson (2007), 182.

36 E. Roesdahl, 'Om Olav Tryggvessons enestående skib og enestående idrætsfærdighed', in C. Paulsen and H.D. Michelsen (eds), *Símunarbok. Heiðursrit til Símun V. Arge á 60 ára degnum 5 September 2008* (Tórshavn 2008), 210–15.

37 J. Jesch, 'Literature in medieval Orkney', in O. Owen (ed.), *The World of Orkneyinga Saga* (Kirkwall 2005), 16.

38 S. Grundtvig (ed.), *Danmarks gamle Folkeviser*, II (Kjöbenhavn 1856), 434.

39 J. Lund, 'Vikingetidens værktøjskister i landskab og mytologi', *Fornvännen* 101 (2006), 323–41.

40 Larsson (2007), 379, 380.

41 Ibid., 379.

42 The great majority of boat or ship graves contain only a single person, but in a few cases several people have been found. In a newly discovered ship burial in Estonia, which has been dated to just before the Viking Age, there were as many as thirty-six individuals – men, obviously killed in battle.

43 M. Warming, 'Ibn Fadlan in the context of his age', in O. Crumlin-Pedersen and B. Munch Thye (eds), *The Ship as Symbol in Prehistoric and Medieval Scandinavia. Papers from an International Research Seminar at the Danish National Museum, Copenhagen, 5–7 May 1994* (Copenhagen 1995), 132 (Ibn Fadlan's text: 136).

44 Larsson (2007), 60–1.

45 A. Andrén, 'Doors to other worlds: Scandinavian death rituals in Gotlandic perspectives', *Journal of European Archaeology* 1 (1993), 33–56.

46 This very far-reaching interpretation, which also connects the word 'fred' (fridr) meaning peace with the fertility god Frey whose symbol is the ship, is referenced in Larsson (2007), 285 and 379.

47 See R. Coates, 'Reflections on some major Lincolnshire place-names, Part Two: Ness wapentake to Yarborough', *Journal of the English Place-Name Society* 40 (2008), 35–95 at 41, 70 and 95, n. 3.

48 B.E. Crawford, 'The churches dedicated to St. Clement in medieval England: a hagio-geography of the seafarer's saint in 11th century North Europe', *Scripta Ecclesiastica Tome 1, Serie Supplementaire a Scrinium. Revue de Patrologie, d'Hagiographie Critique et d'Histoire Ecclesiastique* (St Petersburg 2008).

Roskilde 6

1 J. Bill, M. Gøthche and H.M. Myrhøj, *Nordeuropas største skibsfund. Skibskirkegård under museumsøen i Roskilde* (Roskilde 1998), 136–58.

2 N. Bonde and F.-A. Stylegar, *Roskilde 6 – et langskib fra Norge. Proveniens og alder, KUML* (2011), 253–5.

3 As reconstructed for the exhibition by naval architect Morten Gøthche, who also directed the excavation of the ship.

4 J. Bill, M. Gøthche and H.M. Myrhøj, 'Roskildeskibene', in T. Christensen and M. Andersen (eds), *Civitas Roscald – fra byens begyndelse* (Roskilde 2000), 215–24.

5 O. Crumlin-Pedersen, *Viking-Age Ships and Shipbuilding in Hedeby/Haithabu and Schleswig* (Schleswig and Roskilde 1997); O. Crumlin-Pedersen, O. Olsen, E. Bondesen, P. Jensen, A.H. Petersen and K. Strætkvern, *The Skuldelev Ships I. Topography, Archaeology, History, Conservation and Display* (Roskilde 2002).

6 J. Jesch, *Ships and Men in the Late Viking Age. The Vocabulary of Runic Inscriptions and Skaldic Verse* (Woodbridge 2001), 123–6.

7 N. Bonde and F.-A. Stylegar, *Roskilde 6 – et langskib fra Norge. Proveniens og alder, KUML* (2011), 251.

8 Bonde and Stylegar (2011), 255–8.

9 C. Krag, *Olav 2 Haraldsson Den Hellige – utdypning, Norsk biografisk leksikon* (2009).

10 C. Krag, *Magnus 1 Olavsson Den Gode – utdypning, Norsk biografisk leksikon* (2009), 11-8-2012a.

Conservation of Roskilde 6

1 K. Strætkvern, A. Hjelm Petersen, N. Pokupcic, I. Bojesen-Koefoed, A. Moesgaard and J. Bruun Jensen, 'If only ...! Experiences from the conservation of the world's longest Viking Age shipwreck for exhibition and travel', in the *13th ICOM-CC Working Group WOAM Conference Proceedings* (Istanbul 2013, forthcoming).

2 M. Gøthche and K. Strætkvern, 'Roskilde 6 – Reconstructing the longest warship find of the Viking Age', in B. van Tilburg (ed.), *Proceedings of the Thirteenth International Symposium on Boat and Ship Archaeology Amsterdam 2012*, ISBSA 13 (Amsterdam, forthcoming).

3 A. H. Petersen and K. Strætkvern, 'Til lands, til vands og i luften med – et vikingeskib på vandreudstilling', in I.A. Tank Bronken, S. Braovac, T.M. Olstad and A. Ørnhøi (eds), *Moving Collections; Consequences and Processes* (London 2012), 165–73.

Bibliography

Abels (1988)
R.P. Abels, *Lordship and military obligation in Anglo-Saxon England* (London 1988).

Abels (2003)
R. Abels, 'Alfred the Great, the *micel hæden here* and the Viking Threat' in Timothy Reuter (ed.), *Alfred the Great: Papers from the Eleventh-Centenary Conferences*, (Aldershot 2003), 265–80.

Abram (2011)
C. Abram, *Myths of the Pagan North: the Gods of the Northmen* (London 2011).

Abrams (2001)
L. Abrams, 'Edward the Elder's Danelaw', in N.J. Higham and D.H. Hill (eds) *Edward the Elder, 899–924* (London 2001), 128–43.

Ager and Williams (2010)
B. Ager, and G. Williams, *The Vale of York Hoard* (London 2010).

Aðalsteinsson (1978)
Jón Hnefill Aðalsteinsson, *Under the cloak: the acceptance of Christianity in Iceland with particular reference to the religious attitudes prevailing at the time* (Uppsala 1978).

Alkarp (2009)
M. Alkarp, *Det Gamla Uppsala: Berättelser och Metamorfoser* (Uppsala 2009).

Althoff (1987)
G. Althoff, 'Der friedens-, bündnis- und gemeinschaftsstiftende Charakter des Mahles im früheren Mittelalter', in I. Bitsch *et al.* (eds), *Essen und Trinken in Mittelalter und Neuzeit. Vorträge eines interdisziplinären Symposions vom 10.–13. Juni 1987 an der Justus-Liebig-Universität Giessen* (Sigmaringen 1987), 13–26.

Andersen (1995)
E. Andersen, 'Square sails of wool', in O. Olsen, J. Skamby Madsen and F. Rieck (eds), *Shipshape – Essays for Ole Crumlin-Pedersen* (Roskilde 1995).

Andersen (1996)
W. Andersen, *The Viking Fortress of Trelleborg* (Slagelse 1996).

Andersson (2003)
H. Andersson, 'Urbanisation', in K. Helle (ed.), *The Cambridge History of Scandinavia, I, Prehistory to 1520* (Cambridge 2003), 312–42.

Anderton (1999)
M. Anderton (ed.), *Anglo-Saxon Trading Centres: Beyond the Emporia*, (Glasgow 1999).

Andrén (1993)
A. Andrén, 'Doors to other worlds: Scandinavian death rituals in Gotlandic perspectives', *Journal of European Archaeology* (1993) 1, 33–56.

Andrén, Jennbert and Raudvere (2004)
A. Andrén, K. Jennbert and C. Raudvere (eds), *Ordning mot Kaos. Studier av nordisk förkristen kosmologi* (Lund 2004).

Andrén, Jennbert and Raudvere (2006)
A. Andrén, K. Jennbert and C. Raudvere (eds), *Old Norse Religion in Long-Term Perspectives* (Lund 2006).

Andrén, Jennbert and Raudvere (2001–11)
A. Andrén, K. Jennbert and C. Raudvere (series eds), *Vägar till Midgård: Nordisk Hedendom i Långtidsperspektiv*, 14 vols (Lund 2001–11).

Androshchuk (2008)
F. Androshchuk, 'The Vikings in the east', in Brink with Price (2008), 517–42.

Angenendt (1984)
A. Angenendt, *Kaiserherrschaft und Königstaufe. Kaiser, Könige und Päpste als geistliche Patrone in der abendländischen Missionsgeschichte*, Arbeiten zur Frühmittelalterforschung 15 (Berlin and New York 1984), 215–17.

Anker (2012)
L. Anker, *The Norwegian Stave Churches* (Oslo 2012).

Archibald (2012)
M.M. Archibald, 'Testing', in J. A. Graham-Campbell (ed.), *The Cuerdale Hoard and Related Viking-Age Silver and Gold, from Britain and Ireland, in The British Museum*, British Museum Research Publication 185 (London 2012), 51–64.

Arcini (2005)
C. Arcini, 'The Vikings bare their filed teeth', *American Journal of Physical Anthropology* 128(4) (December 2005), 727–33.

Arents and Eisenschmidt (2010)
U. Arents and S. Eisenschmidt, *Die Gräber von Haithabu* (Neumünster 2010)

Armbruster and Eilbracht (2010)
B. Armbruster and H. Eilbracht (eds), *Wikingergold auf Hiddensee* (Rostock 2010), 184–95.

Asser (1983)
Asser, *Life of King Alfred* in S. Keynes and M. Lapidge (trans. and ed.), *Alfred the Great* (Harmondsworth 1983).

Baastrup (2009)
M. Panum Baastrup, 'Carolingian-Ottonian disc brooches – early Christian symbols in Viking age Denmark', in U. von Freeden, H. Friesinger and E. Wamers (eds), *Glaube, Kult und Herrschaft. Phänomene des Religiösen im 1. Jahrtausend n. Chr. in Mittel- und Nordeuropa* (Bonn 2009), 517–28.

Bäck, Hållans Stenholm and Ljung (2008)
M. Bäck, A M. Hållans Stenholm and J-Å. Ljung, *Lilla Ullevi – historien om det fridlysta rummet* (Stockholm 2008).

Back Danielsson (2007)
I-M. Back Danielsson, *Masking Moments: the Transitions of Bodies and Beings in Late Iron Age Scandinavia* (Stockholm 2007).

Bäcklund (2001)
J. Bäcklund, 'War or Peace? The Relations between the Picts and the Norse in Orkney', *Northern Studies* 36 (2001), 33–48.

Baker, Brookes and Reynolds (2013)
J. Baker, S. Brookes, A. Reynolds (eds), *Landscapes of Defence in Early Medieval Europe* (Turnhout 2013).

Balzer (1979)
M. Balzer, *Paderborn als karolingischer Pfalzort*, in *Deutsche Königspfalzen. Beitrage zu ihrer historischen und archäologischen Erforschung*, Bd. 3, Vol 3 *Veröffentlichungen des Max-Planck-Institutes für Geschichte* (Göttingen 1979) 11/3, 38f 9–85.

Banaszak and Tabaka (2008a)
D. Banaszak and A. Tabaka, 'Der Siedlungskomplex des mittelalterlichen Zentrums auf der Insel Ostrów Lednicki', in I. Boháčová and L. Poláček (eds), *Burg – Vorburg – Suburbium. Zur Problematik der Nebenareale frühmittelalterlicher Zentren* International Conferences in Mikulčice 7. Spisy Archeologického Ústavu Av Čr, Brno, v.v.i. 35 (Brno 2008), 81–2.

Banaszak and Tabaka (2008b)
D. Banaszak and A. Tabaka, 'Relikte der Handwerkstätigkeit im Hinterland der frühpiastischen Burg auf der Insel Ostrów Lednicki', in L. Poláček (ed.), *Das wirtschaftliche Hinterland der frühmittelalterlichen Zentren*. International Conferences in Mikulčice 6. Spisy Archeologického Ústavu Av Čr, Brno, v.v.i. 31 (Brno 2008), 111–15.

Barford (2005)
P.M. Barford, 'Silent Centuries. The Society and Economy of the Northwestern Slavs', in F. Curta (ed.), *East Central and Eastern Europe in the Early Middle Ages* (Ann Arbor 2005), 60–102.

Barnes (2003)
M. Barnes, 'Language and ethnic groups', in K. Helle, *Cambridge History of Scandinavia* (Cambridge 2003), 94–102.

Barrett (2008)
J.H. Barrett, 'The Norse in Scotland' in Brink with Price (2008), 411–427.

Bately (2007)
J. Bately (ed.), 'The source. Text and translation', in J. Bately and A. Englert (eds), *Ohthere's Voyages. A late 9th-century account of voyages along the coasts of Norway and Denmark and its cultural context*, Maritime Culture of the North 1 (Roskilde 2007), 40–50.

Bately (2009)
J. Bately, 'Wulfstan's voyage and his description of *Estland*: the text and the language of the text', in A. Englert and A. Trakadas (eds), *Wulfstan's Voyage. The Baltic Sea region in the early Viking Age as seen from shipboard*. Maritime Culture of the North 2 (Roskilde 2009), 15.

Bately and Englert (2007)
J. Bately and A. Englert (eds), *Ohthere's Voyages. A late 9th-century account of voyages along the coasts of Norway and Denmark and its cultural context*, Maritime Culture of the North 1 (Roskilde 2007).

Bauduin (2005)
P. Bauduin, *Les fondations scandinaves en Occident et les débuts du duché de Normandie. Colloque de Cheisy-la-Salle 2002* (Caen 2005).

Bek-Pedersen (2011)
K. Bek-Pedersen, *The Norns in Old Norse Mythology* (Edinburgh 2011).

Bellows (1936)
H.A. Bellows (trans.),*The Edda*, Voluspa 64 (Princeton 1936).

Biddle and Biddle (1992)
M. Biddle and B. Kjølbye-Biddle, 'Repton and the Vikings', *Antiquity* (1992) 66, 36–51.

Biddle and Biddle (2001)
M. Biddle and B. Kjølbye-Biddle, 'Repton and the 'great heathen army', 873–4', in J. Graham-Campbell, R.A. Hall, J. Jesch and D.N. Parsons (eds) *Vikings and the Danelaw: select papers from the proceedings of the thirteenth Viking Congress, 21–30 August 1997* (Oxford 2001), 45–96.

Bill (2008)
J. Bill, 'Viking ships and the sea', in Brink with Price (2008), 170–80

Bill and Daly (2012)
J. Bill and A. Daly, 'The plundering of the ship graves from Oseberg and Gokstad: an example of power politics?', *Antiquity* (2012), 86 (333), 808–24.

Bill et al. (1998)
J. Bill, M. Gøthche and H.M. Myrhøj, 'Nordeuropas største skibsfund', in *Ni vrag fra vikingetid og middelalder under museumsøen i Roskilde* (Arbejdsmark 1998), 136–58.

Bill et al. (2000)
J. Bill, M. Gøthche and H.M. Myrhøj, 'Roskildeskibene', in T. Christensen and M. Andersen (eds), *Civitas Roscald – fra byens begyndelse* (Roskilde 2000), 215–24.

Binding (1996)
G. Binding, *Deutsche Königspfalzen von Karl dem Grossen bis Friedrich II. (765–1240)* (Darmstadt 1996), 223–34.

Birkeland (1954)
H. Birkeland, *Nordens historie i middelalderen etter arabiske kilder*, Skrifter udgiven av Det Norske Videnskaps Akademi i Oslo. Hist.-filos. klasse, 1954:2 (Oslo 1954).

Blackburn (2007)
M.A.S. Blackburn, 'Coinage and Contacts in the North Atlantic during the seventh to mid-tenth centuries', in A. Mortensen and S.V. Arge (ed.), *Viking and Norse in the North Atlantic* (Tórshavn 2005), 141–51.

Blackburn (2011a)
M.A.S. Blackburn, 'The Viking Winter Camp at Torksey, 872–3', in M.A.S. Blackburn, *Viking Coinage and Currency in the British Isles* (London 2011), 221–64.

Blackburn (2011b)
M.A.S. Blackburn, *Viking Coinage and Currency in the British Isles*, Spink and Son (London 2011).

Blair (2005)
J. Blair, *The Church in Anglo-Saxon Society* (Oxford 2005).

Blair (2008)
J. Blair (ed.) *Waterways and Canal-Building in Medieval England* (Oxford 2008).

Blöndal and Benedikz (1978)
Sigfús Blöndal and B.S. Benedikz (1978), *The Varangians of Byzantium* (Cambridge 1978).

Bolton (2009)
T. Bolton, *The Empire of Cnut the Great: Conquest and the Consolidation of Power in Northern Europe in the Early Eleventh Century* (Leiden and Boston 2009).

Bonde (1990)
N. Bonde, 'Dendrokronologische Altersbestimmung des Schiffes von Nydam', *Offa* (1990) 47, 157–68.

Bonde (1995)
N. Bonde, 'Dendrochronological dating of the Viking age ship burials at Oseberg, Gokstad and Tune, Norway', in A. Sinclair, E. Slater and J. Gowlett (eds), *Archaeological Sciences* (Oxford 1995), 195–200.

Bonde and Stylegar (2009)
N. Bonde and F-A. Stylegar, 'Fra Avaldsnes til Oseberg. Dendrokronologiske undersøkelser av skipsgravene fra Storhaug og Grønhaug på Karmøy', *Viking* (2009), LXXII, 149–68.

Bonde and Stylegar (2011)
N. Bonde and F.-A. Stylegar, 'Roskilde 6 – et langskib fra Norge', *KUML* (2011), 247–62.

Bosworth *et al.* (1995)
C.E. Bosworth, E. van Donzell, W.P. Heinrichs and G. Lecomte (ed.), *The Encyclopedia of Islam, New Edition*, Vol. VIII, NED-SAM, (Leiden 1995), 618-29.

Bradley (1998)
J. Bradley (1988), 'The interpretation of Scandinavian settlement in Ireland' in J. Bradley (ed.), *Settlement and society in medieval Ireland* (Kilkenny 1988), 49–78.

Bradley (2009)
J. Bradley, 'Some reflections on the problem of Scandinavian settlement in the hinterland of Dublin in the ninth century', in J. Bradley, A.J. Fletcher and A. Simms (eds), *Dublin in the Medieval World. Studies in honour of Howard B. Clarke*, (Dublin 2009), 39–62.

Brather (2008)
S. Brather, *Archäologie der westlichen Slawen. Siedlung, Wirtschaft und Gesellschaft im früh- und hochmittelalterlichen Ostmitteleuropa*. Ergänzungsbände zum Reallexikon der Germanischen Altertumskunde 61 (Berlin 2008).

Brather (2001)
S. Brather, 'Polen sect. 3, Historisch-Archäologisches', in Hoops, *Reallexikon der Germanischen Altertumskunde*, vol. 23, 2nd edn (Berlin and New York 2001), 260.

Breuning-Madsen (2010)
H. Breuning-Madsen *et al.*, 'Brønden på toppen af Nordhøjen i Jelling', *Nationalmuseets Arbejdsmark* (2010), 192–203.

Breuning-Madsen et al. (2012)
H. Breuning-Madsen et al., 'The hydrology in huge burial mounds built of loamy tills: a case study on the genesis of perched water tables and a well in a Viking Age burial mound in Jelling, Denmark', *Geografisk Tidsskrift-Danish Journal of Geography* (2012), 112:1, 40–51.

Brink (1996)
S. Brink (ed.), *Jämtlands Kristnande* (Uppsala 1996).

Brink (2004)
S. Brink, 'Mytologiska rum och eskatologiska föreställningar i det vikingatida Norden', in Andrén, Jennbert and Raudvere (2004), 291–316.

Brink (2008)
S. Brink, 'People and land in Early Scandinavia', in I. Garipzanov, P. Geary and P. Urbańczyk (eds) *Franks, Northmen and Slavs: Identities and State Formation in Early Medieval Europe* (Turnhout, 2008), 87–112.

Brink with Price (2008)
S. Brink with N. Price (eds), *The Viking World* (London 2008).

Brockmann (1999)
J. Brockmann (ed.), *Studien und Quellen zur westfälischen Geschichte*, vol. 36, (Paderborn 1999).

Brøgger, Schetelig and Holmboe (1917)
A.W. Brøgger, H. Schetelig and J. Holmboe, *Osebergfunnet*, 1st edn (Kristiania 1917).

Brøgger and Schetelig (1953)
A.W. Brøgger and H. Schetelig, *The Viking Ships* (Oslo 1953).

Brook (2006)
K.A. Brook, *The Jews of Khazaria,* 2nd edition (Lanham MD 2006).

Brooks (1979)
N.P. Brooks, 'England in the Ninth Century: The Crucible of Defeat', *Transactions of the Royal Historical Society,* 5th ser., 29 (1979), 1–20.

Brunhölz (1881)
F. Brunhölz (ed. and trans.), *Karolus Magnus et Leo papa. Ein Paderborner Epos vom Jahre 799,* MGH Poetae 1, (Munich 1881) 367–79.

Buckland (2000)
P.C. Buckland, 'The North Atlantic Environment', in W. Fitzhugh and E.I. Ward, *Vikings: The North Atlantic Saga* (Washington and London 2000), 146–53.

Byock (2001)
J. Byock, *Viking Age Iceland* (Harmondsworth 2001).

Byock (2005)
J. Byock (tr.), *Snorri Sturluson – The Prose Edda* (London 2005).

Capelli et al. (2003)
C. Capelli *et al,* ,'A Y Chromosome Census of the British Isles', *Current Biology* 13, (May 27, 2003), 979–984.

Carlsson (1988)
A. Carlsson, *Vikingatida ringspännen från Gotland,* Stockholm Studies in Archaeology 8 (Stockholm 1988), 19–22.

von Carnap-Bornheim *et al.* (2009)
C. von Carnap-Bornheim, V. Hilberg, A. Radiņş and F. Schopper (eds), *Lettlands viele Völker. Archäologie der Eisenzeit von Christi Geburt bis zum Jahr 1200* (Zossen 2009).

Charles-Edwards (2013)
T.M. Charles-Edwards, *Wales and the Britons, 350-1064* (Oxford 2013).

Christensen and Nockert (2006)
A.E. Christensen and M. Nockert, *Osebergfunnet. Tekstilene* (Oslo 2006).

Clarke (1998)
H.B. Clarke, 'Proto-towns and towns in Ireland and Britain', in Clarke, Mhaonaigh and Ó Floinn (eds) *Ireland and Scandinavia in the Early Viking Age,* 331–80.

Clarke, Mhaonaigh and Ó Floinn (1998)
H.B. Clarke, M. Ní Mhaonaigh and R Ó Floinn (eds), *Ireland and Scandinavia in the Early Viking Age* (Dublin 1998).

Coates (2008)
R. Coates, 'Reflections on some major Lincolnshire place-names, Part Two: Ness wapentake to Yarborough', *Journal of the English Place-Name Society* (2008) 41, 57–102.

Cook and Williams (2006)
B. Cook and G. Williams (eds), *Coinage and History in the North Sea World, c. 500–1250. Essays in Honour of Marion Archibald* (Leiden and Boston 2006).

Coupland (1988)
S. Coupland, 'Dorestad in the ninth century: the numismatic evidence', Jaarboek voor Munt – en Peningkunde (1988), 75, 5–25.

Coupland (1995)
S. Coupland, 'The Vikings in Francia and Anglo-Saxon England to 911' in *The New Cambridge Mediaeval History* (Cambridge 1995), 190–201.

Coupland (1998)
S. Coupland, 'From Poachers to Gamekeepers: Scandinavian war lords and Carolingian kings', *Early Medieval Europe* (1998), 7.1, 85–114.

Coupland (1999)
S. Coupland, 'The Frankish tribute payments to the Vikings and their consequences', Frankia (1999), 26(1), 57–75.

Coupland (2002)
S. Coupland, 'Trading places: Quentovic and Dorestad reassessed', in *Early Medieval Europe* (2002), 11.3, 209–32.

Clunies-Ross (2010)
M. Clunies Ross, *The Cambridge Introduction to the Old Norse-Icelandic Saga* (Cambridge 2010).

Crawford (2007)
B. Crawford, *Scandinavian Scotland* (Leicester 2007).

Crawford (2008)
B.E. Crawford, 'The Churches Dedicated to St. Clement in Medieval England: A Hagio-Geography of the Seafarer's Saint in 11th century North Europe', Scripta Ecclesiastica Tome 1, Serie Supplementaire a Scrinium. Revue de Patrologie, d'Hagiographie Critique et d'Histoire Ecclesiastique (St Petersborg 2008).

Ó Cróinin (1995)
D. Ó Cróinin, *Early Medieval Ireland, 400-1200* (London and New York 1995).

Crumlin-Pedersen (1997)
O. Crumlin-Pedersen, *Viking-Age Ships and Shipbuilding in Hedeby/Haithabu and Schleswig* (Schleswig and Roskilde 1997).

Crumlin-Pedersen (2002)
O. Crumlin-Pedersen, 'Splendour versus duty – 11th century warships in the light of history and archaeology' in Nørgård Jørgensen, Pind, Jørgensen and Clausen (2002), 257–270.

Crumlin-Pedersen and Olsen (2002)
O. Crumlin-Pedersen and O. Olsen (eds), *The Skuldelev Ships I. Topography, Archaeology, History, Conservation and Display.Ships and Boats of the North 4.1* (Roskilde 2002).

Curta (2005)
F. Curta (ed.), *East Central and Eastern Europe in the Early Middle Ages* (Ann Arbor 2005).

Curta and Kovalev (2008)
F. Curta and R. Kovalev, *The other Europe in the Middle Ages: Avars, Bulgars, Khazars, and Cumans* (Leiden and Boston 2008).

D'Amato (2012)
R. D'Amato, *The Varangian Guard 988–1453,* (Oxford 2012).

Dapper (2002)
M. Dapper, *Die ottonische Pfalz Tilleda* in *Die Ottonen* (Petersberg 2002), 266.

Dapper (2007)
M. Dapper, *Die Neuinterpretation der Grabungsergebnisse der Pfalz Tilleda,* in C. Ehlers, J. Jarnut and M. Wemhoff (eds), *Zentren herrschaftlicher Repräsentation im Hochmittelalter. Geschichte, Architektur und Zeremoniell. Deutsche Königspfalzen. Beiträge zu ihrer historischen und archäologischen Erforschung 7, Veröffentlichungen des Max-Planck-Institutes für Geschichte* (Göttingen 2007) 11/7, 151–69.

Dass (2007)
N. Dass (trans. and ed.), *Viking Attacks on Paris – The 'Bella Parisiace Urbis'* (Louvain 2007).

Davidson (1972)
H. Ellis Davidson, *The Battle God of the Vikings* (York 1972), 26.

Davies (2007)
W. Davies, *Wales in the Early Middle Ages* (Leicester 1982).

Dengsø Jessen (2012)
M. Dengsø Jessen, 'The Hall and the Church during Christianization', in N. Johannsen et al. (2012), 133–60.

Dillmann (2006)
F. X. Dillmann, *Les magiciens dans l'Islande ancienne* (Uppsala 2006).

Dobat (2009)
A.S. Dobat, 'The State and The Strangers: The role of external forces in a process of state formation in Viking-Age South Scandinavia (*c.* AD 900–1050)', *Viking and Medieval Scandinavia* (2009) 5, 65–104.

Downham (2007)
C. Downham, *Viking Kings of Britain and Ireland. The Dynasty of Ívarr to A.D. 1014* (Edinburgh 2007).

Downham (2009)
C.E. Downham, 'Hiberno-Norwegians' and 'Anglo-Danes': anachronistic ethnicities and Viking-Age England', *Mediaeval Scandinavia* (2009) 19, 139–69.

Dulinicz (2002)
M. Dulinicz, 'Forschungen zu den Herrschaftszentren des 10. bis 11. Jahrhunderts in Polen', in Henning 2002, 147–60.

Duczko (2004)
W. Duczko, *Viking Rus. Studies on the Presence of Scandinavians in Eastern Europe*. The Northern World. North Europe and the Baltic *c*. 400–1700 AD. Peoples, Economies and Cultures Vol. 12 (Leiden and Boston 2004).

Edgren (2008)
T. Edgren, 'The Viking Age in Finland', in Brink with Price (2008), 470–84.

Eilbracht (2010)
H. Eilbracht, 'Von kurzer Dauer: zur Biografie des Goldschmucks', in Armbruster and Eilbracht (2010), 184–95.

Einhard (2008)
Einhard, *The Life of Charlemagne*, in L. Thorpe (ed. and trans.), *Einhard and Notker the Stammerer: Two Lives of Charlemagne* (Harmondsworth 2008).

Ellis Davidson (1976)
H.R. Ellis Davidson, *The Viking Road to Byzantium* (London 1976), 83–6.

Englert and Trakadas (2009)
A. Englert and A. Trakadas (eds) *Wulfstan's Voyage*, Maritime Cultures of the North 2 (Roskilde 2009).

Etchingham (2010)
C. Etchingham, 'Laithlinn, "Fair Foreigners" and "Dark Foreigners": the identity and provenance of Vikings in ninth-century Ireland', in J. Sheehan and D. Ó Corráin (eds), *The Viking Age: Ireland and the West. Proceedings of the Fifteenth Viking Congress* (Dublin, 2010), 80–9.

Ó Floinn (1998)
R. Ó Floinn, 'The Archaeology of the Early Viking Age in Ireland', in Howard B. Clarke et al. (eds) *Ireland and Scandinavia in the Early Viking Age* (Dublin 1998), 131–65.

Fellows-Jensen (2008)
G. Fellows-Jensen, ‚Scandinavian place-names in the British Isles', in Brink with Price (2008), 391–400.

Feveile (2008a)
C. Feveile, 'Ribe', in Brink with Price (2008), 126–30.

Feveile (2008b)
C. Feveile, 'Series X and Coin Circulation in Ribe', in T. Abramson, ed., *Two Decades of Discovery. Studies in Early Medieval Coinage* 1 (Woodbridge 2008).

Feveile and Jensen (2000)
C. Feveile and S. Jensen, 'Ribe in the 8th and 9th Century', in Stummann Hansen and Randsborg (2000), 9–24.

Fitzhugh and Ward (2000)
W. Fitzhugh and E.I. Ward, *Vikings: The North Atlantic Saga* (Washington and London 2000).

Foote and Wilson (1970)
P.G. Foote and D.M. Wilson, *The Viking Achievement: The society and culture of early medieval Scandinavia* (London 1970).

Frenzel and Ibsen (2010)
J. Frenzel and T. Ibsen, 'In search of the early medieval settlement of Wiskiauten/Mohovoe in the Kaliningrad Region'. *Lietuvos Archeologija* (2010) 36, 51.

Frye (2006)
R.N. Frye, *Ibn Fadlan's Journey to Russia. A Tenth-Century Traveler from Baghdad to the Volga River* (Princeton 2006).

Gai (1999)
S. Gai, *Karolingische Glasfunde der Pfalz Paderborn*, in C. Stiegemann and M. Wemhoff (eds), *799. Kunst und Kultur der Karolingerzeit. Karl der Große und Papst Leo III in Paderborn. Beiträge zum Katalog der Ausstellung* (Mainz 1999), accompanying book, 212–17, catalogue 160–9.

Gai (2004)
S. Gai, *Die Baugeschichte des Pfalzkomplexes*. Analyse und Deutung der stratigraphischen Befunde. Die Gründung der Paderborner Pfalz im Jahre 776, in S. Gai and B. Mecke, *Est locus insignis. Die Pfalz Karls des Großen und ihre bauliche Entwicklung bis zum Jahr 1002, Denkmalpflege und Forschung in Westfalen* 40 (Mainz 2004), 103–14.

Gai (2007)
S. Gai, *Zur Rekonstruktion und Zeitstellung der spätottonischen Pfalz in Paderborn*, in C. Ehlers, J. Jarnut and M. Wemhoff (eds), *Zentren herrschaftlicher Repräsentation im Hochmittelalter. Geschichte, Architektur und Zeremoniell. Deutsche Königspfalzen. Beiträge zu ihrer historischen und archäologischen Erforschung 7, Veröffentlichungen des Max-Planck-Institutes für Geschichte* (Göttingen 2007), 11/7, 121–50.

Garipzanov (2008)
I. Garipzanov, 'Frontier Identities: Carolingian Frontier and the Gens Danorum' I. Garipzanov, P. Geary and P. Urbańczyk (eds) *Franks, Northmen and Slavs: Identities and State Formation in Early Medieval Europe* (Turnhout, 2008), 113–144.

Garipzanov, Geary and Urbańczyk (2008)
I. Garipzanov, P. Geary and P. Urbańczyk (eds) *Franks, Northmen and Slavs: Identities and State Formation in Early Medieval Europe* (Turnhout, 2008).

Gelting (1999)
M.H. Gelting 'Det comparative perspektiv i dansk højmiddelalderforskning. Om familia og familie, lið, leding og landeværn', *Dansk Historisk Tidsskrift* 99.1 (1999), 146–88.

Golden (1995a)
P.B. Golden, 'Rus' in C.E. Bosworth, E. van Donzell, W.P. Heinrichs and G. Lecomte (ed.), *The Encyclopedia of Islam, New Edition*, Vol. VIII, NED-SAM, (Leiden 1995), 618–29.

Golden (1995b)
P.B. Golden, 'Pečenegs', in Bosworth, Donzell, Heinrichs and Lecomte (eds), *The Encyclopedia of Islam*, 289–91.

Golden, Ben-Shammai and Róna-Tas (2007)
P.B. Golden, H. Ben-Shammai and A. Róna-Tas (eds), *The World of the Khazars:New Perspectives* (Leiden and Boston 2007).

Górecki (2001a)
J. Górecki, 'Die Burg in Ostrów Lednicki ein frühstaatliches Zentrum der Piastendynastie', in A. Wieczorek and H.-M. Hinz (eds), *Europas Mitte um 1000*. Beiträge zur Geschichte, Kunst und Archäologie 1 (Stuttgart 2000), 470.

Górecki (2001b)
J. Górecki, 'Waffen und Reiterausrüstungen von Ostrów Lednicki. Zur Geschichte des frühen polnischen Staates und seines Heeres', *Zeitschrift für Archäologie des Mittelalters* (2001) 29, 42.

Gøthche and Strætkvern (forthcoming)
M. Gøthche and K. Strætkvern, 'Roskilde 6 – Reconstructing the longest warship find of the Viking Age', in B. van Tilburg (ed.), *Proceedings of the Thirteenth International Symposium on Boat and Ship Archaeology Amsterdam 2012*, ISBSA 13 (Amsterdam forthcoming).

Graham-Campbell (2012)
J. Graham-Campbell *The Cuerdale Hoard and Related Viking-Age Silver and Gold, from Britain and Ireland, in The British Museum*, British Museum Research Publication 185 (London 2012).

Graham-Campbell and Williams (2007)
J. Graham-Campbell and G. Williams (eds), *Silver Economy in the Viking Age* (Walnut Creek 2007).

Graham-Campbell, Sindbæk and Williams (2011)
J. Graham-Campbell, S.M. Sindbæk and G. Williams (eds), *Silver Economies, Monetisation and Society in Scandinavia, 800–1100* (Aarhus 2011).

Gräslund (2002)
A-S. Gräslund, *Runstensstudier* (Uppsala 2002).

Gregory (2009)
T.E. Gregory, *A History of Byzantium* , 2nd edition (Oxford 2009).

Grewe (2001)
H. Grewe, *Die Ausgrabungen in der Königspfalz Ingelheim* am Rhein, in L. Fenske, J. Jarnut and M. Wemhoff (eds), *Splendor palatii. Neue Forschungen zu Paderborn und anderen Pfalzen der Karolingerzeit. Deutsche Königspfalzen. Beiträge zu ihrer historischen und archäologischen Erforschung* vol. 5, *Veröffentlichungen des Max-Planck-Institutes für Geschichte* (Göttingen 2001) 11/5, 158.

Grothe (1999)
A. Grothe, *Zur karolingischen Keramik der Pfalz Paderborn*, in C. Stiegemann and M. Wemhoff (eds) *799. Kunst und Kultur der Karolingerzeit. Karl der Große und Papst Leo III. in Paderborn. Beiträge zum Katalog der Ausstellung* (Mainz 1999), accompanying book, 209–11, catalogue vol. 1, 144 f.

Grundtvig (1856)
S. Grundtvig (ed.), *Danmarks gamle Folkeviser*, II del (1856).

Gulløv (2000)
H.C. Gulløv, 'Natives and Norse in Greenland', in Fitzhugh and Ward, *Vikings: The North Atlantic Saga*, 318–26.

Gullbekk (2011)
S.H. Gullbekk, 'Norway: Commodity Money, Silver and Coins', in Graham-Campbell, Sindbæk and Williams (eds), *Silver Economies, Monetisation and Society*, 93–112.

Hägg (1991)
I. Hägg, 'Rangsymboliska element i vikingatida gravar. Hedeby – Birka – Mammen', in M. Iversen et al. (eds), *Mammen. Grav, kunst og samfund i vikingetid*. Jysk Arkæologisk Selskabs Skrifter 28 (Højbjerg 1991), 155–62.

Hall (2011)
R.A. Hall, 'Burhs and boroughs: Defended places, trade and towns. Plans, defences, civic features', in D. Hamerow, D.A. Hinton and S. Crawford (eds) *The Oxford Handbook of Anglo-Saxon Archaeology* (Oxford 2011), 600–21.

Halsall (1971)
G. Halsall, *Warfare and Society in the Barbarian West, 450-900* (London 2003).

Hamerow, Hinton and Crawford (2011)
D. Hamerow, D. A. Hinton and S. Crawford (eds) *The Oxford Handbook of Anglo-Saxon Archaeology* (Oxford 2011).

Hårdh (2007)
B. Hårdh, 'Oriental-Scandinavian contacts on the Volga, as manifested by silver rings and weight systems' in Graham-Campbell and Williams (eds) *Silver Economy in the Viking Age*, 135–48.

Hårdh (2008)
B. Hårdh, 'Hacksilver and ingots', in D. Skre (ed.) *Means of Exchange: Dealing with Silver in the Viking Age* (Oslo 2008), 95–118.

Hårdh (2011)
B. Hårdh, 'Viking-Age Silver from Hoards and Cultural Layers', in Graham-Campbell, Sindbæk and Williams (eds), *Silver Economies, Monetisation and Society*, 281–96.

Haywood (1991)
J. Haywood, *Dark Age Naval Power: A Reassessment of Frankish and Anglo-Saxon Seafaring Activity* (Abingdon 1991).

Hedeager Krag (1999)
A. Hedeager Krag, 'Fränkisch-byzantinische Trachteinflüsse in drei dänischen Grabfunden des 10. Jahrhunderts', *Archäologisches Korrespondenzblatt* (1999) 29, 425–44.

Hedeager (2011)
L. Hedeager, *Iron Age Myth and Materiality: an Archaeology of Scandinavia AD 400–1000* (London 2011).

Hedenstierna-Jonsson and Holmquist Olausson (2008)
C. Hedenstierna-Jonsson and L. Holmquist Olausson, *The Oriental Mounts from Birka's Garrison. An expression of warrior rank and status*, Antiquarian Archive 81 (Stockholm 2008).

Heeringen, Henderikx and Mars (1995)
R.M. Van Heeringen, P.A. Henderikx and A. Mars (eds), *Vroeg-Middeleeuwse ringwalburgen in Zeeland* (Goes and Amersfoort 1995).

Heide (2006)
E. Heide, *Gand, seid og åndevind* (Bergen 2006).

von Heijne (2012)
C. von Heijne, 'Danska mynt från tusentalet funna i St Peterskyrkan, Rom', in *Nordisk Numismatisk Unions Medlemsblad* (2012) 2, 46–8.

Helgason *et al.*(2001)
A. Helgason, E. Hickey, S. Goodacre, V. Bosnes, K. Stefánsson, R.Ward, and B.Sykes, 'mtDNA and the Islands of the North Atlantic: Estimating the Proportions of Norse and Gaelic Ancestry', *American Journal of Human Genetics* 68 (2001), 723–737.

Helle (2003)
K. Helle (ed.), *The Cambridge History of Scandinavia.* I. *Prehistory to 1520* (Cambridge 2003).

Henning (2002)
J. Henning (ed.), *Europa im 10. Jahrhundert. Archäologie einer Aufbruchszeit. Internationale Tagung in Vorbereitung der Ausstellung 'Otto der Grosse, Magdeburg und Europe'* (Mainz am Rhein 2002).

Herschend and Kaldal Mikkelsen (2003)
F. Herschend and D. Kaldal Mikkelsen, 'The main building at Borg', in Stamsø Munch et al. (2003), 41–76.

Hilberg (2007)
V. Hilberg, 'Silver Economies of the Ninth and Tenth Centuries AD in Hedeby', in Graham-Campbell, Sindbæk and Williams (eds), *Silver Economies, Monetisation and Society*, 203–2.

Hill (1981)
D. Hill, *An Atlas of Anglo-Saxon England* (Oxford 1981).

Hill and Rumble (1996)
D. Hill and A.R. Rumble (eds) *The Defence of Wessex: The Burghal Hidage and Anglo-Saxon fortifications* (Manchester 1996).

Historisches Museum der Pfalz Speyer (2008)
Historisches Museum der Pfalz Speyer (ed.), *Die Wikinger* (Munich 2008), 151.

Hodges (1982)
R. Hodges, *Dark Age Economics. The Origins of Towns and Trade A.D. 600–1000* (London: 1982).

Hodges (1988)
R. Hodges, *Primitive and Peasant Markets* (Oxford 1988)

Holand (2003)
I. Holand, 'Pottery' and 'Glass vessels', in G. Stamsø Munch et al. (2003), 199–229.

Holke (2009)
P. Holck, *Skjelettene fra Gokstad- og Osebergskipet*, no. 8 edn (Oslo 2009).

Hollander (1964)
L.M. Hollander (trans.), *Heimskringla. History of the Kings of Norway*, (Austin 1964).

Holman (1997)
K. Holman, 'Defining the Danelaw' in J. Graham-Campbell et al. (eds) *Vikings and the Danelaw: Papers from the Proceedings of the Thirteenth Viking Congress* (Oxford 1997), 1–11.

Holmberg and Skamby Madsen (1998)
B. Holmberg and J. Skamby Madsen, 'Da kom en snekke. Havnepladser fra 1000- og 1100-tallet', *KUML* (1998) 1997–8, 197–225.

Hougen (1934)
B. Hougen, 'Studier i Gokstadfunnet', *UOÅrbok* (1934) 5, 1931–2, 74–112, 94ff.

Hudson (1992)
B. Hudson, 'Cnut and the Scottish Kings,' *English Historical Review* 107 (1992), 350–60.

Ibsen (2007)
T. Ibsen, 'Wiskiauten – Bernstein aus dem Samland', *Archäologie in Deutschland* (2007) 5, 34–5.

Ingstad (1995)
A.S. Ingstad, 'The Interpretation of the Oseberg-find', in O. Crumlin-Pedersen and B. Munch Thye (eds), *The Ship as Symbol in Prehistoric and Medieval Scandinavia. Papers from an International Research Seminar at the Danish National Museum, Copenhagen, 5th–7th May 1994* (Copenhagen 1995), 139–47.

Jacobsson (1995)
B. Jacobsson, 'Utgrävningen av Borgen i Trelleborg, Skåne' in G. Fellows-Jensen and N. Lund (eds), *Fjortende Tværfaglige Vikingesymposium*, (Copenhagen: 1995), 12–22.

Jagodziński (2010)
M. Jagodziński, *Truso. Między Weonodlandem a Witlandem. Between Weonodland and Witland* (Elblag 2010).

Jankulak and Wooding (2007)
K. Jankulak and J. Wooding (eds), *Ireland and Wales in the Middle Ages* (Dublin 2007).

Jansson (1987)
S.B.F. Jansson, *Runes in Sweden* (Värnamo 1987).

Jensen (1995)
J.S. Jensen (ed.), *Tusindtallets Danke Mønter fra Den kongelige Mønt- og Medaillesamling. Danish coins from the 11th century in The Royal Collection of Coins and Medals* (Copenhagen 1995).

Jesch (2001)
J. Jesch, *Ships and Men in the Late Viking Age: the vocabulary of runic inscriptions and skaldic verse* (Woodbridge 2001).

Jesch (2002)
J. Jesch, 'Sea-battles in skaldic poetry', in Nørgård Jørgensen, Pind, Jørgensen and Clausen (2002), 57–64.

Jesch (2005)
J. Jesch, 'Literature in Medieval Orkney', in O. Owen (ed.), *The World of Orkneyinga Saga* (Kirkwall 2005), 11–24.

Johannsen, Jessen and Jensen (2012)
N.N. Johannsen, M.D. Jessen and H.J. Jensen (eds), *Excavating the Mind. Cross-sections through culture, cognition and materiality* (Aarhus 2012).

Jöns (1999)
H. Jöns, 'Was the Emporium of Reric the forerunner of Hedeby?', *Bodendenkmalpflege Mecklenburg-Vorpommern, Jahrbuch* (1999) 47, 201–13.

Jørgensen, L. (2003)
L. Jørgensen, 'Manor and Market at Lake Tissø in the Sixth to Eleventh Centuries: The Danish "Productive" Sites', in T. Pestell and K. Ulmschneider (eds), *Markets in Early Medieval Europe. Trading and 'Productive' Sites, 650–850* (Macclesfield 2003), 175–207.

Jørgensen, L (2009)
L. Jørgensen, 'Pre-Christian cult at aristocratic residences and settlement complexes in southern Scandinavia in the 3rd–10th centuries AD', in U. von Freeden, H. Friesinger and E. Wamers (eds), *Glaube, Kult und Herrschaft. Phänomene des Religiösen im 1. Jahrtausend n. Chr. in Mittel- und Nordeuropa*, Kolloquien zur Vor- und Frühgeschichte, vol. 12 (Frankfurt 2009), 329–54.

Jørgensen, Storgård and Thomsen (2003)
L. Jørgensen, B. Storgård and L.G. Thomsen (eds), *Sejrens Triumf. Norden i skyggen af det romerske Imperium* (Copenhagen 2003).

Kähler Holst *et al.* (2012)
M. Kähler Holst, M. Dengsø Jessen, S. Wulff Andersen and A. Pedersen, 'The Late Viking-Age Royal Constructions at Jelling, central Jutland, Denmark. Recent investigations and a suggestion for an interpretative revision', *Praehistorische Zeitschrift* 87(2) (2012), 474–504.

Kalmring (2010)
S. Kalmring, *Der Hafen von Haithabu* (Neumünster 2010).

Kennedy (2004)
H. Kennedy, *The Prophet and the Age of the Caliphates: The Islamic Near East from the 6th to the 11th Century (A History of the Near East)* (London 2004).

Kershaw (2013)
J. Kershaw, *Viking Identities: Scandinavian Jewellery in England* (Oxford 2013)

Kind (2002)
T. Kind, 'Archäologische Funde von Teilen der Reitausrüstung aus Europa und ihr Beitrag zur Kultur- und Sozialgeschichte der Ottonenzeit', in Henning (2002), 283–99.

Kleingärtner (2013)
S. Kleingärtner, *Die frühe Phase der Urbanisierung an der südlichen Ostseeküste im ersten nachchristlichen Jahrtausend.* Studien zur Siedlungsgeschichte und Archäologie der Ostseegebiete 13 (Neumünster 2013).

Kola and Wilke (2000)
A. Kola and G. Wilke, *Brücken vor 1000 Jahren. Unterwasserarchäologie bei der polnischen Herrscherpfalz Ostrów Lednicki* (Toruń 2000), 53.

Korpela (2008)
J. Korpela, *The World of Ladoga: Society, Trade, Transformation and State Building in the Eastern Fennoscandian Boreal Forest Zone, c. 1000–1555.* Nordische Geschichte 7 (Berlin 2008).

Krag (2008)
C. Krag, 'The creation of Norway', in Brink with Price (2008), 645–51.

Krag (2009a)
C. Krag, *Olav 2 Haraldsson Den Hellige – utdypning, Norsk biografisk leksikon* (Store norske leksikon 2009).

Krag (2009b)
C. Krag, *Magnus 1 Olavsson Den Gode – utdypning, Norsk biografisk leksikon* (Store norske leksikon 2009).

Krogh (2007)
K.J. Krogh, *Gåden om Kong Gorms Grav. Historien om Nordhøjen i Jelling. Vikingekongernes Monumenter i Jelling, bind 1* (Copenhagen 1993).

Krogh and Leth-Larsen (2007)
K.J. Krogh and B. Leth-Larsen, *Hedensk og Kristent. Fundene fra den kongelige gravhøj i Jelling. Vikingekongernes monumenter i Jelling, bind 2* (Copenhagen 2007).

Kurnatowska (2000)
Z. Kurnatowska, 'Herrschaftszentren und Herrschaftsorganisation', in A. Wieczorek and H.M. Hinz (eds), *Europas Mitte um 1000.* Beiträge zur Geschichte, Kunst und Archäologie 1 (Stuttgart 2000), 459, fig. 306.

Larrington (1996)
C. Larrington (tr.), *The Poetic Edda* (Oxford 1996).

Larsson (2004)
L. Larsson (ed.), *Continuity for Centuries: a Ceremonial Building and its Context at Uppåkra, Southern Sweden* (Lund 2004).

Larsson (2007)
G. Larsson, *Ship and society: maritime ideology in Late Iron Age Sweden* (Uppsala 2007).

Laurent (1978)
V. Laurent, *Berichte über die Ausgrabungen in Haithabu* (1978).

Lavelle (2010)
R. Lavelle, *Alfred's Wars: Sources and Interpretations of Anglo-Saxon Warfare in the Viking Age* (Woodbridge 2010).

Lawson (1993)
K. Lawson, *Cnut: The Danes in England in the Early Eleventh Century* (London and New York 1993).

Leyser (1993)
K. Leyser, 'Ritual, Zeremonie und Gestik: das ottonische Reich', *Frühmittelalterliche Studien* (1993) 27, 1–26.

Lidén (1969)
H-E. Lidén, 'From pagan sanctuary to Christian church. The excavation of Mære church in Trøndelag', *Norwegian Archaeological Review* (1969) 2, 3–32.

Lindkvist (1988)
T. Lindkvist, *Plundring, skatter och den feodala statens framväxt: organisatoriska tendenser i Sverige under övergången från vikingatid till tidig medeltid* (Uppsala, 1988).

Loe *et al.* (2014)
L. Loe, A. Boyle, H. Webb and D. Score, 'Given to the Ground': A Viking Age Mass Grave on Ridgeway Hill, Weymouth. DNHAS Monograph 22 (Oxford 2014).

Lönnroth (1997)
L. Lönnroth, 'The Vikings in History and Legend', in P. Sawyer (ed.) *The Oxford Illustrated History of the Vikings* (Oxford 1997), 225–249.

Lucas (2009)
G. Lucas, *Hofstaðir: Excavations of a Viking Age Feasting Hall in North-Eastern Iceland* (Reykjavík 2009).

Ludowici (2002)
B. Ludowici, *Die Halle des Königs. Repräsentative Profanarchitektur der ottonischen Pfalzen im Harzraum*, in K. Gereon Beuckers, J. Cramer and M. Imhof (eds), *Die Ottonen, Kunst-Architektur-Geschichte* (Petersberg 2002), 259–65.

Lund (2006)
J. Lund, 'Vikingetidens værktøjskister i landskab og mytologi', *Fornvännen* (2006) 101, 323–41.

Lund (2009)
J. Lund, *Åsted og vadested: deponeringer, genstandsbiografier og rumlig strukturering som kilde til vikingetidens kognitive landskaber* (Oslo 2009).

Lund (1985)
N. Lund, 'The armies of Swein Forkbeard and Cnut: *Leding* or *lið*?', *Anglo-Saxon England* (1985) 15, 105–18.

Lund (1994)
N. Lund, 'If the Vikings knew a Leding – What was it like?', in B. Ambrosiani and H. Clarke (eds), *Developments around the Baltic and the North Sea in the Viking Age.* Birka Studies 3 (Stockholm 1994), 98–105.

Lund (1996)
N. Lund, *Lið, leding og landeværn. Hær og samfund i Danmark i ældre middelalder* (Roskilde 1996).

Lund (2002)
N. Lund, 'If they neglect military service, they shall emend to the king – The Scutage in Danish Charters and Laws', in Nørgård Jørgensen, Pind, Jørgensen and Clausen (2002), 271–5.

Lund (2003)
N. Lund, 'Naval Power in the Viking Age and in High Medieval Denmark', in J.B. Hattendorf and R.W. Unger (eds), *War at Sea in the Middle Ages and Renaissance* (Woodbridge 2003), 25–34.

Lund (2006)
N. Lund, 'Leding, skaldekvad og bønder', *Historisk Tidsskrift* (2006) 106, 243–52.

Lunde and Stone (2012)
P. Lunde and C. Stone, *Ibn Fadlan and the Land of Darkness. Arab Travellers in the Far North*, (Harmondsworth 2012).

McCormick (2001)
M. McCormick, *Origins of the European Economy. Communications and Commerce AD 300–900* (Cambridge 2001).

Maixner (2010)
B. Maixner, *Haithabu. Fernhandelszentrum zwischen den Welten* (Schleswig 2010).

Makarov (2007)
N. A. Makarov, 'The land of the Beormas', in Bateley and Englert (eds) *Ohthere's Voyages*, 140-149.

Malmer (2007)
B. Malmer, 2007 'South Scandinavian Coinage in the Ninth Century', in Graham Campbell and Williams (eds) *Silver Economy in the Viking Age*, 13-27.

Malmros (2002)
R. Malmros, 'Leiđangr in Old Norse court poetry', in Nørgård Jørgensen, Pind, Jørgensen and Clausen (2002), 277–86.

Malmros (2010)
R. Malmros, *Vikingernes syn på militær og samfund. Belyst genmem skjaldenes fyrstedigtning* [with English Summaries] (Aarhus 2010).

Mango (2002)
C. Mango, *The Oxford History of Byzantium* (Oxford 2002).

Marcus (1980)
G.J. Marcus, *The Conquest of the North Atlantic* (Woodbridge 1980).

Meier (2002)
T. Meier, 'Magdeburg zwischen Aachen und Jelling: Repräsentationsarchitektur als semiotisches System', in Henning (2002), 311–22.

Mejsholm (2009)
C. Mejsholm, *Gränsland: Konstruktion av tidig barndom och begravningsritual vid tiden för kristnandet i Skandinavien* (Uppsala 2009)

Meulengracht Sørensen (1983)
P. Meulengracht Sørensen, *The Unmanly Man: Concepts of Sexual Defamation in Early Northern Society* (Odense 1983).

Metcalf (2006)
D.M. Metcalf,' Inflows of Anglo-Saxon and German coins into the Northern lands, *c.* 997–1024', in B. Cook and G. Williams (ed.), *Coinage and History in the North Sea World, c. 500–1250. Essays in Honour of Marion Archibald* (Leiden and Boston 2006), 349–88.

Mikkelsen (1998)
E. Mikkelsen, 'Islam and Scandinavia during the Viking Age', in E. Piltz (ed.), *Byzantium and Islam in Scandinavia. Acts of a Symposium at Uppsala University*, 15–16 June, 1996. Studies in Mediterranean Archaeology 126 (1998), 48–50.

Mikkelsen (2008)
E. Mikkelsen, 'The Vikings and Islam', in Brink with Price (2008), 543–9.

Miller (1990)
W.I. Miller, *Bloodtaking and Peacemaking: Feud, Law and Society in Saga Iceland* (Chicago and London 1990).

Mitchell (2011)
S.A. Mitchell, *Witchcraft and Magic in the Nordic Middle Ages* (Philadelphia 2011).

Moesgaard (2006)
J.C. Moesgaard, 'The import of English coins to the Northern Lands: some remarks on coin circulation in the Viking Age based on new evidence from Denmark', in Cook and Williams (eds), 389–434.

Moesgaard (2010)
J.C. Moesgaard, 'Skattefundene fra Gràgård og Pilhus. Harald Blåtands møntreform', in M. Andersen and P.O. Nielsen (eds), *Danefæ. Skatte fra den danske muld* (Copenhagen 2010), 187–91.

Moltke (1976)
E. Moltke, *Runes and their Origin. Denmark and Elsewhere* (Copenhagen 1976), 203.

Montgomery (2000)
J. Montgomery, 'Ibn Fadlān and the Rūsiyyah', *Journal of Arabic and Islamic Studies* (2000) 3, 1–25.

Montgomery (2008)
J. Montgomery, 'Arabic Sources on the Vikings', in Brink with Price (2008), 55–61.

von zur Mühlen (1975)
B. von zur Mühlen, 'Die Kultur der Wikinger in Ostpreußen', Bonner Hefte für Vorgeschichte 9 (Bonn 1975).

Müller-Wille (1970)
M. Müller-Wille, *Bestattung im Boot. Studien zu einer nord-europäischen Grabsitte* (Neumünster 1970).

Müller-Wille (1976)
M. Müller-Wille, *Das Bootkammergrab von Haithabu* (Schleswig-Holstein 1976).

Müller-Wille (2009)
M. Müller-Wille, 'Emporium Reric', in S. Brather, D. Geuenich and C. Huth (eds), *Historia Archaeologica. Festschrift für Heiko Steuer zum 70. Geburtstag.* Supplements to the Reallexikon der Germanischen Altertumskunde, vol. 70 (Berlin and New York 2009), 451–71.

Myhre (1998)
B. Myhre, 'The archaeology of the early Viking Age in Norway' in H.B. Clarke, M. Ní Mhaonaigh and R. Ó Floinn (eds) *Ireland and Scandinavia in the Early Viking Age* (Dublin 1998), 3–36.

Myhre (1992)
B. Myhre, 'Kronologispørsmålet og ynglingeættens gravplasser', in A.E. Christensen, A.S. Ingstad and B. Myhre (eds), *Osebergdronningens grav* (Oslo 1992), 272–8.

Myhre and Gansum (2003)
B. Myhre and T. Gansum, *Skibshaugen 900 e.Kr. Borrefunnet 1852–2002* (Vestfold 2003).

Näsström (1996)
B-M. Näsström, 'Offerlunden under Frösö kyrka', in Brink (1996), 65–85.

Näsström (2002)
B-M. Näsström, *Blot – Tro och Offer i Norden* (Stockholm 2002).

Nicolaysen (1882)
N. Nicolaysen, *Langskibet fra Gokstad ved Sandefjord – The Viking-Ship discovered at Gokstad in Norway* (Kristiania 1882).

Nielsen (2006)
A-L. Nielsen, 'Rituals and power: about a small building and animal bones from the late Iron Age', in Andrén, Jennbert and Raudvere (2006), 243–7.

Nilsson (1992–6)
B. Nilsson (series ed.), *Projektet Sveriges Kristnande*, 5 vols (Uppsala 1992–6).

Ní Mhaonaigh (1998)
M. Ní Mhaonaigh, 'Friend and Foe: Vikings in Ninth- and Tenth century Irish Literature', in H.B. Clarke, M. Ní Mhaonaigh and R. Ó Floinn (eds), *Ireland and Scandinavia in the Early Viking Age* (Dublin 1998), 381–402.

Noble (2009)
T.F.X. Noble (trans.), *Charlemagne and Louis the Pious. The Lives by Einhard, Notker, Ermoldus, Thegan, and the Astronomer* (University Park, PA 2009), Book 4.

Noonan (1994)
T.S. Noonan, 'The Vikings in the East. Coin and commerce', in B. Ambrosiani (ed.), *Development around the Baltic and the North Sea in the Viking Age.* Viking Congress 12. Birka Studies 3 (Stockholm 1994).

Noonan (1999)
T.S. Noonan, 'Scandinavians in European Russia' in P. Sawyer, *The Oxford Illustrated History of the Vikings*, 134–155.

Nørgaard, Roesdahl and Skovmand (1986)
F. Nørgaard, E. Roesdahl and R. Skovmand (ed.), *Aggersborg gennem 1000 år* (Herning: 1986).

Nørgård Jørgensen, (2002)
A. Nørgård Jørgensen, 'Naval Bases in Southern Scandinavia from the 7th to the 12th Century', in Nørgård Jørgensen, Pind, Jørgensen and Clausen (2002), 125–52.

Nørgård Jørgensen (2009)
A. Nørgård Jørgensen 'Harbours and trading centres on Bornholm, Öland and Gotland in the late 9th century', in Englert and Trakadas (eds) *Wulfstan's Voyage*, 145–150.

Nørgård Jørgensen *et al.* (2002)
A. Nørgård Jørgensen, J. Pind, L. Jørgensen and B. Clausen (eds), *Maritime Warfare in Northern Europe. Technology, organisation, logistics and administration 500 BC–1500 AD*. Papers from an international research seminar at the Danish National Museum, Copenhagen, 3–5 May 2000 (Copenhagen 2002).

Nørlund (1948)
P. Nørlund, *Trelleborg*. Nordiske Fortidsminder IV (Copenhagen 1948).

Norr (2008)
S. Norr, 'Old Gold – the Helmet in *Hákonarmál* as a Sign of its Time', in S. Norr (ed.) *Valsgärde Studies: the Place and People, Past and Present* (Uppsala 2008), 83–114.

Nylén and Lamm (2003)
E. Nylén and J.P. Lamm, *Bildstenar*, 3rd edn (Värnamo 2003).

O'Donoghue (2010)
H. O'Donoghue, *From Asgard to Valhalla* (London 2010).

Olsen (1966)
O. Olsen, *Hov, hørg og kirke* (Copenhagen 1966).

Olsen (1988)
O. Olsen, 'Royal power in Viking age Denmark', in H. Bekker-Nielsen and H. Frede Nielsen (eds), *Beretning fra Syvende Tværfaglige Vikingesymposium*, Odense Universitet 1988 (Århus 1989).

Olsen and Schmidt (1977)
O. Olsen and H. Schmidt, *Fyrkat. En jysk vikingeborg I. Borgen og bebyggelsen* (Copenhagen 1977).

Odess, Loring and Fitzhugh (2000)
D. Odess, S. Loring and W.W.Fitzhugh, '*Skræling:* First Peoples of Helluland, Markland and Vinland', in Fitzhugh and Ward, *Vikings: The North Atlantic Saga,* 193–206.

Page (1995a)
R.I. Page, *Chronicles of the Vikings* (London 1995).

Page (1995b)
R.I. Page, *Runes and Runic Inscriptions* (Woodbridge 1995).

Pálsson and Edwards (1976)
H. Pálsson and P. Edwards (trans.) with an introduction, *Egil's saga* (Harmondsworth 1976).

Pálsson and Edwards (1989)
H. Pálsson and P. Edwards, *Vikings in Russia: Yngvar's Saga and Eymund's Saga* (Edinburgh 1989).

Patton (2009)
K.C. Patton, *Religion of the Gods: Ritual, Paradox and Reflexivity* (Cambridge, Mass. 2009).

Pedersen (1997a)
A. Pedersen, 'Søllested and Møllemosegaard – burial customs in 10th century Denmark', in M. Müller-Wille (ed.), *Rom und Byzanz im Norden. Mission und Glaubenswechsel im Ostseeraum während des 8.-14. Jahrhunderts*, Bd. 1, Akademie der Wissenschaften und der Literatur, Abhandlungen der Geistes- und Sozialwissenschaften Klasse 1997, Nr. 3,I (Mainz 1997), 249–78.

Pedersen (1997b)
A. Pedersen, 'Weapons and riding gear in burials – evidence of military and social rank in 10th century Denmark' in A. Nørgård Jørgensen and B.L. Clausen (eds) *Military Aspects of Scandinavian Society in a European Perspective AD 1–1300* (Copenhagen 1997), 32–37.

Pedersen (2004)
A, Pedersen, 'Schwert', sect. 7, 'Carolingian and Viking Age', in Hoops, *Reallexikon der Germanischen Altertumskunde* (Berlin and New York 2004), vol. 27, 2nd edn, 593.

Pedersen, A. (2008)
A. Pedersen, 'Viking weaponry', in.Brink with Price (2008), 204–211.

Pedersen U. (2008)
U. Pedersen, 'Weights and balances', in Skre (ed.), *Means of Exchange: Dealing with Silver in the Viking Age*, 119–95

Peets (2013)
J. Peets, 'Salme Ship Burials', *Current World Archaeology* 58, April/May 2013, 18–24.

Pentz *et al.*(2009)
P. Pentz, M. B. Baastrup, S. Karg and U. Mannering, 'Kong Haralds vølve', Nationalmuseets Arbejdsmark, (København 2009) 215–32.

Pestell (2011)
'Markets, emporia, wics, and productive sites: pre-Viking trade centres in Anglo-Saxon England', in Hamerow, Hinton and Crawford (eds), *The Oxford Handbook of Anglo-Saxon Archaeology*, 556–79.

Petersen and Strætkvern (2012)
A.H. Petersen and K. Strætkvern, 'Til lands, til vands og i luften med – et vikingeskib på vandreudstilling', in I.A. Tank Bronken, S. Braovac, T.M. Olstad and A. Ørnhøi (eds), *Moving Collections; consequences and processes* (London 2012), NKF-N 2012, 165–73.

Pons-Sanz (2004)
S. Pons-Sanz, 'Whom did al-Ghazāl meet? An exchange of embassies between the Arabs from al-Andalus and the Vikings', *Saga Book* (2004) 28, 5–28.

Price, N. (2002)
N. Price, *The Viking Way: Religion and War in Late Iron Age Scandinavia* (Uppsala 2002).

Price, N. (2006)
N. Price, 'What's in a name? An identity crisis for the Norse gods (and some of their friends)', in Andrén, Jennbert and Raudvere (2006), 179–83.

Price, N. (2008a)
N. Price, 'Dying and the dead: Viking Age mortuary behaviour', in Brink with Price (2008), 257–73.

Price, N. (2008b)
N. Price, 'Bodylore and the archaeology of embedded religion: dramatic licence in the funerals of the Vikings', in Whitley and Hays-Gilpin (2008), 143–65.

Price, N. (2010)
N. Price, 'Passing into poetry: Viking-Age mortuary drama and the origins of Norse mythology', *Medieval Archaeology* (2010) 54, 123–56.

Price, N. (2012)
N. Price, 'Mythic acts: material narratives of the dead in Viking Age Scandinavia', in Raudvere and Schjødt (2012), 13–46.

Price, N. (forthcoming)
N. Price, 'Ship-men and slaughter-wolves: pirate polities in the Viking Age', in L. Müller and S. Amirell (eds), *Persistent piracy: historical perspectives on maritime violence and state formation* (Basingstoke, in press).

Price, T.D. *et al* (2011)
T.D. Price, K. M. Frei, A. S. Dobat, N. Lynnerup and P. Bennike, 'Who was in Harold Bluetooth's army? Strontium isotope investigation of the cemetery at the Viking Age fortress at Trelleborg, Denmark', *Antiquity* 85.328 (2011), 476–89.

Pullen-Appleby (2008)
J. Pullen-Appleby, *English Sea Power, c. 871 to 1100* (Hockwold-cum-Wilton 2008).

Raudvere and Schjødt (2012)
C. Raudvere and J-P. Schjødt (eds), *More Than Mythology: Narratives, Ritual Practices and Regional Distribution in pre-Christian Scandinavian Religions* (Lund 2012).

Redknap (2000)
M. Redknap, *Vikings in Wales. An Archaeological Quest* (Cardiff 2000).

Renaud (2008)
J. Renaud, 'The Duchy of Normandy' in Brink with Price (2008), 453–457.

Renaud (2009)
J. Renaud, *Vikings et noms de lieux de Normandie* (Bayeux 2009).

Reuter (1985)
T. Reuter, 'Plunder and Tribute in the Carolingian Empire', Transactions of the Royal Historical Society, Fifth Series (1985) 35, 75–94.

Reuter (1990)
T. Reuter, 'The End of Carolingian Military Expansion', in P. Godman and R. Collins (ed.) *Charlemagne's Heir: New Perspectives on the Reign of Louis the Pious (814–40)* (Oxford 1990), 391–405.

Reuter (1997)
T. Reuter, 'The recruitment of armies in the Early Middle Ages: what can we know?' in in A. Nørgård Jørgensen and B.L. Clausen (eds) *Military Aspects of Scandinavian Society in a European Perspective AD 1–1300* (Copenhagen 1997), 32–37.

Richards (2008)
J.D. Richards,'Viking Settlement in England' in Brink with Price (2008), 368–375.

Rieck (2002)
F. Rieck, 'The Iron Age Ships from Nydam. Age, Equipment and Capacity', in Jørgensen, Pind, Jørgensen and Clausen 2002, 73–81.

Rieck (2003)
F. Rieck, 'Skibene fra Nydam mose', in L. Jørgensen, B. Storgård and L.G. Thomsen (eds), *Sejrens Triumf. Norden i skyggen af det romerske Imperium* (Copenhagen 2003), 296–309.

Robinson, C.H. (1925)
C.H. Robinson (ed. and trans.), *Rimbert: Life of Anskar, the Apostle of the North, 801–865,* (London 1925).

Robinson, J. (2004)
J. Robinson, *The Lewis Chessmen* (London 2004), 43–55.

Rohrer (2009)
W. Rohrer, 'Wikinger oder Slawen? Die Interpretationsgeschichte frühpiastischer Bestattungen mit Waffenbeigabe', in A. Klammt and S. Rossignol (eds), *Mittelalterliche Eliten und Kulturtransfer östlich der Elbe. Interdisziplinäre Beiträge zu Archäologie und Geschichte im mittelalterlichen Ostmitteleuropa* (Göttingen 2009), 28–37.

Roesdahl (1977)
E. Roesdahl, *Fyrkat. En jysk vikingeborg*, Oldsagerne og gravpladsen, (Copenhagen 1977) II

Roesdahl (1982)
E. Roesdahl, *Viking Age Denmark* (London 1982).

Roesdahl (1985)
E. Roesdahl, 'Review of M. Müller-Wille, Das wikingerzeitliche Gräberfeld von Thumby-Bienebek (Kreis Rendsburg-Eckernförde). Teil I', *Zeitschrift für Archäologie des Mittelalters* (1985) 11/1983, 175–8.

Roesdahl (1998)
E. Roesdahl, 'Cammin – Bamberg – Prague – Léon. Four Scandinavian *Objects d'Art* in Europe', in Wesse (1998).

Roesdahl (2002)
E. Roesdahl, 'Harald Blauzahn – ein dänischer Wikingekönig aus archäologischer Sicht', in Henning 2002.

Rosedahl (2004)
E. Roesdahl, 'En gravplads fra tidlig kristen tid', in N. Lund (ed.), *Kristendommen i Danmark før 1050,* (Roskilde 2004), 153–8.

Roesdahl (2008)
E. Roesdahl, 'Om Olav Tryggvessons enestående skib og enestående idrætsfærdighed', in C. Paulsen and H.D. Michelsen (eds), *Símunarbok. Heiðursrit til Símun V. Arge á 60 ára degnum 5 September 2008* (Tórshavn 2008), 210–15.

Roesdahl (2011)
E. Roesdahl, 'Scandinavia in the Melting-pot, 950–1000', in S. Sigmundsson (ed.), *Viking Settlements and Viking Society. Papers from the Proceedings of the Sixteenth Viking Congress, Reykjavík and Reykholt, 16th-23rd August 2009* (Reykjavík 2011), 347–374.

Roland (1992)
Alex Roland, 'Secrecy, Technology, and War: Greek Fire and the Defense of Byzantium, 678–1204', *Technology and Culture* 33 (4), 1992, 655–679.

Róna-Tas (1999)
A. Róna-Tas, *Hungarians and Europe in the Early Middle Ages: An Introduction to Early Hungarian History* (Budapest 1999).

Røthe
G. Røthe, *Osebergfunnet: en religionshistorisk tolkning* (Oslo 1994).

Sanmark (2004)
A. Sanmark, *Power and Conversion: a Comparative Study of Christianization of Scandinavia* (Uppsala 2004).

Sawyer, B. (2000)
B. Sawyer, *The Viking Age Rune Stones* (Oxford 2000).

Sawyer, P.H. (1971)
P.H. Sawyer, *The Age of the Vikings*, 2nd edn (London 1971), 120–31.

Schilling (2003)
H. Schilling, '[illegible]', *Skalk* (2003), 6, 5–12.

Schledermann (2000)
P. Schledermann, 'East meets West', in Fitzhugh and Ward, *Vikings: The North Atlantic Saga*, 189–92.

Scholz (1972)
B.W. Scholz, *Carolingian Chronicles* (Ann Arbir 1972).

Schramm (1983)
P.E. Schramm, *Die deutschen Könige und Kaiser in den Bildern ihrer Zeit 751–1190*, 2nd edn (Munich 1983).

Schulze-Dörrlamm (2002)
M. Schulze-Dörrlamm, 'Die Ungarneinfälle des 10. Jahrhunderts im Spiegel archäologischer Funde', in Henning (2002), 107–22.

Scragg (1991)
D. Scragg, 'The battle of Maldon', in D, Scragg (ed.) *The Battle of Maldon, AD 991* (Oxford, 1991), 1–37.

Sheehan (2008)
Sheehan, J, 'The longphort in Viking age Ireland', *Acta Archaeologica* (2008) 79, 282–95.

Shepard (1995)
J. Shepard, 'The Rhos guests of Louis the Pious: whence and wherefore?', *Early Medieval Europe* (1995) 4, 41–60.

Shepard (2008)
J. Shepard, 'The Viking Rus and Byzantium', in Brink with Price (2008), 496–516.

Sigurðsson (2008)
G. Sigurðsson, 'The North Atlantic Expansion', in Brink with Price (2008), 562–70.

Simek (1993)
R. Simek, *Dictionary of Northern Mythology* (Cambridge 1993).

Sindbæk (2005)
S.M. Sindbæk, *Ruter og rutinisering. Fjernhandel i Nordeuropa* (Copenhagen 2005), 19.

Sindbæk (2010)
S.M. Sindbæk, 'Close ties and long-range relations: the emporia network in early Viking-Age exchange', in J. Sheehan and D. Ó Corráin (eds) *Ireland in the Viking* Age (Dublin 2010), 430–40.

Sindbæk (2011)
S.M. Sindbæk, 'Silver Economies and Social Ties: Long-Distance Interaction, Long-Term Investments – and why the Viking Age happened', in J. Graham-Campbell, S.M. Sindbæk and G. Williams (eds), *Silver Economies, Monetisation and Society in Scandinavia, 800–1100* (Aarhus 2011), 51–2.

Sjøvold (1974)
T. Sjøvold, *The Iron Age Settlement of Arctic Norway* (Tromsø 1974), 156.

Skre (2007)
D. Skre (ed.), *Kaupang in Skiringssal. Kaupang Excavation Project Publications Series Vol. 1* (Århus and Oslo 2007).

Skre (2008)
D. Skre (ed.), *Means of Exchange: Dealing with Silver in the Viking Age* (Oslo 2008).

Skre (2011)
D. Skre, 'Commodity Money, Silver and Coinage in Scandinavia', in Graham-Campbell, Sindbæk and Williams (eds), *Silver Economies, Monetisation and Society*, 67–92.

Smith (2001)
B. Smith, 'The Picts and the Martyrs, or Did Vikings kill the native population of Orkney and Shetland', *Northern Studies* 36 (2001), 7–32.

Solberg (1991)
B. Solberg, 'Weapon Export from the Continent to the Nordic Countries in the Carolingian Period', in *Studien zur Sachsenforschung* (1991) 7, 241–59.

Solli (2002)
B. Solli, *Seid. Myter, sjamanisme og kjønn i vikingenes tid* (Oslo 2002).

Sørensen (2001)
A.C. Sørensen, *Ladby, A Danish Ship-Grave from the Viking Age*. Ships and Boats of the North 3 (Roskilde 2001).

Sporrong (2003)
U. Sporrong, 'The Scandinavian Landscape and its Resources', in Helle (ed.), *The Cambridge History of Scandinavia.*, 15–42.

Stamsø Munch *et al.* (2003)
G. Stamsø Munch, O. Sverre Johansen and E. Roesdahl (eds), *Borg in Lofoten. A chieftain's farm in North Norway*, Arkeologisk Skriftserie 1 (Trondheim 2003).

Steuer (2007)
H. Steuer, 'Scales and weights', sect. 5, 'Carolingian and Viking Age', in *Hoops Reallexikon der Germanischen Altertumskunde* (Berlin and New York 2007), 35, 2nd edn, 571, fig. 77.

Steuer (2009)
H. Steuer, 'Principles of trade and exchange: trade goods and merchants', in A. Englert and A. Trakadas (eds), *Wulfstan's Voyage*, 294–308.

Stiegemann and Wemhoff (1999)
C. Stiegemann and M. Wemhoff (eds), *799 – Kunst und Kultur der Karolingerzeit 1-2. Karl der Große und Papst Leo III in Paderborn. Katalog der Ausstellung* (Mainz 1999).

Stokes and Strachan (1975)
W. Stokes and J. Strachan (eds and trans.), *Thesaurus Palaeohibernicus: A Collection of Old-Irish Glosses, Scholia, Prose, and Verse*, 2 vols (1901–3), repr. (Oxford 1975).

Strætkvern et al. (2013)
K. Strætkvern, A. Hjelm Petersen, N. Pokupcic, I. Bojesen-Koefoed, A. Moesgaard and J. Bruun Jensen, 'If only ...! Experiences from the conservation of the World's longest Viking Age shipwreck for exhibition and travel', in the 13th ICOM-CC Working Group WOAM Conference proceedings, Istanbul 2013 (forthcoming).

Stummann Hansen and Randsborg (2000)
S. Stummann Hansen and K. Randsborg (eds), *Vikings in the West*, Acta Archaeologica 71/Acta Archaeologica Supplementa II (Copenhagen 2000).

Sturtevant (2013)
P.B. Sturtevant, 'Contesting the semantics of Viking religion', *Viking and Medieval Scandinavia* (2013) 8.

Sundqvist (2009)
O. Sundqvist, 'The question of ancient Scandinavian cultic buildings with particular reference to Old Norse *hof*, *Temenos* 45/1 (2009), 65–84.

Sutherland (2000)
P.D. Sutherland, 'The Norse and Native Americans', in Fitzhugh and Ward, *Vikings: The North Atlantic Saga, 238*–47.

Sutherland (2008)
P.D. Sutherland, 'Norse and natives in the eastern Arctic', in Brink with Price (2008), 613–17.

Svanberg (2003)
F. Svanberg, *Decolonizing the Viking Age*, 2 vols (Stockholm 2003).

Swanton (1996)
M. Swanton (trans and ed.) *The Anglo-Saxon Chronicle* (London 1996).

Szameit (2001)
E. Szameit, 'Fränkische Reiter des 10. Jahrhunderts', in M. Puhle (ed.), *Otto der Grosse. Magdeburg und Europa*, Bd. II, *Katalog* (Mainz am Rhein 2001), 254–6

Thorpe (2008)
L. Thorpe (ed. and trans.), *Einhard and Notker the Stammerer: Two Lives of Charlemagne* (Harmondsworth 2008)

Tolley (2009)
C. Tolley, *Shamanism in Norse Myth and Magic*, 2 vols (Helsinki 2009).

Tolochko (2008)
O.P. Tolochko, 'The *Primary Chronicle*'s 'Ethnography' revisited: Slavs and Varangians in the Middle Dnieper Region and the Origin of the Rus' State', in Garipzanov et al. (eds) (2008), 169–88.

Townend (2002)
M. Townend, *Language and History in Viking Age England* (Turnhout 2002).

Trillmich (1957)
W. Trillmich (ed.), *Thietmar von Merseburg. Chronik.* Ausgewählte Quellen zur deutschen Geschichte des Mittelalters IX (Berlin 1957).

Tummuscheit (2011)
A. Tummuscheit, *Die Baubefunde des frühmittelalterlichen Seehandelsplatzes von Groß Strömkendorf, Lkr. Nordwestmecklenburg.* Early Mediaeval Archaeology between the Baltic and the Mediterranean 2. Research on Gross Strömkendorf 4 (Wiesbaden 2011).

Tyler (1999)
E.M. Tyler, '"The Eyes of the Beholders were Dazzled": Treasure and Artifice in *Encomium Emmae Reginae*', *Early Medieval Europe* (1999) 8/2, 247–70.

Tyler (2005)
E.M. Tyler, 'Talking about History in Eleventh-Century England: The *Encomium Emmae Reginae* and the Court of Harthacnut', *Early Medieval Europe* (2005) 13/4, 359–83.

Valtonen (2007a)
I.Valtonen,'Who were the Finnas?' in Bateley and Englert (eds) *Ohthere's Voyages*, 106–107.

Valtonen (2007a)
I.Valtonen, 'Who were the Cwenas?' in Bateley and Englert (eds) *Ohthere's Voyages*, 108–111.

Varenius (1988)
B. Varenius, *Han ägde bo och skeppslid : om rumslighet och relationer i vikingatid och medeltid* (Umeå 1988).

Varenius (2002)
B. Varenius, 'Maritime warfare as an organising principle in Scandinvian society 1000–1300 AD' in Nørgård Jørgensen, Pind, Jørgensen and Clausen (2002), 249–256.

Vierck (1984)
H. Vierck, 'Mittel- und westeuropäische Einwirkungen auf die Sachkultur von Haithabu/Schleswig', in H. Jankuhn *et al.* (eds), *Archäologische und naturwissenschaftliche Untersuchungen an ländlichen und frühstädtischen Siedlungen im deutschen Küstengebiet vom 5. Jahrhundert v. Chr. bis zum 11. Jahrhundert n. Chr. Band 2. Handelsplätze des frühen und hohen Mittelalters* (Weinheim 1984), 366–422.

Vikstrand (2001)
P. Vikstrand, *Gudarnas platser. Förkristna sakrala ortnamn I Mälardalen* (Uppsala 2001).

Vikstrand (2004)
P. Vikstrand, 'Berget, lunden och åkern. Om sakrala och kosmologiska landskab ur ortnamnens perspektiv', in A. Andrén *et al.* (eds), *Ordning mot kaos – studier av nordisk förkristen kosmologi* (Lund 2004), 317–41.

Vinner (1995)
M. Vinner, 'A Viking-ship off Cape Farewell 1984', in O. Olsen, J. Skamby Madsen and F. Rieck (eds), *Shipshape – Essays for Ole Crumlin-Pedersen* (Roskilde 1995), 289–304.

Waitz (1884)
G. Waitz (ed.), *Vita Anskarii auctore Rimberto*, MGH Scrip. rer. Germ. (Hannover 1884), chs 7–8.

Wallace (2008)
P.F. Wallace, 'Archaeological Evidence for the Different Expressions of Scandinavian Settlement in Ireland' in Brink with Price (2008), 434–438.

Wamers (1985)
E. Wamers, *Insularer Metallschmuck in wikingerzeitlichen Gräbern Nordeuropas. Untersuchungen zur skandinavischen Westexpansion,* Offa-Bücher 56 (Neumünster 1985).

Wamers (1991)
E. Wamers, 'Pyxides imaginatae. Zur Ikonographie und Funktion karolingischer Silberbecher', *Germania* (1991) 69, 97–152.

Wamers (1998)
'Insular Finds in Viking Age Scandinavia and the State Formation of Norway' in H.B. Clarke, M. Ní Mhaonaigh and R Ó Floinn (eds), *Ireland and Scandinavia in the Early Viking Age* (Dublin 1998).

Wamers (2000)
E. Wamers, '... ok Dani gærði kristna ... Der große Jellingstein im Spiegel ottonischer Kunst', *Frühmittelalterliche Studien* (2000) 34, 132–58, Taf. X–XVI.

Wamers (2002)
E. Wamers, 'The 9th century Danish Norwegian conflict: maritime warfare and state formation', in A. Nørgård Jørgensen, J. Pind, L. Jørgensen and B. L. Clausen (eds) *Maritime Warfare in Northern Europe: Technology, organisation, logistics and administration 500BC–1500AD* (Copenhagen 2002), 237–48.

Wamers (2005)
E. Wamers, 'Insignien der Macht. Das Schwert', in E. Wamers and M. Brandt, *Die Macht des Silbers. Karolingische Schätze im Norden* (Regensburg 2005), 54.

Warner (2001)
D.A. Warner (trans.), *Ottonian Germany. The Chronicon of Thietmar of Merseburg* (Manchester 2001).

Warnke (1992/3)
D. Warnke, 'Der Hort eines Edelmetallschmiedes aus der frühslawischen Siedlung Rostock-Dierkow', *Offa* (1992/93) 49/50, 197–206.

Warming (1995)
M. Warming, 'Ibn Fadlan in the Context of his Age', in O. Crumlin-Pedersen and B. Munch Thye (eds), *The ship as symbol in prehistoric and medieval Scandinavia.* Papers from an international research seminar at the Danish National Museum, Copenhagen, 5–7 May 1994 (Copenhagen 1995), 131–8.

Wendt (2007/2008)
A. Wendt, 'Viking age gold rings and the question of "Gefolgschaft"', *Lund Archaeological Review* (2007/2008) 13–14, 75–89.

Wesse (1998)
A. Wesse (ed.), *Studien zur Archäologie des Ostseeraumes von der Eisenzeit zum Mittelalter. Festschrift Michael Müller-Wille* (Neumünster 1998), 547–54.

Westerdahl (2002)
C. Westerdahl, 'The cognitive landscape of naval warfare and defence – Toponymic and archaeological aspects', in Nørgård Jørgensen, Pind, Jørgensen and Clausen 2002, 169–90.

Whitley and Hays-Gilpin (2008)
D.M. Whitley and K. Hays-Gilpin (eds), *Belief in the Past: Theoretical Approaches to the Archaeology of Religion* (Walnut Creek 2008).

Whitelock (1955)
D. Whitelock (ed. and trans.), *English Historical Documents* I, *c. 500–1042* (London 1955).

Wieczorek and Hinz (2000)
A. Wieczorek and H.-M. Hinz (eds), *Europas Mitte um 1000. Katalog* (Stuttgart 2000).

Willemsen and Kik (2010)
A. Willemsen and H. Kik, *Dorestad in an International Framework: new research on centres of trade and coinage in Carolingian times. Proceedings of the first 'Dorestad Congress' held at the National Museum of Antiquities in Leiden 2009* (Turnhout 2010).

Williams, A. (2009)
A. Williams, 'A Metallurgical Study of some Viking Swords', *Gladius* (2009) 29, 121–184.

Williams, G. (2001a)
G. Williams, 'Hákon *Aðalsteins fóstri*: Aspects of Anglo-Saxon Kingship in Tenth-Century Norway', in T.R. Liszka and L.E.M. Walker (eds), *The North Sea World in the Middle Ages* (Dublin 2001), 108–26.

Williams, G. (2001b)
G. Williams, 'Military Institutions and Royal Power, in M.P. Brown and C.A. Farr (eds) *Mercia: an Anglo-Saxon kingdom in Europe,* (London 2001), 295–309.

Williams, G. (2002)
G. Williams. 'Ship-levies in the Viking Age: the methodology of studying military institutions in a semi-historical society' in A. Nørgård Jørgensen, J. Lind, L. Jørgensen and B. Clausen (eds) *Maritime Warfare in Northern Europe. Technology, Organisation, Logistics and Administration 500 BC – 1500 AD* (Copenhagen 2002), 293–308.

Williams, G. (2005)
G. Williams, 'Military obligations and Mercian Supremacy in the eighth century', in D. Hill and M. Worthington (eds) *Æthelbald, Offa and Beonna,* BAR British Series 283 (Oxford: 2005), 101–110.

Williams, G. (2007)
G. Williams, 'Kingship, Christianity and coinage: monetary and political perspectives on silver economy in the Viking Age', in Graham-Campbell and Williams (2007), 177–214.

Williams, G. (2008)
G. Williams, 'Raiding and warfare', in Brink with Price 2008, 193–203.

Williams, G. (2009)
G. Williams, 'Hoards from the northern Danelaw from Cuerdale to the Vale of York', in J. Graham-Campbell, and R. Philpott, R (eds), 2009. *The Huxley Viking Hoard: Scandinavian settlement in the North West* (Liverpool 2009), 73–83.

Williams, G. (2011a)
G. Williams, *Treasures from Sutton Hoo* (London 2011), 20–21.

Williams, G. (2011b)
G. Williams, 'Silver Economies, Monetisation and Society: an Overview', in Graham-Campbell, Sindbæk and Williams (eds) *Silver Economies, Monetisation and Society* (Aarhus 2011), 337–372.

Williams, G. (2012)
G. Williams, 'Towns and minting in northern Europe in the early Middle ages', in F. Lopez Sanchez (ed.), *The City and the Coin in the Ancient and Early Medieval Worlds* (BAR International Series 2402, 2012), 149–60.

Williams, G. (2013a)
G. Williams, 'Towns and Identities in Viking England', in D.M. Hadley and L. Ten Harkel *Everyday Life in Viking Towns: Social Approaches to Viking Age Towns in Ireland and England, c. 850–1100* (Oxford 2013), 14–34.

Williams, G. (2013b)
G.Williams, 'Hack-silver and precious metal economies: a view from the Viking Age' in F. Hunter and K. Painter (eds), *Late Roman Silver: The Traprain Law Hoard in Context* (Edinburgh 2013), 381–94.

Winroth (2011)
A. Winroth, *The Conversion of Scandinavia: Vikings, Merchants and Missionaries in the Remaking of Northern Europe* (New Haven 2011).

Wintergerst (2007)
M. Wintergerst, *Franconofurd*, 1, *Die Befunde der karolingisch-ottonischen Pfalz aus den Frankfurter Altstadtgrabungen* 1953–1993. Schriften des Archäologischen Museums Frankfurt 22/1 (Frankfurt 2007), 46–60.

Woolf (2007)
A. Woolf, *From Pictland to Alba, 789–1070* (Edinburgh 2007).

Wulff (1865)
Wulff [first name unknown], 'Bericht über die Aufdeckung altpreußischer Begräbnisstätten bei dem zum Gute Bledau gehörigen Vorwerke Wiskiauten', Altpreußische Monatsschrift (1865) 2, 641–6.

Youngs (1989)
S. Youngs, *'The Work of Angels', Masterpieces of Celtic Metalwork, 6th–9th centuries AD* (London 1989).

Yorke (1990)
B. Yorke, *Kings and Kingdoms of Early Anglo-Saxon England* (London 1990).

Other sources

S. Toropov, 'Hoards of the Viking Age and Chance Finds of Scandinavian Artefacts in Novgorod Land: the Topography and Composition', Lecture at *Eastward and Westward: inter-ethnic contacts at the time of the formation of Rus' of Novgorod. Culture, Memory and Identity*, St. Petersburg and Novgorod, Russia, 21–24 July 2009.

Les Vikings en France, Dossiers d'Archéologie 277, October 2002.

geschichtsquellen.de/repPers_10094065X.html

www.wiskiauten.eu

List of lenders

The BRITISH MUSEUM
would like to thank all the lenders to the exhibition
for their generosity:

Archäologisches Landesmuseum, Stiftung Schleswig-Holsteinische Landesmuseen, Schloss Gottorf, Schleswig

British Library, London

Colchester and Ipswich Museum Service

Diocese of Sodor and Man, the Parish of the Northern Plain and Andreas Parish Church / Manx National Heritage

Dorset County Council / Oxford Archaeology, Oxford

Gotlands Museum, Visby

Govan Old Parish Church, Glasgow

Kulturhistorisches Museum der Hansestadt Stralsund, Stralsund

Landesamt für Kultur und Denkmalpflege Mecklenburg-Vorpommern, Schwerin

Museum für Vor- und Frühgeschichte, Staatliche Museen zu Berlin

Museum of Archaeology and History in Elblag

Museum of Cultural History, University of Oslo, Oslo

Museum of the First Piasts at Lednica, Lednogóra

National Museum of Denmark, Copenhagen

National Museum of Finland, Helsinki

National Museum of Ireland, Dublin

National Museums Scotland, Edinburgh

Novgorod State Museum, Novgorod

Roskilde Museum, Roskilde

St Andrew's Church, Middleton

State Historical Museum, Moscow

Treasure Trove system for Scotland

Tromsø University Museum, University of Tromsø The Artctic University of Norway, Tromsø

University Museum of Bergen, Bergen

List of exhibits

Each object or assemblage of objects (for instance a hoard or burial) is followed by the find spot, region and country, materials and principal dimensions, museum and registration number (where available) and fig number and page reference if illustrated in this catalogue. The list corresponds in most cases to the order of the exhibits at the British Museum showing.

Details correct at time of printing.

Measurements are given in cm, weights in grams.
L = length, H = height, W = width, Diam. = diameter.

Abbreviations of museums and loaning institutions:

ALM
Archäologisches Landesmuseum, Stiftung Schleswig-Holsteinische Landesmuseen, Schloss Gottorf, Schleswig

Bergen
University Museum of Bergen, Bergen

British Library
British Library, London

Dorset
Dorset County Council / Oxford Archaeology, Oxford

Elblag
Museum of Archaeology and History in Elblag

GF
Gotlands Museum, Visby

GIM
State Historical Museum (Gosudarstvennyi istoricheskii muzei), Moscow

Govan
Govan Old Parish Church, Glasgow

Ipswich
Colchester and Ipswich Museum Service

Lednica
Museum of the First Piasts at Lednica, Lednogóra

M-V
Landesamt für Kultur und Denkmalpflege Mecklenburg-Vorpommern, Schwerin

Manx
Diocese of Sodor and Man, the Parish Church of the Northern Plain and Andreas Parish Church / Manx National Heritage

Middleton
St Andrew's Church, Middleton

MVF
Museum für Vor- und Frühgeschichte, Staatliche Museen zu Berlin

NMD
National Museum of Denmark, Copenhagen

NMF
National Museum of Finland, Helsinki

NMI
National Museum of Ireland, Dublin

NMS
National Museums Scotland, Edinburgh

Novgorod
Novgorod State Museum, Novgorod

Roskilde
Roskilde Museum, Roskilde

Stralsund
Kulturhistorisches Museum der Hansestadt Stralsund, Stralsund

TTS
Treasure Trove system for Scotland

TrM
Tromsø University Museum, University of Tromsø The Artctic University of Norway, Tromsø

UOO
Museum of Cultural History, University of Oslo, Oslo

The Viking homelands

Brooch shaped like a ship, 800–1050.
Tjornehoj II, Fyn, Denmark.
Copper alloy. L 5.5 cm
NMD C37026
Fig. 11, p. 215

Hedeby coin with ship image, *c.* 825–850.
Hollenæs, Lolland, Denmark.
Silver. 0.85 g
NMD FP 5962.1
Fig. 6, p. 209

Model or toy boat, 800–1050.
Haithabu (Hedeby), Schleswig, Germany.
Alder wood. L 58 cm, W 7 cm
ALM KS D 595.038
Fig. 20, p. 226

Model or toy boat, 10th–11th century.
Fishamble Street, Dublin, Ireland.
Wood. L 31.5 cm, W 9 cm
NMI E172:15183
Fig. 19, p. 226

Vessel of Norwegian soapstone, 800–1050.
Hals, northern Jutland, Denmark.
Stone. Diam. 32 cm, H 18 cm
NMD C12529
Not illustrated

Female burial assemblage including a pair of oval brooches and a range of domestic items.
Grave I/1954, Hagbartsholmen, Steigen, Salten, northern Norway. Oval brooches 8.1 x 4.5 cm
Copper alloy, glass, soapstone, bone.
TrM Ts.5281a-b, h-I, m-n, q-r, v
Fig. 14, p. 134

Pin with dragon's head, 950–1000.
Haithabu (Hedeby), Schleswig, Germany.
Copper alloy. L 16.2 cm
ALM KS D 602.098
Fig. 29, p. 50

Double-edged sword, 10th century.
Lake Tissø, north-west Zealand, Denmark.
Iron, copper alloy. L 89 cm
NMD C8727
Not illustrated

Bearded axehead, 9th century.
Øverli, Lom, Oppland, Norway.
Iron. H 16 cm
BM 1891,1021.29
Fig. 18, p. 88

The Viking world

Carolingian disc brooch with equal-armed cross, 9th century.
Marne (region), France.
Copper alloy, enamel, gold. Diam. 3.1 cm
BM ML.4123
Not illustrated

Carolingian trefoil strap-mount, 9th century.
Rome, Italy.
Gilt silver. L 6.2 cm
BM 1847,0207.1
Not illustrated

Anglo-Saxon disc-brooch, 8th century.
Nassington, Northamptonshire, England.
Gilt silver. Diam. 4.1 cm
BM 2012,8034.1
Not illustrated

Anglo-Saxon mount from sword harness, 8th century.
Bawtry, South Yorkshire, England.
Gilt silver, niello. H 1.9 cm
BM 2000,0102.1
Not illustrated

Crozier ferrule (base of a crozier), 8th century.
Ireland.
Gilt copper alloy, amber. L 19.9 cm
NMI P.1019
Fig. 36, p. 53

Irish penannular brooch.
Near Strokestown, Co. Roscommon, Ireland.
Silver. L 24.3 cm
NMI 1939:404-5
Not illustrated

Openwork mount, 8th century.
Phoenix Park, Dublin, Ireland.
Gilt copper alloy. L 8.2 cm
NMI P.782.1
Not illustrated

Pictish brooch with interlaced ornamentation, 8th century.
Rogart, Sutherland, Scotland.
Silver. Diam. 7.7 cm, L 13.3 cm
NMS X.FC.1
Fig. 10, p. 38

Pair of hinge mounts with panels of Celtic interlace, later converted into brooches, 8th–11th century.
Carn a Bhorich, Oronsay, Argyll, Scotland.
Gilt copper alloy. L 7.6 cm
NMS X.FC 183-184
Not illustrated

Composite single-sided comb, complete.
Janów Pomorski/Truso, Poland.
Antler. W 17.1 cm, H 4.5 cm
Elblag MAH 200/2005
Not illustrated

Two handles, possibly for knives or tools.
Janów Pomorski/Truso, Poland.
Antler. L 1.8 cm, Diam. 1.5 cm; L 1.6 cm, Diam. 1.9 cm
Elblag MAH 738/2006; MAH 739/2006
Not illustrated

Two neck rings, two pairs of earrings and a pendant ornament, second half of 10th century.
Hoard, Tempelhof (Swiątki), Poland.
Silver. Neck rings. Diam. 19.0 and 13.2 cm; ear rings: H 6–6.6 cm; pendant: H 8.1 cm
MVF MM II 7278-7284
Not illustrated

Cross pin with chains, 10th–12th century.
Anduln (Zeipen-Görge)/ Ėgliškiai-Anduliai, Rajongem. Kretinga, Lithuania.
Copper alloy, silver. Pin L 38 cm; chains L 71 cm
MVF Ia 462c, Ia 641b
Fig. 13, p. 40

Penannular brooch, 11th or 12th century.
Oberhof/Aukdtkiemiai, Raj. Klaipėda, Lithuania.
Copper alloy. Diam. 5.2 cm
MVF PM OPM 19085
Not illustrated

Arm-ring with animal-head terminals, 10th–13th century.
Oberhof/Aukdtkiemiai, Raj. Klaipėda, Lithuania.
Copper alloy. Diam. 7.7 cm
MVF PM OPM 8256
Fig. 15, p. 40

Flask, 8th–9th century.
Byzantine.
Ivory. H 23 cm
BM 1856,0623.140
Fig. 23, p. 45

Panel depicting a hunting scene from a casket, 9th century.
Byzantine.
Ivory, wood. L 33 cm
BM 1885,0804.1
Not illustrated

Umayyad dirham, 693 (AH 74).
Minted in al-Andalus, Spain.
Silver. 3.82 g
BM 1846,0523.4
Not illustrated

Umayyad dirham, 733 (AH 115)
Minted in Balkh, Afghanistan.
Silver. 2.77 g
BM 1905,1012.7
Not illustrated

Abbasid dirham of Harun al Rahid, 801 (AH 185).
Minted in Madinat-al-Salam, Baghdad, Iraq.
Silver. 2.76 g
BM 1977,0202.25
Not illustrated

Abbasid dirham of Harun al Rahid, 802 (AH 186).
Minted in Balkh, Afghanistan.
Silver. 3.04 g
BM 1977,0202.10
Not illustrated

Abbasid dirham of al'Ma'mun, 814 (AH 199).
Minted in Samarkand, Uzbekistan.
Silver. 2.98 g
BM 1979,0404.22
Not illustrated

Abbasid dirham made in Merv, Turkmenistan, 815 (AH 200).
Minted in Merv, Turkmenistan.
Silver. 4.15 g
BM 1886,0406.37
Not illustrated

Abbasid dirham, 828 (AH 213).
Minted in Misr, Egypt.
Silver. 3.04 g
BM 1976,0208.2
Not illustrated

Limestone with carved Arabic inscription, 10th–11th century.
Hama, Syria.
Limestone, H 24.5 cm, L 25 cm
NMD A 7A527
Fig. 24, p. 46

Walrus skull piece with two tusks, recent.
Greenland.
Walrus bone, ivory. H 47 cm, W 19.5 cm
Private collection
Fig. 5, p. 34

Axehead, 11th–13th century.
Sandnæs (Kilaarsarfik), Nuuk, Sermersooq, Ruin group 64V2-III-511 (V51), Greenland.
Whale bone. L 13.9 cm
NMD D11706.222
Fig. 20, p. 43

Cultures in contact

Graffito of ship, 800–1050.
Winetavern Street, Dublin, Ireland.
Stone. H 31 cm, W 25.5 cm
NMI E81.2839b (replica)
Not illustrated

Graffito of ship, 800–1050.
Jarlshof, Shetland, Scotland.
Stone. H 6.9 cm, W 17.8 cm
NMS X.HSA 790
Not illustrated

Urnes style brooch, *c.* 1100.
Laschendorf, Lkr. Muritz, Germany.
Silver. H 5 cm, W 5 cm
M-V ALM 2005/460, 1
Not illustrated

Slate, decorated in Irish Urnes style, late 10th or early 11th century.
Killaloe, Co. Clare, Ireland.
Stone. L 8.9 cm, W 7.7 cm
BM 1858,0120.1
Fig. 1, p. 30

Berdal brooch and fragments, second half of 9th century.
Finglas, Co. Dublin, Ireland.
Gilt copper alloy. L 8.2 cm, W 6.1 cm
NMI 04E900:254:1-2
Not illustrated

Runic letter on birch bark, 12th century.
Smolensk, Russia.
Bark. L 13.2 cm
GIM 108043, 2648/1
Fig. 11, p. 25

Male burial assemblage with Scandinavian type sword and strap mounts, 9th century.
Jaroslavl, Mikhailovskoe, Russia.
Iron, gilt copper alloy.
GIM 41007, 1641
Not illustrated

Male burial assemblage with battle axe and 'oriental' belt fittings, 11th century.
Grave 3/1935, Barshalder, Grotlingbo, Gotland.
Iron, copper-alloy, fired clay.
GF C 8654:6-18
Not illustrated

East Baltic penannular brooch, 800–1050.
Rakkerbakken, Bornholm, Denmark.
Copper alloy. W 7.2 cm
NMD C33761
Not illustrated

Baltic type firesteel with a handle decorated with a pair of horsemen, 800–1050.
Gyldensgård, Bornholm, Denmark.
Copper alloy, iron. W 7.2 cm
NMD C36050
Fig. 14, p. 40

Pair of Slavonic headdress ('temple') rings, late 800–1050.
Bakkegard, Bornholm, Denmark.
Silver. 2.78 g and 3.85 g.
NMD Dnf. 57/97, 58/97
Fig. 12, p. 39

Denar from the Almoravid-kingdom, adapted as a brooch.
Schleswig, Germany.
Gold. Diam. 2.5 cm
ALM KS D 375.341
Not illustrated

Folded dirham with suspension ring, 10th century.
Grisebjerggård, Zealand, Denmark.
Silver. 0.85 g
NMD Dnf. 228/95
Fig. 3, p. 75

Necklace of beads and Islamic coins, 9th century.
Øster Halne Enge, Northern Jutland, Denmark.
Silver, stone, glass. Necklace Diam. 15 cm; coins Diam. *c.* 2 cm
NMD C5849, C5851, C5852
Not illustrated

Fragments of silk, probably late 10th–early 11th century.
Fishamble Street, Dublin, Ireland.
Silk. L 22 cm; L 19.5 cm
NMI E172:9498, E172:115566
Fig. 25, p. 47

Brooch with runic inscription, *c.* 700.
Hunterston, Ayrshire, Scotland.
Gold, silver, amber. Diam. 12.2 cm
NMS X.FC 8
Fig. 60, p. 67

Hoard of 'Hiberno-Scandinavian' Brooches, *c.* 900.
Flusco Pike, near Penrith, Cumbria, England.
Silver
BM 1991,0109.1, 3-6, 8
Fig. 59, p. 66

Trefoil brooch in the Borre style, first half of 10th century.
Bornholm.
Gilt copper alloy. L 7.3 cm
NMD C20248
Not illustrated

Frankish strap-end with an incised runic inscription (futhark), adapted for use as a brooch, 9th century.
Duesminde 4, Lolland, Denmark.
Silver-gilt with niello. L 7.1 cm, 88.61 g
NMD C35338
Not illustrated

Hogback stone from Glasgow, 10th Century.
Govan, Glasgow.
Stone, L198 cm, H 79cm, W 28cm
Govan
Not illustrated

Female burial assemblage: pair of oval brooches, trefoil brooch and knife, 10th century.
Grave 1, Ladby, Fyn, Denmark.
Gilt copper alloy, iron. Brooch L 10.5 cm; trefoil brooch 5.2 cm; knife L 17.3 cm
NMD C23035- C23038
Not illustrated

Female burial assemblage with a pair of oval brooches, ornaments and whalebone artefacts, second half of 9th century.
Tisnes, Tromsoysund, Nord Troms, Norway.
Copper alloy, bone, glass. Brooches 11 x 7 cm; copper alloy lid 22 cm; copper alloy chain 31.7 cm; bone comb 17 cm; bone cleaver (?) (carved whale-bone object) 12.1 x 9.4 cm; whale-bone weaving batten 84 x 5 cm; whale-bone plate L 39.5, W 28 cm
TrM Ts.791-803
Not illustrated

Pair of oval brooches, 9th century.
Inchicore north, Islandbridge, Dublin, Ireland.
Copper alloy.
NMD R.2420-1
Not illustrated

Female assemblage with oval brooches, pendant and bead necklace, first half of 10th century.
Bolšoe Timerevo, Obl. Jaroslavl, Russia.
Copper alloy, silver, glass, semi-precious stones, bone.
GIM 103949, 2366
Not illustrated

Female assemblage with oval brooches, 'temple' rings, necklace, brooch and pendant cross, second half of 10th century.
Grave 124, Kiev, Ukraine.
Copper alloy, silver, glass, semiprecious stones.
Brooches L 11.0 cm, necklace L 15.5 cm
GIM 33602, 1678/1-2, 4-6, 11-12
Oval brooches fig. 6, p. 23

Female burial assemblage with a pair of animal-head brooches, a round brooch, bead ensemble, buckle and chains.
Grave 218A, Ire, Hellvi, Gotland.
Iron, copper alloy, amber, shell, glass.
GF C 9322:165-176
Animal-head brooch fig. 3, p. 33

Female burial assemblage with a pair of round brooches, chain ornaments, equal-armed brooch, pendants, arm-rings and finger rings, 1050–1100.
Grave C23, Kjuloholm, Kjulo, Finland.
Silver, copper alloy, glass, carnelian.
NMF 8723: 292-294, 266, 302-314
Fig. 18, p. 41

International trade

Carolingian cup, 9th century, used as container for a hoard of hack-silver and coins, 10th century.
Vale of York, North Yorkshire, England.
Silver-gilt, gold, silver. Cup H 9.2 cm, Diam. 12 cm
BM 2009,8027.1–76, 2009.4133.77-693
Fig. 63, p. 69

Silver hoard with local jewellery and Jellinge style ornaments, pendant cross etc., 10th century.
Gnezdovo, Obl. Smolensk, Russia.
Silver.
GIM 108648, 2683
Not illustrated

Silver hoard with local jewellery and Borre-style pendants, 10th–11th century.
Lyuboyezha, Ilmensee region, Russia.
Silver.
Novgorod A 215/1 - 104
Fig. 62, p. 68

Raw amber.
Janów Pomorski/Truso, Poland.
Bead L 2.3 cm
Elblag MAH 737/2006, ME 1117/2663-1155/2701
Fig. 35, p. 52

Spindle whorl, 800–1050.
Scania, Sweden.
Amber. Diam. 3.0 cm
NMD S191
Not illustrated

Jet/lignite arm-ring fragment.
Lagore, Co. Meath, Ireland.
Stone.
NMI E14:1368
Not illustrated

Lignite finger ring, probably 10th–11th century.
Fishamble Street, Dublin, Ireland.
Stone. Diam. 2.3 cm
NMI E172:1964
Fig. 33, p. 52

Glass beads, 800–1050.
Groß Strömkendorf, Germany.
Glass
M-V NMW: 1997/87,412; 1997/87,256e,63; 1997/87,256,59; 1998/125,78,11; 1998/125,556,95; 1998/125,725,30; 1998/126,753d,1a-d; 1998/126, 843,4a-e; 1998/126,10226,105
Fig. 2, p. 161

Beads, 9th century.
Janów Pomorski/Truso, Poland.
Glass. Amber L 2.3 cm
Elblag MAH 1175/03, MAH 1183/03
Not illustrated

Glass, cornelian and rock crystal beads.
Janów Pomorski/Truso, Poland.
Glass, semi-precious stone.
Elblag MAH 192/2005, 549/2005, 293/2002, 43/2002, 52/90, 1723/2008, 4/K/2006, 1431/2008, 1523/2002, 1094/2008, 1616/2008, 1725/2002, 13/G/2006, 1052A/2008, 1177/2003, 1/K/2006, 1440/2008, 1246/2003, 810/2003, 370/90, 2/K/2006, 193/2005, 28/G/2006, 138/2005
Not illustrated

Rock crystal, cornelian and glass beads, 11th century.
Russia.
Stone, glass, silver, gold
NMD OA VIII h 31
Not illustrated

Gaming piece and rough-out, 800–1050.
Fishamble Street, Dublin, Ireland.
Whalebone. H 2.67 cm, Diam. 3.22 cm; H 3.37 cm, Diam. 4.04 cm
NMI E190:3837, E190:2516
Not illustrated

Whetstone, probably 9th–10th century.
Ireland.
Norwegian schist. L 9.3 cm, W 1.4 cm
NMI 1897.480
Fig. 32, p. 51

Incomplete vessel of Norwegian soapstone, 800–1050.
Hals, northern Jutland, Denmark.
Stone. Diam. 32 cm, H 18 cm; Diam. 38 cm, H 19 cm
NMD C12530
Not illustrated

Ankle shackle.
Parchim Löddigsee, Mecklenburg, Germany.
Iron.
M-V ALM LIII 13237.
Fig. 31, p. 51

Slave collar, *c.* 10th–12th century.
St John's Lane, Dublin, Ireland.
Iron. W 15 cm
NMI E173:X119
Fig. 30, p. 51

Transport vessel, 800–1050.
Haithabu (Hedeby), Schleswig, Germany.
Rhenish spruce. H 190 cm, Diam. 100 cm
ALM KS D 595.221
Not illustrated

Buying and selling

Male burial assemblage with folding scales, weights and a padlock, late 9th–10th century.
Grave 50, Kopparsvik, Visby, Gotland.
Iron, copper alloy
GF C 12675:50
Fig. 21, p. 179

Collapsible scales with box and two weights, 11th/12th century.
Rugard at Bergen, Rügen, Mecklenburg Vorpommern, Germany.
Copper alloy. H 38 cm (scales)
MVF II 5134-5136
Fig. 48, p. 58

Steelyard.
Truso, Poland.
Iron, lead. L 19.5 cm
Elblag MAH 1568/2008
Not illustrated

Five Islamic style polyhedral weights and an oblate spheroid (barrel) weight, *c.* 865–900
Yorkshire, England.
Copper alloy, lead. Diam 1.1 cm; H 0.85 cm; H 0.75 cm; H 0.6 cm; H 0.7 cm; H 1.4 cm
BM 2000,0201.2–5, 7; 2000,0206.6
Fig. 49, p. 59

Spheroid weights with pseudo-Arabic inscriptions, 800–1050.
Gedehaven, Møn; Skorrebro, Bornholm, Denmark.
Iron, copper alloy. 204.91 g, 137.69 g
NMD C31656, C37013
Not illustrated

Spheroid weights, 800–1050.
Neble, southwest Zealand, Denmark.
Copper alloy. Diam. 3.7 cm, 2.2 cm, 2.1 cm
NMD C30846, C30855-56
Not illustrated

Weight with pseudo-Arabic inscription.
Menzlin, Lkr. Ostvorpommern, Germany.
Copper alloy. Diam. 3 cm, H 2.5 cm
M-V ALM 1998/999,1
Not illustrated

Three polyhedral weights.
Bornholm/Norholm, Denmark.
Copper alloy.
NMD C33919, C33932, C34502
Not illustrated

Lead weight with inset fragment of insular metalwork, late 9th– early 10th century.
East Yorkshire, England.
Lead, copper alloy. L 1.37 cm, W 1.07 cm, 9.4 g
BM 2000,0101.3
Fig. 52, p. 59

Lead weight with enamelled top, late 9th–early 10th century.
East Yorkshire, England.
Lead, enamel. Diam. 1.24 cm, H 0.8 cm, 13 g
BM 2000,0101.2
Fig. 51, p. 59

Lead weights with coin insets, one with the lettering +DVDD/MON/ETA, *c.* 870–75 and 871–899.
England.
Lead, silver. Diam. 2.95 cm, 71.53 g; Diam. 2.2 cm, 10.6 g
BM 1991,0304.2, 2000,0201.1
Fig. 50, p. 59

Lead weight with inset fragment of insular metalwork, 9th century.
Selso-Vestby, Zealand, Denmark.
Lead, copper alloy. Diam. 3.26 cm, H 1.35 cm, 76.45 g
NMD C37134
Not illustrated

Lead weight with precious metal inset and animal head weight, late 9th century
Berg, Buskerud, Norway.
Lead, gold, silver, gilt copper alloy. L 4 cm, W 3.5 cm; L 3.4 cm, H 1.6 cm
NMD CMXXX, CMXXXI
Figs 7–8, p. 24

Animal head weight, 9th century.
Kilmainham-Islandbridge, Dublin, Ireland.
Lead, gilt copper alloy. L 3.28 cm, W 2.53 cm, H 2.24 cm
NMI R.2413
Fig. 9, p. 24

Nine identical imitations of Harun al Rashid 807/808 dirham, Baghdad.
Haithabu (Hedeby), Schleswig, Germany.
Tin/lead alloy. Diam. 2.2 cm
ALM KS D 604.003 011
Fig. 41, p. 55

Fragmented crucible with partly melted coin.
Janów Pomorski/Truso, Poland.
Fired clay, silver. L 4.3 cm, W 3.8 cm
Elblag MAH 1891/2007
Not illustrated

Mould for ingots.
Egholm, Agersø, Zealand, Denmark.
Soap stone. L 9 cm, W 7.2 cm, H 2.9 cm
NMD C7698
Not illustrated

Grivny of Kiev and Novgorod type.
Hoard, Mikhailovski monastery, Kiev, Ukraine.
Silver. L 6.9–8.2 cm, 152.2–162.28 g; L 11.5–13.5 cm, 194.3–197.34 g
GIM 49878, 1093/5-7; GIM 49878, 1093/56; GIM 49878, 1093/57
Not illustrated

Ingot.
Ireland.
Gold. L 5.34 cm, W 0.7 cm, 28.3 g
BM 1871,0401.13
Not illustrated

Ingot, probably 9th–11th century.
Askeaton, Co. Limerick, Ireland.
Gold. L 4 cm, W 1 cm
NMI 1929:1332
Fig. 45, p. 56

Hoard of three spiral arm-rings, 9th century.
Hoffmanslyst, East Jutland. Denmark.
Silver. Diam. 3.9 cm, 3.9 cm, 3.47 cm
NMD C1074-C1076
Fig. 55, p. 61

Hoard of three silver arm-rings.
Carrowmore or Glentogher, Co. Donegal, Ireland.
Silver. W 7.1 cm, 6.6 cm, 6.4 cm
NMI 1934:388-390
Not illustrated

Hiberno-Norse arm-ring and fragment, 9th century.
Nørre Alslev, Falster, Denmark.
Silver. Diam. 7.2 cm, L 19.8 cm; 50 g, 47 g
NMD Dnf. 6/13, 9/13
Not illustrated

Plain ring money, 10th/11th century.
Unknown provenance, Ireland.
Silver. Diam. 7.5 cm, 38.15 g
NMI 1888:8
Not illustrated

Five fragments of arm-rings, 997–1010.
Burray hoard, Orkney, Scotland.
Silver.
NMS X.IL 271
Not illustrated

Communicating power

Neck ring, 10th century.
Kalmergården, Tissø, Zealand, Denmark.
Gold. Diam. 35 cm
NMD Dnf. 1/77
Fig. 9, p. 129

Hoard of fourteen filigree pendants, spacers, brooch and neck-ring, late 10th century.
Neuendorf/Hiddensee, Rügen, Germany.
Gold.
Stralsund 1873:450, 499a-I, 1874:39a-b; 1874:39a-b, 91, 92, 162, 176
Fig. 12, p. 132

Seven filigree cross pendants, 10th century, part of 12th or 13th century hoard.
Mikhailovski monastery, Kiev, Ukraine.
Silver. H 4.0, W 3.6 cm
GIM 49876, 1091/20/1-7
Fig. 13, p. 132

Hoard of seven arm-rings and one fragment, 11th century.
Peenemünde, Usedom, Germany.
Gold. 390.1 g
Stralsund 1873:a-d,f-g,i, 450; 1874: 39 a-b, 91-92, 162, 176
Fig. 6, p. 128

Gold arm-ring, 9th or 10th century.
Sunderland, Tyne and Wear, England.
Gold. Diam. 7.6 cm
BM 1990,0606.1
Not illustrated

Arm-ring, deposited *c.* 970.
Ballaquayle, Isle of Man.
Gold. Diam 8 cm; 77.8 g
BM 1895, 0809.1
Not illustrated

Arm-ring, 876–950.
Eastbourne, England.
Gold. Diam. 7.3 cm, 82.3 g
BM 1990, 0707.1
Not illustrated

Plaited finger ring, 10th–11th century.
St Aldates Church, Oxford, Oxfordshire, England.
Gold. Diam. 2.6 cm , 12.9 g
BM 1905,1108.1
Fig. 19, p. 136

Finger ring, 10th–11th century.
Hamsey Churchyard, East Sussex, England.
Gold. Diam. 2.6 cm, 7.8 g
BM AF.537
Fig. 18, p. 136

Finger ring, 10th–11th century.
Richnal Green Farm, Essex, England.
Gold. Diam. 2.5 cm, 15.3 g
BM AF.536
Not illustrated

Finger ring, 10th–11th century.
Weston Turville, Buckinghamshire, England.
Gold. Diam. 2.4 cm, 5.5 g
BM 1922,1009.1
Fig. 20, p. 136

Finger ring, 10th–11th century.
West Bergolt, Essex, England.
Gold. Diam. 2.5 cm
BM 1870,0402.77
Not illustrated

Finger ring, 9th–11th century.
Harwich, England.
Gold. Diam. 2.5 cm, 11.6 g
BM 1871,0302.2
Not illustrated

Sword, late 8th–early 9th century.
Kalundborg or Holbæk, Zealand, Denmark.
Silver, iron. L 59.4 cm
NMD C3118
Fig. 37, p. 102

Sword with silver-inlaid guards, 9th century.
Near Kilmainham, Dublin, Ireland.
Iron, silver. L 56.8 cm, W 11.3 cm
NMI Wk5
Fig. 38, p. 102

Sword hilt, 9th century.
Eigg, Scotland.
Bronze, gilt silver, niello
NMS X. IL 157
Not illustrated

Silver-inlaid axehead in the Mammen style, 10th century.
Bjerringhøj, Mammen, Jutland, Denmark.
Iron, silver, brass. L 17.5 cm
NMD C133
Fig. 22, p. 137

Broad-bladed axe with gold inlay in the Ringerike style, 1000–1050.
Botnhamn, Lenvik, Troms, Norway.
Iron, gold. L 14.1 cm, H 14 cm
TrM Ts.11937
Fig. 2, p. 126

Female burial assemblage with a pair of oval brooches, trefoil brooch, arm-ring, glass bead, and knife, 10th century.
Grave 847, Lejre, Zealand, Denmark.
Gilt copper alloy, iron, glass, stone. Oval brooches L 11.3 cm W 7.4 cm, L 11.2cm W 7.5 cm; Treforil brooch Diam. 6.8 cm; Arm-ring L 8.5 cm W 5.9 cm H 0.5 cm; Knife L 12.8 cm; Bead Diam. 1.1 cm; Weight 3.6 cm, H 1.1 cm
NMD C30078-C30084
Not illustrated

Key handle in the Jellinge style, 10th century.
Steensgard, Zealand. Denmark.
Silver gilt. L 5.4 cm
NMD Dnf. 1/98
Not illustrated

Key, early 800–1050.
Tjørnehøj, Fyn, Denmark.
Copper alloy. L 6.4 cm
NMD C35193
Not illustrated

Key, Viking Age/early Medieval.
Tystrupgård, Zealand, Denmark.
Copper alloy. L 3.91 cm, W 1.99 cm
NMD C37188
Not illustrated

Ear spoon with filigree terminal and suspension ring, 10th century.
Gedehaven, south-west Zealand, Denmark.
Gold. L 5.4 cm; 7.67 g
NMD Dnf. 183/90
Fig. 34, p. 141

Chain with animal head terminals in the Jellinge style, 10th century.
Fæsted, west Jutland, Denmark.
Gold. L 62 cm; 67 g
NMD Dnf. 90/11
Fig. 33, p. 141

Chatelaine with ear spoon and nail cleaner in the Jellinge style, 10th century.
Terslev, Zealand, Denmark.
Silver. Ear spoon L 8.3 cm, nail cleaner L 10.6 cm
NMD Dnf. 33/11
Not illustrated

Penannular brooch with mask terminals and pinhead, 10th century.
Høm, Zealand, Denmark.
Copper alloy, gilt and tinned. L 11.9 cm, W 6.5 cm
NMD C6605
Not illustrated

Ball-penannular brooch with engraved terminals and pinhead, 10th century.
Skaill, Sandwick, Orkney.
Silver. L 36 cm. Diam. 20 cm
NMS X.IL 1
Fig. 29, p. 139

Ball-penannular brooch, Scandinavian workmanship, 10th century.
Gorodilovo, Vitebskaya Obl., Russia.
Silver, gold. L 12.9, Diam. 11.1 cm
GIM 77034, 376/55, ZV 5310
Fig. 27, p. 139

Ball-penannular brooch, 10th century.
Rønvika, Bodin, Salten, Norway.
Silver. Pin L 46 cm, Diam. 19.5 cm, 710 g
TrM Ts.2556
Fig. 28, p. 139

Ball-penannular brooch, 900–950.
Flusco Pike, near Penrith, Cumbria, England.
Silver. L 51.1 cm, Diam. 19 cm
BM 1909,0624.2
Not illustrated

Court culture in the Viking Age

Pair of knee-strap buckles and strap-ends, 900–950.
Grave 1058, Lejre, Zealand, Denmark.
Gilt copper alloy. Buckles L 4.3, 4.2 cm; strap-ends L 3.6, 3.5 cm
NMD C30138-41
Fig. 32, p. 140

Carolingian cup and set of small drinking vessels, 8th and 10th century.
Østerby, Fejø (north of Lolland), Denmark.
Silver. Large cup: H 9.6 cm, Diam. 9.6 cm; small cups Diam. up to 7.4 cm
NMD C1458, 1459
Fig. 43, p. 146

Bucket, 10th century.
Bjerringhøj, Mammen, Jutland, Denmark.
Oak. H 29.5 cm, Diam. 29 cm
NMD C154
Fig. 37, p. 142

Mounts for a drinking horn, 10th century.
Unknown provenance, Denmark.
Silver. Max. W 3.3 cm
NMD C24116
Fig. 38, p. 143

Decorated tray linked to Scandinavian tradition, 10th century.
Berlin-Spandau, Berlin, Germany.
Beech. L 47 cm, W 34 cm
MVF If 16215
Fig. 41, p. 144

Die, 800–1050.
Alaug, Furnas, Vang, Hedemarken, Norway.
Bone or possibly walrus ivory. L 3.4 cm, D 2.3 cm
NMD MCLXIX
Not illustrated

Set of 37 gaming pieces, 10th century.
Grave 74, Starigard/Oldenburg, East Holstein, Germany.
Copper alloy with silver, whale and walrus ivory, walrus bone. King's piece H 2.4 cm, Diam. 3 cm
ALM Old. 8 21 065 (1983)
Fig. 44, p. 147

Pair of spurs with strap fittings, 900–950.
Grave 21, Starigard/Oldenburg, East Holstein, Germany.
Copper alloy. Spurs L 14.5 cm, W 7.5 cm; Goad L 3.2 cm
ALM Old. 2 15 29; 2 15 30 (1974)
Fig. 46, p. 148

Pair of stirrups, 10th century.
Ravnholt, east Jutland, Denmark.
Iron, silver. H 25 cm
NMD C20606
Not illustrated

Pair of stirrups of eastern type, middle of 10th/11th century.
Vienhof, Kr. Labiau/Tjulenino, Kaliningradskaja Obl., Russia.
Iron. 12.4 x 12.4 cm; 12.4 x 11.7 cm
MVF PM V, 46, 6828, 15
Not illustrated

Hoard of harness fittings and bridle in the Borre style, 900–950.
Supruty, Upper Oka, Russia.
Iron, gilt copper alloy. Bridle 24.5 x 9.5 cm
GIM 2789
Fig. 47, p. 149

The Viking warship

Ship wreck No. 6, *c.* 1025.
Roskilde harbour, Zealand, Denmark.
Oak. L 3700 cm
NMD C38308
See pp. 228–31, 236–7

Carved fragment from ship wreck No. 6, *c.* 1025.
Roskilde harbour, Zealand, Denmark.
Oak. L 19.8 cm, B 8.6 cm, H 2.8 cm
Roskilde 1482x33
Fig. 1, p. 234

Stick with runes and carved bird's head, associated with Roskilde wreck 6, 1050–1100.
Roskilde harbour, Zealand, Denmark.
Wood, stone. L 46 cm
Roskilde 1482x196
Fig. 10, p. 25

Stepped stem post for a boat, 885–1035.
Laig, Isle of Eigg, Inverness-shire, Scotland.
Oak. L 193 cm, H 30 cm
NMS X.IN 4
Fig, 12, p. 217

Steering oar, 750–1000.
Hevring Flak, East Jutland, Denmark.
Oak. L 230 cm
NMD D268/2007
Not illustrated

Strake with oar port, late 12th century.
Wood Quay, Dublin, Ireland.
Wood. L 170 cm, W 29 cm
NMI TG4
Fig. 13, p. 217

Clinker nails, 9th–10th century.
Lilleberge, Namdalen Nord Trøndelag, Norway.
Iron. L *c.* 2.5 cm
BM 1891,1021.87
Not illustrated

Oars, first half of 9th century.
Oseberg, Norway.
Wood (fir), L 400 cm.
UOO C55000
Fig. 14, p. 218

Block/'maiden', 10th century.
Gokstad, Vestfold, Norway.
Wood. H 59 cm
UOO C10395
Not illustrated

The way of the warrior

Animal figure for a weather vane.
Lolland, Denmark.
Gilt copper alloy. L 9.7 cm
NMD D12128
Fig. 16, p. 220

Weather vane, 1000–1050.
Heggen Church, Buskerud, Norway.
Gilt copper, brass. L 28 cm, H 29 cm
UOO C23602
Fig. 15, p. 219

Stick with ship carvings, 13th century
Bergen, Norway
Wood. L *c.* 25 cm
Bergen
Illustrated on p. 7

Eyebrow ornament for a helmet, late Iron Age/Viking Age.
Gevninge, Zealand, Denmark.
Copper alloy, partially gilt. L. 8 cm, W 5 cm
Roskilde 1994 A124x1
Fig. 53, p. 109

Skull/jawbone showing decorative filing of teeth, *c.* 1000.
Near Weymouth, Dorset, England
Human bone
Dorset
Burial fig. 30, p. 95

Helmet with nose guard (replica), sword with inscription +VLFBERT+H on the blade, silver-inlaid spearhead and pieces of chain mail, 9th–11th century.
Ostrow Lednicki, Kr. Gniezno, Poland.
Iron, silver. Helmet H 18.5 cm, nose guard 6 cm; sword L 72.5 cm
Lednica K.50, MPP/A/31/33/84, MPP/A/93/112/99, MPP/A/93/93/99
Not illustrated

Decorated iron axe, 11th–13th century.
Teterow, Lkr. Ostvorpommern, Germany.
Iron, copper alloy. L 16 cm, W 15 cm
M-V ALM XVI, 15
Fig. 19, p. 88

Shield boss, 9th century.
Bolstad, Sogn og Fjordane, Norway.
Iron. Diam. 14 cm
BM 1891,1021.44
Fig. 22, p. 89

Male weapon burial with broad-bladed axe, late 10th–early 11th century.
Grave 222B, Ire, Hellvi, Gotland.
Iron, copper alloy, bone. Axe L *c.* 16 cm
GF C 9322:177-185
Fig. 25, p. 90

Male burial assemblage, 10th century:
sword with VLFBERH+T inscription, Scandinavian-type spearhead with damascened blade, Thor's hammer ring, and small tools.
Grave 4, Gnezdovo, Obl. Smolensk, Russia.
Iron, copper alloy. Sword L 98.5 cm, spearhead L 52.3 cm, ring L 15.3, W 15.9 cm
GIM 80135, 1071B/67-69, 1798B/66, 1071B/7, 1071B/64-66, 1071B/5
Figs 6–8, p. 81

Single-edged sword, 800–950.
Tude River, Hejninge, Zealand, Denmark.
Iron, brass. L 94.5 cm
NMD C24554
Not illustrated

Carolingian sword, 800–850.
Steinsvik, Tjeldsund, Nordland, Norway.
Iron, copper alloy, silver. Sword L 100.1 cm
UOO C20317a-c
Fig. 36, p. 102

Sword chape in the Borre style, 10th century.
Possibly Suffolk, England.
Copper alloy. L 5.8 cm, W 4.7 cm
BM 1997,0102.1
Fig. 48, p. 107

Sword chape with bird motif, 10th century.
Bjergene, Ballerup, Zealand, Denmark.
Copper alloy. L 9 cm, W 4.4 cm
NMD C34512
Fig. 50, p. 107

Sword chape in the Jellinge style, 10th century.
Selling Hedelod, Ødum, East Jutland, Denmark.
Copper alloy. L 9 cm, W 4.2 cm
NMD C16418
Fig. 49, p. 107

Sword chape in the Borre style, 10th century.
Unknown provenance, former East Prussia.
Copper alloy. H 6 cm, W 4 cm
MVF PM Pr 3370
Not illustrated

Sword chape with Borre style animal head, 10th century.
Korosten, Obl. Žitomir, Ukraine.
Copper alloy. L 7.3 cm
GIM 105009, 2575/1
Fig. 47, p. 107

Decorated axehead, late 11th–12th century.
Humikkala, Masku, Finland.
Iron, silver. L 15.3 cm, W 16.2 cm
NMF 8656:47:5
Fig. 23, p. 137

Inlaid axehead, 1000–1050.
Central Volga area (Kazan region), Russia.
Iron, gold, silver, niello. L 6 cm
GIM 34213, 1959/1
Fig. 20, p. 88

Broad-bladed axe, late 10th/early 11th century.
Ubberup, Ugerlose, Zealand, Denmark.
Iron. L 19.5 cm, W 18.3 cm
NMD C33110
Not illustrated

Axehead of eastern Baltic type, *c.* 950–1100.
Viehhof, Kr. Labiau/Tjulenino, Kaliningradskaja Obl., Russia.
Iron. L 15.5 cm, W 5.5 cm
MVF PM V, 167/169. 7970 14i
Fig. 9, p. 81

Axehead, late 10th–early 11th century.
Löbertshoff, Kr. Labiau/region of Slavjanskoe, Kaliningradskaja Obl., Russia.
Iron. L 24 cm, W 19 cm
MVF PM III, 72. 848,10
Fig. 10, p. 81

Pattern-welded spearhead, 10th century.
Near River Lodden/Twyford, Berkshire, England.
Iron. L 34.7 cm
BM 1955,0506.1
Fig. 51, p. 108

Spearhead, 1000–1050.
London, England.
Iron. L 58 cm
BM 1856,0701.1376
Fig. 41, p. 104

Pattern-welded spearhead, 9th–10th century
River Thames, England.
Iron. L 37 cm
BM 1868,0128.2
Fig. 52, p. 108

Spearhead with decorated socket, 800–1050.
Norway.
Iron, silver
UOO C5613
Not illustrated

Spearhead, 9th century.
Hverven, Ringerike, Buskerud, Norway.
Iron. L 36.6 cm
UOO C769
Not illustrated

Spearhead with silver-inlaid socket, 11th century.
Vilusenharju, Tampere, Upper Satakunta, Finland.
Iron, silver.
NMF 18556:595
Fig. 45, p. 106

Wooden longbow.
Haithabu (Hedeby), Schleswig, Germany.
Yew. L 191 cm
ALM KS D 595.223
Fig. 16, p. 87

Lanceolate (leaf-shaped) arrow-heads, 800–1050.
Sørup, Måløv, Zealand, Denmark.
Iron. L 9–12.5 cm
NMD C24551
Fig. 17, p. 87

Conical helmet, 10th century.
Černaya Mogila, Černigov, Ukraine.
Iron, gilt copper alloy. H 25.0 cm, Diam. 25.0 cm
GIM 76990, 1539/1
Fig. 44, p. 105

Sphero-conical helmet, 10th century.
Gul'Bishce, Černigov, Ukraine.
Iron, copper alloy. H 23.0 cm
GIM 76990, 1540/1
Not illustrated

Dress pin with horseman, 800–1050.
Gedehaven, Magleby, Zealand, Denmark.
Copper alloy. L 7.8 cm
NMD C33382
Not illustrated

Miniature armed horseman, 11th century.
Leissower Mühle / Lisów, Woj. Lubuskie, Poland.
Silver. H 3.5 cm, W 3.2 cm
MVF MM II 20427
Fig. 56, p. 110

Valkyrie figure, 9th century.
Wickham Market, Suffolk, England.
Silver. H 4 cm
Ipswich IPSMG R.2003-12
Fig. 3, p. 79

Valkyrie brooch, 9th century.
Galgebakken, Vrejlev, Vendsyssel, Denmark.
Silver. H 3.82 cm
NMD C37110
Fig. 2, p. 79

Valkyrie pendant, 800–1050.
Kalmergården, north-west Zealand, Denmark.
Silver with niello. H 2.7 cm, W 3.5 cm
NMD KN 855
Fig. 1, p. 116

Valkyrie brooch, 9th century.
Fugledegård/Bulbrogård, north-west Zealand, Denmark.
Copper alloy. H 3.5 cm
NMD FB 1004
Fig. 4, p. 79

Valkyrie figure, *c.* 800.
Hårby, Funen, Denmark.
Gilt copper alloy. H 3.4 cm
NMD
Fig. 3, p. 165

Shield-biting chessmen, *c.* 1150–1175.
Uig, Lewis, Scotland.
Walrus ivory, H 9.2, 8.5, 8.2 cm
BM 1831,1101.123-125
Fig. 27, p. 92

Circular Anglo-Irish mount, 8th–9th century.
Gamborg, Vindinge, Fyn, Denmark.
Gilt copper alloy. Diam. 3.25 cm
NMD C35420
Fig. 14, p. 85

Reliquary, Irish or Scottish, late 8th century.
Unknown provenance, Norway.
Gilt copper alloy, yew wood. H 10.3 cm, W 5.5 cm, L 13.5 cm
NMD 9084
Fig. 31, p. 97

Neck ring with runic inscription, 11th century.
Botnhamn, Lenvik, Troms, Norway.
Silver. Diam. 18 cm
TrM Ts.1649
Fig. 3, p. 126

Hoard of metal and weights, late 9th century.
North Yorkshire, England.
Silver, iron.
BM 2006,1203.1–14, 60, 104–11; 2008,4199.1–10
Fig 3, p. 121

Fragments of metal and weights, late 9th century.
North Yorkshire, England.
Gold, lead, copper alloy.
BM 2010,8014.1–3; 2008,4200.1–26
Fig. 2, p. 121

Silver hoard, selection, *c.* 905–10.
Cuerdale, Lancashire, England.
Silver.
BM 1838,0710; 1841,0711
Fig. 15, p. 86

Hoard of Æthelred II Long Cross pennies, *c.* 1000.
Tyskegård, Bornholm, Denmark.
Silver.
NMD FP395, FP5223, FP5447, FP6249
Fig. 35, p. 101

Skeletons from a mass grave, *c.* 1000
Nr Weymouth, Dorset, England
Human bone
Dorset
Fig. 30, p. 95

Wooden shield, late 9th century.
Gokstad, Vestfold, Norway.
White pine, metal. Diam. 94 cm
UOO C10390
Fig. 23, p. 89

Warriors to soldiers

Free-standing cross, 900–1000.
Middleton, England.
Stone, H 157.5 cm
St. Andrew's Church, Middleton
Fig. 26, p. 91

Male weapon burial: sword, shield boss, axe, spearheads, spurs, bridle, stirrups and soapstone vessel, 900–950.
Asak, Skedsmo, Akershus, Norway.
Iron, soapstone.
UOO C3786-3794
Fig. 57, p. 111

Double-edged sword with VLFBERHT blade, 10th century.
Norway.
Iron. L 90 cm
NMD 780
Not illustrated

Double-edged sword with VLFBERHT blade, Scandinavian type hilt, 10th century.
Schwedt, Brandenburg, Germany.
Iron, silver inlay. L 73.8 cm
MVF If 16773
Fig. 39, p. 103

Double-edged sword with VLFBERHT blade, 10th century.
Wiskiauten/Mochovoe, Rajon Zelenogradsk, Russia.
Iron, silver, copper. L 73 cm
MVF PM V, 145, 7746/1
Fig. 2, p. 73

Double-edged sword with VLFBERHT blade, 800–950.
Peltorinne, Hämeenlinna (Tavastehus), Häme, Finland.
Iron, copper, silver. L 91.6 cm
NMF 18402:1
Fig. 40, p. 103

Set of Frankish sword belt fittings: tongue-shaped strap-end, trefoil mount and three oval mounts, mid-9th century.
Duesminde, Lolland, Denmark.
Silver gilt and niello. L 9.1, 8.7, 5.3, 5.2, 6.2 cm
NMD C35316, C35318, C35342-3, C35361
Not illustrated

Axehead, 950–1050.
Hammersmith, River Thames, England.
Iron. L 21.5 cm, W 20.7 cm
BM 1909,0626.8
Fig. 58, p. 111

The emergence of kingdoms

Rune stone raised by King Harold Bluetooth, *c.* 965.
Jelling, Jutland, Denmark.
Stone. H 243 cm
NMD (replica)
Not illustrated

Bridge pile, *c.* 980
Ravning Enge, Denmark
Oak
NMD
Not illustrated

Athelstan II/Guthrum of East Anglia penny, *c.* 880–6).
Silver. Diam. 2.1 cm, 1.4 g
BM 1838,0710.8
Not illustrated

Sigeferth of Northumbria penny, *c.* 895–900.
Silver. Diam. 2 cm, 1.54 g
BM 1838.0710.1238
Not illustrated

Anlaf (Olaf) Guthfrithsson of Northumbria penny, 939–941.
Silver. Diam. 2 cm, 1.26 g
BM 1862.0930.1
Fig. 57, p. 154

Sihtric II Guthfrithsson of Northumbria penny, mid-940s.
Silver. 1.01 g
BM 1848.0819.169
Fig. 57, p. 154

Eric Bloodaxe of Northumbria penny, 952–4.
Silver. Diam. 2.1 cm, 1.24 g
BM E.5081
Fig. 57, p. 154

Coins of Prince Vladimir Sviatoslavovich (980–1015),
Mogilevskaya, Votnya, Russia.
Silver. Diam. 2.6, 2.7 cm
GIM 77012 111/1-2
Fig. 56, p. 154

Penny of Olaf Tryggvason (995–1000), *c.* 995.
Iholm Island, Denmark.
Silver. 1.07 g
NMD
Fig. 53, p. 153

Penny of Svein Forkbeard (987–1014), *c.* 995.
Unknown provenance.
Silver. 1.29 g
NMD BP 1021
Fig. 52, p. 153

Penny of Olof Skötkonung (995–1022), *c.* 995.
Unknown provenance.
Silver. Diam. 2.0 cm
NMD BP 34y
Fig. 54, p. 153

Sihtric III of Dublin penny, *c.* 995.
Silver. 1.59 g
BM 1957,0612.16
Not illustrated

Liber Vitae, 1031.
New Minster, Winchester, England.
Parchment, L 26 cm, W 15 cm
British Library, Stowe 944
Fig. 60, p. 155

Penny of Cnut (1016–35), Quatrefoil type.
Minted in Winchester.
Silver. 1.48 g
BM BMC II, p. 297, no. 566
Not illustrated

Penny of Cnut (1016–35), Pointed Helmet type.
Minted in Lincoln.
Silver. 1.11 g
BM 1950,0303.34
Not illustrated

Penny of Cnut (1016–35), Short Cross type.
Minted in Axbridge.
Silver. 1.26 g
BM 1850,0620.15
Not illustrated

Danish penny of Cnut (1016–35).
Minted in Lund.
Silver. 1.37 g
BM C1436
Not illustrated

Belief and ritual

Picture stone depicting a sailing ship, 8th century.
Broa, Halla parish, Gotland, Sweden.
Limestone. H 74 cm, W 48 cm
GF A 2089
Fig. 18, p. 224

Remains of boat burial, 10th century
Ardnamurchan, Scotland
Iron, copper alloy, wood. Size of boat *c.* 4.9 x 1.5 m
TTS
Not illustrated

Bent sword from weapon burial, 10th century.
Norderhaug, Loten, Hedmark, Norway.
Iron, silver. Blade L *c.* 70 cm, grip L 12.4 cm
UOO C22138a
Not illustrated

Sword with bent blade, 900–1050.
Löbertshof, Kr. Labiau / region of Slavjanskoe, Kaliningradskaja Obl., Russia.
Iron. L 84 cm, W 12.8 cm, H 13 cm
MVF PM III, 78. 848
Fig. 22, p. 180

Sword with rolled-up blade, 9th/10th century
Linkuhnen, Kr. Niederung, Rževskoe, Kaliningradskaja Obl., Russia.
Iron. L 15.5 cm (folded), W 17 cm, H 11 cm
MVF Pr 7431
Fig. 23, p. 181

Ritually 'killed' sword, 9th/10th century.
Near Kilmainham, Dublin, Ireland.
Iron. L 47.5 cm (folded)
NMI Wk10
Fig. 24, p. 181

Symbols of belief

Dress pin with Odin mask, 800–1050.
Kalmergården, north-west Zealand, Denmark.
L 4.5 cm
NMD KU 2745
Fig. 48, p. 195

Odin or *völva* figure, 800–1050.
Lejre, Zealand, Denmark.
Silver with niello. H 1.75 cm, W 1.98 cm, 9 g
Roskilde ROM 641 op x455
Fig. 14, p. 174

Thor's hammer and miniature strike-a-lights, second half of 10th century.
Hoard, Valse, Falster, Denmark.
Silver. Thor's hammer L 2.8 cm, strike-a-lights W 2.5–2.7 cm
NMD 3538, 3539, 8439
Not illustrated

Thor's hammer with punched cross ornament, 10th century.
Haithabu (Hedeby), Schleswig, Germany.
Silver. L 8.2 cm, W 3.9 cm
ALM KS D 602.074
Fig. 31, p. 187

Set of Thor's hammers and miniature staff, 800–1050.
Fugledegård and Kalmergården, north-west Zealand, Denmark.
Silver gilt, copper alloy, lead, iron.
NMD FG A45
Not illustrated

Cup depicting female figures, 10th century.
Lejre, Zealand, Denmark.
Silver. H 4.4 cm, D 6 cm, 115 g
NMD 11373
Fig. 7, p. 167

Female figure, 800–1050.
Fugledegård, north-west Zealand, Denmark.
Silver. H 4.5 cm
NMD FG 3589
Fig. 6, p. 167

Valkyrie, 800–1050.
Fugledegård, north-west Zealand, Denmark.
Silver with niello, partially gilt, H 4 cm
NMD FG 2234
Fig. 4, p. 167

Valkyrie, 800–1050.
Janów Pomorski/Truso, Poland.
Silver. H 2.7 cm, 2.64 g
Elblag MAH 1578/2008
Fig. 5, p. 167

Seated male figure, possibly the god Thor, Scandinavian, 10th century.
Černaya Mogila, Černigov, Ukraine.
Copper alloy, gilt. L 4.7 cm, W 2.2 cm
GIM 76990, 1539/77
Fig. 1, p. 164

Idol, possibly a Scandinavian deity, late 10th/early 11th century.
Gnezdovo, Obl. Smolensk, Russia.
Lead. H 2.9 cm
GIM 111421, 2778/254
Fig. 2, p. 164

Idol or amulet, 10th/11th century.
Schwedt/Oder (Burgwall), Brandenburg, Germany.
Copper alloy. H 5.5 cm
MVF If 8110
Not illustrated

Magic and belief

Miniature coiled snake, 800–1050.
Denmark.
Copper alloy, L 4.8 cm, W 2.9 cm
NMD 21101
Fig. 19, p. 176

Miniature coiled snake pendant, 9th century.
Hon, Buskerud, Norway.
Gold. L 3.0 cm, W 1.95 cm, 5.6 g
UOO C728
Fig. 18, p. 176

Miniature coiled snake, 800–1050.
Menzlin Lkr. Ostvorpmmern,Tyskland, Germany.
Copper alloy. L 2.5 cm, W 1.5 cm
M-V ALM 2010/1591,1
Fig. 20, p. 176

Bear's tooth and clay paw amulets, 800–1050.
Unknown provenance, Russia.
Clay. Paw L *c.* 7 cm, W *c.* 7.5 cm; tooth L 8.5 cm
NMD OA VIII h 29-30
Figs 16–17, p. 175

Bronze bear's tooth pendants, early 11th century.
Lehtimäki, Kalanti, Varsinais-Suomi, Finland.
Copper alloy, iron
NMF 15131:1-3
Fig. 30, p. 186

Pendant of 'Permian' type with duck's feet, 800–1050.
Tulonen, Karkku, Finland.
Copper alloy. L *c.* 7.5 cm
NMF 5853:100
Not illustrated

Pendant of 'Permian' type, 800–1050.
Drag, Tysfjord, Salten, Norway.
Copper alloy. L 6.7 cm, W 4.9 cm
TrM Ts. 3301
Not illustrated

Sorcerer's staff, second half of the 10th century.
Gävle, Gastrikland, Sweden.
Iron. L 44.37 cm
NMD 9689
Fig. 15 (left), p. 175

Spit, possibly a sorcerer's staff, 10th century.
Fuldby, Zealand, Denmark.
Iron. L 56.12 cm
NMD C192
Fig. 15 (right), p. 175

Burial assemblage, possibly belonging to a female sorcerer: Gotlandic box brooch, pendants, cup, small container; late 10th century.
Grave 4, Fyrkat, east Jutland, Denmark.
Gold, silver, copper alloy, niello, brass, iron.
Brooch Diam. 6 cm; chair Diam. 1.3 cm; cup H 3.8 cm, W 4.3 cm; container H 6 cm; bronze vessel H 6.0, Diam. 9.9 cm; Pendant Diam. 1.3 cm
NMD D162/1966, D165/1966, D167/1966, D168/1966, D169/1966
Figs 1–4, pp. 196–7

Fragment of a stone cross from the Isle of Man, 10th–11th century.
Andreas Parish Church, Isle of Man.
Stone
Manx
Not illustrated

The coming of Christianity

Mould for crosses and Thor's hammers, second half of 10th century.
Trendgården, northern Jutland. Denmark.
Soapstone. L 9.7 cm, W 3.7 cm, H 3.3 cm
NMD C24151
Fig. 33, p. 187

St Peter coin with Thor's hammer, *c.* 921–7.
England.
Silver. Diam. 1.9 cm, 1.12 g
BM 1915,0507.772
Fig. 32, p. 187

Christiana Religio denier of Louis the Pious (814–40), mounted as pendant.
Janów Pomorski/Truso, Poland.
Silver. Diam. 2.1 cm
Elblag MAH 1888/2007
Fig. 26, p. 183

Byzantine milliarense, Emperor Basil II Bulgaroktonos/ Constantine VIII (976–1025), adapted as a pendant with suspension ring.
Unknown provenance, Denmark.
Silver. Diam. 2.1 cm
NMD D361
Not illustrated

Denier of Otto-Adelheid coin, *c.* 1000, mounted as pendant.
Øster Vandet, Thy, Denmark.
Silver. Diam *c.* 2.0 cm
NMD FP 9043
Fig. 41, p. 189

St Edmund memorial penny, East Anglia, *c.* 895–910.
Cuerdale, Lancashire, England.
Silver. Diam. 1.9 cm, 1.52 g
BM 1838,0710,767
Fig. 14, p. 27

Two pennies of Cnut of Northumbria, Mirabilia fecit type, *c.* 900–905.
Cuerdale, Lancashire, England.
Silver. 1.38 g, 1.48 g
BM 1838,0710.1396-7
Fig. 27, p. 184

Byzantine cross reliquary and chain, 1050–1100.
Gundslevmagle, Falster. Denmark.
Silver. Chain L 78.5 cm, ring Diam. 3.4 cm, cross H 9.1 cm, W 6.8 cm
NMD 11690, 11465
Not illustrated

Pendant cross (crucifix), 11th century.
Unknown provenance, Denmark.
Silver. L 3.5 cm, W 2.75 cm
NMD D2355
Not illustrated

Pendant cross and beads, 10th century.
Female grave K/1954 V, Kaupang, Vestfold, Norway.
Silver, glass. Cross L 3.1 cm, beads Diam. 0.9–2.1 cm
UOO C57025/1–8
Fig. 38, p. 189

Cruciform pendant, 10th–11th century
Fishamble Street, Dublin, Ireland.
Amber. L 2.49 cm, W 1.6 cm
NMI E190:6248
Fig. 36, p. 189

Broad-bladed axehead with open blade, late 10th century.
Stenstugu, Hejde, Gotland.
Iron. L *c.* 15.5 cm, W of cutting edge *c.* 14 cm
GF C7642
Fig. 28, p. 185

Arm-ring depicting stylized mounds, trees and crosses, symbolic renderings of the Golgotha drama, 9th–early 10th century.
Råbylille, Elmelunde, Møn, Denmark.
Gold. L 7.7 cm
NMD MMCLV
Fig. 39, p. 189

Penny with stylized adaptation of the Golgotha drama, Danish, second half of 10th century.
Pilhus, Denmark.
Silver.
NMD
Fig. 40, p. 189

Bird-shaped brooch, probably a pelican, 11th century.
Toftegård Syd, south-east Funen, Denmark.
Silver. H 3.8 cm, W 4.7 cm
NMD D 6/1996
Fig. 43, 191

Agnus Dei brooch, 11th/12th century.
Oksholm, Oland, northern Jutland, Denmark.
Copper alloy. Diam. 2.6 cm, H 0.3 cm
NMD D311/2009
Not illustrated

Resurrection egg, Kiev-Russian.
Usedom, Lkr. Ostvorpommern, Germany.
Glazed pottery. H 7 cm, Diam. 4 cm
M-V ALM 1994/500
Not illustrated

Crucifix, *c.* 1100.
Åby, Jultland, Denmark.
Oak, gilt copper alloy. H 59.8 cm
NMD D629
Fig. 44, p. 192

Timeline of the Viking Age

North Atlantic	Britain and Ireland	Western Europe	Scandinavia	Russia and the East
	5th century Beginning of Anglo-Saxon settlement of England from Denmark, northern Germany and neighbouring areas		5th century Helgö on Lake Mälaren already functioning as a centre for production of metalwork, and trade across the Baltic and beyond	
	7th century Similarities in metalwork from Sutton Hoo and other Anglo-Saxon objects indicate continued contact with Scandinavia			
			8th century Development of trading centre at Ribe in Denmark, supporting trade around North Sea	
			c. 725 Willibrord leads short-lived Christian mission to Danes	
			c. 737 Rebuilding of Danevirke earthwork across the southern border of Denmark	
				c. 750 Trading settlement established at Staraya Ladoga
	c. 789 First recorded Viking attack on England, near Portland in Dorset			
	793 Viking attack on monastery at Lindisfarne			
	794–5 Attacks on monasteries in Northumbria, Ireland and Scotland			
		799 Viking raids on Aquitaine		
		800 Charlemagne orders coastal defences to be built against Vikings		
			808 Godfred, king of the Danes, forcibly relocates traders from the Slavic settlement of Reric to Hedeby, and orders repairs to Danevirke	
		810 Godfed raids Frisia	810 Godfred murdered	
			820s Ebo and Ansgar lead Christian missions to Danes and Swedes	
c. 825 Irish monks abandon settlements on the Faeroes as a result of Viking incursions				
		834–7 Repeated raids on Dorestad in Frisia		
	837 Ireland 'devastated' by the raiding of churches, monasteries and shrines			
				839 Envoys of Swedish origin in Constantinople

		Mid-9th century Frisia intermittently granted to Danish leaders by the kings of the Franks		
	841 Viking camps established at Dublin and Linn Duachaill (Annagassan)			
		844 Failed Viking attack on Seville		
		845 Franks pay Vikings 7,000 pounds of silver to avert sack of Paris, but Paris and Hamburg sacked		
	850 Vikings over-winter for the first time in England		850 Ansgar builds churches at Hedeby and Ribe	
	Late 9th century Viking settlement in northern and western Scotland			
c. 860 Exploration of Iceland		859–60 Vikings led by Hasteinn raid in southern Spain and Morocco, and attack small town of Luna in Italy, mistaking it for Rome		860 First Rūs attack on Constantinople
				862 Dynasties of Scandinavian extraction established in Novgorod and Kiev
		864 Charles the Bald orders the construction of bridges to prevent Viking fleets from progressing up the Frankish river systems		
	865 Arrival of 'great heathen raiding army' in East Anglia			
c. 871 Settlement of Iceland begins	871 'Great slaughter' of Vikings at Ashdown by West Saxons under Æthelred I and Alfred. Alfred succeeds his brother as king.			
	876 Settlement of Northumbria by the 'great raiding army'			
	878 Defeat of Vikings under Guthrum by Alfred at Edington. Guthrum adopts Christianity and settles in East Anglia			
		885–6 Siege of Paris by Viking fleet		
		891 Vikings suffer major defeat at the battle of the Dyle		
			c. 900 Harald Finehair establishes some sort of over-kingship in Norway	
	902 Viking rulers expelled from Dublin			
				907 Rūs fleet attacks Constantinople
		911 Viking leader Rollo granted county of Rouen		911 Treaty between Kievan Rūs and Byzantine Empire
		914–36 Vikings occupy Brittany		912–13 Rūs fleet raids on the Caspian Sea, but subsequently destroyed by Khazars
	917 Viking dynasty reinstated in Dublin			
				922–3 Arab emissary ibn Fadlān encounters Rūs in the territory of the Volga Bulghars, and describes them in detail

	927 Athelstan conquers Viking Northumbria to create unified kingdom of England	920s–930s Expansion of territory of counts of Rouen to create Normandy		
	937 Athelstan defeats alliance of Scots, Vikings and Strathclyde British at *Brunanburh*		By 936 Gorm the Old establishes Jelling dynasty as rulers in Denmark	
	939 Death of Athelstan and restoration of independent Viking Northumbria			941 Unsuccessful attack on Constantinople by Rūs followed by treaty between Byzantine Empire and Kiev
				943–4 Rūs occupy and defend Barda'ah in the Caucasus, but abandon the city following an outbreak of dysentry
			948 Bishops recorded in Ribe, Århus and Hedeby	
	954 Death of Eirik Bloodaxe, last king of Northumbria			
			958 Death of Gorm the Old, king of Denmark, succeeded by Harald Bluetooth	
			c. 960 Harald Bluetooth (re-) imposes Danish overlordship over much of Norway	
			c. 965 Harald Bluetooth accepts Christianity	964–71 War between the Rūs and the Bulghars, the Khazars and the Byzantine Empire
			c. 970 Town of Sigtuna established, replacing Birka as the major trading centre in the area	
	970s Viking rulers of the Isle of Man active around the Irish Sea		974–81 Hedeby under German control	
			c. 980 Massive construction programme in Denmark under Harald Bluetooth, including royal complex at Jelling, bridge at Ravning Enge and several ring-forts	980 Establishment of Varangian Guard as a unit in the Byzantine army
986 Eirik the Red begins settlement of Greenland			986 Rebellion against Harald Bluetooth, resulting in his death, and his replacement as king of Denmark by his son Svein Forkbeard	
		987–1006 Normandy becomes a duchy		
				988 Vladimir, prince of Kiev, converts to Christianity
	991 Viking victory at Maldon in Essex marks the beginning of a new phase of large-scale raiding in England			
			995 Olaf Tryggvasson unites Norway, and imposes Christianity by force Olaf Tribute-King unites Sweden for the first time	
	c. 995–1000 Introduction of locally minted coinage in Dublin		*c.* 995–1000 Svein Forkbeard of Denmark, Olaf Tryggvasson of Norway and Olaf Tribute-King of Sweden all introduce coinage carrying their own names and the names of their kingdoms	

c. 1000 Discovery and attempted settlement of Vinland Iceland accepts Christianity		1000 Olaf Tryggvasson killed at Battle of Svolder	
	1013 Svein Forkbeard of Denmark conquers England		
	1014 Battle of Clontarf, between the kings of Munster and Leinster, with Viking allies on both sides		
		1015 Olaf Haraldsson claims kingship of Norway	
	1016 Cnut, son of Svein Forkbeard, becomes king of England		
		c. 1025 Construction of warship Roskilde 6 in southern Norway	
		1028 Olaf Haraldsson expelled from Norway by Cnut, with support from Norwegian chieftains	
		1030 Death of Olaf Haraldsson at Stiklestad in failed attempt to recover Norway	1030–46 Harald 'Hardruler' Sigurdsson of Norway in exile in Russia and Byzantine Empire
	c. 1035 Thorfinn the Mighty, earl of Orkney, extends authority over parts of northern and western Scotland	1035 Death of Cnut the Great, Norway recovers independence under Magnus the Good	
			c. 1040 Expedition of Swedes led by Ingvar to Russia and 'Serkland' meets with disaster
	1042 Death of Harthacnut, son of Cnut. End of Danish rule in England	1042–6 Magnus the Good establishes Norwegian rule over Denmark	1043 Last recorded Rūs attack on Constantinople
		1046 Magnus the Good agrees to share kingdom of Norway with Harald Hardruler in return for half of Harald's treasure	
	c. 1050 Bishopric established in Orkney	1048–64 Harald Hardruler tries unsuccessfully to impose Norwegian rule in Denmark	
	1058 Magnus, son of Harald Hardruler of Norway raids around the Irish Sea		
	1066 Unsuccessful invasion of England by Harald Hardruler of Norway, killed at Stamford Bridge, together with the earls of Orkney. Successful invasion of England under William of Normandy		

Acknowledgements

THE NATIONAL MUSEUM OF DENMARK
would like to thank

The Editors, Gareth Williams, British Museum, London; Peter Pentz, National Museum of Denmark, Copenhagen; and Matthias Wemhoff, Museum für Vor- und Frühgeschichte, Staatliche Museen zu Berlin, would like to thank their co-authors for their contributions to this publication: Professor Jan Bill, Viking Ship Museum, Oslo; Rev Simon Coupland, St Paul's Church, Kingston Hill; Timo Ibsen, Centre for Baltic and Scandinavian Archaeology, Stiftung Schleswig-Holsteinische Landesmuseen, Schleswig; Lars Jørgensen, National Museum of Denmark, Copenhagen; Sunhild Kleingärtner, Deutsches Schiffahrtsmuseum, Bremerhaven; Anne Pedersen, National Museum of Denmark, Copenhagen; Professor Neil Price, University of Aberdeen; Kristiane Strætkvern, National Museum of Denmark, Copenhagen.

Particular thanks are due to Claudia Bloch, Senior Development Editor at The British Museum Press and Thomas J.T. Williams, Project Curator for the Viking exhibition at the British Museum, without whose hard work this book would never have been completed.

Michael Andersen, Sigrid Koch Andersen, Barbara Berlowicz, Jan Birk, Michael Bjørn, Marianne Blank, Inger Bojesen-Koefoed, Maria Baastrup, Kim Carstensen, Mads Danker Danielsen, David Drost, Vibe Edinger, Gerd Elling, Gitte Engholm, Victor Espinoza, Lene Floris, Anita Frigaard, Morten Gøtsche, Søren Greve, Ida N. Gustav, Linea Hansen, Mikkel Hjorth Hansen, Jakob Have, Jan Junge Haugaard, Christian Hede, Dorthe Hedegaard, Berit Heine, Peter Henrichsen, Rune Hernø, Torben Holst, Maria-Louise Jacobsen, Jan Bruun Jensen, Lars Aasbjerg Jensen, Eva Lilja Jensen, Palle M. Jepsen, Lotte Jespersen, Lise Johansson, Maria Kapsali-Ibsen, Marlene Kramm, Andrea M. Kærn, Dorthe Langkilde, Jakob Tue Larsen, Emilie F. Lephilibert, Kirsten Lindhard, Nellie Joy Lindholm, Lars Lindved, Michel Malfilaître, Søren Mikkelsen, Anne le Boëdec Moesgaard, Karin Mygdal, Kim Møller, Mie Maagaard, Anette Nielsen, Hanne Hjetting Nielsen, Poul Otto Nielsen, Stine Raun Nissen, Singe Nygaard, Leif Olsen, Anne Pedersen, Peter Pentz, Anette Hjelm Petersen, Claus Pliniussen, Natasha Pokupcic, Karen Qvist, Dennis Rosenfeld, Susanne Rydahl, Eva Salomonsen, Erik Sauffaus, Henrik Schilling, Henrik Skou, Maruiska Solow, Anders Steenholt, Mikkel Storch, Kristiane Strætkvern, Henning Nørlem Sørensen, John Nørlem Sørensen, Vera Tang, Rikke Tjørnehøj, Trine Wiinblaud.

Christian Adamsen, Zoja Agabalian, Christine Bechameil, Atelier Brückner, Vibeke Boesgaard Brøndel, Christoffer Cold-Ravnkilde, Engelbrecht Construction A/S, Sune Elskær, Mathilde Fenger, Henning Fode, Thorkild Fogde, Kim Minor Funk, Gahrens + Battermann, G4s A/S, Signe Hegelund. Herfølge Kleinsmedie, Jan Michael Jensen, Tom Jersø, Kaels A/S, Carsten U. Larsen, No Parking, Ejvind Nørgaard, Priebe Sceneteknik A/S, Anne og David Robinson, Jane Rowley, Merete Rude, ShiloTV, SpriteLab, System Standex A/S, Anne C. Sørensen, Marie Tarpø, Ivar Tønsberg, Ulfhednir Viking Warrior Group, Ove Ullerup, Vikingeskibsmuseet.

THE BRITISH MUSEUM
would like to thank

Barry Ager, Ben Alsop, Katherine Anderson, James Baker, Colleen Batey, Jane Bennett, David Bilson, Roger Bland, Hannah Boulton, Rosemary Bradley, Lindsey Breaks, Amy Brown, Sue Brunning, Roderick Buchanan, Hayley Bullock, Clio Burroughs, Philip Carley, Jayne Carroll, Lucy Carson, Jago Cooper, Sarah Creed, Vesta Sarkhosh Curtis, Rosie Dalgado, Darrel Day, Stephen Dodd, Tony Doubleday, Stephen Driscoll, Iona Eastman, Chris Entwistle, Alan Farlie, Director, RFK Architects, Daniel Ferguson, Mark Finch, Kirsten Forrest, Allison Fox, Stuart Frost, Paul Goodhead, Pieta Graves, Amanda Gregory, Stephen Harrison, Kathryn Havelock, Coralie Hepburn, Katharine Hoare, Julia Howard, David Hoxley, Katherine Hudson, Caroline Ingham, Bill Jones, Elena Jones, Philip Kevin, Turi King, Louise Loe, Ann Lumley, Joanna Mackle, Jill Maggs, Carolyn Marsden-Smith, Sonja Marzinzik, Katie Maughan, Xerxes Mazda, David McNeff, Beverley Nenk, Nick Newbery, Kate Oliver, Gideon Pain, Helen Parkin, Pippa Pearce, Saul Peckham, Jim Peters, Julianne Phippard, Johanne Porter, Venetia Porter, Neil Price, Susan Raikes, Olivia Rickman, Paul Roberts, David Saunders, Lawrence Schooledge, David Score, Maeve Sikora, Lesley Smith, Jennifer Suggitt, Clare Tomlinson, Will Webb, Rosie Weetch, Patricia Wheatley, Hilary Williams, John Williams, Jonathan Williams, Sam Wyles.

MUSEUM FÜR VOR- UND FRÜHGESCHICHTE,
STAATLICHE MUSEEN ZU BERLIN
would like to thank

Marion Bertram, Ralf Bleile, Nathalie Boes, Hermann Born, Claus von Carnap-Bornheim, Heide Eilbracht, Norbert Goßler, Daniela Greinert, Andreas Grüger, Almut Hoffmann, Angelika Hofmann, Bernhard Heeb, Timo Ibsen, Detlef Jantzen, Horst Junker, Mario Kacner, Sunhild Kleingärtner, Martin Kroker, Mechthild Kronenberg, Tania Lipowski, Birgit Maixner, Bärbel Mucker, Katrin Mundorf, Alexandra Pesch, Claudia Plamp, Elisabeth Rochau-Shalem, Susanne Rockweiler, Petra Rösicke, Geraldine Saherwala, Nina Schepkowski, Jens-Peter Schmidt, Bert Schülke, Gereon Sievernich, Horst Wieder, Sigrid Wollmeiner.

Illustration credits

The publisher would like to thank the copyright holders for granting permission to reproduce the images illustrated. Every attempt has been made to trace accurate ownership of copyrighted images in this book. Errors and omissions will be corrected in subsequent editions provided notification is sent to the publisher.

Pages 6–7

Fig. 1: © The Viking Ship Museum, Denmark. Photo: Werner Karrasch

Fig. 2: © Werner Forman Archives

Introduction

Fig. 1: © Museum of Cultural History, University of Oslo

Fig. 2: G3, FrGC.10 Donated by George IV, King of England. 2006,0204.1 Purchased with assistance from the Art Fund, the National Heritage Memorial Fund, the British Museum Friends, and a number of individual donations © The Trustees of the British Museum

Fig. 3: © The National Museum of Denmark

Fig. 4: © National Historical Museum Stockholm

Fig. 5: © The British Library Board

Fig. 6: GIM 33602 1678/1-2 © The State Historical Museum, Moscow

Fig. 7: © The National Museum of Denmark

Fig. 8: © The National Museum of Denmark

Fig. 9: © National Museum of Ireland

Fig. 10: Photo: Anette Schmidt, Roskilde Museum

Fig. 11: GIM 108043 2648/1 © The State Historical Museum, Moscow

Fig. 12: © The Árni Magnússon Institute, Reykjavík. From AM 226 fol.,f.2v, 17th century. Photographer: Jóhanna Ólafsdottir

Fig. 13: Copyright © York Archaeological Trust 2014

Fig. 14: 1838,0710.767 Donated by Victoria, Queen of England © The Trustees of the British Museum

Chapter 1

Fig. 1: © The Trustees of the British Museum

Fig. 2: © Mark Hannaford/JAI/Corbis

Fig. 3: Photo Raymond Hejdström © Gotlands Museum

Fig. 4: © Science Photo Library

Fig. 5: Photo John Lee © The National Museum of Denmark

Fig. 6: © Ribe Vikinge Center

Fig. 7: © Wikinger Museum Haithabu

Fig. 8: Map: David Hoxley

Fig. 9: 1861,1024.1 Donated by James de Carle Sowerby © The Trustees of the British Museum

Fig. 10: © National Museums Scotland

Fig. 11: © The Trustees of the British Museum

Fig. 12: © The National Museum of Denmark

Fig. 13: © Museum für Vor- und Frühgeschichte, Staatliche Museen zu Berlin, Photo: Claudia Plamp

Fig. 14: © The National Museum of Denmark

Fig. 15: © Museum für Vor- und Frühgeschichte, Staatliche Museen zu Berlin, Photo: Claudia Plamp

Fig. 16: © Museum für Vor- und Frühgeschichte, Staatliche Museen zu Berlin, Photo: Claudia Plamp

Fig. 17: © Museum für Vor- und Frühgeschichte, Staatliche Museen zu Berlin, Photo: Claudia Plamp

Fig. 18: Photo Markku Haverinen, National Board of Antiquities, Helsinki, 2014

Fig. 19: © David Poole/Robert Harding

Fig. 20: © The National Museum of Denmark

Fig. 21: Maxx images / Superstock

Fig. 22: © Reiner Elsen / Mauritius / SuperStock

Fig. 23: 1856,0623.140 © The Trustees of the British Museum

Fig. 24: Photo: Arnold Mikkelsen © The National Museum of Denmark

Fig. 25: © National Museum of Ireland

Fig. 26: © Collection of the Archaeological and Historical Museum in Elbląg. Photo L. Okoński

Fig. 27: Map: David Hoxley

Fig. 28: © Aleksey Goss

Fig. 29: © Wikinger Museum Haithabu

Fig. 30: © National Museum of Ireland

Fig. 31: © Wikinger Museum Haithabu

Fig. 32: © National Museum of Ireland

Fig. 33: © National Museum of Ireland

Fig. 34: © Collection of the Archaeological and Historical Museum in Elbląg. Photo L. Okoński

Fig. 35: © Collection of the Archaeological and Historical Museum in Elbląg. Photo L. Okoński

Fig. 36: © National Museum of Ireland

Fig. 37: © Collection of the Archaeological and Historical Museum in Elbląg. Photo L. Okoński

Fig. 38: 2009,4133.685 The Vale of York Hoard was jointly purchased by the British Museum and the York Museums Trust under the 1996 Treasure Act, with funding from the Art Fund, the National Heritage Memorial Fund, the British Museum Friends and the York Museums Trust © The Trustees of the British Museum

Fig. 39: © Wikinger Museum Haithabu

Fig. 40: Photo John Lee © The National Museum of Denmark

Fig. 41: © Wikinger Museum Haithabu

Fig. 42: © Gabriel Hildebrand/National Historical Museum Stockholm

Fig. 43: 2007,8035.1 Acquired through the Treasure Act. Department for Culture, Media and Sport © The Trustees of the British Museum

Fig. 44: 2010,8016.1 Acquired through the Treasure Act. Department for Culture, Media and Sport © The Trustees of the British Museum

Fig. 45: © National Museum of Ireland

Fig. 46: 1944,0401.56 © The Trustees of the British Museum

Fig. 47: © Museum für Vor- und Frühgeschichte, Staatliche Museen zu Berlin, Photo: Claudia Plamp

Fig. 48: © Museum für Vor- und Frühgeschichte, Staatliche Museen zu Berlin, Photo: Klaus Göken

Fig. 49: 2000,0201.2-5,7 © The Trustees of the British Museum

Fig. 50: 1991,0304.2 and 2000,0201.1 © The Trustees of the British Museum

Fig. 51: 2000,0201.1 © The Trustees of the British Museum

Fig. 52: 2000,0101.3 © The Trustees of the British Museum

Fig. 53: © Gabriel Hildebrand/National Historical Museum Stockholm

Fig. 54: 1878,0509.3 © The Trustees of the British Museum

Fig. 55: © The National Museum of Denmark

Fig. 56: Map: David Hoxley

Fig. 57: 1891,1021.68-74 © The Trustees of the British Museum

Fig. 58: © The National Museum of Denmark

Fig. 59: 1991,0109.1-9 © The Trustees of the British Museum

Fig. 60: © National Museums Scotland

Fig. 61: 1991,0109.2 © The Trustees of the British Museum

Fig. 62: © Novgorod State Museum

Fig. 63: 2009,8027.1-76; 2009.4133.77-693 The Vale of York Hoard was jointly purchased by the British Museum and the York Museums Trust under the 1996 Treasure Act, with funding from the Art Fund, the National Heritage Memorial Fund, the British Museum Friends and the York Museums Trust © The Trustees of the British Museum

Vikings in Arabic sources

Fig. 1: MS. Pococke 375 3v-4r © The Bodleian Library, University of Oxford

Fig. 2: © age fotostock/Robert Harding

Wiskiauten

Fig. 1. Map: David Hoxley

Fig. 2: © Museum für Vor- und Frühgeschichte, Staatliche Museen zu Berlin, Photo: Claudia Plamp

Fig. 3 Photo courtesy of Dr. Timo Ibsen © Zentrum für Baltische und Skandinavische Archäologie Schleswig

Fig. 4: Photo courtesy of Dr. Timo Ibsen © Zentrum für Baltische und Skandinavische Archäologie Schleswig

Reuse of foreign objects

Fig. 1: FOLIO 215v © Bibliothèque nationale de France

Fig. 2: © Gabriel Hildebrand/National Historical Museum Stockholm

Fig. 3: Photo: Arnold Mikkelsen © The National Museum of Denmark

Fig. 4: © Gabriel Hildebrand/National Historical Museum Stockholm

Fig. 5: © Landesamt für Kultur und Denkmalpflege Mecklenburg-Vorpommern, Landesarchaologie, Domhof 4/5, 19055 Schwerin, Germany

Chapter 2

Fig. 1: 1917,1208.71.199 Donated by Nan Ino Cooper, Baroness Lucas of Crudwell and Lady Dingwall in Memory of Auberon Thomas Herbert, 9th Baron Lucas of Crudwell and 5th Lord Dingwall © The Trustees of the British Museum

Fig. 2: © The National Museum of Denmark

Fig. 3: © Colchester and Ipswich Museum Service

Fig. 4: © The National Museum of Denmark

Fig. 5: © Staffan Hyll

Fig. 6: GIM 80135 1071/69 © the State Historical Museum, Moscow

Fig. 7: GIM 80135 1798/66 © the State Historical Museum, Moscow

Fig. 8: GIM 80135 1071/7 © the State Historical Museum, Moscow

Fig. 9: © Museum für Vor- und Frühgeschichte, Staatliche Museen zu Berlin, Photo: Claudia Plamp

Fig. 10: © Museum für Vor- und Frühgeschichte, Staatliche Museen zu Berlin, Photo: Claudia Plamp

Fig. 11: © the Russian Academy of Sciences

Fig. 12: Map: David Hoxley

Fig. 13: © Swedish National Heritage Board, Riksantikvarieämbetet

Fig. 14: Photo: Jørgen Nielsen, Odense Bys Museer, Odense

Fig. 15: 1838,0710.1436, 1442, 1168, 1203; 1841,0711.1-741; 1873,1101.1; Donated by Victoria, Queen of England © The Trustees of the British Museum

Fig. 16: © Wikinger Museum Haithabu

Fig. 17: Photo: Arnold Mikkelsen © The National Museum of Denmark

Fig. 18: 1891,1021.29 © The Trustees of the British Museum

Fig. 19: Copyright Landesamt für Kultur und Denkmalpflege Mecklenburg-Vorpommern, Landesarchäologie, Domhof 4/5, 19055 Schwerin, Germany

Fig. 20: GIM 34213 1959/1 © the State Historical Museum, Moscow

Fig. 21: 1856,0701.1452 © The Trustees of the British Museum

Fig. 22: 1891,1021.44 © The Trustees of the British Museum

Fig. 23: © Museum of Cultural History, University of Oslo. Photo: Eirik Irgens Johnsen

Fig. 24: Photo: Gareth Williams

Fig. 25: Photo © Raymond Hejdström, Gotlands Museum

Fig. 26: Copyright © York Archaeological Trust 2014

Fig. 27: 1831,1101.123-5 © The Trustees of the British Museum

Fig. 28: © The Trustees of the British Museum

Fig. 29: © Museum of Cultural History, University of Oslo. Photo: Eirik Irgens Johnsen

Fig. 30: Oxford Archaeology on behalf of Dorset County Council

Fig. 31: © The National Museum of Denmark

Fig. 32: 1890,0701.3 © The Trustees of the British Museum

Fig. 33: © National Museum Wales

Fig. 34: Map: David Hoxley

Fig. 35: © The National Museum of Denmark

Fig. 36: © Museum of Cultural History, University of Oslo. Photo: Eirik Irgens Johnsen

Fig. 37: Photo: Arnold Mikkelsen © The National Museum of Denmark

Fig. 38: © National Museum of Ireland

Fig. 39: © Museum für Vor- und Frühgeschichte, Staatliche Museen zu Berlin

Fig. 40: Photo Markku Haverinen, NBA, 2014

Fig. 41: 1856,0701.1376 © The Trustees of the British Museum

Fig. 42: 1856,0701.1441 © The Trustees of the British Museum

Fig. 43: © National Museum of Ireland

Fig. 44: GIM 76990 1539/1 © the State Historical Museum, Moscow

Fig. 45: Photo Markku Haverinen, NBA, 2014

Fig. 46: 1891,1021.27 © The Trustees of the British Museum

Fig. 47: GIM 105009 2575/1 © the State Historical Museum, Moscow

Fig. 48: 1997,0102.1 © The Trustees of the British Museum

Fig. 49: Photo: Arnold Mikkelsen © The National Museum of Denmark

Fig. 50: Photo: Arnold Mikkelsen © The National Museum of Denmark

Fig. 51: 1955,0506.1 Donated by G.B. Goffe © The Trustees of the British Museum

Fig. 52: 1868,0128.2 Donated by Capt Oakes © The Trustees of the British Museum

Fig. 53: Photo: Roskilde Museum

Fig. 54: © Historiska Museet, Stockholm, Sweden / Giraudon / The Bridgeman Art Library

Fig. 55: © Museum für Vor- und Frühgeschichte, Staatliche Museen zu Berlin, Photo: Claudia Plamp

Fig. 56: © Museum für Vor- und Frühgeschichte, Staatliche Museen zu Berlin, Photo: Claudia Plamp

Fig. 57: © Museum of Cultural History, University of Oslo. Photo: Kirsten Helgeland.

Fig. 58: 1909,0626.8 © The Trustees of the British Museum

Fig. 59: Map: David Hoxley

Fig. 60: Map: David Hoxley

Fig. 61: © The Viking Ship Museum; Denmark. Photo: Werner Karrasch

Fig. 62: © Swedish National Heritage Board, Riksantikvarieämbetet

The way of the warrior

Fig. 1: © The National Museum of Denmark

Fig. 2: © National Historical Museum (Statens historiska museum) Sweden

Continental defences against the Vikings

Fig. 1: © Getty/ Frans Lemmens

Fig. 2: Map: David Hoxley

Fig. 3: St. Gallen, Stiftsbibliothek, Cod. Sang. 22, p. 140 © Stiftsbibliothek St. Gallen

Viking camps in England and Ireland

Fig. 1: Map: David Hoxley

Fig. 2: 2006,1203.1-14, 60, 104-11; 2008,4199.1-10 © The Trustees of the British Museum

Fig. 3: 2010,8014.1-3; 2008.4200, 1-26 © The Trustees of the British Museum

Chapter 3

Fig. 1: Photo Kjell Ove Storvik/Lofotr Viking Museum

Fig. 2: Photo: Adnan Icagic. Tromsø University Museum

Fig. 3: Photo: June Åsheim. Tromsø University Museum

Fig. 4: © EyeCadcher Media, Lejre Museum/Roskilde Museum and Nicolai Garhøj Larsen

Fig. 5: © Museum of Cultural History, University of Oslo. Kojan & Krogrold.

Fig. 6: Jutta Grudziecki, Kulturhistorisches Museum der Hansestadt Stralsund

Fig. 7: © Roskilde Museum

Fig. 8: Photo: Arnold Mikkelsen © The National Museum of Denmark

Fig. 9: © The National Museum of Denmark

Fig. 10: © De Agostini/The British Library Board

Fig. 11: © The National Museum of Denmark

Fig. 12: © Jutta Grudziecki, Kulturhistorisches Museum der Hansestadt Stralsund

Fig. 13: GIM 49876 1091/20 © the State Historical Museum, Moscow

Fig. 14: Photo: June Åsheim. Tromsø University Museum

Fig. 15: Bohuslen Wikimedia Commons

Fig. 16: © Stockholms läns museum

Fig. 17: 1870,1014.1 © The Trustees of the British Museum

Fig. 18: AF.537 Bequeathed by Sir Augustus Wollaston Franks © The Trustees of the British Museum

Fig. 19: 1905,1108.1 © The Trustess of the British Museum

Fig. 20: 1922,1009.1 © The Trustees of the British Museum

Fig. 21: 1853,0412.71 © The Trustees of the British Museum

Fig. 22: © The National Museum of Denmark

Fig. 23: Photo Markku Haverinen, NBA, 2013

Fig. 24: © Museum of Cultural History, University of Oslo. Photo Mona Knudsen.

Fig. 25: © Museum of Cultural History, University of Oslo. Photo Marianne Vedeler.

Fig. 26: 1991,0109.1 © The Trustees of the British Museum

Fig. 27: GIM 77034 376/55 © the State Historical Museum, Moscow

Fig. 28: Photo: Ernst Furuhatt. Nordlandsmuseet

Fig. 29: © National Museums Scotland

Fig. 30: © National Museum of Ireland

Fig. 31: John Lee © The National Museum of Denmark

Fig. 32: Photo: Arnold Mikkelsen © The National Museum of Denmark

Fig. 33: © The National Museum of Denmark

Fig. 34: © The National Museum of Denmark

Fig. 35: 1967,0609.1 © The Trustees of the British Museum

Fig. 36: Photo: Arnold Mikkelsen © The National Museum of Denmark

Fig. 37: © The National Museum of Denmark

Fig. 38: Photo: Arnold Mikkelsen © The National Museum of Denmark

Fig. 39: © Universal History Archive/ UIG/The Bridgeman Art Library

Fig. 40: © Wikinger Museum Haithabu

Fig. 41: © Museum für Vor- und Frühgeschichte, Staatliche Museen zu Berlin, Photo: Klaus Göken-bearb

Fig. 42: lat. 8085, fol. 61v © Bibliothèque Nationale de France

Fig. 43: © The National Museum of Denmark

Fig. 44: © Wikinger Museum Haithabu

Fig. 45: © Wikinger Museum Haithabu

Fig. 46: © Wikinger Museum Haithabu

Fig. 47: GIM 109343 2712 © the State Historical Museum, Moscow

Fig. 48: © Museum of Cultural History, University of Oslo

Fig. 49: © The National Museum of Denmark

Fig. 50: MS Acc. 2011/5 © The Royal Library (Det Kongelige Bibliotek)

Fig. 51: © The National Museum of Denmark

Fig. 52: © The National Museum of Denmark

Fig. 53: © The National Museum of Denmark

Fig. 54: © The National Museum of Denmark

Fig. 55: © The National Museum of Denmark

Fig. 56: GIM 77012 111/1-3 © the State Historical Museum, Moscow

Fig. 57: 1862,0930.1; 1848.0819,169; E.5081 © The Trustees of the British Museum

Fig. 58: 1957,0612.16 © The Trustees of the British Museum

Fig. 59: © De Agostini/The British Library Board

Fig. 60: Stowe 944, f.6 © The British Library Board

Great halls and palaces

Fig. 1: © Kaiserpfalz Ingelheim, ArchimediX GbR & Holger Grewe, 2002/5

Fig. 2: © Kaiserpfalz Ingelheim, ArchimediX GbR & Holger Grewe, 2002/5

Fig. 3: Photo Museum in der Kaiserpfalz, Paderborn

The royal monuments of Jelling

Fig. 1: Georg Gerster / Panos

Fig. 2: © Carmen Redondo/CORBIS

Fig. 3: © The National Museum of Denmark

Neighbours along the southern Baltic coast

Fig. 1: National Heritage Board of Poland

Fig. 2: Copyright Landesamt für Kultur und Denkmalpflege Mecklenburg-Vorpommern, Landesarchäologie, Domhof 4/5, 19055 Schwerin, Germany

Fig. 3: Copyright Landesamt für Kultur und Denkmalpflege Mecklenburg-Vorpommern, Landesarchäologie, Domhof 4/5, 19055 Schwerin, Germany

Chapter 4

Fig. 1: GIM 76990 1539/77 © the State Historical Museum, Moscow

Fig. 2: GIM 111421 2778/254 © the State Historical Museum, Moscow

Fig. 3: © Odense Bys Museer/Asger Kjærgaard

Fig. 4: © The National Museum of Denmark

Fig. 5: Museum of Archaeology and History in Elbląg

Fig. 6: © The National Museum of Denmark

Fig. 7: © The National Museum of Denmark

Fig. 8: Kenneth Svensson, Arkeologikonsult AB, Sweden

Fig. 9: © SAGNLANDET LEJRE – Denmark

Fig. 10: © The National Museum of Denmark

Fig. 11: © The National Museum of Denmark

Fig. 12: Photo: Arnold Mikkelsen © The National Museum of Denmark

Fig. 13: Photo: Arnold Mikkelsen © The National Museum of Denmark

Fig. 14: Ole Malling, Roskilde Museum

Fig. 15: © The National Museum of Denmark

Fig. 16: © Museum of Cultural History, University of Oslo. Photo Ove Holst

Fig. 17: Photo: Arnold Mikkelsen © The National Museum of Denmark

Fig. 18: Copyright Landesamt für Kultur und Denkmalpflege Mecklenburg-Vorpommern, Landesarchäologie, Domhof 4/5, 19055 Schwerin, Germany

Fig. 19: Photo: Arnold Mikkelsen © The National Museum of Denmark

Fig. 20: Photo: Arnold Mikkelsen © The National Museum of Denmark

Fig. 21: Photo Raymond Hejdström, Gotlands Museum

Fig. 22: © Museum für Vor- und Frühgeschichte, Staatliche Museen zu Berlin, Photo: Claudia Plamp

Fig. 23: © Museum für Vor- und Frühgeschichte, Staatliche Museen zu Berlin, Photo: Claudia Plamp

Fig. 24: © National Museum of Ireland

Fig. 25: © Museum of Cultural History, University of Oslo. Photo: Eirik Irgens Johnsen

Fig. 26: Museum of Archaeology and History in Elbląg

Fig. 27: 1838,0710.1397; 1838,0710.1396 Donated by Victoria, Queen of England © The Trustees of the British Museum

Fig. 28: Photo Raymond Hejdström, Gotlands Museum

Fig. 29: © National Historical Museum Stockholm

Fig. 30: Photo Markku Haverinen, NBA, 2012

Fig. 31: © Wikinger Museum Haithabu

Fig. 32: 1915,0507.772 © The Trustees of the British Museum

Fig. 33: © The National Museum of Denmark

Fig. 34: © The National Museum of Denmark

Fig. 35: © The National Museum of Denmark

Fig. 36: © National Museum of Ireland

Fig. 37: © National Museum of Ireland

Fig. 38: © Museum of Cultural History, University of Oslo. Photo: Eirik Irgens Johnsen

Fig. 39: © The National Museum of Denmark

Fig. 40: © The National Museum of Denmark

Fig. 41: © The National Museum of Denmark

Fig. 42: © Michal Sikorski photography

Fig. 43: © The National Museum of Denmark

Fig. 44: © The National Museum of Denmark

Fig. 45: © Wikinger Museum Haithabu

Fig. 46: © Moesgård Museum, Denmark

Fig. 47: © Westend61 / SuperStock

Fig. 48: © The National Museum of Denmark

The Fyrkat woman

Fig. 1: © The National Museum of Denmark

Fig. 2. © The National Museum of Denmark

Fig. 3: © The National Museum of Denmark

Fig. 4: © The National Museum of Denmark

Fig. 5: ©The National Museum of Denmark

Ritual sites at Lake Tissø

Fig. 1: Photo Per Poulsen © The National Museum of Denmark

Fig. 2: Photo Anne Birgitte Gotfredsen © The National Museum of Denmark

The Oseberg ship and ritual burial

Fig. 1: © Museum of Cultural History, University of Oslo

Fig. 2: © Museum of Cultural History, University of Oslo. Photo O. Væring

Fig. 3: © Museum of Cultural History, University of Oslo. Artist: Mary Storm 1948. Photo: Eirik Irgens Johnsen

Chapter 5

Fig. 1: 1938,0202.1 Purchased with assistance from the Art Fund and the Trustees of the Christy Fund © The Trustees of the British Museum

Fig. 2: © Antwerp City Museums/ MAS / Nationaal Scheepvaartmuseum. Photographer Michel Wuyts

Fig. 3: © The National Museum of Denmark

Fig. 4: © The National Museum of Denmark

Fig. 5: © The Viking Ship Museum, Denmark. Photo: Werner Karrasch.

Fig. 6: © The National Museum of Denmark

Fig. 7: © Ted Spiegel/CORBIS

Fig. 8: © Vikingemuseet, Ladby

Fig. 9: Map: David Hoxley

Fig. 10: Map: David Hoxley

Fig. 11: © The National Museum of Denmark

Fig. 12: © National Museums Scotland

Fig. 13: © National Museum of Ireland

Fig. 14: © Museum of Cultural History, University of Oslo. Photo Eirik Irgens Johnsen

Fig. 15: Museum of Cultural History, University of Oslo. Photo Ellen C. Holte

Fig. 16: © The National Museum of Denmark

Fig. 17: © Martin W. Jürgensen, The National Museum of Denmark

Fig. 18: Photo © Raymond Hejdström, Gotlands Museum

Fig. 19: © National Museum of Ireland

Fig. 20: © Wikinger Museum Haithabu

Fig. 21: Courtesy of the Portable Antiquities Scheme

Roskilde 6

Fig. 1: © The Viking Ship Museum, Denmark. Photo: Werner Karrasch

Fig. 2: © The Viking Ship Museum, Denmark. Photo: Werner Karrasch

Fig. 3: © The Viking Ship Museum, Denmark. Photo: Werner Karrasch

Fig. 4: © The Viking Ship Museum, Denmark.

Fig. 5: © The Viking Ship Museum, Denmark. Illustration: Morten Gøthche

Fig. 6: © The Trustees of the British Museum

Conservation of Roskilde 6

Fig. 1: © The Conservation Department, The National Museum of Denmark

Fig. 2: © Morten Gøthche, The Viking Ship Museum, Roskilde, Denmark

Fig. 3: © The Conservation Department, The National Museum of Denmark

Fig. 4: © The Conservation Department, The National Museum of Denmark

Fig. 5: © The Conservation Department, The National Museum of Denmark

Index

Note: page numbers in **bold** refer to information contained in captions.

A

B

C

D

E

F

J

K

L

M

N

O

P

Q

R

S

T

Þ

U

V

W

Y

Z